THE BATTLE OF THE EAST COAST

Conversation at Harwich between Sherlock Holmes and Dr Watson, from Sir Arthur Conan Doyle's last Holmes story "His Last Bow" (1927):

...Holmes pointed back to the moonlit sea, and shook a thoughtful head.
"There's an east wind coming, Watson".
"I think not, Holmes. It is very warm".
"Good old Watson! You are the one fixed point in a changing age. There's an east wind coming all the same, such a wind as never blew on England yet. It will be cold and bitter, Watson, and a good many of us will wither before its blast".

THE BATTLE OF THE EAST COAST (1939-1945)

by J P Foynes

PUBLISHED BY THE AUTHOR

© J P Foynes 1994
ISBN 0 9521555 2 4

The cover design shows a boat of 1st MTB Flotilla at Felixstowe early in 1940 (front), an East Coast RDF (radar) transmitter tower (spine), and Roughs Tower Maunsell Fort, off Harwich (back).

CONTENTS

Foreword by Captain R D Franks ix Author's Preface x

1. The Nore and 1939 — 1	10. War on the Convoy Route_2 — 212
2. Magnetic Mine Menace — 16	11. Battle with Giants — 239
3. From the Enemy's Grasp — 35	12. Four Years of Air War — 249
4. Invasion Imminent — 55	13. *Beehive, Mantis* and *Midge* — 273
5. War on the Convoy Route_1 — 82	14. Ship Rescue and Salvage — 296
6. The Air Defences — 117	15. Dockyards and Shipyards — 310
7. Coastal Blitz — 136	16. Air-Sea Rescue — 323
8. In Harbour and Ashore — 174	17. To the Far Shore — 346
9. Three British Offensives — 199	18. The Last Eleven Months — 359

Appendices (A–Q) 377 Sources and Acknowledgments 411
Index 417

PHOTOGRAPHS

between pp.

6-7 An East Coast Convoy (3 views, including one from trawler *Sapphire*). Sailors of Polish destroyer *Burza*.

18-19 Magnetic mine victims off Essex; *Simon Bolivar, Blackhill, Terukuni Maru*; the *Gipsy* sinking; the destroyer aground, Lt-Cdr Crossley's funeral.

24-25 *Blyskawica* landing survivors of *Sheaf Crest*; British Type XIV mine; Cap Creasy shooting at a loose mine; *San Calisto* sinking. Early Luftwaffe Blitz on East Coast Shipping; *Tautmila* abandoned, *Reculver* under tow, *Amelia Lauro*'s captain and tail of bomb, damage to East Dudgeon Lightship.

30-31 German destroyer *Karl Galster*, He 115 wreckage on Sheringham Beach, Thames balloon. *Grenville* on her final sortie, and sinking; contact mine blown by Bridlington RMS party, *Cordella*'s crew after blowing a mine.

32-33 Corvette *Mallard* & Paddle Minesweeper *Queen Empress* at Harwich. The German air crash at Clacton (30 April, 1940) _ 4 views. The blocking of Zeebrugge, graves of *St Achilleus* crewmen killed at Dunkirk.

46-47 The Dunkirk Evacuation; photo taken from *Oriole*, tug *Barnes* pulling small boats up the Thames, destroyer *Javelin, Tamzine, Challenge, Waverley*.

PHOTOGRAPHS

60-61	The Brightlingsea Auxiliary Patrol; yacht crews in harbour, patrol boat returning from sailing barge, drifter at Aldous's Jetty, river patrol AA gunners, *Coretta* and *Kongoni, Aquabelle, Marsayru* and trawlers off Mersea.
	Cap Henniker-Heaton and Rear-Adm Harris, three officers of Yarmouth Sub-Command (Fullerton, de Pass, Stoker), RNPS men at Lowestoft.
	Harwich Fixed Defences; loading a 6" gun in Landguard Right Battery, Darrell's Battery and Landguard Fort; Beacon Hill Battery.
71-72	Czech newspaper "Our News". 6" coast artillery guncrew at drill.
	Sq Ldr P Townsend, bomb damage at Colman's Wharf (Yarmouth), parachute mine in Hull garden.
74-75	Cap Bickford's coffin at Immingham, monitor *Erebus;* Sheerness minesweeping trawlers; *Gilt Edge* and *Milford Prince.*
82-83	Ships v. Aircraft; Wells whelker and crew after German air attack, forms of AA defence at sea, M/S trawlermen manning Lewis gun.
	The Port of London continues.
92-93	E-Boats; 1st Flotilla boats, 1st Flotilla officers.
109-110	Upper Thames Patrol, MMS 16; Scene at Garrison Point, Sheerness (1943), remains of Gt Bromley CH station.
120-121	Radar; Bawdsey towers, German air recce. photo of Bawdsey, Walton CHL station.
	German air reconnaissance photos of Chatham & Harwich, wreck of F/O Doulton's Hurricane.
150-151	German Bombers Crashed on the East Coast in 1940: He 111 (Cley), Ju 88 (Aldbrough), Do 17 (Erwarton).
	Italian Air Raids; CR 42 crashed at Orfordness, BR 20 in Tangham Forest, Cr 42 at Corton, 257 Squadron pilots, Harwich Civil Defence Report.
	Official warning on "butterfly" bombs.
160-161	The Blitz of 1940-1; Thameshaven aerial photo, London fireman, *City of Rochester* wreck, *Marmion* wreck, *Fidelia* wreck, Bernard's Factory (Harwich), "Satan" bomb at Gorleston, Middlegate Street (Yarmouth), Riverside Mill and Reckitt's (Hull), St Anne's Home (Bridlington).
178-179	Naval AA Defence at Sheerness; *Royal Eagle, Astral* raising balloon; *Sun* tugs at Southend.
	Two Scenes at Harwich; MTBs & *Whitley, Southdown.*
200-201	The Harwich Submarines; *Sealion,* U36, *Snapper, Snapper*'s POWs. H44; North Coates Beauforts and Beaufighters.

PHOTOGRAPHS

	Operation Outward (Landguard Common); three scenes on *Mallard*; *Bovey Tracey* wreck.
242-243	Minesweepers at Parkeston Quay; ML 150 at Lowestoft.
	12 Feb. 1942; *Scharnhorst*, damage to *Worcester*, *Worcester* at Harwich; SS *Thyra*.
	HMS *Badger* (Harwich); SDO and cricket game.
248-249	The Action Against the German Cruisers; graves of Lt-Cdr Esmonde & *Worcester* crew.
	More Heavy Air Attacks on Ports; Lowestoft, Hull, Grimsby.
256-257	Further Raids on Yarmouth; two Views of "Hermann" bomb, damage at Southtown Maltings.
	The Yarmouth Raid of 25 June 1942; five views of damage & a commemorative plaque.
	Buried Reserve CH station, Gt Bromley; two views of remains.
274-275	Roughs & Shivering Sand Forts; Gt Bromley scope during Cologne raid; recovering V2 engine at Southend.
	MTBs in Felixstowe Basin, 1942 (two views).
282-283	Coastal Forces Heroes; Hichens & Dickens; Bradford & officers.
	15 March 1942; S 111 under tow, S 111 POWS landing at Lowestoft.
294-295	Felixstowe; two MTBs under repair; Wren towing MGB 61.
	MTB 233 repairing at James & Stone's, Brightlingsea; *Gipsy* being refloated.
302-303	Harwich Salvage and Rescue Tugs; *Freija*, *Mammouth*, *Sea Giant*, *Kenia*.
316-317	Amy Johnson; Lt-Cdr Fletcher's grave.
	The Colne Shipyards; Aldous's Brightlingsea (four views), MMS building at Wivenhoe, steam pinnace from James and Stone's of B'sea; MMS 1 launched at Lowestoft; *Ajax* at Chatham.
	HDML at Brightlingsea; Toughs' (Teddington); ML 103 launched. MGB 601 building & on trials, aerial view.
	Air-Sea Rescue HSLs at Gorleston; 108 captured, 2706 burning.
330-331	305 Squadron Wellington wreckage (St Osyth); Airborne lifeboat & Lindholme dinghy.
	The East Anglian Lifeboats; Cromer (2 views), Gorleston, Aldeburgh.
340-341	Air-Sea Rescue at Brightlingsea; 3 ARBs, Clacton lifeboat, Blenheim wreck, ARB personnel, Mustang wreck
364-365	Minor Landing Craft Training at B'sea; 7th Flotilla officers, LCAs under repair; HDML 1383 & frigate Curzon at Harwich; captured Biber.
372-373	Adm Bräuning & E-boat at Felixstowe (3 views); Shotley Cemetary.

MAPS & DIAGRAMS

East Coast convoy & shipping routes	4-5	The Thames Entrance, 1939-45	18
German Offensive Minelaying, 1st 8 Months of war	23	Harwich, 1939-45	18
		Brightlingsea, 1939-45	18
Mine Warfare, 1939-45	27	Lowestoft, 1939-45	19
Evacuations from the Continent, 1940	42	RNPS Badge	19
Routes of Continental Escapers	51	Gt Yarmouth, 1939-45	19
Coast Artillery, 1941	62	Grimsby, 1939-45	19
Harwich Fixed Defences	64	Harwich Submarine Operations	20
Landguard Fixed Defences	65	Operation Outward	21
Darrell's Battery, Landguard	67	Pursuit of E-Bts, 19/20 Nov, 1941	21
Infantry Defence of Thames Estuary & East Anglia, Sep 1940	68	Types of Luftwaffe Bomber Over East Coast	22
Ryder Searchlight	79	Anti-E-Boat Defence	22
Forms of German Attack on Shipping	89	E-Boat Raid of 25 Sep, 1943	23
German explosive anti-M/S float	97	12 February, 1942	24
RDF Plot of Minelaying Planes, 21 Nov, 1940	100	Jamming of Walton CHL, 12/2/42	24
		Action off the Hook & Shell Damage to *Worcester*, 12/2/42	24
German Air Minelaying in Thames Estuary, Dec, 1940	101	AA Defences of Thames Estuary	25
Shipping Losses Graph	102	FW 190 raids on Yarmouth & Lowestoft, May 1943	26
E-Boat Raid of 7/8 March, 1941	112		
CH Station Circuit Diagram	120	2 Night Raids on Ipswich	26
East Coast Radar Chain, 1940	122	V2 Tracking	27
AMES 24, Great Bromley	124	Coastal Forces Ops, Nore Cmd	27
Harwich Air Defences, 1941	126	14/15 March, 1942	27
Bombing Around Gt Bromley CH Sta	131	Combat Motor Craft of 2 Sides	28
German Radar Jamming & Defensive Radar Monitoring	134	E-Boat Raid of 24/25 Oct, 1943	29
		Salvage Problems, Harwich	3
Axis Air Bases Raiding East Coast	140	Sheerness Dockyard & Base	3
Battle of Britain Air Crashes, Thames Estuary	144	B'sea & Oulton Broad Shipyards	3
		Air-Sea Rescue Craft	3
Locations Bombed by the Italians	153	Air-Sea Rescue Organisation	3
		Map Codes	3
Air Attacks on Eastern England, 11/12 May, 1941	165	Felixstowe & N Foreland A/SR	3
Bombing of Harwich area	169	Clandestine Landings in Holland	3
" " Lowestoft	170	Combined Ops, Nore Command	3
" " Gt Yarmouth	171	Ostend Naval Base & Defences	3
" " Hull	172	Situation in North Sea, 9/44-5/45	3
Chatham, 1939-45	177	Midget U-Boat Attacks, 1945	3
		Known E-Bt Sinkings, North Sea	3

In Appendices: Main Types of German Mine 389
Ship Sinkings in Nore Cmd (4 separate maps) 395-6, 401-2

FOREWORD BY CAPTAIN R D FRANKS RN
(the last surviving officer of HMS GIPSY)

I am pleased to write a foreword to Mr Foynes's interesting book. As Captain of HMS *Ganges*, Shotley, in 1957 and 1958, I looked out on one of the harbours (Harwich) which features prominently here. I had had an earlier, much briefer, acquaintance with it in 1939, when my destroyer, the *Gipsy*, triggered one of the early magnetic mines and was sunk.

At that point I dropped out of the "Battle of the East Coast" and for the next two years took part in the Battle of the Atlantic. And what a different battle it was!...Wide ocean, no sandbanks, no mines, no E-boats, virtually no enemy aircraft! I have a great respect for those who fought in the difficult conditions of our East Coast, and yet have figured little in the history books, compared to all the literature about the Atlantic battle.

This book therefore fills a gap and it seems to me the author has filled it well. He has researched British and German records most thoroughly and covered all aspects including those involving the Army and the RAF. Many of the little ships are mentioned (what lovely names many of them had _ *Sweet Promise, Silver Dawn, Waveflower*). Surely many of those who took part in the endless patrols and who still survive, will like to read of those times and perhaps understand a bit more of the whys and wherefores. They can also read of some mysteries and oddities both ashore and afloat, since the author has made it a speciality to probe these. The first faltering attempts to sweep the German magnetic mines, the campaigns against supposed fifth columnists, the peculiarities of the early radar war, are among those which stick in the mind. There is much here on the fast motor craft of Coastal Forces and the Air Sea Rescue. But Mr Foynes also tells us of tragedies, such as the heavy loss of life in *Esk* and *Express*, and later on *Exmoor* and *Vortigern*, and of many deeds of heroism and self-sacrifice. This is a story which I recommend to all those who like to remember "Our Finest Hours".

ROBERT FRANKS

PREFACE

This is an account of that part of the Second World War which was fought along the East Coast of England between Flamborough Head in Yorkshire and North Foreland in Kent. The area coincided with the Royal Navy's Nore Command, and formed a strategic whole in that along it lay the sea route from the wider world to London, and also the frontline for any German attack launched from the occupied Low Countries. Whether ashore, afloat or in the air, the story generally takes place within sight of the coast of the Thames Estuary, East Anglia, or the Humber region. My concern is mainly with the ports, naval bases, warships, coastal shipping and dockyards which kept open that sea route and defended that frontline.

However the book also features the Army, RAF, fishing fleet and such civilians as those of the RNLI and Civil Defence. But I shall *not* be describing those aspects of the war which went on behind the East Coast, nor on the Continent beyond the North Sea: this is neither another history of wartime East Anglia nor of, for instance, the bombing of Germany by Allied airmen based in Eastern England.

In some ways the English East Coast was a backwater of the war_ and ironically, for it lay directly between England and Germany. To the north, the United Kingdom looked out from Scapa Flow on the Arctic convoys. To the west, it faced the U-Boat arena of the Atlantic. To the south (including the south-east, for Dover is surely not in Eastern England) lay the Channel and Dover Strait, scenes of such events as Dunkirk, the biggest combats of the Battle of Britain, the Dieppe Raid, and Normandy. By contrast, the East Coast saw no event big enough to make world headlines, unless one includes the fighting in Holland for brief periods in 1940 and 1944. The best-known combatants to frequent the East Coast of England were the Allied airmen, but they merely hurtled overhead _ except when they came down "in the drink" and needed the local air-sea rescue service.

The distinctive interest of the East Coast in the Second World War is that it saw most of that part of the German offensive against maritime Britain which did not feature submarines and big warships operating far out into the ocean, but which was instead staged by aircraft and small naval craft raiding quite close inshore. It witnessed the largest mine campaign in history, for instance, and the biggest campaign between powered motor boats.

However for me the main interest of the subject is the local, not the national. That a maritime war was fought from or in front of such diverse and familiar places as Yarmouth, Felixstowe, Burnham-on-Crouch, Southend, the London Docks, and even Tower Pier, has struck me as fascinating since I first got to know this coast as a boy and wondered at such things as bomb craters, radar pylons, concrete gun emplacements, and wreck buoys. Exactly what work was done at each military installation or base, and what events occurred at each, and why, could hardly have been settled at that time, even by a historical researcher, since

PREFACE

the official documents involved were closed for thirty or more years. My one regret is that this has meant such a long time lapse that very many of the people with first-hand experience of the wartime coast are no longer with us.

A few more introductory remarks are needed, I think.

First, my facts almost always come from official (and formerly secret) documents in the first instance, and then secondarily from eye-witnesses and only thirdly from the few published books that there are. This is not just for the sake of scholarly rectitude: the primary sources (in spite of my inevitable selecting and interpreting) have a clarity and an immediacy which the secondary material (whatever the skill of its raconteur) lacks. I was not alive during the Second World War, so all rests on research, though my being an East Anglian by origin certainly helped. I have set out my documentary and personal sources as clearly as I can.

Second, a word on the range of things covered. I have tried to sketch the whole war life and organisation of this coast, down to support and administrative work and the smallest bases and vessels. I think I can claim that most of this information has never been published before. In giving this cross-section of the East Coast war, I have had to be brief with some of the major events in order to leave space for some account of the minor ones. But I hope that in these cases my text still makes their relative scale and importance clear. And of course I hope that no one is offended by any omission.

Finally, I have made no mention of the wider war unless to give an explanation of local events which would otherwise be wanting.

J.P.FOYNES

1
THE NORE AND 1939

"DANZIG IST DEUTSCH!" proclaimed German National Socialist propaganda in August 1939. The people of the East Coast of England looked apprehensively at the North Sea, proverbially grey but sparkling under a magnificent sun that summer week. For several years there had been warnings enough, even for those who never read the papers, attended the cinema, or listened to the wireless. New concrete coast gun emplacements had appeared around Sheerness, Harwich and the Humber. The RAF had built numerous bomber and fighter "aerodromes", like Mildenhall and Duxford, and increasingly overflew the fens, the thatched-roof villages, and the sandy coasts of East Anglia with faster and faster aeroplanes. At remote coastal locations every twenty-five miles they had built spectacular clumps of wooden and steel pylons, some taller than Norwich cathedral spire _ a mystery to the local civilians, they were known to their operators to provide electronic early warning of German air attack. (In September 1938 they had tracked the plane on which Neville Chamberlain flew from Heston, Middlesex, to Munich in order to ditch the Czechs and save the world from war). Thousands of Jewish refugee children had disembarked at Harwich that winter, and been lodged in holiday camps at Dovercourt and Pakefield. During the Czech Crisis a partial mobilisation of the Fleet had brought coast artillerymen, naval officers and warships to the Humber, Harwich, Southend and Sheerness, and civilians had tried on gasmasks.

Less than a year later, in August 1939, as Hitler stridently claimed Danzig and the Polish Corridor, the Navy, the RAF, the Coast Artillery, and the Civil Defence services again mustered and stood by. Passenger ferry services from Harwich and Hull to the Continent were suspended, while the thousands of East Coast fishermen and merchant seamen of the Royal Naval Reserve were summoned to Chatham and then posted to their war duties. This time there was no turning back, and for the second time in twenty-one years there was war in the North Sea.

In 1939 the Thames Estuary was still probably the world's busiest waterway, a fact hard to grasp half a century on. The Port of London was Europe's largest, and handled one-third of all Britain's foreign trade _ every dock and berth up to St Katherine's Dock and the Pool, by the Tower, was still in use. From the East End boroughs to Hull coastal towns large and small were still leading their traditional maritime lives, in spite of the 1930s slump. In other words this was before the great decline of East Coast seaports, fishing and shipbuilding.

The focus of the naval and civilian shipping routes was the Nore, the lightship and small sandbank where the Rivers Thames and Medway meet and widen into the North Sea. It gave its name (for "landlubbers" an obscure one even then) to one of the four commands into which the Navy divided Home Waters. The Commander-in-Chief Nore (at the outbreak of war Admiral Sir Henry Brownrigg) was responsible for the Dover Strait and the North Sea between East Anglia and the Low Countries*. His headquarters and shore establishment at Chatham bore the name HMS *Pembroke*, after an old wooden training ship on the Medway. His command was divided into four Sub-Commands, each under a Flag Officer in Charge (FOIC) with the rank of rear-admiral or vice-admiral: Dover (under Ramsay), Sheerness, or the Nore proper (Marrack), London (Boyle), and Harwich (Harris). The respective shore bases were HMSs *Wasp, Wildfire, Pembroke IV,* and *Badger.* In October 1939 a reorganisation made Dover an independent command (under "Vice-Admiral, Dover") and transferred the Humber Sub-Command (FOIC _ Rear-Admiral Pridham) from Rosyth Command to Nore. The limits of the new Nore Command were a line joining Flamborough Head (Yorkshire) to Horn Reef (near the German-Danish border) in the north, and another from North Foreland (Kent) to Walcheren (Holland) in the south.

The Nore Command eventually undertook a huge diversity of activities. But throughout the Second World War its central concern was the East Coast Convoy Route. The need to gather as much merchant shipping as possible into escorted convoys was the most hard-earned lesson of the 1914-18 sea war, and therefore this one at least was remembered in 1939.

The shipping lane most vulnerable _ because it faced Germany across the North Sea _ was that down the East Coast of England to the Port of London. Later, when the German conquest of France all but blocked the Dover Strait, nearly all London-bound shipping had to use that East Coast route, but even in 1939 it was very busy, mainly with colliers supplying London homes and power stations from the mines of the North East. However open to attack, this traffic could not be allowed to stop. London's coal-fired electricity fed not only the vast capital city but, around its periphery, new high-technology industries essential to modern war. To have carried the necessary coal, and also oil, to London by rail or road would have

---

*the southern North Sea has no distinct English name. The Germans consider it part of the "Kanal" (Channel) or call it by the Dutch term "Den Hoofden" (the heads).

THE NORE & 1939

been quite impossible, since it would have demanded every train or lorry in the country.

The first East Coast convoy sailed on 6 September 1939, and initially one passed in each direction every other day. In the south the convoys assembled or dispersed in a commodious anchorage off Southend Pier, safe from U-Boats inside a long net boom, through which the Yantlet Gate could be opened into the outer Thames Estuary or southern North Sea. The northern terminus was the little port of Methil on the Firth of Forth, but most ships left or joined at Blyth, the Tyne, Sunderland, Middlesbrough or Hull, while some worked from Ipswich. Northbound convoys were codenamed FN and southbound FS, both followed by numbers. When a sequence reached 100, another was started at 1. It is therefore possible to read (for instance, in this book) of two convoys with the same number but separated by six months or so. As a simpler code the two FS convoys at sea at any one time were distinguished by the names "Agent" and "Arena", while the FNs were called "Booty" and "Pilot". For part of 1941 faster northbound vessels were separated off into convoys codenamed EC (or "Lunch" and "Bread"): these went straight round into the Atlantic.

In order to facilitate navigation and minesweeping the convoys followed a fixed route, codenamed QZS 148 from Southend to Yarmouth, QZS 288 from there to Sheringham, QZS 152 from there to near the Humber, and QZS 254 further north. (A "QZ" was a mined area, and a "QZS" an Allied safe or swept channel _ though the prefix SCZ was used for the first few months of the war). The channel was under a mile wide, and was minesweept daily. It was marked by large red conical buoys at intervals, purely wartime phenomena which replaced some of the old lights and buoys as "seamarks". From early in 1940 the route between Aldeburgh and Sheringham was made two-lane in order to confuse the enemy and enable convoys to pass each other in darkness in more safety. FS convoys normally took the outer route and FN the inner, but in the event of gales or enemy attacks the FSs could be switched to the inner route (See Map). There was also an inshore channel, narrower and within a few miles of the coast: it was used mainly by barges and coasters plying independently over short distances. All routes were approached from the ports by west-east lanes. Port of London pilot boats met or left convoys in the Barrow Deep. Shipping movements in the Nore Command were thus as complicated as train routes

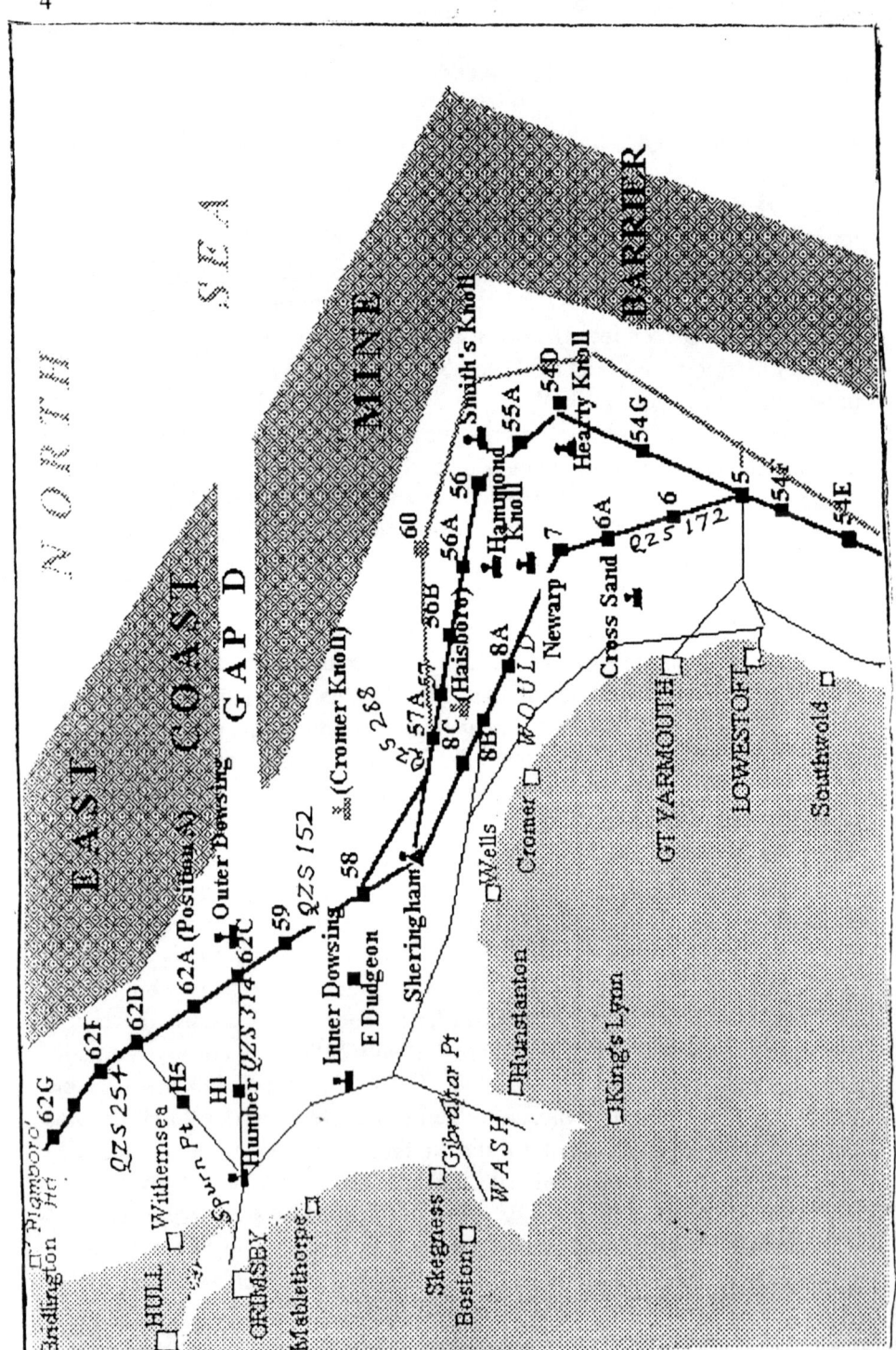

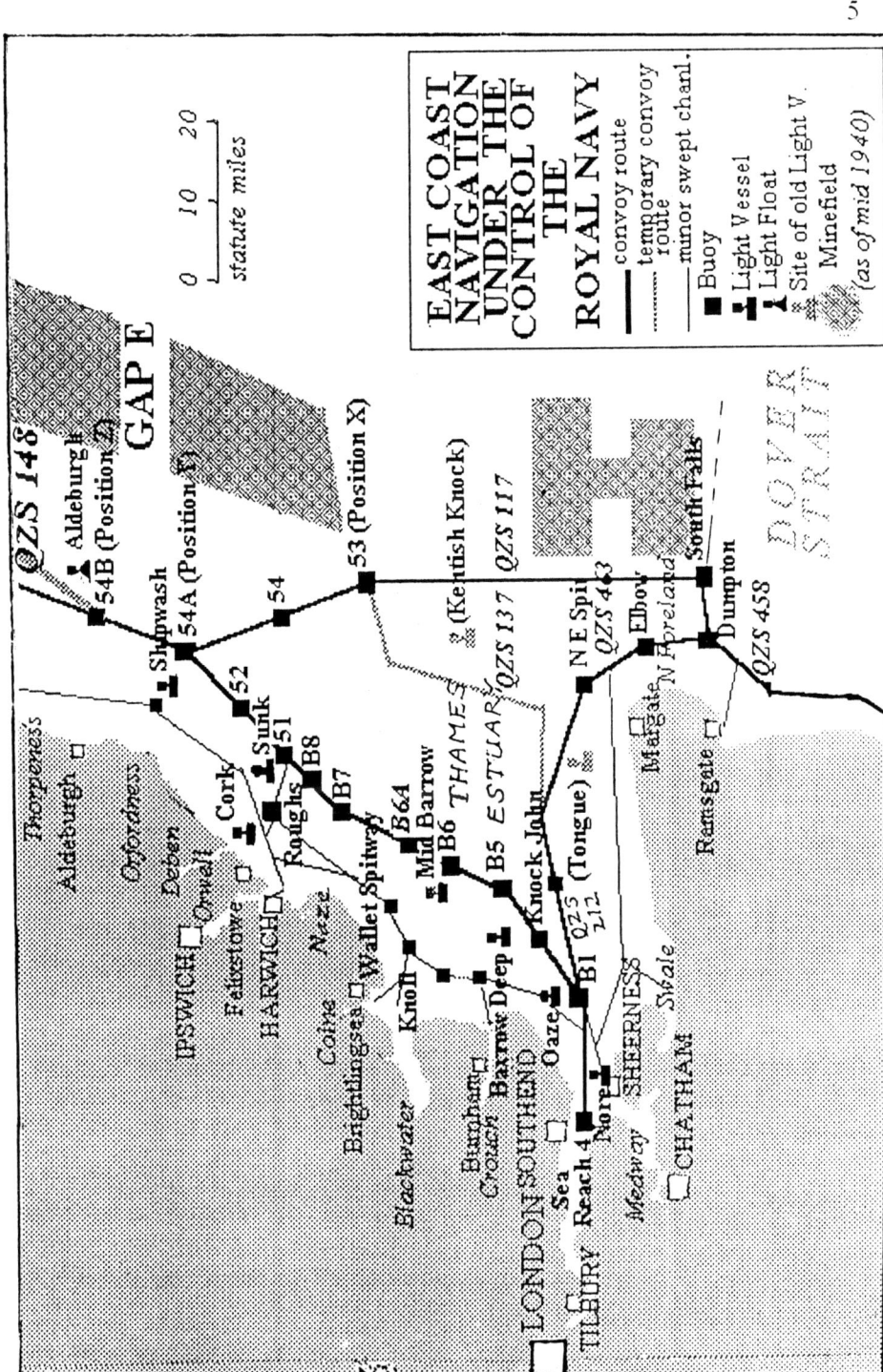

THE NORE & 1939

on a main line. The East Coast convoys were escorted principally by the Rosyth Escort Force, composed of destroyers and sloops and ranging from its base near the Forth Bridge to Harwich, or sometimes the Thames mouth. Additional escort, and all minesweeping, was provided by the naval bases en route, particularly Harwich. The original Rosyth destroyers were eleven of the V/W class, the last to be built in the First World War, and the most numerous ever constructed for the Royal Navy _ plus one famous veteran, the *Broke*. Obsolete for fleet work, these destroyers had been partially rearmed with Anti-Aircraft guns and reclassified as "escort vessels". A "V/W" was easily identifiable at a distance by her tall thin forward and short fat aft funnel. The "REF" also included some slower, but more modern, and depth-charge-equipped, sloops, named after birds or coastal towns. A third East Coast escort ship was the Anti-Aircraft Cruiser. These were survivors of a class of 4,200-ton* First War light crusiers which had been entirely rearmed with "AA" guns, ranging from .303 to four inches in calibre. Six of them _ *Cairo, Calcutta, Carlisle, Coventry, Curacoa,* and *Curlew* _ constituted Rear-Admiral J P Vivien's 20th Cruiser Squadron and worked from Grimsby in the first half of 1940.

Harwich's escort ships were corvettes and anti-submarine trawlers. The former, which arrived early in 1940, were a class of sturdy little five-hundred-tonners nicknamed "Ducks" owing to their waterbird names; *Guillemot, Mallard, Pintail, Puffin, Shearwater, Sheldrake* and *Widgeon*. *Puffin's* commander, Lt-Cdr Earl Beatty, was the son of the famous Jutland admiral. They were organised into two flotillas, the so-called 1st and 2nd Anti-Submarine Striking Forces, and as their title suggests caried depth charges as main armament. However, they never found any U-Boats to sink,

---

*naval displacement. One naval ton=(in effect) about half a gross registered ton, the measurement usually quoted for merchant ships. A 4,200-ton warship is therefore about the same size as a 2,100-ton merchant ship. In this book all warship tonnages are displacements (including those of civilian vessels requisitioned by the Navy), and all merchant ship tonnages are "GRT". The difference arises because displacements are a measure of actual weight, and mercantile tonnage of cubic capacity. I shall not refer to mercantile "net tonnage", but one net ton is about equal to four naval tons. I hope purists will not quibble with my rule-of-thumb explanation.

AN EAST COAST CONVOY

ABOVE: An East Coast convoy seen from the Harwich A/S trawler *Sapphire*. Note the 4-inch & quadruple 2-pdr ("pom-pom") guns.
BELOW: Sailors of the Harwich-based Polish destroyer *Burza*, with the ship's mascot and her offspring. *(IWM)*

THE NORE & 1939

and remained at Harwich for the rest of the war as invaluable convoy escorts and rescue ships. The A/S trawlers were the largest and best-armed of what became a huge fleet of both purchased and requisitioned fishing vessels operated by the Navy's Nore Command. Most of the local A/S ones were named after trees or jewels.

From the outset RAF Coastal Command 16 Group Ansons provided overhead lookout for the convoys from Detling (near Maidstone) and Bircham Newton (near Wells in Norfolk), and from October fighters from Manston (near Margate), Martlesham (near Ipswich), etc, flew escort: indeed for the rest of the war this was to be a major and rather resented chore for most East Coast fighter squadrons.

An East Coast convoy kept a uniform speed of only eight knots, except when anchored during mist which made navigation impossible. It ranged in size from five to sixty ships, with an escort mostly of four or five. In overall command of a convoy was the senior officer of the escort group, but each convoy also had a Commodore, usually an RNR lieutenant-commander, who travelled on a merchant ship and was responsible for mustering, speed and station-keeping. In large convoys there was also a Vice-Commodore, an ordinary merchant captain on a second ship.

In the quieter periods of the war, and in the right weather, the Thames-Forth voyage could be almost a joyride, with sparkling sea and blue sky, and the clear light common in the east of England. But (and leaving aside the human foes) sometimes a ship had to grope through almost impenetrable gloom, nauseously pitched on roller-coaster storm waves, or found herself coated in winter white. Most typically, however, the columns of coal smoke rose so black and so gradually, the ships were so grimy and slow, the sea was so grey and the sky so leaden, as to suggest a still black and white photograph rather than a live scene.

The convoy system was full of hitches at the start, and made many naval officers despair. There were numerous complaints by the Navy about ships straggling, RAF planes coming down low and unannounced and provoking fire, supposedly darkened navigation lights still showing and operational ones not showing, and fishing boats getting in the way. The navigation lights, theoretically supposed to flash simultaneously, in fact failed to synchronise, and this in spite of the BBC time signals. "Obtaining a fix then becomes quite an exciting game", commented the captain of the sloop

THE NORE & 1939

Pelican on 8 April 1940. Some of the merchant captains were also a problem. The commander of the destroyer *Valorous* reported the master of the *Swynfleet* to be "incompetent" that 11 April: "When hailed he said he did not know how to signal". A similar complaint was made by the escort commander of FS 78 on 24 May, who reported that "Vice-Commodore *Westavon* could not read Morse and therefore made a poor Vice-Commodore". This man could not have been very popular with the Navy, for this was the second complaint made about him. On the previous 26 November another escort commander had criticised him for holding up FN 42 by dallying for extra provisions in the Thames. Both *Swynfleet* and *Westavon* were to succumb to enemy action.

It was therefore fortunate for the Nore Command that for the first few weeks of war the enemy rarely showed himself. The Germans were as yet unready for a campaign against British shipping other than by the pocket battleships and handful of U-Boats already at large in the Atlantic. Their airforce had strict instructions to bomb no British town, including London and the East Coast ports, and initially was preoccupied in Poland. Their merchant fleet had shied away from British waters during the fortnight leading up to war, though SS *Pomona* was still at Tilbury Docks at the outbreak _ Captain Siebert and his loyally Nazi crew set fire to her after failing to force an exit through a line of lighters, and were interned in Butlin's Holiday Camp, Clacton. The cargo and passenger trade between Hull and Scandinavia, and Harwich and the Low Countries, was resumed after a few days, though the Harwich ferries (SS *Felixstowe* and *Train Ferries 1-3*) were displaced from Parkeston Quay by the Navy and ran instead from Ipswich.*
The Port of London was undiminished, and the Thames considered safe enough for the OA (West Africa-bound) convoys to assemble there and sail via the Dover Strait.

In the first ten weeks of war twelve merchant ships were sunk by enemy action in the Nore Command _ in every case, apparently, by mines, though oddly none had been swept before or after the sinkings in their vicinities in several of these cases. Some people believed the trouble was due to the torpedoes of U-Boats, and an anxious watch for these craft ensued, bordering at times on a panic like that in the early months of the First World War. Booms, with their numerous attendant vessels, were immediately installed across the Humber and the Harwich entrance as well as the Thames

---

**Train Ferry No 3's master, R R Nugent, died at his native Dovercourt as recently as 1989 _ aged 101.

THE NORE & 1939

mouth. It is now known that the magnetic mines which sank SS *Magdapur* off Aldeburgh and *Goodwood* off Bridlington on 10 September came from U13 and U15 respectively. On that same day, while covering FN 3, *Broke* thought she saw a submarine periscope, dropped depth charges, and optimistically took the resulting column of water and silence as evidence she might have accounted for one raider. By October a barrage of cables, nets and mines had been laid across the Dover Strait (then still in the Nore Command). On the seabed indicator loops were placed _ electromagnetised cables which detected the steel hulls of submerged submarines passing overhead. Atlantic U-Boats had been using the Dover Strait and therefore the Nore Command as a shortcut to and from home, but the barrage and loops put a stop to that. U 12 was sunk on 8 October and U 40 five days later. U-Boats continued for some months to roam the Command, but in order to sow mines and retreat, not to press attacks with torpedoes. Apart from midget-submarines late in the war, U-Boats only sank two ships in the Nore Command by direct attack _ one on 4 December 1939, the other (the tanker *British Councillor*) on 2 February 1940, and both off Withernsea near the northern edge of the area. The several sinkings by U-Boat torpedo listed, for example, in Rohwer's history are fictitious, or, rather, were due to U-Boat *mines*. Many of the alleged U-Boat sightings by British ships seem to have been imaginary, and plenty of depth charges were released onto harmless flotsam. On just the one occasion there was no mistake: on 31 May 1940, during the Dunkirk Evacuation, the Rosyth sloop *Weston* destroyed U 13 off Lowestoft. However most of the mines which sank ships in the Nore Command at this early period *had* come from U-Boats, including those which accounted for three foreign vessels (one French, one Greek, and one Norwegian) near the Outer Dowsing, east of the Humber, in October.*

Apart from U-Boat torpedoes and mines, the Luftwaffe gradually brought its power to bear on East Coast shipping, in imitation of tactics briefly tried by German planes in 1917. In the first attack of the new war, on 29 September 1939, three bombs were unsuccessfully aimed by a single enemy plane off the Humber. On 21 October a bold and full-scale raid was attempted, and failed disastrously. Four Heinkel He 115 seaplanes out of a force of nine, probably carrying torpedoes, were shot down by RAF Fighter Command's 46 Squadron off Withernsea in broad daylight, and fell like so many wounded ducks. The convoy which was to have been attacked, and its

---

*most of the U-Boats mentioned in my first two chapters were of the smaller, 250-ton "coastal" varieties _ i.e. Types IIB and IIC.

escorting AA cruiser, had also briefly opened fire. One three-man German crew was rescued three days later by the destroyer *Gurkha* and landed at Parkeston Quay, and another trio was washed up dead at Happisburgh (Norfolk) on 2 November. Probably partly as a result there were no more major air raids on convoys until the following summer. There were some minor attacks. The sloop *Auckland* was strafed by an He 111 on 11 January 1940 without effect. On 6 March the Harwich corvettes *Mallard* and *Puffin* were ineffectively bombed and machine-gunned while escorting a convoy near 54E Buoy, off Southwold. On the following day FN 12 was attacked some after leaving the Nore, but the raiders were driven off by the destroyer *Whitley*'s guns.

At this period the enemy much preferred to make air attacks on ships sailing independently and well away from the coast, in waters outside the range of British low-altitude RDF (radar) and the normal Fighter Command air cover. Indeed in the winter months of 1939-40 these raids mounted into a ferocious little campaign.

The first such attack was on 7 October 1939. The Harwich minesweepers *Niger* and *Selkirk* were near Brown Ridge, fifty miles east of Yarmouth, and having been promised a special RAF escort by their FOIC, paid no heed when a plane approached from the west. They were therefore lucky to avoid the bombs of a Dornier Do 18 flying boat. Rear-Admiral Harris had failed to obtain the escort but also to inform them. The Admiralty criticised him and the minesweepers, which had not fired recognition signals. Yet on 10 November almost exactly the same thing happened. The Harwich-based Polish destroyers *Blyskawica* and *Grom* had gone out to the same area to look for reported drifting lifeboats. Because two British aircraft were involved in the search the destroyers did not challenge two He 115s, one of which narrowly missed *Blyskawica* with a torpedo. Ten days later the Harwich destroyer *Boadicea* was missed by a few bombs from one of a group of eight German planes, flying very high up. That same day *Gipsy*, another Harwich destroyer, found three survivors from a German reconnaissance plane which had been shot down in the Galloper area by RAF 74 (fighter) Squadron.

Two hundred Yarmouth and Lowestoft fishing boats were still working the sandbanks off Norfolk at this period, and making an important contribution to the nation's food supplies. On 17 December the Luftwaffe

THE NORE & 1939

made a sudden attack on several of these, and others from the Humber and the Forth working further north. Several boats were sunk, including the Grimsby-based *Pearl*, fishing seventy miles north-east of Yarmouth _ the first fishing vessel to be lost from enemy action in the Nore Command. In January 1940 the Blitz on vulnerable shipping intensified. On the 9th, flying at minimum height above freezing mist in order to avoid detection, several He 111s climbed a little way into clear visibility when they neared the East Coast "QZS", spotted the upperworks of various scattered ships, and attacked with bombs tumbling and machine guns blazing. North of Cromer two small merchantmen, the *Upminster* of London and the *Oakgrove* of Glasgow, were sunk. To their east SS *Chrysolite* was damaged. The Trinity House tender *Reculver* was one her way out from Yarmouth to the Cockle and other nearby lightships with relief crewmen when she was repeatedly blasted with bombs and raked with bullets. Her captain, W J Lees, and thirty-one more of the forty men on board were wounded, of whom two (including one of the lightship men) died. The Grimsby A/S trawler *Hammond* towed her back to base, while the Gorleston lifeboat landed the crew. That evening German radio broadcast triumphally, each bulletin ending with the spirited song "Wir Fahren Gegen Engelland" (We Sail Against England).

Off the Humber two days later, aboard SS *Keynes*, Radio Officer C A Coleman continued to transmit the SOS though wounded by a shower of bullets and bomb fragments, while Seaman S L Brown retaliated against the raider with the ship's only gun. She sank, but her gallant crew were rescued: Coleman won the OBE and Brown the BEM, and both were given the Lloyd's War Medal _ the first such decorations for the Merchant Navy on the East Coast. On the 13th the Hammond Knoll Light Vessel was repeatedly shot up and the Cromer lifeboat had to land her two shell-shocked survivors.

This early Blitz came to a head on the last three days of that January, over a sea now studded with ice floes and off a coast buried in snow. On the 29th the merchantman *Stanburn* was sunk off Flamborough Head, and the East Dudgeon Light Vessel off Skegness _ her eight crew had to abandon her in a gale, and when their lifeboat survived only one man (John Sanders of Yarmouth) survived. On the Latvian *Tautmila*, attacked in spite of the national emblems painted on her sides, bombs killed seven men. The captain (ironically a Baltic German), his wife and thirteen more crew made shore in a boat while the wreck drifted ashore at Walcot, near Cromer, with one additional survivor still aboard. Next day a 7,200-ton tanker, *Voreda*, was sunk and two more ships were damaged near Hearty Knoll, off Caister. *Larwood*, of the trawler group to which *Hammond* belonged, was near-missed alongside Yarmouth, while her crew shot steadily though unsuccessfully back. Nearby SS *Royal Crown* was badly damaged and abandoned, but beached herself at Covehithe: the attacking pilot, Feldwebel Moldenhauer, was acclaimed in German propaganda. Meanwhile SS *Highwave* had broken down, straggled from a convoy, and been spotted by a German reconnaissance plane. While awaiting assistance from Harwich she was bombed and sunk near the Kentish Knock Light Vessel, which was herself attacked.

Seventy air attacks had been experienced by vessels of all kinds in the Nore Command in those three days. The Yarmouth fishing fleet had taken many of them. For a time the Navy sent out its own armed trawlers from Grimsby to escort them, but an angry meeting of fishermen claimed that not only did these afford no protection but *attracted* German planes. RAF Coastal Command Ansons at Bircham Newton were already flying cover over the fishing grounds against U-Boat attacks: some Blenheim fighters were now posted to that base to guard against bombers. Both types of mission were inevitably dubbed "Kipper patrols". The Germans were not interested in Battle of Britain-type aerial combat at this period, and the Luftwaffe attacks fell away somewhat.

The British Government claimed that attacking lightships had been in violation of International Law, because they were for the safety of ships from all nations and not to support the war effort (Drax, the C-in-C Nore, had angrily vetoed an ungentlemanly suggestion that Trinity House should report German air activity to the Navy and RAF). An MP, Sir Archibald Southby, described the German tactics as "on a par with shooting a hospital nurse in the back". The press revived the language of 1914-18, and spoke of "atrocities", "villainies", "frightfulness" and "piracy". *Punch* printed a cartoon showing a giant Nazi vulture swooping on a lightship. Over the next few months the East Dudgeon, Kentish Knock and Edinburgh Light Vessels were replaced by buoys and the Outer Dowsing, Hammond Knoll, Smith's Knoll, Aldeburgh and Cross Sand by red light floats. The Newarp, Spurn, Bull, Cromer Knoll, Outer Gabbard, Galloper, Tongue, Haisborough and Corton Light Vessels were removed altogether. In 1941 most of the lightships

THE NORE & 1939

still remaining were withdrawn after a fresh round of attacks.

The bombing of neutral ships also caused moral outrage. The Germans had even, and on more than one occasion, attacked their Italian allies (though Italy was still neutral as yet). On 9 March the *Amelia Lauro* was reduced to a floating scrapheap near Smith's Knoll: though she reached the Humber she was too damaged to sail again and was eventually used as a harbour blockship. Survivors were rescued by *Pintail* from Harwich and the Rosyth sloop *Londonderry*. Two of her crew had died: after they were buried at Yarmouth her captain, Lepaci, delivered an impassioned speech against their killers.

The Germans maintained that British lightships were marking the routes of warships and war convoys, and were therefore fair game. As for the neutrals, they either accused them of supplying the British war effort, or claimed that they had mistaken them for Allied ships.

The bombing, U-Boat forays and mining by the enemy coincided with intelligence reports of an imminent German invasion of the Low Countries, and in November 1939 Hitler did indeed intend to launch such an attack, to be dissuaded by his generals and the worsening weather. Consequently strong forces of modern destroyers (as distinct from the itinerant and antique V/Ws of the REF) were brought to Harwich and Immingham. For instance *Cossack* and five more of the Tribal class visited Harwich in October, and at the end of the month no less than seventeen destroyers from four flotillas put into that harbour in the soace of twenty-four hours. In November the Harwich destroyer force was fixed as the 1st Flotilla, made up of the leader *Codrington*, a varying number of G class, and three Polish vessels recently escaped from the Nazis in their native Baltic _ *Blyskawica* (Lightning), *Burza* (Storm) and *Grom* (Thunder). At Immingham were the eight J class of the 7th Flotilla, commanded by Captain Mack, and the various J and K class of Captain Lord Louis Mountbatten's 5th Flotilla. All these destroyers were employed on routine patrols of from one to three days each, between them covering the whole North Sea and Dover Strait. One major duty was to check merchant shipping running down the coast of the Low Countries, thereby enforcing the Allied blockade of the German North Sea ports. Any merchantman suspected of being German or trading with Germany was "arrested" and taken to the Downs anchorage off Ramsgate. The Harwich destroyers, aided by the trawlers *River Clyde, Stella*

THE NORE & 1939

Leonis and *William Wesney*, took in thirteen of these, one of which turned out to be the German SS *Phaedra*.

For readers interested in the proper Royal navy nomenclature, these destroyer flotillas were officially known by the abbreviations D1, D7 and D5, and their senior officers as Captain D1, etc.

Frequently in and out of the various East Coast bases at this period were the five specially converted minelaying destroyers of the 20th Flotilla: *Esk, Express, Icarus, Intrepid* and *Ivanhoe*, plus the brandnew minelayer *Princess Victoria*. They were laying a huge mine barrier along the seaward flank of the convoy route. This eventually came as far south as the Dover minefields, and was fifteen miles wide. At first it was in fact a huge bluff, since in spite of being declared to the shipping of all nations it consisted only of shading on a chart _ this was because it took eight months to manufacture and lay all the one hundred thousand mines needed (one third of them for Nore Command). The mines were laid at a density of ten or eleven to the square mile (so much for the cartoon impression of minefields!), meaning that a submarine crossing the barrier stood a prohibitively dangerous three-to-two chance of striking one. When a mine was torn from its moorings by heavy seas its detonators were automatically disconnected _ at least in theory! The field had two levels. Moored well underwater, to stop U-Boats and large warships, were the round H2 (First World War-surplus) Types or (new) "belted" Type XIVs: specimens of both can still be seen as red-painted charity money boxes at East Coast ports. Motor boats with shallow draughts could pass over these deep mines. At the lesser depth were the small antenna mines, for sinking E-boats. As may be imagined the mine barrier had a number of lateral channels for British warships. Gap A was off the Forth, B off Blyth in Northumberland, C off the Tees, D off the Humber, and E off Aldeburgh and linking through to Harwich.

"D20" had also made some offensive minelaying forays. These had had little impact until 22 February 1940, when they paid off in an extraordinary way. German destroyers were leaving the Heligoland Bight for "Operation Wikinger", their first raid on the Humber fishing fleet, then busy on the Dogger Bank. They were mistaken for British vessels by some He 111s from the unit which had recently been bombing Allied and neutral ships off the East Coast. As the destroyers *Leberecht Maass* and *Max Schultz* zig-zagged to avoid their own side's bombs they left the swept channel and ran on

THE NORE & 1939

British mines: both sank, and with the loss of almost six hundred lives. There were no more attempts by German destroyers to get at the East Coast fishing fleet.

The New Year of 1940 saw a big buildup of Royal Navy strength in the Nore Command, especially at Harwich. Minelayers, patrol destroyers, escort corvettes and trawlers, motor torpedo boats, submarines and AA cruisers were all present. But by now everything was eclipsed by the minesweepers and their campaign.

2
MAGNETIC MINE MENACE

On the morning of 13 November 1939 the Harwich-based destroyers *Blanche* and *Basilisk* were escorting the large minelaying cruiser *Adventure* from Grimsby down to Portsmouth. The three ships lay stopped near the Tongue Light Vessel, about ten miles north of Margate, owing to fog and problems *Blanche* was having with her paravanes (a form of anti-mine gear). As they began to edge out of the misty dawn gloom at 0514 an explosion was heard and seen in the sea well ahead and to starboard. Eleven minutes later there was a blast right under *Adventure*, and no fewer than sixty-two of her crew were injured (at least three of them fatally) by being hurled down hatchways or against bulkheads. The ships stopped and waited for the Ramsgate tug *Fabia*, which took *Adventure* in tow while *Basilisk* conveyed her casualties to Sheerness and *Blanche* stood guard against possible U-Boats. No sooner had everyone got under way just after 0800, than *Blanche* was blasted aft, splitting her deck, buckling a bulkhead, and letting the sea into her engine room. The bridge was wrecked by the shock, which hurled the wheel and instruments about, stunned Lt-Cdr Aubrey and all his officers, knocked out the radio and internal telephones, and turned on the sirens at full blast _ so that shouted orders were drowned out. One crewman was killed and ten were injured. It seemed that *Blanche* might be towed in by another of the Ramsgate tugs, but as she waited she began to heel over dangerously, and it was decided to abandon her, soon after which she sank.

While warnings were radioed to other shipping, the Harwich patrol destroyer *Glowworm* stationed herself east of the Tongue Light Vessel to redirect Thames-bound shipping, and the trawler *Myrtle* did likewise for vessels coming out of the river. But meanwhile a merchantman, *Ponzano*, had also gone down only a few miles to the south-east. Yet a third ship, the large *Matra*, was lost that evening in the same area, in spite of a thorough search for mines and U-Boats. Over the next month fourteen vessels of various types were to be sunk around the Tongue Lightship, including a second warship _ the Sheerness trawler *Mastiff*, while scouring the seabed for mines with nets on 20 November _ and the 8,800-ton Dutch liner *Spaardam* on the 27th.*

---

*There is insufficient space in this book to list every wartime ship sinking in the text, but all the names and locations can be traced in the list and charts in Appendix I.

MAGNETIC MINE MENACE

Of course mines were suspected, but none were at first swept or even seen. None had actually come into direct contact with any ship. This came on top of twelve unexplained sinkings in September and October, starting with that of *Magdapur* near the Aldeburgh Napes on 10 September. Were the mines being triggered at a distance by, for instance, the hull magnetism of the ships? Complicating the picture was the many German contact mines near the Humber, which originated from an undetected offensive foray by steam torpedo-boats and destroyers (commanded by Rear-Admiral Lütjens*) on the night of 17-18 October. It was eventually realised that all the seven sinkings in the area between *Orsa* (on the 21st) and *Juno* (on the 30th) inclusive were due to these mines. Two hundred loose enemy mines were washed up on the Yorkshire coast alone, having broken away from their moorings in the autumn gales. The international press first heard of magnetic mines on 19 November, when the master of the Danish SS *Canada* informed a public inquiry in Copenhagen that his ship had been sunk by such a weapon off the Humber on the 3rd.

On 18 November the 8309-ton Dutch passenger liner *Simon Bolivar*, of the Royal Netherlands Steamship Company, was bound for Rotterdam to Tilbury, and thence was to go to the West Indies. When, at 1230, she was approaching Longsand Head, twenty-five miles off Harwich, she was rocked by a severe underwater explosion. She lay stopped and wirelessed for assistance, but within fifteen minutes there was a second blast immediately beneath the bridge. The hull was torn open and the liner went down amid escaping steam and oil with the loss of 130 lives, including Captain Voorspuij, though the sea was sufficiently shallow for her funnels and masts to remain clear of the water.

A destroyer, a trawler and Captain Bonser's train ferry from Harwich brought 140 survivors, mostly women and children, to Parkeston Quay, while others were placed on board passing London-bound ships. The Walton and Clacton lifeboats put out and circled well into the night in a vain effort to find more survivors. A clearing station for the wounded was set up in Parkeston railway Hotel by Harwich Civil Defence group, led by C M F Bernard. Local newspapermen arrived and were amazed to see survivors coated in black oil sitting amid the gleaming sliver cutlery and white table cloths of the hotel dining room. The wounded were taken to Shotley naval hospital and the Essex County Hospital in Colchester. The most pathetic sight were the

---

*later lost on the battleship *Bismarck* in the Atlantic.

children, some of whom had lost their parents either temporarily or permanently, and who screamed hysterically or clung, dazed, to their rescuers. A story went the rounds that one child had been put with a black woman on the assumption that she was his mother, but on being scrubbed was found to be white. Civil Defence workers cleaned up the victims and provided them with tea and new clothes. While this humanitarian work was in progress the air raid sirens sounded and everyone had to take shelter underground.

Over the next five days six more ships went down off Harwich, all of them between the Shipwash in the north and Longsand in the south. A Yugoslav vessel was lost in the former location only half an hour after *Simon Bolivar*. A large British tanker, the *James L Maguire*, was damaged but towed into Harwich. The largest sinking was, of all nationalities, Japanese _ the passenger liner *Terukuni Maru*, of Tokyo, went down ten miles off the Naze on the 21st. Holed to starboard, she listed for a long time before capsizing, so that all her occupants escaped, including W J Mark, a British pilot taken on at Ramsgate. As she healed over the lookouts at Landguard Fort, opposite Harwich, saw the huge rising sun painted on her side to ward off attackers. The captain, Matukura, gave an interview to the British press, which also published photographs of the rescue and the passengers' praise for the Japanese crew. Pearl Harbor and the Burma Railway still lay in the future.

That evening was mild and calm, as 1st Destroyer Flotilla prepared to leave Harwich Harbour on a U-Boat hunting sweep around the Cork Lightship. At about 1900 two enemy floatplanes (variously identified as He 59s or 115s) came in over the harbour entrance at less than 150 feet, dropped what Landguard Fort reported as "objects apparently attached to parachutes", machine-gunned the fort's observation post, and made off. The defences cannot be described as having been ready. The crews of the examination boat and pilot boat had merely waved at the approaching planes, under the impression that they were seaplanes from RAF Felixstowe. The intruders were too low for the heavy AA guns, while the light AA crews were apparently too stunned at seeing their first raiders to respond; and perhaps it seemed wrong to fire on planes from which parachutes were coming.

The Navy sent out light craft to search all round the Landguard Peninsula, and they reported nothing to the Operations Room. Accordingly,

MAGNETIC MINE VICTIMS OFF ESSEX:

(from top to bottom)
Dutch liner *Simon Bolivar*
British collier *Blackhill*
Japanese liner *Terukuni Maru* **(rescue in progress)**
(WI)

THE *GIPSY* SINKING

ABOVE: The destroyer aground in Harwich Harbour entrance, after triggering the magnetic mine. *(WI)*

BELOW: Boys of HMS *Ganges* bringing the body of *Gipsy*'s captain, Lt-Cdr Crossley, to Shotley Naval Cemetary. *(East Anglian Daily Times)*

MAGNETIC MINE MENACE

as planned, the Polish destroyer *Burza* slipped from Parkeston, followed in turn by *Griffin, Gipsy, Grom,* the leader *Keith,* and *Boadicea*. At 2123 *Gipsy,* then just inside the boom gate and level with the fort, was rent by a terrific explosion. The 1340-ton ship broke in half just astern of the bridge, her boilers torn out and one funnel crumpled over the port side like a flimsy cardboard tube.

Fifty-three years later her last surviving officer, Lt R D Franks, recalled how she had only been back at Parkeston for two hours after rescuing the three German airmen (mentioned in Chapter 1), when ordered to sea, and how he and the captain were on the bridge, talking about the mine threat, when they were thrown over onto "B" gun deck by the explosion.

At least fifty of her complement of 150 were lost. Other destroyers, the army launch *Viking* (which was moored close by at the fort jetty) and numerous harbour launches came to the rescue and landed survivors at both Harwich and Felixstowe. Franks found the captain, Lt-Cdr Crossley, injured on the foredeck, but he later died in Shotley Hospital. His grave, along with those of eight other *Gipsy* dead, can still be seen in the naval cemetery up on the hill by Shotley Church. Daybreak revealed *Gipsy* awash up to the bridge, but with her bows jutting out of the water at a sharp angle from the stern, which was entirely underwater. Felixstowe Police records show that floating corpses continued to wash ashore for the next four months.

At 1330 on 22 November the enemy discovered his success when an He 115 reconnointred the harbour from 20,000 feet. Winston Churchill, then First Lord of the Admiralty, was baffled and furious at the loss of a ship inside a defended harbour. That day he personally came to Parkeston and interviewed Rear-Admiral Harris. Churchill wanted to know why the AA guns had not fired, and why so many destroyers had navigated a channel just overflown by enemy minelayers. Someone's head had to roll _ in this case that of the garrison commander (in charge of harbour forts and AA), Lt-Col Ward, for within days he had resigned his command. Churchill's descent on Harwich was not entirely negative, for it was Admiralty pressure which led the RAF to raise the first barrage balloons for the protection of the harbour on 23 November _ and on 3 December a larger "floating", i.e, shipborne, barrage was raised on the Thames mouth between Sheerness and Southend.

22 November was a day of crisis at the Admiralty. In addition to the two Harwich destroyers a dozen merchantmen had been lost, all without

the exact cause being determined. All traffic in and out of the Thames was temporarily stopped. FN convoys were held at Southend, and FS diverted to the Downs anchorage. All navigation lights in the Thames Estuary were extinguished. To by-pass the two danger areas a new channel (QZS 137) was buoyed via the Edinburgh Channels and Knock Deep, and had to be used for the next eight months.

Apart from the *Gipsy* mines, nobody but Germans had witnessed any of the actual minelaying so far. Only since the war have the details concerning it come to light. Captain Bonte's destroyers *Karl Galster, Wilhelm Heidkamp, Hermann Künne,* and *Hans Lüdemann**, covered by a light cruiser and torpedo-boats (more or less the same force that Lütjens had taken to the Humber Sub-Command the previous month), laid the Tongue field on the night of 12/13 November. Commander Hartmann led *Hermann Künne, Berndt von Arnim* and *Wilhelm Heidkamp* to lay the Harwich field on the night of 17th/18th. These were the closest approaches by German warships of such size to the British coast during the war. As yet there was no standing offshore patrol or low-level radar to detect them. Seaplanes had sown forty mines on 20 November, and U-Boats had also been involved: U 15 sowed off Lowestoft on the 15th, U 19 off Orfordness on the 24th, and U 58 off Lowestoft again on the 28th. That the Humber approach was also a target was soon proved by the loss of four or five ships there, including the 14,000-ton Polish liner *Pilsudski* on the 24th, the largest ship to be sunk in the Nore Command throughout the war. Three destroyers led by Commander Bey had been responsible.

On the evening of 22 November Captain A S May, the Southend CSO (second-in-command) gathered thirty-five sailors with nineteen Lewis machine-guns and put them on motor boats and the Pier ready to forestall another *Gipsy* disaster right at the Thames mouth. Enemy planes duly appeared, but according to May sheered away when his improvised barrage opened up. Meanwhile, three miles east, at Shoebury, Captain Lloyd, of the Army's 518 Coast Artillery Regiment, engaged the same raiders with his own Lewis, counting three, one of which he claimed to have downed off Sheerness on the Kent coast opposite. One mine, dangling from a parachute, was seen falling, and then found on the mud at Shoeburyness by Lloyd and his men.

Awaiting such a contingency at the Admiralty in London was a party

---

*The British soon had their revenge on this flotilla. In April 1940 the Royal Navy sank most of it in Narvik Fjord and killed Bonte.

MAGNETIC MINE MENACE

from HMS *Vernon*, Portsmouth, the Navy's Torpedoes and Mines Branch. In charge was Lt-Cdr J G D Ouvry, who had been one of those rescued from the *Mastiff* only two days before. At 10.30 p.m. he, Lt-Cdr Roger Lewis, CPO Baldwin, and Able Seaman Vearncombe left for Southend by car, driving flat out down the A13. At the Palace Hotel, the Southend naval headquarters, they picked up Cdr G T Bowles, of the NOIC's staff, and a press photographer, who was the only person on hand with a flash-equipped camera, and had been sworn to secrecy and to hand over his films of the mine before developing. At Shoeburyness they found Cdr R F P Maton, from the nearby Naval Ordnance Depot, and Lloyd's military guard. Ouvry went out onto the mud and inspected the mine by Aldis lamp while Lewis took an impression of the top of the fuze so that Maton could have brass (i.e, non-magnetic) tools made (they were hacked out overnight in his workshop). Meanwhile the photographer took flash pictures of the mine, which was then lashed down so that it would not be disturbed by the rising tide. An inquisitive civilian then appeared through the gloom further up the beach: in going to head him off troops chanced upon the mine parachute, which had come adrift. As dawn broke the party adjourned to Maton's house for breakfast.

By now the flash photographs had been sent to the Admiralty: a second and better set were now taken with the benefit of daylight. Back on the scene Ouvry and CPO Baldwin, working to beat the next tide, started to defuse the mine while Lewis and Vearncombe watched from a safe distance, making notes for future use in case of disaster. The mine was an aluminium cylinder, eight feet long by two feet one and a half inches in diameter, resting on its side. Ouvry identified the fuze as lying under a copper strip. Bending this aside, he saw a circular plate held in place behind a screwed ring and made watertight with tallow and sealing wax. With his brass screwdriver and brass rod he removed all this, and drew out two explosive discs, "an object resembling a hydrostatic valve" (presumably the magnetic mechanism), and a recognisable standard mine detonator. After the mine had been rolled over he removed similar fittings from a hole on the other side, but then, underneath, found an unexpected cylindrical casing containing a third mechanism, joined by five leads to the interior of the mine. When yet a fourth fitting had been pulled out and brought ashore it started to tick. The party fled but there was no explosion, and when Ouvry crept back the ticking had stopped: it turned

MAGNETIC MINE MENACE

out to be from a clockwork delay mechanism. Ouvry was joined on the foreshore by Dr Wood, a *Vernon* scientist, and they immediately came to a conclusion about the basic principle of the mine. It was not designed to float, but sank onto the seabed, where an oncoming ship raised a pivoted needle which closed a battery-powered detonator circuit, the explosion ensuing after the clockwork delayer had allowed the approaching ship to come overhead. The principle was, in fact, nothing new, since Britain herself had started to manufacture such mines at the end of the previous war.

That afternoon Ouvry called at the Admiralty, and found Churchill and a huge room full of senior officers waiting for him to make a brief technical speech. Next morning (the 24th) Ouvry took the dismembered mine to Woolwich Arsenal, where the fuzes were X-rayed: he then removed them to *Vernon*, where he showed them to a visiting King George VI. Meanwhile his colleague Lt Glenny, aided by Baldwin and Vearncombe, was dealing with the *second* mine dropped by that same plane at Shoeburyness. It was so imbedded that a tractor had to be used to free it. These mines were each 1128 pounds in weight, including 650 pounds of Hexanite explosive. They had small external horns, but these were for anchoring them on the seabed, not detonation. This first type of magnetic mine was christened simply "Type A".

Ouvry was appointed to head a new "Enemy Mines Section" at *Vernon* and put in charge of training disposal personnel. He was in particular contact with the Nore Command HQ, where a new C-in-C, Admiral Drax, took over on 1 December, and with the Nore Minesweeping Officer, Captain J V Wotton. On his visit to Portsmouth the King awarded Ouvry and Lewis the DSO, Glenny the DSC, and Baldwin and Vearncombe the DSM. Baldwin was to be killed tackling another such mine a few weeks later.

Not all the Southend mines had been found by the *Vernon* party, but more soon turned up. On 23 November one spontaneously blew right in the middle of the Thames entrance, due south of Shoeburyness. Two days later two fishermen accidentally detonated one each, the first east of Gravesend, the second on Mucking Flats _ amazingly neither man was hurt, though the first, one Shuttlewood, had been in nothing sturdier than a 30-cwt boat. So far no German contact mines had been found in the southern part of the Nore Command, but in the second half of December several of the enemy's round Type-Xs were swept in the Sunk area, having apparently been laid by a U-

MAGNETIC MINE MENACE

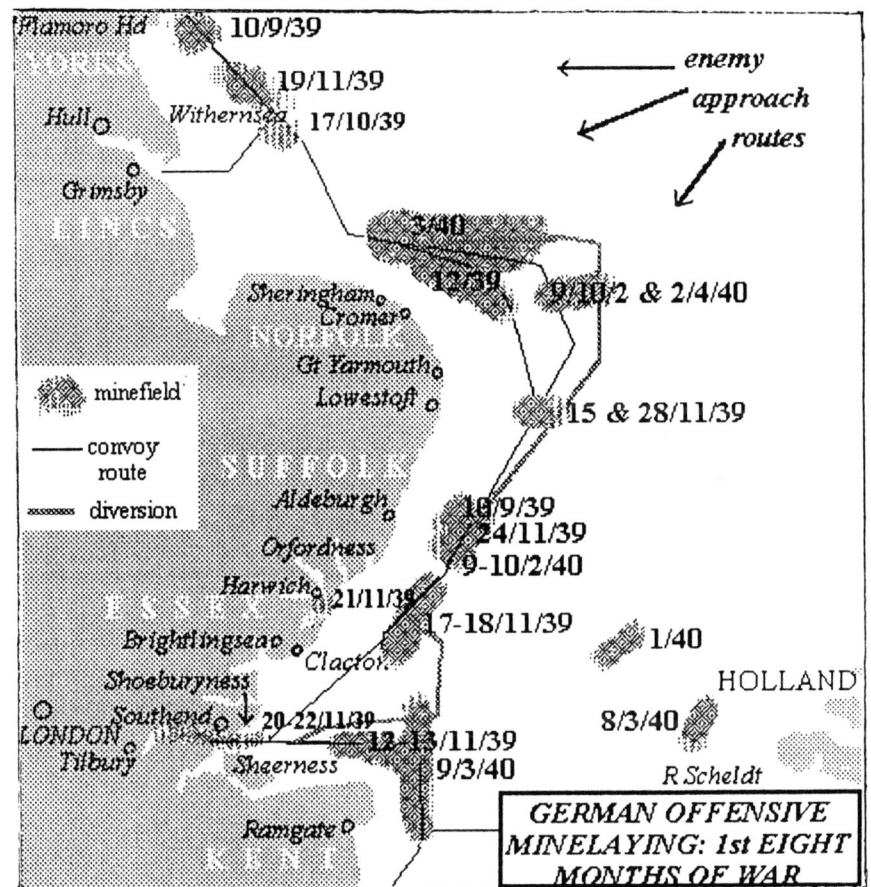

GERMAN OFFENSIVE MINELAYING: 1st EIGHT MONTHS OF WAR

Boat.

Early in December enemy destroyers, U-Boats and aircraft began to scatter magnetic mines off Norfolk, which soon combined with the bombing described in Chapter 1 to make this hitherto safe area as dangerous as the Thames Estuary or the Humber approaches. Double-sized Type-B mines, each of 2107 pounds (about one ton), including 1500 pounds of charge, made their debut. U 59's cargo, off Caister, sank the minesweeping trawler *Washington* and the small merchantman *Marwick Head*. U 60's sank the larger SS *City of Kobe* near Cross Sand. Some weeks later U 56's accounted for the freighters *Onto* and *Portelet* near Smith's Knoll. The mines which sank *Corea* and *King Egbert* off Cromer had been laid by two destroyers on the night of the 7th. When these raiders were challenged by the Immingham destroyer *Jersey*, one, the *Erich Giese*, torpedoed her before fleeing into the darkness. The British ship lost ten crewmen killed, was almost flooded, caught fire in several places, and had to jettison all her explosives. But her sister ship *Juno* towed her home. As soon as the raids started the Admiralty closed the Would Channel between Cromer and the Norfolk sandbanks.

An He 115 involved in this minelaying crashed on Sheringham Beach on the 5th, having struck the tip of one of the tall RDF (radar) towers at West Beckham. The wreckage was hauled ashore and examined by RAF experts, and the body of a crew member named Rödel was given a full military funeral at RAF Bircham Newton.

The day of that crash the Admiralty coincidentally sent out to all Commands a rough description of the Type-A mine, an account of the crude counter-measures so far taken, instructions on safety procedure, and a request for further information. These questions are revealing of the incomplete state of knowledge at this juncture:

_Was there more than one type of aircraft-laid mine? (There were, by now, two).
_Did the submarine-laid mine differ from the aircraft one? (It did not, at least in 1939).
_What were the weights and mechanisms? ((These were being determined at HMS *Vernon*).
_Were there such things as floating "influence" mines, and/or acoustically-detonated ones? (No, not yet).
_Why were ships mined at spots other ships had just crossed? (The mines had delayers, or only fired on repeated magnetic attraction).
_Why had a humming or buzzing been heard for a few seconds before the blast in some cases? (The delayer working).
_Why was there sometimes a bump or a scrape under a ship followed by explosion at a distance? (The ship's bottom touched the mine but it did not blow until after the delay).

Meanwhile the British had been struggling with counter measures. The main *passive* measure was "degaussing". The Shoeburyness mine

TOP LEFT: Harwich-based Polish destroyer *Blyskawica* landing survivors of SS *Sheaf Crest*, mined in the Thames Estuary on 30 Nov, 1939. *(WI)*

TOP RIGHT: British Type XIV contact mine of the kind used in the East Coast Mine Barrier.

LEFT: Capt. Creasy shooting at a loose mine. *(WI)*

The Eagle Line's SS *San Calisto* sinking in the Tongue magnetic minefield on 1 Dec, 1939. Note the armament on her stern. *(WI)*

EARLY LUFTWAFFE BLITZ ON EAST COAST SHIPPING
from the top left:
Tautmila abandoned at Walcot.
Reculver being towed by *Hammond*.
On board the *Royal Crown* wreck.
Amelia Lauro's Capt. Lepaci & a naval officer with the tail of one of the bombs which hit the ship.
Damage to the East Dudgeon Light Vessel.

(*WI*)

MAGNETIC MINE MENACE

mechanism had shown that the German detonators responded to the North-South (or so-called "blue") magnetic fields of ships built in the Northern Hemisphere, where such is the natural polarity, and not to the South-North (or "red") polarity of ships built south of the Equator. Now, acting on this principle, it was possible to reverse the magnetism of ships (the strength of which can be predicted by what physicists call Gauss's Law), and thereby to immunise them by means of electric cables powered from dynamoes and encircling the hulls just above the waterline. Because it was impossible to run exactly the right current through every steel fitting in a ship, degaussing could only give partial protection in practice. And it played havoc with ships' compasses. The huge numbers of vessels (naval and commercial) involved, and the vast mileages of electric cable needed, made the degaussing of all shipping a process lasting months. A temporary substitute was found in "wiping" _ demagnetising a ship by linking it for some hours with a powerful generator ashore or on another vessel (the effect lasted a few months).

Of active measures one that obviously would not work was the towing of gear for snaring and cutting the cables by which conventional, floating or "contact" mines were anchored to the seabed. The existing minesweepers, such as the two *Halcyon*-class flotillas based at Harwich and the Humber respectively, had only this *Oropesa* or "O" gear (as it was called in honour of the first vessel to carry it in the First World War). Magnetics were ground mines _ that is, rested on the seabed instead of floating _ and therefore could not be cut adrift, brought to the surface and blown up by gunfire in the traditional way. Initially some attempts were made to trawl up the new mines with nets, but these perpetually became snared on irrelevant underwater obstacles yet brought up no mines. On the day after the *Gipsy* disaster the Harwich destroyer *Wivern* tried to clear the harbour approach by steaming along it at full speed with a skeleton crew all ready to take to the lifeboats, but (fortunately?) found nothing.

Some scientists not employed by the Admiralty heard about the magnetic mines crisis and offered to help. They should have known better! Larnder, the Air Ministry radar expert who had built the first "RDF" transmitter at Bawdsey and since become head of the Fighter Command Operational Research Section at Stanmore, wrote to Rowe, the head of the Air Ministry Research Establishment, suggesting that motor boats with magnets rushed past the mines "before (they) reached the surface". He assumed that the *whole* mine was magnetic and stuck itself to its victim! He asked Rowe to help him improve his proposal by asking the Admiralty if the mine exploded only "on contact" with a ship or while it was making its "ascent". Rowe's advice to him speaks volumes:

> "...although I have no wish to curb the output of your fertile brain, I really do not think it is possible for us to concern ourselves with the details of the magnetic mine...details of the German mine are very difficult to get hold of _ i.e, the Admiralty is keeping all this to itself. Though I can sympathise with your point of view, Harrogate (the Air Ministry) might well infer that your real job takes insufficient of your time".

Tackling the trouble at source proved unsuccessful. It was known that many of the mines had been sown by seaplanes based on the German Frisian islands of Borkum and Sylt. The RAF repeatedly raided these places, but without result. In any case the Germans had already made their big effort, and the British problem was *existing* minefields.

The most promising methods were clearly going to be those in which the mines were blown from a safe distance by towing or placing large magnets near them. Actually dragging magnets along the seabed had already been tried on the West Coast, and was now tried from Grimsby and Harwich on the East, but the six-foot bar magnets seldom blew mines, and their cables always became entangled _ hence the nickname "Bosun's Nightmare".

There was also the "skid", an electromagnetic coil mounted on a towed raft. One of these achieved the first sweeping of a magnetic mine off Holehaven, the creek west of Canvey Island, on 30 November. Skids could be quickly and cheaply built, and for the best part of a year small shipyards knocked them up while better equipment was in the pipeline. The first skid-towing flotilla, made up of the former pleasure launches *New Prince of Wales* and *Southend Britannia*, started work from Gravesend in December. Skids unfortunately exerted so little magnetic pull that they had to pass right over mines in very shallow water to work, and in so doing destroyed themselves.

A dramatic minesweeper was the SS (now HMS) *Borde*, the mine destructor ship, a converted merchantman with an electromagnet on her bow as heavy as three express locomotives. At Manston airfield, near Margate, three Wellington bombers were fitted with "DWI" (Directional Wireless

MAGNETIC MINE MENACE

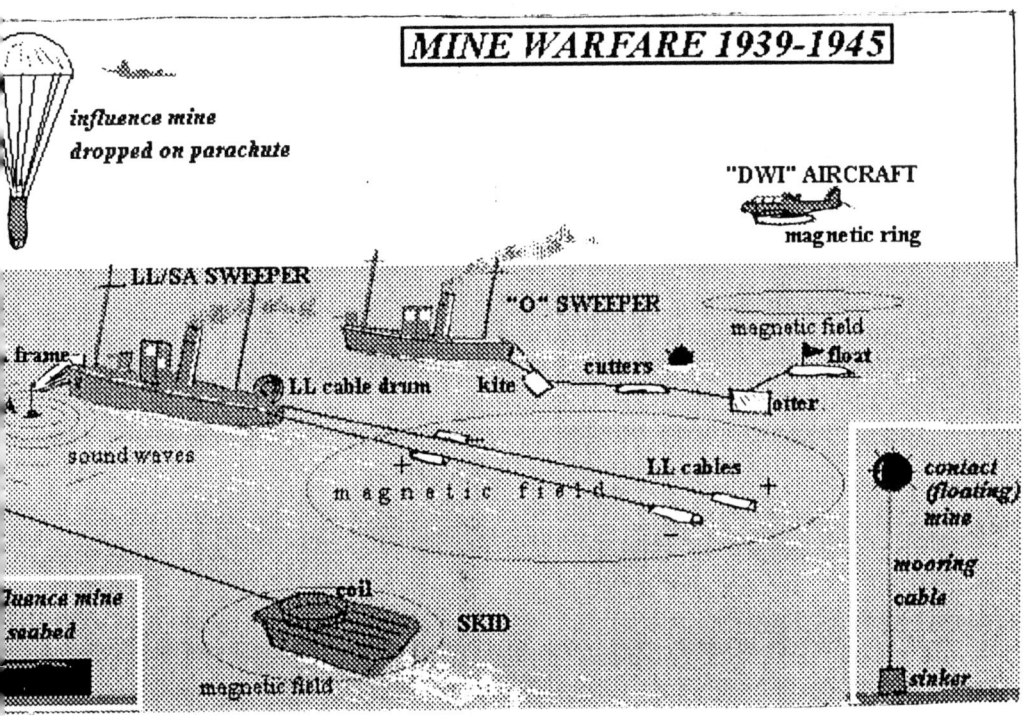

Installation), or, without the codename, magnetic loops under the fuselages for mine detonating. From Professor Haigh, of Greenwich Royal Naval College, and the Admiralty Research Labotarory at Teddington, had come "LL" (pronounced "Double L), two pairs of electric cables, towed parallel on floats, which gave out powerful pulses every few seconds and thereby generated magnetic fields much greater than those of the ordinary, non-pulsing, electromagnets. HMS *Vernon* fitted out an experimental flotilla with these. It included the requisitioned Lowestoft fishing drifters *Evening Primrose, John Alfred, Renascent, Sea Holly* and *Sweet Promise*, and the small tugs *Servitor, Shako, Slogan, Solitaire* and *Souvenir*. Cdr Peterson was in charge, with Lt-Cdr Lewis of Shoeburyness fame as technical adviser. Because the heavy LL cables were being kept afloat with transverse wooden floats they had to be kept stretched out when not in use. In the busy harbour at Sheerness, where the flotilla had assembled, they were cut through night after night by passing ships. Consequently Peterson found a quieter base at

MAGNETIC MINE MENACE

Brightlingsea in the New Year.

To recover mines for defusing and research *Vernon* fitted out eight more locally-requisitioned drifters at Lowestoft; *Achievable, Fisher Boy, Formidable, Lord Cavan, Ray of Hope, Scotch Thistle* and *Silver Dawn*. With Lt-Cdr Cubison in charge most of this Mine Recovery Flotilla based itself on Ramsgate and began the perilous work of netting its samples in December. On the 10th half this force was at work in the original Tongue field, around North East Spit Buoy, near Margate, in the course of Operation "TM2". Cdr Hamond, the bluff and bearded seadog in charge of *Vernon* mine recovery, was on *Ray of Hope*, and Lt Glenny, who defused the second Shoeburyness mine, was on *Silver Dawn*. At 1130 the former drifter was blown to bits: Hamond, the skipper and the mate survived only because the explosion hurled the entire wheelhouse into the sea.

A huge fleet of minesweepers was now assembling in the Thames Estuary. Harwich alone had sixty-eight requisitioned wooden fishing vessels (compared to a mere three, plus six of the larger Halcyons, in the first two or three months of war). No better use could be found for fifty-seven of these than as mine lookouts. At Yarmouth and Lowestoft were fifty more trawlers and drifters, all lookouts. That the mine clearance campaign had scarcely begun is shown by the total swept in Harwich Sub-Command up to the end of 1939 _ precisely zero. (Sheerness had removed a few).

In the New Year two old types of auxiliary minesweeper, both employed locally during the First World War, returned to Harwich waters. In January a flotilla of "Hunt" minesweeping sloops, which had been laid up or converted into survey ships in the 1930s, reappeared in their original role _ *Dundalk, Dunoon, Elgin, Fitzroy, Kellett, Selkirk* and *Sutton* (each 710 tons) were based at Yarmouth and later transferred to Harwich itself. The "Hunts" were known as "Smokey Joes" in the Navy because of the clouds of black smoke churned out by their coal furnaces. At the end of February the first three requisitioned PMSs (paddle minesweepers) of the 12th Flotilla arrived at Harwich. These extraordinarily antique-looking vessels had been employed in peacetime as ferry or pleasure boats on the Thames or the Clyde. They were coal-fired, had primitive pre-turbine engines and sported wooden paddle wheels amidships which gave them a peculiarly wide appearance when seen end on. Their suitability for their wartime job lay in their very shallow draft. These three vessels were *Duchess of Fife, Marmion* and *Waverley* (all built

MAGNETIC MINE MENACE

around the turn of the century): later *Oriole, Queen Empress, Duchess of Rothesay* and *Princess Elizabeth* joined. Three similar craft, *Thames Queen, Queen of Kent* and *Queen of Thanet*, had been stationed in the Thames mouth since December as Army AA ships for engaging the German minelaying planes. The Navy rated the performance and morale of this unit as low, and in April 1940 Cdr Cordeaux, until then Staff Intelligence Officer with the C-in-C Nore, fitted out and led a naval AA flotilla, comprising yet three more paddle ships _ *Crested Eagle, Golden Eagle* and *Royal Eagle*. Each carried a crude gunlaying "RDF" (radar), for locating her targets. Many of the craft just listed, including the three "Eagle Ships", had been familiar in peacetime for taking holidaymakers down the Thames to Margate and Clacton, and at the outbreak of war had ferried evacuee children from the capital to East Anglia.

In December 1939 the tracking of minelayers (which inevitably worked at night) was made easier by the arrival of the first two CHL (Chain Home Low) RDF (radar) stations at Foreness (Kent) and Walton-on-Naze (Essex) respectively. CHL had a much higher frequency than the existing RDF, enabling it to detect warships _ and planes descending to low levels to release their mines. Walton and Foreness both claimed, on occasion, that they had actually seen the echoes of the mines themselves, as they floated down on their parachutes. In fact these were freak successes, because the minelaying planes nearly always dropped their cargoes at below five hundred feet, below the "horizon" (except for big steel ships) of any early RDF, i.e, in the zone blanketed by echoes back off the sea and sandbanks.*A conclusive experiment was carried out at Worth Maltravers, Dorset, in June 1940. Numerous oil drums, representing mines, were dropped five miles from a CHL especially instructed to spot them, but "not the smallest change in the echo" was detected, even though the splashes were visible through binoculars.

In the New Year the magnetic minesweeping experiment began. On 1 January *Borde* (with Captain R Hudson) left her Downs anchorage, attended by the "O" (*Oropesa*) trawler *Myrtle*, the danlaying trawlers *Solon* and *Edwardian* (danlayers marked the edges of swept channels with buoys), and the rescue drifter *Renascent*. The flotilla resembled a mother hen with her chicks, or should I say a duck with her ducklings? A week later *Borde* blew her first mine in the Barrow Deep. She found the process alarming. Hudson gaped at a column of black water two hundred feet tall, followed by a yellow

---

*...nor could CHL estimate height, and thereby detect when a minelaying plane was descending towards its target area, or distinguish it from a bomber.

spout (coloured by sand) of thirty feet. Powerful as the magnet was, the mine did not blow until the ship was appallingly close; the shock shattered windows, injured crewmen by throwing them against bulkheads, and peppered the ship with leaks, forcing her to retire to Chatham Dockyard. When the electromagnet had been switched on it had *permanently* ruined all the ship's more delicate instruments, including the radio, compass, and even the crew's watches. Flying over the Tongue minefield the same day a DWI plane was also, surprisingly, successful: there really was something in the idea that a very fastmoving magnet could get clear in the few seconds it took the clockwork delayer to click into action.

Operations were restricted by the coldest winter in forty years. Harbours were iced up, the sea was studded with small icebergs, and cables froze to windlasses. But between 8 and 10 February a coordinated attempt began to clear the minefield around the Sunk Lightship, off Harwich, into which all the approach channels but one were still blocked. *Borde*, now based at Harwich and attended by the trawlers and drifters *James Lay, Larch, Nogi, Sea Holly, Solon* and *Waveflower,* swept for a week until reduced to such a shambles that she had to retire again to Chatham. Commodore Benson, onetime pioneer of the "Oropesa", and now in charge of Harwich minesweepers, came out personally in a yacht, leading four trawlers towing skids in line abreast. He accounted for one mine. The Experimental LL Flotilla emerged from an almost icebound Brightlingsea, and *Salvo* blew one mine, though her cables were so mangled she had to return to Aldous's Shipyard for repairs. Next day the trawler *Rose Hilda* swept the first magnetic mine in the northern sector by towing a skid from Yarmouth.

While the Brightlingsea drifters moved up to Norfolk on 23 March the tugs blew no fewer than four mines back in the Thames Estuary. That same day *Cordella* and *Earl Kitchener*, the first two operational (as opposed to, experimental) LL trawlers, arrived at Harwich, and five days later the first operational LL flotilla, comprising *Lichen, Monarda, Tilly Duff* and *Vernal*, established itself at Sheerness. *Borde* came back to Harwich and blew two more mines on 31 March, but was again damaged and forced back to the Dockyard.

By that date the respective "scores" of the rival magnetic minesweepers were as follows: *Borde* 19, DWI 14, skids 8, LL 7 and "Bosun's Nightmare" 1. But already the Admiralty had taken the decision to

ABOVE: The German destroyer *Karl Galster*, which led the magnetic minelaying raid off Margate on 12/13 November, 1939.

BELOW: Wreckage from the He 115 crashed on Sheringham Beach on 5 December, 1939. *(WI)*

The Harwich destroyer Grenville on her final sortie--a press photographer happened to be on board. *(WI)*

ABOVE: A few hours later *Grenville* had been mined and was sinking.

BELOW LEFT: A contact mine blown by the Bridlington RMS party.

BELOW RIGHT: HMT *Cordella*'s crew painting a chevron on her funnel to mark the LL sweeping of another magnetic mine (Harwich, mid-1940). *(WI)*

A balloon of the Thames Floating Barrage, Dec 1939. *(WI)*

MAGNETIC MINE MENACE

favour LL and begun to equip a vast fleet of vessels with it.

There had been a fortuitous lull in German minelaying while this sweeping breakthrough was being pioneered: the enemy had not manufactured enough of the mines to follow up his victories at the end of 1939.

During this lull one mine nevertheless inflicted on the Nore Command its worst loss of this period. On 19 January 1940 the destroyer *Grenville* (Captain G E Creasy), led other G-class of her 1st Flotilla out from Harwich to check Dutch coastal shipping for German blockade runners. That afternoon, on their way back, *Grenville* blew a mine (laid a fortnight before by a German destroyer) near the North Hinder Lightship. The 1485-ton vessel turned on her side and sank sternfirst. The crew faced a brief but agonising ordeal in the near-freezing water before most were picked up by the other destroyers. While some packed onto the ship's boats until they were nearly swamped, others clung to the gunwales. The captain (later a famous admiral) kept up morale by leading songs. These were of little help to some men still in the water, for many died of exposure _ it happened to be the coldest day of that Arctic winter. In all seventy-seven died and 122 were rescued. One able seaman had a remarkable escape. When the ship was hit he was near the bow, which lifted so high that as a non-swimmer he could not bring himself to jump. Eventually the whole ship submerged except for a few feet of bow, leaving him clinging to the porthole. There he hung desperately for over an hour until seen and rescued. He was very definitely the last to leave *Grenville* alive.

On the night of 9-10 February, during the first magnetic sweeping bout, the enemy surface-ship minelayers made their last major foray, faced as they now were with British radar and lookout trawlers. Captain Berger's 1st Destroyer Flotilla sowed more magnetic mines off the Shipwash, Captain Bey's 4th Flotilla did likewise off Cromer. The first seems to have claimed no victims, but in the north there was a new run of losses, beginning with the tanker *British Triumph* on 13 February and the Italian ship *Giorgio Ohlsen* next day, and ending only with the Norwegian *Burgos* at the end of March.

On 11 March the enigmatically-named *Schiff II* contact-mined the area between the Kentish Knock, South Falls and North Goodwin sandbanks, where the shipping passed between the Thames Estuary and the Dover Strait. The Greek merchant ship *Niritos* had already been lost when a Harwich

MAGNETIC MINE MENACE

Oropesa trawler group, led by *Waveflower*, arrived and charted the field. One trawler, the *Maida*, was blown up while danlaying _ only six of her crew survived. In all, this field sank four vessels. It was cleared by the Harwich paddlers.

On 2 April the motor coaster *Ulm* laid another contact field off Smith's Knoll, near the Norfolk coast, and managed to regain her base in spite of being chased by a Harwich submarine. *Ulm*'s mission was the last German surface expedition close to the English coast for some months. Her mines sank Lt D H Swift's Yarmouth minesweeper *Dunoon* on the 30th.

A fresh batch of magnetic mines now reached the Luftwaffe, however. They were "red" or reversed-polarity types, which ignored Borde-type electromagnets yet responded to degaussed ship hulls. Some were Type Cs, superceding the Bs, and Type Ds, superceding the As. Cs and Ds were the standard German ground mines for the rest of the war*. Before release from their aircraft all these mines had their parachutes folded inside "cones" (in appearance actually bowl-shaped) at the ends. The parachute cords were attached to the mines by tallow plugs which dissolved in sea water. A Type C parachute was twenty-eight feet in diameter, big enough to cover the roof of a house. For camouflage both parachutes and mines were often sea-green in colour. On 17 April German planes began to scatter the new mines along the whole length of the East Anglian coast. They did not lack audacity. Some seaplanes actually set down on the sea so close to the shore they could be heard restarting their engines by local civilians. On 22 April four planes flew right up to within earshot of Felixstowe and Walton-on-Naze to mine the Harwich approach. Some machines even crossed the coast. This had a dramatic result on the night of 30 April/1 May. An He 111, probably from Marx airfield, near Oldenburg, and with two mines on board, came too low over Clacton-on-Sea, and crashed into the town at the junction of Victoria and Skelmersdale Roads, a pleasant, suburban, spot two hundred yards from the seafront. There was silence, civilians came to their windows to look, and then a terrible explosion blew the plane to pieces, flattened three houses and damaged fifty more, and killed two onlookers and injured as many as 156 more. The blast was heard as a dull thump as far away as Ipswich. The corpses of the four Luftwaffe crewmen were scattered about in the wreckage.

---

*See Appendix E for all German mines.

ABOVE: The corvette *Mallard* in Harwich Harbour (Felixstowe in the background). *(Tyler)*

BELOW: The paddle minesweeper *Queen Empress* in Harwich Harbour, with Parkeston Quay in the left background and Shotley on the right. The ship has a Type 286P RDF aerial on her masthead. *(IWM)*

THE GERMAN AIR CRASH AT CLACTON, 30 April, 1940
ABOVE: The tail section of the Heinkel He 111.
BELOW: Damage to houses nearby.

ABOVE: One of the He 111's engines.   *(Odhams)*
BELOW: Lt-Cdr R J H Ryan RN, of HMS *Vernon*, supervising the removal of the unexploded C-Type magnetic mine.   *(Derek Johnson)*

ABOVE: British blockships in the Zeebrugge Harbour entrance, during the operation mounted by Sheerness and Harwich warships on 27 May, 1940. *(Odhams)*
BELOW: Shotley_ the graves of four men from the Harwich-based trawler *St Achilleus*, killed at Dunkirk. The Gaelic inscription on Seaman MacLeod's gravestone means "Until day breaks and the shadows flee".

MAGNETIC MINE MENACE

Nevertheless, one of the mines survived intact: Civil Defence workers took it to be a water cylinder from a ruined house and were using it as a seat when HMS *Vernon's* party arrived at the scene. The Navy now had possession of its first red mine, a fact (in the words of the Nore Command War History) "of the utmost importance and an exceptional piece of good luck".

Another minelaying plane, this time an He 115, crashed on woodland at Eyke in East Suffolk on 7 June. It was blasted into thousands of fragments, yet one crew member was found hanging alive in a tree, though he later died in hospital.

HMS *Vernon* was not able or willing to defuse and analyse all the contact mines (some of them cut loose from our own defensive fields) being washed ahore. In 1939 a Bridlington-based naval team had tackled many on the nearby coast. Since then a Yarmouth-based RMS (Rendering Mines Safe) Party of twelve men under Lt-Cdr Roy Edwards had been responsible for eliminating all the beached mines in the Nore Command. In March 1940 the coastline was split into five sections and four smaller RMS parties, still under Edwards's overall control, were based at Bridlington, Mablethorpe, Brightlingsea and Chatham.

Compared with the secrecy later in the war, this whole mines crisis received great publicity in the press, only the locations of the incidents and the new magnetic counter-measures being withheld. Indeed, even the formerwere sometimes betrayed by photographs and obvious allusions. Eighty ships had been sunk off the East Coast by German mines in the period to May 1940, at a cost of some six hundred lives. Even so there seemed remarkably little rancour _ at least compared to that engendered by the bombing attacks. When the four German airmen at Clacton (Vagts, Sodtmann, Fresen and Koch) were buried just outside the town they had a full and dignified military funeral; and although this was normal, what was unusual was the large and sympathetic crowd. Nevertheless, the mining of such neutral passenger ships as *Simon Bolivar*, though unintentioned, seems even now a sheer war crime. The Germans must have known full well that magnetic mines tended to be triggered by the largest ships, and that the largest ships in the area *were* passenger liners, some of them neutral.

The Nore Command had weathered its first great crisis: indeed, though it was not knowable at the time, shipping losses on the East Coast were never to be so severe again. Since the New Year the German offensive had been losing its bite, to the point where its only mercantile victims in May were the small freighter *Henry Woodall* off Withernsea on the 10th and the tiny Maldon fishing smack *Teaser* off Tollesbury Pier in the Blackwater on the 22nd. A real respite had been won. But many grave anxieties soon crowded in.

3
FROM THE ENEMY'S GRASP

Early in April 1940 all the destroyers in the Nore Command _ that is, 5th and 7th Flotillas and half of 1st Flotilla, from Immingham, and the other half of 1st Flotilla from Harwich _ left for Scapa Flow. They were to escort a big minelaying operation against the German iron ore traffic in Norwegian waters. In the event Hitler struck first, by invading Denmark and Norway on 9 April. The East Coast destroyers, together with the Harwich submarines, were brought into the resultant campaign and lost some of their number.

From the Humber went many of the transports and escort vessels which moved Allied troops from port to port in North Norway and finally back to Britain. Mr Tom Higgins, originally a Grimsby fisherman and in 1940 a seaman on the naval trawler *Hammond* (which had helped the unfortunate *Reculver* at Yarmouth), was good enough to send me his recollections of one such odyssey. Via Grimsby, Aberdeen and Lerwick he sailed for Andalsnes, a small port 230 miles north-west of Oslo as the crow flies. He was himself at the wheel when the snow-capped heights of Norway came into view on 20 April. Inside the fjord his own and the other ships were assailed by air raid after air raid, three or four planes at a time. She dodged one attack by zig-zagging under cover of the mountains, but then hit a reef and sank. Higgins and his comrades clambered off onto a tiny island, and then swam to the mainland and sheltered from the bombing in a wood. Next day *Hammond*'s old friend *Larwood* was seen burning out in the fjord _ she too had been bombed, and her survivors now fled to the same wood. Rescued by boats, the two crews were taken to Molde, where they slept in a garage until the bombing and machine-gunning roused them at dawn. They were joined by some British artillerymen from Andalsnes, which the enemy had overrun, and nearby Higgins found three more wounded sailors. The casualties were treated at the local hospital, while a café proprietress cooked for the whole party without payment before locking up and abandoning her premises. Next day, after more air raids on Molde, the British party led the wounded and the nurses out of the hospital, through the burning town, and down to the shelter of woods near the water, where another German plane tried to strafe them. The cruiser *Glasgow* and two destroyers then arrived, and Higgins and his friends boarded her along with other refugees, who inclded King Haakon of Norway. As the ships left the fjord three aircraft vainly attacked them, one falling in flames. *Glasgow* landed the King at his new base at Tromsö, in the far north beyond the Arctic Circle, and a port familiar to Higgins and other Humber men from their prewar fishing days. Thence the cruiser sailed for Scotland with 168 British army and naval survivors. It had been a long fortnight since Higgins and his East Coast friends left the comparative quiet of the Nore Command.

On 1 May the Admiralty warned Admiral Drax, at Chatham, that Germany was about to invade the Low Countries. On the 3rd Vice-Admiral Edward-Collins of 2nd Cruiser Squadron brought *Arethusa* and *Galatea* (each 5,220 tons, six 6-inch guns) to Sheerness. Meanwhile four H-class destroyers of the 2nd Flotilla and three K plus one J of the 5th arrived at Harwich. On the 5th the Felixstowe MTBs (motor torpedo boats) were brought to half an hour's notice. On the 9th the rest of 5th Destroyer Flotilla with Captain (D) Lord Mountbatten, coming south to Harwich, was instead diverted into a sweep of the Heligoland Bight, along with the 9,100-ton cruiser *Birmingham*. An E-boat (German motor torpedo boat) torpedoed Mountbatten's flagship the *Kelly*, which had to be towed back to the Tyne. The same day *Galatea* and the 20th Flotilla destroyers *Esk, Express* and *Intrepid*, plus the minelayer *Princess Victoria*, came to Harwich in order to lay mines off the Dutch ports in case, as in Norway, the Germans should invade them by sea.*

This buildup was certainly timely, for in the early hours of 10 May the Germans began to pour into Holland and Belgium by land and air. The world knew at once that the long-awaited Battle in the West had opened.

From the outset it was obvious that the Low Countries were tumbling headlong into Hitler's grasp. The Allied armies began to move north from France, plunging into the same trap. The Royal Navy on the English East Coast immediately set off for the same tragic scene, and three weeks of grim rescue. Admiral Drax assumed overall responsibility for the naval operations, while on-the-spot direction at the Dutch ports was provided from 13 May by Captain T E Halsey, senior officer of the Dover-based 16th Flotilla and the destroyer *Malcolm*. Over the next few days destroyer reinforcements entered the Nore Command from Scapa Flow, Rosyth, Dover and other bases.

When news of the German attack was received on the 10th Captain Bickford's 20th Destroyer Flotilla left Harwich to mine the approaches to

---

*this had no effect on the Dutch campaign, but that 27 July three German "M"-class sweepers were sunk by the mines.

FROM THE ENEMY'S GRASP

Ijmuiden* and Den Helder. Cruisers and destroyers left the Humber for Terschelling, while *Galatea* and *Arethusa* sailed from Sheerness that afternoon to load the Dutch gold reserve at Ijmuiden. *Codrington* (with Captain Creasy) and *Griffin*, coming south from Scapa, headed straight for Scheveningen, the seaside suburb of the Hague, and shot at enemy seaplanes trying to put down there and land troops.

On 11 May all available Nore destroyers patrolled before the Dutch ports, awaiting calls for assistance. A Dover destroyer landed two hundred Chatham Royal Marines at Flushing as an advanced party for French troops coming by land through Belgium. The Luftwaffe was almost omnipresent and bombed everything it sighted. A Dutch ship, the *Prins Willem van Oranje*, was set on fire off Flushing and was towed into the Thames and saved by six London firefloats. *Codrington* and *Griffin* reported that enemy bombers had been aiming at them at frequent intervals for ten hours!

On the 12th *Prinses Juliana*, a Dutch troop transport, was bombed and abandoned. *Havock*, from Harwich, helped in the rescue and removed her secret papers. The Germans were now at the gates of all the main Dutch cities and evacuation began, without a moment to lose. The three Harwich H-class destroyers, operating separately, each performed evacuation and escort work from Ijmuiden, refuelled at Parkeston, and left again for the Hook in the early hours of the 13th. Three V/Ws, two from Harwich and one from Sheerness, patrolled off Scheveningen while Dover destroyers began the Hook of Holland evacuation. Overnight *Codrington* ferried Princess Juliana, her husband Prince Bernard and their baby daughters Princesses Beatrix (now the Queen of the Netherlands) and Irene from Ijmuiden to Harwich. En route the destroyer triggered a magnetic mine ahead, but without damage to herself.

Another V/W destroyer, *Walpole* (Cdr Bowerman) steamed at full speed from Harwich to Ijmuiden that same night, and landed a secret party of one British Intelligence officer and two Dutch civilians. This trio were greeted by a nightmare: within minutes they saw the liner *Van Renselaer* sunk by bombs, a trawler mined and obliterated in the harbour mouth, frantic Jewish refugees committing suicide by driving cars over the quayside, and a neat stack of dead German parachutists behind a fish shed. Having prevented a young Jewess from driving into the sea they persuaded her to take them to

---

*The strict Dutch spelling is IJmuiden. The older English spelling was Ymuiden. The pronunciation is not the regular Dutch "eye-moyden", but the irregular "Ay-mowden".

FROM THE ENEMY'S GRASP

Amsterdam. There, armed with documents from Churchill and the Dutch Legation in London, they saved a sackful of industrial diamonds from capture by the enemy. Regaining Ijmuiden and *Walpole*, within thirty-two hours of leaving Harwich they were back with their prize.

Meanwhile the three H-class were approaching the Hook. The whole area was under continual air attack and on the eastern horizon sinister columns of smoke rose from Rotterdam, where such ships as the liners *Statendam* and *Veendam*, the pride of the Dutch merchant marine, lay bombed and burning to destruction in the Nieuwe Maas river. *Hyperion* (Cdr Nicholson) returned escorting the refugee ship *Dotterel*. *Hereward* (Lt-Cdr Greening) embarked Queen Wilhelmina and berthed alongside Parkeston Quay that evening. The Queen boarded a special train (with a military guard made up of 5 King's Liverpools from the Harwich garrison) and was met at Liverpool Street Station by King George VI and her own family.

The invasion had caught some of the Harwich-Hook London North Eastern Railway ferry ships in Dutch harbours. All were made evacuation ships and promptly returned to Parkeston, except for *St Denis*, broken down at Rotterdam _ as the Germans overran the city she had to be scuttled at her berth.

On the morning of the 14th six Harwich destroyers left for the Hook in an eleventh hour attempt to evacuate some of the Dutch Army. Three, plus *Malcolm*, took off the last of the civilian refugees, while the rest waited off Schevningen for news of the Dutch General Staff, falsely reported to be there, and then moved north to try Ijmuiden. Numerous fires from sabotaged oil tanks were visible along the coast as they steamed north. Meanwhile the Dover-based *Wild Swan*. stood off the Hook while a four-man party from Chatham set off on a pilot boat for Rotterdam to take on twenty-six tons of gold. The launch hit a mine in the Nieuwe Waterweg and all aboard perished.

The destroyers were not the only Nore warships active. The MTBs at Felixstowe Dock were also involved, and greatly distinguished themselves. On 12 May Lt-Cdr Cole took MTBs 22, 24 and 25 of the hitherto Channel-based 3rd Flotilla over to Ijmuiden, along the Noordzee Canal, through Amsterdam, and into the Zuider Zee. His force acted as a reconnaissance group for the destroyers off Ijmuiden. The three MTBs were cheered by the Ijmuiden guardship crew and parties of schoolchildren lining the canals. They were considerably helped by the Dutch, which made possible the evacuation

FROM THE ENEMY'S GRASP

to British destroyers of the Amsterdam consular staff and a Royal Navy landing party aboard three tugs. Cole had a Dutch rear-admiral aboard MTB 22 to advise him. On the afternoon of the 14th the three MTBs were due to leave. Cole later recorded: "I informed Rear-Admiral Vrede that I must leave forthwith and told him what I had learned of the situation. He took our departure very well but I know he realised his cause was hopeless". As they set out from Ijmuiden at 2000 the MTBs were attacked by two German seaplanes. Able Seaman Stanley Aldridge, the gunner of Lt Parkinson's MTB 24, shot down an He 115 while the gunners on the other two boats hit and damaged a Dornier Do 18.

MTBs 15 and 16 left Felixstowe for the Hook at 1230 on 14 May to take off demolition parties. 15 broke down and had to return to base, but 16 (Lt Gould) entered the Hook late that afternoon, after all the bigger British craft had left, and waited for two hours. The town was burning and the Germans were only a few miles away. At one stage a shell fell in the harbour. To the east there were dreadful fires in Rotterdam, lit by the He 111s which had killed nine hundred citizens of the city of Erasmus. Gould tried to telephone the American consul in Rotterdam for information on missing British nationals _ not surprisingly without success. He later wrote; "Many (Dutch) soldiers remained on the quayside. When I asked some of them if they wished to be taken to England they replied 'No, we're Germans now. We are staying'. They were quite friendly and gave my crew cigars". Eventually a Dutch family of four, one Dutch naval officer ("he had no sleep for six days, and was in an exhausted and semi-hysterical state") and five British soldiers were rescued by MTB 16. At 2030, on her way home, she:

> "passed a British destroyer (probably *Malcolm*) which appeared to be making for the Hook. I made by V/S* 'Have evacuated all remaining British troops'. To this the destroyer replied 'Am going in for the army'. Taking this to refer to the Dutch Army, I made 'None remaining wish to leave'. The destroyer continued on her course".

Midnight of 14/15 May found nine out of eleven Harwich destroyers waiting in three groups off Den Helder, Ijmuiden and the Hook in the hope of rescuing the Dutch Army. But, unknown to them, Holland had just surrendered. By daybreak, with bombing a looming threat, all had called off

---

*visual signal

their vigil and were returning to base.

Before the surrender some of the Dutch Navy had pulled out. The cruiser *Heemskerk* reached the Downs and *Sumatra* the Humber. The minesweeper *Birkja*, the gunboats *Brinlo* and *Grunlo*, the world's most powerful salvage tug *Zwarte Zee*, a schuyt (coaster), three motor boats and four naval trawlers turned up at Harwich. Many more schuyts and larger merchant ships were safe in, or escaped to, the Thames, Several Fokker Tviii-W seaplanes got away to RAF Felixstowe.

Early on the morning of 16 May, after the official arrival of all other vessels from Holland, FS 70 passed a sailing dinghy with five Dutchmen aboard near the Shipwash Light Vessel; they had fled Scheveningen the previous day. Notwithstanding the spring weather two of the escapers had exposure: the convoy landed them all at Sheerness.

Three days later, returning to the Humber from her work off Holland, the minelayer *Princess Victoria* (Captain J B E Hall) was mined and sunk. Between that day and the 25th the undersea telephone cables to the Continent were pulled up; these had run from Mundesley and Bacton (Norfolk) and Lowestoft to Borkum (Germany), from Lowestoft and Benacre (Suffolk) to Zandvoort (Holland), and from Aldeburgh to Domburg (Holland).

The focus of activity shifted south-westwards along the Continental coast. The northern Allied armies, including most of the BEF (British Expeditionary Force), were now cut off in an ever-diminishing area of Northern France and Western Belgium, and seemed doomed to destruction or capture. On 24 May the Germans encircled and stormed Boulogne and Calais. The Navy was sent to evacuate both ports, but succeeded (up to a point) only in the first instance. Harwich recalled the destroyers *Burza*, *Grafton* and *Greyhound* from their patrol east of the Aldeburgh Light and sent them to help the Dover destroyers. *Burza* was divebombed and lost most of her bows. Sheerness sent *Venetia*, *Vimy*, *Windsor* and *Wolfhound*. The first suffered a direct hit from a German shore battery and two of her officers were wounded, and the captain of *Vimy* was killed by a bomb.

That night the Nore Command blocked the port of Zeebrugge, then being hastily evacuated by the Allies. Three of the Harwich "Duck" corvettes and the Sheerness destroyer *Vega* brought five blockships full of cement, re-

FROM THE ENEMY'S GRASP

enacting the dramatic and bloody operation of 1918. (The plan had existed and the blockships had been waiting in the Medway since the previous autumn). Ostend was also to have been sealed up, but the Germans got there first, having paved the way by savagely bombing the town for a week, and killing 160 Allied troops and civilians.

All thoughts then turned to Dunkirk, the last Continental North Sea port in Allied hands. The great "Operation Dynamo" evacuation began on 27 May. It primarily concerned Dover, and secondarily and in the same command, Ramsgate _ Vice-Admiral Ramsay of Dover was in charge. But I shall sketch the contribution of the Nore Command, that is, East Coast, ports and craft.

In the Dunkirk legend every small boat-owner in South East England spontaneously set out from his home port and returned thither laden with soldiers from the beaches. This is in fact an ideal amalgamated out of many half-truths. First, though 2,500 offers of private boats were made, only about a tenth of these were taken up; on the East Coast amateurs' craft were almost exclusively from the River Thames. Second, only about half the vessels involved can be classified as small craft, and of these only a minority were manned by civilians, some of whom were in any case tugmen, bargees, lifeboatmen, pilots and other professional sailors. Third, vessels did not cross straight from their home ports, but went via Sheerness, Harwich and/or Ramsgate. Many were towed by larger vessels. And, Dover excepted, troops were landed only at Ramsgate, Margate, to a lesser extent Harwich, and from just a few ships, Sheerness. Fourth, the small craft did not usually bring troops back to England, but ferried them from the beaches or Dunkirk harbour to the ships offshore. Most of the small craft had fuel and provisions for only one day of this, and since most started on the fourth day of the evacuation, and took three days to do a complete round trip, this single day was all most saw of Dunkirk _ many were recalled near the end while en route to a second day's operations.

Each East Coast port made its contribution. Sheerness must be mentioned first. There, on 14 May, the Navy started the Small Vessels Pool, under Admiral Lionel Preston. This was charged with registering, after appeals had been made via the BBC, every seaworthy private motor boat of between thirty and one hundred feet in the Thames Estuary, mainly with the object of requisitioning the best of them for harbour duties with the existing

FROM THE ENEMY'S GRASP

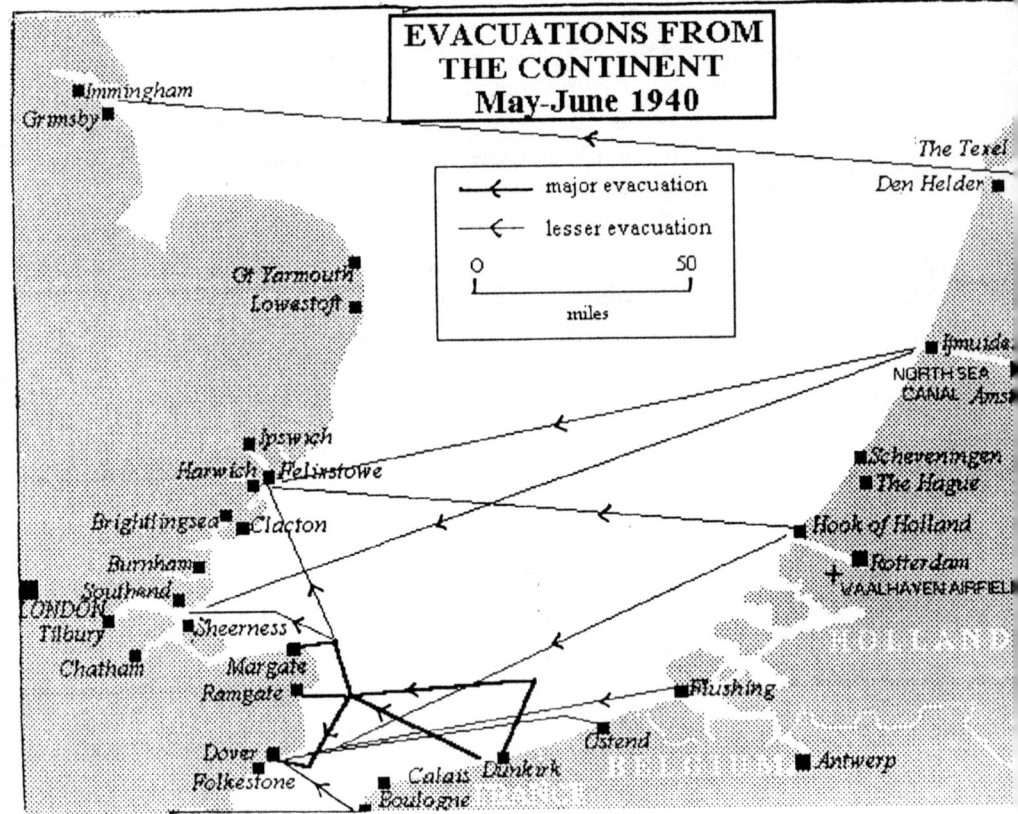

minesweeper, and proposed patrol, fleet on the East Coast. On 26 May the Pool was given more urgent work: its officers hastened round all the yachting harbours and boatyards in the Estuary to requisition so far unregistered but suitable craft _ over forty were found. At Pool HQ Paymaster-Lt-Cdr H Garrett RNVR spent sixty almost continuous hours on the telephone contacting boat owners, potential crews, and Dover, so as to bring into the operation over one hundred small craft from the Upper Thames. If possible officers from the RNVR training base at Hove (HMS *King Alfred*) were put in charge of the boats. A form, "T 124", was hastily cyclostyled _ it bound civilian volunteers to serve under naval orders and discipline for one month. Such was the urgency that only a hundred men had signed it at Sheerness before being rushed to sea.

Craft of very diverse sizes, shapes and ages arrived at Sheerness,

FROM THE ENEMY'S GRASP

some of which had never been out in the open sea, most of which had not been run for many months, and none of which had adequate fuel. Making them all seaworthy was the work of Rear-Admiral A H Taylor and his engineers _ this "Maintenance Officer, Operation Dynamo" only arrived at Sheerness on 27 May. His second-in-command, Cdr Troup, managed to make himself maintenance officer on the spot, and went out to Dunkirk in an army motor boat, setting himself up as Piermaster of the West Mole (western harbour entrance pier) and supervising the evacuation of ten thousand French troops. The Harwich AA cruiser *Calcutta* landed a tenth of these at Sheerness, where a young Malcolm Muggeridge, in the guise of Field Security Police officer, treated them to a propaganda lecture (which fell flat) and to cigarettes (which were cheered).

From Sheerness the destroyers *Vega, Vimy, Windsor* and *Wolfhound* left for the operation, and early on the 30th seven Dover-based destroyers refuelled there, having been pulled out owing to bombing _ dozens of dead and wounded were taken from *Ivanhoe* to Gillingham, to the naval hospital and/or the cemetary. *Vimy* took out Captain Tennant, Senior Naval Officer Dunkirk, and his staff.

Three notable Sheerness vessels to join "Dynamo" were Captain Cordeaux's "Eagle ships", which had been providing the Estuary with AA cover against magnetic minelayers. *Crested Eagle* was bombed near Dunkirk harbour entrance and burned out. To rescue survivors Cordeaux himself jumped into the sea from *Queen Eagle*, and had to be hauled out unconscious (he was given the DSC). There was anxiety that the gunlaying RDF set on the wreck would fall into enemy hands, but it was found to be have been burned beyond recognition. Three other paddle steamers of the peacetime Thames pleasure fleet also joined from Sheerness, including *Medway Queen*, which rescued seven hundred troops, and *Queen of the Channel*, which was sunk on 28 May.

Also from Sheerness was the 250-ton merchant coaster *Lady Sheila* (property of Watson and Company). The Extended Defences (i.e, harbour defence) Flotilla sent four of its armed yachts; *Amulree, Caleta, Christobel II* and *Glala*, and the Insect-class shallow-draft gunboats *Locust* and *Mosquito*. *Locust* towed back the sloop *Bideford*, which would otherwise have been abandoned: her crew also found a stray puppy on the East Mole and adopted it as a mascot. *Mosquito* was sunk. The minesweeping trawlers

FROM THE ENEMY'S GRASP

Monarda and *Strathelliott* went. The former, commanded by Lt Lovelock RNVR (who received the DSC) went from rescue to rescue. As nearby bombs caused her whole fabric to shudder, she picked up five French sailors, 120 British soldiers, and fifteen wounded from a sinking French trawler. She then saved Squadron Leader McGregor, an RAF Hurricane pilot, from the sea, and went on to rescue twenty-five men, then another forty from a sinking naval cutter. Another Sheerness naval yacht involved was *Alouette II*, which had been employed echo-sounding for mines.

At Sheerness, Tilbury and Gravesend the Navy requisitioned twenty-one schuyts on 26 May. These fuelled and provisioned at Sheerness and mostly left for Ramsgate evacuation base next morning. The crews for these craft were not Dutchmen, but came from the Royal Naval Barracks at Chatham. From there also originated "Party Number 3", which reinforced the civilian crews of several British and Dutch ferry ships lying at Dover. They found some of these civilians keener to get ashore than to sail for Dunkirk: three ships had to put under armed guard to prevent this, while the occupants shouted back panicky abuse*. From Chatham a large medical party joined "Dynamo" via Folkestone: it saw some terrible sights in the next four days. From the two Medway naval dockyards went the tug *St Clears* and nine lighters.

From Rochester and Sittingbourne, conveniently close to Sheerness as they were, most of the Thames sailing barges used at Dunkirk were taken. They went out with their normal two- or three-man crews, and were mostly used for ferrying out stores, not for rescuing. *Lady Rosebery* was blown up with two of her three crew killed. *Ena* and *Beatrice Maud* were abandoned, but later boarded by stranded Allied troops (French in the latter case) and steered to Kent. Other notable barges were *Pudge* (requisitioned at Tilbury), and *Tollesbury*, an Ipswich vessel taken from Erith.

At Southend the various craft being requisitioned and stored by Sheerness did brief trials and also tested their compasses before being adopted and sent into action. *Greater London*, the Southend lifeboat, went out _ she towed the minesweeper *Kellett* out of Dunkirk harbour after she had got stuck with two hundred French troops aboard. Other Southend contributions included *New Prince of Wales*, the naval skid-tower and former pleasure boat (she was bombed with two dead and three wounded), the

---

*One was the Harwich railway ferry *Malines*. These ships had already done important work at Dunkirk, in fact.

FROM THE ENEMY'S GRASP

pleasure launches *Southend Britannia* and *Shamrock* (who had her Canvey Island owner aboard), and six cockle "bawleys" from Leigh, some of the smallest craft to set out, and of which one, the *Renown*, was lost. Several *Sun* tugs went from their wartime base at the Pier, while two more well-known tugs, the *Persia* and *Challenge,* were brought from the Thameshaven oil piers nearby.

Up river London itself provided most of the civilian motor boats called forth by the Pool at Sheerness. These (too many to list) were assembled initially at Toughs' Yard, Teddington, or, within a mile of the Admiralty, at Westminster Pier. They had come from such leafy and prosperous suburbs as Richmond, Kew, Teddington and Hampton Court. On board several were their peacetime owners, untrammelled by naval officers, the Chatham Barracks men, or T 124. *Sea Roamer,* a mere forty-footer, rescued French soldiers from a wreck, survived collisions and snarled propellers, and was towed home by a paddle steamer. *Minotaur,* once the pinnace of a cruiser which fought at Jutland, was sailed from Mortlake by a crew of sea scouts. *Sundowner,* from Chiswick, was skippered by the son of her owner, Cdr Lightoller RNR, the senior surviving officer of the *Titanic* _ she ferried 130 men to the evacuation ships. *Chelmondesleigh*'s skipper-owner was the comedian Tommy Trinder. *Marsayru,* skippered by Lt G D Olivier, elder brother of the film actor, helped rescue over four hundred Frenchmen: *Constant Nymph*'s score was nine hundred; *Silver Queen*'s one thousand. *Quisiana* came from as far up river as Chertsey. The London glass-sided pleasure boats *Hurlingham, King, Marchioness** and *Viscountess,* some of which still exist, participated. Among the more workaday London small craft was the firefloat *Massey Shaw* (skippered by A J May), which rescued seven hundred.

Burnham-on-Crouch was the furthrest north from which a purely civilian contingent came _ it sent the oyster-dredger *Vanguard*, the smack *Seasalter*, the motor-barge *Viking* and the yacht *Ma Joie*. The motor boat *Dab II* sailed from Heybridge Basin, and the Navy manned the yacht *Margaret Mary* at West Mersea and took her out via Sheerness. From Brightlingsea the naval drifter *Renascent* and the civilian-manned former Clacton pleasure launches *Grace Darling* and *Britannia IV* took part. All three had been assisting the Experimental LL Flotilla. *Renascent* went out via

---

*sunk with heavy loss of life near Southwark Bridge in a collision in 1989.

FROM THE ENEMY'S GRASP

Sheerness with *Monarda*, passed through an air raid by eighty planes, and rescued first from the beaches, secondly from the harbour. She saw the Portsmouth yacht *Grive* blown up right in front of her, and rescued four of her crew. In view of statements that the British left behind thousands of French soldiers, it is interesting that those invited by *Renascent* refused to come. Also at Brightlingsea* many Colne fishing smacks were provisioned at naval expense and sailed to Ramsgate by their normal crews, but were not in the event required. From Colchester the sailing barges *Queen, Unique* and *Ethel Everard* participated, though I cannot be sure that they were not in the Thames or Medway when summoned. *Ethel Everard* was abandoned on Dunkirk beach, where, with sails tattered but still spread, she attracted a German official photographer. An unnamed lifeboat was brought from Rowhedge Shipyard.

From Clacton the lifeboat, *Edward Z Dresden*, was taken to Dunkirk via Ramsgate by part of her RNLI crew, but skippered by W P Trotter, a civilian with naval experience. A few miles along the coast *EMED*, the Walton and Frinton lifeboat, was remanned by Lt Mead RNVR and a naval crew. On 1 June she was near-missed by a shell, Mead was hit in the chest by shrapnel and killed, and she was listed as missing. Two days later, although crippled by a rope twisted round a propeller, she was found drifting, towed into Dover, cleaned up, and sent back for one more run to the beaches. Two private yachts were also taken by the Navy from Walton _ in this case the Backwaters behind the town. These, *Singapore* and *Singapore III*, belonged to a local businessman named Bostock. The second yacht broke down en route and did not take part.

Harwich was the only harbour outside Kent to undertake all aspects of Operation Dynamo, albeit on a much more modest scale than Dover. The Navy gathered up the local sailing barges *Mizpah, Aldie, Barbara Jean, Cabby, Hilda* and *Spinaway* (all except the first from Ipswich), and sent them off. The private launch *Pelagia* was brought down from Woodbridge and sailed via Harwich by her Army-officer owner and the headmaster of Framlingham School. From Harwich Harbour came the Army launch *Vulture*.

But Harwich's main contribution was in warships. The AA cruiser *Calcutta*, six destroyers, five PMSs, five corvettes, fourteen trawlers and drifters, three salvage craft, three tugs, eight launches, two MTBs, two

---

*mistakenly given as "Bridlington" in the official report.

THE DUNKIRK EVACUATION

Top Left: Photographs of the evacuation in progress are extremely rare, and this one, widely published at the time, was later taken to be a fake. It has, however, recently been authenticated by a junior officer of the Harwich paddle minesweeper *Oriole*, who took it from on board while she was beached.

Top Right: The river tug *Barnes* towing private boats back to Toughs' Yard, Teddington, after the operation. This same group of craft were photographed many times on their way up river.   *(Odhams Press)*

Below: The destroyer *Javelin*, which arrived at Dunkirk from Harwich, rescuing some of the *Abukir*'s survivors en route. Along with other J-class, she was mainly based at Immingham during the first year of war.   *(WI)*

Above Left: *Tamzine*, the smallest craft in Operation Dynamo (other than ships' boats). *(IWM)*
Above Right: *Challenge*, one of the London tugs at Dunkirk, preserved in St Katherine's Dock.
Below: The ill-fated Harwich PMS *Waverley*, sunk at Dunkirk with heavy loss of life. *(The Times)*

FROM THE ENEMY'S GRASP

MASBs (motor anti-submarine boats), and ML 100 (the only vessel of her type then operational) left the harbour for Operation Dynamo _ fifty vessels of all types. Seven *Halcyon* and *Hunt* auxiliary minesweepers from North Shields, and six paddlers from Rosyth, coaled there en route to Dunkirk. The trawlers *Argyllshire* and *St Achilleus* were lost: the four sailors from the latter who still lie in Shotley Cemetery may well be the only Dunkirk fatalities to be buried on the East Anglian coast. The smaller craft included the launch *Plover* and two cutters from HMS *Ganges*, Shotley. The MTBs were participating in their second evacuation in a fortnight. MASB 6 was used to ferry the C-in-C of the BEF, Gort, back to Dover.

Since the fall of Holland HMS *Badger*'s destroyers had been reorganised into two groups to keep enemy warships out of the southern North Sea. Force A comprised *Codrington, Grenade, Jaguar* and *Javelin* and was led by Captain Creasy. Force B comprised *Blyskawica, Greyhound, Gallant*, and *Grafton* and was led by Cdr Marshall A'Deane. During the Calais operation Force B surrendered these last two ships to Dover Command. On the night of the 27th its other two ships were on patrol between Yarmouth and Ijmuiden. Even at that distance the fires and gunflashes on the French coast were clearly visible. The two destroyers were ordered to Dunkirk, but on arrival next morning were sent back to the West Hinder out of sight of enemy bombers. Overnight Force A had transferred from Harwich to Dover. Near the North Hinder *Javelin* found twenty-six survivors from the ferry boat *Abukir*, sunk by E-boat while escaping from Ostend. *Jaguar* (Lt-Cdr J P W Hine) took a woman, six men and a dog from a raft between the North Goodwin Lightship and Kwinte Bank.

On the 29th all the Harwich and ex-Harwich destroyers entered Dunkirk waters for evacuation duty, and all came under ferocious attack. *Blyskawica* had to zig-zag to avoid U-Boat torpedoes, and even as she did so was divebombed and strafed by one plane, though the damage was slight. Minutes later *Greyhound* was also bombed and brought to a halt by smashed engines and a gaping hole underwater. *Blyskawica* towed her into Dover and then returned for her second load of troops that day. Meanwhile *Grafton* was sunk off Bray-Dunes by one of the first E-boats to reach the area, while *Gallant* was sunk and both *Grenade* and *Jaguar* were damaged by bombing in the same attack which set fire to *Crested Eagle*. *Jaguar* had thirteen dead and nineteen wounded _ one of the former (a stoker) was a suicide. The salvage vessel *Forde* took her back to Harwich and surveyed her for underwater damage. *Forde* also towed to safety the bombed and sinking ferry boat *Royal Daffodil* next day

Five of Harwich's seven "anti-submarine" corvettes participated in Dynamo; *Guillemot, Mallard, Shearwater, Sheldrake* and *Widgeon*. Their job was to fend off small enemy warships, but *Widgeon* also rescued some of the crew of the sunken French destroyer *Sirocco*.

On the night of 28 May Harwich's 12th Minesweeping Flotilla of paddle steamers was ordered to stop sweeping the Would, to coal at Lowestoft, and to head for Dunkirk. Entirely officered by reservists, its aged craft carried only one 12-pdr and some machine guns apiece. At La Panne, next morning, *Marmion* picked up survivors from the lifeboat of a mined French ship and brought troops from shore with her own boat in the afternoon. *Oriole* ran herself aground amid fierce bombing and acted as a bridge for troops to reach the larger ships. She then rescued seven hundred men herself. The flotilla leader *Waverley* rendered valuable service and then met disaster. On 29 May she began to rescue with small boats, eventually taking six hundred men back to Dover. Two days later, again loaded to capacity with troops, she came under repeated attack by up to twelve He 111s at a time. Near misses killed four soldiers, wounded many others, and made her unmanageable. Then a direct hit holed her. Within one minute of the order to abandon she sank with the loss of 360 soldiers and sailors, over half those on board. The remainder, including her captain, Lt S F Harmer-Elliott RNVR, were rescued by a French destroyer, the *Golden Eagle*, some drifters, and a tug.

6,900 troops were disembarked at Harwich by destroyers and minesweepers. Eight special trains took them from Parkeston Quay to the Midlands. When one minesweeper berthed she had scuppers running with blood, according to onlookers. In another example of the demoralisation that went on in Dynamo alongside the heroism, when another minesweeper arrived her three hundred soldier-passengers were made to leave their ammunition on board, and were marched from the gangway to the sheds between a double row of Welsh Guards, who shielded them and the onlookers from any mutual communication.

Further along the East Anglian coast Aldeburgh sent both its lifeboats, *Abdy Beauclerck* and *Lucy Lawers*. The Southwold boat *Mary*

FROM THE ENEMY'S GRASP

Scott also went. Lowestoft sent a contingent: the Army launch *Haig*, the private motor boat *Elvin* (with retired Lt-Cdr Buchanan in charge), and the lifeboat *Michael Stephens*. Yarmouth naval base sent the A/S trawler *Thuringia* and M/S trawler *Thomas Bartlett* (both were bombed and sunk on arrival), and thirteen M/S drifters. Some say the Yarmouth base "flagship" (the large motor launch *Watchful*) also went, but this remains unproven. Gorleston despatched the lifeboat *Louise Stephens*. The thirteen motor-boats and ex-lifeboats which set out from Sheringham, Wells, Blakeney and Brancaster, with some well-known local sailors on board, only got as far as the Thames Estuary. Grimsby was the northernmost Nore Command port to send assistance _ the Army launch *Pidgeon* and the minesweepers *Dundalk, Fitzroy, Salamander* and *Sutton*. On the 28th *Fitzroy* took from a Belgian boat eight Belgian officers, two French soldiers, and two Jewish refugees. (One cannot help wondering what unusual friendships must have been struck up in small boats in this whole vast ordeal!)

Of the third of a million Allied troops landed in England during "Dynamo" over two-thirds disembarked at Dover (and Folkestone). Neverthless 42, 211 came ashore at Ramsgate and even more, 46,772, within the Nore Command and Thames Estuary at Margate. This last place was also notable for its lifeboat, the *Lady Southborough*: skippered by a civilian, C D Parker, who won the DSM, she ferried many hundreds of troops to larger craft. A tiny wooden boat called *Tamzine*, now preserved in the Imperial War Museum in London, came from Margate and is supposed to have been the smallest craft in "Dynamo", though the reader will appreciate that she would have been towed to Dunkirk and used merely as a short-range ferry. Altogether fifty-three vessels, ranging from destroyers to motor boats, landed troops (many of them French) at Margate. The last to arrive should have been the French minesweeper *Émile Deschamps*, but as she approached the North Foreland on 4 June a magnetic mine dragged her to the bottom with over four hundred "Poilus", the worst loss of life in a single incident in the Nore Command throughout the war.

Twenty-seven of their compatriots meanwhile steered a fishing boat from Dunkirk to Clacton, arriving late that night _ probably the last escape before the French rearguard hauled down the Tricolor. Yet, eleven days later, eight French and four British soldiers reached Southend from Boulogne in an open boat, and reported that there were still many unsurrendered Allied troops but comparatively few Germans in that northern corner of France. The Frenchmen included Captain Bouvier d'Yvoire, the son of a Haute Savoie baron. Within another week France had surrendered. On 3 July three of her naval trawlers, still at Sheerness, were seized by the Royal Navy, and unusually most of their crews volunteered to join the Allies.

The whole Western Continental Coast was now in German hands, and the English East Coast was locking and bolting itself in. After Dunkirk there was relief nationally, and mourning locally _ for the many sailors who had *not* returned. With the enemy no longer "round the corner" in Heligoland Bight, but right opposite (and between forty and 150 miles away), there must obviously be foreboding. Invasion, bombing and surface raiding had to be next.

After the great evacuations a trickle of brave refugees continued to escape Nazi-occupied Europe and head for the East Coast of England in small boats and occasionally even aircraft. The "Englandvaarder" (sailors to England) as the Dutch called them, had to face air and naval patrols, unpredictable and often violent seas, concentration camp if they were caught, and even aggressive and prolonged interrogation (as possible spies) if they arrived.

As early as July 1940 Dutchmen Karel Michielsen, Kees van Endenburg and Fredi van Nunes reached Lowestoft from Scheveningen after four nights and three days in the rowing boat *Duck*, to be acclaimed by the Dutch in exile in England on their Radio Orange.

But in 1941 the escapes came thick and fast. On 19 March the Ipswich patrol trawler *Vindelicia* ("Windy Lizzy" to her crew) found two Dutchmen in a motor boat near the Shipwash, and took them to Harwich. Six days later the Sheerness destroyer *Meynell* found three of their compatriots drifting towards the Sunk Lightship in another small boat: she transferred them to the Harwich minesweeper *Leda*, which landed them at her base. On 4 April L J van der Veen, J M De Niet and W A Giel (from the Hague) J E Woltjer (Rotterdam), E Klein (Amsterdam) and H W Keesom (Leiden) came ashore at Pakefield (Lowestoft) and handed themselves over to the coast artillerymen. They had crossed from the Harlingvliet in a twelve-foot motor boat in twenty-three hours. They brought photographs and German literature of value to MI5, who questioned them, and even produced bouquets of tulips

FROM THE ENEMY'S GRASP

for Queen Wilhelmina and Queen Elizabeth.

On 2 May two Dutch naval officers made landfall in a sail and motor dinghy near Southwold, after a very rough crossing. Three days later there was a double escape more like fiction than reality: four Dutch civilian employees of the Fokker aircraft company near Amsterdam (which was now working for the Germans) took off in two light aircraft (two men in each) and headed out to sea before the Luftwaffe were alerted. One plane forcelanded at Covehithe, near Southwold (although hit by British Army rifle fire), the other off Broadstairs on the Isle of Thanet in Kent. In June there were three Dutch escapes in as one week. The Sheerness M/S trawler *Wardour* rescued three men from Ijmuiden near B7 Buoy, off Frinton, on the 20th, and took them back to her base. At 54B Buoy, two days later the Harwich M/S trawler *Stour* rescued two Katwijk men, R F Burgwal and R F Van Daalen Watters, from a rubber kayak in which they lay half-dead from *twelve days* of exertion. She landed them at Lowestoft. And on the 25th the Harwich destroyer *Eglinton* brought two ex-army officers in from a boat off

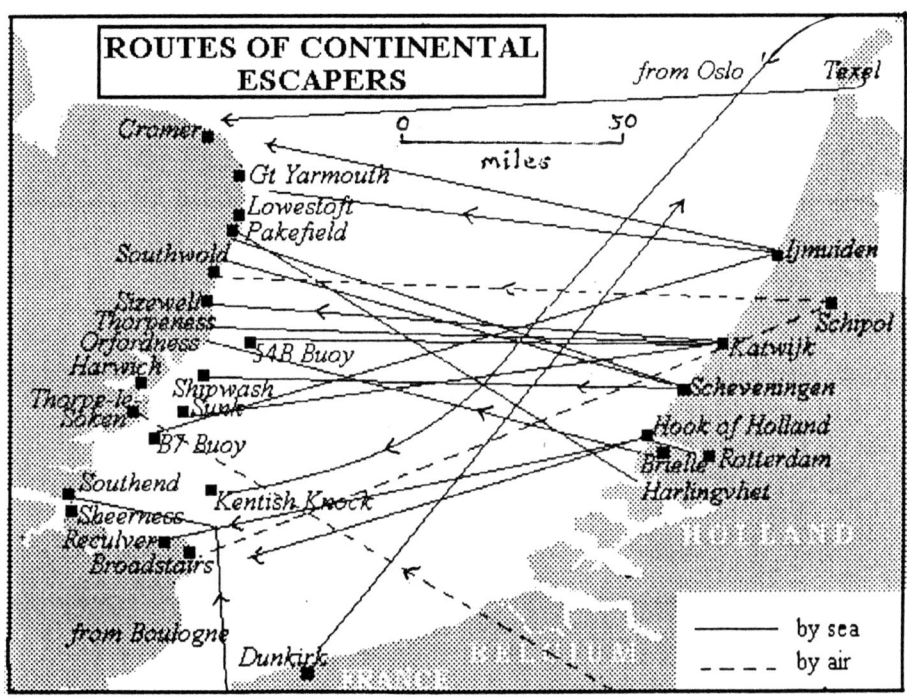

FROM THE ENEMY'S GRASP

Southwold.

September 1941 was also a record month for "Englandvarder", hoping to make the run before the autumn weather. On the 4th eight Dutchmen landed at Orfordness from a motor boat which they had brought from the little moated port of Brielle. On the 19th the Yarmouth M/S trawler *Solon* found five Dutchmen and three Norwegians (two of them dead) in a small craft forty miles east of her base. Two days later the Peteri brothers, Katwijk students, reached the fantasy village of Thorpeness in another tiny canoe. And on the 27th two Delft men named van Rietschoten and Naassen sailed from Katwijk to Sizewell in Suffolk.

The Germans at the exit from the Nieuwe Waterweg must have been "roasted" by their superiors on 23 October, for that day two of the most audacious groups of escapers got by them. Eight men and one woman had stolen a German Red Cross launch at Rotterdam, then bluffed their way out of the canal and crossed the North Sea to Reculver in Kent. Five more men, from the Hook, also slipped over and were landed at Sheerness by the destroyer *Hambledon*.

Five equally daring escapers came into Immingham with the Dutch coaster *Nautilus* and one German prisoner on 10 May 1942. The crew of a merchantman in German service, they had overpowered their guard while carrying timber from Norrkoping, Sweden, to Cuxhaven, Germany. All had seemed lost when they ran into a German convoy, but they faked engine trouble so as to have an excuse to drop out, and then headed for England. The captain had indeed risked his life, for although of Dutch birth, he was a German citizen.

By the end of the war seventy-five Dutch citizens (including a woman), five Danes, four Soviet Georgians (to be dealt with in a later chapter) and two Belgians were brought into Yarmouth alone. The Belgians were the only survivors of a party of seven who had left Dunkirk in a small boat on 22 November 1941. They had been strafed by Messerschmitts which smashed their engines, and had drifted right down the Belgian and Dutch coasts until found by Sub-Lt Leaf's MGB (Motor Gunboat) 89 from Lowestoft, by which time they were semi-conscious and close to death. Two of their compatriots, airforce sergeants named Divoy and Donnet, sneaked across from Brussels to Thorpe-le-Soken (near Harwich) in a light aircraft on 5 July that year, surrendering to local Special Constable Percy Brown.

FROM THE ENEMY'S GRASP

Many Danish fishing vessels came into the Humber. Banned by both Germans and British from areas outside their home waters, they frequently defied this in search of catches. Several had no intention of coming as far as England, but were brought in by force. The Rosyth destroyer *Vanity* found no fewer than fourteen near the Dogger Bank on 19 September 1942, sank one (which tried to resist), and seized the others, three of which were taken to Grimsby, the rest to Rosyth. Of the genuine Danish refugees, two sailed from Ribe (near Esbjerg) to Bridlington on 21 October 1940.

Few escapers had such a sea ordeal as the Norwegian Oluf Olsen and his two friends. On 29 September 1940 the Tribal class destroyer *Bedouin*, in transit to Scotland, found them bearded and emaciated on a storm-battered fifty-foot smack, *Haabet* ("Hope") near the Kentish Knock. They had left Oslo with her over a fortnight before. Having almost reached Aberdeen, they were blown back to within sight of Denmark by the worst storm of the year. Dodging inquisitive German ships and planes, and gradually succumbing to cold, hunger and seasickness, they struggled across the Heligoland Bight, all the way down the Dutch coast, and across to Kent, making a total journey of 1,200 miles.

A French arrival gave the Nore Command its own *Marie Celeste*. On 17 January 1942 the Calais fishing lugger *Ave Maria* was found beached at Margate, with no signs of life aboard. It transpired that she had been torn from her moorings by a gale and blown across the Dover Strait.

Not all the refugees arriving on the East Coast by sea and air were genuine. It was apparently known in advance that the fourteen Dutchmen and Dutch East Indians who arrived at Yarmouth in two boats on 8 April 1942 would include several spies _ for local troops were so warned. On the 18th of the next month the Harwich M/S and patrol trawler *Carena* found three Dutchmen in a dinghy and landed them at Parkeston Quay, whence Detective Constable Leonard Chaplin and Military Police took them to "Fairhaven", the Army Field Security office on Marine Parade, Dovercourt. Having slept the night at the Police Station (Main Road), they were removed to London, and like all "Englandvaarder", "grilled" at the "Royal Patriotic School" by the Dutch Intelligence colonel Oreste Pinto. Two were genuine, but the third, named Dronkers, was already suspect for such exaggerated behaviour as kissing the ground on his disembarkation, and on the last day of the year was hanged at Wandsworth Prison as a spy. In a less grim if more bizarre

FROM THE ENEMY'S GRASP

incident two men landed a light plane at Scratby, on the coast north of Yarmouth, on 24 November 1941. Claiming to be Dutchmen, they produced identity cards which satisfied local troops. But, having been moved to Horsham St Faith aerodrome, the pair were arrested by RAF police. They had escaped from a prisoner of war camp in Cumberland and stolen their plane, a Miles Magister trainer, from Carlisle airport!

4
INVASION IMMINENT

The overrunning of Holland in May 1940 first raised the spectre of invasion on the East Coast. With British forces still tied up in Belgium and Norway there were very understandable fears that the enemy might sidestep France and rush Eastern England with parachutists and light naval craft. At this period there was nothing resembling a continuous coast defence system by Army or Navy: mile after mile of shore lay quite open and unguarded. Even the "Strongpoints" were weak; for instance at Harwich and Felixstowe, apart from the coast and AA artillery, and the harbour boom, the defences comprised only one infantry battalion (about nine hundred men) and one field artillery battery (of eight guns).

On 15 May the Navy formed "Anti-Invasion Striking Forces" at the Humber, Harwich, Sheerness and Dover. The Harwich one consisted of Creasy's 1st Destroyer Flotilla, the AA cruiser *Calcutta*, three MASBs, and several old submarines. Some of its men were inspected on Parkeston Quay by Churchill on 26 May. That the speech he made did not impress some of his listeners was perhaps because he was preoccupied with the Admiralty's pessimistic estimate of the numbers likely to be rescued from Dunkirk.

Bombing, the threat of invasion, and the lack of space for the swelling numbers of servicemen combined to make evacuation the great civilian event of the year on the East Coast. Among those moved out in May and June were the boys from HMS *Ganges* (Shotley) and *Arethusa* (Chatham), all the London children brought to the area at the outbreak of war, and most of the women and children of Sheerness, Southend, Harwich, Felixstowe, Lowestoft and Yarmouth. By August the civilian populations of each of those towns had fallen by three-fifths, and at the end of that month all but 15% were scheduled to go, a plan cancelled at the last minute. For most of the war there were more servicemen in such places than civilians, and whole streets were taken over for billets.

Under new security precautions control of civilian movements became much stricter. Checkpoints kept all but local residents and servicemen out of every East Coast town with a naval base and beyond a half a mile from RDF stations and airfields. The seaside resort and the yacht station were completely abolished. All the piers from Margate via Clacton and Felixstowe to Skegness were breached, except for Southend, already occupied by the Navy. All seafront cafés and hotels closed down and practically every premises facing the sea was requisitioned, boarded up and sandbagged. In June all beaches were mined, scaffolded against landing craft, entangled with barbed wire and studded with concrete obstacles. The Army began to extend similar barriers around all the ports and coastal towns by land. The minefields took a considerable toll from now on, though not of the enemy. At nearly every coastal locality civilians (often children), troops and untold animals were killed on wandering astray. In the bloodiest incident seven soldiers of the 5th Buckinghamshires were blown up at Thorpeness in September 1942. However, the biggest explosion rocked Southwold on 26 September 1940: a German bomb triggered the whole field of several hundred mines around 327 Coast Artillery Battery, wrecked huts, tore away barbed wire and camouflage netting, and injured troops _ yet caused no deaths.

With "Dynamo" over the Admiralty planned to concentrate a great force of destroyers at Harwich. Some were anti-invasion vessels, others escorts for the highly exposed convoy route, which the REF alone was now inadequate to protect. No fewer than forty destroyers from five flotillas (5th, 8th, 16th, 18th and 21st) were nominally assigned to Harwich. In fact only four of these ships were actually present, the rest being scattered as far away as Scapa and Narvik. These four themselves left on 10 June, and the concentration at *Badger* was postponed in view of momentary priorities elsewhere. Norway and France having been abandoned, a more regular deployment was ordered, and at the end of June Harwich received most of the 16th and 18th Flotillas, respectively comprising *Malcolm* and three A class and *Montrose* and eight V/Ws. At the end of July four minelaying destroyers of 20th Flotilla and six modern J and K class of the 5th were also temporarily with *Badger*, giving it a total of seventeen available destroyers plus seven en route or refitting. Harwich destroyers were responsible for the periodic anti-invasion "Patrol T" east of Mine Barrier Gap E. "K", "O", "C" and "D" were Harwich anti-E-boat patrols off Southwold, Yarmouth, Cromer and Sheringham respectively.

In August 20th and 5th Flotillas moved to Immingham, where they had been before Norway. The light cruisers *Aurora* and *Galatea* joined them. Meanwhile 21st Flotilla, made up of *Campbell* and some V/Ws, was sent to Sheerness, whence it patrolled in front of Dover on alternate nights (with the Portsmouth destroyers). Also at *Wildfire* were *Birmingham* and *Manchester*, of 18th Cruiser Squadron, and the gunboat *Locust*. Sheerness warships ran a

INVASION IMMINENT

periodic "Patrol S", off Margate.

A whole new section of the Navy appeared on the East Coast the week after Dunkirk. The Admiralty was reviving the First World War Auxiliary Patrol, whose duty was to protect coastal and inshore waters against invaders and sea-raiders _ and it also incorporated minewatching. Extra trawlers, drifters, yachts and motor boats were requisitioned for this purpose, or transferred from minesweeping. The manpower came largely from the RNR and RNVR in the case of officers, and the Royal Naval patrol Service's drafting base at HMS *Europa* (Lowestoft) in that of ratings. (The latter, in spite of its name, had been established in 1939 to crew the A/S and M/S trawlers and drifters). The "Soap" (Senior Officer Auxiliary Patrol) at a base would be professional RN or RNR, his Group Officers (a group comprised from three to five vessels) RNR or more often RNVR, and the individual vessel skippers invariably RNR. The skippers, crews, trawlers and drifters, as in the minesweeping fleet, originated from the fishing ports of the Humber, East Anglia and Eastern Scotland. The yachts and motor boats were mainly from the Sheerness Small Vessels Pool and the Dunkirk operation _ and to man them the big backlog of T 124 volunteers, drafted after "Dynamo", were "invited" to stay on indefinitely as members of the Patrol Service (the real alternative was conscription).

By the spring of 1941 there were 746 light naval craft in the Nore Command (apart from a few MTB- and ML-type craft all taken from civilian owners), as compared to 432 in Western Approaches, with double the coastline. Nearly half the Nore total were former fishing vessels, and another quarter former pleasure boats. About one third were Auxiliary Patrol.

Reference to so many warships, of diverse functions, as "trawlers" or "drifters" may have mystified readers. These were, of course, the two larger general types of prewar fishing vessel. Trawlers were relatively big (200-650 ton), long-distance, deep-draught vessels, which fished waters as distant as the Arctic with "trawls" or bag-shaped nets. In peacetime most had been based at Grimsby, Hull, the North East Scottish ports or sometimes Fleetwood in Lancashire. Drifters were smaller, shallow-draught vessels, (of 50-150 tons), which fished the North Sea sandbanks with "drift nets" hung vertically downwards like curtains. They had mostly been based at Yarmouth, Lowestoft or the small Fifeshire ports. Owing to their size and range only trawlers were used for A/S (i.e, convoy escort), boom and "O" minesweeping work, but both types did LL sweeping and patrol, while for inshore duties such as examination, barrage-balloon mooring and store-loading drifters were usual. And so the terms "trawler" and "drifter" give only a partial indication of an ex-fishing vessel's wartime job.

Many had already served in the First World War, and nearly all were coal-fired, with what today seem weirdly antique high wheelhouses and tall funnels.

Most of the East Coast trawlers and drifters had originated locally. A trawler with the prefix "Lord" was likely to have been requisitioned from Pickering and Haldane, of Hull, though the "Lord" drifters were from the Lowestoft Steam Herring Drifters Company. Trawlers named after native tribes (like *Basuto*) were from Hellyers', and those with the prefix "Cape" from Hudsons', both Hull firms. The suffix "Wyke" indicated an Ernest Robbins (West Dock Steam Fishing Company) vessel, also of Hull. Names starting with "R" mostly meant Sleight's, and those with "S" the Standard Steam Fishing Company, both of Grimsby. But the largest requisitioning source was Sir John Marsden's Consolidated Fisheries, Grimsby, which had 135 vessels according to the prewar Lloyd's List.

Some of the naval fishing vessels were foreign. There were Dutch, Belgian and French craft, some of which had come via Dunkirk. At Harwich the 30th Danlaying Flotilla consisted of five Antarctic whalers (all with names beginning with "S"), with high bow decks for harpoons.

At sea each AP vessel had a patrol line some five to eight miles long, along which she shuttled every few hours (some lines had double patrols). Each patrol line had a code letter and number (H for Harwich, G for Grimsby or Humber, N for Nore or Sheerness, Y for Yarmouth). Mostly (at least for the first year) there was a double set of lines. A sea patrol vessel kept station for about six days at a time and then put into harbour for two or three days to coal, provision and give the crew leave. River patrols mostly operated only at night, though in the wide Blackwater and Wash a routine of three whole days on, three off, three on, three standby was standard. The Auxiliary Patrol was armed, according to the size of craft, with 12, 6 and 3-pdr guns, Hotchkiss and Bren machine guns, rifles and Holman projectors (compressed air tubes for throwing hand grenades), and even cutlasses for hand-to-hand fighting! Slightly later on a common if odd weapon was the PAC (parachute and cable), a compressed air launching tube which threw a canister containing

INVASION IMMINENT

parachutes, cable and hand grenades at enemy aircraft _ the cable was meant to wrap round the wings until the grenades made contact!

The Auxiliary Patrol, at least in its early days, was in some ways a slovenly affair. With the connivance of skippers and even officers crews carried fishing nets in the hope of passing the time, supplementing their rations, and making money ashore. They tended to stay put at their patrol positions instead of moving around. The first uniforms were simply fishermen's clothing. Ships were seldom cleaned. The officers struggled to tighten up, especially by remaining aboard their little "flagships" in harbour and by actually commanding them in place of their usual fisherman-skippers. On *Evening Primrose* Lt Laine RNVR, then a Group Officer at Brightlingsea, met

> "one Skipper C, a really grubby old man who had been a skipper in drifters in the 1914-18 war and was loved by NOIC because he had won the DSC at Dunkirk. His ship was filthy, and the old man, with whom one was obliged to take ones meals in the primitive wardroom, where we also slept, wore an old cloth cap with which he wiped his face after eating. He always removed his false teeth and put them beside his plate after meals with quite a flourish _another off-putting habit. But luckily I have a cast-iron stomach".

Against this negative picture, the patrol crews were a hardy lot, philosophical about exchanging the perils of Arctic voyages for the dangers of mines and bombs nearer home. They became adept with their AA weapons, and though mostly unable to see the nighttime enemy minelaying. sometimes reported it and saved many lives on other ships. Their losses were considerable.

A special part of the Patrol was the Examination Service, which stopped and checked all craft approaching East Coast harbours. This operated from the Danzig Crisis of 1939 off the Thames, Harwich and Humber (with drifters), where it dealt with vessels up to ocean-going size and boarded ships to search for contraband, enemy personnel, etc. It was now extended to the minor ports _ the River Crouch, Brightlingsea (for Colne and Blackwater), Lowestoft, Yarmouth, King's Lynn, Boston and Bridlington _ but here it dealt mostly with small craft and had no search powers. To communicate with their examination boats, or directly to approaching ships, naval bases set up signal stations on top of suitable structures like coastguard stations, forts or Martello Towers. The signallers were equipped with Aldis (Morse code) lights and flags. Their stations were classified into PWSSs (Port War Signal Stations), manned by sailors, and at major harbours, and

INVASION IMMINENT

MWSSs (Minor Stations), run by Royal Marines and later sometimes by "Wrens" (Womens' Royal Naval Service).

To help safeguard the estuaries from raiders or invaders the first physical precautions were taken in July 1940. "Observation" minefields were laid at Yarmouth, Lowestoft, across the Colne below Brightlingsea, at Holehaven, Coalhouse Point (across the Thames below Tilbury), and across the Medway at Sheerness. They consisted of Great War-surplus torpedo heads on which the detonators were "dead" until switched on along a single continuous electric cable by an "observer" on shore. To seal up other openings _ the Wash, Ore (Suffolk), Hamford Water and River Crouch (Essex) _ "booms" or barriers of chains, cables, nets or small yachts were laid. No fewer than two hundred of the latter were scattered about the Crouch and Roach to block enemy seaplane landings. The Thames, Harwich and Humber anti-submarine booms were strengthened with a finer mesh. These booms were now major undertakings, with many vessels needed on each to guard and open the gates, do repairs and maintenance, and ferry personnel back and forth. For instance the Sheerness, or Thames, boom base operated fourteen trawlers and tugs, five unpowered lighters, and five civilian-manned launches, and employed over four hundred people _ the boom between Shoeburyness and Sheppey was six miles long. Boom departments also installed and tended lines of underwater obstructions laid off potential invasion beaches. Indicator loops lay on the seabed off each boom, and to these Asdic (in today's parlance Sonar) sets were now added. Three torpedo-tubes were rigged up at Harwich Shipyard, three at Thameshaven Oil Pier, and six at Sheerness _ and near the latter it was even proposed to put some on the 1820-vintage hulk *Cornwallis*, until her timbers were found to be too weak. Blockships were anchored inside harbours, to be towed into entrance channels in the event of succesful enemy landings _ the *Amelia Lauro* wreck in the Humber, the *Como* at Yarmouth, the *Vina* at Lowestoft, the *Frederika Larsen* at Harwich (for the Orwell). The Army dotted nineteen old ships along the Thames between Barking and Canvey and mounted one 12-pdr and one Lewis gun on each.

At the beginning of July 1940 the Nore Command was considerably reorganised. An additional Sub-Command, Yarmouth, was carved out of the northern part of Harwich and the southern of the Humber _ its jurisdiction ran from the Wash and the latitude of Mablethorpe to the Minsmere River

THE BRIGHTLINGSEA AUXILIARY PATROL
ABOVE: Yacht crews assembled in harbour.
BELOW: Patrol boat returning from a check on a Thames sailing barge.
(Ashcroft)

BRIGHTLiNGSEA
(continued)
this page from top left:
1) Drifter at Aldous's Jetty, January, 1941.
2) River patrol crew manning Hotchkiss guns during a morning air raid alert.
3) *Coretta* (crewed by Wivenhoe man P O Ernie Vince) coming alongside *Kongoni*.
4) The brand-new *Aquabelle*.
above right: *Marsayru* (Patrol Boat 25) and trawlers in Brightlingsea Reach (Mersea in background). *Marsayru* was formerly the property of G D Olivier, the film-actor's brother and himself a Coastal Forces officer on the East Coast. All the patrol boats shown here had been at Dunkirk. *(all Ashcroft)*

Above Left: Captain Henniker Heaton, NOIC Brightlingsea (left) with Rear-Adm Harris, FOIC Harwich, touring the Blackwater on the yacht *Kongoni* during the invasion scare of 1940.
(Ashcroft)

Above Right: Officers of Yarmouth Sub-Command. L to R: Adm Fullerton, FOIC Yarmouth; Cdre de Pass, of HMS *Europa*, & Capt Stoker, NOIC Lowestoft.

Left: RN Patrol Service recruits at the Sparrows' Nest, HMS *Europa*. *(Ford Jenkins)*

HARWICH FIXED DEFENCES

TOP: Landguard Right Battery, Felixstowe. Men of 515 (Suffolk) Coast Artillery Regiment loading a 6-inch gun. *(IWM)*

ABOVE LEFT: Darrell's twin-6-pdr Battery (note the BOPs) and Languard Fort (War Signal Station top right) seen from Landguard Right Battery, 1974. Harwich is across the water in the distance.

RIGHT: Beacon Hill Battery, Harwich. In order from the front the structures are 1) Steel window shutters of Cornwallis Battery BOP, 2) Old A1 6-inch gun site, 3) New A1 gun site, 4) 6-inch battery BOP, 5) A2 6-inch gun site, 6) Radar tower.

INVASION IMMINENT

(between Dunwich and Sizewell, Suffolk). The FOIC, replacing a more junior NOIC* subordinate to the Harwich FOIC, was a distinguished retired admiral, Sir Eric Fullerton. Lowestoft (apart from HMS *Europa*) was upgraded from being an annex of Yarmouth to a base in its own right, with the title HMS *Minos* and a NOIC, Captain H H G D Stoker DSO, though minesweeping there was yet another establishment called HMS *Martello*. *Minos* was responsible for the whole seagoing Auxiliary Patrol in Yarmouth Sub-Command. In Harwich Sub-Command Brightlingsea and Felixstowe became semi-autonomous bases under the names HMSs *Nemo* and *Beehive*, the former mainly an Auxiliary Patrol base, the latter responsible for MTBs. Brightlingsea had an NOIC, Captain A Henniker-Heaton, who was also RNO+ Frinton.. Felixstowe came directly under the Harwich FOIC, Rear-Admiral Harris. From July Ipswich was an overspill base accommodating the Auxiliary Patrol for the northern half of Harwich Sub-Command: from September it was termed HMS *Bunting*. Its SOAP, Cdr Cubison, formerly of *Vernon*'s Mine Recovery Flotilla, came under Harwich.

So far in this book I have concentrated on the Royal Navy. But the invasion threat equally concerned the Army. The oldest Army defences on the East Coast were the Coast Artillery fortifications, which originated from Tudor times and had been repeatedly rebuilt since to resist the threat of Holland, France and Germany in turn, These "Fixed Defences" were to be seen round the Thames and Medway mouths, Harwich, Lowestoft, Yarmouth and the Humber. Between the wars they had normally been unmanned save for a few caretakers and maintenance men. In 1932, in one of the earliest rearmament moves, a command called HQ Coast Defences, Eastern Ports, was set up at Sheerness. In the 1939 Danzig Crisis the batteries were quickly manned by local (county) Territorial Army Heavy Artillery Regiments. These were given numbers and the title "Coast Regiments (Royal Artillery) _"coastal" is a misnomer.

Their guns were two and occasionally three or four to a battery. The larger calibres were 9.2, 6 and 4.7 inches. They were mounted on rings of

---

*Naval Officer in Charge.

+Resident Naval Officer. To recap all these titles: a FOIC ran a Sub-Command, an NOIC a subsidiary base within a Sub-Command, while an RNO did not normally command vessels, but represented the Navy on a section of coast with little or no base.

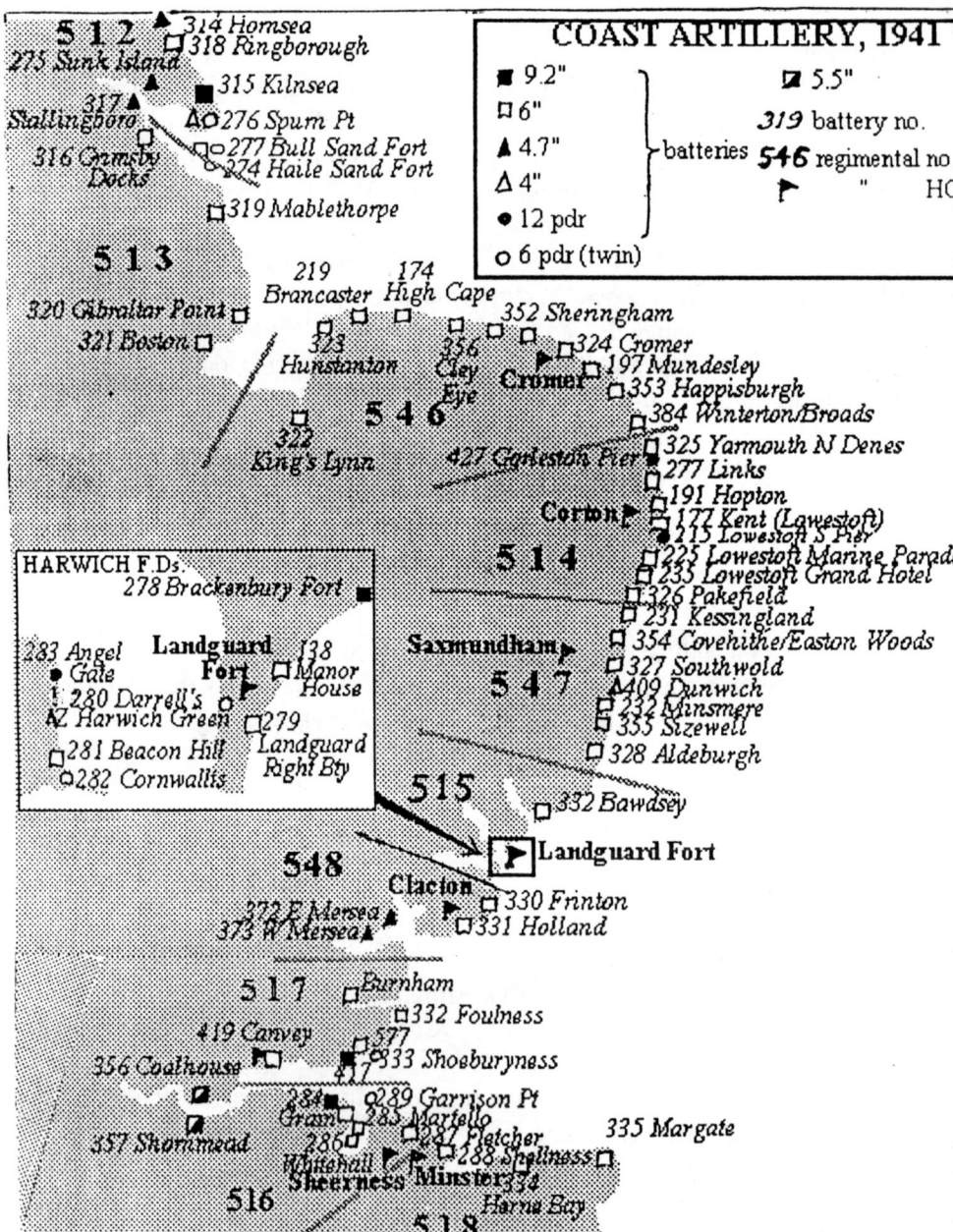

INVASION IMMINENT

steel bolts set in the floors of concrete wells, so that when horizontal the barrels just cleared the ground. The 9.2-inch fired a 380-pound shell to a maximum range of seventeen miles. The original light weapon, for defence against E-Boat raids primarily, was the 12-pdr (calibre 3-inch). In 1940 this was replaced or supplemented by the twin 6-pdr quick-firer (calibre, 2 inches), which fired up to two rounds a second when expertly handled, being fed straight from the magazine by whole trays of ammunition raised on lifts and swung out to the breaches. There were three pairs of these guns at Harwich Harbour, where, at the battery named after Darrell, who in 1667 saved Landguard Fort from capture by the Dutch, two pairs replaced two 4.7-inch weapons, which had just been removed, shipped to Norway, and sunk en route.

In May 1940 Coast Artillery was suddenly expanded. The guns were "housed" in steel front shields and ferroconcrete side, rear and overhead cover, to a thickness of fourteen inches. On the coastline between major harbours many additional batteries, mostly 6-inch, appeared. The total number of guns rose to a maximum of some 130, including twenty-eight on the Humber, eighteen at Harwich Harbour and twenty-nine on the Thames and Medway. Many of the new guns were Navy-surplus, and for a few weeks were manned by sailors, but soon all but "Z" Battery on Harwich Green (two 4-inch pieces operated by Royal Marines) had all been transferred to the Army.*

The manpower of a two-gun coast battery ranged from about seventy to 150. Since only about six to eight men were needed to work a single gun at a given moment, this seems a high figure. But each battery had a "BOP" (Battery Observation Post) _ a concrete tower with steel shutters for lookouts and rangefinders, two searchlights, one or two sentry posts for inland defence and security, a magazine, an electric generator room, and machine guns for local (including AA) defence, and all these needed relief watches. With barrack huts, storerooms, cookhouses and so on the Fixed Defences sites sprawled across sizeable areas _ those at Harwich covered over two hundred acres, and the Landguard compound was over a mile long. Initially the original Coast Regiments had charge of the new, temporary batteries along the shores away from the harbours. 515 Regiment, at Landguard, at one time included all the guns from West Mersea to Thorpeness, and a manpower of 1,500. In December 1940, however, the new guns to left and right of the

---

*Z Battery moved to Egypt in February 1941. Note that the term "Z Battery" has no connection with the anti-aircraft rockets also installed at Harwich.

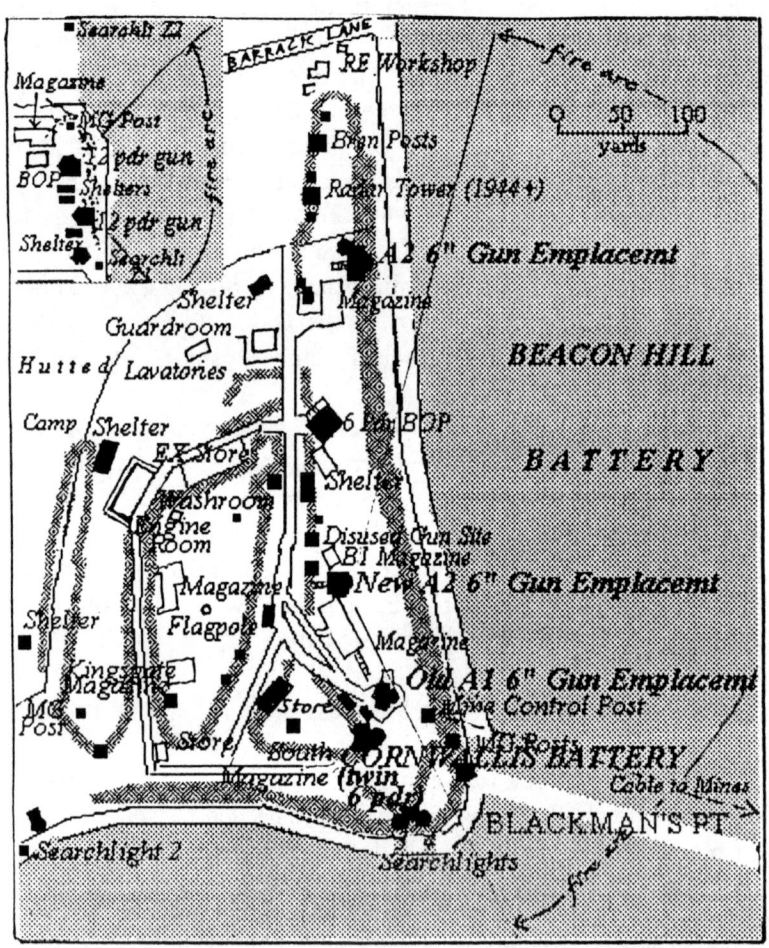

FIXED DEFENCES AT BEACON HILL & (inset) ANGEL GATE, HARWICH

immediate Harwich-Felixstowe area were split off under separate regiments _ 547 (centred at Saxmundham) and 548 (Clacton) respectively. 546 was the new regiment on the North Norfolk coast, centred on Cromer. In 1942 the Lowestoft guns were separated from those at Yarmouth, as 544 Regiment, and those at Harwich proper from those at Felixstowe, as 572 Regiment.

These defences incorporated some old forts, like Grain on the Medway, Coalhouse on the Thames, and Landguard at Felixstowe. At

INVASION IMMINENT

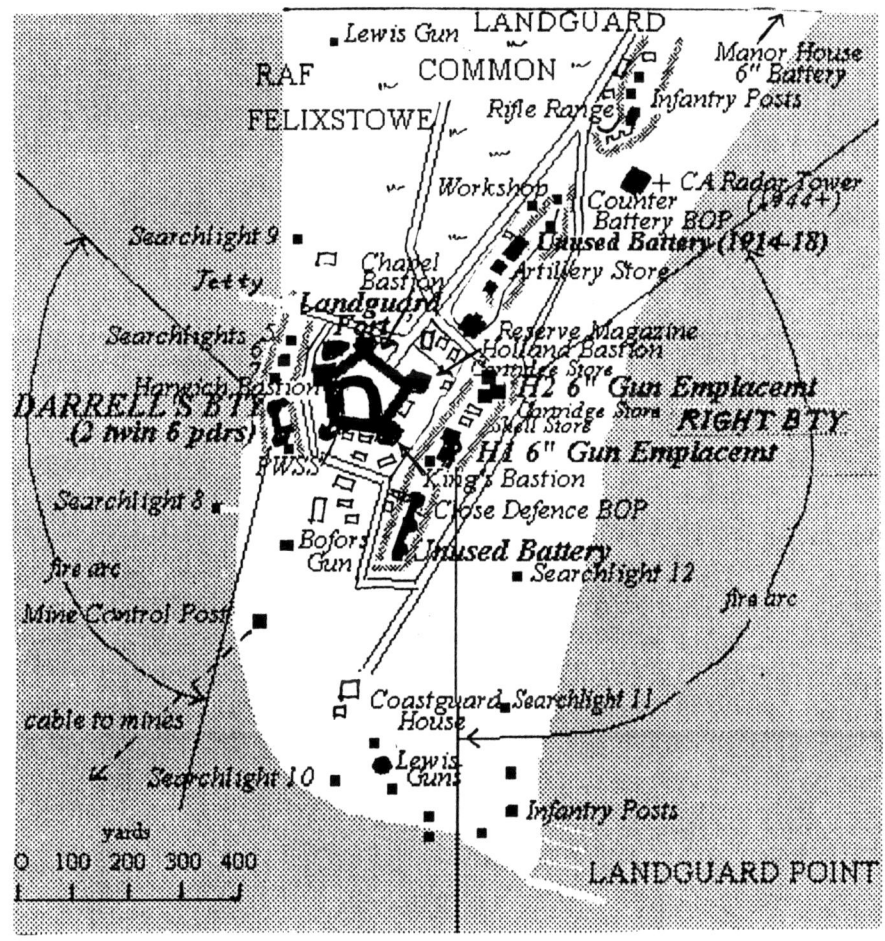

FIXED DEFENCES AT LANDGUARD (Felixstowe)

Sheerness two BOPs and two guns were built onto Garrison Point Fort. Landguard Fort, a similar great Victorian brick pentagon aptly known as "The Tomb", was an important headquarters for the Harwich area. It housed Fixed defences HQ and initially the Operations Room for the AA guns, till this was transferred to the even older Q Tower, a Martello Tower in Felixstowe Town. It was also the PWSS for Harwich Harbour: from an observation post on the roof naval lookouts and signallers checked incoming shipping and could activate guns, searchlights and minefield if necessary. On boards above the windows buoys, lightships and church towers were neatly painted together with their distances and bearings. Garrison Point and Spurn Point Forts were the equivalents on the Medway and Humber. From these eyries dramatic events were seen amid the cold and dark monotony; ships blowing up on mines, bombing attacks, planes crashing. By night there were awe-inspiring and mysterious pyrotechnics. Sudden flashes out to sea might be bombs or mines exploding, convoys shooting at E-boats or aircraft, British warships on night-firing exercises, ships signalling by Aldis lamp, or men adrift and firing distress rockets. Frequently a red glow, particularly in the direction of London, signalled incendiary- bomb fires. From as far north as Harwich it was occasionally possible to see the flash of the German big guns at Cap Gris Nez (firing into Kent) or the searchlight beams over Dunkirk, both eighty miles away. Sometimes the observation posts became as light as day from the greenish glare of aircraft flares, whereupon flak and tracer would erupt on all sides.

The Fixed Defenced had many limitations until late in the war. Their emplacements were of rather feeble construction (mere brick in the case of the new batteries), proof only against the lighter shells and bombs. The guns were hand-traversed and elevated. There was no gunlaying radar until 1944, though AA had it from as early as 1941. Several batteries (e.g, Brackenbury, Happisburgh, Cromer) were built on crumbling sandstone cliffs, which meant that they had to practice with half-charge ammunition for fear of undermining themselves. The camouflage of the sites was poor, and one can still see a BOP, painted with fictitious doors and windows to resemble a house, in spite of standing alone in the middle of Beacon Hill Battery, Harwich. Inadequate for general coastal coverage, the guns did protect the harbours, however, and the Germans actually had few big warships or heavy bomber planes with which to have "cracked" them. Many of the concrete emplacements and towers remain to this day, at least at the prewar permanent sites, though the last of them were abandoned by the Army in 1957.

Separate from Coast Artillery were the mobile guns brought up to cover particularly important stretches of coast during the invasion threat. 43 Royal Marine Battery mounted eight 12-pdrs on three-ton lorries at Catton, Norwich, to support the coast defence of Norfolk. Pairs of 9.2-inch Great War howitzers, remeniscent of the Somme or Ypres, were stationed some five

INVASION IMMINENT

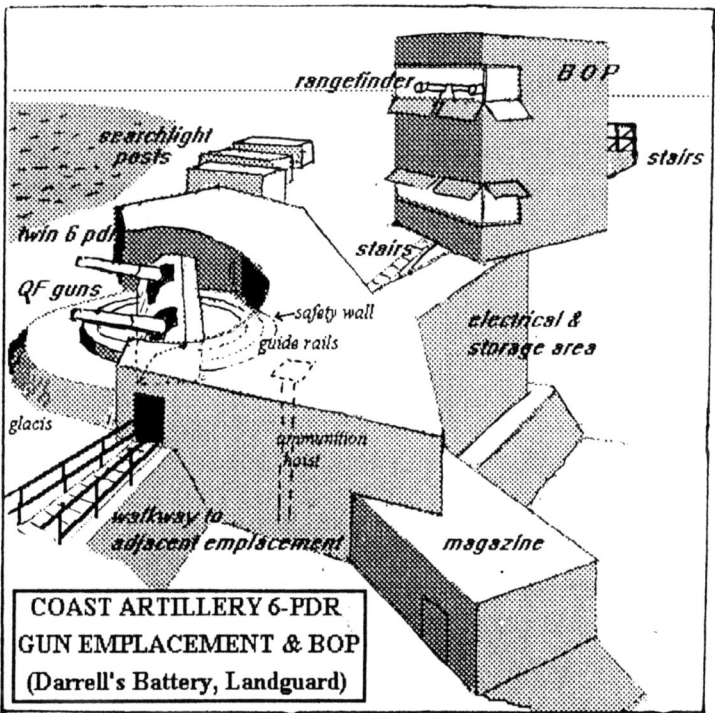

COAST ARTILLERY 6-PDR GUN EMPLACEMENT & BOP (Darrell's Battery, Landguard)

miles inland at various points. And 1st Super Heavy Regiment trundled two 12-inch railway guns onto specially built sidings at Levington Bridge and Walk Gate Farm, Trimley St Martin, and two more to Tollesbury (later shifted to Holland-on-Sea), to cover the Harwich sector. On practice shoots the Levington and Trimley shells (each a third of a ton) passed right over Felixstowe and hit the sea several miles off Brackenbury Fort.

The coastline was continuously defended by infantry divisions (subdivided into brigades and battalions), with field and anti-tank artillery regiments attached. These also safeguarded against attacks from inland by parachutists, who had proved so dangerous in Holland and Belgium. These infantry divisions, none of which had been in action on the Continent, first took up station on the East Coast in June 1940, when still very deficient in weapons, transport and ammunition. At that time invasion was expected on the East rather than the South Coast _ until enemy shipping began to move through into the English Channel in September. XI Corps, with HQ at Althorne near Burnham-on-Crouch, had 15th (Scottish) Division on the

INVASION IMMINENT

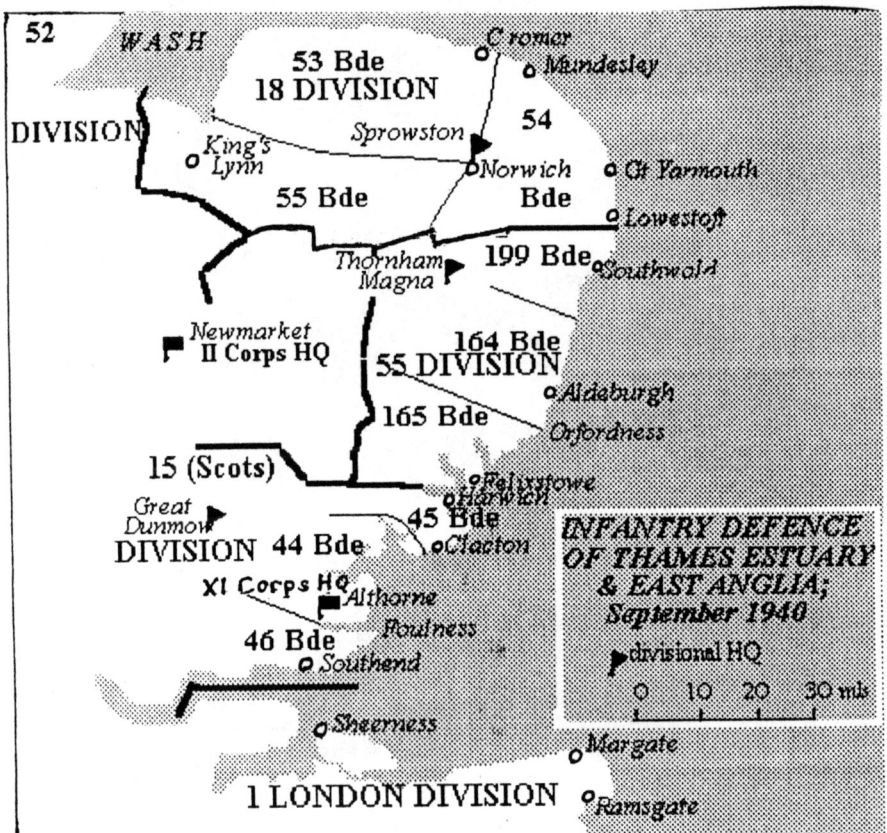

Essex coast and 55th on the Suffolk. II Corps had 18th Division* in Norfolk and 1st in Lincolnshire. XII Corps had 1st London Division in North East Kent. As a first priority, they built concrete or brick pillboxes all along the shore and also on the inland sides of ports (an average on one every fifth of a mile), and supplemented these with about twice that number of sandbagged weapon pits. The same frontages were entangled with barbed wire. Explosive charges, or "Bosche Bumps", were placed under all roads and even tracks leading to the coast. All side roads were stopped with huge concrete blocks. At quaysides were "flame fougasses", tanks of fuel which could be opened up and ignited if the enemy landed there. These kinds of defences helped offset the initial lack of all modern weapons except rifles. When engaged in a mock invasion exercise near Harwich on 24 September 1940 the 10th Cameronians were briefed; "Red band on enemy rifle means Bren gun and blue band means

---

*later captured by the Japanese at Singapore.

INVASION IMMINENT

anti-tank rifle". An impressive expedient were the half-dozen armoured trains (for all their protection feeble in firepower), which could reach many remote ports by rail, and which were manned by exiled Poles.*

In view of the lack of up-to-date artillery pieces (only a few 18-pdrs were available), three types of First War gun were distributed _ the 4-inch static (for landward defence of ports), the 6-pdr (small enough to be carried inside a lorry and run down on planks, necessary in view of the lack of suitable tractors), and the French 75-mm (equivalent to 3-inch, and a classic gun indeed), a stock of which Churchill had just imported from America. These had to double as anti-tank weapons, firing solid, armour-piercing, shot, as only a very few of the rather ineffective 2-pdrs were available. Church towers were fitted as artillery spotting posts.

Security and sentry work at naval and airforce bases was provided by miscellaneous unbrigaded units made up boy soldiers or men too old or unfit for combat _ a company for a naval or large air base, a platoon or two for an RDF station. 9th and 70th Suffolk Battalions, based at Ipswich, were examples of these units.

Other services were required to help defend the coastline _ RAF and Royal Navy bases organised their own defence schemes and kept stocks of rifles. Finally, there was the Home Guard, or "LDV" (Local Defence Volunteers), as the generals preferred to call them. This weekend civilian army was inaugurated at Churchill's personal insistence on 25 May 1940. On the following day public enrolment meetings were held at all the East Coast towns. The Home Guard was organised into units of up to battalion size. Its normal routine was training on one or two evenings a week and relieving army sentries at weekends at such secondary strategic points as railway stations, gasworks, water towers, electricity sub-stations, telephone exchanges, hospitals and searchlight sites. In invasion alerts it was, according to Army orders of June 1941, to man pillboxes, put villages in states of all-round defence, keep lookout for parachutists, man roadblocks, direct traffic, and run errands. Until 1942 the only transport available was requisitioned buses and vans, and all supplies, especially ammunition, were very scarce.

There were three states of readiness, short of actual combat; "Normal", "Alert" and "Invasion Imminent". Arrangements varied, but typically one fifth of defenders manned their posts under the first. At naval bases the rest were at two hours' notice by day (primarily for beach landings)

---

*Train "C" caused a stir at Aldeburgh on 2 November, 1940, by shooting down a raiding Dornier. "D" mostly inhabited a siding at Mistley, just up the Stour from Harwich.

and half an hour by night (mainly for harbour raids and parachute drops). Elsewhere it was sufficient for four-fifths to be at four hours' notice day and night. "Alert" meant a two-fifths manning, with notice for the rest cut to half an hour. "Invasion imminent" meant the cancellation of all leave, the total manning of defences in misty weather, three quarters by night, and half in daylight. "Alert" was continually being occasioned by rumours, unidentified ships and official intelligence, sometimes as many as three times a day. By night the defence perimeters were continuously patrolled by troops equipped with indispensible maps of the minefields and with pyrotechnics for signalling, while motor boats did likewise on the estuaries and creeks as from 22 June. A green rocket meant "I have sighted enemy ships", a Golden Rain "SOS, enemy landing", a red "Enemy have landed", and a white "I require assistance". Any strange vehicles on the roads or boats on the rivers and creeks were to be challenged, and if challenged to answer, with four blasts on the horn or four light flashes. The peculiar list of telephone and radio codewords read:

Toadstools = beachmines
Blackbirds = have sighted enemy ships
Gallipoli = enemy landing from ships
Parasols = enemy parachutists
Caterpillars = enemy landing tanks
Pepper air = being attacked by aircraft
Purge = landing about to take place.

The many exercises were not always strong on realism and official reports of some make comic reading today. One can imagine the banter between troops with plain rifles and those with the magical coloured bands. The same exercise included an imaginary German naval attack. Said the report; "Two E-boats struck mines on nearing the shore, a third landed and all its crew were rounded up and destroyed" (presumably "and" here meant "or"!),"...one prisoner states that the mouth of the Thames is in German hands and it won't be long before Harwich is too". In another Harwich-area exercise, in January 1941, there was a fanciful scenario: "England is a portion of the globe of which Italy is in temporary possession. The population is unarmed but loathes the WOP and is pro-British in its sympathies"*. Meanwhile, at Southend, "Oberleutnant Adolf Stuggenheimer and thirty fanatics" landed from a Dutch schuyt and linked up with local fifth

---

*10 Cameronians War Diary.

LEFT: The Czech Army newspaper "Our News", produced at Dovercourt in 1943 (and previously at Lowestoft). *(Cummings)*

BELOW: The crew of a 6-inch coast artillery gun doing drill at the outbreak of war _ probably at Shoeburyness. As yet the emplacement has no front shield or overhead cover. *(Sport & General)*

ABOVE: Sq Ldr Peter Townsend, pictured at Martlesham Heath in July 1940. *(WI)*

WINTER 1941, & THE LUFTWAFFE WAR AGAINST NORTH SEA SHIPPING SPILLS OVER ONTO THE EAST COAST

Top Right: bomb damage to Colman's Wharf, Great Yarmouth, after the attack on 14 February. *(Box)*

Above: an unexploded German Type-C mine in a Hull garden a few days later. Note the parachute draped over the fence. *(Geraghty)*

INVASION IMMINENT

columnists, clad in British uniforms procured from the treacherous Quartermaster of the 11th Highland Light Infantry in exchange for his beloved whisky and haggis _ the rest of that battalion had to crush this coup de main before the "main invasion".*

Just as absurd, to us now, are some of the warnings about fifth columnists, which were thought (largely falsely) to have helped the invaders of Norway, Holland, Belgium and France. In the summer of 1940 troops and police were told to regard the following people as "suspicious"; men holding their hands above their heads (possibly armed with bombs), those unable to speak English, men armed with sub-machine guns, men looking like women in disguise. With heavy but unconscious irony some divisional Intelligence officers expressed extra suspicion of such wandering persons as commercial travellers because they were "obviously Jewish"! Another document is tinged with the sinister as well as the absurd: "Maldon is known to have a large Fascist element", it said. The manager of the Maldon flour mill was suspected of weakening the local Home Guard by enrolling boys in it and rejecting men. A friend of Mosley lived at Colchester. A night watchman at Feering had a German wife, and had refused to pass on an LDV message. There was a German woman at Jaywick. A searchlight generator cable had been "deliberately cut" at Frinton. Entirely bogus LDV telephone calls had been made. There was suspicious behaviour by the owner of a West Mersea beach hut, rendered doubly significant by the "repeated cutting" of the Mersea telephone cable over the Strood (causeway). On 13 June a "steady light" was seen from Brightlingsea Creek. When a flashing light was seen from a house at Point Clear a "careful watch" was ordered...+

There had been a very similar scare around the same Essex estuaries in the First World War: The Army and Navy at Brightlingsea had spent years chasing suspicious lights to no avail, and right through to the Armistice had sworn that a nest of traitors existed nearby, probably on Mersea Island.

In his memoirs *Most Secret War* R V Jones, Scientific Adviser to the Government, gives a fascinating account of a visit he, RAF investigator Group Captain Blackford, and two RAF policemen paid to Norfolk early that July. The "C O" at Bircham Newton airfield claimed that fifth columnists were guiding in enemy bombers with fireworks, as well as jamming West Beckham RDF station. The suspects were the local electrical engineer, a

---

*Admiralty Report on Counter-Invasion Measures (PRO ADM 199/687).
+15 Division War Diary (PRO WO 166/448).

INVASION IMMINENT

former Mosleyite Blackshirt, and his father, the local stationer, who had mislaid a map with the West Beckham towers pencilled on. Armed with a warrant from Chief Constable Box of Norfolk, Jones and co. raided the two men's houses and found a small electrical device hidden at the electrical engineer's. However, this turned out to be a hair-remover belonging to his wife, while the stationer was found to be a scoutmaster, and his map one used for pointing out landmarks to the boys. Jones concluded that the whole thing was nonsense, to the disappointment of his fellow investigators. He concluded a hectic, not to say crazy, twenty-four hours by spending the night up one of the West Beckham towers with a device used for detecting the (very real and very dangerous) German radio navigation beams.

Meanwhile 18th Division troops in the same county were being told to look out for a strange code fifth columnists and German parachutists were "known" to mark out on fields or scratch on walls and telephone poles (I show part of it in Appendix G).

One can see how any state, in a war situation, develops unpleasent fantasies _ change the placenames and these could all be secret police utterances from Stalin's Russia! I believe that in the case of the East Coast of England in 1940 they had three main causes: 1)the authorities were aware how weak security and public vigilance still were and therefore deliberately fostered the rumours, absurd or not; 2)few could accept the humiliating thought that Germany might be winning the war so far for straightforward military reasons, and therefore resorted to conspiracy myths; and 3)British Army Intelligence mistook the easygoing and indifferent attitude towards the war effort of some East Anglian civilians for enemy sympathies.

Some of the security worries were, of course, justified. At the period of maximum invasion danger in September 1940 the commander of 1st London Division, in North- East Kent, rated his own men's sense of secrecy "deplorable". He was mostly concerned about loose telephone talk _ in such verbal communication the division used a jargon called "Code Ridiculous", but often so carelessly and lazily as to tell a wire-tapper all he needed to know. Yet one cannot help thinking that the name given to the code had been asking for trouble!

Behind the absurdity and occasional panic a grim determination took hold. Defenders of harbour areas in particular were to do everything in their power to deny them to the Germans. Standing orders were of the following

INVASION IMMINENT

kind:

"The Felixstowe battalion will defend the battalion area against any form of attack, with every means at its disposal and with the cooperation of all supporting arms, and to the last man and the last round. There will be NO withdrawal".*

Those who had experienced the Blitzkrieg first hand can have harboured few illusions about the likely effectiveness of obsolete guns, feeble pillboxes and thin barbed wire against tanks and crack infantry _ indeed XI and II Corps were soon saying their divisions had built too many static defences and had picked up the dangerous Maginot mentality. While the Navy at Harwich, Chatham and Sheerness had elaborate plans to beach and immobilise its ships, and to evacuate all personnel by rail, in the event of successful invasion, the Army was briefed to demolish the port installations. Dock cranes, jetties, quays, dry docks, approach roads and railways, gasworks and petrol tanks, were all to be blown up. At Harwich alone official lists noted for destruction fifty civilian installations alone, unknown to their owners. Every Army division had maps of the roads in its area set aside for the mass flight of civilian refugees. Once the coast was in German hands there were only the handfuls of almost literally underground fighters organised by Intelligence and so secret as to be unknown even to the three regular services _ to put up a guerrilla resistance. These units, collectively the so-called 202 Battalion, maintained underground hides in woods and fields, where weapons were stored and there were even bunks. David Lampe gave details of these in his book *The Last Ditch*, describing, for example, the unit based at Weeley, nine miles south-west of Harwich, and commanded by the local squire, also called Weeley.

Round the clock the British infantry patrols trudged the shore and back areas open to parachutists. By day little more met the eye in many places than the bleak North Sea, and, to landwards, pools of brackish water, marsh grass, telegraph poles and mud tracks stretching away in desolation. The blacked-out night was sometimes so dark as to merge land, water and sky. Then sounds became accentuated. When the tide was down birds twittered on the mud: when it was up there was a continuous hiss of sea on shingle. On such nights the scuttle of a rabbit, the yowl of a stray dog, the momentary light-flash from a ship or a house adjusting its blackout, the slapping of waves on a wooden groyne, could seem menacing. Panicky

---
*212 Bde War Diary (PRO WO 166/1065).

fingers might fumble with Very pistols and rifle bolts. A frightened challenge might ring out, or even a startled rifle shot, but only the rustle of unknown wildlife, or the usual sound of wind and waves, would come back to the straining ears.

Officers of the East Coast divisions were told that there were 8,400 barges in Belgium and 18,000 in Holland, from which 4,700, totalling ten million tons, might be used by the enemy to invade East Anglia with ten divisions. On 13 August _ what the Luftwaffe called "Eagle Day", there was a rumour of invasion from Norway, and all Nore Command ships were put on half an hour's notice. It was a complete false alarm. On 18 August all coastal units were ordered to watch very studiously for "unnatural fog", since the enemy were said to have a scheme to produce this all along the invasion coast to cover his crossing. A week later such an omen was reported all the way from Beachy Head to Yarmouth, and the most widespread alert so far was ordered. The fog turned out to be natural sea mist, and to extend from Beachy Head not to Great Yarmouth, but the much nearer Yarmouth Isle of Wight. On 26 August Nore Command issued "Operational Order P2", warning bases that

"on receipt of the signal "Purge!"...Auxiliary Patrol vessels in the ____proceed to attack the enemy's transports forthwith."

On 31 August there was a firm report of an enemy fleet emerging from the Zuider Zee and steaming west. The whole Nore Command was put on alert. 5th Destroyer Flotilla was sent from the Humber to attack the invaders. Three cruisers were moved from Scotland to the Humber. Harwich destroyers went out on patrol, and Sheerness ones came to the Aldeburgh Light Float to back them up. Submarine H34 came out from Harwich. 20th Destroyer Flotilla, then Immingham-based, steamed with its mines through Mine Barrier Gap D, heading for the Frisian Islands _ there to meet disaster in an uncharted enemy minefield. *Express* (the flotilla leader), *Esk* and *Ivanhoe*, making up the whole of "39th Division", were all mined off the Texel, on the north-west shoulder of Holland, shortly after 2300. According to some official sources the ships had already dumped their own mines in order to be able to fight an action, while others say that they were "made safe" at this point. *Esk* almost immediately sank with the loss of her captain (Lt-Cdr R J H Crouch) and all but one of her 150 or more crew. *Express* had

ABOVE: Captain (D) Bickford, of 20th Destroyer Flotilla, leaving Immingham for his funeral after the disaster of 31 August-1 September, 1940. *(IWM)*

BELOW: The monitor *Erebus*, based in the Medway during the 1940 and 1941 invasion alerts. Note the 15-inch guns. *(IWM)*

SHEERNESS MINESWEEPING TRAWLERS
Above: *Gilt Edge* heading out to sea. Garrison Point Fort in the left background and Thames barges distant right. *(IWM)*
Below: The *Milford Prince* _ later based at Ipswich as a danlayer. *(Mrs A Miller)*

INVASION IMMINENT

her whole fore section blown off back to the bridge, and Captain(D) J G Bickford and ninety other personnel were killed or fatally wounded: it was suggested, though never proved, that a mine had triggered her magazine. *Ivanhoe* had hit one mine with a paravane and been only slightly damaged, and began to take off *Express's* wounded, but a second mine then broke her back and left fifty-three of her crew dead or dying and most of the rest injured to greater or lesser degree.

Captain Mountbatten's 5th Flotilla came to the rescue. His flagship *Jupiter* went to help *Express*, and was joined by two small destroyers of 21st Flotilla, from Sheerness, the *Garth* and *Hambledon*, which had been near the Shipwash Light Vessel when news of the disaster was heard and had come through Gap E. Another 5th Flotilla destroyer, *Javelin*, went on a vain search for *Esk*. The Grimsby minesweepers *Leda* and *Saltash*, three tugs, and Felixstowe MTBs 29, 30 and 31 were also sent to *Express*, and six Blenheim fighters took off to provide air cover. A third 5th Flotilla destroyer, *Kelvin*, headed for *Ivanhoe*, and was later joined by *Garth* and the REF destroyer *Vortigern*.

When Mountbatten went alongside *Express* she piped a formal salute and all those crew who could stand to attention did so. He later confessed himself moved. The towing operation took the whole of 1 September. At noon, while rescuers and rescued were still much nearer to Holland than to England, two Dornier seaplanes appeared but did not attack _ Mountbatten mused that perhaps their crews were "not Nazis"(!) That night a Blohm and Voss HA 138 did drop one bomb which missed. Meanwhile *Jupiter* quite fortuitously rescued three more men, the crew of a Fleet Air Arm 812 Squadron Swordfish biplane bomber, which had crashed while raiding the Vlaardingen oil tanks, near Rotterdam, from North Coates aerodrome in Lincolnshire. At last, early on the 2nd, *Express* was pulled safe into the Humber. Men of all ranks wondered at Mountbatten's nerve in plunging into the same uncharted minefield as the three victims. For him it was a repeat of the previous May, when he had brought back the damaged *Kelly* over an even longer distance.

Meanwhile, at dawn on the 1st, a Hudson aircraft from North Coates flew over *Ivanhoe*, and signalled that four MTBs were coming from Felixstowe to take on the wounded. Three hours later they arrived: MTBs 14, 16, and 17 duly sped away with the injured while 15 stayed to help. Though

INVASION IMMINENT

the destroyer was still firmly afloat, her captain, Cdr P H Hadow, had already let himself be persuaded by his inexperienced Engineer Officer, Lt(E) Mahoney, that she should be abandoned. Repeated scuttling efforts nevertheless failed. *Kelvin* took survivors from boats and rafts, and at the request of Hadow, now on MTB 15, sank the wreck with a torpedo. A Dornier flying boat circled in the distance, but as if in response to the crew's audible prayers, no bombers appeared _ apparently those on the nearby Dutch bases were getting ready to raid the Thames mouth. Before *Ivanhoe* disappeared Hadow had himself left the scene. Some liferafts full of survivors had disappeared during the night: they had drifted in to the Dutch coast and their occupants were by now in German hands.

Altogether the death toll on the three destroyers was almost three hundred, but with wounded and prisoners the full casualty figure was well over four hundred: only during Dunkirk did the Nore Command suffer worse losses in a single day. Captain Bickford was buried at sea. An Admiralty Board of Inquiry at Hull three weeks later concluded that 20th Flotilla had had no way of avoiding the disaster, but criticised the unfortunate Hadow on three counts _ scuttling his ship rather than trying to have her towed, taking so long to sink her, and leaving the scene while she still floated. But I must record that the Department of Naval Construction later disagreed with the first charge, arguing that *Ivanhoe* had been doomed and that Mahoney and Hadow were right.

And what had the Nore Command achieved on 31 August and 1 September, beyond these rescues? In a word, nothing. It was announced next day that the "invasion fleet" had beenonly a German coastal convoy bound from the Elbe to the Maas, and that the whole alert had been a false alarm.

But with the peak of Battle of Britain in the skies, the "Alert" state became almost continuous. Early that September things came to a head. In one week the number of barges at Ostend, only eighty-six miles from Harwich, had risen from eighteen to 205. Four real spies had been captured after landing from a small boat in Kent, and another had been found after parachuting into Northamptonshire. On the 6th the scheduled FS convoy was ordered into the Humber out of harm's way. On the afternoon of the 7th the Luftwaffe flew en masse up the Estuary to make its first daylight raid on London. That evening the Chiefs of Staff learned that barges were now in Channel as well as North Sea ports, and at 2100 the "Invasion Imminent"

INVASION IMMINENT

codeword "Cromwell" was issued to all East and South Coast units. An hour later patrol vessels on standby at the Nore bases put to sea, while coast gunners, infantrymen and demolition parties stood to at their post with loaded weapons and gasmasks.

But the word was "Invasion Imminent", not "Invasion". Although "Cromwell" was misinterpreted by some troops in Sussex, who that night rang church bells and machine-gunned sheep in a field by mistake for parachutists, nearly all troops understood that although the enemy was now ready to move, he had not yet begun to do so. That night and the next the cruiser *Aurora* and three destroyers from Sheerness combed Calais Roads and saw no sign of the enemy putting to sea, and *Galatea* and three more destroyers had the same experience off Boulogne, which they were set to bombard until the visibility deteriorated. For these and two more nights the Harwich destroyers scoured right up to the Flemish sandbanks, off Ostend and the Scheldt, and encountered only one tug towing a barge, which they sank. On 10 September the shore defences reverted to "Alert". The naval bases circulated rumours, recalled to this day by many a person on the East Coast, that a German invasion fleet had been destroyed by pumping oil onto the water, and that the Channel was now full of charred enemy corpses _ but it had been *told* to spread them as a morale-booster!

On the 15th, after a day and a half of low cloud, storms and rain, fine weather returned. That night (while a harvest moon lit up the East Coast) the BBC broadcast the reassuring claim that over 180 German planes had been shot down in the day's air battles over London and the South East. Though serious night raids on London continued, there was little daylight Luftwaffe activity for the next two days.

Yet by 22nd there was again cause for alarm. Air activity had begun to pick up again. News was received that some of the 1,600 barges and other craft accumulated by the enemy in Dutch, Belgian and French harbours were in groups at sea off Calais and Emden. Admiral Drax, at the Nore, sent the following inaccurate message to his bases:

> "In the past two thousand years there have been only two successful invasions of Britain, Julius Caesar and William I in 1066. Another attempt may shortly be expected, but the defence will be far stronger than ever before".*

The Great War monitor *Erebus* was brought to Sheerness and on the nights

---

*PRO ADM 199/821

INVASION IMMINENT

of 29/30 September and 15/16 October shelled Calais and Dunkirk with her pair of mighty 15-inch guns, in attempts to add to the toll of sunken invasion barges already claimed by the RAF. The aged tankers *War Nizam* and *Oakfield* were fitted out at Sheerness and Chatham Dockyards to serve as fireships in the same cause. The desperate operation to run these into enemy harbours, codenamed "Lucid", was thrice initiated that autumn, to be called off each time when the alert was lifted.

There was no great event that signalled the passing of the danger, but as the autumn drew on, anxiety gradually lessened.

An invasion was, nonetheless, fully expected to come in the spring or summer of 1941. During the intervening winter some major defence preparations were carried out. The garrisons at the major naval bases were roughly doubled in numbers and, with extra guns of all types, trebled in firepower. They completed inland defences as strong as those to seaward. A more flexible Army deployment now took place. Much of the coastline was given to static, second-grade, divisions such as the Lincolnshire, Norfolk and Essex County, while the mobile and tougher field divisions withdrew inland to train _ from there they could rush to the rescue of their comrades on the coast if necessary.

The Navy replaced the "observation minefields" of simultaneously-activated old torpedo heads with "controlled" fields of new mines which could be selectively fired under invaders. *Plover, Hawfinch* and the Dutch *Van der Zaan* were some of the vessels responsible for laying most of both the earlier and later fields. Many miles of electric cable had to be laid for each, and in some cases the public electricity supply extended. The control stations were in the War Signal Stations, i.e, forts and Martello Towers, or in concrete bunkers built for the purpose. To assist the controllers small RDF sets, and Ryder searchlights, each of which illuminated a square mile of sea by burning flares in front of concave steel mirrors, were installed. Including the existing Royal Marine signallers, each minefield party was about twenty-four strong. From the New Year the new controlled fields were placed at Harwich, Yarmouth, the Medway entrance, Lower Hope Reach (on the Thames), and Holehaven, and on the Crouch, Blackwater, Colne, Deben and Humber. Harbours with minefields, signal stations and examination boats were classified as "Defended Ports". Incidentally, the whole scheme was thought unnecessary and wasteful by some admirals, such as Harris at Harwich.

INVASION IMMINENT

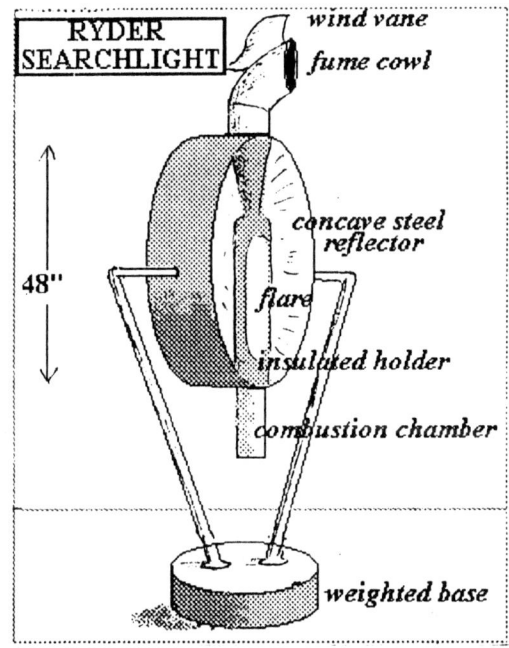

Meanwhile *Adventure* laid 4,500 moored magnetic mines along the outer edge of the East Coast barrier from Blyth southwards. A plan to lay the same number of antenna contact mines along the inner edge was scrapped because they would have stopped British MTBs crossing the barrier at points other than the Gaps. However the Humber-based *Teviot Bank* continued to superimpose shallow "BS" minefields over the deep-laid barrier.

In January there were large-scale Army manoeuvres in East Anglia, in response to a hypothetical landing by five German divisions on the Norfolk coast: the reports luridly describe the imaginary devastation of Lowestoft and Great Yarmouth. Churchill was rather peeved by this "Operation Victor", since he disliked the Army's assumption that the Navy and RAF might not be able to stop an invasion happening in the first place. *Erebus* carried out another bombardment on the night of 10/11 February, this time against Ostend, which was air-raided simultaneously.

With Hitler's embroilment in Russia that summer the invasion fear largely disappeared. The East Coast continued to be lined with static infantry divisions, punctuated by the occasional field formation, for the rest of the war. In 1943 and 1944 a memorable feature of the area were the brigades of Continental exiles _ Czechs at Harwich, Walton-on-Naze and later Southend, Belgian in Thanet , Dutch at Lowestoft and later Harwich. Serious invasion alerts continued until as late as 1942. However thereafter indifferent morale and lax security among troops, and awkwardness by some of the civilian population, seemed to concern the officers more than what the enemy were doing a hundred miles away in the Low Countries. The Intelligence Officer of 54th Division, centred on Thornham Magna, near Eye in Suffolk, has left us

INVASION IMMINENT

some unintended humour symptomatic of the period. In April 1942 a certain Suffolk knight (whom I shall not name) was found with a German Spandau sub-machine gun and an abundance of armour-piercing and tracer ammunition. He claimed to be a former MI5 agent, apparently by way of excuse. He was not prosecuted, even though he turned out never to have been an MI5 agent and to have been warned about his behaviour before by no less a person than the Chief Constable. Around the same time two men of 2/7 Queen's Regiment, stationed at Shrublands Camp near Ipswich, were given captured German uniforms to dress in so that these could be shown at a training parade. They sneaked out of the camp and swaggered about in the road until troops from another unit came up and seized them. At Ipswich Police Station they kept up the act and pretended not to understand English. No doubt the local security forces were disappointed when the truth dawned, What punishment the pair received is not recorded.

In view of the many British commando raids on the Continental coast it seems odd that the Germans never tried the equivalent, in Eastern England or anywhere else on the British shores. But whereas the British raided the Continent in the frame of mind that they could not yet invade but hoped eventually to do so, the Germans had let the whole invasion strategy lapse. There have been stories about German raids on the East Coast, such as the recent one about an attempted landing at Shingle Street, beside the RAF's Kings Marshes weapons experimental site near the mouth of the Ore, in Suffolk. (In this case German submarines and burned corpses have featured). But I am pretty confident that all such tales are bogus. There are complete, long-declassified, war diaries for all three services on the wartime Suffolk coast, and none give so much as a hint of any German shore raid or landing. Of course they could all be falsified, but I hardly think this likely.

It *may*, however, be the case that an E-boat or E-boats carried out a close reconnaissance of Orfordness and the nearby Bawdsey RDF station on the night of 2 December 1940 and the following misty morning. A motor boat was spotted flashing a light only five hundred yards off North Weir Point, and then heard and seen near Bawdsey and off the Naze. Engines could still be heard at daybreak, by which time it had been established that no British craft were in the area, but the search mounted was blocked by the mist, and when this cleared nothing was to be seen.

It is now known that Hitler never did give a clear and final go-ahead

INVASION IMMINENT

for the invasion plans he called "Operation Sealion", nor did they involvelandings north of Ramsgate _ i.e, on the East Coast. Moreover his postponement on 17 September 1940 (due only in part to the failure of the Luftwaffe two days before) was a permanent one. This means that in one sense the East Coast invasion watch was all for nothing. But for long the alarm was real, and without that watch an opportunity would have been presented to the Germans which, their Russian campaign notwithstanding, they might have been tempted by.

5
WAR ON THE CONVOY ROUTE, PART 1

Though there was at first a distinct lull in the East Coast sea war, it was obvious that it would be enormously intensified by the recent German conquest of Western Continental Europe. The new strategic equation facing the Nore Command had two pluses _ after their losses in Norway the Germans were extremely weak in major surface warships, and their U-Boats were all by-passing the North Sea for the Atlantic. But there were several minuses. The E-boats were based in Holland, Belgium and France. So was the much more formidable Luftwaffe, which, though its main business was not the sea war, seriously menaced East Coast shipping. The convoys and the warships supporting them would soon have to face a recharged campaign of bombing, machine-gunning and air minelaying. The eastern sky was to be darkened with columns of smoke from burning ships, and not for the first time this coast would become a graveyard of wrecked ships. The war in the North Sea was never comparable to the Battle of the Atlantic, but it was real enough.

For a few weeks after Dunkirk the maritime pattern of the first eight months of war continued: ocean convoys came into London via the Dover Strait, and enemy minelaying, surface-ship raids, and bombing, were minor. But the anti-invasion measures and the call-up of boats and men into the Auxiliary Patrol brought Yarmouth and Lowestoft fish-drifting almost wholly to an end. Over the summer, in spite of British propaganda to the contrary, the traffic of the Port of London was greatly reduced. Only a small fraction of its shipping used the vulnerable Strait of Dover route after July*. But since the East Coast route handled all the rest, it assumed, if anything, an added importance.

German minelaying was now mainly done by He 111s of KG (Kampfgeschwader[+]) 4 at Gilze-Rijen, and to a lesser extent Ju 88s of KG 30 at Soesterberg (both in Holland), rather than by the Heligoland Bight floatplanes. Some of the magnetic mines were bi-polar, with both "blue" and "red" mechanisms, doubling the workload of the British sweepers. "Actuation" delays meant that mines would not be blown by repeated

---

*4,919 ships passed Southend in the last quarter of 1939, but only 1,719 in the last quarter of 1940. In the first half of 1941 500,000 tons of shipping used the Channel route as opposed to 16,500,000 on the East Coast, plus 4,000,000 going into the Humber.   [+]Literally "Battle Squadron", but actually a force of about a hundred bombers.

SHIPS VERSUS AIRCRAFT

Above: Cyril and Roland Grimes, and Joseph Barnes, on board their 25-foot whelker at Wells. They were machine-gunned by the Luftwaffe in the first direct attack on British coastal shipping since Dunkirk.
Left: Forms of air defence at sea. 1.Pom-pom (2-pdr) guns, 2.Holman projector, 3.PAC, 4.Type 285 RDF aerial, 5.Type 286P RDF aerial.
Below: M/S trawler crew manning a Lewis gun, probably during a gunnery course at HMS *Europa*, Lowestoft. (W.I.)

THE PORT OF LONDON CONTINUES, as merchant ships head out to sea past the Royal Naval College at Greenwich early in 1940. British propaganda continues to announce that the port was in full swing until that summer, but enemy activity then forced major cutbacks. *(WI)*

WAR ON THE CONVOY ROUTE _ 1

sweeping, yet explode days later when unsuspecting ships passed.
Early in June the enemy scored his first mine victory of this period, a little prelude for the big campaigns ahead. On the 1st he dropped several mines right off Harwich Harbour, probably to catch warships returning from Dunkirk. On the 3rd one was triggered by the Harwich examination drifter *Ocean Lassie*, anchored two miles south-east of Landguard Point _ she sank in one minute with the loss of seven of her thirteen crew. Two days later, very nearby, another mine destroyed the useful if unlovely *Sweep II*, the Ipswich Corporation sewage-disposal boat, while she was discharging her noxious load. Two of her four crew perished. On the 12th a third mine accounted for the Harwich LL trawler *Sisapon*, near the Cork Lightship, along with twelve of her twenty-one crew. Lt J P Kelly RNVR, aboard the trawler *Lord Irwin*, had taken both vessels into an area known to be mined, and was blamed for the loss and nearly court-martialled.

Also on 12 June an He 111 minelayer crashed near the North Foreland, the first to fall into the Thames Estuary. Almost a month later, on 7 July, the body of an He 111 crewman was found by one of the barrage balloon vessels off Sheerness, and taken to RAF Eastchurch for examination and burial. 952 Balloon Squadron's record book describes the dead man as "Ober Leutnant in the 2nd Scaffel Kampf Geschwader General Waver" (sic). ("General Wever" was KG 4).

Out to sea, east of the Shipwash, SS *Haytor* was sunk on 26 July. On the 30th *Clan Monroe* had her back broken and twelve men killed near Southship Head, but was towed to Hollesley Bay by Harwich rescue tugs and beached in shallow water. *Moidart* was also lost nearby. The Harwich destroyer *Whitshed* (Cdr E R Conder) had her bows practically torn off when she was mined almost on the same spot at five o'clock that morning. Thirteen men were killed and fifteen wounded. The stokers' messdeck hatch was jammed while the deck below flooded with oil and water. Rapid work by a Surgeon-Lieutenant and two ratings released the hatch in time to save three men. *Whitshed* steamed back to Parkeston sternfirst under her own power escorted by the destroyer *Ambuscade*, the corvette *Puffin* and two MTBs. As she rounded Beach End Buoy the trawler *River Clyde*, leaving harbour, nearly collided with her, provoking Cdr Conder to report "From the conduct and appearance of the CO of the *River Clyde* I cannot believe that he is a fit person to command one of HM ships". Within the week *River Clyde* too had been sunk by mine (with twelve dead). The big Ellerman freighter *City of Canberra* was also mine-damaged on 1 August but was towed to Hollesley Bay under fighter cover and later repaired.

Responsible for these losses were, for a change, moored (i.e, contact) mines. All the available *Oropesa* sweepers went to work. From Harwich came the 4th (Auxiliary) and 6th (Fleet) Flotillas; the latter had recently transferred from Yarmouth and had been clearing Gap E. 12th (Paddle) Flotilla was brought down from Lowestoft. And many trawlers asssisted. Around Position X, on the 137 QZS convoy-route diversion where *Haytor* had been sunk, the paddle steamers swept several of the standard GX (German Type X) mines. *Queen Empress* also found a small unidentified type, which the Harwich Captain of Minesweeper's launch *Epping* towed in and beached just inside Landguard Point, after a line had been tied to it by the courageous Lt C W S Goss RNVR. This, and a second of the same type, were defused on the spot by *Vernon*, and with one of the sinkers used to anchor such mines to the seabed, transported to that base. Altogether thirty-eight mines were disposed of, including nineteen Type Xs, some magnetics, several of the small new type, a Type Y (also new at this period), and a French mine, probably not laid by the enemy but brought by the tide from the fields of our former ally in the Dover Strait. There may perhaps have been even more types. The rather confusing official records speak of "conical floats", the anti-sweeping devices which became really evident only some months later, Type Ws (which were perhaps the small new mines), and even five mines of Russian manufacture, defused at Landguard on 29 July, and which must have been sold to Germany as part of the Nazi-Soviet Pact. But on the subject of the Type W the Nore Command War Diary (not a 100 per cent reliable source) records that the Lowestoft trawler *Euclase* recovered the first of these on 6 August.

HMS *Vernon* was continually being called to the East Coast. On 3 August it took away a mine which fell unexploded at Reculver (Kent): on arrival a booby trap inside this went off and killed four men, *without* detonating the main charge.

On the convoy route the mine danger was now too great to be held at bay by one sweep per day. The Admiralty directed that there must be two. Since sweeping needed to be done around low tide, and there are two such tides in twenty-four hours, one sweep would sometimes (and in the shorter

WAR ON THE CONVOY ROUTE _ 1

autumn and winter months always) have to be done at night. That August this procedure began: when the first magnetics were blown in darkness the explosions in the water reminded the LL crews of glowing pink jellies.

Meanwhile magnetic mines had brought bad luck to the newly founded base at Brightlingsea. The NOIC, Captain Henniker-Heaton, reported to the FOIC at Harwich as follows:

"Sir,

I regret to have to report the loss of HM trawler *Staunton* on the night of 26th/27th July in the following circumstances:_
HM trawler *Staunton* left her anchorage off Brightlingsea at 1800 on 26th and proceeded to her patrol between Wallet Spitway Buoy and North Buxey Buoy. She was last sighted by Motor Yacht *Sarawara* at 2200 steaming on this patrol. She failed to return on the following day, 27th inst, and all skippers of trawlers and drifters in her vicinity were interrogated as to whether they had sighted her or heard any explosion in her area, and it was ascertained that no explosion had been heard.

The motor yacht *Giroflée* was cruising as examination vessel two miles from *Staunton*'s patrol during the whole of the 27th, and reported that nothing was to be seen of her. All trawlers, drifter and motor boat patrols were ordered to keep an especial lookout for her when they again proceeded to sea at 1800. I proceeded out in M Y *Giroflée* to search for her on the morning of the 28th, and at 1130 in dead low water sighted the tops of two masts showing four feet above the water, S 50^0 E, 8 cables from Knoll Buoy. I sent a boat to investigate, and they reported that they were trawler masts _ the foremast being still firm in the ship and the aftermast having broken away _ they brought this spar back with them. I buoyed the position and reported this on my return to harbour. During the night of 26th/27th there were several severe lightning and thunder storms, accompanied by torrential rain, and great enemy air activity, and it appears that these circumstances may be the cause of no explosion having been heard in *Staunton's* vicinity.

I regret to come to the conclusion that HM Trawler *Staunton* was blown up by enemy mine, and that there are no survivors. Deck Hand Clarke of *Staunton* had been given special leave and was not on board on the night of 26th/27th."*

---

*Reports of Sinkings by Mine (PRO ADM 199/220)

WAR ON THE CONVOY ROUTE _ 1

Petty Officer Hazell White, then commanding the yacht *Triton*, remembered seeing *Staunton*'s crew going out to their ship on the liberty boat at the same time as he himself set forth. The skipper was proudly wearing his RNR cap and jacket, with brass buttons gleaming, for the first time. He also recalled one of the several German aircraft which overflew that night coming down low and dropping an object or objects near Knoll Buoy, and said he signalled this information back to HMS *Nemo*. The Army and RAF, incidentally, reported that a German plane had been shot down in this area that night, and that earlier another one had overflown Brightlingsea Creek itself, firing three cannon shells. The loss of life on *Staunton* was probably eighteen. Many of the crew, who like their ship came from Grimsby, had brought their wives down to share their billets at Brightlingsea. These women were in the habit of meeting their husbands on the Causeway when they returned from patrol. On the 27th they were there in a state of agitation that can be imagined, and begged White's and every other crew coming ashore for news.

Staunton had not been degaussed or wiped, and nor had three more of Henniker-Heaton's trawlers, including the *Drummer*. He kept these off patrol until the mobile wiping drifter had come from Harwich and treated them. To fill the gap, and to reassure his men, he himself went aborad *Giroflée* and supervised the Position HB (Knoll) night patrol. *Drummer* was the ship which then took over at that spot. By an uncanny and frightening coincidence she suffered the *Staunton*'s fate, only a hundred yards east of the same place, and only eight nights later. She had just arrived on station when the magnetic mine blast was clearly heard from Brightlingsea. Four of the crew were killed. When the rest reached Brightlingsea they crowded into the bar of the Anchor Hotel, which also housed the NOIC's offices, cursed those who offered them tea, and demanded whisky.

As a result of these losses deep-draught trawlers were withdrawn from the shallow Brightlingsea waters in favour of drifters. As in other cases a special fund was collected in the town for the families of the dead from the two trawlers. A service at sea was conducted, and wreaths were put on the wrecks. Later local fishermen accidentally hauled up bodies, and there were rumours that these were put back as fish bait _ perhaps merely the black humour of war.

WAR ON THE CONVOY ROUTE _ 1

The Luftwaffe's pursuit of Allied ships during Dunkirk took it as far north as the latitude of Harwich. On 31 May the merchantman *Fulham IV* was towed in by rescue tugs and beached at Shotley Spit after being bombed. The same day three trawlers of the 19th A/S Group were attacked by aircraft thirty miles east of Orfordness, *Greenfly* being damaged by bomb splinters and machine-gun bullets.

To limber up for the assault on RAF airfields the Luftwaffe bombed coastal convoys and naval bases during July and the first half of August. Fighter battles of considerable scale and ferocity were visible from Suffolk and Essex, as well as Kent, in this first phase of the Battle of Britain.

There had been very few fighter combats on the East Coast so far. In the most recent, on 2 April 1940, three Martlesham Heath Hurricanes had driven a pair of He 59s away from a convoy. On 7 July 85 (Hurricane) Squadron, led by Squadron Leader Peter Townsend (in later years Princess Margaret's suitor), arrived at Martlesham. During its first patrol the following morning Flight Sergeant Allard, already something of an ace with eleven victories claimed over France, dived onto the tail of a solitary He 111, flying from Rosières in Picardy, and sent it crashing into the sea six miles south east of Felixstowe. This was the first confirmed *daylight* air victory close to this coast.

That day a tiny whelk fishing boat from Wells (Norfolk) was machine-gunned off her harbour. Typically the censors released the story to the press, which suggested that the attack was deliberate terrorism. Rather, it marked the resumption of the enemy bombing campaign against East Coast shipping, more or less suspended early that spring. On the morning of the 9th He 111s attacked Norwich and convoy FS 18, then ten miles east of Lowestoft. Douglas Bader's 242 (Hurricane) Squadron, from Coltishall, intercepted and claimed two of the raiders. In the afternoon the bombers returned and tried to spot the convoy through occsional breaks in a cloudy sky. One plane caught a glimpse of it near Thorpeness and aimed two bombs in vain. Another damaged a straggler, *Polgrange*, by bombing and machine-gunning. As the raiders headed home one was chased and destroyed by three 17 Squadron Hurricanes from Debden (Essex) over the North Hinder.

On the 10th nine He 111s dropped a hail of bombs on the Harwich fleet minesweepers *Halcyon*, *Harrier* and *Speedwell* east of Lowestoft without hitting them. Later that was officially designated the first day of the

WAR ON THE CONVOY ROUTE _ 1

Battle of Britain. For the next month hardly a day passed without an air attack on a convoy or warships in the North Sea.

On the morning of the 11th Squadron Leader Townsend was patrolling above thick rain cloud east of Harwich when he spotted a Do 17 flying south (it had just raided Yarmouth* and was returning to St Leger in France). He damaged the Dornier and wounded three of the crew, but his own machine was hit and he had to bail out. The Harwich A/S trawler *Cap Finisterre* rescued him and landed him at Felixstowe _ he was airborne in a new Hurricane within twenty hours. Later that day FN 19 was bombed near the Aldeburgh Light Float without result. The Harwich destroyers *Venomous* and *Wivern* were the target for six aircraft, but saved themselves by the violent zig-zag steering known in the Navy as "evasive action". Later that day, off Cromer, Bader made fleeting contact with a Dornier in the ubiquitous cloud and it was later confirmed as his first victory.

The morning of the 12th brought the first major convoy battle. At 0825 about nine German aircraft divebombed a Harwich Trinity House lightship near Roughs Buoy, missing with all their bombs. Then an hour-long series of attacks commenced on a southbound convoy north-east of Orfordness. Some thirty British fighters from 17, 85 and 151 Squadrons battled with more than forty German bombers. The Harwich trawler *Carena* gallantly held her own against repeated attacks. The collier *Hornchurch* was sunk and two Hurricanes shot down at a cost to the enemy of four aircraft. The *Badger* corvette *Widgeon* rescued the whole crew of the *Hornchurch*, while a trawler picked up three German fliers amid falling bombs.

At noon next day (the 13th) the crack German Raiding Group 210 of Messerschmitt Bf 110[+] fighter-bombers, led by Hauptmann Rubensdörffer, flew from St Omer to attack FN 21 south of the Aldeburgh Light Float. The ships evaded the dozen large bombs dropped. A second attack in the afternoon also failed.

The enemy was luckier on the 15th. Bombing FN 23 near the Shipwash at two o'clock in the afternoon during lashing rain, he hit and set on fire the collier *Heworth* and the Polish ship *Zbaraz*. The Rosyth destroyer *Valorous* saved the crew of the former, which broke her back and sank near

---

*not Lowestoft, as Townsend later wrote. He expresses admiration for the raider's daring escape, but it had killed four civilians.

[+]the official German designation, but henceforth I shall stick to the familiar British "Me 110" (and, for the Bf 109, "Me 109").

WAR ON THE CONVOY ROUTE _ 1

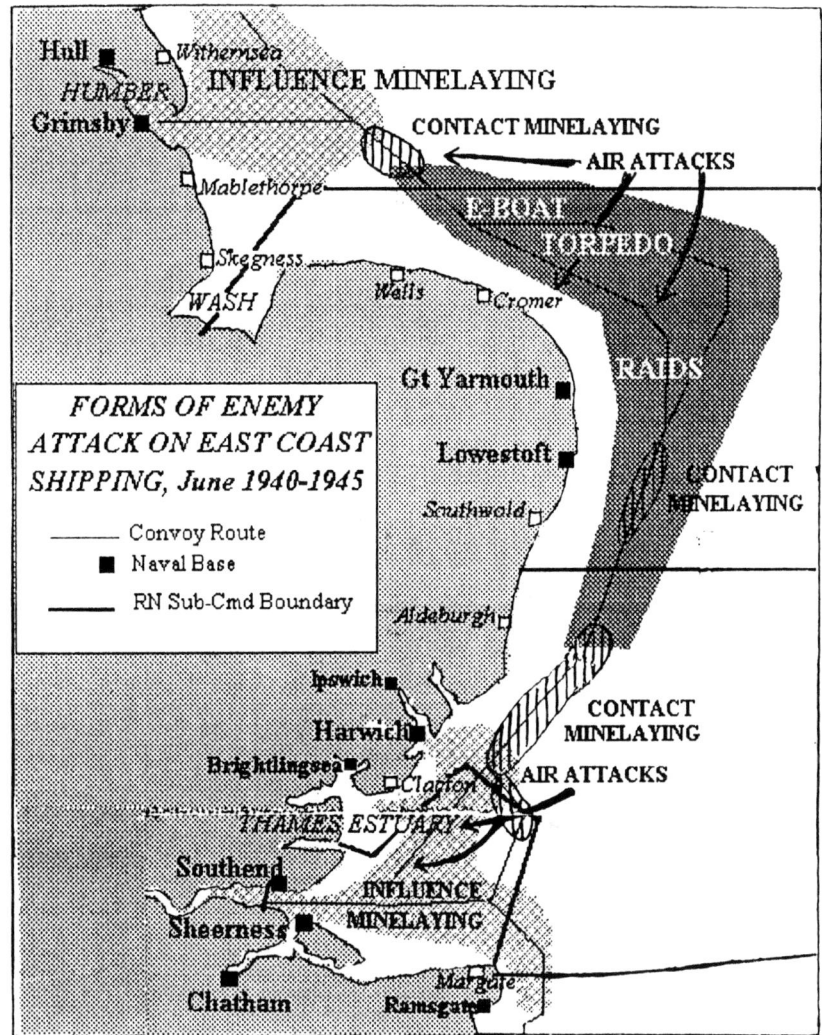

FORMS OF ENEMY ATTACK ON EAST COAST SHIPPING, June 1940-1945

North Ship Head while under tow by the Harwich rescue tug *St Olaves*. The same fate befell the *Zbaraz* at the opposite end of the Shipwash, in her case the trawler *Vidonia* and the tug *Muria* being the would-be rescuers. The two wrecks remained rearing out of the water like eerie sentinels to the Harwich approach.

On 18 July numerous small craft were bombed and machine-gunned in Harwich Sub-Command, around Kentish Knock in the south and the Shipwash and Sunk further north. The trawlers *Fleming, Sphene, Sapphire,*

WAR ON THE CONVOY ROUTE _ 1

Stella Leonis and *Turquoise* were attacked: some of their dead have graves at Shotley. One plane strafed the Sunk Light Vessel, while as many as ten others rained bombs on a Felixstowe MTB off Bawdsey without effect, an incident which gave rise to Navy protests to the Army about the failure of the RDF Station's AA guns to lend support. On 24 July *Fleming*, then in company with *Berberis* on 137 QZS, east of Longsand, took a bomb down the funnel and sank with the loss of nineteen out of twenty-two crew.

On 27 July the destroyers *Montrose* (Cdr C R L Parry) and *Wren* (Lt-Cdr I W G Harker) of the Harwich-based 16th Flotilla were escorting the *Halcyon* and six M/S trawlers forty miles east of their base in Mine Barrier Gap E. At 1700 they were divebombed by fifteen planes. *Montrose* survived innumerable near-misses. One bomb missed by as little as a foot and disabled the ship, though it caused no casualties or structural damage. Another was destroyed right overhead by a flak shell. The concussion of such near-misses had remarkable effects _ one prone officer was thrown back into a standing position. In all, three strikes were made at *Montrose*, during which she blazed away with all guns and claimed to have shot down two of her attackers. When the smoke had cleared, nothing was to be seen of the *Wren*. Her precise fate was only pieced together later by survivors in Shotley Hospital. Apparently she had been bombed at the same time as the first attack on *Montrose*. At least twenty bombs had fallen near the ship and two holed her below the waterline. Her bulkheads had collapsed and she had gone down sternfirst within two minutes except for the stem, which remained exposed until the tide covered it. Thirty-seven of the crew died, among them Harker, whose grave may still be seen at Shotley Churchyard. The trawlers shot the tail off one raider and rescued *Wren*'s survivors.

Two days later twenty of Rubensdörffer's Me 110s, and twenty more from ZG*2, bombed an FN convoy off Orfordness. 151 Squadron, from North Weald, engaged the raiders. Two ships and a fighter were damaged before the Germans withdrew. Next day Flight Sergeant Allard destroyed an Me 110 after chasing it away from the next convoy at almost wavetop height.

On 1 August Ellerman's *City of Brisbane*, having accidentally gone aground on South Longsand Head, was divebombed and set on fire. Sixteen days later, in situ, she was bombed again and completely gutted. When the Navy inspected her they found a wrecked German aircraft on board. Meanwhile, on the 2nd, a German bomber found *Cap Finisterre*, to which

---

*Zestörer Geschwader ("destroyer squadron", literally);

WAR ON THE CONVOY ROUTE _ 1

Townsend owed his life, and blew her to pieces with a direct hit.
 The East Coast convoys were marginally less exposed after 5 August, when the long easterly diversion through Knock Deep was abandoned and they were re-routed onto QZS 148, through the Barrow Deep. Likewise the outermost lane off Norfolk was given up, and convoys either used the original route past Hearty Knoll or the inshore, Would, route.
 The fiercest of the convoy battles took place off the Naze during a north-westerly gale on the morning of 11 August. 17 and 85 Squadrons of Hurricanes (Debden and North Weald) and 74 Squadron of Spitfires (Manston), in all twenty-four aircraft, engaged about twice that number of German machines. The enemy target was FN 49, in which the empty 5,500-ton tanker *Oiltrader* was badly damaged _ a bomb hit her aft, exploded her magazine, killed two men and injured two others, and wrecked her steering. She staggered out of the line near the Shipwash Light and was towed to Harwich by rescue tugs. SS *Kirnwood* took two bombs in the engine room, and was towed, still burning, to Yarmouth, where the fire was eventually dowsed on the River Yare by the local fire brigade. In the air battle four Me 110s were shot down and two damaged, and two Ju 87 Stuka divebombers destroyed, for the loss of two Spitfires and two Hurricanes. Several British "aces" were involved in this combat, Townsend damaging two planes, and Pilot Officer Manger, who had two victories over the area to his credit, losing his life.
 Not all the fatal air attacks were in Harwich waters. That same day the Sheerness trawler *Edwardian* was bombed off Kent, with three killed and three wounded, though she was saved by being beached at the North Foreland. Next afternoon Stukas led by Hauptmann Brauchitsch, son of the Chief-of-Staff of the German Army, swooped on the Sheerness M/S Group 2 north of Margate and sank the trawlers *Pyrope* and *Tamarisk* (thirteen were killed, and the rest rescued by the Margate lifeboat). On 21 August, while one bomber raided the naval training camp at Skegness, another sank the netlayer *Kylemore* off Sheringham. One or other of these planes was then downed off Yarmouth by Bader.
 Lowflying bombers were now common over the Dover Strait, and to help deter them a Mobile Balloon Barrage was formed at Sheerness by Lt-Cdr G H F Owles. Its ships, which included *Astral, Fratton, Gatinais,*

Oiltrader, back in service, was finally sunk by German bombing fifteen miles east of Corton on 29 March, 1941 _ without loss of life.

WAR ON THE CONVOY ROUTE _ 1

Pintade and *Ramier,* sailed alongside the weekly Channel convoys, ringing them with balloons and kites. Owles's flotilla was unique in being solely so armed, and operationally he came under an RAF officer of lower rank, Flying Officer Puckle of Balloon Command. The CW and CE convoys, which were also escorted by Sheerness's 21st Destroyer Flotilla, nevertheless came under intense attack from Stukas, as well as E-boats and heavy guns, as they passed Dover.

Throughout that summer and autumn the sea threw up a grisly harvest of dead airmen along the East Coast. There were bodies without limbs and without heads, though often identifiable from uniforms and documentation.

It was now the turn of the third German weapon in the North Sea _ the "E-boat". This was the term applied by the Admiralty to the fast diesel-powered, torpedo- and mine-equipped, motor boats which the Germans called "Schnellboote" (fast boats). In May they began to arrive in Dutch harbours. During the Boulogne evacuation they torpedoed and sunk a French destroyer off that port, and during "Dynamo", a week later, they attacked Harwich and Dover warships as near the Kent coast as South Falls and the West Hinder. Attempting their first two raids on East Coast convoys, some had clashed with the Rosyth destroyer *Vivien* off Lowestoft on 10 June and unsuccessfully aimed torpedoes at a merchantman at Smith's Knoll the following night _ invariably their sorties were in darkness. For the next several weeks they operated from Boulogne towards the South Coast, but at the end of July it was they who laid the destructive contact minefield off Harwich. On 14 August Harwich and Felixstowe vessels vainly chased them near the Dutch coast, and two nights later there were more sightings near the Shipwash. There was, in fact, only one flotilla involved at this stage _ the 1st, under Kapitänleutnant* Birnbacher, which had successively shifted its base from Flushing to Boulogne to Ijmuiden (the latter was the North Sea outport of Amsterdam, 120 miles east of Lowestoft).

On 4 September this force pulled out the stops and mauled a convoy near the Haisborough Sands, north-east of Yarmouth. S 18 (Leutnant-zur-See Christiansen) torpedoed and sank SS *Joseph Swan* (killing fifteen of her crew) and the Dutch *Nieuwland,* S 21 (Lt z S Klug) sank *Corbrook* and *New Lambton,* and S 22 (Lt z S Grund) disposed of *Fulham V.* S 54 damaged a sixth ship. Another Dutch vessel, the *Stad Alkmaer,* succumbed to Lt z S

---

*equivalent to Lieutenant-Commander.

E-BOATS

Above: Some of 1st Flotilla alongside their prewar depot ship. S 21, commanded by Lt z S Klug, sank two ships off Yarmouth on the night of 4 September, 1940. Later E-boats had raised foredecks, hiding the torpedo tubes.
Below: Four officers of 1st Flotilla, all prominent off the East Coast. Left to right--Töniges, Fimmen, Klug, von Mirbach. Note the abundance of Iron Crosses.

AN INTERNATIONAL WAR – DEAD OF FOUR NATIONS

The graves of a British RN captain, a Chinese and a Danish merchant seaman, and a Dutch naval rating. The second man is buried at Dovercourt, the other three at Shotley.

WAR ON THE CONVOY ROUTE _ 1

Popp's S 33 a few miles south three nights later. As a result of these losses, and the simultaneous air raids on the London Docks, the Admiralty banned all merchant ships of over 6,500 tons from the East Coast on 11 September, though from the 30th exceptions were allowed.

The Yarmouth section of the convoy route now came to be called "E-Boat Alley". Henceforth destroyers shot at these craft night after night, Auxiliary Patrol vessels were vigilant for their approach, and motor boats hunted them right over to the Dutch coast. But for long, as a later chapter will show, the speed and elusiveness of the E-boat made her an almost invulnerable phantom.

On 23 September E-boats appeared among the five-trawler Ipswich Auxiliary Patrol group off Aldeburgh. *Edwina*, at Position HW2, engaged in a long-range machine-gun skirmish with two E-boats firing tracer: a gunner claimed (falsely) to have sunk one enemy, while a lookout said he saw a U-Boat surfacing, but the trawler was unable to report because her radio had failed. *Loch Inver* at HV seemed to have disappeared, and at dawn Group Officer J P T Cockley RNR, on *Lady Shirley*, found a hammock and a Carley float belonging to her. She had been sunk with all twenty-three crew (including Sub-Lt Metecalf RNVR) _ whether by the E-boats' torpedoes or mines was unknown.

The merchantman *Continental Coaster* fell victim to S 30 west of Smith's Knoll Lightship the same night. Nearby three merchant ships in FN 11 (*Hauxley, PLM 14* and *Gasfire*) were torpedoed and badly damaged on 17 October, with twenty-three dead between them, though only the firstnamed actually sank.

Four Harwich destroyers, *Montrose, Walpole, Whitshed* and *Worcester*, were converted for anti-E-boat work by the replacement of their for'd main guns with twin 6-pdr quick-firers of Coast Artillery type. Between then and the end of the year most of the other Nore Command V/Ws were replaced by small, new, Hunt-class destroyers; each with four 4-inch and five 2-pdr dual-purpose, quick-firing, anti-ship/AA guns. 21st Flotilla, at Sheerness, received *Cattistock, Cottesmore, Garth, Hambledon, Holderness* and *Mendip*, and 16th, at Harwich, received *Cotswold, Exmoor, Quorn* and *Southdown* (the latter bore Cdr Conder and the former *Whitshed* crew). Sheerness and Harwich escort vessels ran from their own bases to Flamborough Head and back (thought to be the maximum reach of the E-

WAR ON THE CONVOY ROUTE – 1

boats), while Rosyth craft covered the whole convoy route against bombers and U-Boats. 18 Destroyer Flotilla and the Sheerness and Humber cruisers left the Command by Christmas, since their role had been anti-invasion.

Starting with *Southdown*, the escort destroyers were fitted with Type 285 ASV (Air-Surface Vessel) RDF (radar), a smaller-scale and weaker version of CHL in that both operated on 1.5 metres. The aerials, which were fixed and therefore gave no directional information, formed an ungainly "birdcage" on the foremast. This was much inferior to the later, 10-cm, ASV which revolutionised the hunting of U-Boats. It detected E-boats at no more than two miles, because beyond that distance the back-echoes from the sea swamped any desired signals. Warships using it had to stand further away from their convoys than was otherwise desirable in order to avoid the huge echo from so many steel ships. (Together with its very similar successor, the Type 286M, it was more useful against aircraft, of which it could give several minutes' warning). As for the CHLs on shore, they could easily detect the convoys on their route about ten miles out, but could not pick up the small, low-built, E-boats and in any case had no direct phone links to the Navy (via Harwich) until well into 1941.

The escort craft also had HE (hydrophone equipment _ underwater microphones for picking up engine noise) and Asdic (sonar), which the operator turned from side to side with a car-like steering wheel. The E-boats were rarely audible to the unaided ear, because as they approached their prey they switched from their two main Diesel engines to a special quiet-running motor, and often they would stop just off the route ahead of the convoy with no engines running at all. The fans, wash and rattle of sparks in funnels of the British ships muffled any German-made sound still further. For visual detection the Royal Navy fired starshells, but as the main armament had to be used for them, they interrupted the firing of high-explosive. The smaller craft were issued with Schermuly rocket flares with a range of just over a quarter of a mile. Early starshells and flares gave, by later standards, a rather poor light.

On the night of 19-20 November occurred the first confirmed destruction of an E-boat in the Alley. She (apparently S 23) was rammed and sunk off Southwold by the Sheerness destroyer *Campbell*, nineteen Germans being captured. It was an isolated victory, though.

WAR ON THE CONVOY ROUTE - 1

Occupied with the Battle of Britain, the Luftwaffe largely kept out of the sea war from mid-August till October. On 6 September four Me 110s strafed the Felixstowe MTB 32 near Foulness, punching holes in the hull, wheelhouse and torpedoes without hurting the crew _ but she must have been a mere target of opportunity. On the 30th the corvettes *Mallard* and *Pintail* were returning to Harwich after a night patrol. A Do 17 dropped a stick of four bombs so close to *Mallard* as to damage her underwater and force her to stop dead. Seeing the plane turn to make a second run, both ships opened 4-inch AA fire and made it drop its four remaining bombs prematurely. The plane circled and made off to the north-east. While *Mallard* was being towed in by the tug *Kenia* another hostile plane passed right overhead without apparently spotting them.

November suddenly brought the heaviest bombing of all. The most remarkable incident for the Navy occurred on the 1st. The Harwich corvette *Pintail*, while escorting a convoy near Yarmouth with the REF's *Watchman* and *Verdun*, was the target for four bombs from a lowflying He 111. There was a direct hit on the bridge, which killed the captain, Lt Brunton RNR, and wounded most of his officers, and another which penetrated the port side and flooded the engine room. The ship's power, lighting and wireless immediately failed. The Heinkel made a machine-gunning attack before leaving. In circumstances ideal for panic, the crew remained calm enough to see that, in spite of the damage, their little ship was perfectly seaworthy. They shored up the sagging superstructure, pumped out the engine room, and soon had the vessel underway for Yarmouth, which she reached safely. Three of the crew were mentioned in despatches, for much larger ships have been abandoned after being hit by only one bomb. The casualties had been ten killed and nine wounded.

That month the Luftwaffe again attacked shipping in formation. Also on the 1st, over twenty Ju 88s and Me 109s attacked just outside the Thames mouth. SS *Letchworth* was sunk, the Mid Barrow Lightship was near-missed by bombs and bullets, the Oaze Lightship was blown up with all hands, and the Sheerness M/S trawler *Tilburyness* went down with ten dead. The AA paddle ship *Royal Eagle* and the tug *Salvo* valiantly threw up protective fire and rescued survivors. Next day FN 25 warded off no fewer than four bombing attacks between the Sunk and Aldeburgh Lights. The merchantman *Astrologer* and the tug *Muria* were sunk in the Sheerness Sub-Command on

WAR ON THE CONVOY ROUTE _ 1

the 7th, while the Rosyth sloop *Egret* shot down a Stuka in Barrow Deep.

Next afternoon the air campaign came to a peak with a raid by twenty-four Stukas, covered by as many as sixty Me 109s, on FN 29 in the Barrow Deep. Four merchant ships were hit, of which one, the Dutch *Agamemnon*, sank with the loss of three lives _ her survivors were taken off by Thames Pilot Cutter No.6. The Rosyth destroyer *Winchester* claimed to have downed two of the raiders, having taken bomb damage herself. Simultaneously some Me 110s bombed the Medway entrance at Sheerness, witthout hitting anything of note. Overhead a huge air battle raged, the fiercest on the East Coast for two months. 17 and 257 (Hurricane) Squadrons, from Martlesham, set about the ponderous Stukas of III/StG3 (Third "Gruppe", Third "Stuka Geschwader"), and, without loss to themselves, gave them a very unpleasant time. RAF 11 Group credited 17 Squadron alone with thirteen shot down, and Dowding (AOC-in-C Fighter Command) sent special congratulations to Martlesham. (German sources do not specify the losses). Yet the raiders returned on the 11th, damaged three more merchant ships, and shot down two Hurricanes of 17 Squadron. And on the 18th they damaged three further ships between Harwich and Southend.

Though air attacks continued in the Barrow Deep and East Swin they were by only a few planes at a time, and the Stukas had left for good. Another unusual aircraft put in an appearance, and was shot down, on 9 December, though. The Rosyth destroyer *Vortigern* fired back at a Blohm and Voss 138 (a three-engined reconnaissance seaplane) when this attacked FN 53 near the Aldeburgh Light Float. The same aircraft type, and various other rare German seaplanes, were also encountered in 1941.

All in all direct German air attacks had made a limited impact, in spite of the wonderful propaganda film being screened in Germany at that time in which Stukas clear the North Sea of British shipping. The great threat had once again become mines. In late September and October four Felixstowe MTBs had been sunk or damaged by blowing mines a considerable distance away, in spite of their own shallow draft, small size and largely wooden construction, and thorough LL sweeping. The blame was put on acoustic (nicknamed "green") mines, which were detonated by the engine noise of ships. After two months with very few minings, these occurred at an average rate of one a day from 5 October onwards, beginning with the cement coaster *Adaptity* in the East Swin off Clacton. The Sheerness

WAR ON THE CONVOY ROUTE — 1

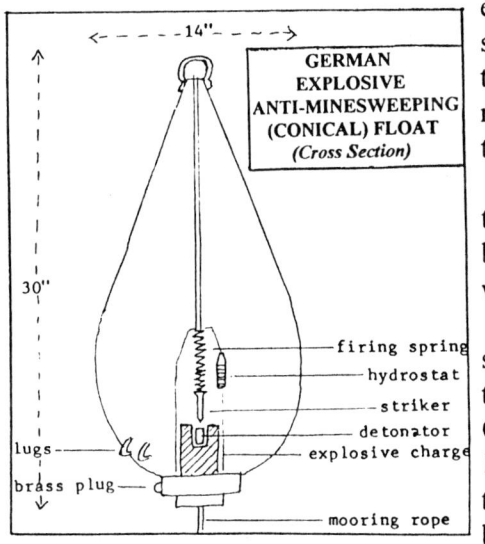

GERMAN EXPLOSIVE ANTI-MINESWEEPING (CONICAL) FLOAT
(Cross Section)

examination vessel *Danube III* was sunk on the 13th, the Trinity House tender *Reculver* (which featured in my first chapter) in the Humber on the 13th.

From their locations all the "green" mines were undoubtedly being air-dropped (by the Luftwaffe's IX Corps, based in Holland) _ but the E-boats now laid their second major contact minefield off the East Coast. On the night of 11 October the Harwich corvette *Widgeon* and Yarmouth patrol trawlers reported glimpsing E-boats. Next morning *Berberis*'s Harwich-based trawler group swept a mine and the C-in-C Nore ordered in 4th Minesweeper Flotilla and the paddle steamers. 148 QZS was searched from the North east Swin, off the Naze, to Position Z, off Aldeburgh, and six more of the mines were found. Fleet minesweepers working ahead of convoys found more over the next two days, but on the 15th the Danish merchant ship *Frankrig* and the British collier *George Balfour* were mined within two miles of each other near 54 Buoy. *Frankrig* was lost, though the destroyer *Holderness* saved her crew. On the 17th the Harwich Hunt-class minesweeper *Dundalk* was lost close to Bawdsey. That same day troops guarding Yarmouth beach investigated several black, round-bottomed cones (described by some men as pear-shaped), each two-and-a-half feet long and lying on the tidemark. When moved, one of these exploded and killed four soldiers. The objects were not mines, but anti-minesweeping floats. They contained small explosive charges for sundering *Oropesa* sweep wires when these tugged at them and disturbed their hydrostats.*

On the night of 18-19 October the Ipswich patrol trawler *Velia*, then off the Sunk Light Vessel, anchored because of fog. When the crew hauled

---

*Not everything washed ashore at Yarmouth was hostile. Two strange items were a) a message in a bottle _ "Greetings from Kaunahr Spa", and b) a Gothic-lettered signboard originating from the German Navy at Cologne _ it must have washed down the Rhine and across the North Sea.

up the anchor next morning they saw a contact mine hanging by its cable on one fluke. The chain was immediately played out but the mine exploded and blew off the entire fore part of the vessel. Everyone had retreated astern in time, and before the ship sank had been rescued by the trawlers *Hekla* and *Stella Carina*.

On the night of the 21st RNVR Lt W J Curtayne's group of "O" trawlers was east of the convoy route off Orfordness on a "Dagger Patrol" _ i.e, watching over the channel during the night which they had swept by day. *Waveflower*, which was Curtayne's ship, fell behind the other three, and in trying to catch up ran into a mine and sank. The other three trawlers, of which Lt M Gardner RNVR on *Joseph Button* was in effective charge, heard an explosion, did not worry unduly, and anchored for the night. At first light, with no sign of *Waveflower*, Gardner's ships dispersed to look for her, and then *Joseph Button* too was mined and sunk with five dead. Later *Thomas Leeds*, also in this group, found Curtayne and six more survivors from *Waveflower*. The Admiralty wrote to Admiral Drax; "I am to acquaint you that their Lordships concur that these inquiries reveal a deplorable state of affairs. Neither...officer seems to have shown any initiative or power of command". The FOIC Harwich wrote that these officers had shown a "complete lack of a sense of responsibility".*

Forty mines in all were swept in this field, including some magnetics and a Type Z contact, but most were of the small Type W, whose lightness gave the "O" Sweeps difficulties. The last mine victim was SS *Sheaffield*, abandoned and burned out near the mouth of the Deben on the 28th.

Due not to this contact field, but to an air-dropped influence mine, the 21st Flotilla destroyer *Venetia*, returning to Sheerness from a Dover Strait patrol, was mined at Knob Buoy (in the Thames approach) and immediately broke in two. The captain (Lt-Cdr D L Craig) and some forty crew were lost. From "green" mines ships were no longer safe even in dock. The Port of London Authority tugs *Lea* and *Deanbrook* were both blown up in Tilbury Basin on 1 November, with twelve men dead between them.

On the 7th, in addition to two vessels sunk by bombs, three were lost to mines _ all in the Outer Thames Estuary. Near the Nore Lightship the merchant ship *Herland* was sunk. By 51 Buoy six men died on the Harwich "O" trawler *William Wesney* (which had been in the Curtayne-Gardner group) _ two of the survivors rescued by other "O" trawlers and the corvette

---

*Admiralty Board of Inquiry Report; PRO ADM 1/10891

WAR ON THE CONVOY ROUTE _ 1

Sheldrake died on the way into Harwich. The destroyer *Vega* was damaged nearby. The Brightlingsea patrol drifter *Reed* was blown up off Holland-on-Sea: all fourteen ratings were killed and though the Group Officer on board, Lt K Empson RNVR, was rescued by HMS *Nemo*'s rescue boat and landed by the Clacton lifeboat, he died in hospital. Brightlingsea had hit another bad patch. Only the previous day four men were wounded, one fatally, by an air attack on its patrol drifter *Reids*. Two weeks later *Xmas Rose* was blown up with three dead (including Skipper Merson) and eight wounded at North East Gunfleet Buoy, and two days after that *Sailor King* was damaged while recovering a mine only just below Brightlingsea Creek entrance.

The mines sewn by German aircraft at dawn on 21 November (see map overleaf), which caused the last of these incidents, probably also destroyed ML 127 in the East Swin on the 22nd. One of my informants, Lt Barette RNVR, who had planned to travel aboard her on her maiden voyage from Brooke Marine's building yard at Oulton Broad to the fitting-out base at Chatham, said he owed his life to his superior officer, who the night beforehand banned him from making the journey. Two Yarmouth-based MLs were sunk close to this date in the Humber (see Chapter 13), also by mines _ the three were the first MLs to be lost.

Meanwhile, in Sheerness Sub-Command, the month's mine losses included the Trinity House tender *Argus* (on the 12th, and only one of her thirty-three crew survived), the A/S trawler *Amethyst* (on the 19th), the merchantmen *Ryal* (23rd) and *Alice Marie* (24th) and the M/S trawler *Kennymore* (25th).

Sailor King (mentioned above) was part of the *Vernon* Mine Recovery Flotilla, the 2nd Division of which, under Lt-Cdr M W Griffiths RNVR*, had been based at Lowestoft. During the last three months of 1940 this scoured the Thames Estuary for specimens of the new acoustic mines: in order to save travelling time, it shifted its base to Brightlingsea in the New Year.

Meanwhile a commercial road drill, trade-named the "Kango Hammer", was found to emit its loud noise at the same frequency as the average marine engine, and (therefore) as the acoustic mines. When put inside a steel cyliner and lowered into the water from a ship's bow, it blew mines at a safe distance. On 24 November the Sheerness trawler *Capricornus* became the first ship to achieve this feat. The Admiralty bought up all available

---

*also a noted sailing author, and later a resident of West Mersea.

WAR ON THE CONVOY ROUTE _ 1

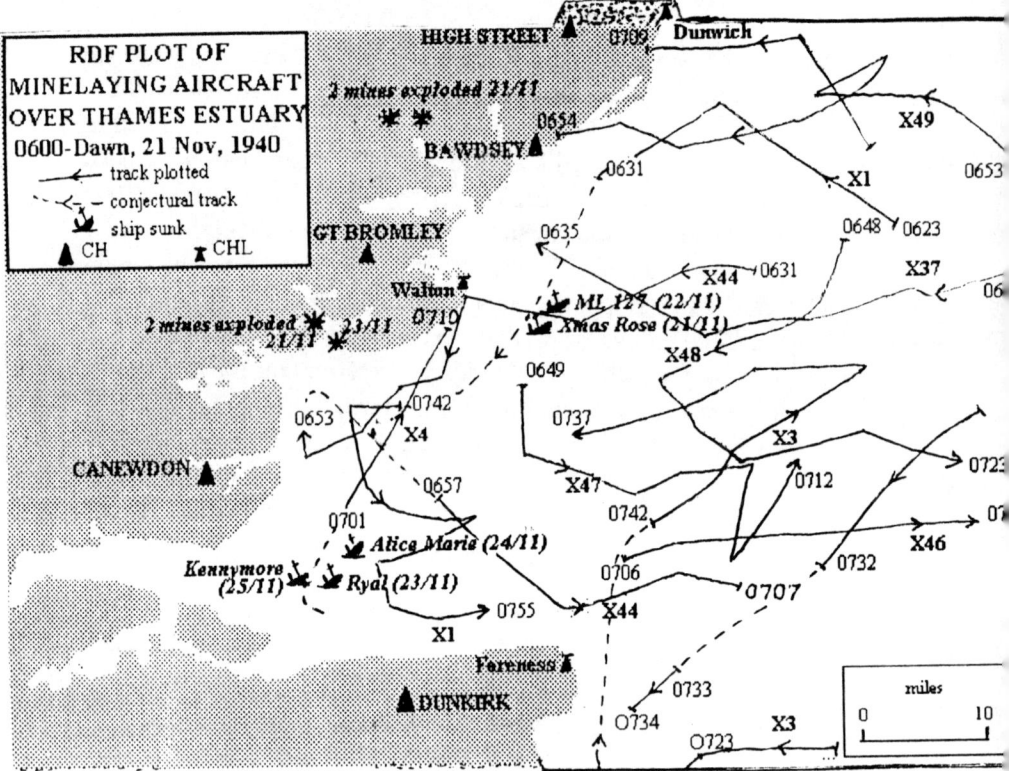

Kango hammers, which were officially dubbed "SA" (Sweep Acoustic) equipment, and began to instal them in trawlers and drifters.

This did not occur in time to prevent a disaster in the very mouth of the Thames, in the convoy-mustering anchorage right between Sheerness and Southend Pier. In the week between 8 and 15 December some 350 IX Luftkorps aircraft headed for this area with two mines apiece. On the night of 12-13 December (according to the German naval historian Röhwer) an unprecedented ninety-three were sent. British observers saw a quarter of the load fall inside the boom; others fell on land in Essex and Kent _ one fell as far inland as Stock Church (which it wrecked) near Chelmsford. Most had six-day delay mechanisms. That the threat was acoustic was proven when *Vernon* examined stray mines dropped at Whitstable and on Foulness Sand. The London river was closed to shipping while a disappointing total of nineteen mines were swept. It was reopened on the 16th, but a great many more unlocated mines were suspected, and ships were told to move

WAR ON THE CONVOY ROUTE _ 1

only on low engine revolutions. Next day no fewer than seven ships were sunk, including the boom trawler *Thomas Connolly* and barrage balloon drifter *Carry On*. Of the men on the merchant ships *Aquiety, Belvedere, Beneficient, Inver* and *Malrix* nineteen died and thirty-six were rescued by the Southend *Sun* tugs. The run of losses continued right into the New Year _ a commercial and a naval tanker, a Royal Mail ship, a barge, three tugs, another balloon drifter...in all sixteen vessels were lost. The worst incident was probably the loss of the tanker *Arinia*, on 19 December. Approaching Southend Pier after safely running the whole length of the East Coast she burst from end to end into a single terrible sheet of flame. As her own, and a nearby Channel, convoy watched helplessly all but two of her sixty-nine crew were burned to death or drowned.

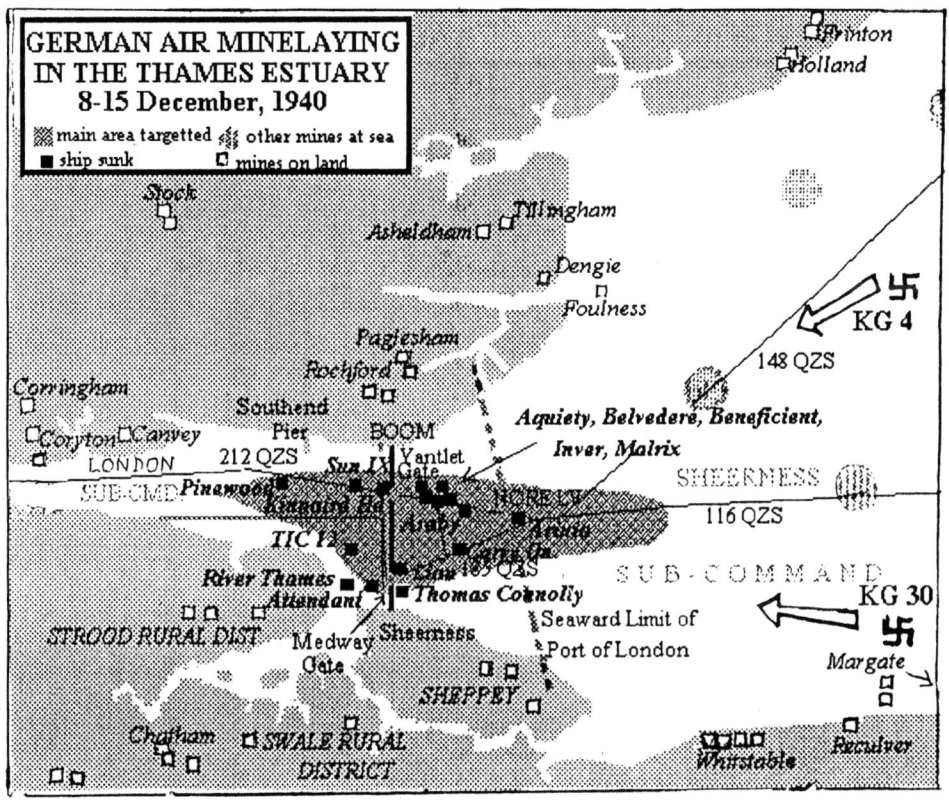

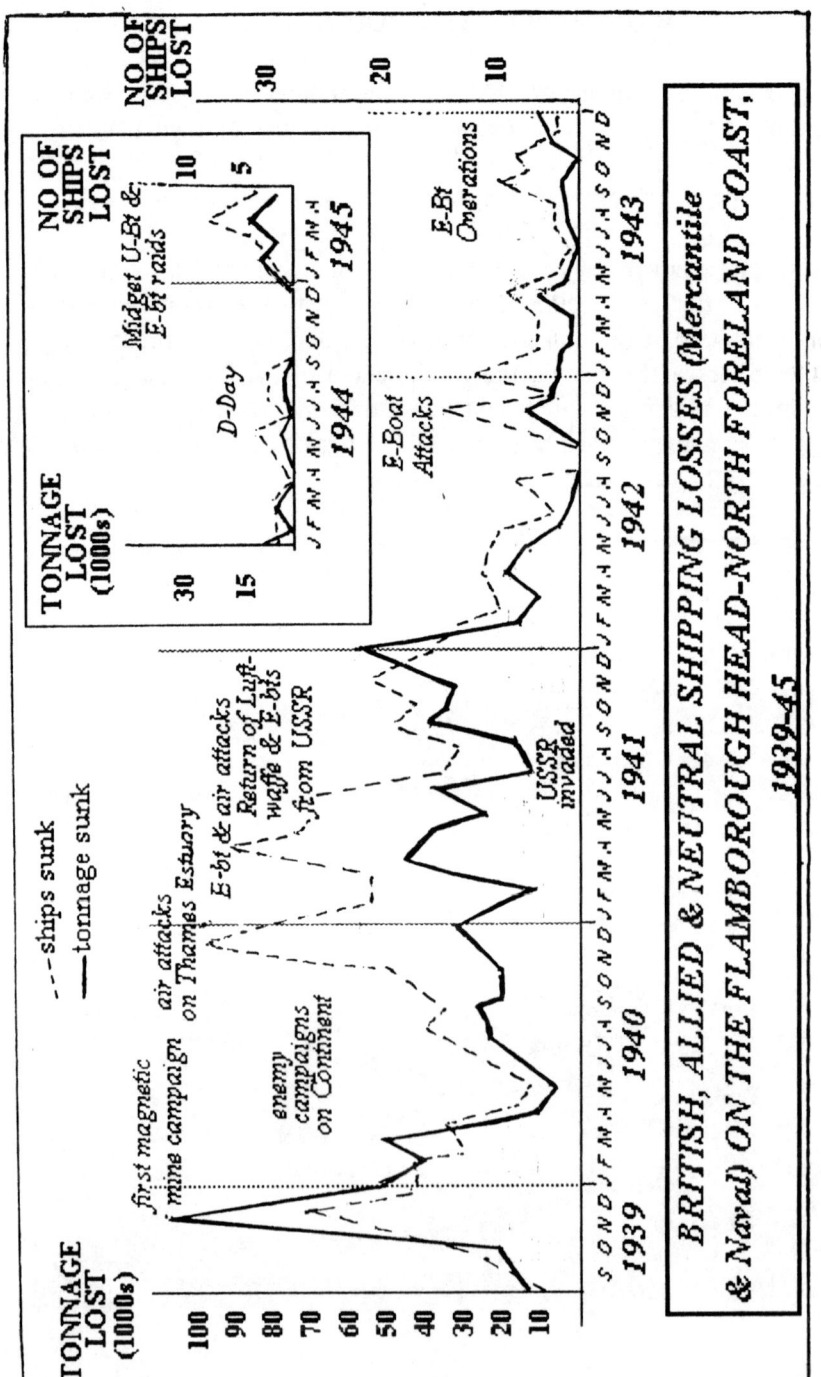

BRITISH, ALLIED & NEUTRAL SHIPPING LOSSES (Mercantile & Naval) ON THE FLAMBOROUGH HEAD-NORTH FORELAND COAST, 1939-45

WAR ON THE CONVOY ROUTE _ 1

On 15 December seven of Birnbacher's E-boats reappeared near 54G Buoy, off Yarmouth, and sank *N C Monberg*. Their last foray of the year was on Christmas Eve, from off Orfordness to off Corton, where the Coast Artillery saw the starshells and gunflashes and went on the alert. The Dutch *Stad Maastricht*, in FN 66, was torpedoed by Lt Klug's S 28 and eventually went down while under tow near the North East Gunfleet, her crew having been removed by *Shearwater*. While Rosyth destroyers engaged the raiders the Lowestoft trawler *Pelton* was also hit (by Lt Müller's S 59) and blew up. MAC (Motor Attendant Craft) 5 was sunk with all hands by a mine next day when she came out from Harwich to inspect the wreck of the *Stad Maastricht*. As if to desecrate 25 December still more, a conical float killed a soldier a few miles away on the beach at Frinton.

So ended 1940. 190 vessels of all types had been sunk on the East Coast between Flamborough Head and the North Foreland, 116 by mines, the rate of sinkings reaching a whole-war peak of thirty-six in November. But minesweeping and escort had gone smoothly enough for ports to be closed and convoys to be halted on only a handful of days. In spite of the number of ships lost the tonnage sunk (and especially the cargo tonnage) was proportionately much lower than in late 1939, as the graph opposite shows. 503 enemy mines had been swept during the year in the Nore Command, 277 of them magnetic, 32 acoustic, and 194 contact.

Although massed attacks were over, Luftwaffe bombing of East Coast shipping came to a peak in the winter of 1941. The enemy planes, operating one after another but singly in order to slip through the air defences, either picked on lone vessels or dived from cloud onto the heads or rears of convoys. They were apparently encouraged rather than deterred by the weather, which snowed up the coastal districts for the second time in the war.

On 4 January SS *Coity Castle*, in FS 77, was damaged by bombing and machine-gunning, while other German aircraft bombed FN 75 in Barrow Deep. Next day the Dutch timber ship *Alioth* was damaged near the Cork Lightship, and *Tower Grange*, the FN 76 Vice-Commodore's ship, was unsuccessfully attacked near the Sunk Lightship. On the 19th the *Bonnington Court* was bombed and sunk one mile west of the latter marker. That month the Shipwash and Sunk Light Vessels were repeatedly attacked, and had to be abandoned, while, inshore, attacks were also made on the Harwich and Lowestoft examination vessels.

26 January was a dramatic day.

In the morning a Ju 88 of III/KG 30 was shot down by the Lowestoft M/S trawler *Galvani* (Skipper Peck), then off Caister. The plane crashlanded at Somerton, a mile inland. The four survivors were remarkably cooperative. As they were carrying their rubber dinghy towards the sea they surrendered to two unarmed civilians without hesitation, let alone resistance. If the local press is to be believed one officer actually declared "We are in good old England at last. We feel at home now"(!) When interrogated by the RAF they were most forthcoming. They explained how from their base at Schipol (in peacetime Amsterdam Airport) they had mined all round Britain, how they navigated with the help of the radio beacon on the Dutch island of Schouwen, how they avoided British harbours when there was low cloud, because it hid barrage balloons above, and how they could position their cargoes into areas half a kilometre square. It was assumed that such helpful Germans would have left their logbook intact on the plane, but to the RAF's annoyance they were found to have burned it.

In the afternoon the Luftwaffe bombed two straggling convoys as they passed each other off Essex. First the heads of both FS 95, then off Foulness, and FN 92, off the Naze, were attacked out of the low cloud and sleety drizzle. In the former convoy three ships were damaged. A plane missed one ship in the latter and flew off trailing its target's kite balloon without apparent damage to itself. A second plane hit and set ablaze the Swedish freighter *Belgia*, carrying ballast and a small cargo of coffee. Six of the ship's crew were killed and the remaining twenty (including a stewardess) were rescued by the Harwich destroyer *Cotswold*, which towed the burning ship to Frinton Beach, where she ran aground. She had been bound for Blyth, where she was to have picked up 120 Swedish merchant ship survivors and taken them home under a safe conduct from the Germans. A third plane, a Ju 88, overflew Clacton and was then shot down in the Colne mouth by the Brightlingsea drifter *Fisher Boy*, which fired a mere six bullets before both her machine guns jammed. One survivor, Oberleutnant Kurt Frohlieb, was captured. The officer on the drifter, Lt Plomer RCNVR*, had the extra satisfaction of proving the Admiralty wrong in its usual claim that it was always dirty guns and never defective ammunition which caused such

---

*Royal Canadian Volunteer Naval Reserve.

WAR ON THE CONVOY ROUTE _ 1

jamming.

Half an hour later, over the Barrow Deep, two more planes went for the tail of FS 95, then being escorted by the Rosyth destroyer *Wallace* and (temporarily) the Brightlingsea patrol drifters *Reids* (Skipper Ovenstone) and *Lord St Vincent* (Skipper Alexander). Gunner Fraser Guy, on *Reids*, shot down a Ju 88 (for which he received a DSM), and Gunner Buchan on *Lord St Vincent* destroyed a Do 17 (and got a Mention in Despatches). Both were certain kills as *Wallace* and *Reids* recovered wreckage from the Dornier and *Wallace* captured two survivors from the Junkers.

The *Sultan*, a lead carrier, broke down and dropped out of her convoy on 2 February. No sooner had *Lord St Vincent* radioed this news back to Brightlingsea _ unfortunately, in plain language _ than a German bomber appeared and struck *The Sultan's* stern. She sank in flames on Sunk Sand. *Lord St Vincent* lay alongside and thereby saved the twelve survivors (two men, including an Army gunner, had died). While the Harwich FOIC praised Skipper Alexander, and his Group Officer, Lt Garland RNVR, who was also on board, the C-in-C Nore said that the uncoded radio message had probably given the Germans their opportunity in the first place.

Another *Nemo* drifter, *Eager*, shot down one of two attacking Ju 88s on 12 February: this time Gunner Loftus and Commando Corporal Bowles (who was training aboard) received DSMs. Bowles, however, died of wounds in Clacton Hospital before he could receive the news. The Brightlingsea drifters were attacked about twenty times that winter and spring, but none of them was lost or badly damaged and they gave better than they got. In April their score was four aircraft certainly destroyed (including three in half an hour on 26 January), two more probably, and four possibly. The Admiralty expressed "their Lordships' pleasure" and the base, especially gunnery instructor CPO John Blake _ though not the incompetent radio arrangements, was mentioned in the Harwich FOIC's half-yearly awards recommendations.

On 27 February three merchantmen _ *Old Charlton, Blacktoft* and *Newlands* _ were bomb-damaged off Harwich. Two were towed to safety, but *Old Charlton* sank, though SS *Catherine Hawksfield* rescued all her crew. 3 March saw the sinking of the Lowestoft patrol trawler *Cobbers* off her base _ eleven of her crew died. In the space of the next ten days the Yarmouth M/S trawlers took thirteen attacks and definitely brought down four planes: two were claimed by *Nadine* and *Orizaba*, and Group Officer J W G Price RNR and Seaman J J Hall on the former won the DSC and DSM

WAR ON THE CONVOY ROUTE _ 1

respectively. On the 7th a Dornier was shot down only a thousand yards south-east of Gorleston: two of its crew were captured at sea, one drowned, and one (Oberleutnant Kuntz) swam ashore and surrendered to 514 Coast Artillery Regiment. The trawler *George Robb* and a Yarmouth Bofors gun hd both hit the plane. Two hours later, escorting FS 28 near 52 Buoy, off Harwich, the corvette *Guillemot* shot down an He 111: one survivor was brought in by ML 180. On the 12th the Yarmouth trawler *Milford Queen* claimed a Do 17 near 8C Buoy, off Cromer, with a PAC, probably the first success at sea of this weapon. SS *Fireglow* put in another claim soon afterwards, but one must discount G Pawle's story that a coaster master brought down a German plane off Essex by *accidentally* tripping over his PAC firing lanyard!

Two big ships were next to be hit. *Artemisia* was bombed and sunk in the Would on 14 March _ and, a new departure, at night. On 6 April the Liverpool general cargo ship *Glenfinlas* was damaged near the Sunk Lightship. Hit in the engine room and stokehold, she was kept afloat and towed into Harwich. Her mainly Chinese below-decks crew had taken heavy casualties, and the following names mark eight Commonwealth War Graves Co mmission headstones in Dovercourt Cemetary; Ling Yang, Ta Wan, Lan Ki, Ling Sang, Chan Yee, Hu Hee and Ling Choy. More night attacks followed in May, sinking, for instance, SS *Royston* off Cromer on the 4th and *Fowberry Tower* off the Humber on the 12th _ apparently in moonlight the Luftwaffe could pick up coalburning ships from their high plumes of dark smoke.

There were about three hundred air attacks against vessels of all types in the Nore Command in the first half of 1941, and during the rest of the year, plus the first two months of 1942, another 350. They only began to decline after mid-1941, and at first slowly. During this fourteen-month period there were thirty-one attacks on warships in Sheerness Sub-Command, sixty-seven in Harwich, 169 in Yarmouth, and seventy in Humber. The bombing retreated northwards, because it virtually ceased in the Sheerness area in February 1941, in Harwich in July, and in the northern two after February 1942.

In 1941 there was no doubt that the Humber was taking the brunt of German minelaying. In the early hours of 22 January some twenty German aircraft were over the estuary. Next day the LL trawler *Luda Lady* was sunk

WAR ON THE CONVOY ROUTE _ 1

passing through the boom gate, and the same fate befell the tug *St Cyrus* when she went to help her _ all seven of her crew were killed. Over the next week thirty-six mines were safely blown _ seventeen acoustics, three magnetics, the rest of indeterminate type _ mainly by the trawlers *Fitzgerald* and *Aiglon*. Hardly had the estuary been made safe when, on the night of 4 February, the biggest minelaying force yet flew over. In a rare (though not unique) incident one mine fell right onto SS *Gwynwood*, standing in the convoy anchorage and still patching up the damage inflicted by a bomb in the Barrow Deep on her previous voyage. She sank with thirteen dead. The port was closed while the sweepers got to work. Over the next fortnight no fewer than ninety-four mines (twenty-eight magnetic and sixty-six acoustic) were swept. The total was swollen with some more dropped on the 9th. *Fitzgerald* (again), *Strathborve* and *Cayrian* were mainly responsible for the good work. Another forty mines were accounted for in other ways _ unfortunately some by sinking ships; the fishing trawler *Thomas Deas* on the 6th, the naval trawlers *Remillo* on the 27th and *St Donats* on 1 March. Several were dealt with on land by *Vernon* parties led by Cdr Hamond, Lt-Cdr C W A Chapple DSC and Sub-Lt Wadsley GM RNVR. One mine was defused in Alexandra Dock, Hull, on 14 March. Four days later another was to be "knocked out" in St Andrew's Dock by means of a carefully placed small charge to smash the detonator circuits without blowing the mine itself. The C-in-C Nore, FOIC Humber and other senior officers had come to watch the proceedings from a safe distance. In fact the whole mine blew and wrecked the Hull Fish Market, nonetheless without harming half the "gold braid" of the Nore Command.

The Humber minesweepers blew 171 mines in February 1941. This was indeed unparallelled: Harwich Sub-Command, for instance, only swept a hundred mines in the whole *year*. The peak day on the Humber was 14 February, when thirty-five mines were dealt with _ including fourteen acoustics by *Fitzgerald* and twelve by *Aiglon*. On the 29th *Rolls Royce* (Skipper Romyn DSC) and another SA trawler set a record by blowing twenty-eight acoustics in eighty-three minutes. The aptly-named *Rolls Royce* reached her century (actually 102) that Christmas Eve, and went on to another record by sweeping a total of 196 mines for the whole war. Captain Bardwell DSC was in charge of the Grimsby-based minesweepers.

Inevitably some mines were missed until it was too late. Mistakes were also made. *Fitzgerald* sank the little net vessel *Gloaming* and the Civil

WAR ON THE CONVOY ROUTE _ 1

Defence smack *Joan Margaret* by inadvertantly triggering an acoustic near them on 20 March. Incidentally next day AA guns brought down a German bomber on Haborough Road, Immingham. The two captured survivors refused to tell their interrogators whether they had been minelaying or not. The trawler *Lord Selborne* was lost with seventeen crew off the estuary on the last day of that month. A harbour defence drifter, *Bahram*, was sunk nearby on 3 April, and on the 11th the boom defence vessels *Othello* and *Yorkshire Belle* were destroyed on station with all hands.

On 10 June the Harwich corvette *Pintail* and the merchant ship *Royal Scot* were sunk by acoustic mines on the convoy route east of the Humber. Lt-Cdr Heber-Percy, captain of the Harwich destroyer *Quantock*, who was passing with another convoy, later reported of *Pintail's* sinking; "It was the most dreadful sight that I have ever seen...It did not seem possible that there could be any survivors". In fact there were twenty-two, rescued by his and another ship, but this was only one third of the crew.

In more southerly waters a needless sinking was the new Harwich Trinity House vessel *Strathearn*, which on 8 January 1941 went into the Wallet off Clacton to replace a damaged buoy in ignorance of the FOIC's warning not to venture into this dangerous area without minesweeper escort. Fifteen of the crew were killed and six wounded because they were down in the for'd hull eating dinner when an acoustic mine went off under the bow. That night the Luftwaffe made an attempt to repeat its intensive mining of the Yantlet Channel, through the Thames boom, following it up three nights later. What the Admiralty dubbed "the third Thames mine offensive" came on the nights of 8/9 and 10/11 March, and the "fourth" on 4/5 April. Though several dozen planes were involved each time, the Sheerness SA craft now had the measure of "green" mines, and total losses were at most one sailing barge and one tug. The worst incident in Sheerness waters in 1941 was in fact the mining of the AA-equipped convoy leader (formerly Dutch minelayer) *Van Meerlant* near the Girdler Light Vessel on 4 June _ forty-two sailors died.

On the beaches the conical floats, in spite of warnings, continued to take a toll. On 3 January two privates of the King's Own Rifles tried to load one onto a wheelbarrow below Gunton Cliff, Lowestoft, and were blown to pieces. Two days later two civilians died tampering with another at Happisburgh. On the 29th a soldier was killed by one at Felixstowe. Next

Right: **Upper Thames Patrol being inspected by its commander, Rear-Admiral Brooke (ret). These tiny craft were manned by Home Guards, suitably clad in naval-style uniforms.**
(Odhams)

Below: **MMS 16, built at Wivenhoe in the spring of 1941 and based at Gravesend. Note the SA gear on her bows and the LL cable drum astern of the superstructure.**
(IWM)

Above: **SHEERNESS, 1943**
Seldom do all three wartime armed services feature in one photograph, but is the case here. On the left, the Army are manning a Bofors light anti-aircraft gun. To its right is the Army Coast Artillery's Garrison Point Fort, but on top are the Navy's Port War Signal Station and radio mast. From overhead the RAF are bringing to earth a barrage balloon, and in the right foreground they have an air-sea rescue seaplane tender up on a cradle. *(RAF Museum)*

Below: The remains of Great Bromley CH radar station R (receiver) site, in 1989. The smaller concete blocks are the bases of the 247-foot wooden towers, demolished in 1958, and the large one (centre right) is the R block.

WAR ON THE CONVOY ROUTE _ 1

day a research physicist from the Army Small Arms Experimental Establishment at Foulness found one on the beach nearby and enterprisingly carried it to his laboratory for examination. He left it in the care of a sixteen-year old assistant, whom it promptly killed. Two Army sappers were killed by another one at Dunwich on 28 April. Surprisingly each of these floats bore an explosive charge of less than one kilogram. The floats were being scattered on the convoy route by the hundred from E-boats which, curiously, were now doing little more contact-minelaying. The winter gales had been tearing them from their mooring cables and washing them ashore, especially around Lowestoft. Some of the RMS (Rendering Mines Safe) parties were very busy, as these figures* for the period October 1940-June 1941 show:

RMS Party	German & British mines dealt with	German floats dealt with
BRIDLINGTON	62	149
MABLETHORPE	15	60
YARMOUTH	152	630
BRIGHTLINGSEA	4	34
NORE	34	unknown

In May 1941 the Germans introduced a new groundmine, known to them as the "Bomb-Mine" and to us as the Type G. It had no parachute, weighed a full ton, and ignored the ten-second pulse frequency of LL _ until this was altered.

A new type of minesweeper was now being built _ the MMS (Motor Minesweeper or "Micky Mouse"); wooden, shallow-draught, with SA on an A-frame on the bow and an LL cable drum astern. The first two (Nos 1 and 8) left Richards' Shipyard at Lowestoft in March, and were the first of the Sheerness flotilla.

The tactics of the enemy minelying aircraft had become predictable, though thereby little easier to counter. The planes came in all weathers and phases of the moon, but usually (though not invariably) by night, along two distinct corridors from Holland and one from Northern France via Ostend. They flew most of the way at five to eight thousand feet, meaning that RDF saw them at about seventy-five miles, but then they started spiralling down, often crossing the convoy route, approaching a prominent coastal feature like

---
*Nore Command War Diary (PRO ADM 199/407)

the North Foreland, Clacton Pier, or Spurn Point, and then turning back towards the shipping channel. By this time, frustratingly, they would be under five hundred feet and the CHL horizon. June 1941 was one of the peak months of their campaign: RDF counted 334 minelaying sorties on the East Coast, distributed over seventeen nights, with fifty on the busiest night _ and half as many sorties again may have gone undetected.

So far the interception of these minelayers had scarcely begun, for reasons I will mention elsewhere. At a rough estimate thirty percent of enemy mines were swept soon after sowing (including those that sank ships), ten percent spontaneously blew and a similar proportion fell on land, and fifty percent went unlocated for the time being, through falling wide of the convoy routes.

Early 1941 marked a furious phase of the E-boat war, with three German flotillas available in Holland. On the night of 23 January FN 85 was attacked by these raiders near 54F Buoy, off Lowestoft. Among the escort were the Harwich A/S trawlers *Tourmaline* and *Turquoise*. In the hectic ensuing action *Tourmaline* (Lt Ashmore RNVR), using a 12-pdr, Savage guns, twin 0.5-inch machine guns and Lewis guns, claimed to have destroyed one E-boat and damaged another. Such claims were common and usually mistaken. But this one was confirmed four days later, when the bodies of Walter Laube, Paul Friese, Alfred Thiel and one other German naval rating were washed ashore at Aldeburgh and their effects brought to Harwich and scrutinised by Naval Intelligence. Typical of war, *Tourmaline*'s celebrations were shortlived. Within a fortnight she had been sunk by bombing near the North Foreland.

On 25 February E-boats again attacked near 54F Buoy. The Harwich Hunt-class destroyer *Exmoor* was escorting FN 17 towards No 5 Buoy when she was jolted by an explosion. There were five officers on the bridge at that moment; Lt-Cdr Lampard (the captain), Lt Hamilton, and Sub-Lts Barr, Beckwith and Thorp. Hamilton later told an inquiry:

> "There was no indication of E-boats. The best Asdic operator was in the hut, but he heard nothing...there was an explosion aft. I have no idea what caused (it). I am certain it was not the ammunition...
> Whatever it was that hit the ship, it probably hit the pom-pom deck, which blazed at once and the whole thing was a twisted wreck. The pom-pom ammunition started going off and the ship listed over to port at about 20° with the whole of the after part...ablaze. She

WAR ON THE CONVOY ROUTE _ 1

blazed from aft as far as the searchlight platform and then took a list to port".*

He went on to describe *Exmoor* rolling flat onto her side, and continued: "I saw the captain standing on the side of the ship by me and he said that he was alright, and when we went into the water I lost him. He did not show up any more after we left".

Sub-Lt Thorp said that:

"I could see all hands standing on the side of the ship, and as the stern went under they slid down into the water: the ship was then standing on her stern with her bows right out of the water, and oil fuel was burning on the water on the starboard quarter, the flames from which lit up the surrounding area like daylight and burned for about twenty minutes".

On shore the Corton Coast Artillerymen noted a "large fire at 090°", and supposing it to be a crashed aircraft, called for the Lowestoft air-sea rescue boats.

Meanwhile, in *Exmoor*'s sick bay, Surgeon-Lt Hughes also had no idea his ship had been torpedoed. The impact was not loud, nor did it even knock him off his chair. He only realised the situation was serious when the listing began. Emerging from the forecastle aft door he also saw the whole aft end ablaze, pom-pom ammunition exploding, and a patch of oil alight on the surface and spreading aft. He was amazed to see all *Exmoor*'s lights still burning as she sank. The Harwich corvette *Shearwater* had reached the scene and took off thirty-two survivors, including Hamilton, Thorp and Hughes. The latter gave three hours artificial respiration to one rating in vain, then picked a lump of brass out of another's cheekbone, stuffing the hole with cotton wool soaked in iodine in lieu of any other antiseptic. The Board of Inquiry witnesses, or at any rate the report incorporating their testimony, said nothing about the worst horror of that night, which is that the oil fire engulfed many men while they tried to swim or paddle to safety. 106 *Exmoor* personnel, including Lampard, lost their lives, the highest death toll in any 1939-45 Nore Command warship crew.

The survivors were at first unaware that any E-boat had been involved. Some said they had heard a plane fly over just before the disaster, and therefore blamed a parachute mine. But others faintly recalled a "rushing" or "slushing" noise immediately before the explosion _ a typical torpedo sound. One of *Exmoor*'s merchant ship flock, *Minorca,* was

*Board of Inquiry Report in PRO ADM 199/670.

WAR ON THE CONVOY ROUTE _ 1

definitely sunk by this means off Sheringham a few hours later. At the Admiralty, after the file was closed, someone pencilled on the cover "probably torpedoed by E-boat". It was decided that the torpedo must have hit on the port quarter at the top of the fuel tank which lay just below the seamen's mess. It is now known that the torpedo was fired by Lt Feldt's S 30, of 2nd Flotilla. It was her second destroyer victim, for she had sunk *Wakeful* at Dunkirk. It was also Feldt who had sunk a small convoy straggler on 6 February _ she had been bound from Ipswich to Newcastle and, uniquely, her wreck was never found.

7 March must, however, rank as the E-boats' greatest victory. They sank (or in one case drove ashore and wrecked) seven merchant ships as two convoys passed each other off Norfolk.

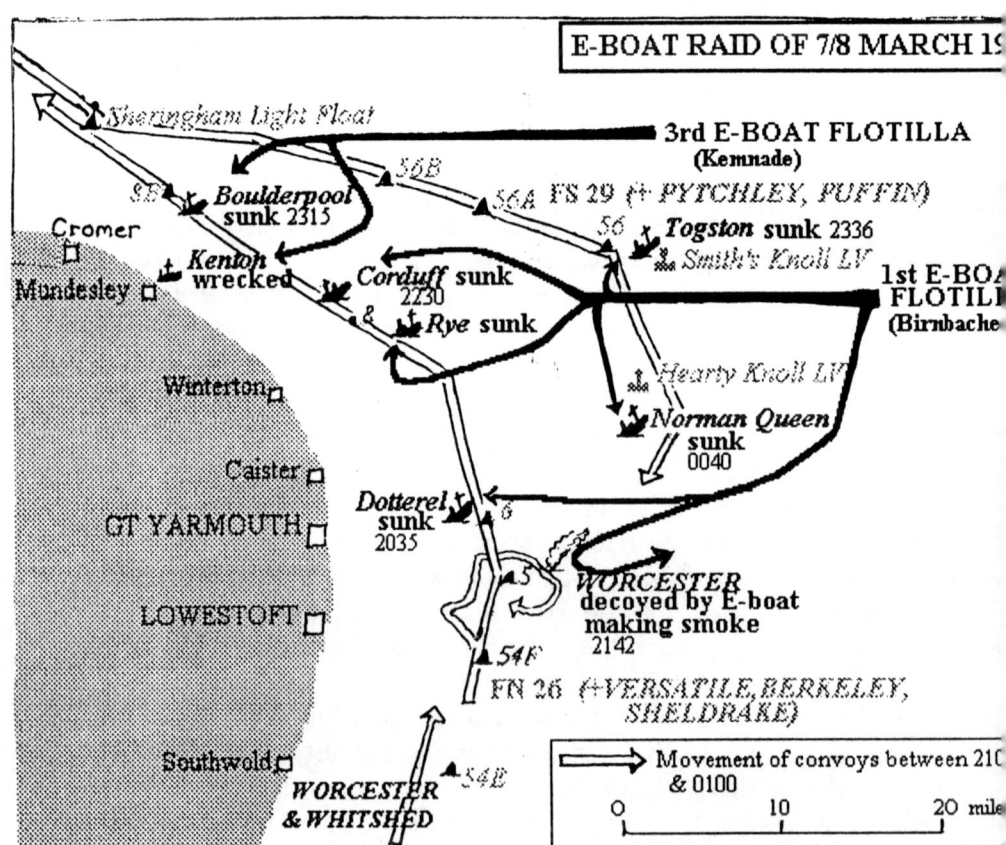

WAR ON THE CONVOY ROUTE _ 1

FS 29 had forty-two ships in two columns, with the Sheerness Hunt-class destroyer *Pytchley* and the Harwich corvette *Puffin* as the only escorts. FN 26 had twenty-nine ships, also in two lines, with the Rosyth destroyer *Versatile* in the van, the Sheerness Hunt-class *Berkeley* to starboard of centre, and the Harwich corvette *Sheldrake* in the rear. Further south, hurrying north to overtake FN 26 and meet FS 29, were *Worcester*, with Captain(D16) Halsey on board, and *Whitshed*, both of Harwich. There had been intense enemy air activity all along the East Coast during the two days before the E-boats struck. From one hour past Blyth, on the 6th, FS 29 had been regularly bombed and shadowed from the air. On both the 6th and 7th there were raids on coastal towns and ships in the Harwich, Lowestoft and Yarmouth areas, in which FN 25 had been caught up. On many ships nerves were badly frayed. By nightfall on the 7th FS 29 was level with Cromer and FN 26 with Lowestoft (see map), and the E-boats were ready to pounce. Lt-Cdr Kemnade's 3rd Flotilla, of six craft, was concentrated off Mundesley (Norfolk), while Birnbacher's 1st, also of six, was scattered between there and a point off Lowestoft.

At 2035, at this southernmost location, the first torpedo slammed into SS *Dotterel*, streaming alongside *Sheldrake* at the rear of the starboard column. The corvette went alongside and put on a boarding party, but then a second torpedo (from Lt z S von Mirbach's S 29) passed right underneath her and blew the merchantman in half. The glare, together with a cascade of starshells, was seen on land by the Coast Artillery at Corton, ten miles west. Eight merchant seamen, and from *Sheldrake* Lt Checcucci and two ratings, died on *Dotterel*. *Sheldrake*, only slightly damaged, rescued nineteen survivors and took them to Yarmouth, while the stern half of *Dotterel* sank. FN 26 continued past Yarmouth, along the Would route (QZS 171/215) and from about 2200 was subject to a second attack. Raiders of both German flotillas had got on both sides of the channel, though it seemed to the convoy as if some were darting from side to side. 1st E-boat Flotilla's gauntlet was run first. Its torpedoes came from both the shore and seaward directions, and SS *Rye* and her nineteen crew disappeared and were presumed lost. (She had been sunk by Oblt. Büchting's S 27). SS *Corduff* (like all these merchantmen with names beginning with *Cor* a William Cory ship) had heard many torpedoes explode either side astern when, near No 8 Buoy, at 2230, she was hit from seawards by Lt z S Klug's S 28. Seven of her crew were killed, two were left injured on the sinking ship, and fourteen, including Captain D E Rees, fled in a boat. This was intercepted by Klug, who asked if any of the occupants were officers (fearing capture, they replied that none were), said that the two wounded men had been taken prisoner, gave them a bearing to the coast, and sped away into the night. Rees and his men made SOS signals at two in the morning and then after dawn, and at 0745 were rescued by the inimitable Cromer lifeboat. On shore Rees had an uneasy interview with the local RNO, Captain Tudor. Why had he and his men left their two friends to die or be captured? Rees pleaded that his crew had been demoralised: hours of the Luftwaffe droning overhead had so worn them down that when *Corduff* was hit they had panicked.

3rd E-boat Flotilla opened its attack as soon as 1st left off. At 2320 *Berkeley* found the survivors of *Boulderpool*, just sent to the bottom by Oblt. von Gernet's S 61, while after an attack by Oblt. Mayer's S 31 *Kenton*'s crew abandoned their sinking ship and let her drift ashore near Cromer.

Between the times of the two German attacks just described *Worcester* and *Whitshed* passed what was left of the *Dotterel* wreck, which *Whitshed*, apparently unaware of the rescue by *Sheldrake*, boarded. At 2142 *Worcester*, whose ASV was defective owing to penetration by rainwater, was delayed and decoyed by one E-boat trailing smoke and dropping smokefloats. The two V/W-class destroyers continued on the outer shipping lane, in order to meet FS 29 before harm befell it.

They were too late. FS 29 first saw ominous E-boat flares ahead at 2115. An hour or so later, as it passed 56B and 56A Buoys, it could see the attack on FN 26, as this passed in the opposite direction twelve miles south. Around midnight FS 29 began to round the 56 Buoy bend of QZS 288, twenty-five miles off Winterton and the furthrest from the coast either convoy went that night. At 0035 the first of Birnbacher's torpedoes was heard exploding. The two escort vessels opened a barrage of starshells (many of which seemed to splutter out quickly in the steady drizzle), and "DA" (delayed action explosive shells). *Pytchley* was at the head of the convoy and *Puffin* near the rear _ but this was ten miles apart! *Pytchley* clearly saw one raider and sprayed her whole vicinity with Oerlikon and machine-gun fire: she thought damage had been caused but the E-boat escaped. SS *Togston* was torpedoed and sunk, with nine dead, near Smith's Knoll Lightship. The convoy once caught sight of her eleven survivors, in the lifeboat, by the light

WAR ON THE CONVOY ROUTE _ 1

of starshells, but for the moment they were not resighted: *Puffin* finally saved them at 0120. SS *Norman Queen* also sank, with eight more dead. At 0150, twenty miles off Caister, *Worcester* met FN 26. The raiders were already on their way home: without loss to themselves they had killed fifty-four Britons and captured two that night, though I should record that the combined gross tonnage of the seven ships sunk was only 13,134, equivalent to one large ocean-going merchantman.

This was only one of many E-boat actions that month, in which SS *Trevethoe* was sunk on the 12th and the Norwegian *Daphne* on the 18th. Six destroyers and a corvette from Harwich and Sheerness were all engaged within the space of sixteen days, *Worcester* four times. In most cases all that had been actually seen of the enemy was a tiny, fleeting black silhouette against the starshell glare, a white wake or the faintest and briefest flicker on the ASV "scope". In fifty actions with E-boats in 1941, the Nore Command only sank two, and much paper was wasted trying to write coherent reports with useful tactical conclusions on confused melées. But reading these reports can still send a shiver down the spine. Take, for example, Captain Halsey's account of the *Trevethoe* action:

> 0030. Sighted torpedo running on the surface on starboard bow on a nearly opposite course to the ship. Almost as soon as sighted a slushing noise was heard from it, exactly as described in Cdr Dechaineux's letter reporting survivors' accounts of *Exmoor*'s loss. A second torpedo track was almost simultaneously sighted on a parallel course down the port side...running submerged. *Steadied ship between the tracks.* *

The next E-boat victory came on 17 April. As usual 2nd Flotilla lay in wait, engines stopped, this time at No 6 Buoy, off Corton. The merchantmen *Effra* and *Nereus* (a Dutch ship) were sunk and *Ethel Radcliffe*, the FS 64 Vice-Commodore's vessel (a grain carrier) was damaged but towed to Yarmouth. Twelve nights later *Ambrose Fleming* was sunk by 1st Flotilla's S 29 (von Mirbach).

British communications and RDF (radar), both ashore and afloat, and starshells, had not been very effective in these actions. The escorts had been too few compared to the size of convoys. Some new defensive measures were beginning, however. "Snowflake" starshells were found to light up areas one to two miles in diameter. HMS *Minos* (Lowestoft) now had the MGBs

---
*PRO ADM 199/670. Dechaineux was captain of *Eglinton*. Author's italics.

WAR ON THE CONVOY ROUTE _ 1

(Motor Gunboats) with which to maintain the standing "QE" patrols (sometimes stiffened by a destroyer or two) to the east of the Alley, a forerunner of the continuous "Z Line" of the later war years. Other MGBs, based there and at Felixstowe, began the difficult game of trying to intercept the E-boats on their return from raids. But as yet no MGB carried RDF or effective illuminants. On the escort destroyers the first "Headache" operators appeared, German-speakers who listened in to the E-boats' radio talk. There was already a shore equivalent known as the "Y" Service, which I shall discuss elsewhere.

The simplest way to have forestalled the E-boats would have been to have sailed the convoys through the Alley in daylight. But this would have meant their leaving and reaching the Thames in darkness, when the necessary navigation and signal lights would have invited German minelaying and bomber planes to *the* strategic East Coast spot. On 10 March, as a compromise, FN convoys were ordered to leave as soon after dawn as possible, and FS to stop and anchor for a while off the Humber the night before they reached the Alley _ so as to have daylight as far as Sheringham Buoy.

RAF Coastal Command was asked to seek out the E-boats at sea (raids on their heavily AA-defended bases were ruled out): there were to be "QA" operations (bombing), "QB" (flare-towing) and "QD" (reconnaissances along the raiders' usual approach routes). They were singularly unsuccessful.

On 22 June 1941 the Germans invaded Russia, and by diverting most of the Luftwaffe and (temporarily) three E-boat flotillas out of four from the West, brought the hardest round of the East Coast war to an end. About 365 ships of all sizes and kinds, naval and civilian, had so far been sunk from all causes on the Bridlington-Margate coast. An examination of the figures shows that the Nore Command experienced no clearcut turning-point or obvious breakthrough in mid 1941. Nevertheless the worst *was* over, and it was already evident that if their goal was to strangle East Coast shipping the Germans had failed.

6
THE AIR DEFENCES

The East Coast was not new to air raids in 1940. Indeed it had undergone their debut in warfare. On the night of 19 January 1915 Zeppelins L3 and L4 dropped fourteen small bombs the length of Great Yarmouth, from Albermarle Road in the north to Nelson's Pillar in the south, killing two civilians and opening the first "Blitz" on Britain. In 1917 Gotha aeroplanes replaced Zeppelins, and, in between bombing London, made raids on East Coast ports as lethal as Göring's. On 4 July Felixstowe Air Station was hit, with the loss of a seaplane and seventeen lives. On the 22nd sixteen aircraft dropped fifty-five bombs on Harwich Harbour and Felixstowe, killing thirteen servicemen and civilians. On 3 September 120 sailors were killed by bombs on Chatham Naval Barracks. These raids alone killed more people in these three towns than all the attacks of 1939-45 put together.

Such events, together with the enormous improvement in bomber aircraft since 1918, convinced many between the wars that, in Baldwin's words, "The bomber will always get through". With the air defences of the time, these words were quite justified, and not least on the East Coast. Feeble aero engines and biplane construction gave fighters, in spite of their lightness, little margin of speed over bombers. Great War East Coast airfields had been abandoned. Early warning consisted of giant microphones and sound-collecting concrete walls, useless because they smothered any distant aeroplane noise picked up with the swish of wind and sea.

The formation of the Luftwaffe in 1934-35 was indeed the mother of invention, however. Fighter bases reappeared in the East _ apart from the ring round London, at Manston (Kent), Rochford, Debden (Essex), Martlesham Heath (Suffolk), Duxford (Cambridgeshire), Digby and Kirton-in-Lindsay (Lincolnshire). The Hurricane and Spitfire, with supercharged engines and monoplane design, first flew in 1936. Martlesham especially played a vital role as the RAF's test field for new planes and their armaments.

But the special connection of the East Coast was with radar, or "RDF" (radio directionfinding) as it was codenamed at the time. The Air Ministry Research Establishment, led by Robert Watson-Watt, and staffed by such brilliant technicians as Bainbridge-Bell, Bowen, Larnder, Minnis and Wilkins, pioneered the very first British version of this device at Orfordness, and then Bawdsey, on the Suffolk coast, in 1935. By 1937 the (Thames) Estuary Chain of five AMESs (Air Ministry Experimental Stations _ the

THE AIR DEFENCES

name was a cover) was operational _ at Bawdsey, at Great Bromley and Canewdon in Essex, and the prophetically-named Dunkirk and Dover in Kent. That year the Air Ministry started another fifteen stations to constitute the *CH* (Chain Home), lining the coast from Sussex to Scotland. North of Bawdsey the next few stations were High Street (Darsham, Suffolk), Stoke Holy Cross and West Beckham (Norfolk), Stenigot (Lincolnshire) and Staxton Wold (Yorkshire).* Most were very rural locations, without mains water and sewage, or, more to the point, mains electricity _ it had to be extended to the sites.

The scientists were sorry to leave Orford, with the cosy "Crown and Castle" and "Jolly Sailor" pubs, picture-postcard village square and castle keep, and mysterious ferry over to the gravel peninsula called "The Island". But they soon liked Bawdsey too. Here both the researchers and the operational CH station occupied the extensive house and grounds of a remote clifftop manor, purchased from the Quilter family. From the outside world this could either be reached via the narrow country lanes which led past Sutton Hoo, where archaeologists were making a famous discovery of their own, or across the mouth of the Deben from Felixstowe on the ferry run by a hook-handed civilian called Brinkley. The brilliant but opinionated Watson-Watt went to London in 1938 to head the Air Ministry DCD (Directorate of Communications Development), leaving his imperious and unpopular assistant A P Rowe in charge until the "AMRE" was driven from Bawdsey by the outbreak of war.

In the words of the novelist Len Deighton:
"There was a unique atmosphere at Bawdsey...the old manor house by the sea. It had extensive grounds that included a cricket pitch, peach trees, and the biggest bougainvillaea in the country. The high-grade academic physicists lived and worked in the manor house.

There was no red tape and they stopped work for a swim if they felt like it. On the other hand, it was not unusual for the laboratory to be in full operation long after midnight. Visitors came from the famous Cavendish Laboratory at Cambridge to sit by the fire and talk shop. These sessions grew into what Bawdsey men called 'Soviets', in which visiting civil servants, air marshals _ and eventually even air crew straight from operations _ could say anything they liked to anyone they chose. An Assistant III was often actively abetted in

---
*The local civilians did not know their purpose, dubbing them "pylons" (after the electricity ones) and speculating that the stations were for shooting death rays at enemy bombers.

THE AIR DEFENCES

arguing with an air marshal, said an unrepentent Watson-Watt, who was often fomenting such excitement".*

The distinguished visitors included Air Chief Marshal Sir Hugh Dowding, chief of Fighter Command, and Dr R V Jones, later head of British Scientific Intelligence. On his visit Churchill peered through a telescope guided by RDF onto a ship approaching Harwich: he growled "I can't see a bloody thing", but was told that the directionfinding was so precise that the ship was hidden behind the cross hairs of his lens. The Germans were of course not invited, but General Martini, head of Luftwaffe signals, came and spied on the Manor from a Zeppelin.

As in all radar, Watson-Watt's *transmitter* broadcast, not an even signal, which would have been too weak, but in *pulses* powerful enough to echo back off aircraft. The CH of 1939 made twelve and a half fifteen-microsecond pulses per second. And as in all radar, his *receiver* was built round a *cathode ray tube*, the flat-ended glass bulb invented for electrical research several years earlier and already on sale to the public in miniscule numbers in the first television sets. The tube was named after the cathode or "gun" at its narrow end, which shot electrons through a vacuum and onto a flourescent "*scope*" (screen) at the other, wider, end, causing a glowing spot to appear there. Since transmitter and receiver were linked, every time the former pulsed, it triggered the firing of the latter's cathode and made a spot on its scope. It also activated "horizontal deflection coils", which swung the beam across the scope, thereby turning the spot into a glowing line called the *trace*. The tiny period of cathode-firing, or beam-swinging, was known as the "*time base*". When the receiver aerial picked up a faint echo it activated "vertical deflection coils" to pull down the cathode beam, thereby causing a little depression or "*blip*" in the trace. Now this echo reached the receiver very slightly earlier or later according to how far the radio pulse had to travel to the aircraft and back (slightly, because the speed of radio waves is 186,000 miles per second _ an echo from ninety-three miles away would be received 1/1,000 of a second later than from an object right beside the station, or, in the jargon, one millisecond along the timebase). And so, the nearer the blip to the start (i.e, left-hand end) of the trace the nearer the aircraft, and the further along the further away. Here then, was a system of *rangefinding* as well as mere detection.

---

*Len Deighton; *Fighter* (Jonathan Cape)

THE AIR DEFENCES

The curvature of the earth (rather than the weakening of the signal over distance) limited maximum range, of course. In 1939 an East Coast CH station could detect a plane at 20,000 feet at 110 miles, on at 10,000 feet at eighty miles, and one at 3,000 feet at forty-four miles.

Separate aircraft, flying at different distances, showed up as multiple blips and could be counted, but it was very hard to count planes in formation. Then the echoes were so close together that the distinct blips were replaced by a flickering fuzziness on the trace: the bigger this patch of shimmering light, the bigger the formation. It was a matter of guesswork, and this could be very misleading; for one thing, ten twin-engined bombers in formation resembled twenty single-engined fighters.

In retrospect the design of CH was very odd. Each station, and none was complete until 1940, had three or four 358-foot steel T (transmitter) towers and four 247-foot wooden R (receiver) towers. Yet Germany's equivalent installations, which remained unknown to British Intelligence till 1941, consisted of one quite small and modern-looking grid and one dish,

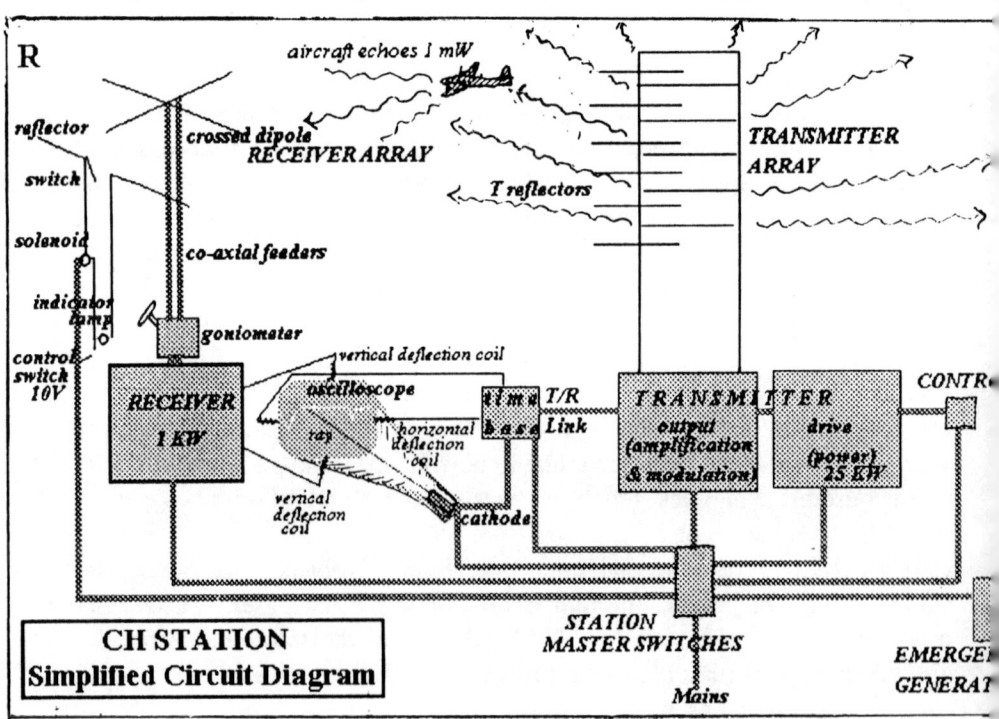

RADAR

Top Left: Bawdsey CH Station, at some date after 1943. Four wooden R towers in the background, & four steel T towers in front, with a CHL array on the 200-ft platform of the leftmost tower, and a CD on the rightmost *(Kinsey)*

Left: Bawdsey photographed by the Luftwaffe in July 1942 *(Elliott)*

Top: A CHL array on the former Walton-on-Naze lighthouse, at a date after 1941 *(Derek Johnson)*

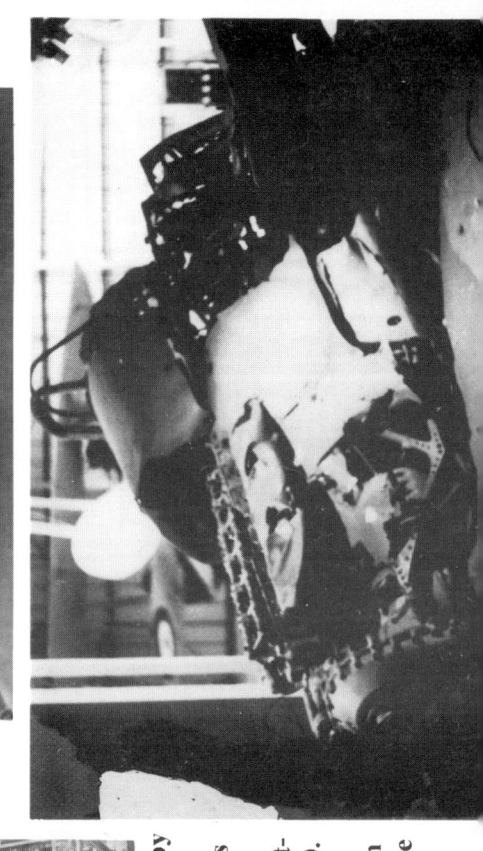

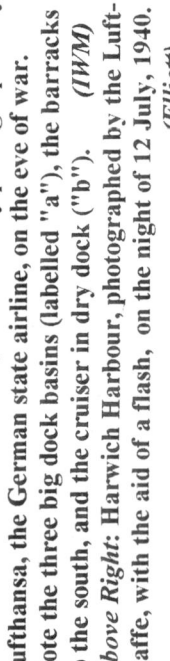

Above: Chatham naval area, clandestinely photographed by Lufthansa, the German state airline, on the eve of war. Note the three big dock basins (labelled "a"), the barracks to the south, and the cruiser in dry dock ("b"). *(IWM)*

Above Right: Harwich Harbour, photographed by the Luftwaffe, with the aid of a flash, on the night of 12 July, 1940. *(Elliott)*

Right: The remains of F/O Doulton's Hurricane, shot down into Walton Backwaters on 31 August 1940, and now in the RAF Museum. *(RAFM)*

THE AIR DEFENCES

mounted not on a tower, but at ground level. Whereas the British aerials were fixed, and transmitted to and received from the whole sky simultaneously, the German rotated to concentrate on one small area at a time. In performance the British aerials had longer range on highflying raiders, but not in proportion to their much greater height _ and only the Germans could detect lowfliers. There was one underlying reason for these differences. The British, alarmed by the sudden rise of the Luftwaffe, rushed a system ahead which was based on 1935 radio valves, which (at the required power) were merely of *HF* (High Frequency) and not *VHF* (Very High Frequency), and therefore of long (initially 13.22 metres) wavelength. This meant T and R aerials of half this length (i.e, about nineteen feet) _ ones so unwieldy they could not be turned in specific directions. Such a relatively low frequency was swamped by *ground echoes* if mounted close to the earth, hence the lofty towers. But these were obviously very visible, and thus likely to be bombed or jammed. As insurance against this, there were to supposed to be four sets of T and R aerials (of differing wavelengths) at each station _ hence the many towers. Had the Air Ministry been able to wait for just three more years, they could have had VHF valves giving wavelengths one-eighth as long, rotating aerials, concentrated transmission and reception, lower-altitude detection, and lower and fewer towers _ the system actually used with *CHL* (Chain Home Low) from 1939! In the event bombing and jamming were not serious, and no CH station maintained more than three wavelengths.

Until 1940 the Chain Home used a single 13.22-metre wavelength and had all its aerials on the wooden towers, pending the appearance of somewhat more modern T and R sets and of the steel T towers.* The former was known as the Intermediate and the latter as the Final CH _ and this was not ready until the Battle of Britain had begun. Intermediate was kept on for some time as a standby for Final.

Being fixed, and incapable of *directional* transmission and reception, it might seem as if the CH aerials had no direction-finding ability. This was partly overcome by an ingenious if ponderous trick. Two horizontal R dipoles (two-ended aerials) were mounted crosswise, and linked to a rotary switch (the "*goniometer*") which dimmed one as it boosted the other. Therefore, for instance, if a blip came to a maximum with the eastfacing dipole fully on and

---

*Henceforth there were three wavelengths in normal use, and each station used one, repeated every three stations along, thus: Dunkirk 13.22m (Wavelength W), Canewdon 11.95 (O), Great Bromley 11.38 (T), Bawdsey 13.22 (W), etc.

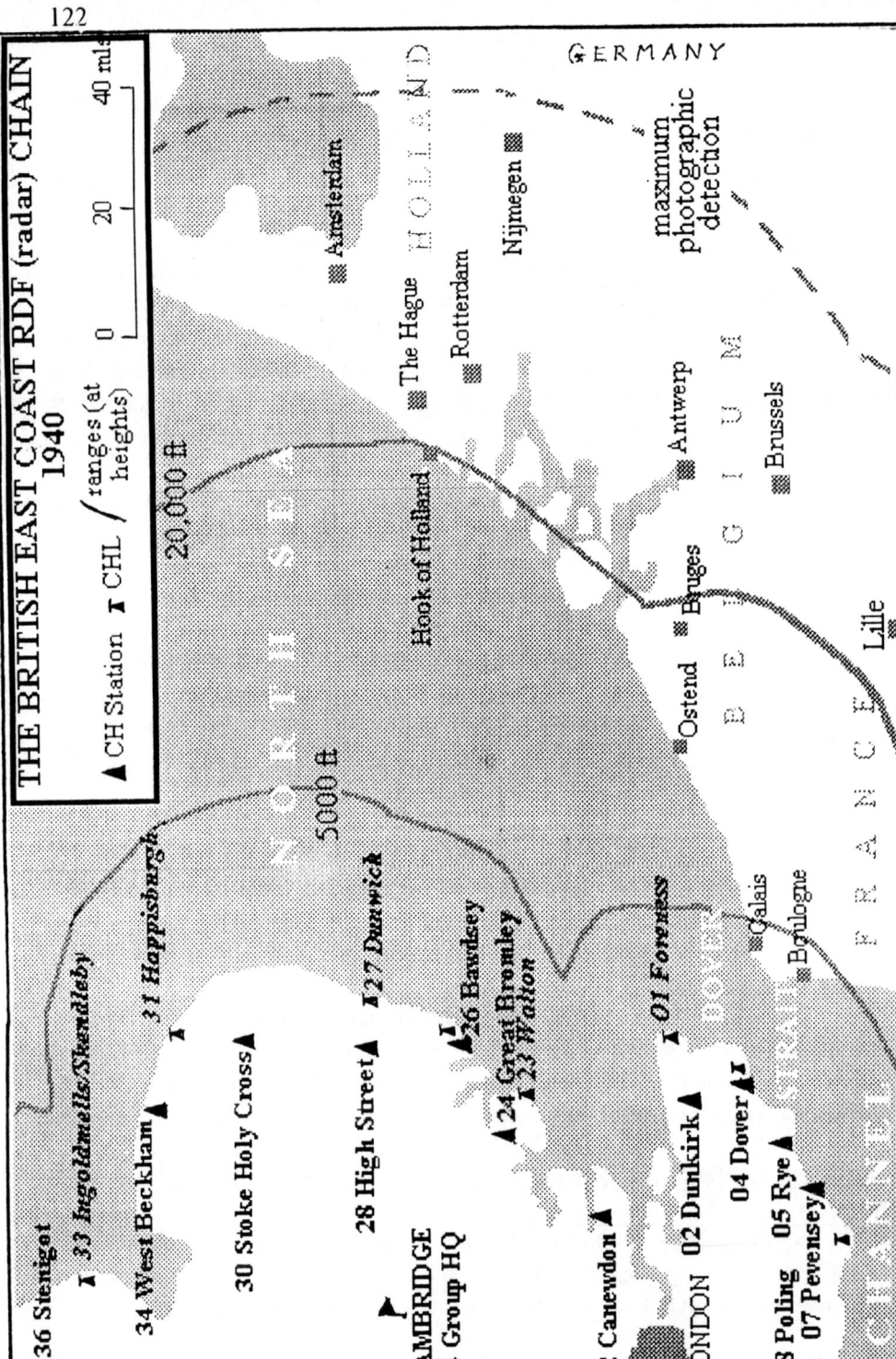

THE AIR DEFENCES

the southfacing off, it indicated a plane to the east; if each dipole was half-on at maximum echo, the plane was in the south-east. To shut off unwanted inland echoes *reflector* dipoles were mounted on those sides of the R towers. Because an R-aerial "*array*" could either gather echoes from medium or high elevation but not both, two were needed for detection, and range and direction finding. A third was added to help with height finding _ its echoes were compared with those of the high- and medium-level arrays to assess heights at the appropriate bands. CHL, when it was installed, had to supply the low-altitude information.

Setting up the aerial arrays, feeders and leads on the towers was a lengthy affair. The AMESs was "calibrated" (accuracy-checked) with the help of the primitive little Duxford-bases autogiros (helicopters), which flew around them on predetermined courses transmitting to the R towers with "squegging oscillators", miniature transmitters which put out a distinctive fluctuating pulse. Once operational, many stations developed faults, and indeed these caused more disruption than enemy action. Most were due either to "false" echoes from steel objects in the neighbourhood, or, less tolerably, to distortions in the goniometer readings caused by the various R dipoles not responding evenly to echoes. The Final equipment at AMES 24 (Great Bromley) became progressively more useless through 1941 until it was switched off in May, not to be reinstated until September, and then only after two inquiries by the TRE (Telecomunications Research Establishment), the first of which chased red herrings.

At ground level an AMES consisted of two compounds, each about three hundred yards square and scattered with nondescript huts and earth-and-concrete bunkers. But overhead loomed the weird and almost intimidating latticeworks of steel or pinewood, swaying against the scudding clouds, and festooned with huge spreads of wires and aerials humming in the wind. To distant observers the towers scarcely looked the same twice. Seen in line the three or four T-towers resembled one, at an acute angle they seemed to be graded in different heights, from the side they looked spaced apart and of equal heights. They might look blurred or horizon blue, or sometimes sharp and black or silver; occasionally the tops disappeared into low cloud.

Under earth and concrete, as if unrelated to the towers, were the radio rooms entered only by the initiated. The T and R sets were as big as double wardrobes, containing banks of glowing glass valves the size of milk bottles.

AIR MINISTRY EXPERIMENTAL STATION 24 (GREAT BROMLEY), 1942

NOTE
'Gee' was a bomber command RDF navigation system monitored and directed from Gt Bromley in 1941 & 1942.

THE AIR DEFENCES

Soundproofed, half dark, cut off from the daylight world, and furnished around a glowing screen, an R room was like an esoteric cinema. Though the picture shown was no more than a single flickering green line, it stretched the imagination of its small and informed "audience".

The latter consisted, at any one time, of a watch of seven men (or from 1941 mostly WAAFs). The Operator manipulated goniometer and interaerial switches, watched the blip on the trace, and announced his readings of aircraft range, bearing, elevation and numbers to his or her colleagues. The Converter combined these into actual locations by hand-manipulating a spotlight over a map in 1939, and from 1940 by means of the "Uniselector" Converter, Electric Calculator, or "Fruit Machine", a primitive computer "programmed" by the Operator setting dials and pressing buttons. The Plotter noted down readings and worked out tracks on the map. Via a continuously open telephone line the Teller announced the team's conclusions aloud to the Filter Room at Fighter Command HQ at Stanmore (Middlesex), where they were compared with information from other stations to update a huge map. The "PBX" operator controlled the phone switchboard, not only for the Teller's calls, but so that the team could talk to the T personnel (in a separate block), the RAF airfields, and the local AA defences. The Radio Operator provided an alternative communication link. And the Officer or NCO of the Watch was in charge. Each station had four watches, later cut to three, then raised to three and a half. It also had engineers to tend the equipment, clerks, gate guards, cooks, drivers, etc.

Though I have implied that the British radar of 1939 was crude, it already had some fascinating refinements. One coating of phosphor on the scopes caused persistent blips to show up red and stand out from the green flicker of meaningless intereference which lit up the other coating. Coloured scope filters helped rest the observers' eyes, and fade jamming and interference. At the T block, a switch could vary the pulsewidth (pulse duration) _ lengthening helped show up faint echoes from long range, shortening separated overlapping and therefore confusing signals. The IFRU (Intermediate Frequency Rejector Unit) suppressed some jamming without also eliminating desired signals. It was fitted just after the outbreak of war, largely because, on the very first day, nearly all East Coast stations were affected by interference, of a purely coincidental nature, from radio stations in America and Russia _ at one time Dover, Dunkirk, Canewdon and

THE AIR DEFENCES

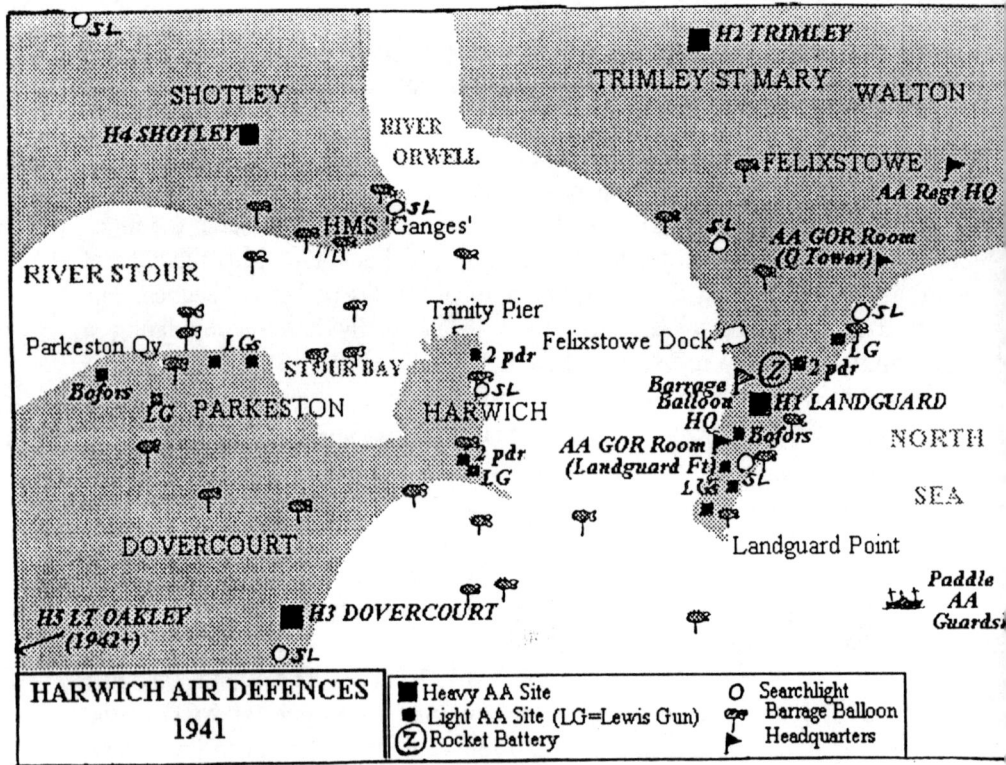

Bawdsey reported their receivers as "nearly useless". Around Christmas 1939 the CHL (Chain Home Low) started up on 1.5 metres, for tracking of ships as well as lowflying aircraft, with ad-hoc stations at Foreness (near Margate), Walton-on-Naze, Bawdsey (the only one to share a CH site), Dunwich, Hopton (near Lowestoft) and Happisburgh.

Incidentally until the 1960s it was commonly believed that till about 1941 the Germans neither had radar of their own, nor knew of ours. Neither is true, but till then German radar did not form a proper defensive chain, and the crudity of our stations misled the enemy into underestimating them.

In the Danzig Crisis of August 1939 Heavy (3.7-inch) AA, and Searchlight, Batteries arrived at the eastern ports. Numbers of guns varied as the enemy's targets changed, but in late 1940 settled at about seventy "Thames and Medway South" (including Chatham and Sheerness), forty-four "Thames and Medway North" (including Tilbury, Thameshaven and

THE AIR DEFENCES

Southend), twenty-four Harwich (including also Ipswich and Martlesham) and thirty-eight Humber. These included some old 3-inch medium guns standing in as heavies. Light AA weapons, useful against lowflying raiders, were old and scarce at this period, and at naval harbours largely lacking. The Army argued that warships could provide the necessary cover. Rear-Admiral Harris, at Harwich, was one FOIC to protest, pointing out that whereas there were no light guns at his own base there were no fewer than fifty-two quadrupally-mounted Lewises around Wrabness and Copperas Wood Mine Depots. (On 6 November 1939 twelve of these were accordingly shifted to Parkeston Quay). By contrast each CH station already had three of the superior Swedish-designed 40-mm repeat-firing Bofors. In 1940 a few of these same guns reached each of the major naval bases, where they operated alongside the Lewises. The most remarkable item in the AA arsenal was the "Z" or "UP" (unrotated projectile), i.e, rocket battery, of which two of the first four were installed in 1940 at Sheerness and Harwich, mainly to deter divebombers.

Balloon barrages were raised around London, the Medway, and the Humber, at the outbreak of war. The only one in East Anglia, at Harwich, was begun on 25 November in reaction to the *Gipsy* mining, only to be destroyed by lightning a few days later _ by the start of the bombing it consisted of twenty-four balloons, ten of them raised from barges on the harbour. Air minelaying also brought into existence a floating barrage of eighteen balloons in the Thames mouth, flown from old drifters and maintained from Sheerness. These balloon barrages, flying at six thousand feet, were visible in clear weather from twenty miles away. In the roughest weather they had to be lowered _ innumerable balloons were lost from gales, ice and lightning. After a stormy day there were ragged gaps in them, with some balloons punctured and floating in harbour, others broken free and wandering out to sea or far inland, possibly with cables dangling dangerously and snagging power lines and church spires. Though they destroyed a very few enemy bombers, the balloons were more of a menace to the RAF. Six British planes came to grief on the one at Harwich. Two crashed in June 1940 alone: on the 4th a 44 Squadron Hampden from Waddington (Lincolnshire) crashed in the Orwell off Trimley with only one survivors among four crew. Nine days later another Hampden from the neighbouring 144 Squadron at Helmswell came down on Marriage's Mill, Felixstowe

THE AIR DEFENCES

Dock, setting light to the mill, five railway trucks and four grain barges and killing its five crew and a local civilian.

Since the start of the war some RAF bases had had "Q", or decoy, sites whither lights and dummy canvas huts were meant to divert the Luftwaffe. The Navy now discussed building some of its own for the protection of harbours. Rear-Admiral Harris, of Harwich, drew Admiralty attention to the many bombs and mines falling around Brightlingsea (for instance, many between Maldon, Foulness and Great Bentley on 16 October, and two mines on the south side of Brightlingsea Creek on the 18th), and to a Schipol-based reconnaisance Ju 88 crashing at Brightlingsea on the 2nd). He argued that the enemy must be mistaking the Colne/Blackwater mouths for the similarly-shaped estuaries of the Orwell and Stour off Harwich. He called for a decoy "Harwich base" at Bradwell to lure even more bombers astray. His idea was initially rejected, because the RAF planned to start a base at the proposed site, and because only the most inexperienced pilots could decoyed by so wide a margin. Having shifted his tack to arguing that Mersea was a possible site, he evoked more interest. As a result Q sites were built at East Mersea (representing Parkeston Quay) and at Sandy Point, St Osyth (for Felixstowe), followed by others at Bradfield and Thorpe-le-Soken. These were soon imitated around Sheerness, Yarmouth, etc. It is doubtful if these sites ever achieved anything. Unlike the civilian "Starfish" sites outside major towns, which were lit up to during raids to suggest incendiary bomb fires, they were too dim to be obvious to pilots. Incidentally there is evidence that the blackout at East Coast towns, including Harwich, Brightlingsea and those on the North Kent coast, was so poor that they showed up better than the Q sites.

The Blitz brought civilians as well as servicemen into the frontline _ the organisations being the Police, Fire Brigades (which incorporated many amateur, auxiliary, units), and the ARP (Air Raid Precautions), coordinated by Civil Defence, plus the Observer Corps. Poice duties included not only crowd and traffic control, but also assistance with rescue, reporting bomb positions, and taking temporary charge of German prisoners. They also had the continual and extraordinary job of picking up objects fallen from the skies. A list of such items kept by Inspector Rush of Felixstowe includes .303 and .50 ammunition, ammunition drums, bomb casings, smoke bombs, target drogues, parachutes, jettisoned petrol tanks, and even cockpit covers and

THE AIR DEFENCES

aircraft doors. The part-time ARP volunteers were charged with the blackout, sirens, shelters, reporting bombs (both exploded and unexploded), rescue and the treatment of light casualties at first aid posts. It had been carrying out full-scale exercises since March 1939. Its wardens, some of them by no means young men, saw a more more hectic than many servicemen's. These civilian services did not have responsibility for military, naval and RAF areas, which had their own ARP arrangements.

The (Royal) Observer Corps plotted enemy planes inshore and overland, where the radar of 1940 could not function. Along the East Coast it had one post about every six miles, some perched on Martello Towers and disused lighthouses. A post was no more sophisticated than a ring of sandbags, containing a map table, a crude sighting device for bearingss and heights, and a pair of binoculars, all provided by the volunteers themselves, usually. Post reports went to Group HQs at Bromley and Maidstone in Kent, Colchester, Cambridge, Bury St Edmunds, Norwich, Lincoln and York, and thence to the Stanmore Filter Room. Inevitably they were tardier than the RDF reports, and of course those made in mist or darkness gave little information.

In the biggest prewar defence exercise, held on 8 and 9 June 1939, the performance was mixed. On the CH side the Bawdsey transmitter broke down for a time, Dover was rated as disappointing, and Stoke Holy Cross and High Street gave such poor coverage over Lowestoft that the experts spoke of a "hole" in the chain _ on the other hand Great Bromley was described as a "precision instrument". Dedben fighters intercepted 76% of the "attackers", and Biggin Hill 69%. This was, of course, against an "enemy" who did not fire back, bomb the defences, or come in overwhelming strength. A year later, in the real thing, much lower interception rates were certainly achieved.

But the Germans did the defences, and Britain, an enormous favour by not launching their Blitz, as feared and forecast, until long after war was declared. By the start of the Battle of Britain in the summer of 1940 Final CH, CHL, extra balloon barrages and operational Spitfire squadrons had all arrived.

On the first afternoon of war, in addition to the radar interference already mentioned, the air defences were put on their first alert and sirens wailed round the Thames Estuary. This has been ascribed either to a civil

THE AIR DEFENCES

aircraft coming into Croydon airport without notification, or an official test. Either way it was evidence of efficiency. The same cannot be said of the obscure incident, on the fourth day of war, nicknamed the "Battle of Barking Creek". AMES 22 (Canewdon) accidentally left "out" the reflector behind its R array, which caused it to read British aircraft on a practice flight inland as Germans out to sea. East Mersea searchlight site then mistook some overflying RAF planes for enemy. The Essex fighter bases scrambled their Hurricanes, and Canewdon duly read these as more Germans. When pilots saw some planes flying in from the coast off a patrol, they opened fire, and three Hurricanes crashed in the Ipswich-Mistley area. RDF, Stanmore and the pilots were presumably all at fault and no doubt all benefited from the experience.

This affair helped expedite the debut of IFF ("Identification Friend or Foe"), which had been under test at Bawdsey to enable RDF to distinguish between Allied and enemy aircraft. IFF Marks I and II, small transmitters fitted in planes, broadcast a wave which appeared on R scopes as noticeably "stretched" or "square" blips, with different degrees of stretching for fighters, bombers and SOS signals. Mark I went on the air in February 1940.

As many air historians have written, the reporting system was quite crucial to the defence in the Battle of Britain, for without RDF and the Stanmore Filter Room Fighter Command could not have responded in time to more than a very few of the hundreds of Luftwaffe sorties daily, and strategic objectives, starting with its own bases, would have been smashed. (This leaves aside the question of whether all three of the German armed services were ready to follow this up with an invasion).

The Germans made scant attempts to bomb the RDF stations, except on 12 August 1940 on the Channel coast. They did make some attempt, of course. At Bawdsey two personnel were killed on 17 April and three on 6 May, 1941, and one in 1943, without operations being effected. AMES 24 (Great Bromley) was a target six times in 1940, two or three in 1941, and was also nearly hit once in 1942. Two parachute mines fell within three hundred yards of it on 13 November 1940. It was never hit. High Street had perhaps also been the intended target of a little mine-dropping campaign that autumn. On 5 November 1940 a stick of bombs exploded right between the T towers at West Beckham, and cut one of the two main electric cables _ the station was operational again on the other within eight minutes. AMES 23,

THE AIR DEFENCES

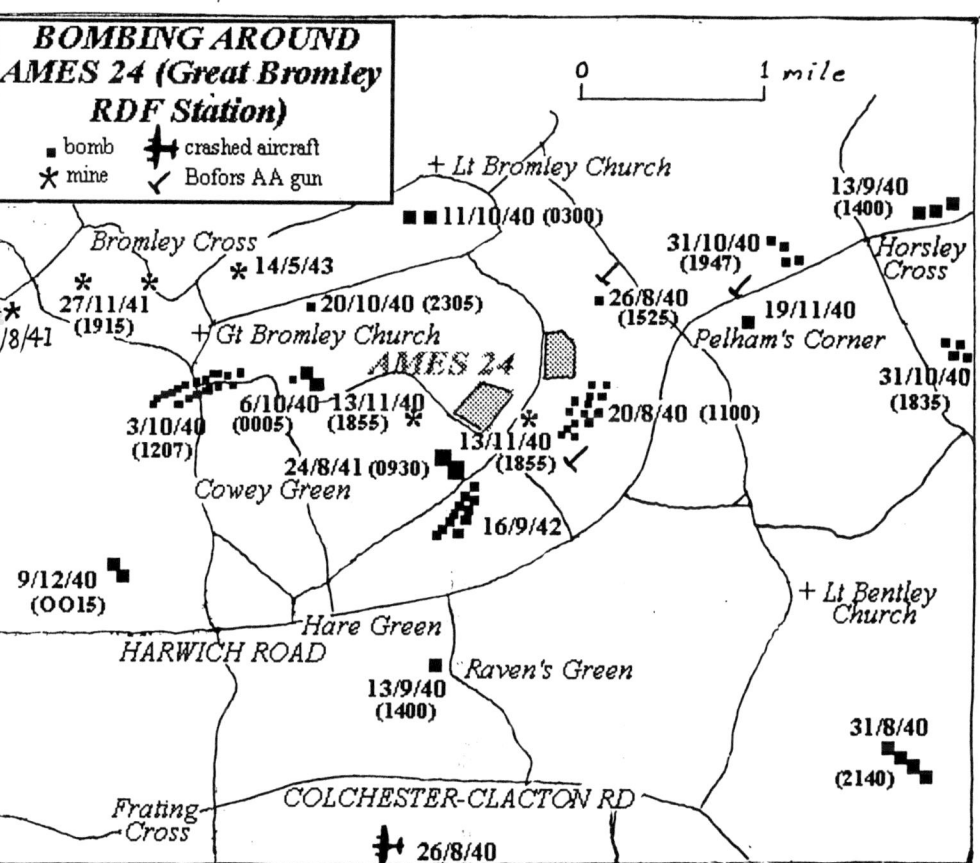

the Naze CHL, was in the path of two fierce Focke-Wulf fighter-bomber raids in 1943, but the attackers preferred to bomb nearby Walton and Frinton. A ship-tracking station at Bard Hill (Norfolk) was destroyed by a plane on 15 January 1945, but the offender was a British Lancaster, which accidentally crashed onto the site.

Such was the number of stations _ by 1940 there were twelve, or one every eleven miles, between Dover and the Wash _ that early warning enjoyed overlapping coverage except on very lowflying planes and inland. But what if the enemy suddenly changed tactics and blitzed all the stations simultaneously? To dispel this nightmare 60 Group (Fighter Command), in charge of all defensive RDF, organised so-called MRUs ("Mobile Radio Units"). Each consisted of a transmitter and receiver on lorries, and a collapsible 87-(later 105) foot mast with aerials, operating on the "shortwave" around seven metres. In the Battle of Britain some of thse had been used to plug holes on the South Coast: just after it others went to the obscure East Coast locations of The Avenue (to cover Stoke Holy Cross), Cedars Farm (Bawdsey), Frating (Great Bromley) and Loftman's Farm (Canewdon). Removed at the end of the year, they were reinstated in the summer of 1941.

In an attempt to detect at longer range and lower altitude, a camera device called "Photo Freddie" now took repeated long-exposure photographs of the R scope, revealing otherwise invisible aircraft but eliminating interference. It was first tested at Walton CHL, the trying to track lowflying minelayers, in March 1940, and by 1941 was in general use, increasing ranges by up to 70%.

Overhead, the night fighter became a reality for the first time with the invention of the AI (airborne interception), a miniaturised RDF set, carried in the plane's cockpit and capable of tracking a raider at two miles. A crude prototype of this had been built at Bawdsey as early as 1936, by E G Bowen, and tested by the aircraft of "D" Performance Testing Flight, Martlesham. (Bowen also tested the related ASV, against such Harwich-bound shipping as the butter boat from Esbjerg). In 1940 controllers were sent to some of the CH and CHL stations, beginning with Bawdsey (then commanded by Squadron Leader Tester and civilian technical supervisor Cole), and tried to direct fighters to within AI range by direct R/T link, by-passing plotters, filter rooms, and airfields. On 12 May 1940 a Martlesham 25 Squadron Blenheim made a Bawdsey-guided interception of one of the He 111s attacking the Dutch coast. Flight Lt C D S "Blood Orange" Smith (he was very red-headed), formerly of the "D" Testing Flight, was the pilot, and Flight Lt W R Farnes, of North Weald, was the ground controller. Both planes were damaged, and the Blenheim crashed at base, with both crew wounded: apparently the Heinkel also landed intact. But this contact was a freak (partial) success, achieved in any case in daylight. Existing RDF was too ponderous to guide night fighters, who only located bombers in bright moonlight.

But a substitute appeared in GCI (Ground Control Interception). Its very short (half-metre) wavelength arrays rotated to *beam* their transmissions. As they turned, the time-base and trace rotated with them

THE AIR DEFENCES

around the PPI or Plan Position Indicator, a scope with a map painted over it. The blip automatically showed up as a bright spot at the correct map location, eliminating converter and plotter. In short, this was modern radar. Furthermore, GCI stations were radio-linked direct to fighters, which the operators "talked" to their targets. On the East Coast the first station was at Waldringfield (near Felixstowe), opened in January 1941. This later moved to nearby Trimley, and other stations appeared at Foreness, Foulness, Neatishead (near Norwich), Langtoft (near Spalding) and Hampston Hill in Yorkshire. The Waldringfield station was originally commanded by Flying Officer Tibbenham. It was said to be ideally sited, except for the huge permanent echoes from the steel barrage balloon cables at Harwich and T towers at Bawdsey. It consisted merely of one T array and one R array, each attached to a trailer (of which the second doubled as the Ops Room), a VHF radio trailer, and a generator hut. At any one time the duty watch in the Ops trailer numbered five.

The bases for the East Coast's AI Beaufighters were Hundson (Herts), West Malling, Manston and Gravesend (Kent), Rochford, Debden and later Bradwell Bay (Essex), Castle Camps (Cambs), and Digby and Kirton-in-Lindsay (Lincs). One of the West Malling pilots was Guy Gibson, later the "Dambuster" bomber squadron commander, who flew with 29 Squadron.

GCI, improvements in their little RDF sets, and practice, boosted the fighter crews' confidence in their AI, which they initially despised, referring to "things" and "boxes". In the winter of 1940-41 the night fighters performed lamentably. But in March the GCI-AI tie-up was made. That month the night fighters put in twenty-four claims nationally: fifty-two followed in April and 102 in May. Nor were they much inflated, though the dramatic breakthrough did not stop the minelaying planes, which were too low for AI, which swamped itself with an awful "Christmas Tree" (ground echo) when flown below its own range of ten thousand feet.

Meanwhile German jamming of East Coast RDF stations, like the bombing, was very intermittent and almost all weak. Owing to greater proximity to the Continent the Channel coast suffered worse. Jamming did not become at all a common thing until late in 1941. To monitor its origin, technological and geographical, a mobile team called the "J Watch" toured the East Coast stations. As analysis of the bearings of the jamming (see map)

Bawdsey
Hook of Holland
Great Bromley
HOLLAND
Dunkirk
Bruges
Swingate
BELGIUM
Rye
Calais
Pevensey
MONT COUPLE
Boulogne
FRANCE
J WATCH REPORTS
27/7-1/8/42
=

MONITORING OF GERMAN DEFENSIVE RADAR:
Nov-Dec 1943
British J Station
German radar station (proven postwar)
"hoarding" ---- Freya
SALZHERI
HERIN
ZANDER
BIBER
HOLLAND
Holland
SCHMETTERLING
HAMSTER (Domburg)
Foreness
BREMSE
BELGIUM

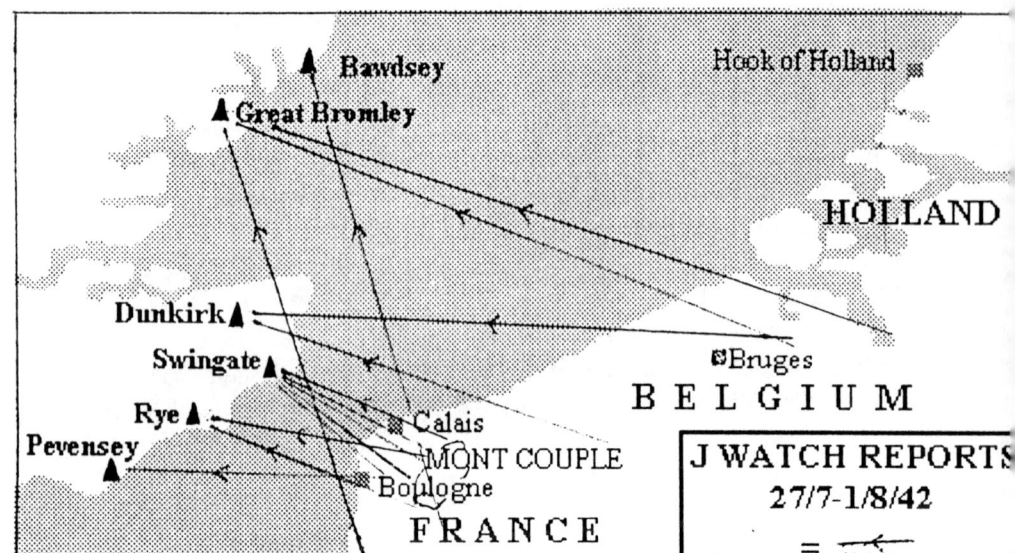

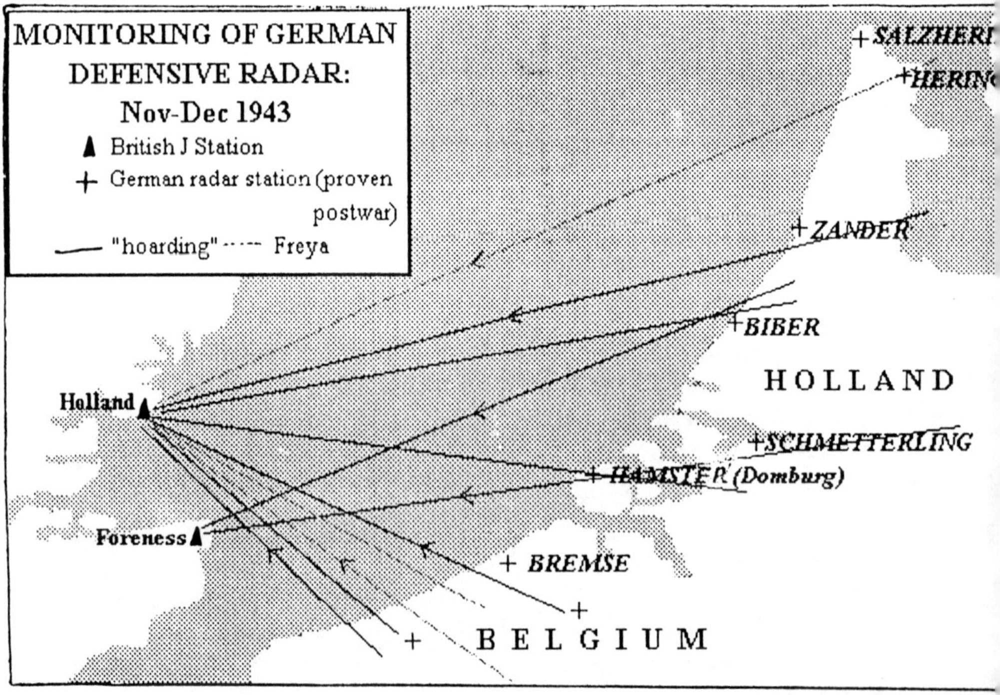

THE AIR DEFENCES

proved that the main jamming transmitters were on Mont Couple near Calais, though there were others in Belgium and Holland.*

In 1943 stations were set up at Foreness and Holland-on-Sea monitor the transmissions of German defensive radar _ stations with the 240-cm "Freya" and "Mammut" (known to the British as "Hoarding"), the equivalent of the British GCIs, and forming part of the Kammhuber Line for the night air defence of the Reich. At Sizewell and the North Foreland the RAF put jammers to disrupt these enemy stations, especially the major one at Domburg, opposite Harwich.

It was over the Norfolk coast in 1940 that the RAF first detected the radio navigation beams along which the Luftwaffe sometimes flew. As these beams multiplied and diversified in type, a chain of small stations was extended by Bomber Command's 80 Wing to jam or bend them. In the Eastern Area Braintree (Essex) was the HQ. Early beam monitoring was done at Bawdsey, Brentwood, Canewdon, Drayton (Norfolk), High Street, Little Waltham (Essex), North Foreland and West Beckham, and at Braintree there was an "Aspirin" station to bend the beams and at Scole (Suffolk) a "Meacon" to jam them.

---

*On the eve of the Normandy Invasion Bomber Command reduced this to a mass of scrap metal.

7
COASTAL BLITZ

The German air minelaying campaign of November 1939 could be regarded, in the broader sense, as the beginning of the Luftwaffe "Blitz" on England (there had already been air raids on naval bases in Scotland). If so the *Gipsy* fatalities were the first English air raid victims. Harwich experienced its second "raid" on the night of 7 December, wh en two German seaplanes, probably minelayers, machine-gunned Landguard Fort; HMS *Cyclops*, trawlers and light AA let fly but the intruders droned right round the harbour and out to sea again without bombing. Ten days later a plane aimed unsuccessfully at merchantmen waiting in the Humber to join a convoy. Bombing aimed at convoys and warships came within a few miles of the coast in the spring of 1940, before Dunkirk. Ships off Margate reported attacks from the air on 20 April. Three sailors were killed when the 6th Flotilla minesweeper *Hussar* was bomb-damaged off Orfordness on 15 May. In the early hours of the 22nd of that month five or six salvoes in the Harwich harbour approach shook Felixstowe seafront, with one stray bomb at Butley, near Orford _ the first to fall on land in East Anglia.

While the fighting in France still raged the bombing of English land targets began, though on a small scale. On the nights of 24/25 May and 5/6 June airfields around the Wash and Humber were targets, though on the first night one HE (high explosive) bomb struck Wickford, and on the second incendiaries burned at Grays, both in South Essex.

While France surrendered the Luftwaffe first raided ports in Eastern England. On the bright moonlit night of 18/19 June the oil tanks at Killingholme (near Immingham), Harwich, Thameshaven, Sheerness and Chatham were attacked, and those at Saltend (near Hull) were targetted the following night. The bombing was mostly very scattered and inaccurate, but at Thameshaven twelve thousand gallons of oil were burned, and the whale factory ship *Southern Express*, moored offshore, was hit by a bomb which bounced off. One civilian was killed at Holland-on-Sea (part of Clacton), another at Shoeburyness (part of Southend). In a deceptive early RAF night fighter victory (achieved without AI) five He 111s were shot down _ one near Sheringham, one off Felixstowe, one at Margate, one near Cambridge, and one near Chelmsford (this last by the South African "Sailor" Malan, subsequently one of the top-scoring fighter aces of the Western Allies), for the loss of two British Blenheims. From the first crash the Cley Beach

COASTAL BLITZ

Coastguard captured four prisoners, one of whom was taken to Cromer Hospital.

On the night of 21/22 June about a hundred aircraft raided Derby, Hull, Grimsby, Lowestoft, Ipswich, Felixstowe, Harwich, the Brightlingsea area, several airfields, but above all the Thames oil depots. Owing to the moonlight and British fighter patrols the AA, which had shot away with profligate inaccuracy two nights earlier, remained silent. Three civilians died at Ipswich, but no strategic damage was done anywhere. During the raid a Blenheim from Wyton (Hunts) made the first-ever detection of a German "Knickebein" (radio navigation beam), laid from Cleves in Germany to Derby via Beccles and Spalding.

An East Coast port was first damaged by a single He 111, flying (unusually) from Norway, on the afternoon of 1 July. No fewer than five of the very first George Medals were won by staff and firemen at the Shell-Mex and Anglo-American oil tanks at Saltend (Hull): these men sealed off tanks and fought the fire even though flames almost surrounded them and their clothes were soaked with oil. The raider was shot down into the North Sea by a 616 Squadron Spitfire, and its crew were (apparently) rescued by a Harwich destroyer or corvette.

Two days later a larger daylight raid was mounted against the East Coast. Do 17s simultaneously aimed at Manston airfield, Clacton, Frinton, Bramble Island explosives factory (behind the Naze), Dovercourt, Felixstowe, Ipswich, Bawdsey and Lowestoft. Curiously, most salvoes fell about a hundred yards offshore, but at Ipswich a civilian was killed, and at Clapham Road, Lowestoft, four. That night the British Xylonite factory at Brantham, and Brook's malthouse, across the Stour at Mistley, were bombed. Brooks and the sailing barge *Bijou,* moored alongside, were burned out.

There was also activity in the North. On 8 July RAF 249 Squadron downed an LG1* Ju 88 into a cornfield at Aldbrough, on the East Riding coast: armed only with the peremptory manner of a Yorkshire farmer's wife Mrs Cardwell took a crewman prisoner, and won an OBE. Three days later a plane bombed Bridlington Railway Station, and two workers courageously moved to safety an ammunition waggon which theatened to catch fire. That same day Cromer experienced its first four air raid deaths. On 18 July the Medway towns were first hit, with five dead at Gillingham. Two days later a Brussels-based Ju 88 crashed at St Osyth (Essex) and its four crew were

---

*"Lehrgeschwader" literally= "Instructional Squadron"

captured; it was the latest in a series of planes to reconnoitre the nearby Thames Estuary.

And so the Blitz on the East Coast began. It was a rather different story from the bombing of the big cities. It began earlier and continued later. It involved very frequent low-intensity activity rather than a few spectacular raids. Nearly all the East Coast raids were by forces of less than twenty planes per objective, and many were by single machines only. No more than half a dozen raiders usually found their target. (I exclude Hull from all this). A secondary strategy for the enemy, it was intended continually to disrupt the Nore Command naval bases from which the London-bound convoys were supported. (There were also intermittent raids on airfields). This harbour raiding, which merged into a great deal of minelaying, was mainly done at night or under cover of mist and cloud. It was usually rather dispersed in place and time, with single raiders overflying at average intervals of half an hour and bombing a mile or two apart (and therefore mostly off target). Most of the German bombs fell almost unnoticed on empty sea, estuary and marshland, though sometimes a ship or a port would be hit with serious casualties. The Luftwaffe flew to East Coast targets mainly by visual observation, dead reckoning and guidance from ground radio directionfinding stations. The "Knickebein" system of flying *along* radio beams to their intersection with other beams was reserved for the bigger targets.

I have never read a publication giving the relevant statistics for Luftwaffe bombing accuracy. But it can be statistically estimated from the studies* made by the RAF just after the war, on the basis of comparisons between German and British records. Even against the vast target of London 45% of the German bombload fell outside the Metropolitan Civil Defence Region. 19% of the tonnage aimed at Hull in its seven largest raids fell within the city boundary: in Yarmouth's seven biggest raids the proportion was the same. To use my own research, the trio Norwich-Yarmouth-Lowestoft (plus a few nearby minor targets) took about 25% of the bombs within fifteen miles of each; in the analogous case of Ipswich-Colchester-Harwich the percentage was about seventeen. Errors of thirty miles were not uncommon. (RAF bombing till 1942 was even worse). On the East Coast the broad rule was that four out of five bombs missed the towns and harbours they were meant for. Moreover even this is misleading, because hitting a town did not

---

*Secret *RAF Fighter Command History; Vol III _ Night Air Defence, 1941* (PRO AIR 41/17).

COASTAL BLITZ

necessarily mean hitting a target area.

The "Red Alert" air raid warning, when sirens sounded and AA gunners stood to, was a daily occurence on most parts of the East Coast for most of the war. At both Yarmouth and Lowestoft there were over 2040 such alerts _ one for every day of the war, and at the peak the sirens were going there a nerve-shattering six times daily. Orfordness and Chatham each had over 1300 Red Alerts, London over 1200, Harwich 1144, Brightlingsea 917, Hull 815. But about 90% of Red Alerts were false alarms at most places, in that the enemy stopped short of the coast and attacked ships or laid mines, flew on to more inland targets, or confined themselves to reconnaissance. London took 334 actual raids, Yarmouth 97, Hull 76, Lowestoft 74, Harwich 52 and Brightlingsea 12. These figures refer to bombs dropped within the town and harbour limits of those towns, and exclude those which fell on adjacent countryside and sea, as well as machine-gunning attacks. If these are added Yarmouth's total (to take one instance) rises to 126. Some of these raids were trivial (a few incendiaries dropped or bullets fired, with no damage done, for example). But some were not.

Though very frequent, German overflying on the East Coast was on only half the scale of that on the South. The number of Red Alerts, however, was as great. This can be explained: most were triggered, not by bombers, but by minelayers. The highest number of Red Alerts on the East Coast was at Yarmouth and Lowestoft, yet overflying here was of only half the scale of that by the Thames Estuary. There were two reasons for this paradox: i)three frequent targets (Norwich and thes two ports) were so close together that they picked up most of each others' alerts, and ii)this coastline collected not only the minelaying tracks into Yarmouth Naval Sub-Command, but most of those (and there were many) into Humber. This is supported by the 1500 Red Alerts for Cromer, which, lying "behind" Yarmouth (with its 2040), escaped the latter's level of bombing yet still registered most of the Humber minelaying alerts. As clinching evidence that the great bulk of enemy air activity off East Anglia stopped short of land, and that overflying locally was not vast, consider Cambridge's total of 329 Red Alerts. The number of minelaying and bombing attacks *off* East Anglia vastly outweighed the number of attacks *on* East Anglia.

The overflying bombers were mostly making for targets beyond East Anglia, some as far away as Merseyside, Belfast and Scotland. About one

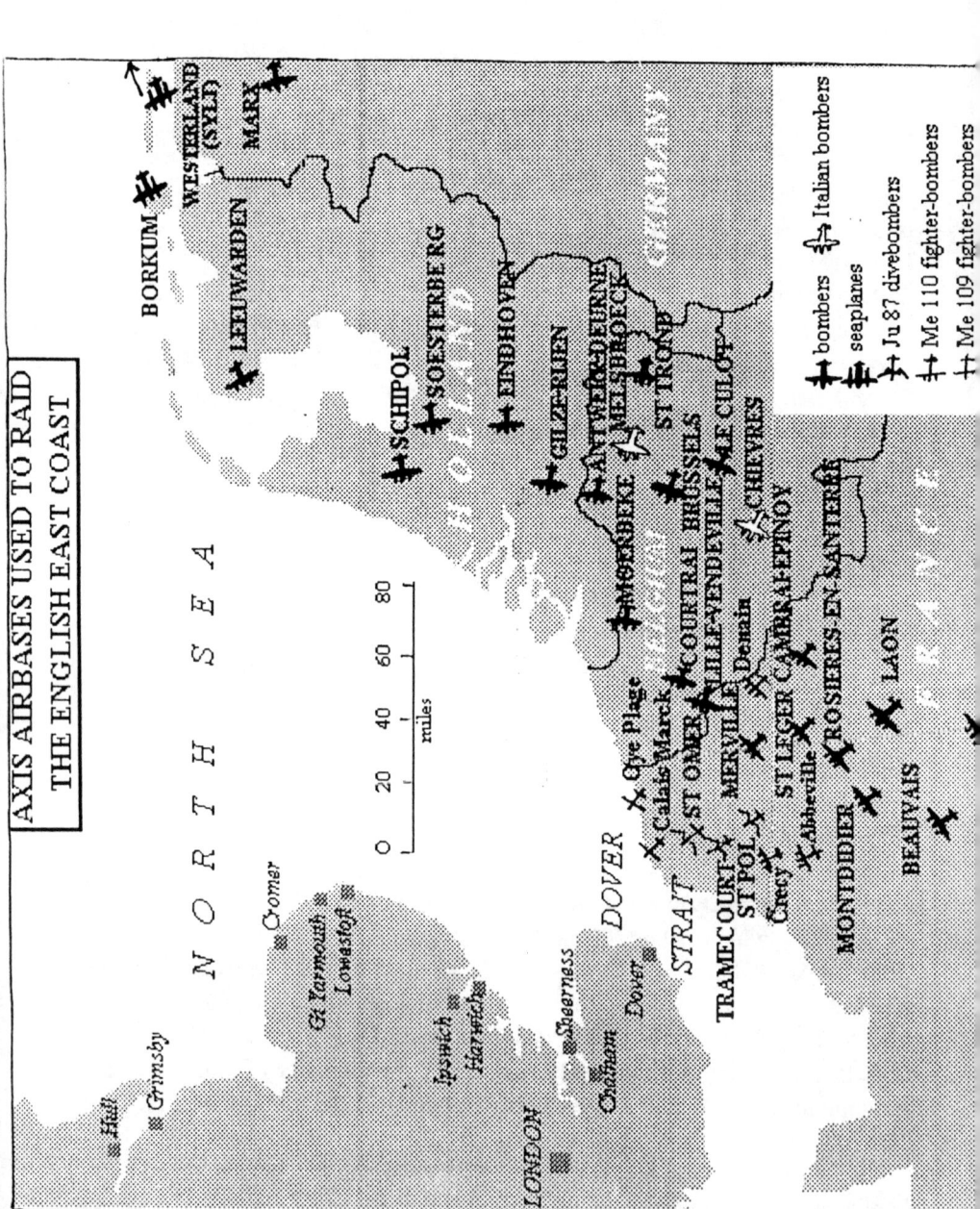

COASTAL BLITZ

third of enemy aircraft raiding the United Kingdom in the first two years of war came via the East, as opposed to the South, Coast. The overflying decreased going northwards: Essex and Suffolk were overflown twice as much as Norfolk, Lincolnshire and Yorkshire but half as much as Kent. (By far the most overflown county was Sussex, which heard more hostile aircraft than the whole East Coast from the Thames to John O'Groats. Only a fraction of raiders headed for London came in north of the Thames; during the Blitz the proportion rose from one-seventh to one quarter. Most raiders crossing South Essex and Kent were either bound for London or Thames Estuary targets, though in order to avoid the AA guns many London-bound planes came in north of Clacton and even as far up as Orfordness. From there northwards to Norfolk overflights were mostly bound for the Midlands and Merseyside, but in 1941 there was a tendency to come in over Lincolnshire to shorten overland flying. Similarly Hull raiders preferred to approach from the north-east rather than the direct south-east route, since the latter took them too near the defences along the Norfolk coast.

Most of the German bombers crossing the East Coast came from Dutch bases such as Schipol, Leeuwarden, Soesterberg and Gilze-Rijen, though some were from Belgium and Northern France.

The weight of bombing on the East Coast was not, of course, comparable to that on big targets like London. However, while over Britain as a whole an average of three HE bombs fell on each square mile, on the East Coast the average was *ten*, and at Hull, Yarmouth, Lowestoft and Harwich *between fifty and a hundred,* just as high a ratio as on Greater London (though not Central London). These concentrations show that, though some of the bombs were randomly dumped by damaged or lost aircraft, most were aimed (albeit inaccurately) at Nore Command ports and bases.

The overwhelmingly main target was London. The overspill from the Blitz on the capital, and its port (which extended downriver to Tilbury and Thameshaven) accounted for most of the bombs on North Kent and South Essex. Between the Blackwater and Orfordness most of the bombing was Harwich-Ipswich overspill. The Lowestoft-Yarmouth-Norwich "spread" was Dunwich-Sheringham, and Hull-intended bombing stretched at least as far as Skegness and Bridlington. Yarmouth, Lowestoft and Hull were the most bombed places on the East Coast, apparently because of their exposed positions and relatively weak defences. *In proportion to their populations* the first two were the most bombed boroughs in England*. The attacks on them were inappropriately heavy, because they were neither major ports nor front-rank naval bases. The convoy-escorting, minesweeping and operational direction in the Nore Command came mainly from Chatham, Sheerness (which also had big dockyards), Harwich and Grimsby. Yet these bases escaped remarkably lightly overall. In the case of Sheerness and Harwich there were two reasons for this beyond the enemy's preference for softer targets: the powerful defences at those ports, and the absorption of most bombs dropped by the large surrounding stretches of water. For example, though Lowestoft suffered ten times the damage and casualties of Harwich, the total bombload *aimed* at the two places was about the same.

In August and September 1940 the continuing small harbour raids were overshadowed by the Battle of Britain, aimed at the RAF airfields from Martlesham southwards. Many of the famous "aces" of "the Few" were based near the East Anglian coast, such as Townsend at Martlesham, Stanford Tuck at Debden, Beamish at North Weald, Malan at Rochford and Bader at Coltishall (and later Duxford).

The mind's eye sees a bright blue sky etched with white vapour trails, and a bright yellow landscape, with the ripe corn rustling right up to the edges of the airfields and the fences of the AA sites and CH stations. But in fact the first week's overland combat had to be fitted between cold fronts and rain showers. Switching from the raids on convoys, Luftflotte (Air Fleet) 2 bombed, among other places, Manston airfield and Dunkirk CH station on 12 August; the former took a hundred bombs from Rubensdörffer's Me 110s, in the first major attack on any home airfield of RAF Fighter Command (and it was to be raided another eight times during the Battle of Britain).

Next day was Göring's "Adlertag" (Eagle Day), the start of his main offensive against Fighter Command. IV/LG 1's Stukas, from Tramecourt in the Pas de Calais, and KG 2's Do 17s, from Cambrai, heavily blasted the airfields at Detling (near Maidstone) and Eastchurch (Isle of Sheppey), and in all killed at least seventy personnel and destroyed twenty-three aircraft. Every Eastchurch hangar was hit, and the Detling mess turned into a slaughterhouse. Unbeknown to the Germans, however, these were Coastal,

---

*In Scotland Clydebank was more intensively bombed. In England Dover suffered more than the two East Anglian boroughs if the German shelling is included.

COASTAL BLITZ

not Fighter, Command bases. When the bombing started Admiral Drax was addressing a conference of merchant ship masters on Southend Pier _everyone rushed for shelter underneath. Two days later there was drama over Felixstowe as Rubensdorffer raided Martlesham and then beat off an interception force on his way back. The airfield was badly battered without any aircraft, save an obsolete visiting Battle light bomber, being disabled, but in the air combat the enemy downed six Hurricanes without loss to himself. Meanwhile thirty Do 17s of KG 3 (at Montdidier) wrecked the satellite fighter field and part of the Short's aircraft factory at Rochester, thereby delaying the proptotypes of the Stirling four-engined bomber. Far to the north, in the Yorkshire East Riding, Ju 88s from Aalborg, Denmark, destroyed ten Whitley bombers on Driffield airfield but at the price of six of their own number down in the North Sea.

16 August was another hectic day. Prevented by cloud from bombing the Essex fighter bases, two units of He 111s flew back out to sea and bombed two major ports as they went. In Tilbury Docks the big cargo liner *Clan Forbes* was hit, with three crewmen and a docker killed (though the ship was repairable), while a direct hit on a Northfleet factory, just across the river, killed sixteen workers. Some hours later bombs fell near Shotley Naval barracks, in harbour round the light cruiser *Cardiff*, on Harwich Hard, and in Felixstowe town, where several buildings were destroyed but the only casualty was listed as "one cat". *Cardiff* and the other cruisers were wisely withdrawn from the Thames Estuary next day

In the early afternoon of the 18th a dozen Me 109s (mistaken for "He 113s" by the defenders) strafed Manston and destroyed two Spitfires on the ground. A few hours later fifty He 111s and twenty-five Me 110 escorts, briefed to attack North Weald but in the process of turning back owing to low cloud, were intercepted by the North Weald, Debden and Martlesham squadrons off Foulness. Five British fighters, four German bombers and four German fighters crashed. The raiders dumped their bombs in spectacular fashion _ mainly in the sea, though one load fell on Shoeburyness and killed three civilians. One dead and one wounded German airmen were found immediately afterwards on the beach nearby. Out to sea a Hurricane pilot was rescued by the Barrow Deep Lightship and landed by a Felixstowe MTB. An Me 110 dived into a sandpit at Clacton and disappeared without trace. Another British pilot bailed out on Whitstable Golfcourse, and stood

BATTLE OF BRITAIN
AIRCRAFT CRASHED
IN & AROUND THE
THAMES ESTUARY

+ German bomber
⚔ German fighter
O British fighter

O Halstead 31/8

COASTAL BLITZ

bleeding at the bar while a member complained that the noise of the battle had put him off his game.

The next few days were too cloudy for full-scale raids and the Luftwaffe resorted to scattered coastal incursions, some at night. On the 19th Chatham Dockyard was hit for the first time, when a plane dived unannounced out of low cloud and bombed the sawmills and smithies, where five workers were killed and twenty-four injured. About the same time Wrabness Mine Depot was near-missed. Next day Southwold, Gorleston, and Great Bromley CH were attacked by one plane each, and on the 21st three sailors were killed at the naval training camp at Ingoldmells (in peacetime the Skegness Butlin's Holiday camp) and six civilians at Lowestoft. Northerly Bridlington took several nasty little attacks at this time: local ARP man Thomas Alderson won one of the very first George Crosses for crawling into burning and collapsing buildings to save their occupants.

The 24th brought more mass airfield attacks. North Weald was a target, and ten soldiers died there in their shelter. From an He 111 wreck at Heybridge a treasure trove of items was recovered, including leather brief cases, a camera. purses full of French money, maps, an Iron Cross First Class, passports, ration cards and a logbook. Another Heinkel crashed at Southend, where the General Hospital tended two injured survivors. Meanwhile Manston had been reduced to a blazing shambles: the Margate Fire Brigade helped fight the fires. (Four days later Churchill came to see the damage, and the airfield ceased to be an operational fighter station for the rest of the battle).

That night Hull, far beyond the battle zone proper, reported its first air raid deaths: one plane killed seven civilians off Rustenburg Street. The target had been Immingham. But the more significant event was the failed raid on Thameshaven: in the course of it one plane bombed what is now the Barbican area in the City of London and another caused a fierce fire in two West India Docks warehouses, which it took eight firefloats and 170 pumps to quell. The Germans had accidentally broken their own (politically-inspired) rule never to bomb London. It was in direct response to this that Churchill ordered an immediate retaliation raid on Berlin (also never attacked hitherto), and, as the next consequence, Hitler downgraded the telling raids on RAF fighter bases and ordered a massive Blitz on London. This outcome took a fortnight to emerge.

COASTAL BLITZ

Meanwhile, on the 26th, "Raid X20", as Stanmore called it, was missed by the fighters after RDF had tracked it to the coast at Foulness. The raiders hit Debden and killed five there, while half the station's planes were away escorting a convoy. North Weald's 111 and other squadrons caught the flank of the raiders over Maldon, and in the ensuing struggle six German and four British planes fell. Next day brought the worst civilian casualties so far, when bombs dumped on Gillingham killed twenty people at the Bus Depot. On the 28th Rochford airfield, only three miles from Southend town centre, was heavily though inaccurately bombed. One enemy machine crashed onto the base within yards of an RAF doctor, who pulled out one corpse, caught sight of a second German pointing a gun at him, and then saw that he was dead as well, though propped up with his finger still on the trigger. A stray bomb killed two women in Victoria Avenue, Southend.

On the morning of the 31st Debden was again the target. "X29" split into two groups, and while Debden's own squadrons engaged one rather unsuccessfully over Brightlingsea, the other hit the airfield with a hundred bombs and wounded fourteen RAF personnel, two fatally. A *Nemo* patrol boat saved three airmen from the River Colne _ a Hurricane pilot and the two crewmen of an Me 110, who were taken to the base's little hospital in Church Road. Four more Hurricanes had also crashed: the wreckage of one is now on display at the RAF Museum at Hendon, after being disinterred from the Walton Backwaters mud in the 1970s. Further south Detling and Eastchurch were again (mistakenly) bombed.

During the first six days of September Luftflotte 2 concentrated heavily on airfields, docks and oil refineries around the Thames Estuary, but no higher up than the London Royal Docks. On the 1st Tilbury Docks and RAF Hornchurch were heavily hit: at the former the Harland and Wolff Shipyard and several sheds were hit, and six men were killed, while bombs fell beside the Admiral Superintendant's office in Chatham Dockyard without exploding.

If the encounter over Essex on 18 August could be called "The Battle of Foulness", and that on the 31st "The Battle of Brightlingsea", that on 3 September would have to be "The Battle of Burnham-on-Crouch", for in the struggle overhead between ZG 2 and ZG 26 Me 110s and several Essex-based RAF squadrons six planes from each side were seen to fall around that town, including two at Canewdon and one each at Creeksea, North Shoebury,

COASTAL BLITZ

Stow Maries, South Fambridge, Mundon and the Pyefleet.

On the night of the 4th Chatham, Tilbury and Harwich were raided by between eight and ten planes each. At, and near, the former some two hundred (mostly small, 50-kg) HE bombs fell: one salvo destroyed part of the naval storage yard. Two ships caught fire at Tilbury. There was no damage at Harwich, though there was a nasty moment when two bombs dropped right alongside a shed full of gun cotton at Bramble Island factory but failed to explode*. Lt W A Feather, of the Army's 4th Bomb Disposal Company, won the George Medal for defusing both this bomb and one of those dropped at Wrabness a fortnight earlier.

On the afternoon of 5 September the industrial Essex bank of the Thames was attacked. A pulp warehouse at Tilbury, and the Thames Board Works and Jurgens margarine factory at Purfleet (hence the whaling ship bombed previously) were set on fire. More seriously, all three oil refineries (Thameshaven, Coryton and Shellhaven), were hit. They blazed for five nights and four days, and ten thousand tons of oil went up in a mile-high column of smoke, which could be seen halfway across the North Sea and by night provided a bright beacon for the Luftwaffe, which returned three times to stoke up the fires. Two men died, including a fireman who fell into the flames. The mayhem continued on the 6th, with fresh fires and twenty-four people killed across the river at Dartford.

Then, on the early afternoon of the 7th, the London Blitz began. Until nightfall and beyond over six hundred bombers, heavily fighter-escorted, assaulted the capital in waves, navigating with ease along the south bank of the Estuary in daylight and then by the light of the hundreds of fires by night. At Surrey Docks alone the London fire brigades were using five hundred pumps by late afternoon, as twenty-five acres of timber yards burned. Cranes sagged and heeled over in the heat, and passing ships had their paint scorched off. Downstream, fires around the Royal Docks completely severed the roads into Silvertown, and some of its population had to be evacuated by water. Thirteen merchant ships were sunk or disabled in the dock basins, and a tug was destroyed off Beckton Gasworks. One wharf in the East India Dock was wholly burned out. Firemen were rushed into London from half a dozen surrounding counties. It was said that the smoke, smell and (after dark) the glare were detectable as far afield as Suffolk. The searchlights were so obscured by smoke around the Thames mouth as to be

---

*this incident at the Great Oakley factory is distinct from the accidental explosion in 1942 which killed three workers and after which three others won medals for rescue work.

useless. Nonetheless, this day cost the enemy some forty aircraft, including an He 111 which crashed on the Isle of Grain opposite Sheerness, and from which four injured survivors were taken to Chatham naval hospital.

From then until November London had not twenty-fours' respite. The Docks continued to be hit both by day and night, with a large merchantman (*Minnie de Larrinaga*) wrecked on the 9th, all the buildings on the St Katherine's Dock East Basin gutted on the 10th. But, though it is conventionally said that the Docks were the Luftwaffe's main target, after the first week the focus shifted to *Central* London, and overall Westminster, Holborn, the City and Lambeth received heavier bombing than the East End. Furthermore, it is a curious fact that the bombing of the London Docks was largely without decisive point or serious strategic effect (I leave aside the thousands of civilian lives lost in the surrounding boroughs). The Port of London was no longer a prime national channel for food and raw materials, while the big coal and oil cargoes went to the Thames power stations and refineries, not the more famous docks. Although many ships were bombed in dock, the proximity of onshore fire hydrants and the shallowness of the water prevented virtually all of them from being lost. Much more damage was done to London's seaborne trade by the far less publicised minelaying out in the North Sea.

The Port of London bombing did not stop at the eastern edge of the Metropolitan area but continued to extend down river. On the morning of 11 September one plane bombed the Navy's oil tanks at Port Victoria, opposite Sheerness. Civilian labourers Steadman and Sale very bravely ran among the tanks, plugging holes made by bomb splinters to stop the fuel reaching a fire. On the 18th there were two separate daylight raids on Tilbury, which killed at least eight people, destroyed the dockside hotel, and made much of the small town's population homeless. The Port Victoria tanks were again targetted. Simultaneously eight civilians died at Rochester and Gillingham, as bombs fell all around, but not on, the Chatham naval zone. Almost uniquely, some *four-engined* Luftwaffe bombers were seen over the Medway.* In all the Essex oil refineries were raided eight times that month. The Luftwaffe were paying a price, though. On the 8th an He 111 crashed in the river off Grays, with three dead and two captured. A week later, on "Battle of Britain

---

*There is also evidence that on the night of the 16th a four-engined Ju 89 had flown south past Harwich and aimed bombs at Sheerness.

COASTAL BLITZ

Sunday", a second bomber crashed at Woolwich Arsenal, a third at Orsett, and a fourth in Barking Reach _ downed by the guns of SS *Port Auckland*. Nowhere was AA fire heavier than round the lower London River: it was not unusual for several hundred unexploded shells to be picked up after a night's raid. Almost inevitably British AA fire killed eight civilians at Southend (for instance), in four separate incidents.

In the last fortnight of September parachute mines began to fall on land as well as sea. The size of these, and their exploding *on* rather than *in* the ground, caused enormous blast damage. Most of these mines had conventional rather than magnetic or acoustic mechanisms (though coincidentally the latter appeared in sea mines that very same fortnight). Ipswich, Holland-on-Sea, Maldon, Burnham-on-Crouch (where six people were killed), Foulness and the Medway area all reported them, as well as London. At Ipswich (Cemetery Road) it proved impossible to defuse an unexploded one, and it had to be blown up on the spot, destroying sixty-two houses! Next day five soldiers and a policeman were blown up while investigating another mine at Worlingworth (East Suffolk).

Within hours of the first mine incidents the Ministry of Home Security (in overall charge of Civil Defence) issued this warning to all regions:

"Last night and tonight suspected magnetic mines dropped by parachutes in urban areas. Many unexploded. Admiralty advice no metal be brought near, and all vibration be avoided in vicinity. Admiralty urgently investigating as possible new weapon"*.

Though they were in other respects the standard Types C and D, most of the mines were not magnetic (or acoustic), in fact. HMS *Vernon*'s "Land Incidents Section" coped with the crisis, for the Army did not deal with mines. Phenomenal courage was shown. Lt-Cdr Ryan and CPO Ellingworth, who had defused the first "red" magnetic mine at Clacton, dealt with one of the new "land mines"[+] at Hornchurch airfield, and were then killed tackling another in a Dagenham warehouse on 21 September. These two men had been professionals but the other heroes of the hour were RNVR amateurs, some of whom had been civilians but a few weeks earlier. One such, Lt

---

*PRO HO 198/1518.   [+]Note the dual meaning of "land mine": i)large mine dropped on land from a plane, and ii)small Army defensive mine.

COASTAL BLITZ

Armitage, defused a mine hanging in a tree at Orpington. Sub-Lt Babington dealt with another one down a deep pit at Chatham Dockyard. Sub-Lt Danckwerts and his team defused sixteen mines in forty-eight hours, almost without rest, and unauthorised. Two Australians, Lts I S Mould and H R Syme, later also became prominent. All the officers just named received the newly instituted George Cross, a bravery award second only to the VC.

That autumn had an unforgettable atmosphere for those who stayed near the Thames Estuary and were not posted or evacuated elsewhere. When night came down and, perhaps, the mist crept up the rivers and creeks, a sort of Erskine Childers-Baring Gould mystery became tangible. Then, from out to sea, came the drumming heartbeat of the Heinkels and Junkers bringing mines and bombs to the Estuary and to London. The gruff stutter of the Light AA on the "Eagle Ships" would be joined by the door-slamming thump of the 3.7s and 4.5s on shore, like bad theatrical effects "out of sync" with the continual yellow flashes reflecting in the water.

Though London was now overwhelmingly the bombing target, lesser ports were occasionally hit. The first strategic damage at Lowestoft came on 29 September, when two planes bombed across the harbour area from North Pier to Beach Road. Twelve men were killed, including four sailors and four soldiers on the pier, and one of the several wounded civilians had to have an arm amputated. The bombs triggered beach mines which injured troops at their posts. On 5 October ten civilians were killed at Gillingham and the Ordnance Street area of Chatham, where Charles Dickens had lived. A fourteen-year-old girl trapped under wreckage protected a younger child and an infant with her body, and was later presented with a watch by the mayor. Four nights later six men were killed at Chatham naval barracks, scene of air raid carnage in the previous world war. Seven died at Rochester and Strood on the 17th, and a Type-C mine fell on Sheerness power station but did not go off.

The Harwich air defences were probably the most active and successful on the East Coast. On 14 September an He 111 was shot down by Debden fighters at nearby Harkstead, across the Stour in Suffolk. On the night of 12 October the crew of a Ju 88, machine-gunning a Landguard searchlight down the beam, were dazzled and crashed into the sea. Four nights later another Heinkel fouled a balloon cable and fell in flames on Shotley Spit, killing all four crew but not detonating its two mines. On the

GERMAN BOMBERS CRASHED ON THE EAST COAST IN 1940

Above: He 111 shot down at Cley beach, Norfolk, early on 19 June. *(Odhams)*

Right: Ju 88 shot down at Aldbrough, Yorkshire, on 8 July. *(WI)*

Below: Abandoned Do 17 bellylanded at Erwarton on 21 October (Harwich Harbour and Parkeston Quay in the background).

ITALIAN AIR RAIDS

Upper photos show CR 42 crashed at Orfordness, BR 2 in Tangham Forest, and CR at Corton, all on 11 Nov, 19

Below: 257 Squadron pilots with trophies from the BR 2 wreck. Tuck is the figure in the peaked cap below the Hurricane's nose.

(WI & Ford Jenkins

Below: Civil Defence report on the Italian raid on Harwich on 21 December, 1940 *(Bernard)*

A.R.P./M.3.

7999

MESSAGE FORM

Date	Time at which receipt or despatch of message was completed	Telephonist's Initials
21.12.40	10·54	a.v

ADDRESS TO:— Divisional Control Colchester

TEXT OF MESSAGE:— Minor Bombing report stop Enemy bombers from 1747 to 1810 stop 6 H.E. in Sea stop No damage no casualties stop 2 H.E. Bombs at High House Farm Road A 136 stop no damage no casualties stop One H.E. Bomb Junction Kings Head St. and Market Street Harwich stop One Severe casualty 9 minor stop Services damaged water/gas. Sewers stop Lock up shops and houses damaged about 15 Serious approximately 30 minor stop

TIME OF ORIGIN OF MESSAGE

ADDRESS FROM ——CH REPORT CENTRE

SIGNATURE (of official authorising the despatch of an "out" message)

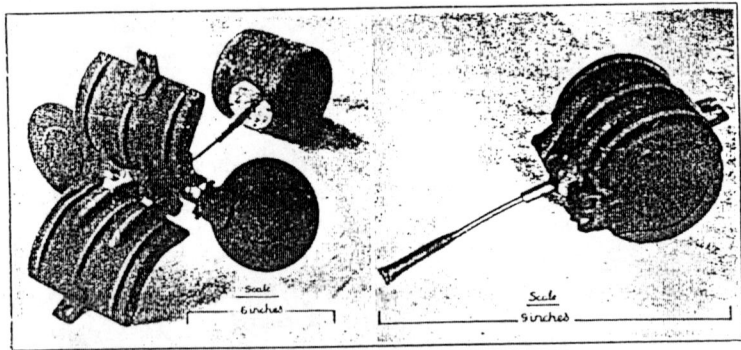

Official warning notice issued after the SD2 ("butterfly") bomb introduced in raids on East Anglian airfields and Ipswich (27-29 October, 1940)

COASTAL BLITZ

18th the flak at Bawdsey claimed to have caused another Harwich raider to crash off the Colne mouth. The 29th saw a bomber shot down off Parkeston Quay en route to attack airfields _ one crewman was saved from the Stour; the other four had bailed out and surrendered to the Clacton police at Beaumont, five miles south.

The Do 17 which bellylanded on the river mud at Erwarton, opposite Parkeston, soon after midnight on 20-21 October was a mystery. It had come down during a raid on Harwich, yet in spite of exhaustive searches no trace of the crew was found. In fact the plane, owing to electrical failure in a magnetic storm, had been abandoned by its crew over Salisbury Plain while en route to bomb Liverpool. Engines still running, it had flown on for another two hundred miles and, in spite of attracting flak from many counties, only come down of its own accord.

We now come to one of the war's least-known unusual episodes: the brief bombing campaign against the East Coast naval bases (mainly Harwich) by the *Italians*. Mussolini, anxious to claim some part of the credit for the expected defeat of Britain, offered the services of the Regia Aeronautica (Royal Airforce) to Hitler. A force known as the CAI (Corpo Aereo Italiano) accordingly arrived at airfields in Belgium _ a fact duly notified to the troops on the East Coast by British Army Intelligence. No Italian had attacked English soil since the Romans. All the Italian operations were failures, though in all early wartime strategic bombing this is a relative term. At the time East Coast civilians had no way of distinguishing the nighttime Italian raids from German.

The first combat mission of the CAI was against Harwich on the night of 24 October 1940. Sixteen Breda BR 20 bombers from the 13th and 43rd Stormi, based at Melsbroek and Chièvres, were sent. One crashed on takeoff and two lost their way and were abandoned over the Continent when their fuel ran out. None of the rest hit their objective, contrary to a bombastic claim in the Italian postwar air history. A few found vaguely the right area; bombs fell at Trimley, Wrabness, Beaumont, Pye sands (off the Naze), and near a drifter off Clacton. Others seem to have gone on to Yarmouth, near which bombs were reported at the appropriate time.

Meanwhile the Luftwaffe had not entirely given up its daylight attacks on airfields. On 27 and 29 October it made two raids on RAF bases in East Anglia, which were notable for the introduction of the "Butterfly", a

2-kg anti-personnel bomblet about the size of a paint tin, so called because it was steadied in flight by two metal wings on a protruding rod. On the 27th a large force bombed Martlesham airfield, while a stray plane from another operation attacked the nearby dock area of Ipswich, where seven civilians and a naval officer were killed when they mistook the "butterflies" for the more harmless incendiaries. A Lewis gunner at the Nacton Heavy AA site shot down a Do 17 into the Stour at Holbrook. Two days later Me 109s and 110s bombed North Weald: in the resulting fighter battle three raiders crashed (on the Tillingham seawall, off Goldhanger, and at Langenhoe), and West Mersea was bombed.

In daylight that same day the Italians aimed their second raid at Dover*, though the eight Royal Marines killed by it were at Deal. On 5 November eight BR 20s achieved no more than timely fireworks around Harwich, though Landguard Fort counted several explosions in the sea and flares were dropped.

For 11 November the Italians planned an elaborate daylight raid on Harwich. Nine BR 20s of 43 Stormo were to be escorted by twenty-two Cant CR 42 fighters from 95 Squadriglia at Eecklo near Bruges. Two other forces, one of five Cant Z 1007-Bis from 172 Squadriglia at Chièvres, the other of twenty-four GR 50s from 20 Gruppo at Ursel, were to launch preliminary diversions off Foulness and Yarmouth, and to sustain these feints for the maximum time made use of the forward airfields at Coxyde and Raversyde on the Belgian coast. Still more diversionary cover was promised by German raids on London and a convoy in the Thames Estuary.

In the event the plan was ruined by the presence of British fighters, and their superiority over the obsolete CR 42 biplanes, though the later Italian attempt to blame the Germans, who called off their London raid and made inaccurate intelligence and weather forecasts, had some validity. The Foulness feint failed because the GR 50s, having lost their way in thick cloud, unenterprisingly returned to base. Although 17 RAF Squadron was grounded at Martlesham for refuelling after a convoy patrol (as the attackers had calculated) two other Hurricane squadrons were on hand. 257 had, unknown to the Axis, just been transferred to Martlesham from Debden. Its "ace" commander, Squadron Leader Stanford Tuck, was delayed at base, but Flight Lt Blatchford immediately led it into the air. Meanwhile 46 Squadron,

---

*not Ramsgate, as has been said in the past. This is confirmed by the Dover Command War Diary (PRO ADM 199/360).

COASTAL BLITZ

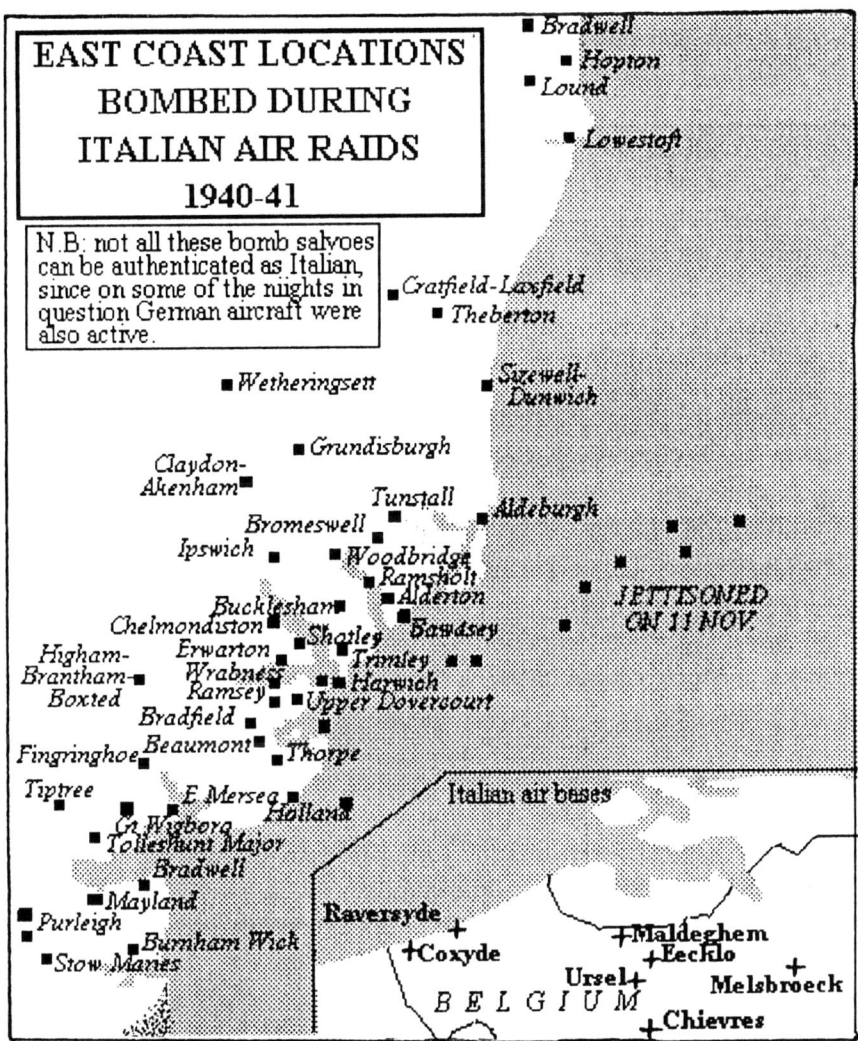

temporarily commanded by the ironically-named Flight Lt Rabagliatti, was on patrol off Clacton. Therefore twenty-five British fighters converged on the Italians off Felixstowe. After "a large vic formation of seven, led by two others a considerable distance ahead" had been sighted "a general dogfight followed which resulted in the complete rout of the Italian aircraft"*. These flew up the Suffolk coast away from their target, jettisoning their bombs, and then fled for Belgium. Between them the two British squadrons claimed

---

*46 Squadron Operational Record Book (PRO AIR 27/460).

fourteen enemy planes shot down, plus two probables _ Blatchford and six other pilots (including two Poles) claimed at least two each. Blatchford, having run out of ammunition, ripped the top wing of one CR 42 with his propeller. In fact the Italian loss was six _ three BR 20s and three CR 42s, though nineteen of the fighters were damaged by having to crashland (owing to lack of fuel) on return. Three victims fell on land in Suffolk. A BR 20, peppered with bullet holes, minus a prop blade and with an engine wedged under a wing, crashed on Bromeswell rifle range, in the forests east of Woodbridge. Its captain, Affriani, was killed, three crew members were wounded _ one of whom died, and a fifth man was unhurt. The prisoners included a photographer. Tuck and other Martlesham officers drove to the scene and recovered such trophies as two steel helmets, a bayonet sheath, two crested flying jackets and two bottles of Chianti. Sergeant Pilot Lazzari, after being chased north along the coast and flying at rooftop level across Lowestoft, crashed his CR 42 at Corton. Although he had run over a railway line he was rescued unhurt. He claimed that he had been forced down by an engine fault, and local troops found only one bullet hole in his plane. Another CR 42 was crashlanded on its nose on Orfordness Beach by Sergeant Pilot Salvadori, and is nowadays in the Hendon RAF Museum. He had eluded the Hurricanes but crashed owing to an oil failure.

A BR 20 hit by the Pole Pniak came down in the sea off Aldeburgh after one man had bailed out but ripped his parachute on the tail and fallen to his death. The plane later sank with its remaining occupants. Another BR 20 plunged into the sea off Orfordness. Two men were seen to bale out but the Aldeburgh lifeboat found only an Italian parachute. A CR 42 fell in the same area. A German He 59 rescue seaplane came out looking for survivors, but, in the no-nonsense fashion Churchill had authorised, was shot down twenty miles off the Naze.

The British press and film news, who came to Martlesham next day, somewhat sensationalised the battle, for instance claiming that Tuck himself had taken part (this no doubt to make a good "ace" story). The Italian air historian General Santoro was to claim nine British fighters were destroyed (none were), but gave himself away with an agonised post-mortem. The CAI never approached these shores in daylight again.

Martlesham mistakenly reported it on 17 November, apparently because of the superficial resemblance between BR 20s and Me 110s. A

COASTAL BLITZ

force of the latter divebombed Felixstowe Dock, killing a soldier and a civilian "casual netmaker" employed by the Boom Department. The Anglo-Austrian Count Czernin, of 17 Squadron, bailed out at Ufford and his Hurricane crashed at Bredfield, both near Woodbridge, after he had been hit by the famous Adolf Galland, commanding the covering Me 109s. Next day nine men were wounded at HMS *Europa*, Lowestoft, while three soldiers and three civilians simultaneously perished outside. This was the first of only two occasions when the Patrol Service Depot, with its hordes of personnel a fine target, was hit.

The remaining Italian raids were on Harwich (nights of 17/18 and 20/21 November, 14, 21 and 22 December), Ipswich (20/21 and 29 November, and 2 January 1941), and Yarmouth and Lowestoft (29 November). In reality this bombing was largely dispersed onto other areas, with all the 20 November "Harwich" bombs falling around the Blackwater and some later salvoes as far away as *Grimsby*! Some of these raids did do damage. The Lowestoft one killed three people at the Coop Canning Factory, though damage at Richards shipyard next door was confined to a buckled crane and quay and some splinter holes in the coaster *Empire Sound*. On 21 December the bombs at Harwich were fairly well concentrated, falling just outside the harbour boom, near Shotley Barracks, near Upper Dovercourt, and on Harwich Town, where the International Stores in Kings Head Street were demolished and one civilian lost a leg. That these were Italian raids was confirmed by bomb fragments, such as by C M F Bernard, the Harwich Civil Defence Controller, after the lastmentioned raid. In the New Year the CAI was broken up and the Luftwaffe regained its monopoly.

During the Italian pseudo-Blitz an extraordinary event was reported from Kent. On the night of 19-20 November several explosions occurred at intervals in fields at Rainham and Bearsted. An off-target raid on Chatham? Possibly, but no *bombs* had fallen, instead artillery shells had been fired from occupied France! For some months German heavy guns had been shelling the Dover area, but could they really reach as far as Chatham? In fact the Germans had just two guns capable of this feat, their K12(E)s, each with 109 stupendous feet of 21-cm (8.2-inch) calibre muzzle, weirdly braced with rods and railway-mounted on myriad wheels. Having shelled the Maginot Line they had been trundled up to secret sidings near Gravelines, and thence fired right over the Dover Strait and East Kent to a maximum range of seventy-one miles. In fact Chatham was just beyond this limit, making RAF Detling a likelier target. Remarkably, the K 12(E)'s range extended as far as the line Hastings -Hawkhurst- Isle of Grain- Southend-Burnham- Colne Point-Little Clacton-Walton _ i.e, it included parts of Sussex and Essex as well as Kent. Yet this seems to have been the only occasion they fired into an area bordering the Nore Command. And the only proven instance of a German land-based gun stretching into this area was on 28 June 1943, when a Margate factory was hit by a 28-cm (11-inch) shell from the Grosser Kurfurst Battery at Cap Gris Nez, firing at its maximum of $38\frac{1}{2}$ miles. Of course at these great distances guns could neither be visually sighted nor remotely accurate, which no doubt explains why they were not used more.

That December sporadic German raids continued against the Nore Command bases. Chatham's two worst raids were at this period: on the 3rd ten men were killed and fifty-two injured in the Dockyard and Naval barracks, while seven civilians died in the town, and on the 14th one of the stray Thames mines destroyed sixty houses in Ordnance Street and Boundary Road, killing fifteen and injuring 123 people. On both the 4 and 5 December bombs on Hamilton Dock, Lowestoft, caused only slight casualties, though on the first occasion another bombload killed a Coast Artillery officer at Pakefield.

The largest night raid of the whole year struck London and surrounding counties on 8/9 December. The whole interior of the PLA Building, on Tower Hill, which contained the FOIC's office, was wrecked. Gravesend and Sheerness were also considerably damaged and a trail of misplaced bombs was scattered right across Essex. A mine fell on London Bridge Station and would have brought much of the railway transport of South East England to a halt had it not been defused by *Vernon*'s Lt J B P Miller RNVR. One of the raiders, a Ju 88, was brought down on the A13 road at Grays, and scattered itself over many acres.

That winter's daylight raids on shipping sometimes extended to the nearby shore. The Wrabness Mine Depot was near-missed again on 6 January. On the next two days Ipswich Docks were raided: on the 8th two people were killed there _ while another plane aimed at the Brantham plastics factory. Clacton and Lowestoft seemed to be favourite targets of opportunity. At the former five soldiers died at Connaught Gardens searchlight site on 19 January 1941. Until now only nine people had been killed in air raids on

COASTAL BLITZ

Yarmouth, but the New Year heralded approaching danger. On 25 January, in a bold daylight foray, a single Do 17 bombed across the River Yare and on both banks: seven people were killed, including two seamen on the trawler *Their Merit,* moored at South Quay. On 4 February three naval ratings were killed in the NAAFI canteen at Waveney Dock, Lowestoft: the offending plane was shot down in the sea off Corton, one crewman being saved by a boat from the Yarmouth examination vessel. Next night four civilians were killed in Yarmouth town centre. In daylight on the 7th a hail of HE wrecked the Lowestoft harbourmaster's house, Customs House, railway goodsyard, and swing bridge _ eleven people were killed, including the bridge operator.

Meanwhile, on the night of 5/6 February many Thames and Medway towns were bombed, including Southend, though the fifteen dead in Southend's worst raid perished in the High Street's London Hotel the previous night. The Luftwaffe now gave up the regular Blitz on London, and began its "Tour of the Ports". It was now that the East Coast harbour towns, which were included in this, came in for their worst raids.

On the night of 17/18 February the targets appear to have been Harwich and Yarmouth. Perhaps eight planes went for the former (but only one bombed near, at Dovercourt) Of about sixteen meant for Yarmouth six hit the borough. One destroyed the Walrond Institute, which housed the FOIC's office, though he and his staff escaped with a dusting through being on the ground floor. The gasworks caught fire, but firemen prevented any explosion. Surpisingly only one person was killed.

Four nights later Chatham had extraordinary luck in escaping casualty-free as an equally large raid dissipated itself on and around the Medway.

One of the most alarming periods at Harwich and Felixstowe was the three consecutive nights of 24-26 February. At least a dozen planes were over on the first: one salvo landed perilously close to the Parkeston oil tanks, another killed five people and injured seven on the Harwich Town-Dovercourt parish boundary, and an unexploded bomb buried itself under the police station in Main Road, which was also the Civil Defence Report Centre (the staff carried on working). On the 27th, in daylight, several East Coast ports were attacked at the same time as a convoy. One plane bombed Cleethorpe Road, Grimsby, very near the Docks and naval base, and killed eleven civilians. Two more civilians were killed at Yarmouth, six at

Lowestoft, and one each at Felixstowe and Ipswich, where a bomb broke open one of Cranfield's granaries and spilled its contents onto the quayside.

On 6 March a raid on offshore shipping doubled as one on Lowestoft. The Public Library and much of the rest of Clapham Road was destroyed, and the trawler *Evesham* was damaged in Inner Harbour, total deaths numbering five _ three aircraft had been involved. Next day, and again on 22 March, the little base at Brightlingsea was bombed by two Me 109s. On the 7th the NOIC's office was near-missed, four of Stones's shipyard workers were injured, and a sailor was reported as suffering from shock after screaming hysterically. Another Me 109 killed three civilians in Clacton the same afternon. On the 22nd bombs fell right across Aldous's Shipyard, narrowly missing MLs awaiting launch, but sank the LL drifter *Jeannie Leask* and killed a stoker and a shipyard worker on board (this vessel was under repair after being damaged by simultaneously detonating a magnetic and an acoustic mine a week before).

Meanwhile anti-shipping parachute mines were causing deaths in the Medway area. On 5 March the tug *Silverstone*, towing a petrol barge three miles above Rochester Bridge, had one fall on top of her, sinking her and the barge and killing all seven crew from the two craft. Five days later Sheerness reported that two people had been killed by one of the many mines aimed at the Thames mouth that night. These were the only air raid deaths it ever suffered _ extraordinary, considering it was one of the two chief operational naval bases of the Nore Command.

That same day a specially adapted Ju 88 of I/NJG*2 crashed at Terrington, by the Wash in West Norfolk. Throughout the main 1940-41 Blitz such night fighter-bombers made "intruder" attacks on air bases in Eastern England, in which they posed as RAF bombers coming into land and thereby got clsoe to the runways and the planes landing on them. Not far away, on the 13th, bombs on Bentinck's Dock, King's Lynn, wrecked a coal hoist, sank a barge and killed four soldiers.

That night, and the following, Clydeside was the main enemy target, and the East Coast raids were diversions. About eighteen planes were sent for such an operation against Yarmouth on the second night. Not untypically, only one bomber hit the town, while bombs fell just inland, at Hull, Lowestoft, near Harwich and on SS *Artmesia* at sea.

Another oddity of the Blitz so far was that Hull, by far the largest

---

*Nachtgeschwader=literally "Night Squadron".

COASTAL BLITZ

town and port on the East Coast (unless London is counted), had suffered only the sort of minor attacks common to the lesser harbours. But within a week in mid-March 1941 143 inhabitants were killed. Most died on the night of the 18th/19th, when some thirty planes hit the town: postwar RAF research was to show that another two hundred had set out to bomb it, only to waste their loads over a huge area of Yorkshire, Lincolnshire, and the sea.

The following night the Luftwaffe suddenly returned to the London Docks in force. The Navy's Victoria Dockyard, by the river at Deptford, was absolutely smothered by at least eleven HE bombs and a plane-load of incendiaries. Thirty-three out of forty-three storage buildings were destroyed along with oil, stationery, soap, alcohol and tools. Six civilians, including an Admiralty Police inspector and sergeant, were killed, and six injured. Though the fire brigade sent fifty engines, the streets of London were in such chaos that the first took over two hours to arrive. The Dockyard staff were officially much praised, and one man won the George Medal. Nearby, in Surrey Docks, bombs sank the AA paddle ship *Helvelyn* and near-missed and rocked her sister the *Goatfell*. Three ratings from the latter jumped onto the former, although she was burning and sinking, and saved six injured men, one of whom died ashore later. These rescuers received BEMs. Across the river at Shadwell and the commercial Victoria Dock two merchant ships, eight barges and a tug were damaged. The whole port was closed next day. The death toll throughout Greater London was 750. At least five delayed action mines fell, unplotted, in the Docks and river. Next morning SS *Lindenhall* was sunk at her berth as the first of them detonated. A policeman had been told that a mine had been seen coming down in the area, but had blockheadedly refused to believe it or pass on the report. A day later SS *Halo* sank off Barking Creek on the second mine, while a skid towed by the launch *Colette* blew a third nearby. On the 29th SS *Grenaa* approached a berth at Rotherhithe just vacated by another ship. She blew a fourth mine, was torn apart, and had seven men killed. The blast ripped off the bows of the Colchester sailing barge *Emma* nearby. That same night the fifth mine went off harmlessly in the East India Dock. As a result of all this the FOIC stationed thirty-two (later raised to fifty) minewatching barges every quarter of a mile along the Thames from Dagenham to Gravesend. Ninety-five medically unfit naval ratings were sent to man them, and another fifty-three were stationed on shore by the Docks. There was also a £5 reward for civilians reporting mines, though apparently it was hardly ever claimed.

Hull was now taking severe damage from parachute mines, which were quite additional to those being aimed at the Humber. On 31 March twelve fell, killing fifty-two people. One mine shattered the Shell-Mex Building, housing Civil Defence Control, on the corner of Ferensway and Spring Bank, and killed a doctor and a policeman.

April and May 1941 marked the worst phase of the East Coast Blitz. The night of 7/8 April brought the Luftwaffe to most of the eastern ports. Two mines on Rochester killed eleven people, and damaged the Shorts factory again. Five bombloads fell in the general Harwich-Ipswich area, indicating an attempt to hit one or both ports. But the six planes which hit Yarmouth and Gorleston inflicted on East Anglia the most destructive raid it had experienced so far. For the first time here many incendiaries _ up to four thousand _ fell. There were sixty major and 150 minor fires, compared with only thirty-four pumps in the whole district. On South Quay and Southgates Road the Royal Navy's Coastal Forces base office, the Trinity House depot, and the Eastern Counties Farmers' cattle-feed mill were among the buildings destroyed, and behind them most of the shops in King Street blazed. The sky glowed lurid red as far away as the opposite side of the county. As his shore office burned Lt-Cdr Lewis ordered his 13th ML Flotilla, moored alongside, to hose themselves down and escape to sea. Lt Lightoller, the Dunkirk veteran, saved ML 195 by personally picking incendiaries off the wooden deck and throwing them into the river. On shore four mines between them killed seven people, including five special constables at a police post. The total death toll was at least seventeen. "Human memory is short", wrote Norfolk Chief Constable and ARP Controller C G Box, "but I shall never forget the appalling sight Yarmouth presented that night". As visitors can still see from the age of the rebuilt houses, the left bank of the Yare between the Town Hall and the Fish Wharf had been quite devastated, almost to a City of London degree.

Next night at least seven more aircraft returned, to do more damage and kill six people at Gorleston. Bombs also fell from three planes at Parkeston, Harwich Quay and Felixstowe. A single bomb at Trinity Pier sank the paddle minesweeper *Marmion*, the examination drifter *Darcy Cooper*, and the Army launch *Falcon*, moored side by side, and killed nine sailors and soldiers (twenty-two more were wounded, of whom one died later _ a

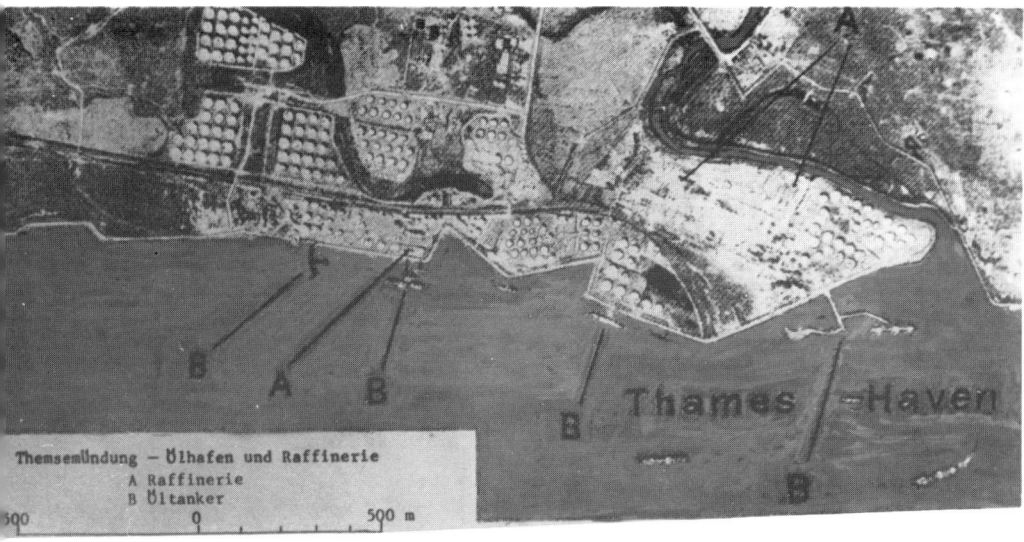

THE BLITZ OF 1940-41

Above: **THAMESHAVEN** German reconnaissance photo of the Thameshaven oil tanks. This key strategic area was bombed eight times in September 1940 alone.

LONDON
Fireman at work in the Surrey Docks on the morning of 8 September, after the first major raid. *(WI)*

ROCHESTER
The paddle minesweeper *City of Rochester*, sunk off the Acorn Yard on 19 May, 1941. *(E D G Payne)*

HARWICH

TOP LEFT: The paddle minesweeper *Marmion*, sunk at Trinity Pier early on 9 April, 1941. *(Galbraith)*

BELOW: Bernard's Factory, gutted by incendiaries on 9 May, 1941. Note how the heat has twisted the roof girders. *(Bernard)*

LOWESTOFT *(TOP RIGHT)* The blockship *Fidelia* sunk in Waveney Dock, on 5 May, 1941. *(Ford Jenkins)*

GORLESTON *(ABOVE)*: Unexploded "Satan" bomb in Frederick Road, 12 June, 1941.
YARMOUTH *(BELOW)*: Middlegate Street after the raid of 7/8 April, 1941.   *(Box)*

HULL: Riverside Mill (*above left*) and Reckitt and Coleman's factory (*above right*) on the morning of 9 May, 1941.
BRIDLINGTON (*right*): St Anne's Home, where seven people were killed on 18 June, 1941.

COASTAL BLITZ

gravestone at Shotley tells us). The force of the explosion hurled a chunk of *Darcy Cooper's* boiler as far as Bathside Gasworks, half a mile away, where it was roped off on suspicion of being an unexploded bomb.

Duly filed with all the Admiralty's own official air raid reports were two letters from Mr Leonard Rose, a Dovercourt farmer, Independent parliamentary candidate, and regular litigant and protester. He alleged that during the 25 February raid the artillerymen at Beacon Hill, Harwich, had freely entered and left their huts, so that the light streamed out of the doors and invited the bombers. Of the 9 April raid, he claimed that the AA had failed to respond, and that the

> "naval doctors, as before, created a most distressing impression and would appear to be deserving of the most severe censor (sic)...one wonders at the outcome of our Nation's struggle, if the local contingent represents a fair cross-section of the Country's effort".

Rear-Admiral Goolden, the Harwich FOIC, wrote;

> "The allegation that the Naval Ambulance was engaged in transport in connection with cocktail parties is a malicious fabrication...No useful comment can possibly be made on this statement, which would appear to be on a par with the general tone of Mr Rose's letter throughout".*

That same night about a dozen aircraft made a serious attempt to wreck the Essex oil refineries. At least twelve parachute mines, besides bombs, fell on Thameshaven and adjacent Corringham and Stanford-le-Hope. Eight people were already dead on shore when next afternoon one of the mines exploded under the tanker *Lunula* at Thameshaven No 4 Jetty. Thirty-seven crewmen died, and the wreck burned for four days before sinking.

On the night of 9/10 April three or four raiders accurately delivered some large HEs and incendiaries to Ipswich Docks. The Auxiliary Patrol office, workshop and sickbay, and an adjacent timber yard, were burned, the Ransom and Rapier engineering works, Paul's granaries and Jepson's shipyard were damaged, and three old barges used as firefloats were sunk. On one of the latter a fireman was drowned, and a firewatcher was killed by British AA splinters. Two Leading Seamen, A A Cozens and J W Abbot, won BEMs for running into the naval magazine, where 3-inch shells were stored and small arms ammunition was already going off, and dowsing the fire.

---

*PRO ADM 199/1173

COASTAL BLITZ

The following night it was Lowestoft's turn: about seven planes scattered forty-five HEs and nine hundred incendiaries in many separate areas of town, destroying the Coastguard Station, a fish yard and several houses, and killing twenty-two civilians and injuring thirty-nine. In Old Nelson Street a week later one of those HEs not to explode went off and killed the two Colchester bomb disposal men who were tackling it. During this raid a single lowflying plane had bombed the quayside and sheds at Parkeston, and injured three naval ratings _ the only time this principal part of HMS *Badger* was ever hit. The same night another single aircraft killed thirteen civilians at Yarmouth.

On 15/16 April Hull took six more mines. One destroyed a shelter off Holderness Road, slaughtering all sixty of its occupants and making five hundred other people homeless. Meanwhile five bombers (out of some eighteen sent) struck close to the heart of Yarmouth, which was "fortunate" to lose only two more lives. Another two were lost at Una Road, Parkeston _ the only air-raid fatalities at that small town.

Next the Luftwaffe in France and the Low Countries gathered together every bomber for the two biggest raids ever mounted on London, one on 16/17, the other on 19/20 April _ over seven hundred planes flew in the second. The more northerly East Coast towns had a breathing space, but London overspill hit wide areas around the Lower Thames. For instance, in the second raid three people died at Southend (two mines hit Leigh), four at Rochester (where the cement ship *Montalto* was sunk at Blue Boar Pier) and thirteen at Dartford, and over fifty mines landed in Essex alone. Much fresh damage was done in the London docks, and two days later mines sown in the river sank the tug *Regency* off Dagenham and the barge *Coronation of Leeds* off Thameshaven.

Next day there was a much smaller, but for this period most unusual, raid: five Me 110s divebombed Harwich Harbour in broad daylight. They hit nothing, and flying back over the Shipwash, one was shot down by the trawler *Bassett*, for which Lt H S Heriot RNVR won the DSC and Seaman Turner the DSM. On the 21st, during a Lowestoft night raid, the thatched church at Pakefield was burned out by a single incendiary.

After London and Hull, Yarmouth had suffered worst that April. It had had eighteen raids, in which fifty-one people were killed _ more than in the whole of the rest of the war so far. Incidentally, several of the Coltishall

COASTAL BLITZ

RAF fighter pilots who had tried to counter this Blitz lost their lives when a bomb hit the "Ferry Inn" pub, at Horning, on the Broads, on the 27th of that month.

May was also everywhere an unpleasent month. On the night of the 2nd several planes raided Lowestoft and nearby Oulton, and wrought havoc all along the railway line into Central Station, though only three people were killed. Next night delayed action bombs fell at this port, and also two mines, one on the sea wall, the other onto the trawler *Ben Gairn*, berthed on the north wall of Waveney Dock. With remarkable faith Cdr Cubison, now the Lowestoft SOAP, ordered everyone else to evacuate the docks, told all vessels to stay put in case the noise of their leaving triggered the mine, and then went back to sleep on his yacht *Martello,* although she was moored next in line to the *Ben Gairn.* At daybreak the mine blew, sinking the trawler and her sister-ship the *Niblick* without casualties. On *Martello* the blast did no more than rattle the ship and awaken the crazy Cubison! Meanwhile several aircraft had bombed the Harwich area _ apart from wrecking the railway yard at Parkeston they demolished a large house in Cliff Road Dovercourt and killed four civilians. Two pathetic Civil Defence messages stand out from the rest: soon after midnight the rescuers telephoned "Please send mortuary van for the body of a child", and at 0645 on the 4th it was announced that a terribly injured woman had been dug out of the wreckage after nine hours _ she survived in hospital for one week.

Next night (4th/5th) there was a widespread raid. At Roughs Buoy, off Harwich, the minesweeper *Selkirk* and patrol trawler *Franc Tireur* were damaged by near misses. Seven or eight planes attacked Ipswich (four people died) and the adjacent industrial village of Nacton, on the Orwell, where Wrinch's, Adlard's and Crane's factories were damaged. At Lowestoft a plane sank the blockship *Fidelia* by the harbour entrance and scattered other bombs across the town centre which destroyed Woolworths' Store.

Then, on the nights of 7/8 and 8/9 May Hull endured that common German tactic, a double Blitz. Contrary to several local accounts, this was not comparable to the previous main raids on Coventry, Merseyside, Clydeside or Plymouth. And, even combined, the two May raids did not equal the largest enemy *attempt* on Hull, on 18/19 March. On the first night about thirty planes bombed Hull, on the second fifty, though on each occasion three-fifths of the raiders sent missed the city.

COASTAL BLITZ

Nevertheless these two raids were Hull's worst. The naval offices (no longer the HQ of the FOIC Humber) were destroyed. Riverside Quay was burned out from end to end. Rank's Flour Mill and Reckitt's Factory (home of the household "Brasso") were destroyed. Hammond's department store was gutted and opened to the sky. The City hall roof was burned, two theatres and the "Valiant" Seaman's Mission were demolished, and the whole Prudential Insurance Building was levelled except for the tower, which stood alone until felled for safety reasons next day. The Paragon (main) Railway Station was damaged and the Main Bus Station burned out _ at daybreak its vehicles were one blackened and twisted mass of iron.

Dozens of mines came down on, and to landward and seaward, of the city. One hit a public shelter at Staniforth Place, Hessle Road, and wiped out several entire families. The LL drifter *Justifier* and nineteen barges and lighters were sunk in the Docks. Three mines fell in the dock basins. As the LL trawler *Silicia* was approaching St Andrew's Dock from the Humber next day a mine exploded under her stern and blew her to pieces. Seven men were killed and three wounded _ Lt-Cdr Marson was thrown in the air and broke both legs. The survivors were saved by ML 211. Two hours later LL tugs swept two more mines on the same spot.(During the whole war 122 mines struck Hull, about 30% of its total bomb tonnage, and an exceptionally high proportion).

Well over two hundred people were killed on each of those two nights. A communal grave was dug and an official mass funeral held at North Cemetary, but so terrible were the emotions displayed and so greatly did the authorities fear for public morale that no such ceremony was ever staged again. Over eight thousand homeless were evacuated from the city, and such was the alarm that whole neighbourhoods fled to camp out in the country (not entirely wisely, as Holderness and Beverley Rural Districts received hundreds of bombs intended for Hull), and finally thirty thousand citizens left with official backing.

By comparison the other East Coast raids on the night of 8/9 May seem minor. Three planes bombed Yarmouth, straddling the *Ethel Radcliffe* wreck and killing six people ashore. Several overflew Lowestoft, though only one bombed the town, killing two. Out to sea another plane sank the base's patrol drifter *Uberty*. A bomber hit another beached shipwreck, the *Clan Monroe*, in Hollesley Bay, off Shingle Street. About four more attacked

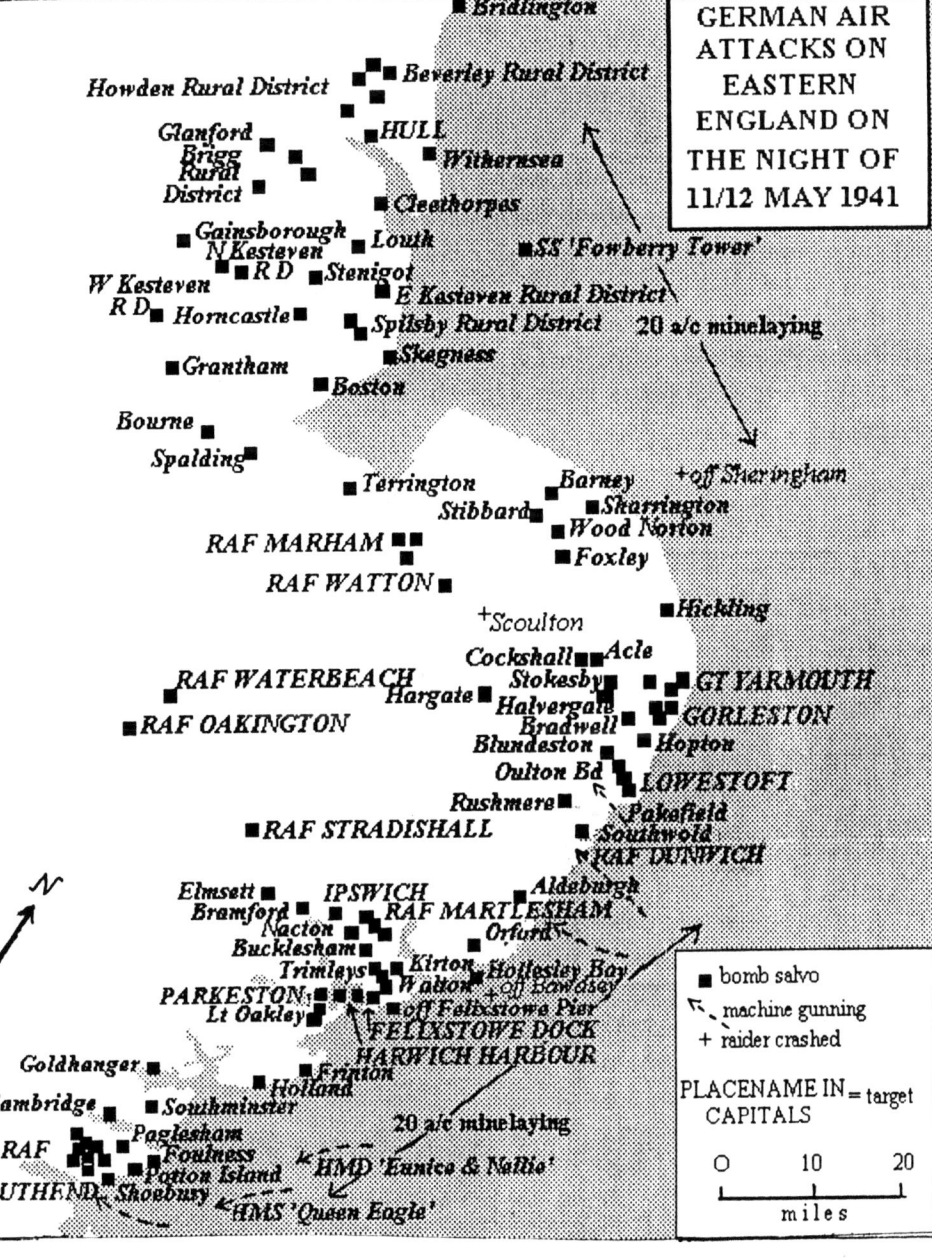

COASTAL BLITZ

Ipswich and Nacton, hitting one of Fison's factory buildings at Cliff Quay and killing four civilians on the nearby council estate. Six or seven raiders were over Harwich and Felixstowe. The clothing factory belonging to Civil Defence Controller Bernard was destroyed, and a train in Harwich Station damaged, by a load of incendiaries, while two one-ton "Hermann" bombs caused severe damage, but only a few slight casualties, in Felixstowe Town.

In the last big raid of the London Blitz, on the night of 10/11 May, over 1,400 people were killed. It was the worst raid ever experienced in Britain. There was much fresh damage to the Docks. A bomb destroyed Tower Pier (the London Auxiliary Patrol base), the accommodation yacht *Gypsy*, and some patrol boats: four naval personnel were killed and eight injured.

The night of 11/12 May saw the largest and most widespread attack on the East Coast apart from those aimed at London and Hull. About a hundred aircraft attacked at various points between Flamborough Head and the Thames, while forty more mined the convoy route. Just after dark on the 11th JG*26 Me 109s made the biggest fighter-bomber raid since the Battle of Britain. While the main force attacked Southend (Rochford) airfield, small groups struck (in vain) at Oulton Broad, Pakefield, Dunwich CHL. Southwold, Aldeburgh, the Brightlingsea patrol drifter *Eunice and Nellie*, and the Sheerness AA ship *Queen Eagle*. A few hours later the bombers proper were heard. One hit Hull and killed two people (the rest of this force missed the city). Yarmouth was lucky in that the six planes which bombed it killed no one. At Lowestoft the four bombloads which hit the town centre north of the harbour killed six. About seven aircraft bombed on and around Ipswich, aiming at Martlesham too. An RAF man was killed at Ipswich airport, and ten civilians died at Elmsett, west of the town. Even more planes attacked Harwich, but in that town and base there were no casualties or damage, though across the harbour one bomber wrecked HMS *Beehive*'s Warhead and Depthcharge Store without detonating the seven tons of explosive inside, and another killed a soldier and three civilians (including a newborn baby) at Walton (Felixstowe).

Two nights later the examination drifter *M A West* was sunk at Yarmouth. On 16/17 May a Type-G mine on Harwich Town brought down the Ordnance Buildings, near the High Lighthouse, and demolished seventeen dwellings and damaged as many as seven hundred _ two civilians were killed,

---

*Jagdgeschwader (literally "Hunt Squadron").

COASTAL BLITZ

including the leader of a first aid post. Next night two planes hit Southend: a direct hit wrecked the Nore Yacht Club and near the airfield ten soldiers died in their billet. The following night the paddle minesweeper *City of Rochester* was sunk at the Acorn Yard, at the place of her name, with four men dead. On the 24th the important Lowestoft Brook Marine shipyard was direct hit, yet without serious casualties or damage, but two days later two bombs on the edge of town left ten dead.

That month was also costly for the Luftwaffe, for evidence that the defences were at last fully hitting back was plentiful. At least a dozen German bombers were shot down on or near the East Coast (not counting others inland). On the 3rd a Ju 88, damaged over Skegness, ditched in the shallows at Dead Man's gap, between Palling and Winterton (Norfolk): the four crew were captured by troops. Next day the Harwich destroyer *Southdown* (the first destroyer to carry radar, yet attacked from the air more often than any other Nore Command ship) destroyed a plane at 62 Buoy, off the Humber, and very early on the 5th another Ju 88 crashed near Sheringham _ one crewman died and three others were taken to hospital at Norwich. In the early hours of the 12th 257 Squadron claimed a Ju 88 and an He 111, and 25 Squadron a Ju 88, all over the water, while the Martlesham and Bawdsey Bofors guns brought down a fourth raider. On the 15th, as one small revenge for Hull's recent ordeal, shore and warship AA shot down a Ju 88 near the Humber Boom Gate _ two Germans were captured. At noon on the 19th, in a late and unusually northerly foray by Erpr.Gr. 210 (once Rubensdörffer's group), an Me 110, having dropped two bombs near the Lowestoft PWSS, was shot down by the light shore guns within half a mile of the Coast Artillery Fire Command Post at Corton; a Lt Hasse was captured. That night the Bawdsey flak put in a second claim, but the He 111 downed off the Cork Lightship was probably hit by the Harwich guardship (and former paddle minesweeper) *Princess Elizabeth*, and possibly by a night minesweeping patrol of four trawlers. The mutilated body of the pilot, Herbert Lindemann, was found.

Before that May was up the bombing had greatly eased, for the Luftwaffe was moving east ready for the invasion of Russia. Indeed it had virtually finished from Harwich southwards, until the V-Bombs late in the war. Northwards it continued, and it was to turn out that most of the air raid deaths at Ipswich, Lowestoft, Yarmouth, King's Lynn and Hull still lay in the future. The main 1940-41 Blitz went on for about three months longer at the enemy's three favourite targets, Lowestoft, Yarmouth and Hull, than most of the rest of Britain.

On 13 June the new Lowestoft blockship, *King Henry*, was sunk (there was reason to think this harbour entrance the most dangerous spot on the East Coast), while fifteen soldiers were killed in their Whapload Road billet nearby. On 22 July the same number of civilians perished in the southern part of town. 16 August brought another "incident" in Waveney Dock: naval offices were hit, the canteen was wrecked for the third time, and the tug *Ness Point* was sunk.

At Yarmouth twenty people were killed on 7 July, mainly in a Kitchener Road shelter which was direct-hit. Three more died in that town on the 8th/9th, when as many as fifteen planes staged a diversion to cover a Birmingham raid and destroyed an unprecedented 120 houses. Six more people died on the 14th. In three of the June and July attacks at Yarmouth and Gorleston 1,800-kg (i.e, 1.8-ton!) "Satan" bombs were dropped, two of which failed to explode. On 22 August the netlayer *Tonbridge* was sunk with thirty-two dead just as she was approaching harbour past Britannia Pier and ready to take on the pilot.

At Hull twenty-two people were killed on 10-11 July, twenty-five on 14th/15th, 150 on 17th/18th (mainly in East Hull), twenty-nine on 17th/18th August, and forty-one on 31 August/1 September.

Other places to suffer after the main Blitz were King's Lynn (sixteen killed on 12 June), and Bridlington (seven on 18 June).

There was one curious exception to the enemy's abandonment of southerly targets. On the night of 14 June no fewer than twenty-nine mines (mostly Type-Gs), and a few bombs, were scattered in North Kent, at places as diverse as Gravesend, Maidstone, Sittingbourne (where the only two fatalities occurred), and Eastchurch. So many mines had never fallen on land during enemy minelaying operations, and this was not overspill from some huge London raid. From enemy sources the RAF later learned that the thirty tons of ordnance had been meant for Chatham (where one "Hermann" had fallen).

The economic and strategic effects of this year of coastal Blitz, together with the raids of 1942-45 (which I shall describe later), were

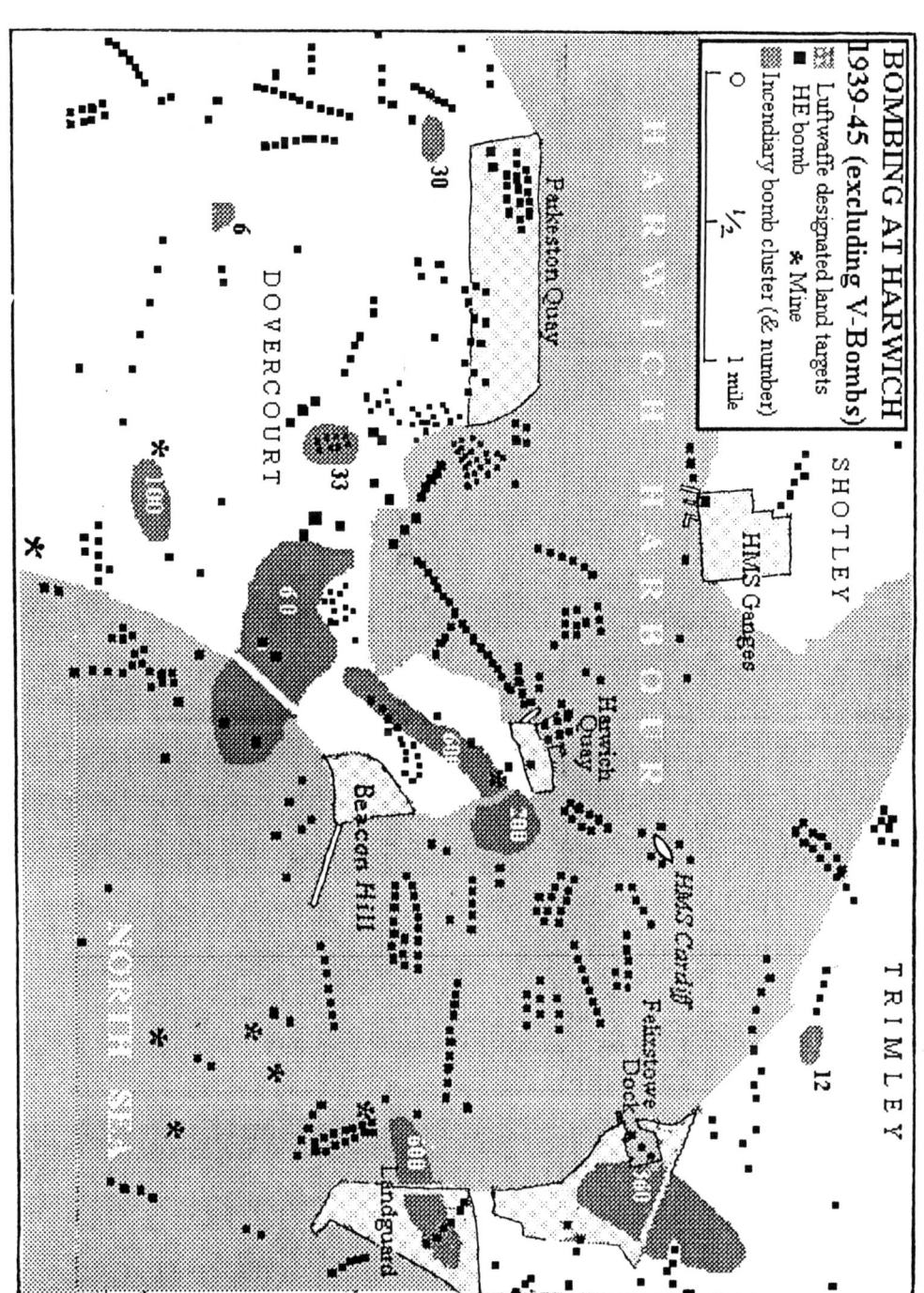

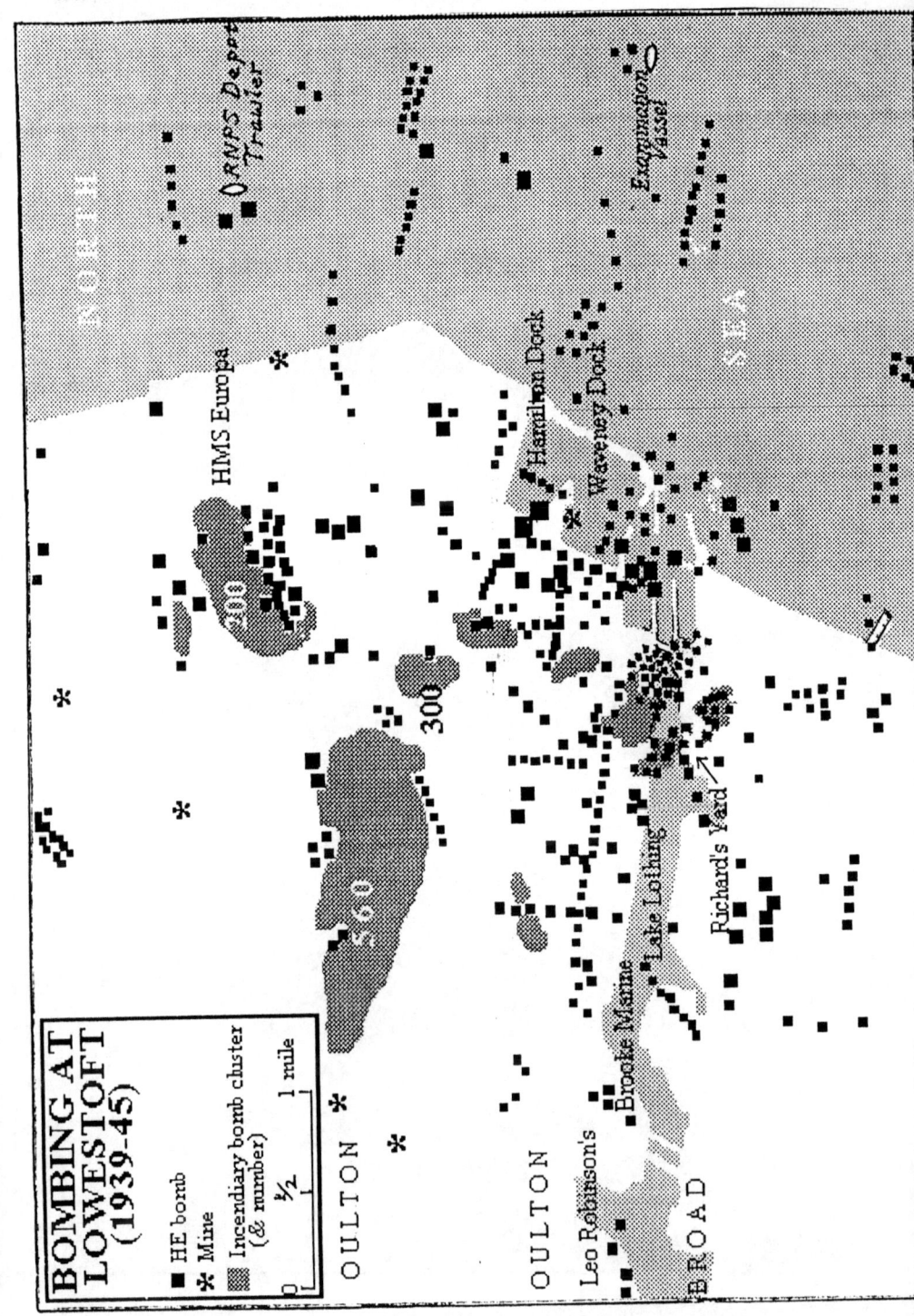

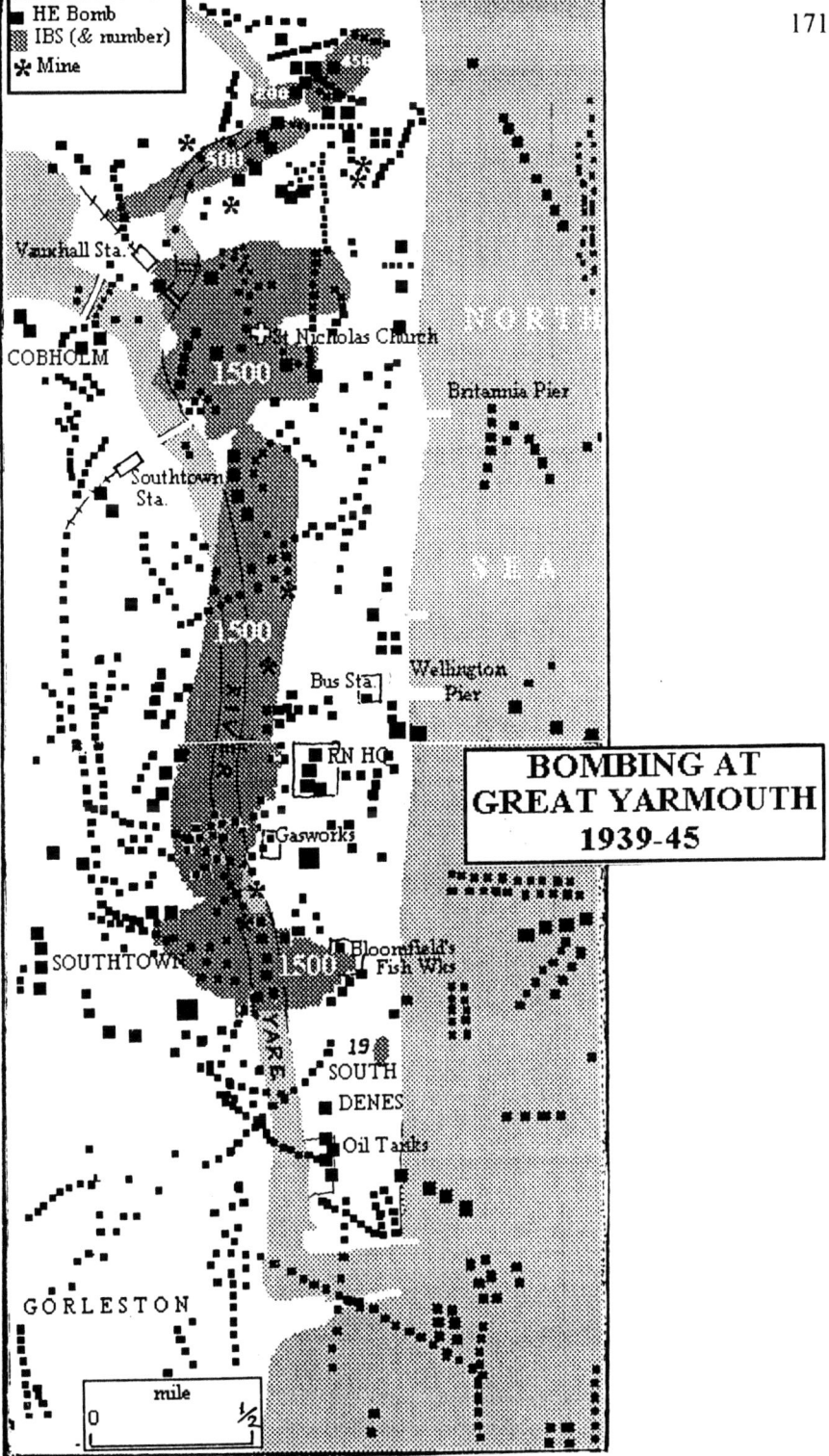

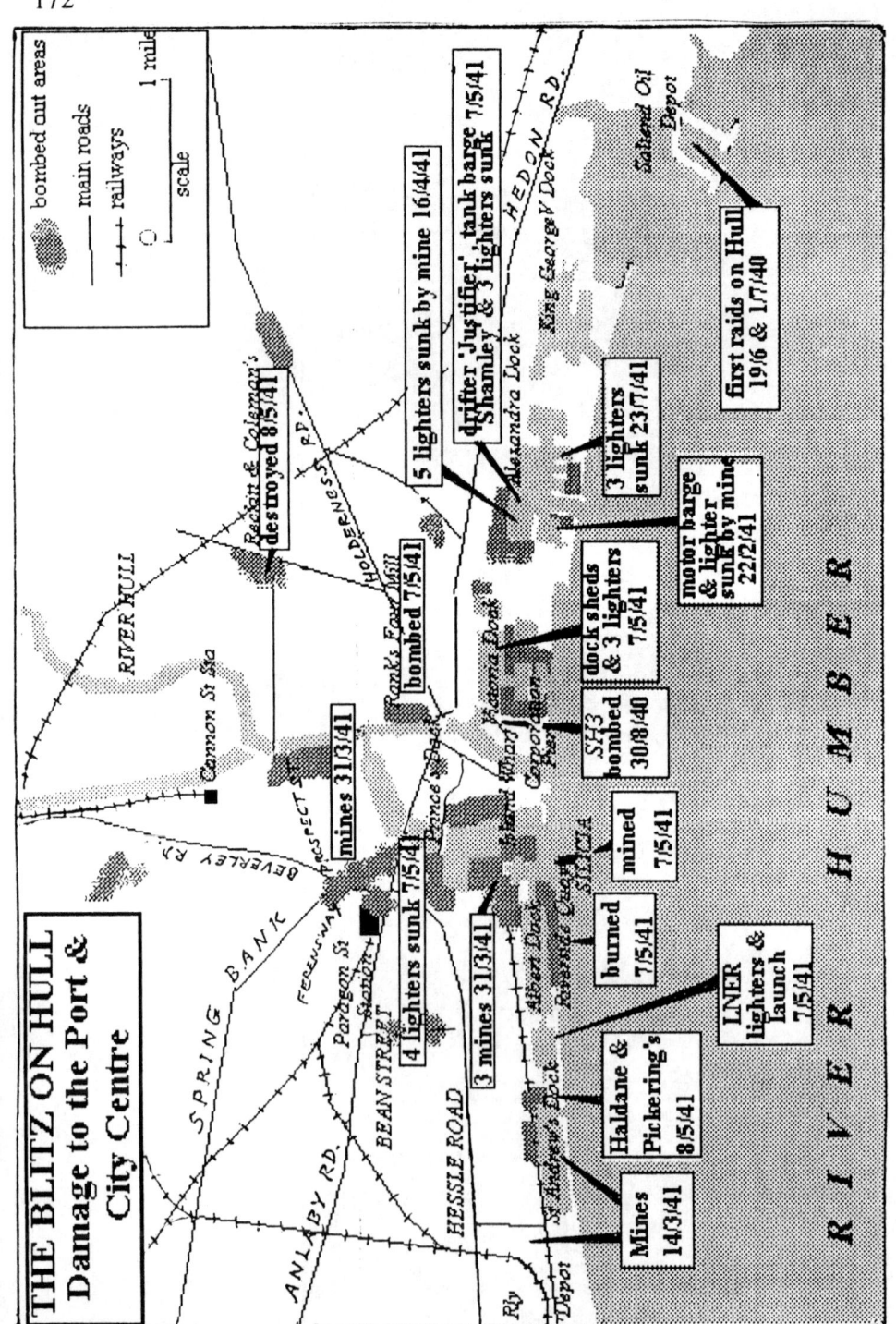

COASTAL BLITZ

modest. The Nore Command's permanent loss of warships bombed in harbour, was, after repair and salvage, no more than three paddle ships, six trawlers or drifters, and three MGBs. In the merchant fleet permanent losses included half a dozen freighters, a similar number of tugs, and rather more barges and lighters. One fishing smack was sunk at West Mersea. London aside, some 2,700 people died at saltwater locations between Bridlington and Margate (over 40% of them at Hull), out of a national total of 65,000. The Luftwaffe expended some twenty thousand HE bombs on this coastline, about one-fifteenth of its Blitz grand total. If the eventual losses among the raiders are also noted the whole campaign may be seen as a double failure. Of course the same applies to the RAF's bombing in the first half of the war at least.

8
IN HARBOUR AND ASHORE

Before the war there were four naval establishments in the Nore Command; HMSs *Pembroke* (Chatham), *Wildfire* (Sheerness), *President* (Victoria Embankment, London), and *Ganges* (Shotley). Only Sheerness accomodated operational warships. It was the magnetic mine crisis of late 1939, and the invasion threat of 1940, which swelled the manpower of the Command from some twelve thousand to over fifty thousand, and its craft of all types from some one hundred to nine hundred. Eventually the number of bases reached thirty-five, some sharing the same harbours _ though one was a hundred miles inland! According to naval custom each was given a ship name; old ships, local allusions, furry animals and insects predominated. The new bases had to requisition hotels, schools, warehouses and shipyard buildings as offices and storehouses. Personnel of shore bases and those vessels without bunks and galleys were accommodated in old ships or shore billets. A surprising number lodged ashore with their families, who often moved into rented accommodation to join them.

The extra personnel were re-employed retired men, RNR (ex-Merchant Navy and, on the requisitioned fishing vessels, ex-fishermen), RNVR (ex-civilians _ the officers were very often businessmen or solicitors in peacetime), T 124 volunteers (civilians serving under naval orders), conscripted HO (Hostilities only) ratings, and Wrens. Ultimately, in this Command, these temporary wartime recruits outnumbered the professional Royal Navy twenty to one (nationally the ratio was five to one). The smaller the base the higher the ratio. For example, among the 650 sailors at Brightlingsea in 1941 there were only three professional RN officers (two of them returned from retirement) and a few equivalent Chief Petty Officers. Usually RNR and RNVR officers were officially entitled "Temporary" and did not rise above the rank of Commander, or command a ship of more than five hundred tons or a base. They wore "wavy" instead of "straight" rank insignia; RNR waves were double and criss-crossed. The WRNS had to be reinvented in 1939, having been abolished after the Great War. Rare until 1941, by 1943 they numbered 37% of Nore Command shore staff, and, though they did not go to sea, provided most of the shore signallers, plotters, writers (clerks), drivers and domestics. They had distinctive rank titles _ for instance First Officer was equivalent to Lieutenant-Commander and Third Officer to Sub-Lieutenant. The wartime Navy also had many civilian

IN HARBOUR & ASHORE

employees _ the dockyard workers, the dockyard police, the crews of most harbour craft, and the VAD (Voluntary Aid Detachment) nurses.

At Chatham the Commander-in-Chief, the Nore, had a large staff of specialists of every kind for overseeing all major warship operations and all convoys outward-bound from the Thames as well as indirectly supervising the localised work of the five Sub-Commands. At the latter level minesweeping and shorter-distance escort were the principal concerns. Auxiliary patrol was run at this but also the NOIC and more active RNO level, together with air-sea rescue. Training bases were until 1943 for most purposes directly under the Admiralty and not the local naval authorities. The C-in-C and FOICs were assisted by CSOs (Chief Staff Officers), with all technical works on ships delegated to Maintenance Captains and all other shore duties to Base Captains. NOICs were assisted in these respects by Commanders or Lieutenant-Commanders. SOAPs ran the Auxiliary Patrol for NOICs, while RNOs were their own SOAPs. SOOs (Staff Officers Operations) were, in spite of their name, charged not with directing combat operations, but with routine ship and harbour craft movements. NCSOs (Naval Control Service Officers) were the overlords of merchant ship movements _ including convoy mustering, the examination service, harbour tugs and berthing, and marine rescue and salvage. Navigation Officers (usually RNR) were pilots for warships, and also directed the docking of ships and tested compasses and issued or updated charts. There was an Intelligence Officer with the C-in-C and each FOIC, in charge, not of espionage(!) but disseminating Admiralty intelligence to those requiring it; he also supervised the bombing decoys. Working with the one at Chatham was the MLO (Military Liaison Officer), a soldier who passed on naval information needed by the Army. XDOs (Extended Defence Officers) were in command of the offshore drifters, launches and boats which protected bases from sea raids: there were of course also Boom Officers in some places. The onshore Gunnery Officers supervised the repair and testing of guns, the issue of ammunition, and the gunnery training of personnel.

Signalling was the work of up to 10% of the Nore Command shore staff, and eventually was almost wholly done by Wr ens. Sixty signallers were employed at Chatham alone, and dealt with two thousand messages a day. V/S (Visual Signalling) meant Aldis (Morse-code) lamps or sempahore flags, and was used by War Signal Stations and examination vessels. R/T

IN HARBOUR & ASHORE

(radio telephony) _ a recent invention _ meant spoken radio communication, and with a simple code, was the link between patrol vessels, rescue craft, and operations rooms. W/T (wireless telegraphy) meant radio Mores communication, and was usually donein cypher and between escort vesels or minesweepers and shore bases. By mid 1941 all escort vessels also had Air Ministry R/T sets to talk to their accompanying fighter aircraft. Ordinary telephones were numerous enough to employ 284 Wren operators by VE Day. Every base had a switchboard via which internal and external calls were relayed. All calls between naval personnel, including ones on different bases, passed through the Admiralty's enclosed telephone network, and not the public exchanges _ many of the cables ran from harbour to harbour on the seabed. Scrambler devices were switched on for calls meant to be kept secret from the Wren operators and naval signals engineers.

About a fifth of the vessels in the Nore Command were small non-combat harbour craft. Harwich had thirty-two (see Appendix D) and Brightlingsea eight in September 1941. Liberty boats took crews to and from shore ("liberty" is naval slang for leave). Harbour duty boats bore food, fuel, ammunition and water. Harbour launches carried officers on official business. Harbour tugs berthed vessels. "Admirals' barges" were FOIC's launches. "Trotboats" or "tenders" (a "trot" was a mooring buoy) accompanied particular ships or flotillas in harbour, providing all their ship-to-shore transport. Except for officers' launches, all these craft were usually civilian-manned. In addition unmanned and unpowered storage barges and RAF-manned barrage balloon vessels were dispersed around the Thames, Medway, Humber and Harwich Harbour.

The two bases on the Medway _ Chatham and Sheerness, were the originals of the Command, and harked back to the eras of Pepys and Nelson. HMS *Pembroke*, Chatham, in war as in peace, was the C-in-C's HQ, the major dockyard for larger vessels, the Royal Marine centre, the personnel drafting depot and barracks, and also RAF Coastal Command 16 Group HQ. This complex lay north of the town in a great bend in the river, along Dock Road and behind the grassy hill (topped by a white war memorial column) called "The Lines". Area Combined HQ, mostly an underground bunker, was the operations and plotting centre for both the Navy's Nore Command and 16 Group RAF. Located off Medway Road, it was alongside Admiralty House,

IN HARBOUR & ASHORE

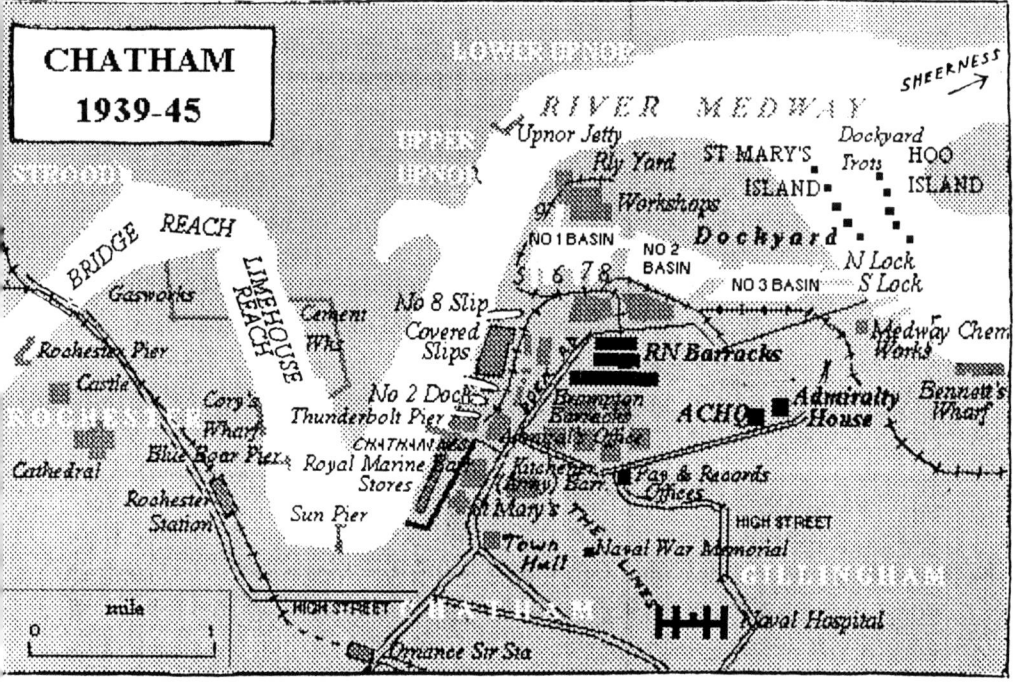

the naval C-in-C's offices.

The RN Barracks was a huge area of buildings, permanent and temporary, for drafting new recruits for the whole Navy (and not just this command): it shared this work with Plymouth and Portsmouth. The "Chatham War Division", as it was officially known, held up to twelve thousand men at one time (though the average was about eight thousand) and was commanded successively by Commodores Bennett and Nicholson. The Royal Marines also used Chatham as a manning and training base; their smaller barracks was by St Mary's Church. Chatham also had a big naval hospital and a prison. The former, on the edge of Gillingham and today the Medway (civilian) Hospital, was so large as to have thirty-eight naval doctors and forty-one nursing sisters. Surgeon-Rear-Admiral Dudley, in charge, had more letters after his name than any other officer I have heard of. For the last four years of the war there was a Nore Passive Defence Organisation, which ran the Command's air raid shelters, anti-gas measures and firefighting. It was headed by Lt-Cdr Hardcastle RNVR, formerly head of the fire brigade at Tientsin, China. The most unusual part of HMS *Pembroke* was its *farm* on St Mary's Island, the wasteland along the Medway north of the Dockyard, where flowers (for naval churches), onions, tomatoes, chickens and pigs were raised. Indeed a naval town, Chatham at one time housed sixteen thousand sailors and marines, including some seven hundred officers.

There were four Cs-in-C at Chatham during the course of the war. The second, Drax, held the post throughout 1940. In full he was Admiral Sir Reginald Aylmer Ranfurly Plunket-Ernle-Erle-Drax. The son of an Anglo-Irish baronet (his elder brother had taken the title and estate), Reginald Drax had served with Beatty on his flagship, the battle cruiser *Lion,* at Jutland, and no doubt partly in consequence, had rapidly gone through such lofty postwar apppointments as Director of the Naval Staff College, President of the Allied Naval Control Commission in Germany, and ADC to King George V. He was considered the intellectual of the interwar Navy. C-in-C Plymouth at the time of Munich, in 1939 he went to Moscow as head of the British military and naval mission to Russia, but was unable to prevent Stalin's regime from making its pact with Hitler and therefore the destruction of Poland and, in effect, the Second World War. Sent to the Nore at the end of 1939, Drax coupled the appointment with that of ADC to King George VI, presumably because Chatham was the closest major naval base to Buckingham Palace and Windsor. Drax was not the most energetic of officers (for instance, he seldom visited the bases in his command, notwithstanding the invasion crisis of 1940). But he was more than a courtier and diplomat. He strenuously argued the case for the strongest possible naval forces on the East Coast, and used his contacts in the highest circles to obtain them. Unlike most other admirals, he actually believed a German invasion probable _ and in turn that it was likeliest in his Command area. On the whole the Admiralty thought he was grabbing too many of the destroyers and trawlers needed to combat the triumphant U-Boats in the Atlantic, and even seem to have taken pleasure in criticising some of the slackness in his Command.

Drax was retired at sixty early in 1941 (after a spell as a Home Guard in Dorset he became an adviser on policy to the Admiralty), and was succeeded by Vice-Admiral Sir George Lyon, a former England Rugby player and until recently C-in-C of the West Africa Station: Lyon soon toured the whole of his Command.

Apart from some dockyard boats and the eight small motor-boats of the Medway Patrol, Chatham was not a ship base. Its outport was Sheerness,

Above & Left: **NAVAL AA DEFENCE AT SHEERNESS** The AA "Eagle Ship" *Royal Eagle (IWM)* & a balloon being raised on the Channel Mobile Balloon Barrage Vessel *Astral,* whose cat seems unimpressed. *(RAFM)*

Below: **SOUTHEND** *Sun* tugs alongside the Pier *(Herbert)*

TWO SCENES IN HARWICH HARBOUR
ABOVE: 1st MTB Flotilla fitting temporary depth charge racks at Parkeston Quay during the 1940 invasion danger. The destroyer *Whitley* is moored in the background. (Note the false bow wave to deceive enemy aircraft). Erwarton shore in the distance. *(IWM)*

BELOW: The Hunt-class destroyer *Southdown* moored off Shotley in 1943. Note the pennant (identification) number "L25", the single 2-pdr and twin-6-pdrs on the bow, and the "X"-shaped Type 286P radar aerial on the masthead. *(IWM)*

IN HARBOUR & ASHORE

or HMS *Wildfire*, ten miles downstream at the Medway-Thames corner of the Isle of Sheppey, and like Chatham the site of a big dockyard. In November 1939 *Wildfire II* was established at Queenborough, two miles south, as the minesweeping base: in July 1941 it was renamed *St Tudno*, after the old steamer moored there as an accommodation ship. It operated about forty-five vessels, originally trawlers and drifters, eventually motor minesweepers. Meanwhile *Wildfire* itself became the base for 21st Destroyer Flotilla, seven drifters, six motor fishing vessels and four Harbour Defence MLs for defence and patrol of the Thames entrance, seven AA paddle ("Eagle") ships, fourteen Thames boom vessels, three examination boats, and some forty barrage balloon vessels (including the mobile ones). In all Sheerness had some three thousand personnel afloat and 1,300 ashore, not counting the Dockyard civilians. Officially it remained the Chatham outpost: therefore its Sub-Command was entitled "Nore" and its commanding officer "Commodore-in-Charge" instead of FOIC _ the "flagship" being *Pembroke*.

Wildfire was largely contained within the famous dockyard* which, though founded in the Second Dutch War, had been built in its present form in 1823 by Rennie, the architect of Waterloo Bridge. The northernmost naval post at Sheerness was the PWSS, on top of Garrison Point Fort, at the corner of the Medway and the open sea. To the south, warships were moored in the two tidal basins, called the Lower and Middle Camber, and beyond, in the caisson-enclosed Great Basin. The Lower Camber contained the Small Vessels Pool (of Dunkirk fame), and Dry Docks 4 and 5 also opened from it. Directly behind the Middle Camber was the Quadrangle, said to be the largest single brick building on the East Coast, and containing Naval Stores: a railway track ran into this from the rear. Behind the Great Basin were Dry Docks 1, 2 and 3, where destroyers and sometimes submarines were repaired. Further back lay Captain D21's office, the Boom Defence office, and many electrical and other workshops. The general base office, HMS *Wildfire*, lay between the entrances of the Middle Camber and Great Basin. The Chief Engineer's office and the Sick Bay were south-east of the Great Basin, and the wooden hulk *Cornwallis* was moored in the river by the south-west corner. Sheerness vessels fuelled at the Medway Oil Depot, across the estuary at Port Victoria, on the southern side of the Isle of Grain, which had not yet become the site of an oil refinery.

With an eventual total of 14,940 naval personnel (in 1943) London

---
*See Chapter 15 for a map of this.

was the largest base in the Nore Command, though a very dispersed one. Initially all its establishments came under the name HMS *Pembroke IV*. Its FOIC shared the Port of London Authority Building on Tower Hill with J D Ritchie, the PLA General Manager, who ran the whole civilian aspect of the vast dock system. Both the successive FOICs, Rear-Admirals E C Boyle and M Dunbar-Nasmith, happened to be First World War submarine aces with VCs. The dock network had its own NCSO, Cdr Lord Teynham: no merchantman berthed or sailed without his orders. On the other side of the Tower, on the floating Tower Pier, was the office of the Thames Auxiliary Patrol (under former PLA harbourmaster Cdr A M Coleman DSC RN), which operated down to No 4 Sea Reach Buoy, off Southend, and berthed its craft at Greenhithe, Cliffe, Tilbury, Holehaven and Dagenham. One boat, *Water Gipsy*, was commanded by Petty Officer Sir Alan (A P)Herbert', the MP and writer, a rather unlikely-looking sailor with his spectacles and owlish face. In the upper reaches of the Thames, above Westminster, the retired Rear-Admiral Sir Basil Brooke commanded a Home Guard *naval* unit made up of amateur river sailors and their boats. Gravesend was the minesweeper base. It started late in 1939 with skid-towing launches, but in the spring of 1941 was greatly enlarged with LL drifters, tugs and MMSs, and with Cdr C S Lockhart in charge. Opposite, Tilbury was from March 1940 a degaussing and degaussing-test centre, and also a kite balloon depot.

In 1941 *Pembroke IV* was renamed *Yeoman*, while the Thames patrol was separated out as *Tower* (the allusions, of course, are to the Tower of London). Gravesend became HMS *Gordon*, for the hero of Khartoum had been a local man.

London was the main drafting and training base for Wrens. These came under HMS *Pembroke III* and stayed in hostels at Mill Hill, Golden Square (Soho), Barkeston Gardens (Earls Court), Crosby Hall (Highgate), Woodford Green and New College Oxford. The London Docks, including Tilbury, were much used for repairs and refits on warships, and at Deptford was the old-established storage or "victualling" yard (in fact it held few "victuals"). Nearby Greenwich Royal Naval College was also part of this Sub-Command. Outside it, and responsible to the Admiralty directly and not to the C-in-C, the Nore, was HMS *President*, the London Division depot of the RNVR, on board an old ship of that name, plus HMS *Chrysanthemum*, both moored alongside Victoria Embankment off the Temple. *President* was

IN HARBOUR & ASHORE

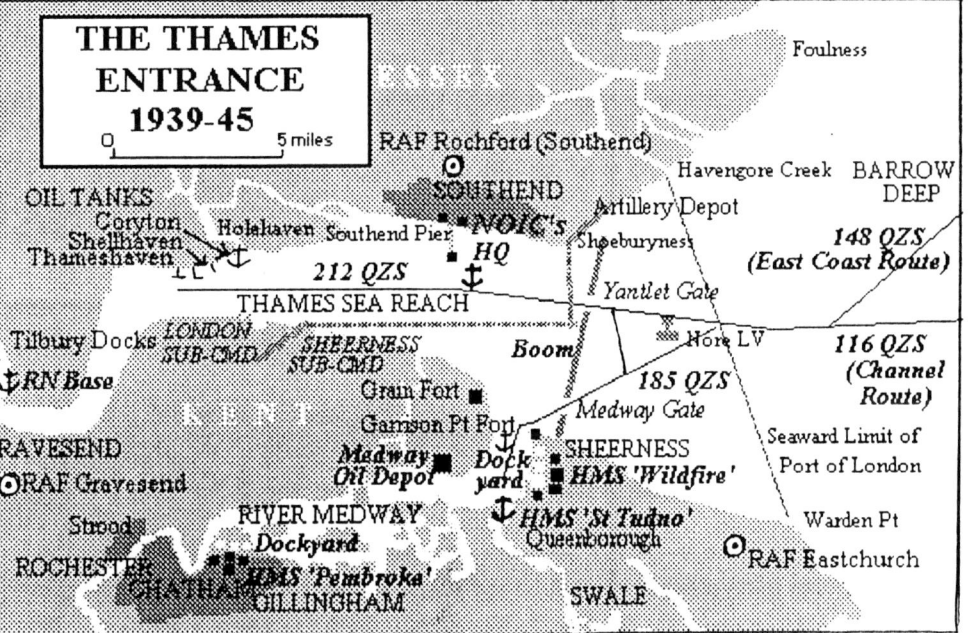

mythically also the "base ship" of the all the officers (up to Admirals) serving at the Admiralty in the Mall, as a glance at the wartime Navy Lists shows.

Southend was responsible for the mustering, briefing and Commodores of the FN and less frequent EC and CW (outbound Channel), and the reception of the FS and CE (inbound Channel) convoys. Between thirty and a hundred merchant ships *in each direction* had to be cleared by it daily. At the main shore offices, the ornate Palace Hotel and later three houses on nearby Royal Terrace, extremely complicated arrangements had to be made and endless signalling done. From here Boarding Craft (launches) went out to communicate with ships' masters. From the Pier the *Sun* tugs helped manoeuvre the ships and tow in ones that had broken down or were damaged. To the "Solarium" at the pier head, one and a quarter miles out from shore, ships' masters were at first brought for conferences at which they reported on their needs and were given sailing instructions; but increasingly a system called "buttoning" was used, in which the launches took out orders to the ships themselves _ this greatly speeded things up and was practicable once the Merchant Navy had got used to the convoy system. When an FN convoy was cleared to leave the estuary a square red flag was hoisted over the pierhead; a traingular red pennant allowed FS convoys to enter.

Along the Pier ran the narrow-gauge railway beloved of holidaymakers in peacetime. It proved useful in war, and between 1939 and 1945 carried nearly half a million servicemen out to warships and landing craft. There was also a pipeline along the Pier which pumped fifty thousand tons of water to ships. By war's end 3,367 convoys of 84,297 ships had been assembled off Southend Pier. As a potential enemy target in its own right the Pier bristled with machine guns, and had its own Defence Officer, the elderly Lt-Cdr Whittle, a former Navy diver and sprinter. Not untypically of the Luftwaffe's Blitz, of more than eighty salvoes of bombs dropped on Southend only two fell near the Pier, which was never hit.

Southend originally had an NOIC, responsible for minefields, signal stations and other activities on the Essex shore of the river, as well as an NCSO for merchant shipping. But late in 1940 the two posts were combined in the person of Captain J P Champion, who remained in charge until 1945 except for a period in 1941 when Captain Goff was NOIC/NCSO. By March 1940 the staff of the Southend Naval Control was 106 officers, including FN convoy Commodores, and two hundred signallers and messengers. For a long time there was nothing short of a feud between Southend and the FOIC's office in London over control of the convoys, since the the former claimed that independent control of the convoys had been vested in it by the Admiralty Trade Division, but the FOIC had the seniority. Time, paper and signalling channels were wasted informing Rear-Admiral Boyle of the daily Southend routine and obtaining his official approval for steps of which he knew little. Eventually the problem was solved by granting Southend operational autonomy, and, in October 1941, the formal name HMS *Leigh*.

Burnham-on-Crouch, in peacetime a sort of East Coast lesser Cowes, was, until its sudden expansion into a landing craft training centre late in 1943, the smallest base in the Nore Command. Before mid 1940 the only naval presence was the small motor yacht *Pteromys*, stationed in the Crouch as an examination boat by the NCSO Southend, and the "RNO Foulness", Captain Dane (RN retired), with an office in the Royal Burnham Yacht Club. In July 1940 the Crouch was transferred to Harwich Sub-Command, and the FOIC sent two extra patrol yachts, the *Irma* and *Ona*, followed by four more in August, when a Patrol shore base was started. At

IN HARBOUR & ASHORE

that time Burnham was under the NOIC Brightlingsea. In September an RNVR lieutenant was sent to assist Dane, and in October Burnham returned to *Pembroke IV* (London) and was classified as an MDP. During the second half of 1940 the base was in charge of two hundred moored civilian yachts, forming an invasion barrier in the Crouch and Roach. In March 1941 an MWSS (manned by four Royal Marines) was opened at Foulness Point, in April and undersea phone cable was laid to Harwich, and in June thirty-three controlled mines were placed at the Crouch entrance, with Ryder serachlights and a command post at Holiwell Point. The little base received its first R/T set in November. The total number of personnel was then no more than sixty.

HMS *Badger*, Harwich, was established during the Danzig Crisis of 1939.*At first it operated only six fleet minesweepers, twelve A/S trawlers, and some boom and examination vessels, and provided an anchorage and refuelling base for the Rosyth Escort Force. But by the end of the year it had leaped into prominence as a destroyer, submarine and MTB base, as well as having the largest minesweeping force in the country. Initially the shore staff was twenty-nine officers and forty-five ratings, with about one thousand personnel afloat. By mid 1940 it grew to some 150 officers and 1,200 ratings, with four thousand afloat.

The FOIC's and Base Captain's offices, along with most of the base facilities, were not at the crumbling little town of Harwich itself (which Pepys and Nelson knew), but one mile up the broad Stour at Parkeston Quay, the peacetime property of the London North Eastern Railway and port for Continental ferries. The Navy took over the Station Hotel and large cargo sheds, along with most of the civilian dock workforce, though curiously public passenger trains continued to pass through its territory to Dovercourt and Harwich. In 1940 the main naval offices were moved from the Hotel to Hamilton House, a redbrick former Customs building, where an underground opeartions room was opened in 1941. *Badger* gave its name to the *Westwood*, a requisitioned, German-built, four-masted sailing ship moored at the east end of Parkeston Quay for ratings' accommodation. She was said to have only been moved once, and then to face round the other way, and to be aground on her own beer and whisky bottles _ but a precisely similar story was told about *St Tudno*. Before the war oil tanks with a capacity of twelve thousand tons had been dug into the slopes just above the west end of Parkeston village. Nearby were W/T and R/T masts. Parkeston Quay was the

---
*Harwich had last been a major naval base pre-1920, and especially during the Great War, with Rr-Adm Tyrwhitt. The HQ/offices had been mainly on the Shotley (Suffolk) side of the Stour.

IN HARBOUR & ASHORE

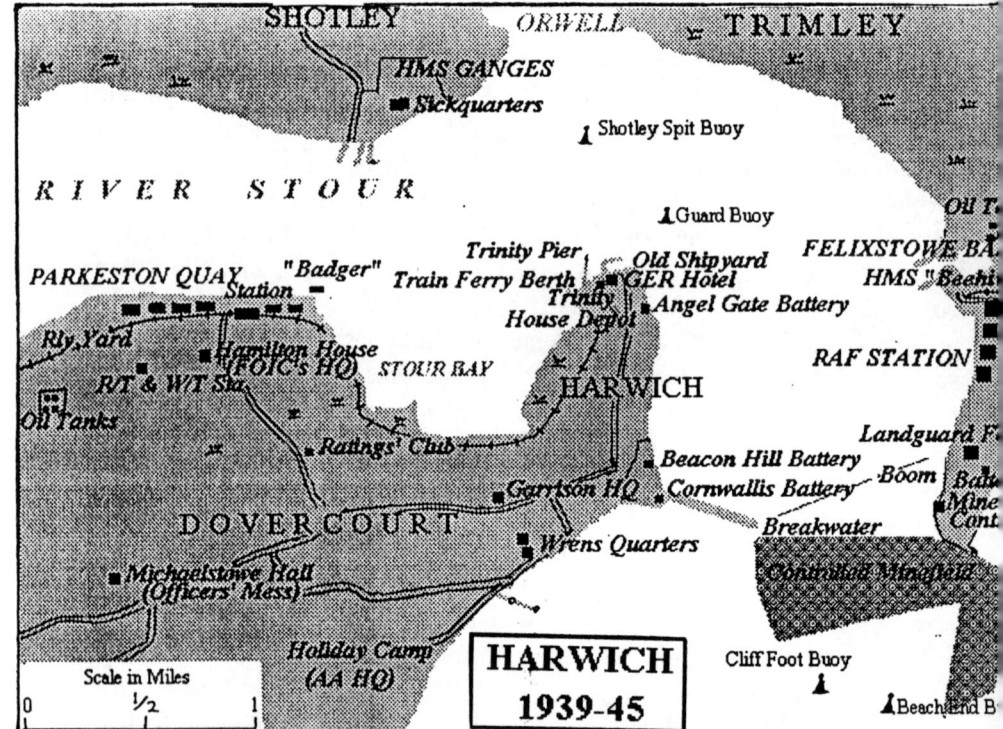

base for almost all Harwich warships. In spite of being a mile long it was often so crowded that ships berthed three or four deep, with others out on mooring buoys. In mid 1941 *Badger* accommodated eight destroyers (16th Flotilla), eight corvettes, five fleet minesweepers (4th Flotilla), nine auxiliary and six paddle minesweepers, fourteen A/S trawlers, thirty-four M/S trawlers and drifters, five danlayers, three examination and two torpedo-recovery vessels, three harbour-defence boats and seven salvage craft. In 1942 all minesweeping was put under an autonomous base called HMS *Epping*, after the trotboat used locally and in peacetime as a railway harbour ferry. Its commander, Captain T W Marsh, was unusual in being a former lower-deck man.

In 1943 the NCSO, for most of the war Cdr Champion de Crespigny, moved from Parkeston to the onetime Great Eastern Railway Hotel at Harwich Quay, nearer the harbour mouth. Already there, and using the nearby Train Ferry Berth and the eastern side of Trinity Pier for their vessels,

IN HARBOUR & ASHORE

were the Salvage and Rescue Tugs Departments, the Examination Service, and the Local Defence (AA paddler) Flotilla. The Old Shipyard (today the "Navy Yard") had been requisitioned (and in 1943 was purchased) for tug-berthing. Round in Stour Bay at Gas House Creek was from June 1943 the High-Speed Target Service, with its former MTBs and RAF launches. In October 1942 Harwich Town became a semi-separate base, with the Examination Officer, and peacetime harbour master, Cdr Froud RN (retired) as Senior Officer.

Of course Trinity Pier took its name from the Trinity House depot there and on shore nearby. With the aid of sub-depots like Yarmouth and Bow Creek this was responsible for the remaining lightships and buoys all along the East Coast. Then as now brightly painted specimens of both met the eye coming down West Street. The elegant yellow-funnelled, black-hulled maintenance ships continued to frequent the Pier; the Trinity House flagship *Patricia* (paid off as late as the 1980s, and with her wheel preserved in Harwich Church), *Ready, Alert, Strathearn* (till mined), *Pathfinder, Triton, Beacon*, and the ex-Antarctic survey ship *Discovery II*, which went to Normandy to buoy channels for invasion shipping.

Badger was reckoned to be well served with shore facilities. There were Anglican and a Roman Catholic chapels at Parkeston, sports fields at Parkeston and Shotley, and numerous pubs in Harwich Town (one, which I had better not identify, had a "red light" reputation). There was a theatre in one of the Parkeston dock sheds. Bikes could be hired for excursions into the countryside. The Maintenance Captain, Ryan, turned Michaelstowe Hall, Ramsey, into a very comfortable officers' club, and there was a ratings' club in the old County School buildings at Parkeston. Most of Cliff Road, Dovercourt, with the nearby Cliff Hotel and Elco Café, were requisitioned for Wrens' accommodation _ the number of Wrens on the base reached 380 by 1943.

One or two sailors based at Harwich were unusual. The first FOIC, Harris, had two months' sick leave in 1940 and finally retired six months after that. Lt-Cdr Lombard-Hobson, of *Southdown,* alleges that he (he does not actually name him) had a nervous breakdown and that once, during an air raid, came onto his destroyer raving and firing off a revolver. The strain on all the early FOICs was considerable; they began with almost no office staff, had limited air defence over their bases, and had to read and pass on news of lost warships at the rate of several a week. On the corvette *Guillemot* was Lt Nicholas Monsarrat RNVR, later the author of *The Cruel Sea*. Lombard-Hobson, who was at one time his captain, said that Monsarrat was reserved and unpopular but that he himself liked him.

Harwich claimed to be the busiest naval base in the country. According to Rear-Admiral Rogers, then FOIC, 487 warships used the harbour between mid-July and mid-August 1943, as compared to 271 at Londonderry, 193 at Scapa Flow and 126 at Portsmouth.

Across the Stour from Parkeston was HMS *Ganges*, Shotley. In 1899 a wooden hulk of that name, once a ship of the line, had been anchored of that Suffolk village and appointed as a training ship for Royal Navy boys. Three years later the base moved ashore, though the name remained. For three-quarters of a century it was a mainstay of Royal Navy seaman recruitment. Before the Second World War life there was at best tough, at worst wretched. Many of the boys were orphans sent straight from Dr Barnardo's Homes, with no possible choice in their careers. Instructors were notorious for brutality. Boys learning to swim were literally thrown in at the deep end, and while rowing on the Stour were swiped with towropes when they made mistakes. But for many the most dreaded part of the training was climbing the 140-foot mast, which can still be seen at Shotley. Many boys fell from this, some to their deaths when they tried to lunge for guy-ropes and propelled themselves clear of the safety net. The commanding officer at Shotley in 1939 was Captain F W H Goolden. He and a predecessor, Captain H H Rogers (1933-35) were to be among the wartime Harwich FOICs.

When hostilities began *Ganges* was on summer leave, an many of its older trainees went straight to sea without returning for a final term. The sickquarters on the site which became a small but important naval hospital, and received many wounded survivors from mined, bombed and shelled ships. In March 1940 boys' training began to close down, and a number were sent elsewhere. 264 HO ratings arrived and trained alongside the 1,500 remaining boys in April, and in May most of these latter were evacuated to Liverpool, Devonport and the Isle of Man. From then on *Ganges* gave a three-month basic training course to some three thousand fresh conscripts at a time, ultimately turning out sixty thousand, or one-tenth of all HO men. During the summer of 1940 half the trainees were posted away to a camp at Highnam Court, Gloucester, to which everyone else would have evacuated

IN HARBOUR & ASHORE

had invaders made Shotley untenable. Between then and 1944 Captain Fallowfield commanded *Ganges*, and for the last year of the war Captain Gibbs. In peace and war Shotley was also the depot of a naval Officer of Works, S S B Simeon, responsible for building work at all the East Anglian bases.

Higher up the Stour, on the Essex side, was another establishment of peacetime origin, the Wrabness Mine Depot. This stored naval mines before they were loaded onto minelayers at Parkeston _ a railway linked the two places. It had a wartime annex nearby at Copperas Wood. The combined depot had a staff of between 140 and 180 civilians.

From the start of the war there were naval personnel opposite Harwich Town at Felixstowe. Landguard Fort included the Harwich PWSS, and Felixstowe Dock was the home of the Boom Department (under Lt-Cdr Pollard and later Cdr Swayne). Early in 1940 Felixstowe Dock and Quay also became an MTB base, and in July this separated off from *Badger* as HMS *Beehive*, though it still remained in the FOIC's domain for various purposes. It had encroached on the premises of, and remained cheek by jowl with, RAF Felixstowe. Before the war the RAF's experimental seaplane base, this remained in use as a store for old flying-boats, an RAF rescue launch base, and HQ of the Harwich balloon barrage.

Up the Orwell at Ipswich was another overflow from *Badger*, eventually named HMS *Bunting*. It accommodated the twenty auxiliary patrol trawlers and eleven motor boats for the northern half of Harwich Sub-Command. In 1941 the Lowestoft-based 6th ML Flotilla refuelled there, and in the middle years of the war some of the Harwich fleet minesweepers also used it. The senior officer was only a SOAP of Commander rank, the first being Cubison, formerly of *Vernon*. His shore office was on Cliff Quay: the yacht *Bunting* was used as an accommodation ship and the launch *Freelance* was an officers' transport. The "Navydrome", in Fore Street, was the sailors' canteen and club. Numbers based at Ipswich never exceeded five hundred.

Captain G I S More RN (retired) was RNO Aldeburgh and Felixstowe, and lived in the Brudenell's Hotel on Aldeburgh seafront. He was in charge of a handful of patrol boats on the Rivers Deben and Ore, plus obstruction yachts, later replaced by a controlled minefield, on the latter. The Aldeburgh PWSS, on top of the big quadruple Martello Tower, was used to

IN HARBOUR & ASHORE

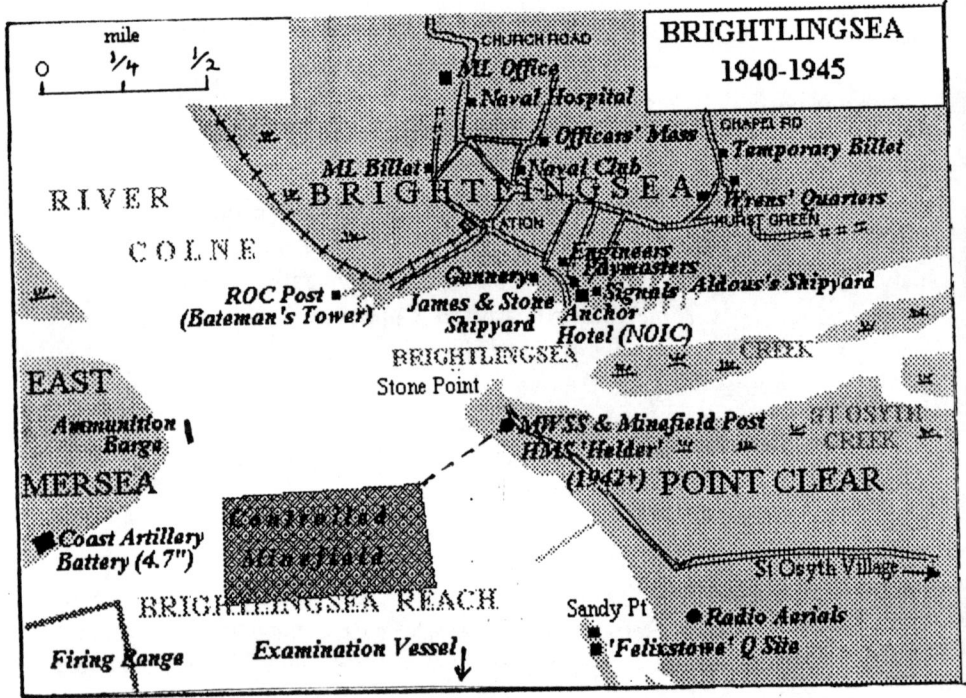

communicate with convoys.

Also under the Harwich FOIC was the NOIC Brightlingsea, with responsibility for naval activities in the Colne and Blackwater, Walton Backwaters, and the Wallet. His base, HMS *Nemo*, was an enlarged continuation of the *Vernon* experimental LL flotilla transferred from Sheerness in the winter of 1940. Before the war Brightlingsea had been a sprat and oyster fishing port and, with nearby estuary villages, a nursery of professional yachtsmen, such as those who had sailed the Americas' Cup entries of the millionaire grocer Lipton and the aircraft manufacturer Sopwith. It treasured a connection with the Medieval Cinque Ports. The NOIC's and SOAP's offices, including a tiny Ops Room, were in the half-timbered Edwardian Anchor Hotel, on the Hard. Behind, at the entrance to Aldous's Shipyard, lay a brick signals office, various store huts, and some jetties. On the other side, below Stone's Shipyard, the base used Mack's Amusements Hall and some huts as a Gunnery Depot. A little wooden customs house became the Paymasters' Office, and a Coastguard House the

IN HARBOUR & ASHORE

Engineers' Office. Inland were houses for the Officers' Mess (Regent Road), the small hospital ("Ashmore", Church Road), and the Ratings' Club (New Church Hall). The Colne Yacht Club, then a wooden building opposite James's Shipyard, was a bar and venue for officers. Across on the south (St Osyth) side of Brightlingsea Creek Stone Point (No 1) Martello Tower became in 1941 the V/S and Controlled Minefield Post, and Point Clear (No 2) Tower mounted the R/T aerials _ cables under the Creek linked these towers back to the Anchor.

The Captain ML, originally separate from and independent of the NOIC, was installed in April 1941 at the Manor House, one mile inland on the edge of town, though on the merger of ML and the main base this became the Officers' Mess.

Nemo was a microcosm of Nore Command naval activities. In mid-1941, in addition to ML-equipping, its duties included patrol, examination, minesweeping, mine recovery, repairs, rescue and minor landing craft training. For these purposes it operated up to twenty drifters and fifty motor yachts and boats. Several MTBs, MGBs and MLs were always to be seen there, but these were visitors. The personnel ashore and afloat totalled some 650 at maximum, though from mid-1942 until the end of the war the average was 250 (excluding visitors). The river part of the patrol was, as on the Suffolk and Norfolk rivers, transferred to the Royal Army Service Corps at the end of 1941 (their Blackwater base was West Mersea), and the drifter part moved to Sheerness the following May.

The first Brightlingsea NOIC was Vice-Admiral Campbell VC, a "Q ship" hero of the Great War, but he soon fell ill. His replacement, Captain Henniker-Heaton, was a gentlemanly, reticent and easygoing character _ liked rather than feared. The driving force of the base was Cdr C D Campbell RNVR, in peacetime a City banker and owner of a large steam yacht. He started the local air-sea rescue service, organised sports and fundraising activities, and handled public relations. There was some tension between the ML department and the "Anchor", occasioned by Captain (ML) Farquharson's unsociability and professional intolerance towards Henniker-Heaton and some of his gentlemanly but amaterish officers. Lax security and unpunctuality were two of the sins the "Anchor" was notorious for tolerating.

Some young officers, restless to see action, big ships, and the world, chafed at life at *Nemo*. Others found it a friendly place. The former President

IN HARBOUR & ASHORE

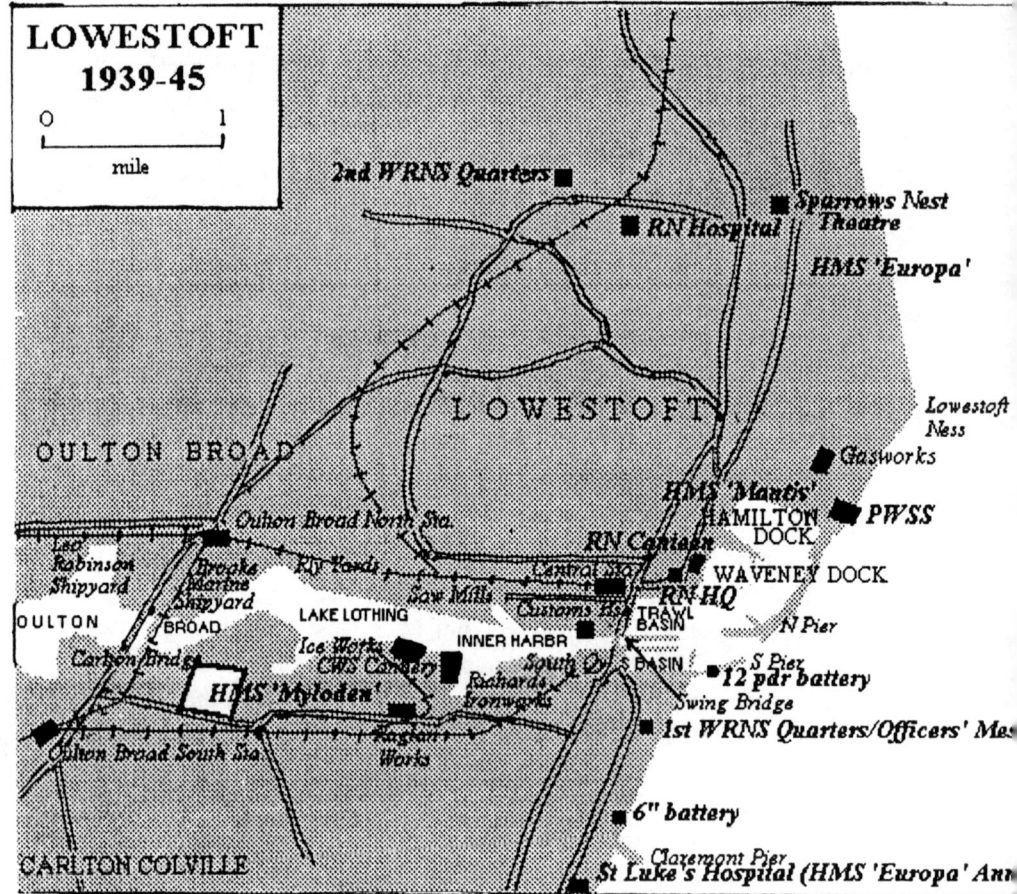

of the MTB Officers' Association described it to me as "a charming backwater" (he visited it in the later war years).

Lowestoft, in peacetime a big herring-drifting port with a seaside resort at either end, eventually featured no fewer than five distinct naval establishments, together more populous than the nearby Sub-Command HQ at Yarmouth. Lowestoft base was an annex for Yarmouth minesweepers in 1939, but in 1940 was set up in its own right as HMS *Minos*. Its duties were then all seagoing auxiliary patrol in Yarmouth Sub-Command, and minesweeping in the southern one-third of that zone. It was commanded by an NOIC, Captain H H G D Stoker DSO, and from mid-1942 to early 1945, Rear-Admiral Knowles. Its PWSS and Controlled Minefield Station, the

IN HARBOUR & ASHORE

former Coastguard Station near Lowestoft Ness, was the easternmost military post in the United Kingdom. The Examination Officer, Lt-Cdr H B Phillips RNR, was also effectively second-in-charge. In April 1941 its patrol and minesweeping departments were merged (the same happened at Harwich) and separated off under the name *Martello*, after the yacht of the "Captain M/S and P", now Cdr Cubison, formerly of Ipswich. Initially he commanded about thirteen M/S trawlers and twenty patrol trawlers and drifters. His successor, from early 1942 until war's end, was Captain F G A Theobald OBE DSO. The *Minos/Martello* base was Waveney Dock, just inside the harbour entrance and to starboard. Beyond, in Hamilton Dock, *Minos II* was started in August 1941, under Cdr K M B L Barnard, and was the MTB, MGB and ML base. To avoid confusion with *Minos* proper it was renamed *Mantis* in July 1941.

The *Minos* shore office was in Suffolk Road, just off Waveney Road and within a stone's throw of the Docks. The Ratings' Club for this base and *Martello* was in a Waveney Dock shed, together with a canteen. The Royal Hotel, on the seafront south of the harbour, was at first the "Wrennery", and then the Officers' Mess _ the Wrens moved to St Margaret's School towards the north of town. The base hospital was nearby in St Nicholas's Nursery School, St Margaret's Road (of course all the local schoolchildren had been evacuated).

Above the swing bridge and the railway station were the large sheets of water called Oulton Broad and Lake Lothing: here were extensive yards for the building of motor minesweepers and power launches.

The numerically largest contingent at Lowestoft, one mile north of the harbour and usually devoid of vessels of its own, was HMS *Europa*. Briefly entitled *Pembroke* X at the start of war, this was the personnel depot and training base for the Royal Naval Patrol Service _ i.e, it supplied the crews for all the Navy's trawlers, drifters, yachts, motor minesweepers, smaller air-sea rescue boats, and HDMLs. In spite of its name (of Great War origin) the RNPS began by crewing, not patrol vessels, but A/S and M/S craft, as its badge stated. But "fishery protection" trawlers followed and from 1940 it was of course the mainstay of the Auxiliary Patrol. Its HQ, also used as a temporary billet, was a prewar seaside theatre called the "Sparrows' Nest", though this had taken its name from an old cottage on the clifftop above. The last "bill" of the theatre, the comediennes Elsie and Doris Waters, were sunning themselves on the lawn in front when the Navy arrived. *Europa* also requisitioned houses on and below the cliff and put up numerous temporary huts. It trained its sea cooks (in what style of cuisine one dare not ask) in the Church Road School, and its stokers and enginemen at the old St Luke's Hospital, on Kirkley Cliff. Its billets were scattered all over the town, some as far away as three miles. Some were notoriously grubby and overcrowded. *Europa*, with six thousand trainees at its peak, provided a wartime livelihood for thousands of landladies, or "mas", as the sailors called them _ indeed they saved the whole town from total penury. Commonly the trainees, having been assembled into crews and given such basic training as "square-bashing" and gunnery, picked up their vessels at Hull, where most were fitted out. The three Commodores successively in charge were Piercey (1939-41), de Pass (1941-44) and Duke (1944-5). *Europa* trained seventy thousand men in all, including James Callaghan, then a conscript seaman, later a prime minister. Its site is now marked by a conspicuous white memorial, commemorating the 2,385 RNPS men who lost their lives in all waters. Behind the old theatre is a small museum featuring honour boards naming all those *Europa* men who were decorated.

BADGE OF THE RN PATROL SERVICE

Some men recall *Europa*, its billets, and the "mas", with affection. But former Ordinary Telegraphist Marshall described it to me as "this horrible dump", and went on to say:

> "It was a poverty-stricken set-up, and enough to break the spirit of the most hardy of types, let alone a greenhorn landlubber fresh out of training, which was heaven by comparison. Any ship or billet would be better than the 'Nest', even the dirtiest drifter or the scruffiest trawler imaginable...There were matelots in every room, and three or four to a bed if you could find a bed. The teenaged skivvy who opened the door to me welcomed me with 'For Christ's sake not another bugger!' Table manners were unheard of; if you didn't grab, ten others did".

Callaghan himself was once quoted as saying he had spent the most miserable night of his life sleeping on the floor of one billet in Carlton Road, but later denied saying it, and returned to take part in a reunion at the Nest.

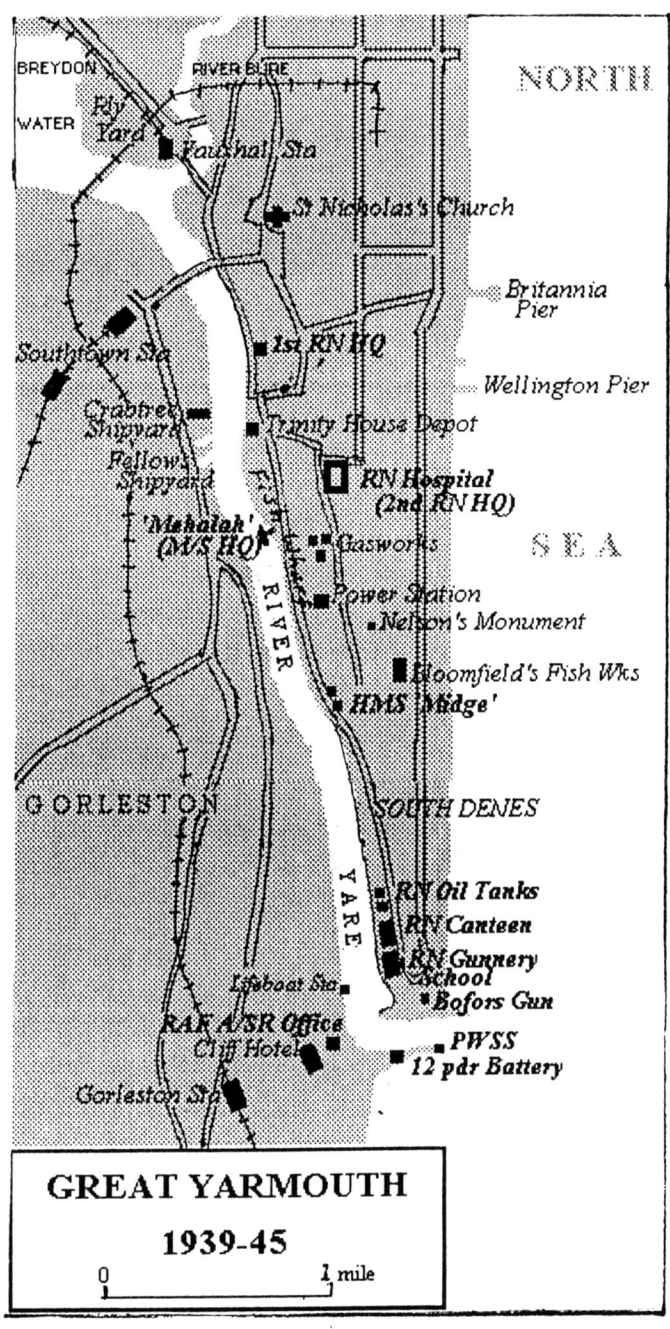

GREAT YARMOUTH 1939-45

IN HARBOUR & ASHORE

The WVS (Womens' Voluntary Service) were invaluable in helping to staff the canteens and running the more gentle entertainments for the sailors. Lady Somerleyton, of the stately home near the town, could be described as the patroness of the base, and was often seen serving in the canteen with Mrs Stoker, wife of the NOIC.

In 1943 some two hundred officers and seven thousand ratings were based at Lowestoft (including one of the country's largest Wren contingents), of which *Europa* accounted for one third of the officers but three-quaters of the ratings.

Yarmouth base, or HMS *Watchful,* was originally the home of an NOIC and minesweepers subject to the FOIC Harwich. In July 1940 it was upgraded to an FOIC's base, with Admiral Fullereton in command: at that juncture it berthed thirty-two "O" trawlers and fourteen LL trawlers and drifters. The base, like the old (and formerly walled) town and the fishery wharfs, faced the River Yare, not the famous beach. The FOIC's office was in the Walrond Institute, on the quayside, until this was bombed out _ he then moved to the staff quarters of the RN Mental Hospital, which had moved to Lancaster. In January 1941 HMS *Midge*, the ML and MTB base, was started by Cdr E R Lewis DSO DSC; its officers' quarters were in Shaddingfield Lodge, another part of the old hospital. Minesweepers were separate almost from the start, first under Captain Cronyn, then Captain Caspar Swinley DSO DSC, a former Dover destroyer commander, who lived aboard an old sailing barge, the *Mehalah,* moored at the Fishwharf. Swinley was a public relations man, who ensured civilian goodwill for the base. The minesweeping base name was *Miranda*. Between them *Watchful, Midge* and *Miranda* averaged about 220 officers and 2,200 ratings in the middle part of the war.

Unlike Lowestoft, Yarmouth berthed its vessels along river quays, not in docks, though at both places many were anchored offshore in the "Roads" in fair weather. The unpopulated southern end of the peninsula on which Yarmouth stands, the South Denes (site of a Zeppelin-terrorising seaplane base in the Great War), provided space for fuel tanks, AA gun sites, etc. The PWSS and a 12-pdr coast battery were on Gorleston Pier, at the harbour entrance. Inland Yarmouth supervised the RNO Wroxham, who ran twenty-six small motor boats as a Norfolk Broads patrol _ Wroxham, Acle, Brundle, Ormesby, Potter Heigham and St Olaves were their moorings. Ormesby was also the site of Yarmouth's naval W/T station.

IN HARBOUR & ASHORE

It now seems almost unbelievable that warships, even small ones, were formerly to be seen on the Broads and River Waveney. But MTBs, MGBs and MLs were built, and repaired, locally (mainly at Oulton Broad), and sometimes passed from Yarmouth to Lowestoft via the inland route, on which the "The Ship" pub at Haddiscoe Bridge was a favourite halfway house.

The Wash was supervised initially from King's Lynn, but mostly from Boston, Lincolnshire _ nets, tended by one ship, and two or three yachts, being the only naval defences. The first RNO Boston was Cdr C B Vacher DSO, formerly CSO at Harwich; later Captain K N Humphreys took over. In 1943 a landing craft base was added, and Boston became known for a time as HMS *Arbella*. It originally controlled an RMS party at Mablethorpe, a signal station south of Skegness, and RNOs at King's Lynn and Mablethorpe. It was in Humber Sub-Command. Some eighteen miles north-east, right on the coast at Ingoldmells, was HMS *Royal Arthur*, a huge HO ratings' training base at the old Skegness Butlin's Holiday Camp. Opened at the outbreak of war, its permanent staff was some 750 strong, including up to 110 officers, headed by Rear-Admiral F A Buckley, and it held up to four thousand trainees.

The FOIC Humber "set up shop" at Hull on the outbreak of war. His shore base, HMS *Beaver*, administered trawler-equipping, RDF-fitting, repairs and a Naval Control Service, initially from Savile Street. After the May 1941 Blitz the *Beaver* office moved to the New Manchester Hotel, and its W/T office to an LNER ferry boat at Corporation Pier. Later it moved to three houses in Sunny Bank, but had to shift to three more after a bomb fell in the rear. Because Hull continued to be a major seaport in spite of the war, most of the Humber organisation was from the outset established across the estuary at *Beaver II* _ i.e, Immingham and Grimsby.

Immingham berthed cruisers and destroyers when these were Humber-based in 1939 and 1940. Its most famous sailor was Captain Lord Louis Mountbatten, of the 5th Destroyer Flotilla. His royal connections and wealthy style jarred incongruously with the grimy coal docks, but he did know how to lead. The base had few recreational facilities until he used his influence to equip a cinema. When Holland fell, and invasion first threatened, he had three hundred Guardsmen brought to the area as a stopgap until other troops arrived. He knew almost everyone in his flotilla, of whatever rank, by

IN HARBOUR & ASHORE

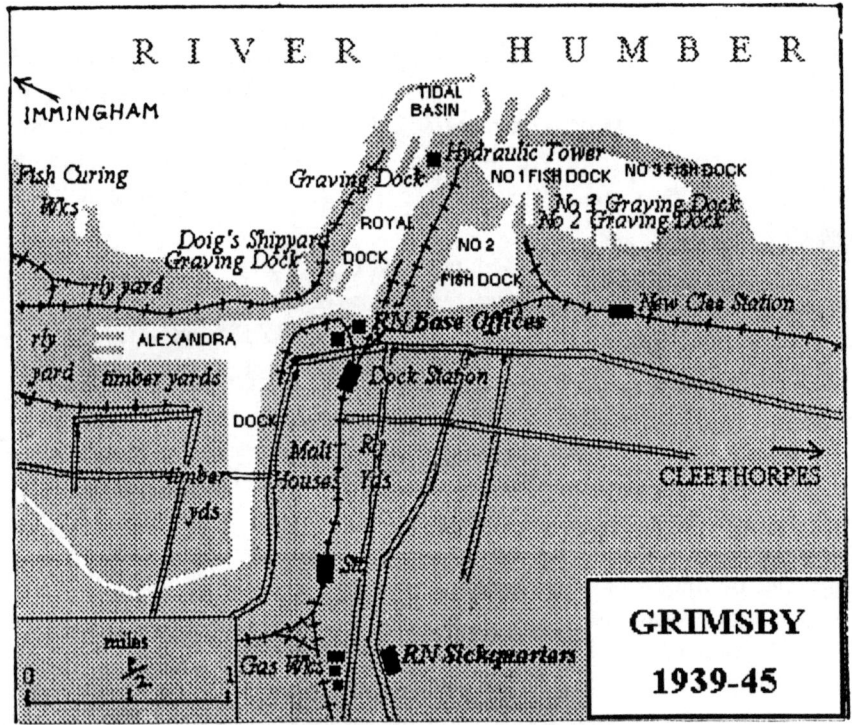

name and by sight, yet is said to have had his blindspots about the class divide: when he visited an officer billeted in one of a row of terraced houses he went to the wrong door and, when told his mistake, exclaimed in puzzlement "There can't be more than one hosue here!"

In November 1940 Vice-Admiral R V Holt CB, the FOIC Humber, moved to Immingham from Hull. The NOIC Grimsby, Captain W K E Coulen, thereupon exchanged his status for that of Holt's CSO. The Grimsby naval offices were in the Pekin (Dock) Buildings. Beneath the extraordinary landmark of the Hydraulic Tower, the Grimsby Fish Docks and Royal Dock provided much abundant berthing space, and in mid-1941 accommodated two mine-destructor ships, forty-five M/S trawlers and drifters, eighteen patrol trawlers, twelve harbour defence patrol vessels, seven boom vessels, five examination and eight river patrol craft, and nine balloon drifters. The Humber sickquarters was inland in the old YMCA building in Heneage Road. The W/T station was at Cleethorpes, and the oil tanks and mine depot were at

IN HARBOUR & ASHORE

Killingholme. The Humber PWSS was at Spurn Point (with a second under command at Flamborough Head, the rocky promontary overlooking Bridlington, where Nore jurisdiction gave way to Rosyth).

Beaver III, at Immingham, was an ML and MGB base started in 1942: it was shortlived. Immingham also housed the RMS party which resulted from the merger of Bridlington's and Mablethorpe's in 1943.

The total Humber shore staff was about 1,200, with some 2,500 afloat _ discounting those on the larger warships which left in the autumn of 1940.

Immingham, like Parkeston, was no more than a village. Grimsby struck even many of the sailors as rough and dingy, though for long it seemed safe from air raids, unlike Hull up river. The Navy particularly patronised two of its pubs, the "Lincoln Arms" and "Sheffield Arms" _ they were phenomenally crowded and squalid.

The war did not completely stop the huge fishing industry of the Humber. Though most of the boats and men had been taken by the Patrol Service, some shifted to Scotland or the West Coast. Eighteen Grimsby fishing boats, *other than naval ones*, were lost in the war, and with them 144 lives. In 1943 the Hull trawler-owners chartered small craft left in the Humber but not used by the Navy and brought in fish from Iceland. There they exchanged pianos, prams, coal and even a car for fish. Only one ship on this run, the large *Rother*, was refrigerated. The chief organiser of this, Owen Helyer, made a profit of £500,000 which he denoted by prior agreement to the Ministry of Food. In 1944 the faroes fleet came into the Humber, with large catches of national nutritional importance.

In the summer of 1943 Vice-Admiral Sir Hugh Binney toured the Nore Command to recommend manpower economies. He advised the takeover of Harwich Sub-Command by Yarmouth and the demotion of the former's FOIC to NOIC, the removal of all estuary minefields, the closure of the examination service at lesser ports, and the merger of HMS *Nemo* with the new landing craft base, *Helder*, on St Osyth Stone, and the demotion of its NOIC to RNO. Other RNOs he wanted paid off. His proposals were inevitably unpopular, and significantly few of them were carried out. However, the minelfields were "weighed" in August and at the end of the year the posts of NOIC and Captain ML Brightlingsea were merged.

IN HARBOUR & ASHORE

I have concentrated on the naval bases in this chapter. But I ought to include the bases of 16 Group RAF Coastal Command _ at various times North Coates, Donna Nook and Strubby in Lincolnshire, Bircham Newton, Docking and Langham in Norfolk, and Detling, Eastchurch and Manston in Kent. All these were on or very near the sea, and their planes by definition operated over the North Sea. It has always taken a disproportionate number of ground personnel to keep aircraft flying compared to those ashore at naval bases. North Coates had nearly as many personnel as Yarmouth naval base for most of the war, and there were more airmen at Manston than sailors at Dover. Previous chapters have alluded to some of the host of radar, barrage balloon, AA, coast artillery, searchlight and infantry sites and bases along this coast. In 1941 over 120,000 troops were posted beside it, more than double the manpower of the local Navy. In 1943, though there were perhaps thirty thousand RAF and WAAF personnel based within sight of this coast, the total number of airmen and airwomen in the Eastern Counties exceeded a third of a million, three-fifths of them Americans: this was five times the Allied naval strength in the region.

All three services depended on the East Coast for weapons training and testing. The various training camps, firing ranges and testing grounds formed an almost unbroken chain. On the North Kent coast were the Margate Light AA practice camp and the Reculver bombing range. In Thames Sea Reach was a trial area for Coastal Forces' boats built up river. On the Essex shore, in succession, were Shoeburyness artillery, Foulness small arms, Dengie aircraft strafing, the USAAF Blackwater, and the Middlewick (Colchester) machine gun ranges. There was another Coastal Forces' trials area off Mersea, nearby parts of the Blackwater Estuary were used for landing-craft training, and the Clacton Butlin's was another big Light AA camp. The Naze was used for anti-aircraft training and experiments, including early attempts to guide rockets by radar. In Suffolk Brackenbury Camp, Felixstowe, was a base for artillery practice shooting. At Orfordness the RAF tested more radio-controlled rockets, while the Navy used the nearby sea for practice firing and the Army employed the remote heaths and woodlands around Sudbourne, immediately inland, as a training area. (I have already dealt with the prewar electronic warfare research at Orfordness and Bawdsey). On the North Norfolk coast Weybourne was a major Heavy AA range, and in the Wash Wainfleet Sands were pounded incessantly by Bomber Command, so heavily concentrated in adjacent Lincolnshire.

9
THREE BRITISH OFFENSIVES

Most of the warfare described so far has been defensive. During the first half of the war there was no possibility of a serious British surface-ship or amphibious attack upon Occupied Europe. Stealthier, and, frankly, less telling, tactics had to be used, and with whatever imperfect weapons were available. I shall now turn to three such limited offensives, one from under the North Sea, two from above it.

The fame of the German "Unterseeboote" in both world wars has disguised the activities of the Royal Navy's own submarines. During the 1914-18 War Harwich was an important submarine base, as one of the monuments in Shotley Naval Cemetery testifies. In 1939 there were only two British submarine bases in the North Sea _ Rosyth, and Blyth in Northumberland, where the boats were best positioned to act in support of the Home Fleet and to intercept warships trying to break out of the Heligoland Bight and Skagerrak. However, well-founded rumours of German plans to invade the Low Countries, and the activity of U-Boats in the southern North Sea, prompted the Admiralty to activate Harwich as a third base.

Early in November 1939 3rd Submarine Flotilla was transferred there from Malta, where it was superfluous now that Italy appeared to be staying neutral for the time-being. The flotilla had six boats; *Salmon* (Lt E O Bickford), *Sealion* (Cdr B J Bryant), *Shark* (Lt P N Buckley) and *Snapper* (Lt W King) from Malta, and *Sterlet* (Lt G H S Haward) and *Sunfish* (Lt-Cdr J E Slaughter) from home bases. These S-class craft, built between 1933 and 1937, were smaller than most previous British submarines, though larger than most of the early wartime U-Boats, but were mechanically reliable and well armed with six bow torpedo tubes, one 3-inch deck gun and one machine gun apiece. Each crew was from thirty-eight to forty.

3rd Flotilla was based on the depot ship *Cyclops*, formerly the merchantman *Indrabarah*, at 11,300 tons and 460 feet long a huge ship by Harwich standards. "Cycle-box", as she was for some reason known, and her six charges berthed near the west end of Parkeston Quay, where the LNER provided shore space including a lare transit shed. The submariners were among the most efficient sailors at Harwich and converted this shed into an HQ and store within three weeks. There was no skilled labour to be spared from work on the surface ships, and the Admiralty expected the flotilla commander, Captain Sir P Ruck-Keene, to arrange refits at Sheerness. However he took the unusual step of advertising for labour in the newspapers, thereby enrolling 120 civilian workers from all over the country within three weeks. His second-in-command, Cdr G W G Simpson, organised recreational facilities which became the envy of the rest of *Badger*. Part of the huge transit shed was converted into a theatre to seat a thousand, complete with scenery, props and curtain. Entertainers (such as Gracie Fields) were hired from the West End to give performances, and attracted packed audiences on winter evenings.

3rd Flotilla's patrol areas were in Heligoland Bight and initially also off the Dutch coast. The submarines went out on the surface by night and then lay submerged amid the enemy minefields and convoy routes, scanning the horizon through periscopes for German warships or blockade-running merchantmen, which they both reported to base and themselves attacked with torpedoes. The submarines remained in enemy waters for up to five days at a stretch, and nightly resurfaced to recharge their batteries. A complete patrol round-trip could last up to ten days.

The first patrol took place on 2 December 1939. Lt Bickford's *Salmon* was sent to a point eighty miles west of Jutland. The opportunity was used to test the recall arrangements from Harwich pubs and cinemas adopted by HMS *Badger*. Two days later *Salmon* sighted U 36 cruising on the surface, and closed in and destroyed her by torpedo. At this stage of the war the sinking of a U-Boat was still a rare event. On her next patrol, on 12 December, *Salmon* came across the famous German blockade-running liner *Bremen*, much sought after by the British and now making her final homeward dash after coming from New York via Murmansk. Bickford could have stayed submerged and despatched his massive target with torpedoes, but obeyed International Law, surfaced near the liner, and ordered her to stop. However at that moment a Do 18 flying-boat appeared, and *Salmon* had to dive and lose her prize. But the submarine's patrol was not quite over: at dawn next day, on her way back from the Bight, she sighted the German six-thousand-ton light cruisers *Leipzig* and *Nürnberg* returning from minelaying off the Tyne. She fired a wide salvo of torpedoes and gained one hit on each vessel. Bickford surfaced in order to radio for aircraft or other submarines to come and finish off the targets, but the cruisers fired a hail of shells at him and forced him to submerge. By the time he had got out of range and

(this page & overleaf)
THE HARWICH SUBMARINES

ABOVE:
    Sealion in Harwich Harbour in January 1940 _ the LNER ferry *Vienna* in the background.
(Lt-Cdr Bryant)

LEFT:
    U 36 (Kplt. Fröhlich), sunk by *Sealion* in November 1939. U 36 was one of the early "coastal" U-Boats which mined along the East Coast at this period.
(Pictorial Press)

LEFT:
Snapper coming alongside her depôt ship, *Cyclops*, at Harwich (Parkeston) after her victorious cruise in Danish waters, April 1940.
(Daily Mirror)

BELOW:
Snapper's prisoners being led along Parkeston Quay.
(News Chronicle)

ABOVE: H 44 leaving Parkeston. HMS *Ganges* (Shotley) in background.
BELOW: Aircraft from North Coates. In the upper photo 22 Squadron Beauforts are loading torpedoes, in the lower Strike Wing Beaufighters are raiding a German convoy off Borkum. *(all photos IWM)*

RIGHT: **Operation "Outward"** Incendiary balloons being released from Landguard Common, Felixstowe. Landguard Fort, with its PWSS on the roof, is on the far right, and the mine control tower is right of centre.
(PRO)
BELOW LEFT: The crew of the corvette *Mallard*, assembled in Harwich Harbour.
BELOW RIGHT: Officers of the same ship beside the stern 2-pdrs.
(Professor Tyler)

LEFT: Mallard, **looking towards the stern.** *(Tyler*

BELOW: SS *Bovey Trace* **bombed and sinking off Lowestoft _ 17 Nov, 1941** *(RAF Museur*

THREE BRITISH OFFENSIVES

resurfaced, both had disappeared towards the German coast. But his torpedoes were not wasted: both cruisers were badly damaged underwater, had to go into dock for months, and missed the Norwegian campaign.

Bickford received a hero's welcome at Harwich. He was promoted to Lieutenant-Commander and given the DSO. He later had other successes off Norway, and just before taking his final leave of Harwich in May once again made the newspapers by getting married (at Dovercourt Church).The young submariners were glamourised by press and public in the way the Battle of Britain pilots were later to be.

However, a typical British submariner's life was far from being a roll call of victories. The Rosyth flotilla suffered disastrous losses in the winter of 1940, including some sister-craft of the Harwich S-class. The average Bight patrol was gruelling and hazardous but hardly eventful. In February Cdr Simpson, relieving the captain of *Sunfish* for a leave, took her out in response to an invasion alarm. For three days he hovered around a mysterious green light twenty miles west of Heligoland, rumoured to be a mustering buoy for enemy warships, without seeing, let alone sinking, so much as a rowing-boat.

At the end of that month 3rd Flotilla received extraordinary orders _ to prepare to enter the Baltic to support the Finns fighting the Winter War against Russia. The First Lord, Churchill, was an exponent of the proposed expedition and the move was almost certainly his own idea. Stores were gathered in the Parkeston transit shed and Baltic charts were studied, but on 13 March the order was cancelled owing to the Russo-Finnish armistice.

Ten days later 3rd Flotilla was joined by part of the French 10th Submarine Flotilla, which was to take over the Dutch coast patrols in order to relieve the British for the planned operations off Norway. For five weeks Parkeston flew the Tricolor and White Ensign side by side, and a two-nation submariners' football team was started. This was, of course, still in the pre-Vichy days of Entente Cordiale. The French boats, the last of which did not arrive till early May, were *Achille, Amazone, Antiope, Calypso, Casablanca, Circe, Doris, La Sibylle, Orphée, Pasteur, Rubis* (a minelayer), *Sfax* and *Thetis*. Their depot ship was the aptly named *Jules Verne*, and the flotilla commander Captain Belot.

On 5 April Cdr Bryant's *Sealion* got into trouble for failing to report "a small darkened vessel (which) swung to port stern on...(and) seemed to have a suspiciously keen lookout" until after her return from the Skagerrak patrol for which she was headed. The evasive ship was the minelayer *Ulm* (see Chapter 2). This matter was soon pushed into the background, however, for on 9 April Germany invaded Denmark and Norway by land, sea and air. The rest of 3rd Flotilla immediately followed *Sealion* to Scandinavian waters.

Sealion's report for that dramatic month continues:

"9 April...a most unpleasent day. Glassy calm, surrounded by fishing boats, and enemy aircraft continually flying low and close...Our periscope was used most judiciously.

11 April. First day of the sink on sight German ships policy. Tried to intercept German battle cruiser in swept channel at 56°20'N, 11°35'E*.

Let two ships go _ assumed neutral, then torpedoed third (German *August Leonhardt*) _ trawlers and aircraft in area so no attempt to rescue survivors.

12 April. First day of unrestricted warfare..."+

Lt King's *Snapper* sank a petrol carrier on 12 April and then two ships in convoy with a single salvo at dawn on 15 April. She returned to an enthusiastic welcome at Parkeston with four German seaman prisoners on board _ two others had died en route and been buried at sea, after one of the other prisoners had made a passionate Nazi oration over them. *Sunfish* sank no fewer than four ships. *Shark*, patrolling west of Jutland, found no targets. But she was fortunate compared with *Sterlet*, which was depth-charged by German trawlers and sunk with all hands in the Skagerrak on the 18th.

When his five remaining submarines returned to Parkeston Ruck-Keene invited his civilian workers on board for morale purposes. Cdr Simpson later commented; "This simple act was important; our civilian technicians rightly considered themselves part of the flotilla".

At this juncture the French boats all left for Scotland in order to join the Norwegian campaign themselves. Between 20 and 27 May Ruck-Keene, *Cyclops* and 3rd Flotilla finally pulled out of Harwich to take part in the Narvik operation. They left behind Cdr Simpson and a small nucleus staff to organise an anti-invasion flotilla with five H-class ex-training submarines sent from Portland and Portsmouth on 15 May in reaction to the fall of Holland.

Simpson and his staff had to make bricks without straw. They had no

---

*=between the Danish island of Anholt and the Great Belt. +PRO ADM 199/1835.

THREE BRITISH OFFENSIVES

depot ship and lost their transit shed to the destroyer base. They had to set up HQ in the Customs offices at Parkeston Station, siting their mess in the inspection room. The H-class were veterans of 1918 and thoroughly weak and obsolete. Incredibly, their wireless sets were contemporary with the boats themselves, possessing so short a radius (sixty miles) that signalling back to base while on patrol was impossible. They also lacked echo-sounders, so that entering harbour in darkness they had to rely on lead soundings made by a rating who, standing on the open deck, was in no small danger of drowning in rough weather.

But "Shrimp", as Simpson was known, was a shrewd and energetic organiser. He obtained new W/T sets and echo-sounders by "diverting" unused stocks from the RAF and Admiralty respectively. Typical of his efficiency were the preparations for evacuating the base in the event of invasion (see Chapter 4). When Admiral Sir Max Horton, then head of the Submarine Service and himself a celebrated submariner of the Great War, visited Harwich in August and asked to see these precautions, Simpson

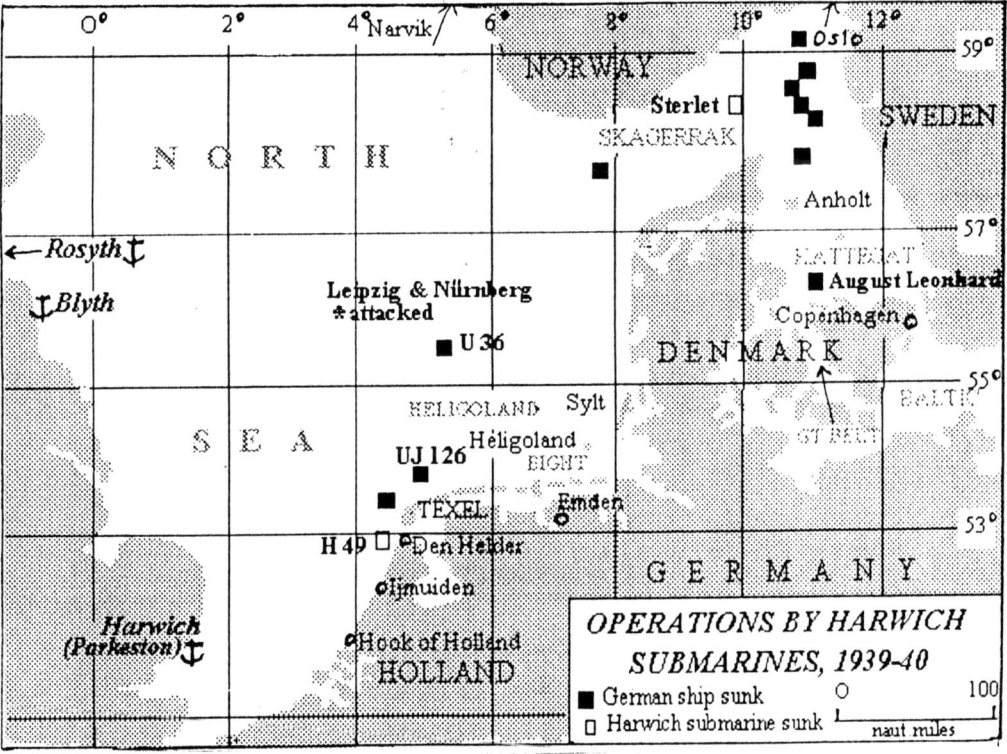

THREE BRITISH OFFENSIVES

summoned a train from a hidden siding in three minutes. On board were stores, ammunition, torpedoes, living accommodation, radio sets, food and water _ all the essentials, in fact, for starting up a fresh base wherever ordered. Simpson commanded the Harwich submarines from mid-May to late-September 1940, going on to lead the Malta-based 10th Flotilla, which did so much to harry Rommel's supply lines. After the war he, Bryant, and King all published memoirs with brief accounts of the Harwich submarine base.

The five original vessels of the ad-hoc Harwich flotilla were H 28, 34, 44, 49 and 50. H 31, commanded by Lt M D Wanklyn, subsequently an "ace" in the Mediterranean, and H 69, joined later. One of H 28's officers, Sub-Lt Edward Young RNVR, was to include yet another account of the Harwich base in his book *One of Our Submarines*.

For the first fortnight of June L 23 and 26 were also stationed at Harwich. Although as old as the H-class, they were still among the best-armed (two 4-inch guns on each plus torpedo tubes), fastest (up to seventeen knots) and largest (1,150 tons) in the Navy. They dated from a time when the submarine was regarded as a submersible destroyer or cruiser rather than a light raiding or patrol craft. One further, equally unusual(!) type of submarine came to Harwich. As a bombing and air reconnaissance decoy four 150-foot wooden dummies were built at Wivenhoe Shipyard and moored on buoys off the west end of Parkeston Quay. Each had a dummy sailor complete with cap and white jersey, and a dummy gun. The wooden submarines remained long after their real counterparts had left, but were eventually abandoned after breaking loose in a gale.

The patrol areas of the H class were off the Dutch coast. A two-boat standing patrol was maintained until September 1940 off the Texel. In addition to reporting enemy shipping movements and acting as an outer screen against invasion, the submarines began to attack the German equivalent of our East Coast Convoy Route, running between Emden, Ijmuiden, and Rotterdam. On 18 July Wanklyn's H 31 sank the German anti-submarine boat UJ 126 north-west of Terschelling. On 27 September Lt Langley's H 49 sank a two-thousand-ton merchantman in the same area. But H 49 soon paid for this _ on 18 October she was depth-charged and destroyed with all hands (thirty officers and ratings) by German patrol craft near Den Helder. Captain G Philips, Simpson's successor, assembled all the

THREE BRITISH OFFENSIVES

rest of his base on Parkeston Quay and made a quiet and dignified announcement.

After Simpson's departure the Harwich submarine base was soon run down. Three boats left for other bases in October, leaving only H 28 and 49. After the latter's loss H 28 lingered alone in harbour until the beginning of November, when she too was withdrawn. The history of Harwich submarine base had lasted almost exactly a year. The RAF and the Navy's MTBs took over its Dutch-coast reconnaissance and raiding functions.

A proper account of the offensive waged on the enemy coast by the East-of-England based aircraft of RAF Bomber and Coastal Commands would vitiate my policy of focusing on the English East Coast itself. However, in view of the Luftwaffe attacks on this coast, and the considerable scale of the RAF's North Sea operations, it is necessary to say something in the interests of balance.

During the first two years of war the RAF probably aimed more bombs at the enemy on the western seabord of the Continent than on the cities and factories of Germany. In 1939, before it was allowed to raid a single land target, Bomber Command struck at the German fleet in Heligoland Bight. Blenheims of 2 Group, based at Wattisham (Suffolk), Wellingtons of 3 Group from Mildenhall and Honington (Suffolk) and Feltwell (Norfolk), and Hampdens of 5 Group, in Lincolnshire, were involved _ flying in formation in daylight. Twenty-four Wattisham Blenheims of 107 and 110 Squadrons raided Schillig Roads as early as the second afternoon of war. They hit the pocket battleship *Admiral Scheer* with three bombs which failed to explode. The only German casualties and serious damage were caused when one plane crashed onto the bows of the light cruiser *Emden*. Seven bombers, including some in a Wellington squadron which also took part, failed to return. In the worst of these suicidal raids, forty-four 3 Group Wellingtons lost twelve of their number off Wilhelmshaven on 18 December. The formation was carved up by Me 109s which were (unbeknown to the British) guided by "Freya" radar _ the RAF air gunners did well to destroy two of their tormentors. Two of the damaged bombers almost reached the English coast before ditching. A 9 Squadron plane crashed off the Humber and its crew were saved by a Grimsby trawler. A 149 Squadron machine came down off Norfolk, but though its crew were seen struggling with their inflatable dinghy by other returning aircraft, the Cromer and Sheringham lifeboats found nothing after a long search.

In September 1940 the RAF again concentrated on North Sea targets when it threw its bombers against the invasion shipping in the ports of the Low Countries and Northern France — what the airmen called "Blackpool front". This nighttime offensive came to a head simultaneously with the Battle of Britain. In scale, spread, and accuracy, it resembled the German offensive against British East Coast ports the following year. In September over three hundred British Blenheims, Wellingtons, Whitleys and Hampdens raided Ostend, attacking it on twenty-five nights out of thirty, and dropping as many tons of HE (all in small 250- and 40-lbers) and incendiaries. The other main targets were Antwerp, Dunkirk, Boulogne and Calais. The British were optimistic. Bomber Command Intelligence Reports speak of every Ostend dock being hit, some repeatedly, and of fires visible fifty miles away and a pillar of smoke two miles high. Later it estimated eighty barges sunk at Ostend on the 13th/14th (a quarter of those counted on recent reconnaissance photographs of the port), and eighty-four destroyed at Dunkirk on 18/19th.

These claims were, however, as exaggerated as those made at this period by Fighter Command. Since the War British historians have claimed the destruction *or damaging* of only a more modest ten per cent of the enemy's two thousand invasion craft (up to the point when they began to disperse, on 21 September) and German historians record that two-thirds were merely damaged. Belgian Civil Defence reports remark on no great damage at Ostend, which would have been devastated had most of the RAF bombing not been highly scattered and inaccurate. Hitler did not call off "Operation Sealion" because of RAF night raiding of the invasion ports, though it probably did cause him to reflect on the likely German losses once his fleet was out in the Channel in daylight. But the courage of the aircrews was undeniable. Sergeant Hannah of 83 Squadron won a VC during the 14th/15th Antwerp raid, when he used his bare hands to put out a fire on his damaged Hampden and brought her home. He was eighteen.

Less intensive bombing of these potential invasion ports continued for the rest of the year and right through 1941, coming to a head again in the autumn of the latter year, when there were fears that if the Germans captured Moscow, or broke off their Russian advance owing to the winter, they might resurrect "Sealion". Early in 1942 Emden, the closest German seaport

---

*my estimate of one bomb in five being delivered to British towns and harbours by the Luftwaffe also seems to fit the RAF raids on Ostend.

THREE BRITISH OFFENSIVES

to Britain, began to come under heavier RAF attack than the French and Belgian ports (ultimately 56% of its was destroyed, compared with 10% of Ostend). That year, and during early 1943, small daylight raids were made on Ijmuiden, Rotterdam, Flushing, Zeebrugge and Ostend, but with factories and power stations, not ports, as the targets. Sharing in part of this campaign the US Eighth Air Force made its debut.

The enemy's coastal merchant shipping was always an objective. By night, for almost the whole war, Bomber Command apportioned a sizeable proportion of its sorties to "gardening" _ influence minelaying in the Bight, Skagerrak, Kattegat and Baltic. 2 Group, whose aircraft could not reach the interior of Germany, concentrated on "nomads" _ low-level strikes at the convoys both by day and night, and suffered as high a rate of loss as any part of the RAF in consequence.

Fighter Command, using bombs as well as strafing, joined in this same campaign in 1941. Most of its attacks were made from Manston, on the Isle of Thanet promontory pointing towards Ostend. 601 Squadron, and from mid-year also 242, were involved in "roadstead" attacks on shipping leaving port between St Valéry and Ostend. 242's commander, Squadron Leader Whitney-Straight, was very soon shot down off the former place and taken prisoner. By September squadrons based at, or using, Manston, had attacked seventy-four ships of over one thousand tons each, plus hundreds of small craft, and claimed to have sunk 44,600 tons for the loss of thirty-three planes. Manston boasted, somewhat prematurely, of the Channel being closed to the enemy in daylight.

Further north the anti-shipping work was increasingly undertaken by 16 Group, Coastal Command, from Bircham Newton and later North Coates, Langham (Norfolk) and Manston. 22 (Beaufort) Squaudron had started to use North Coates, a new airfield by the sea six miles from Grimsby, for minelaying in April 1940. On 12 May five of its aircraft bombed Waalhaven, the Rotterdam airfield just seized by German paratroops. In mid-year 812 Fleet Air Arm Squadron's Swordfish biplanes joined the base, and helped with the bombing as well as convoy-escorting. On 15 September 22 Squadron claimed to have sunk a four-thousand-ton ship entering Ijmuiden, and four days later launched torpedo attacks on invasion craft off Den Helder. On 21 December six of its Beauforts were sent to raid the giant battleship *Tirpitz* (sister of the *Bismarck*) at Wilhelmshaven: they bombed but did not catch sight of their target, which was not to succumb to the RAF for another four years. In the summer of 1941 407 Canadian Squadron, of American-built Hudsons, started operating from North Coates, carrying out air-sea rescue searches and raids on the Dutch coast convoys. On 22 January 1942 one Hudson, captained by Pilot Officer Dann, crashed on the emergency airfield at Donna Nook, beside the Humber entrance, killing its whole crew and thirteen ground staff _ a total of eighteen. That 15 May, soon after moving to the huge dirt airfield of Bircham Newton, 407 Squadron suffered utter disaster on a Dutch coast raid. Four Hudsons were lost, a fifth was destroyed along with all its crew by crashlanding at Docking (Norfolk), and a sixth was wrecked landing at Coningsby (Lincs). Twenty-one airman died. Flight Lt Christie, who led the operation, won the DSO.

Coastal Command could be ruthless. 206 (Hudson) Squadron, of Bircham Newton, was certainly quick on the trigger. On 24 July 1940 it attacked a flotilla of Soviet tugs and salvage craft off the Texel, and on 2 October it aimed at a hospital ship, despite her illuminated Red Crosses, because she failed to answer wireless signals.

I shall give one more example from Bircham Newton to convey a little of the flavour of such operations. On 30 January 1942 500 Squadron sent five Hudsons to raid a small convoy near Sylt. One plane was lost in the sea and not located by an air search from its home station. A second was damaged and forcelanded at Winterton. A third divebombed the convoy, then moving through ice floes with navigation lights showing, and claimed one bomb hit on a ship's stern. Flying back with the altimeter showing two hundred feet, it nevertheless struck a rock with its starboard propeller. Feathering that engine caused all electricals to fail, including the gyro-compass and airspeed indicator. The Hudson was continually picked out by searchlights and flak, and apparently braved all five or six AA barrages of the major German North Sea ports. It was unable to steer and was buffeted by dense snowstorms. After two and a half hours it reached Norfolk, circled a village and vainly tried to get an answer on its radio and to lower its undercarriage. It then fired seven Very lights and bellylanded in a field. The crew were lucky, since only the observer was (slightly) injured, with cuts, a black eye, and a tooth knocked out. Meanwhile another Bircham Newton Hudson, from 279 Squadron, was searching for this plane. It twice hit the sea accidentally _ the escape hatch was torn off and the logbook and charts were

THREE BRITISH OFFENSIVES

blown out. With its radio dead the aircraft survived the snowstorms andlanded at base after three gruelling hours.

Incidentally a young RAF officer based at Bircham Newton in 1945, just before returning to Oxford, in time became more famous than anyone else on the wartime East Coast: his name was Richard Burton.

Late in 1942 the North Coates "Strike Wing", made up of 143, 236 and 254 Beaufighter and "Torbeau" (Torpedo Beaufort) Squadrons, was formed. In time it became the most effective of *all* Allied weapons against the enemy in the North Sea. After a disappointing start it suddenly began to sink a string of enemy craft from April 1943, subjecting the Dutch coast convoys to a storm of torpedoes, rockets and cannon shells. By VE Day it had sunk seventy-one ships, and assisted in sinking at least as many more _ most of these within the Nore Command area. Its total included ten U-Boats, eight midget U-Boats, four E-boats, five R-Boats (three of the former and one of the latter in a single raid on Boulogne on 13 June 1944), a destroyer, a dozen minesweepers and a score of flak ships. It had accounted for the bulk of the eighty-six ships sunk by Coastal Command in the Nore Command. Unfortunately its score also included the Lowestoft MTB 734, accidentally strafed and sunk three weeks after D-Day.

One of Strike Wing's new Beaufighter XIIs was wrecked in an unusual way on 4 April 1943. Two mechanics, AC2 Robinson and LAC Walton, then on a charge in the Guard Room, escaped, boarded the plane, and tried to take off for Eire. They crashed, yet survived and ran off towards Grimsby. Captured at Cleethorpes hours later, they were brought back for court martial, with (one assumes) a serious outcome.

In 1944 the Anzac (second) Strike Wing was formed with Australian and New Zealand squadrons, and based at Langham.

The strangest part of the British East Coast air offensive involved no planes at all _ it was the incendiary *balloon* campaign "Operation Outward". For the origins of this we must return to the night of 16/17 September 1940, when violent gales over England tore loose most of the barrage balloons (next morning Harwich reported only having one left), and took them out out over the North Sea. Next day scores of them were over Denmark, Sweden and even Finland. Their trailing cables brought down power and phone lines, paralysed the Swedish west coast railway (which was electric), and blacked

THREE BRITISH OFFENSIVES

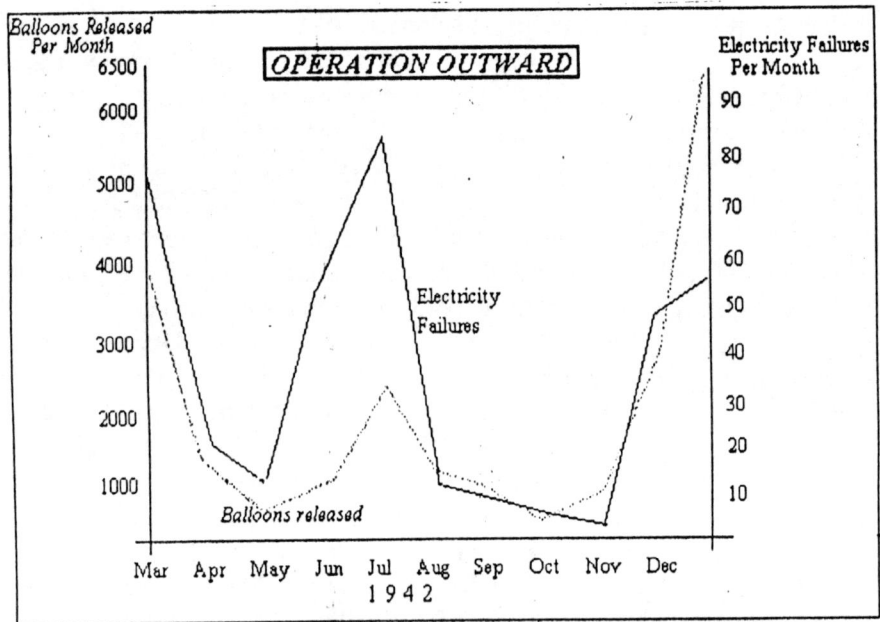

out much of Southern Sweden. The British learned all this in detail from the Stockholm newpapers and radio. This set experts thinking, and in November a map was drawn which showed that if balloons were released from Yarmouth on the prevailing west wind most would descend in *Germany*. Next March the Navy (not the RAF, as one might assume) produced a plan to send the balloons from the Dover and Felixstowe Boom Depots, with the aim of firing the German forests as well as destroying power lines. The balloons were to be like those used in weather forecasting, and each was to trail an "incendiary sock" which, on wrapping round a wire or branch would snap a phial of flammable chemicals inside. It was almost another year later, however, before four Royal Navy and Royal Marine officers and 110 ratings set up the first, most-secret, "Outward" base on Landguard Common, Felixstowe. After a false start, the campaign proper began in March.

On the 29th the Army's 54 Division reported:

"The appearance of a number of strange-shaped balloons over Felixstowe (forty was the number quoted) with trailing ropes to which were attached white metal canisters, caused great curiosity and some trepidation amongst the local population...in Maidstone Road, Felixstowe, the sight of the balloons caused two women to commence screaming hysterically

THREE BRITISH OFFENSIVES

that the invasion had commenced and Nazi parachutists were coming down. Their uproar was promptly quelled by the local ARP warden".*

Further along the coast, the balloons became a perpetual nuisance at Lowestoft and Yarmouth: the air-sea rescue unit at Gorleston protested about the number of false alarms caused by reports of these apparent "parachutes". The balloons, incidentally, were not very dangerous to life and limb: the Air Council vetoed the Navy's suggestions for explosive bombs, which might kill neutrals. Later "Outward" was extended to bases at Yarmouth (for a time moved to Waxham) and at Oldstairs, near Dover. It continued intermittently until September 1944.

The campaign must have been a mere pinprick to the enemy, of course. No overall assessment of its modest effects seems to have been made by either side. However, British records on it do survive from 1942, and are of interest. During that year from about six hundred to six thousand balloons were released per month, according to weather conditions. And, each month (according to postwar intelligence), they caused between seven and ninety electricity failures in German-dominated Europe: i.e, one balloon in eighty was effective. Within the first month the Swiss and Hungarian authorities were issuing solemn warnings to their publics, and once again considerable disruption was reported from Sweden. This gave some indication of the effects in Germany, where official silence was maintained. That year the peaks in electricity power cuts in Germany coincided with the peaks of "Outward", as my graph shows. Postwar analysis of German power company records indicated that in May Pomerania had thirty-nine electricity failures due to the balloons, and East Prussia thirty-five. These two German regions were about seven hundred and nine hundred miles respectively from Felixstowe.+

---

*54 Division War Diary (PRO WO 166/6380).

+Incidentally "Outward" was not unique, as the Japanese tried a similar campaign against the Western United States _ it killed one man in Oregon.

10
WAR ON THE CONVOY ROUTE _ PART 2

The transfer of most of the Luftwaffe to support the invasion of Russia, while greatly reducing the overall threat to Britain, did not much diminish the peril of East Coast shipping. A gradual decline in enemy air activity, and therefore in both mining and bombing, and a corresponding improvement in British air defence, convoy protection and minesweeping begun in about March 1941 and continued for a full year. Only then, in the spring of 1942, did shipping loses quite abruptly die away, and a breakthrough could be said to have occurred.

In fact, just as the Germans were beginning their invasion of Russia in June 1941, they struck heavily at North Sea shipping.

During the week of the 21st-28th ten vessels were badly bombed, of which eight sank. The colliers *Cormount* and the Norwegian *Skum* (both bound for Ipswich power station) were bombed within sight of Harwich, but the former was beached for repair on Shotley Spit and the latter towed to Southend. An Army gunner on *Cormount*, Bombardier H Reed, posthumously won the George Cross and Lloyd's War Medal for an act of unusual courage. Although the ship was flooding from an aerial torpedo hit, and had also been sprayed with machine gun bullets which had torn open his stomach, he refused first aid until he had carried the ship's wounded Chief Officer down two steel ladders to the sick bay. He died uncomplaining in his own entrails and blood, and was landed at Harwich.

In this Blitz three M/S trawlers were sunk _ *Nogi** (off her Yarmouth base), *Tranio* (of Harwich, off Cromer) amd *Force* (near 8A Buoy). Two of the sunken merchantmen were Dutch _ *Schieland* and *Montferland*. E-boats cooperated with the Luftwaffe, and in the same week sank *Hull Trader* and *Trelissic* off Cromer, while a mine disposed of *Kenneth Hawksfield* off Southwold.

On 1 July the Luftwaffe sowed a large acoustic minefield in the Thames Estuary. Some of the mines overshot into North Kent. As Lt Cliff RANVR defused an impact-damaged Type-G at Leysdown, on Sheppey, it gave him electric shocks and hissed and sparked spitefully. He had to keep

---

*Like many requisitioned Humber fishing trawlers she bore a Japanese name. Apparently the Japanese had sent charity money after Hull fishermen were killed on the Dogger Bank by panicky sailors on board the Russian fleet bound for the war with Japan in 1904.

WAR ON THE CONVOY ROUTE _ 2

the mechanism covered because the Type-G included a booby trap detonated by photo-electric cell. Afloat the Sheerness drifters *Devon County* (LL) and *Receptive* (Patrol), the sailing barges *Rosme* and *Blue Mermaid*, and a private launch in the Crouch were among the victims. The Brightlingsea patrol drifter *Lord St Vincent* was mined near North East Gunfleet Buoy. Her crew, under Group Officer Lt Jenkins RNVR and Skipper Alexander RNR, tried to drift ashore on a Carley float with the tide, but it changed and threatened to carry them out to sea. They were eventually saved after attracting the attention of the Harwich examination boat by waving a shirt tied to a paddle. One man died in agony aboard the float, a second died in Shotley hospital.

Far to the north, that same week, the Grimsby "O" trawler *Akranes* was bombed and sunk off Bridlington. Lt Harvey RNVR, the Group Officer on board, was rescued, and for the second time, since he had been sunk with another Grimsby "O" trawler, *Sea King*, the previous October.

To help guide their bombers and E-boats to shipping targets the Germans commonly sent over the Ju 88s of Reconnaissance Group (F)122. One of them prowled near FS convoys off Bridlington, and was accordingly dubbed "Flamborough Fannie": another located northbound convoys off Suffolk at dusk before they disappeared into the night.

Squadron Leader Stanford Tuck had shot at, and shot down, many a German plane over the East Anglian coast over the previous year. He fought against the Luftwaffe from an unusual angle that July, however. Convalescing from the air crash described in Chapter 16, he was off Cromer en route from Southend to Canada on a ship in EC 38, when a Ju 88 attacked. One of its bombs bounced off the sea, flew right over his head, bounced again on the other side of the ship, and then struck SS *Homefire*, which burned out and sank! Tuck grabbed an unmanned deck machine gun and fired back in vain. That night, near the Dudgeon, a motor boat approached his ship and, in Oxford English, asked her identity. The convoy Commodore having given it, she was subjected to a hail of tracer shells _ from an E-boat. Lt Monsarrat, on *Guillemot*, recalled a similar trick being played on a convoy he was escorting in 1942: his corvette replied with all guns and (incorrectly) claimed an E-boat sunk.

On 7 August the first MMS was lost: No 39 was mined near Longsand Head. Considering their numbers, these craft suffered remarkably few losses. Sheerness minesweepers, which worked down to the Naze (excluding the Wallet), were now second in importance only to Grimsby's. On the 30th four such LL drifters, *Monarda, Internos, Forerunner* and *Vernal* blew eleven acoustic and three magnetic mines in just over an hour on the North Thames foreshore off Southend. Acoustics were prone to go off in batches by chain reaction; five exploded simultaneously, and then the blowing of two nearby magnetics triggered another pair. *Forerunner* and *Monarda* were both sunk within the next ten weeks.

On 24 August Harwich witnessed a disaster reminiscent of that of the *Gipsy*. A minelaying plane had flown over four nights earlier and been taken for a bomber. Its true mission was revealed when the Norwegian collier *Skagerrak*, bound from Newcastle to Ipswich Power Station with a cargo of coke, detonated two mines, about two hundred feet apart in three fathoms of water, in the Orwell one mile above Harwich Harbour. The ship was blown clean in two and sank with the loss of all but five of the twenty-three crew on board, who included Danes, Swedes, Mexicans, and five Britons _ two Army and two Navy gunners, and the Ipswich pilot. (Some of the dead were buried at Shotley).

An innovation at this time were the moored influence (as opposed to moored contact and ground influence) mines. Types P and T were air-laid cylinders, but there was also an influence version of the ship-laid, round, Type V.

Among the mine victims in September was HMS *Corfield*, the second of the mine-destructor (*Borde*-type) ships to be fitted out _ she was lost off the Humber on the 9th. The worst incident that month, however, was the mining of the tanker *Vancouver* near Sunk Head Buoy on the 21st. She had come all the way from Halifax Nova Scotia en route to Shellhaven. So quickly was she engulfed in flames that only three could be rescued by the Rosyth destroyer *Valorous*. The death toll of forty-five was the highest on any cargo ship in Harwich waters.

One area the enemy rarely bothered to attack, owing to the scarcity of shipping, was that supervised by Boston _ i.e, the Wash and inshore waters off Lincolnshire outside the Humber. On 3 November 1941 Boston suffered its only loss in a vicious moment. Its patrol yacht *Ouzel* had embarked three soldiers, in addition to her naval crew of seven, to survey the Army beach defence camouflage at Skegness and Mablethorpe. Just off the

WAR ON THE CONVOY ROUTE _ 2

latter place the boat was mined with the loss of all on board. How unlucky they were may be judged by the fact that only two other enemy mines had ever been swept within eight miles of Mablethorpe.

No odder incident occurred off the wartime East Coast than that on 28 October 1941, when the coaster *Roslea* left Lowestoft for Hartlepools but ended up in the opposite direction, captive with the Germans in Belgium. Her steering had apparently jammed, and she passed right through the Mine Barrier. The official records seem to contain but two bare mentions of her loss. All very puzzling.

After a lull, that autumn saw another fierce upsurge in bombing attacks. Between late October and mid-November these sank the merchantmen *Antiope* and *Friesland* (off Cromer), *Nicholaos Piangos* and *British Fortune* (off Orfordness), *Brynmill* and *Marie Dawn* (off the Humber), *Corhampton* (off Withernsea), and *Bovey Tracey* (off Lowestoft), as well as the "O" trawler *Francolin*, off Cromer. To sink so many ships within three weeks, most of them in strongly-escorted convoys, was probably the heaviest blow struck against East Coast shipping by German bombers. On 22 November SS *Bestum*, like *Skagerrak* a Norwegian collier bound from the Tyne to Ipswich Power Station, was also sunk (on Cork Spit), but salvaged. On the 24th, in one of the last of this run of attacks, *Ardenza* was bombed off Orfordness but reached Yarmouth safely.

The E-boats put in some dramatic appearances in the second half of 1941. On 20 August they damaged SS *Dalewood* and sank the Polish freighter *Czestochowa* off Wells. Next month *Duncarron*, the Norwegian *Eikhaug*, and *Teddington* were sunk further east. Von Bätge's 4th Flotilla was responsible in all these cases. He was undoubtedly helped by the continual R/T tuning and chatter emanating from the British escorts. Cdr Coats, the new captain of the Harwich destroyer *Worcester,* protested strongly about this practice. After the *Teddington* sinking he wrote: "On the night of 17/18th a voice with a very slight foreign accent shouted 'Hello, hello, hello!' on the exact wavelength. If anyone had answered he would have been D/Fed"*. But on the night of 12/13 October FN 31 was attacked on the outer route between 56B and 57 Buoys, and the small freighters *Chevington* and *Roy* were sunk by 2nd E-boat Flotilla, newly returned from the Baltic. According to their pursuers, which were the Rosyth destroyers

---

*PRO ADM 199/670. "D/Fed"=direction found.

WAR ON THE CONVOY ROUTE _ 2

Westminster and *Wolsey*, the Harwich destroyer *Cotswold*, and some MGBs, the raiders numbered nine or ten.

On the night of 19-20 November 2nd Flotilla executed a bold torpedo foray against FS 50 near 55A Buoy, north-east of Yarmouth. Two of the usual small colliers, *Aruba* and *Waldinge*, were sunk by S 41 and S 105 respectively. But the third victim was HMS *Badger*'s oiler *War Mehtar*, on her way back to base with a supply of fuel from Grangemouth, on the Forth. At 11,680 tons displacement she was the largest ship ever to fall victim to an E-boat (in this case Lt Rebensburg's S 104) on the East Coast. FS 50 had numbered as many as fifty-eight merchant ships, but unlike some earlier convoys, its escort had not been weak, comprising the Rosyth destroyers *Verdun, Vesper* and *Wolsey*, the D21 (Sheerness) destroyers *Campbell, Garth* and *Hambledon*, the D16 (Harwich) destroyer *Quorn*, the Harwich corvettes *Kittiwake* and *Widgeon* and trawler *Kingston Olivine*, two Grimsby MLs, and MMS 553. *Vesper* and *Garth* (see map) had been very near *Aruba* when she was torpedoed just past 56 Buoy, and had chased three raiders due east. *Garth* was damaged by cannon shells and towed to Parkeston: at Shotley one can still see the grave of the eighteen-year-old Leading Seaman who died of his wounds that night. *Waldinge* and *War Mehtar* had been side by side when hit near 55A Buoy, and *Wolsey* had been just astern. She, and *Campbell*, out in the van, had chased several E-boats north-east, and claimed one hit. (See map).

Over the next few nights a smaller tanker, *Virgilia*, was lost to 4th E-boat Flotilla near Hearty Knoll Buoy, and with thirty-five burned to death or drowned. Other E-boat victims were the Dutch collier *Groenlo* (off Southwold), the *Asperity, Cormarsh* and *Empire Newcomen*, all on the same night in the Dudgeon area, and the Greek *Rokos Vergotris* at Smith's Knoll on 23 December. During the *Virgilia* raid a CHL RDF first played an E-boat finding role _ Happisburgh plotted the approach of up to thirteen, though all had helpfully come within a dozen miles of it.

For most of that autumn, by contrast, there had been a perceptible lull in mine sinkings; for instance in October and November in the four southernmost Nore Sub-Commands the only sizeable merchantmen so lost were the *Empire Ghyll* and *Mahseer*, both on 18 October near B7 Buoy (East Swin). But in December the mine danger again flared up, sinking fourteen vessels in the Nore Command, all but one merchant ships, and

WAR ON THE CONVOY ROUTE _ 2

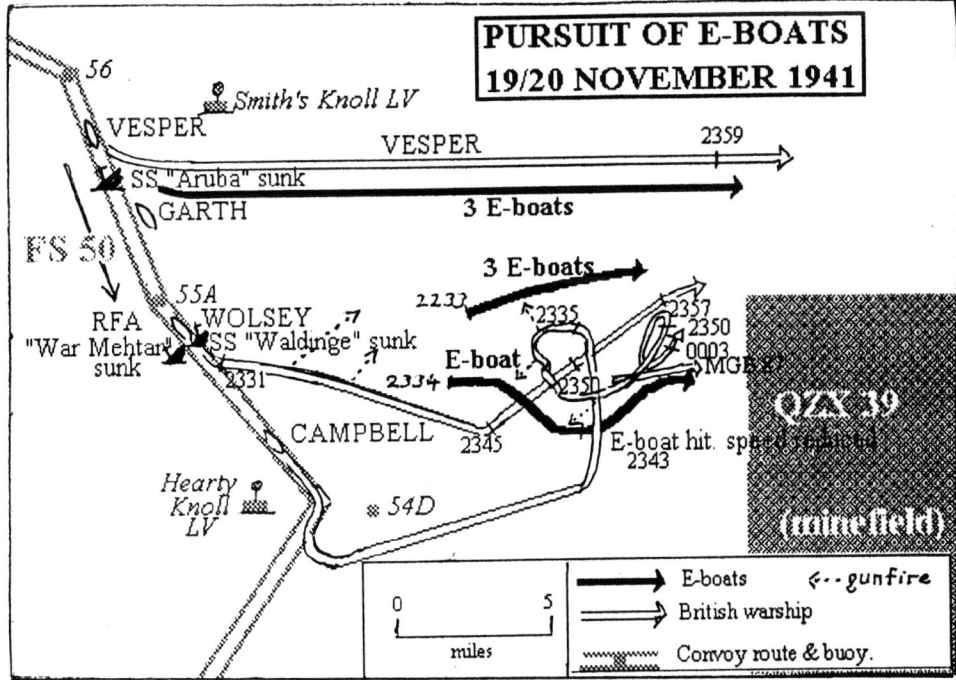

including the seven-thousand-ton oil tanker *British Captain* off Aldeburgh on the 2nd and the 4,468-ton creosote tanker *Stanmount* off Yarmouth on Christmas Eve. Humber Sub-Command was mined by 2nd E-boat flotilla on 29-30 November (while 4th hunted *Asperity's* convoy with torpedoes), and by forty aircraft the following night: no doubt these operations sank the big merchantmen *Dromore Castle, Ben Macdhui* and the Greek *Stephanos Chandris* that December. On the nights of 20 and 21 December RDF plotted the largest numbers of enemy minelaying aircraft over the Thames Estuary since June. On the second occasion at least thirty-five were counted: three flew over Ramsgate, one over Sheerness, two over the Swale, three close to Margate, and two across Shoeburyness, where the mines actually fell on the beach; others came within a mile of Dengie, Clacton and Frinton. and one flew right over Parkeston.

The tonnage of shipping sunk on the Nore Command part of the East Coast that month was the second highest of the whole war. The mercantile tonnage lost in the whole second half of 1941 was about 77,000, as opposed to 45,000 in the first. However the total tonnage for 1941 was slightly less than the 130,000 for 1940, and neither figure approached the 199,000 tons sunk in less than four months in 1939, when many of the victims were of a size now banned from the East Coast. Nevertheless 1941 had been the year both of the heaviest German minelaying and, as the following table shows, of the most intensive British minesweeping:

MINES SWEPT IN THE NORE COMMAND*

	ground	contact	totals
1939	4	81	85
1940	309	194	503
1941	1257	28	1285
1942	707	157	864
1943	373	86	459
1944	432	178	610
1945	137	30	167
	3219	754	3973

Humber and Sheerness Sub-Commands had taken the brunt of the mine war in 1941, apparently because the E-boats did not wish to run into their own acoustic mines during their raids on Yarmouth and Harwich Sub-Commands. 199 minesweepers were based in the Nore Command in the middle of 1941, of which thirty-four were fitted with LL only, fifty-five with LL and SA (acoustic sweeps), and thirty-six with O and SA. They were sweeping a total of 515 miles of channel, of which 240 made up the main convoy route.

Considerable but entirely manageable mine losses continued into early 1942. The new problem was twin-mechanism mines, in which magnetism "switched on" the detonators and sound fired them. By contrast to a year earlier the Humber was now fairly free of mines and had no sinkings.

But on 6 January three ships were mined off Suffolk. The tanker *Scottish Musician* and the freighter *Largo*, both in ballast with FN 97, were damaged near 54E Buoy, but towed to Harwich, where *Largo*'s seven injured were treated in Dovercourt Hospital. The coaster *Norwich Trader*, independently bound from London to Yarmouth, was blown up with all hands between Roughs and the Shipwash. When the Harwich drifter *Three Kings*

---

*Nore Command War Diaries (PRO ADM 199/407).

WAR ON THE CONVOY ROUTE _ 2

arrived on the scene she could find only two corpses and floating wreckage.
 The worst incident was the mining of the Rosyth destroyer *Vimiera* three days later. She was sunk leading an FS convoy within sight of Sheerness. The whole ship forward of the aft funnel disintegrated, and over seventy died. Two particular acts of heroism were recorded. Surgeon-Lt Kidd RNVR jumped into the water and dragged his captain, Lt-Cdr Mackenzie RNR, and four ratings (all badly wounded) onto a Carley float, which he paddled to an MMS. PO Chapman was one of three injured men caught below deck in a pitch-dark mess in the sinking wreck. He found an exit by striking matches and dragged his two comrades to safety.
 Quickstep sank near B7 Buoy on the 12th, with the loss of thirteen crew, the other fifteen being taken to Harwich by the Brightlingsea drifter *Lord Keith*. On the 25th the collier *Swynfleet*, heading for Ipswich Gasworks and approaching Harwich Harbour, left the safe channel by steering to the wrong side of Beach End Buoy and thereby triggered a magnetic mine. She sank within a stone's throw of Landguard Point. Efforts at salvage failed, and the wreck remained for the rest of the war, its funnel, still above water, providing a target for Harwich warships testing their guns. Much the biggest mined ships of early 1942 were the Greek *Atlanticos* (5,446 tons) on 21 February and *Frumenton* (6,675) on 3 March. The former sank near B8 Buoy, the latter near 54E _ after the Harwich corvette *Shearwater* had saved all forty-three of her crew and tried to tow her to Yarmouth.
 Early in 1942 the Luftwaffe bombers made many ferocious attacks, then virtually abandoned East Coast shipping targets for good. On 16 January 1942 the Yarmouth M/S trawler *Irvana* was bombed and sunk close to base, followed on the 30th by the Grimsby trawler *Loch Alsh*, near 59 Buoy.
 When air-attacked warships were required to record the type of plane involved. Though they carried identification silhouettes, this was not always an easy task. For instance, with their twin tails and narrow bodies the Do 17 and Me 110 could easily be confused. The previous 2 November FN 40 had reported its attackers as having "tails like Do 17s and noses like Ju 88s". Three months later, off the Humber, warships reported Me 110s, though this was beyond their range. On both, and other occasions, the bombers were of the new Do 217 type, which bore twice the bombload of the old Do 17s. The sketches overleaf illustrate the confusion.

WAR ON THE CONVOY ROUTE _ 2

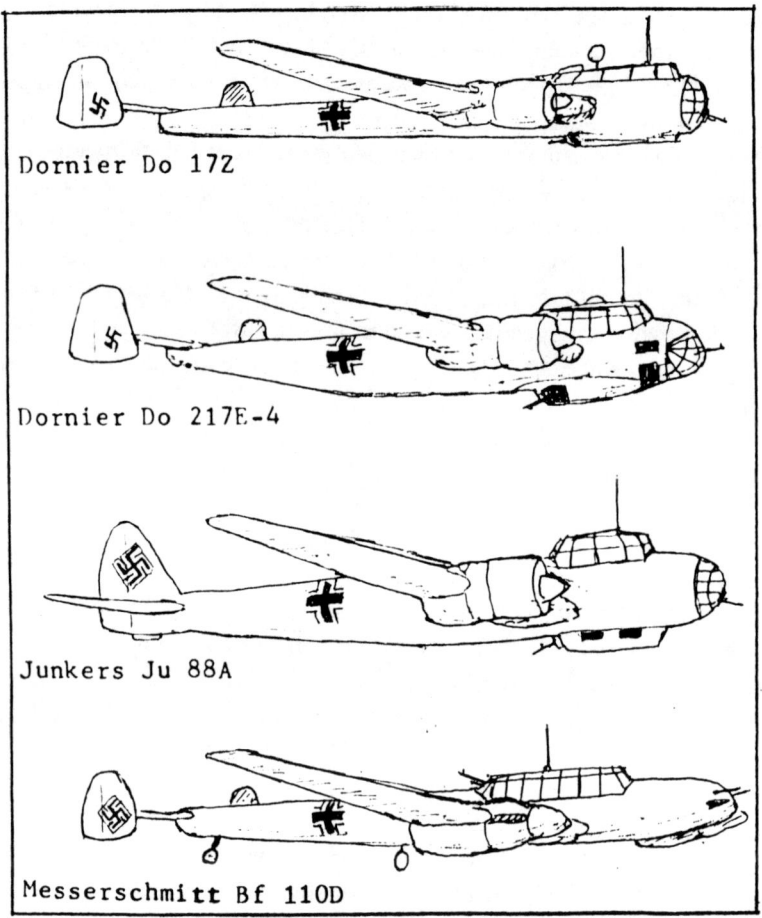

Dornier Do 17Z

Dornier Do 217E-4

Junkers Ju 88A

Messerschmitt Bf 110D

That February was indeed the Luftwaffe's swansong over the shipping routes, for it carried out more attacks in Nore Command waters that month (fifty) than since the previous May. All but one were in the Humber and Yarmouth Sub-Commands. The 2nd and the 5th were the worst days. On the former the Grimsby and Yarmouth M/S and patrol trawlers were attacked on station by at least twenty planes, and Grimsby's *Cape Spartel* and Yarmouth's *Cloughton Wyke* were sunk. On the latter a convoy as well as scattered warships were targets. The Harwich A/S trawler *Kingston Olivine* was strafed near 54G Buoy, without damage or casualties.

On the 17th, in the last such operation anywhere near Harwich, two

WAR ON THE CONVOY ROUTE _ 2

raiders flew as near that harbour as Andrews Buoy, only half a mile off Landguard Point, to attack but miss the trawlers *Caswell, Firefly* and *Stella Rigel.* Next day the aged Grimsby patrol trawler *Warland* was sunk near the *Loch Alsh* wreck.

British warships and merchantmen had claimed many Luftwaffe bombers shot down since the middle of 1941, but only the finding of aircraft wreckage, corpses or survivors confirms these. On these grounds we can accept the following:

_a **Do 17** shot down by Grimsby trawlers near the Humber Light Vessel, and a **minelayer** by the paddle ship *Balmoral* in the Thames Estuary, both on 6 July;

¬an **He 111** by the Ipswich patrol trawler *Norland* at 54B Buoy on 4 August;

_a **bomber** by the Grimsby M/S trawler *Wellsbach* near Withernsea on 9 August (a PAC was used, and Feldwebel Markert, the pilot, was picked up by the trawler *Grey Mist;*

_a **Ju 88** by the Lowestoft trawler *Euclase* at No 5 Buoy, on 15 September, with all four crew captured by the trawler *Alfredian;*

_a **Do 217**, off Yarmouth on 12 November, by accidentally striking the topmast of the trawler *Francolin* while sinking her;

_the **Ju 88** which sank *Irvana* in Yarmouth Roads on 30 January 1942, from that ship's fire, all four airmen being captured;

_another **Ju 88**, by the Lowestoft trawler *Fyldea* near 54G Buoy, during a snowstorm that same day _ one body was found and buried at sea...

...and on 5 February SS *Helder* brought down a plane east of Spurn Point. Lt-Cdr Unwin, of the Sheerness destroyer *Pytchley,* later saw the bodies being recovered and wrote to *Helder's* master: "It might interest you to know that one German body was found completely decapitated, the very best way to deal with all Huns".* Many a postwar historian has written of the mutual respect and even comradeship in arms between 1939-45 British and Germans, as if they had been on the same joint NATO exercise. But this was not the mood of 1942: Unwin and sailors like him had seen innumerable compatriots killed, mutilated and blinded by German bombs and mines, and reacted to any small triumph in the way I have described.

In March the bombing abruptly declined, and then stopped, though apparently for some months the Luftwaffe continued unsuccessfully to search

---

*PRO ADM 199/1314

out convoys by night. On 5 March the crew of the Harwich rescue tug *Superman* suffered two seriously injured from a near miss off Yarmouth, and a fortnight later the Brightlingsea drifter *Lord Keith* avoided two bombs from a Thames Estuary minelayer. These were the last direct air attacks at sea reported by Nore Command bases.

Meanwhile, after a short break, the E-boats returned. On the night of 19/20 February 1942 there was a major battle, composed of four separate actions, between them and Sheerness (21st Flotilla) destroyers near Hearty Knoll. *Mendip* and *Pytchley* were providing additional escort for FS 29, while *Holderness* was on a standing patrol. "Headache" (radio monitoring) and shipborne RDF had given warning of the Germans' approach, when a barrage of starshells silhoutted several raiders. 21st Flotilla opened up with 4-inch, 2 pdr pom-pom and 20-mm Oerlikon guns, and two E-boats were believed definitely sunk and a third probably. *Holderness* spotted S 53, minus her bows, and closed in to capture her. As Lt A J R White brought the destroyer alongside, Lt Ditcham RNR jumped on board with ropes, whereupon the E-boat captain blew his demolition charges, killing himself, blasting off the roof of his wheelhouse, and setting fire to his vessel. Ditcham was not stopped from fixing his lines, and the rest of his boarding party jumped across. Flames were lapping round the *loaded* torpedo tubes of S 53 when Leading Seaman W R Read turned a water hose on them, even though ammunition was bursting all around him. Eighteen prisoners were taken; "all very frightened on arrival aboard but...very impressed with their treatment and food". The E-boat proved unsalvable. The captains of *Mendip* and *Pytchley* (Lt-Cdrs Rolfe and Unwin) were awarded bars to their existing DSCs; Ditcham also received the DSC, and Read was one of five to get the DSM.

E-boats only sank two ships by torpedo on the East Coast in the first quarter of 1942. The second of these was the Rosyth destroyer *Vortigern*, near 57D Buoy seventeen miles north of Cromer, in the early hours of 15 March. Oberleutnant Roeder's S 104 (of 4th Flotilla) torpedoed her. She had been escorting FS 49. In view of the number of E-boats on the loose Lt-Cdr Lombard-Hobson's Harwich corvette *Guillemot* ignored survivors in the water and continued her task of covering the convoy till daybreak. She then turned back and found the wreck, with two survivors clinging to the stern: the destroyer had been torn open forward and had immediately plunged down

WAR ON THE CONVOY ROUTE _ 2

end-on till her bow hit the bottom. According to Nicholas Monsarrat, one of the corvette's officers, she later found a Carley float with "a handful of black-faced, oil-soaked men, surrounded by prone figures sprawling in the lazy attitudes of death". One man weakly raised an arm, another grinned in spite of his shattered leg. As live and dead men were lifted onto *Guillemot* a Spitfire circled overhead _ "guard, spectator and mourner, all in one"*. The sea all around was strewn with floating corpses, several of which were later recovered by the Cromer and Sheringham lifeboats. In spite of hours more searching *Guillemot* found no more live men, and steamed on to Harwich to land the survivors. Since there were only fourteen in all the death toll must have been at least 110, the worst in any wartime incident off the East Coast. Lombard-Hobson and seven survivors attended a Board of Inquiry at Parkeston which found that, contrary to recommended practice in "E-boat Alley" *Vortigern's* liferafts had been lashed down and most of her crew had not been wearing lifebelts.

This sinking was only part of that night and day's widespread operations, extending to 54E Buoy (off Southwold) and the Dutch and Belgian coasts, and involving the Sheerness destroyers *Holderness* and *Pytchley*, the Rosyth destroyer *Wallace* (then the young Prince Philip's ship), four MLs, eight MGBs, and many aircraft. In Chapter 13 I shall describe the capture of one of the raiders and the sinking of another _ a victory which to some extent offset the *Vortigern* tragedy.

Operating from a new base at Ostend, 4th E-boat Flotilla was responsible for mining the Swedish merchantman *Scotia* near the Aldeburgh Light Float on 12 April. Her crew having been saved by the *Badger* corvette *Puffin*, she sank near 54F Buoy, off Lowestoft. On the night of 20-21 April six Ostend E-boats laid a contact minefield around 54B Buoy, off Aldeburgh. A Harwich "O" trawler group, escorted by the Hunt class destroyers *Cotswold* and *Quorn,* was then at work ahead of FS 80. But some of the scattered and drifting mines by-passed the sweeps and got amid the following ships. Two merchantmen, *Plawsworth* and the Belgian *Vae Victis*, were sunk, though all on board were rescued. Then *Cotswold* and *Quorn* also hit mines. *Cotswold* was severely damaged near the bow, and the forward compartments, including a boiler room and magazine, were flooded, the bulkhead subdivisions being vitiated by the passage for water offered by the ventilating system. Five were killed and twenty-three injured. For a while

---

*Monsarrat; *Three Corvettes.*

WAR ON THE CONVOY ROUTE _ 2

Cotswold seemed doomed to sink. Lt-Cdr Hichen's Felixstowe-based MGB flotilla broke off its pursuit of the E-boats to help evacuate the destroyer. Then four Harwich tugs arrived, towed her to Shotley, and beached her. Meanwhile *Quorn* was towed in by the corvette *Shearwater*, with two dead and one wounded.

But now the extraordinary respite came. In May only four craft of all types were lost in the Nore Command, the lowest in any wartime month so far. For the next eight months only four vessels were sunk in Harwich Sub-Command, only three each in Sheerness and Humber. In August no ships at all were sunk _ SS *Kyloe* was mined off Yarmouth but beached. In September nothing was so much as war-damaged. I must now break off my narrative to explore what had happened.

Aggressive British MGBs were now operating in strength from Yarmouth, Lowestoft and Felixstowe, and more closely pursuing the E-boats, but they had so far not actually sunk any. The RAF was also chasing them more, though with little success. Counter-offensive strategy is therefore not the answer. So the answer must lie in British defensive weapons and measures.

From the middle of 1942 the anti-E-boat patrol system called the "Z Lines" was instituted. Some thirty miles out from the coast, just inside the Mine Barrier, and from off Wells to off Harwich, stretched a line of mooring buoys, one every four miles, and each with a "Z" prefix and a number. On any given night about one third of these would be occupied by a unit (each identified by a letter) of two Coastal Forces craft _ MGBs, MLs, occasionally MTBs, sometimes even R(rescue)MLs. As a backstop there was a much sparser Z Line about ten miles behind this. In all the Z Lines had over thirty positions and ten units. There were also seven destroyer and corvette standing patrol positions. All this represented an extension of the thinner and less systematic patrols of 1941. (See map opposite).

As a ruse to confuse enemy radio monitors the numbering of some of the convoy route buoys was now altered. 54E Buoy (off Dunwich) became 3A, 54F (off Corton) became 4 (with a 3B and 3C added in between), 54D and 56A were interchanged, as were 56 and 57, and 55A became 54G. I do not know if this actually fooled the Germans, but it certainly confused me when I started my research!

WAR ON THE CONVOY ROUTE _ 2

Another factor working for the defence was improved ship plotting. Some account of this is probably overdue. Since early in the war plots _ with staff, maps and telephones _ had been kept at Area Combined HQ, Chatham, and at Harwich, Yarmouth and Immingham. The senior officer involved was Lt-Cdr Kerr, of the Chatham "NPR" (Naval Plot Room). The sources of information about the positions of friendly, neutral and enemy shipping were many; Naval Control Service Officers (who supervised all merchant ship movements in, from and into major harbours), PWSSs, warships at sea, port authorities, RDF, aircraft, Coastguards, plot rooms in adjacent commands, and now also the Maunsell Forts (see Chapter 12).

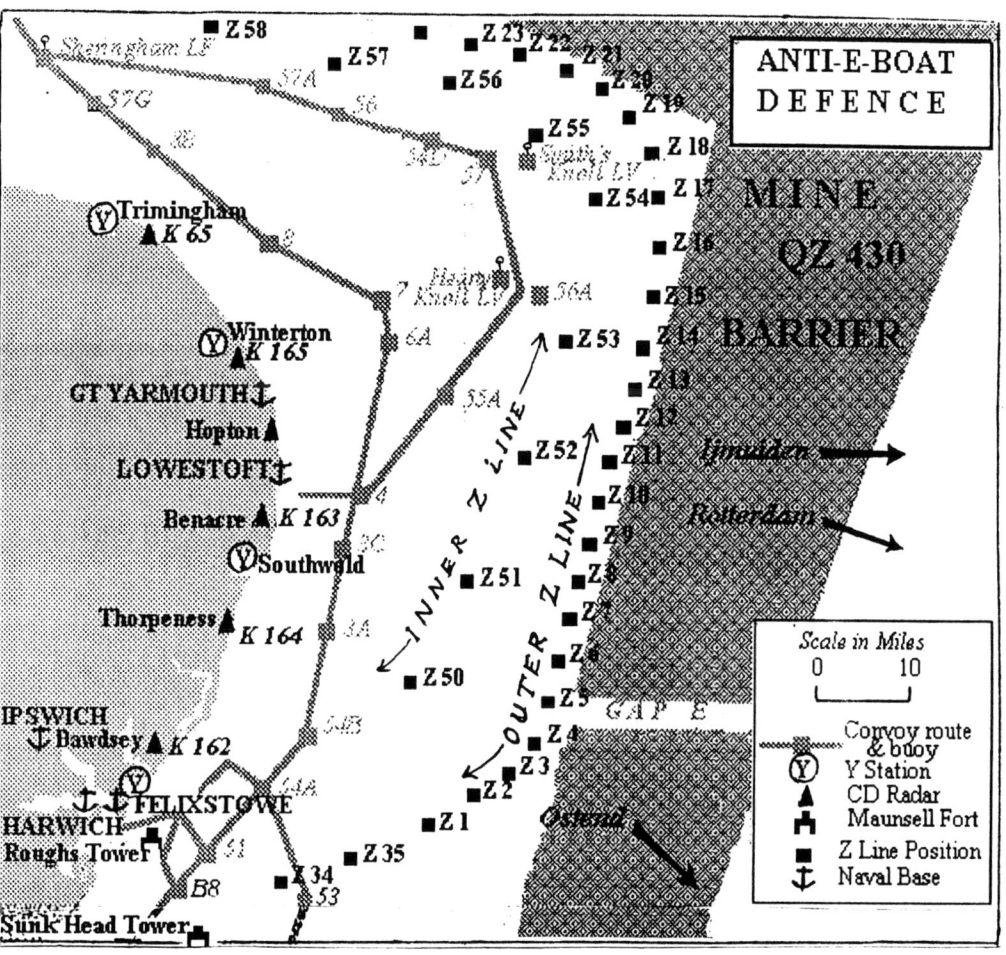

WAR ON THE CONVOY ROUTE _ 2

The Sub-Command plot rooms fed one digest of their local information to the Chatham HQ every six minutes. In return it informed Harwich and Yarmouth of ships coming their way from the Sheerness area, and also from the Dover Strait. Yarmouth forewarned Humber, which in turn informed Tyne Sub-Command in Rosyth Command, and relayed plots from Tyne to Chatham. Information was shared with RAF Fighter Command and 16 Group Coastal Command on request. NCSOs, and at minor ports the local Customs, informed their Sub-Command Plot Rooms of the names, types, departure times, proposed routes, speeds and destinations of all departing vessels.

But keeping track of Allied and neutral shipping was one thing, warning of the evasive E-boats and Luftwaffe another.

A full chain of RDF (radar) stations had been in existence for some time, without providing much help to the Navy and to shipping. In spite of the GCI-AI breakthrough described in Chapter 7 the mine and torpedo raiders, moving on (or only a few hundred feet above) the sea, could not usually be seen by the RAF. CHL alone could detect ships, but usually only large steel vessels, which E-boats were not, nor was its "horizon" low enough for minelaying planes.

Just before the end of 1941 CHL had been joined by a new and potentially superior system. This was the CM (centimetric), CD (coast defence) or CHEL (Chain Home Extra Low) variety, of which the initial equipment was termed CD Mark IV or Type 271 by the Navy and Type 14 by the RAF _ what would today be called a microwave radar. Its frequency of 3 GHz (wavelength=10 cm.) enabled it to locate small objects virtually down to sea level at fifteen miles _e.g, E-boats on some parts of the convoy route. Its transmissions were made possible by the British invention of the Magnetron, a copper cylinder no bigger than a teacup in which the electrons from a cathode were trapped into electromagnetised cavities, where the accumulation of energy made them vibrate at this enormous frequency. (Secret and brandnew military technology in 1941, but today found, with a different application, in any microwave oven!) The first such stations on the East Coast were North Foreland (codenumbered 5), Dengie (140), Bawdsey (162), Bleed Hill, or Winterton (135), Trimingham (65), Bard Hill (134). Type 271 also appeared on a few destroyers in 1942, supplementing Type 286 (see Chapter 5), and in the air a 10 cm AI appeared in night fighters. But

WAR ON THE CONVOY ROUTE _ 2

whatever its value in the Battle of the Atlantic and to Fighter Command, this first 10-cm RDF disappointed the Navy's Nore Command. It was underpowered, did not reach the further sections of the convoy route, and even closer in did not give warning of E-boats or lowflying planes until these were about to strike, or had struck.

These 10-cm RDF sets were too bulky _ and too scarce _ to fit onto the Z Line motor craft themselves. Some now had Type 286 (1.5 metre) sets, but these had so small a range than the odds were much against any MGB or ML detecting an E-boat.

A more valuable source for the Plot Rooms was the "Y" Service, the organisation which listened in to German radio. This had been set up in the summer of 1940 to give warning of invasion, and had operated from mobile vans. By May 1941 it had been accommodated in buildings at Withernsea, Winterton, Trimingham, Southwold and Felixstowe's Cliff Hotel, with another station to follow at Sheringham and an RAF section which among other duties detected minelaying planes at Gorleston. Some equipment ("Headache") was also put on destroyers. The "Y" reports were gathered by filter rooms at Harwich and Immingham. Its German-speaking (mainly Wren) operators occasionally read messages indicative of enemy strength and intentions, but even if less lucky (and at first some of the operators said they could hardly understand a word) it was useful, because it could pinpoint the enemy by means of directionfinding aerials, and, when this had been done repeatedly, work out a track and probable target. Nevertheless both the E-boats and Luftwaffe minelayers moved at such speed, and on such irregular courses, that the Z Line units in the one case, the nightfighters in the other, still failed to intercept in most cases.

In fact the British defence improvements of 1942 were the stepping stone to more effective systems in 1943, but were not responsible for the respite in the East Coast sea war in the former year. This had three real causes. First, the enemy was hampered by the long hours of spring and summer daylight, though he had been less deterred by these in 1941. Secondly, and more importantly, his Dutch-based E-Boats transferred to the Channel that summer. Thirdly, that spring Hitler insisted that most of the Luftwaffe bombers in the West concentrate on the strategically irrelevant retaliation attacks on British cities known as the Baedecker Raids, two of which battered Norwich and killed nearly 230 of its citizens late that April.

WAR ON THE CONVOY ROUTE _ 2

This did not take away the minelaying planes, which made more sorties in April than in either of the previous two months, but it accounts for the sharp falling-off in bombing attacks on shipping.

The 1942 lull was not without a few shocks. The Yarmouth Hunt-class minesweeper *Fitzroy* was sunk by mine on 27 May with twelve dead and ten wounded. The Felixstowe-based Harwich boom trawler *Tunisian* was blown up by another mine right off Landguard on 9 July, with the loss of all twenty-nine crew; she had been on her way to repair a line of underwater obstacles off Shingle Street.

Two tiny Essex fishing smacks were also victims _ *Little Express* from Tollesbury on 4 May and *Maggie* from West Mersea on 17 June. All three crew were killed on the first and both (a married couple) on the second. The Tollesbury fishermen had been running some terrible risks. In 1941 their smack *Thistle* had been sunk by a mine in the Wallet, by an odd coincidence on the *same* day as a naval examination drifter with the *same* name suffered the *same* fate off Lowestoft. On 12 August that year the *Express* was sunk on Whitstable Flats without loss of life, but her owners, in spite of their experience and the ban on fishing in the area, bought another boat (*Little Express*) and sneaked out to the very same waters, with the result just mentioned.

At this period Corton Beach, north of Lowestoft, was the scene of grim and heroic mine recovery work. On 13 May Sub-Lt Nickson, of HMS *Vernon*, towed in one of the deadly little Type R contact mines from ML 253's dinghy, and then defused it. A week later Cdr Hamond and Lt Mould arrived from *Vernon* on the yacht *Esmeralda* and drifter *Fisher Boy*, and recovered some more of these mines at sea, while their divers brought up one of the "sinkers" which clamped the mine cables to the seabed. On 11 June a Lowestoft Operations Duty Officer, Lt A C D Coombes RNR, volunteered to help, and went out in ML 152 to tow in a Type T magnetic mine for experts to examine. He and two ratings brought the mine ashore at Corton, but it contained a trick contact detonator, and the veteran Yarmouth RMS Officer, Lt-Cdr Edwards (see Chapter 2), and an American, Ensign Howard, were killed as they worked on it. Two days later Lt-Cdr Armitage (see Chapter 7), from *Vernon*, landed another Type T, and it was successfully dismantled by Mould, who received the George Cross as a result. All these mines had been

WAR ON THE CONVOY ROUTE _ 2

laid by E-boats as a parting shot before moving to the Channel.
RMS (Rendering Mines Safe) parties did not have to be led by commissioned officers. Edwards's assistant PO Wood travelled to almost every stretch of the East Coast to defuse or destroy mines washed ashore. In the first two months of 1942 he dealt with 109 British contact mines (mainly broken loose from the Barrier in rough seas), plus six German. He won the BEM for defusing a British Type XIVA right in the middle of a beach minefield near Felixstowe Pier in March 1943.

Extraordinary ingenuity as well as courage was expended on mines. At Seasalter, near Whitstable, one was winched out from under the seabed in 1943 after being buried thirty-one feet deep for two years. A large brick wall had been built above and around it to keep out water and mud, and a light railway(!) had been taken out to the spot on a causeway of scaffolding.

By the end of the war 698 mines were "rendered safe" on the Norfolk coast alone.

With the lengthening nights of autumn E-boat Alley once more lived up to its name, for those marauders were back in Holland. On 19/20 September the Harwich destroyer *Hambledon* and corvette *Mallard* engaged them off Yarmouth and (falsely) claimed one destroyed. On 6-7 October twelve E-boats from the familiar 2nd and 4th Flotillas raided FN 32 off Sheringham and sank with torpedoes the merchantmen *Sheafwater, Ilse* and *Jessie Maersk*, the Yarmouth ML 339, and the Harwich rescue tug *Caroline Moller*. The "holiday" was over. A week later a new E-boat flotilla, Korvettenkapitän Obermaier's 6th, broke in half SS *George Balfour*, and sank the Norwegian *Lysland*, near Dudgeon Shoal on the northern edge of Yarmouth Sub-Command. (In fact nearly all sinkings by E-boats were in that Command, with just three others in Harwich and one in Humber: the norhernmost E-boat sorties reached no further than twenty miles due east of Spurn Point).

On 9 November 2nd Flotilla sank SS *Wandle* and damaged the Norwegian SS *Fidelio* near Lowestoft. And nearby on 12 December Korvettenkapitän Bätge's 4th Flotilla disposed of four ships in FN 89, though none was of more than 2,300 tons. On this occasion the Winterton and Southwold Y Service did some useful tracking.

And so into 1943...Again off Lowestoft, in the early hours of 18 February, the D21 (Sheerness) destroyer *Garth* destroyed S 71 (of 6th

Flotilla), the first E-boat to fall to Nore Command for eleven months. Thirteen E-boats (according to a prisoner) had slipped through the Z Line due east of Corton because of the ineffectiveness of the local RDF and because the MGBs at Z12 and Z52 had been forced back to harbour by bad weather. Southwold Y first detected the foray, which was a contact mining operation, and then *Garth* picked up the enemy on her Type 286 ASV (RDF) and heard German voices through her "Headache" radio.

She made the following cyphered W/T (Morse) signals:

Intermediate Confidential Code, to Yarmouth W/T Station...

0051. Three E-boats bearing 010° one mile distant my position 3C Buoy.

0059. E-boats driven off in general direction course 180°. My position 130° 3C Buoy one mile.

0125. One E-boat heavily damaged and on fire. Have lost touch with remainder. My position 170° 4 Buoy eight miles.

To C-in-C Nore...

0205. Have seven prisoners on board. E-boat left on fire in position 158° 4 Buoy seven miles. Intend to investigate at daylight.

To *Kittiwake*...

0208. Am closing you. My position 3C.

Intermediate Secret Code, to C-in-C Nore...

0310...E-boats minelaying, each carrying six mines. No information yet as to whether mines had been laid before boats were flushed in Position 000° 3C Buoy by one and a half miles.

To Harwich...

0905. Have seven German survivors to land on arrival _ one seriously wounded, remainder minor wounds, eleven killed and two critically wounded including two officers were left on board E-boat.*

...One of the survivors was in fact a dog(!) for *Garth*'s captain later reported that "a bitch in the family way...swam to the boat".

Mines sank several craft in the winter of 1942-43, but all were small. Among them were six Thames sailing barges. Like the fishing smacks, these had been vulnerable mainly to acoustic mines, because they moved very slowly along the shallow inshore route on chugging auxiliary motors. Dunkirk excepted, twenty-one were sunk on the East Coast, all between Hollesley Bay and Rochester. The list runs (chronologically): *Herbert* (lost

*PRO ADM 199/536

WAR ON THE CONVOY ROUTE _ 2

in storm), *Yampa* (storm), *Bijou* (bombed), *Glencœ*(storm), *Globe* (mined), *Martinet* (Storm), *Emma* (bombed), *Rosme, Blue Mermaid, Golden Grain, Britisher, HKD, Unique, Bankside, Gertrude May, Ailsa* (all mined), *Castanet* (collision with *Skagerrak* wreck), *Resolute* (mined), *Tam O'Shanter* (storm), *Wouldham Court* (struck by crashing aircraft) and *JBW* (mined).

Mostly under a hundred tons and of turn-of-the-century date, these craft, with their distinctive rust-coloured sails, carried grain, four and malt from small creeks to the Estuary ports. Each had a crew of two or three only, with no armament save rifles. The majority of them had been requisitioned as minewatching and storage craft _ almost every East Coast naval base had several, and the largest company, the London and Rochester Trading Company, parted with 108 out of 160. But others doggedly carried on, though they were not allowed to move by night. The barges of the Everard company were some of the best known: their senior master, Will Uglow, made 147 wartime voyages on the *Will Everard*.

On 13 March 1943 Francis and Gilders' *Alaric*, bound from Burnham-on-Crouch to Felixstowe, suffered the most unusual of all attacks on sailing barges. Just out of the Crouch she was strafed by six Focke-Wulf FW 190 fighters, returning from an unsuccessful raid on Bradwell airfield. One crew member was killed, but the barge was towed to safety by Brightlingsea Air-Sea Rescue Boat 3.

British shipping losses on the East Coast in 1942 had fallen by two-thirds over those of 1941, and in 1943 were halved again. In the latter year they totalled less than those in the peak *month* of 1940 (November). In 1943 improved British defences *were* largely responsible, though the Luftwaffe's preoccupations on other fronts had a big effect on their North Sea minelaying.

British minesweeping was now mainly undertaken by purpose-built modern vessels instead of by aged requisitioned fishing craft. In place of the "O" trawlers there were big (850-ton) *Algerine* and *Bangor*-class minesweepers, with 4-inch and 20-mm guns and crews of eighty-five. 18th Flotilla (*Algerines*) arrived at Harwich that May. It was replaced by 9th Flotilla (*Bangors*) in November, which in turn gave way to the 15th by the end of the year. From October the familiar 4th Flotilla, of "Smokey Joes", was again present, to be replaced by 6th and 7th Flotillas (*Algerines*) in

WAR ON THE CONVOY ROUTE _ 2

March 1944. The smaller "influence" MMSs had first appeared in the spring of 1941, but until now had been scarce. A second whole class of them, longer in build, now joined, while the British Yard Minesweepers (BYMSs) were purchased from the USA. One Harwich MMS flotilla, the 139th, was Dutch; each vessel being named after an island of that country as well as having a number. (Off duty their crews lived on the accommodation ship *Hydrograaf*). By 1944 the minesweepers in the Nore Command were distributed thus:

	FLEET M/S	MMSs	BYMSs	M/S TRAWLERS & DRIFTERS	PATROL VESSELS HELPING WITH M/S
London				10	
Sheerness		39			
Harwich	25	15	10	8	17
Brightlingsea				4	
Lowestoft		10	6		21
Yarmouth		8	8	33	
Grimsby	8		10	56	
	33	72	34	111	38

Grand Total=288

The AA defences around the Thames mouth, including the Maunsell Forts, made that area too dangerous for minelaying aircraft, and no doubt explain why only two ships were sunk there by this cause in the last two years of war.

In 1943 the Magnetron-based centimetric radar at last came into its own, and relieved CHL of its ship-tracking role. CD Mark VI** ("double star), or Type 277 (for the RAF, "Type 55") was much more powerful than Mark IV (Type 271), superceded it, and formed a complete chain. It was installed at North Foreland, Dunkirk, Whitstable, Warden Point, Dengie, Bawdsey, Orford, Thorpeness, Benacre, Hopton, Winterton, Trimingham and Bard Hill. An extra set went to Great Bromley in 1944. Concentrated reception at these stations was assisted by modern-looking rotatable paraboloid (dish) aerials, and tracking by the PPI. Normal range on an E-boat was about thirty miles. This kind of radar put out so much energy, with

WAR ON THE CONVOY ROUTE _ 2

such high-amplitude (strong, pronounced) waves that the desired echoes received overrode the irrelevant echoes off the sea and sandbanks which had so limited range in the past. The transmissions deflected off a smooth sea and away from the receiver, and bounced back only from upright surfaces and planes, though therefore a very rough sea could send back echoes and shorten effective range. Occasionally, with a glass-smooth sea and the kind of atmospheric conditions which refracted radio waves around the earth's curvature, amazingly long ranges could be achieved on Type 277. On 11 May 1944 Hopton and Benacre tracked six British MTBs out to ninety-six miles _ almost the Frisian Islands, and that 14 September Benacre plotted six E-boats at sixty miles. Such ranges were more often attainable on big steel ships, so that some of the more southerly CDs could detect the enemy coastal convoys off the Low Countries.

These stations were telephonically linked straight to the Nore and Sub-Command Plot Rooms. A high level of speed and efficiency was demanded of their operators, since scattered E-boats or minelaying planes could present up to ten tracks at once, each of which had to be reported every two minutes.

In 1943 a scaled-down 10-cm radar, Type 291, appeared on some Z Line craft, and even on patrol trawlers: this did not give the big ranges mentioned above (for the sets were lower-powered and much lower-mounted), but did in theory mean that nothing could now sneak through the patrols without being spotted.

The first naval vessel to be lost in 1943 was the Lowestoft "O" trawler *Moravia*, mined off Orfordness on 14 March. The largest merchantman to be lost was the Finnish tanker *Josefina Thorden*, bound from Curacoa in the West Indies to Shellhaven on the Thames. A mine broke her in two, but half of her plus the valuable cargo inside was towed to safety, and her crew were also saved.

A notable feature of that year was the occasional but dramatic incursions by the E-boats. One torpedoed and sank the big patrol trawler *Adonis* off Lowestoft on 15 April. Felixstowe and Southwold Y had heard the approaching raiders' radio, an RAF plane had sighted them, and there had been MLs at Z4, 7, 19 and 22, and MGBs at Z50, 51, 54 and 55, but the E-boats outflanked them, going via the empty Z3 and 54 Buoy and then turning north. On the night of 4/5 August seven boats of the 2nd and 6th Flotillas laid a minefield on the convoy route east of Harwich. Bawdsey CD radar was in the course of changing over from Type IV to Type VI and missed them. When the Ipswich patrol trawler *Red Gauntlet* appeared, S 86 torpedoed and sank her with all hands. The mines, though, were all promptly swept.

On the night of 24/25 September no fewer than twenty-nine E-boats carried out "Operation Probestick", the laying of 110 mines on the Harwich stretch of the convoy route. Four flotillas participated (2nd, 4th, 6th, and Korvettenkapitän Zymalkowski's new 8th), and it was the largest E-boat raid ever. Rotterdam was the attacker's starting point.

The Germans approached in three groups; "A" (as the plotters dubbed it) came in towards Orfordness, "B" towards Harwich, and "C" towards the Naze. Five MLs, three RMLs, eight MGBs and two MTBs were on the outer and inner Z Lines. Near to the raid were:

> Unit T (the Lowestoft MGBs 82 and 91 at Z9),
> Unit V (the Lowestoft MLs 113 and 116 at Z7),
> Unit N (the Yarmouth MTBs 624 and 628 at Z50),
> Unit W (the Lowestoft MLs 145 and 150 at Z4),
> Unit Y (the Felixstowe MGBs 61 and 67 at Z34).

...and along the convoy route was the five-trawler Ipswich Patrol Group 78.

(See map).

CD radar stations K162 (Bawdsey) and K164 (Thorpeness), newly equipped with their high-performance Type 277 sets, detected echoes and at 0045 Harwich put out the warning signal. At 0050 Southwold Y (under Wren Second Officer Pelloe) and Felixstowe Y (Third Officer Gill) heard Group A. A voice identifying itself as "von Quatsch" said "We have laid (mines?)" and then reeled off several routine messages. A "von Walther" and a "von Jasper" were heard, followed by signals from Groups B and C. The former's leader was heard to say"...reports that he has finished minelaying". Voices called themselves "Martin, Georg, Klaus, Hugo, Alle, Walter, Heinz", giving some idea of the number of raiders. 45.6 and 45.7 MHz were the frequencies. Only snatches of conversation could be heard through the whine made by radar and the "mush" of interference. The "loudest" boat was the southernmost one, belonging to "Nikko", apparently Oberleutnant-zur-See Baron Nikko von Stempel. All the radar, Y and ship wireless messages poured into a tense

WAR ON THE CONVOY ROUTE _ 2

Harwich (Parkeston) Plot Room.
Unit N, with its two powerful D-Type MTBs, was almost in the path of Group A, but failed to hear the warning signal. Only three minutes later the Ipswich patrol trawler *Carena* (which had once landed the spy Dronkers) sighted Group B at 54B Buoy, ten miles east of Orfordness. These E-boats were laying their minefield around 52 Buoy, near the Shipwash (twelve miles east of Harwich), when at 0050 the Ipswich trawler *Franc Tireur* intervened. Oberleutnant-zur-See Ritter von Georg's S 96 torpedoed and sank her; fifteen of the crew died and the other four were found by other trawlers and then landed by a Felixstowe RAF launch. Her sister-trawler *Donna Nook*, hurrying to the scene, collided with another trawler, *Stella Rigel*, and also

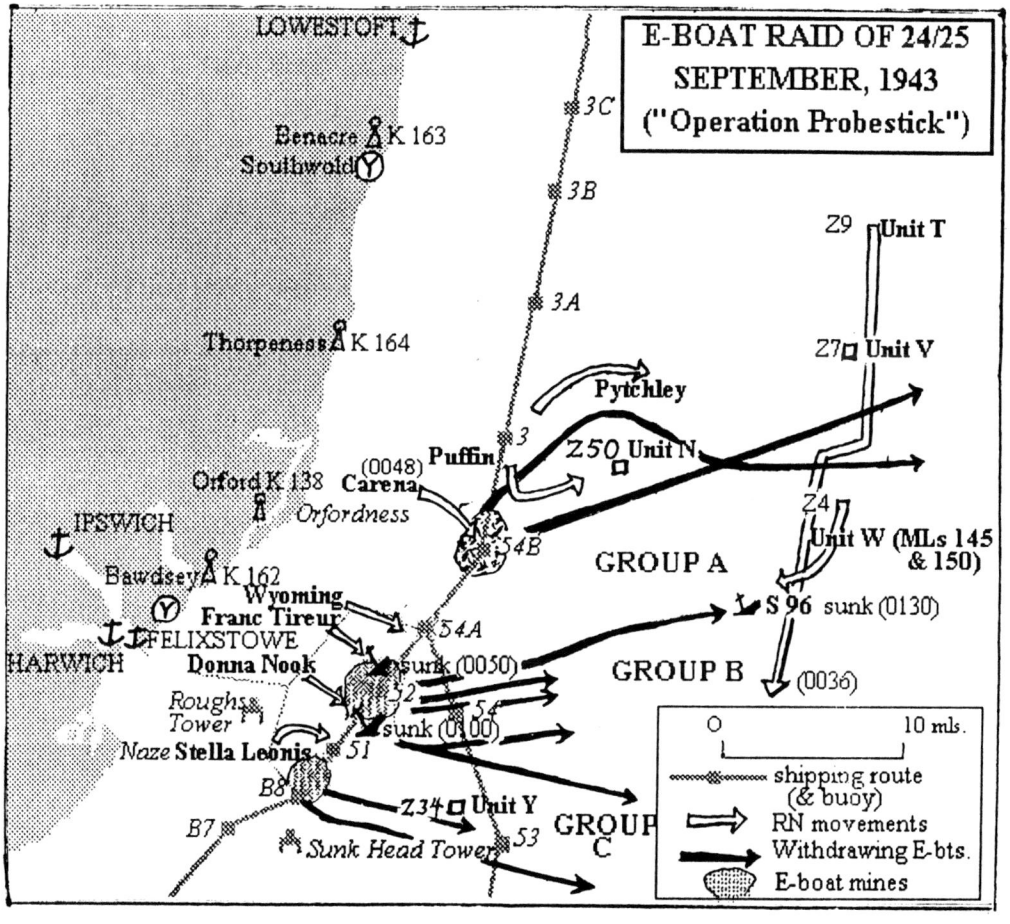

sank, though without loss of life.

Meanwhile, in the south, Group C had minelaid between 51 and B8 Buoys, eleven miles east-south-east of the Naze. They were clearly seen on the radars of the Roughs and Sunkhead Maunsell Forts.

Soon after 0100 the three groups scattered and began to withdraw east-north-eastwards. The Harwich corvette *Puffin* and Sheerness destroyer *Pytchley* closed in from the north but were soon outrun. Unit N belatedly woke up to the chase and briefly pursued one raider. Unit T's two MGBs tore south from Z9 in an attempt to head off Group B, but Unit W's two MLs were closer to hand, and by an odd coincidence found themselves right in the path of von Georg's S 96. They were too slow to pursue, but RNVR Lt J O Thomas's ML 150 most courageously avenged the *Franc Tireur* by ramming the E-boat, which was crippled and scuttled by her crew. RNVR Lt R F Seddon's ML 145 rescued two German officers and eleven ratings, but heavy seas doomed the rest. Both MLs limped back to Lowestoft, though 150 had lost her bows in the collision. The RNVR took great pride in the two ML captains, both of whom were unquestioned amateurs, having been until recently a student and an actor respectively.

Some of the mines began to detonate spontaneously, and eventually the rest were swept without loss.

Exactly a month later an almost equally large E-boat raid miscarried off Cromer, but since this was (from the British side) mainly an MGB action, it will be described in Chapter 13.

Not until November, after nearly a year without sinking a merchant ship, did the North Sea E-boats gain further successes in that respect. On 4/5 November they torpedoed two vessels off Cromer for the loss of one of their own boats, and a week later they laid an extensive minefield by the Sunk Lightship, only ten miles from Harwich. Because of poor weather, apparently, neither radar nor patrol craft spotted them. On 13 November SS *Cormount*, repaired after her earlier ordeal, was sunk on wandering out of the swept channel, followed by *Morar* a fortnight later. On 2 December the *Bangor*-class minesweeper *Ardrossan* was holed and partly flooded, but was pumped out and reached Parkeston. On 21 December a third merchant ship, the Norwegian *Norhawk*, was lost. Two days later the destroyers *Worcester* (from Harwich) and *Holderness* (Sheerness) were damaged.

With all the Z Line and other warships, and radar and Y, available, it

WAR ON THE CONVOY ROUTE _ 2

was disappointing to some that more E-boats could not be caught and sunk. But progress *had* been made since 1941 and 1942: the raiders could no longer creep up on convoys or sow mines undetected, thereby sinking several ships in one go and escaping scot free.

Meanwhile in Humber Sub-Command there had been only one major German attack in the second half of 1943. On the night of 21/22 September aircraft laid magnetic Type G mines in the Humber approach. One machine, carrying two of these mines, crashed at the hamlet of Out Newton, near the village of Easington above Spurn Point. The Immingham RMS party was tackling one mine from the wreck when it exploded, killing Lt Tanner. Thirty-four mines were eventually blown: one sank the "O" trawler *Meror* on 3 October, though without casualties. The Out Newton plane, incidentally, attracted a crowd of children from Withernsea, who stole guns and ammunition from it and were prosecuted by the RAF.

In 1944 the German shipping offensive collapsed almost totally. It accounted for a mere *four* vessels. The first two fell victim to E-boats. On 13 February Zymalkowski's 8th Flotilla sank the Grimsby M/S trawler *Cap d'Antifer* near the Dudgeon, just inside Humber Sub-Command; there were no survivors and only oil and a piece of the ship's nameboard were ever found. Eleven nights later thirteen from 2nd and 8th Flotillas made a determined attempt to smash a southbound convoy at Hearty Knoll. They sank only the merchant ship *Philipp M.* CD radar tracked them _ Thorpeness saw them at up to 42,000 yards east-north-east. The Y stations found it hard to monitor these raids, because the enemy had wisely cut down the range of his radio.

The onceformidable and ubiquitous mines were now a rarity. They sank only two vessels, both on 20 May 1944 off Harwich _ the patrol trawler *Wyoming* and the Dutch MMS 227, though on 14 April they had damaged the destroyer *Cotswold* a second time. E-boats returning from the May minelaying raid were spotted from the air off Orfordness, and, almost incredibly, an antique Manston-based 819 Squadron Swordfish biplane bombed and sank S 87.

Apart from one final fling in 1945, the German offensive against British shipping may be regarded as spent before the Normandy Invasion of June 1944. I shall, therefore, now review the East Coast part of it. Some six hundred vessels of all types were sunk during the war near the home shores of the Nore Command (i.e, not counting losses near the Continental coast). The losses in Yarmouth, Harwich and Sheerness Sub-Commands were almost equal, but in the descending order given. Humber area losses were of about half this order, while only a few vessels were actually *lost* in the London river. Some three hundred craft were sunk by mines, 130 by bombs, seventy-odd by E-boats, and ten by U-Boats. The balance succumbed to storms, accidental fires, collisions, etc.

Some East Coast shipping firms lost heavily. Everards' (of London and Greenhithe, ship names ending in *ity*), had seventeen coasters and two sailing barges sunk, all on this coast save for one of each lost at Dunkirk. William Cory of London owned twenty-one ships pre-war (all with *Cor* name prefixes): thirteen, including two under naval requisition, were sunk on the East Coast. Two Tyneside firms, France Fenwick (names ending in *wood*), and the Gas, Light and Coke Company (names usually referring to those products), each lost nine locally. Ellerman Wilson of Hull (names ending in *o*) was the only oceangoing line I shall mention, but of their many losses only two happened on this coast. The Harwich railway fleet lost five ferry ships (*St Denis, Train Ferry No 2, Bruges, Amsterdam* and *Archangel*) but all were on government service elsewhere. Of the sailing barge firms Francis and Gilders of Colchester suffered the highest loss; six. Not far away the little Mistley firm of Horlocks' was unlucky to lose two more locally (*Blue Mermaid _* the last sailing barge to be built, and *Gertrude May*), plus a coaster off the Tyne.

The human casualties, including merchant seamen of twenty nationalities, Royal Navy personnel, soldiers, tugmen, pilots, fishermen and civilian passengers, amounted to at least 3,600 dead, besides wounded and even a few prisoners.

Not a Battle of the Atlantic, but a severe campaign by any other standards. High as the losses seem, they were for the enemy a measure of failure. Over the war as a whole, for every ship and cargo lost another six hundred got through, and even at the relatively shortlived blackest periods, another thirty. The Germans' goal of denying sustenance to the world's largest city was always beyond their reach.

11
BATTLE WITH GIANTS

Throughout the war no great fleet battle, of the classic Camperdown or Jutland type, occurred in the North Sea. On just a single occasion German major warships entered the Nore Command, and that had no decisive outcome. However this "bolt out of the blue" was such as to call for a brief description.

In 1941 the German 35,000-ton battle cruisers *Scharnhorst* and *Gneisenau* and 14,000-ton heavy cruiser *Prinz Eugen* broke out of the North Sea and, via Iceland waters, into the Atlantic to raid British shipping. Subsequently they took refuge in the German-occupied French port of Brest, at the western entrance to the English Channel. Persistent RAF attempts to bomb them in harbour, the ominous example of the *Bismarck* (with whom *Prinz Eugen* had sailed), and his fears for an Allied invasion of Norway, pressed Hitler to demand their recall to Germany. British strength in the Atlantic made the German Navy run the calculated risk of rushing the three great warships straight through the Channel, Dover Strait and southern North Sea, as opposed to the long voyage round the west and north of the British Isles.

On intelligence that this was about to happen, the Admiralty ordered various precautions. One was "Operation QO", the sweeping of two additional gaps through the British minefield (QZ)X 384 and the German (QZ)X 403, south of Gap E, for the greater convenience of Nore warships coming out to intercept enemies leaving the Dover Strait. This was carried out by the Harwich-based 13th Fleet Minesweeper Flotilla, reinforced by *Blyth* and the 9th Flotilla, sent round from the West Coast. Another measure was the transfer between 3 and 5 February 1942 of three 21st Flotilla destroyers from Sheerness to Harwich (nearer these gaps) _ *Vesper, Vivacious* and the leader *Campbell*, which bore Captain (21D) Pizey. Both 21st and HMS *Badger*'s own 16th Flotilla were placed on an alert to last while tides and moonlight were suitable for a German breakout.

12 February was the last day of that alert. At 0915 six torpedo-equipped destroyers put out of Harwich on the orders of Vice-Admiral Lyon, now C-in-C Nore*. From 21st Flotilla were *Campbell* and *Vivacious*, and

---

*Several accounts of 12 February 1942 have been published which give slightly varying versions of British movements. Mine is based on Captain Pizey's official reports, composed over his signature within a few days of the events.

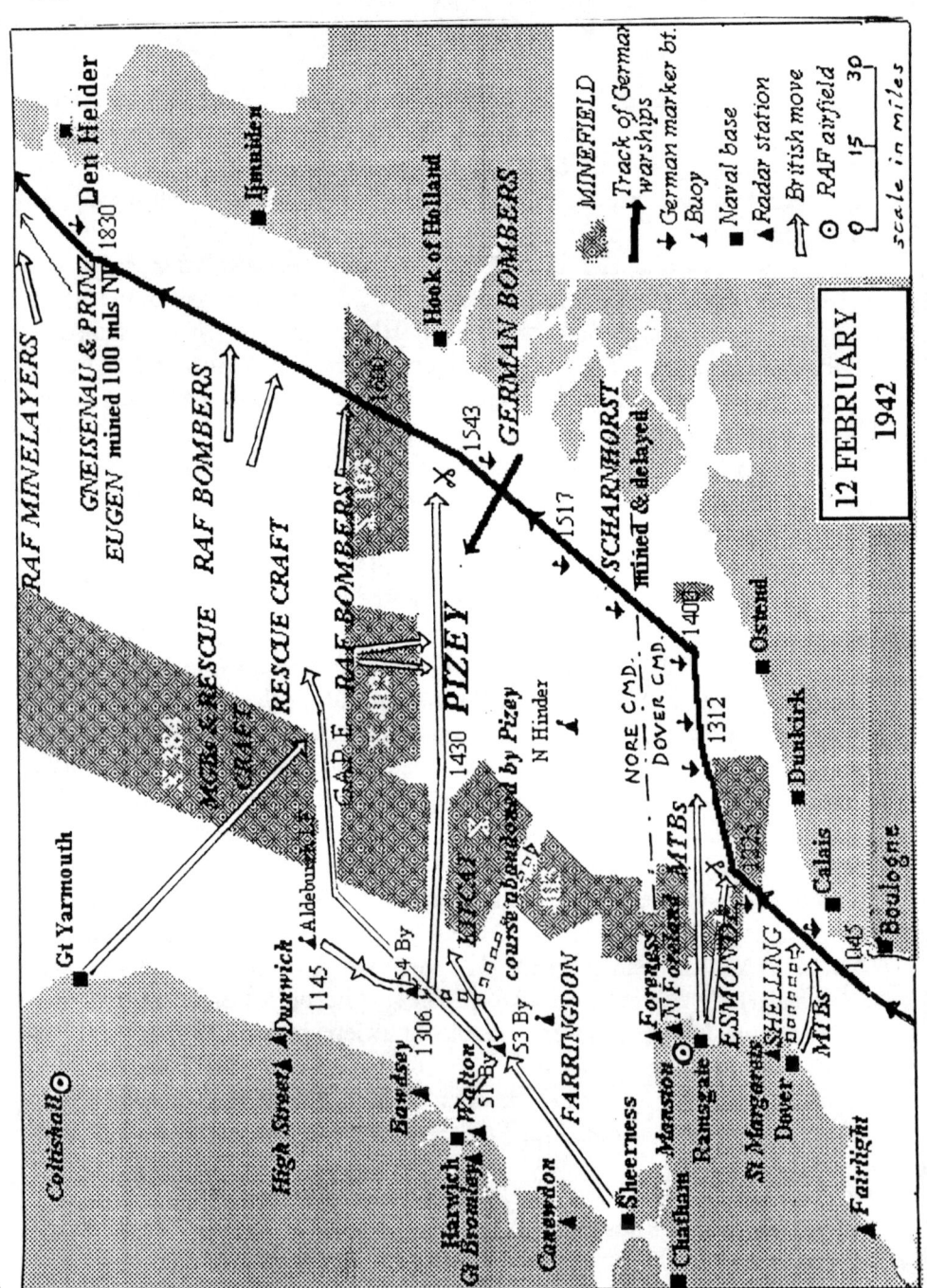

BATTLE WITH GIANTS

from Captain J P Wright's 16th *Mackay, Walpole, Whitshed* and *Worcester*. They were to stand by at the Aldeburgh Light Float.

Unknown to Pizey or anyone else in Britain, the German warships, commanded by Admiral Ciliax aboard *Scharnhorst*, had slipped out of Brest during the night and run almost the whole length of the English Channel. Coastal Command's standing ASV (radar) night air patrols had been called off for rather feeble technical and meteorological reasons. On a cloudy, almost moonless, night the enemy had flown no overhead air cover for British RDF to detect. When this cover had appeared at dawn, and been noticed, Fighter Command at Stanmore had misinterpreted the orbiting echoes as an air-sea rescue search, and when fighters actually saw some of the German light warships but (owing to bad visibility) *only* them, the impression of merely routine enemy Channel activity seemed confirmed. By then the CM (CHEL) RDF stations at Beachy Head and St Margaret's (Dover) should have seen something, but were being jammed, yet did not think this especially significant because it had been happening to the Dover Strait CM chain for three months! Only at 1045, with the German warships approaching Boulogne, did M7 CM station on the cliffs at Fairlight (near Hastings), though only on maintenance, make the first sighting of the battle cruisers. Soon afterwards Group Captain Beamish and Wing Commander Boyd, of Kenley, who had not been briefed about the warships and were merely on a routine sweep (or private jaunt?) in their Spitfires, also saw the enemy. They did not report till their return to base, and indeed it was another half an hour before any of this RAF information reached the Admiralty. They in turn informed Vice-Admiral Ramsay, at Dover, and, at 1137, Lyon at Chatham.

For its part the RAF had already earmarked up to 250 Bomber Command aircraft for this contingency, but it would be four hours before even the first of these could be briefed, fuelled and bombed up, and flown south from their bases in the North, by which time the German runaways would be far up the Dutch coast. Nor had Bomber Command trained in attacking moving ship targets, and the winter cloud was likely to force its planes down so low that their bombs would not pierce the enemy's armour.

Six obsolete Swordish biplane torpedo bombers of 825 Squadron, Fleet Air Arm, under Lt-Cdr Esmonde DSO RN and temporarily based at Manston, were the only suitable attack planes immediately to hand _ suitable since they had torpedoes and had attacked the *Bismarck* the previous spring.

BATTLE WITH GIANTS

Within three-quarters of an hour they were to be armed, while 11 Fighter Group at Uxbridge sent 72, 121 ("Eagle" _ i.e, American-manned) and 401 Squadrons from Hornchurch and Biggin Hill as escorts.

As they sat in their cockpits awaiting these fighters Esmonde and his crews could hear the boom of the Dover heavy guns, vainly firing at the enemy under RDF guidance _ this was certainly not one of those bright days when France could be seen from Kent! As the allotted moment for take-off approached, Esmonde was told that his escort would be delayed but also that the Germans had increased speed. His Swordfishs' range was so small that he decided to wait no longer. At 1220 Wing-Commander Gleave, a former Battle of Britain pilot with a burned face, and now Manston CO, watched as the six biplanes, so reminiscent of the Taranto raid, "flew out on Track 140". 72 Squadron's Spitfires were appearing and circling above the Swordfish: the two other fighter squadrons were not far away but failed to link up.

Twenty minutes later the Swordfish met the enemy off Gravelines. 72 Squadron, and Esmonde's own plane, were set upon by Me 109s and FW 190s, and lost touch with the rest of the Swordfish. Veering back out of control towards Kent, Esmonde and his two crew crashed into the sea and died. (His body was recovered by a Sheerness trawler, and his grave can still be seen in the naval cemetary at Gillingham). As the other five Swordfish flew on into the wall of flak from the warships all were lost: only five of the eighteen 825 Squadron peresonnel on this mission were rescued. Gleave put together the first report on this suicidal and vain attack, and in it recommended Esmonde for the VC, three other pilots for the DSC, and two more crewmen for the DSM. Vice-Admiral Ramsay wrote of Esmonde: "Such bravery as his is in keeping with the highest naval traditions and will remain through generations to come a stirring memory".*

Straight after the Swordfish attack MTBs from Dover and Ramsgate (though the latter had originated from Felixstowe) fired torpedoes but only from beyond the enemy's escort screen. They held on to a point thirty-two miles due east of the North Foreland. At 1312, which was about the same time, Ramsay watched the enemy blip fade from the scope at St Margaret's CM station. The Germans had passed right through his command area unscathed.

Meanwhile, off Orfordness, Captain Pizey had at 1145 been relayed

---

*PRO ADM 1/12459

ABOVE: Bangor-class fleet minesweepers and trawlers at Parkeston Quay *(IWM)*
BELOW: ML 150 in Hamilton Dock, Lowestoft, after ramming and sinking an E-boat off Harwich on 25 September, 1943. *(Scott)*

12 FEBRUARY 1942

ABOVE FAR LEFT: *Scharnhorst* at Kiel early in the war.
ABOVE NEAR LEFT: *Worcester*'s bow damage under repair at Chatham Dockyard.
BELOW LEFT: *Worcester*'s superstructure damage.
ABOVE: *Worcester* in Harwich Harbour after returning from Chatham. Note the Type 286P RDF at the masthead. Harwich Church and GER Hotel visible in the left distance. *(IWM)*

BELOW: The Swedish SS *Thyra*, pictured at Harwich pre-war. On 28 Feb, 1942, she was mined off that port and beached on the Shipwash. *(Hitchman)*

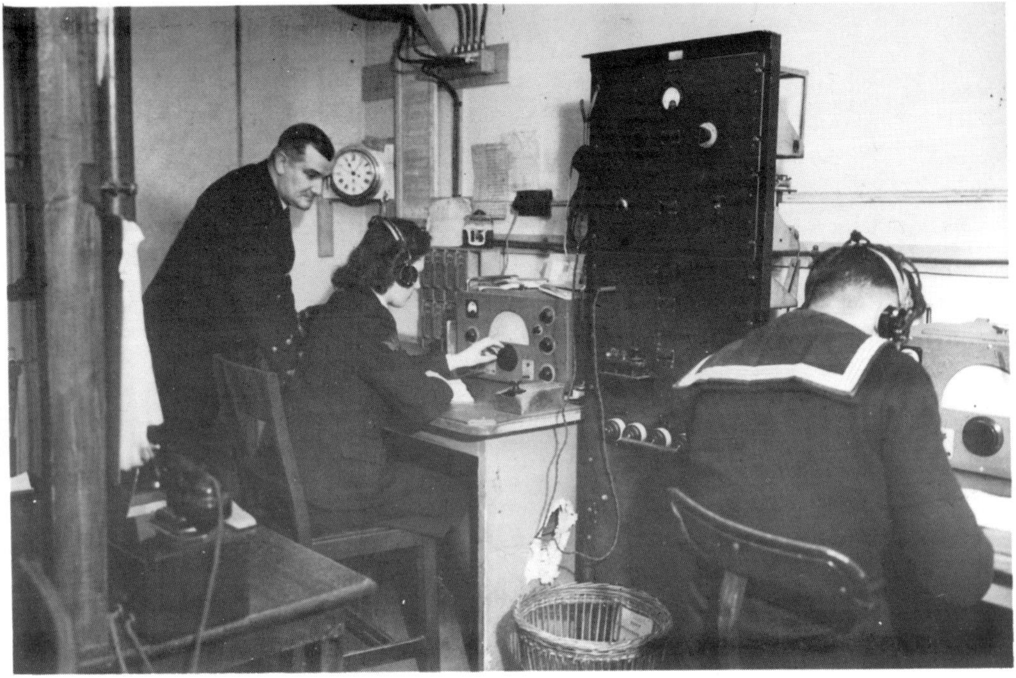

HMS *BADGER*, HARWICH

ABOVE: Radio operators in the Signals Distributon Office at Parkeston. *(IWM)*
BELOW: Luminaries of the base meet a Wren cricket team on the Parkeston playing field. The FOIC, Rear-Admiral Hugh Rogers, is second from the right. The Parkeston Quay Hotel and cranes are visible in the background. *(IWM)*

BATTLE WITH GIANTS

an order from Dover to join in the hunt. He had been put under Ramsay's orders for the moment. Taking command of 16th as well as 21st Destroyer Flotilla, he began to head for the southern "QO" gap through the German minefield to intercept Ciliax near the North Hinder. He reorganised his force into two battle divisions, the first led by himself in *Campbell*, and also comprising *Vivacious* and *Worcester*, the second led by Wright on *Whitshed*, with *Mackay* and *Walpole*.

His six ships were but Davids to the enemy Goliaths. They carried only 4 or 4.7-inch guns compared with their opponents' 11 and 8-inch. They were all First World War veterans with tired engines, weak armour, hand-worked torpedo tubes and inferior gunnery control systems. Even the German destroyers, E-boats (2nd, 4th and 6th Flotillas) and aircraft escorting the big warships were a severe threat to them.

Meanwhile all the Hunt-class destroyers in the Nore Command were ordered out to sea. Seven had been standing by _ *Berkeley*, *Fernie* and *Garth* at Sheerness, and *Eglinton*, *Hambledon*, *Quorn* and *Southdown* at Harwich. They were sent first to 51 Buoy, and then on to a position forty miles east of the Naze, in case the enemy light forces attempted to cut in between Pizey and the English coast. Cdr Kitcat, on *Eglinton*, took charge. Lt-Cdr Farringdon, on *Meynell*, was later sent from Sheerness to 51 Buoy with *Cattistock*, *Cottesmore*, *Holderness* and *Pytchley*. Subsequently it was argued that these Hunts would have been more useful to Pizey as AA cover, but it took two hours for them to raise steam and none could have joined him in time. In expectation of a sea and air battle eleven MGBs were sent from Yarmouth to the far end of Gap E at noon, and two hours later the Harwich and Yarmouth rescue tugs and Felixstowe and Gorleston RAF rescue launches were ordered out.

Pizey had been heading for the southernmost "QO" minefield gap, but soon after 1300 he was told that the Germans were increasing speed, and altered his course to meet them off the Hook of Holland. This meant switching to the more northerly of the gaps. I have often read that he took a deliberate gamble in crossing the minefield _ in some books a British one, in others (e.g. the official history) a German. But in reality he was using a gap already swept for him, and in any case would have had charts of all British mines.

At 1411 the hunt was transferred from Dover's control to the Nore's, after Ramsay said he was unfamiliar with the North Sea minefields. The German ships were now beyond the British RDF range, but CHL and the longer-range CH were able to estimate their position from the echoes of the escort planes circling overhead. Enemy jamming transmitters on the Pas de Calais were busy, and all the RDF from Sussex to Suffolk was affected by so-called "spiky railings" travelling across their scopes. Yet mostly the interference was too weak to hide the genuine blips. In the morning, and again towards evening, Walton CHL (AMES 23) was almost saturated by railings only a mile apart along the whole timebase, yet now, with the enemy opposite, was unaffected. Plots were telephoned straight to the Nore and Harwich Naval Plot Rooms as well as RAF Stanmore from there, and from Dunkirk, Canewdon, Great Bromley and Bawdsey.

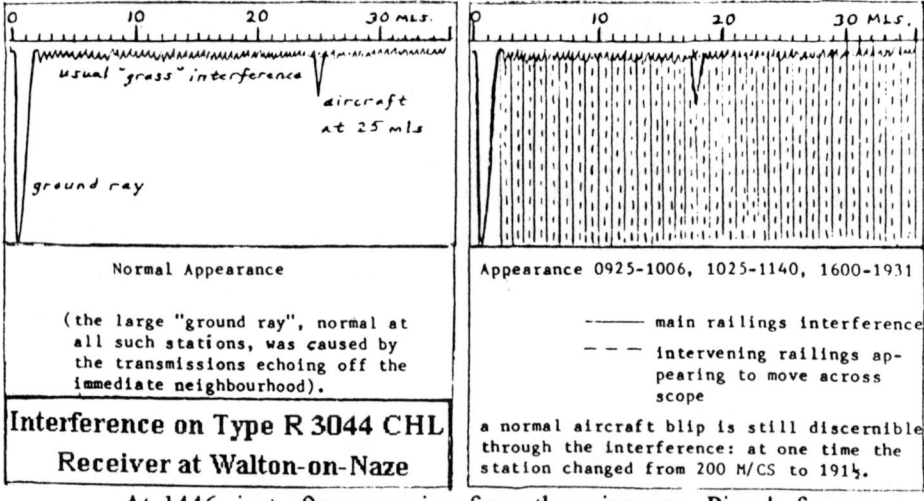

At 1446, just after emerging from the mine gap, Pizey's force was mistakenly bombed by RAF Hampdens, which aimed first at *Mackay* and then at *Worcester*. The destroyers held their fire in the hope of showing the planes their error. Fortunately no damage was incurred. Many other British aircraft flew overhead in search of the enemy, which few spotted owing to low and unbroken cloud. At 1507 *Walpole*'s engines started to give out and she was sent back.

Ten minutes later *Campbell*'s Type 271 (10 cm) RDF, then the only centimetric set on a Nore Command warship, located some of the German warships. Unknown to the British, the enemy convoy had split into two parts

BATTLE WITH GIANTS

three-quarters of an hour earlier, when *Scharnhorst* had exploded an old British mine, damaged her hull, and fallen behind, whereupon Ciliax had moved to a destroyer. At this juncture one formation of Stukas and another of Ju 88s attacked *Mackay* _ without success. At 1531 Pizey sighted the grey blurs of *Gneisenau* (in the van) and *Prinz Eugen*, surrounded by the black dots of light craft and escort planes, and steered in to the attack in fan formation. His destroyers met with a thundering barrage of heavy shells but closed to ranges of between 2,500 and three thousand yards before loosing their torpedoes and turning, *Worcester* going nearest. The sea conditions were bad, with the ships rolling and spray breaking over the torpedo tubes and guns. None of the torpedoes struck home _ in spite of claims made, and as the five destroyers turned they came under a storm of steel.

Worcester was the unlucky ship. Confronting *Gneisenau*, she was hit by eight shells in three minutes _ three from the battle cruiser and five from *Prinz Eugen*. The devastation was frightful. The 8 and 11-inch shells tore holes up to ten feet across below the waterline and on the bows and deck. A mast and a funnel were shot away. The lower bridge, wardroom and radio room were wrecked. Ammunition lockers amidships exploded and the whole crew of a 12-pdr gun were killed when shells fell on either side of the nearby torpedo tubes, though miraculously the crews of these survived. The deck was spattered with blood from end to end, with an arm or a leg lying here and there. If anything it was all too numbing for panic. One shell bored a hole from the middle of the upper deck to the side of the hull below the waterline, flooding No 1 Boiler Room. The ship took on a $20°$ list and came to a halt.

At that moment just one or two more shells, or a torpedo or bomb, would have finished her, while the survival of the other ships was only due to luck. But the Germans, in the half-light of a winter's afternoon, believed their attackers to be cruisers and were therefore unwilling to pursue. Moreover they had seen *Worcester* disappear in a cloud of smoke and spray and therefore felt confident in claiming one enemy definitely sunk. They therefore continued on their course, so that the action was broken off at 1556 after only eleven minutes, whereupon Pizey's four undamaged vessels were able to come to *Worcester*'s aid.

But as *Campbell* and *Vivacious* drew alongside to remove her wounded, they were mistaken for German by a 42 Squadron (Coastal Command) Beaufort, and only narrowly escaped torpedoes. 42 Squadron had

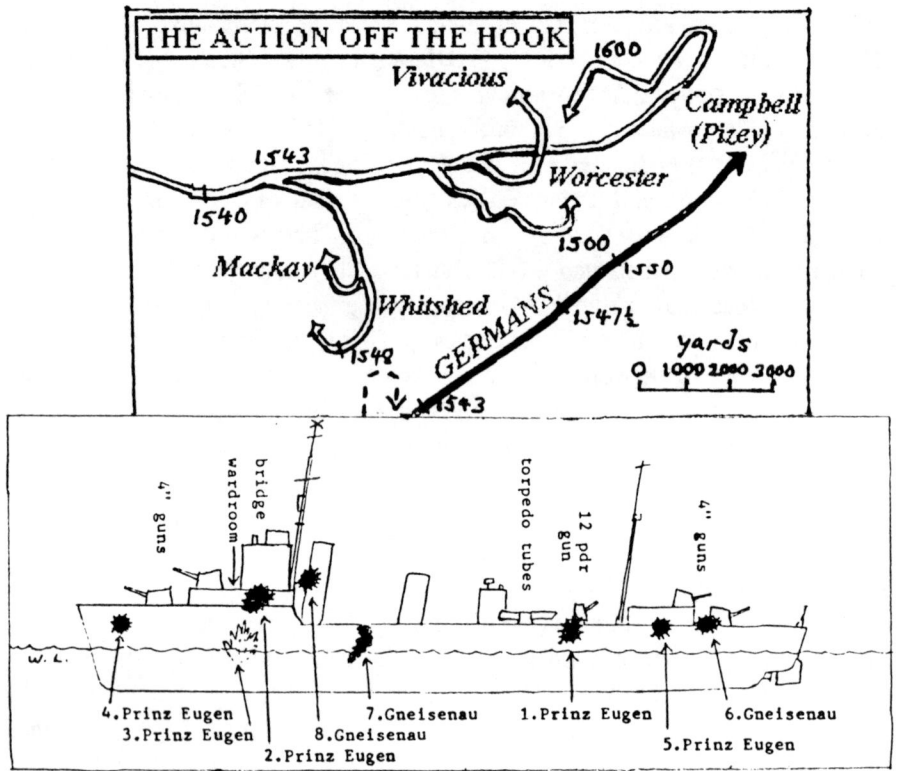

SHELL DAMAGE TO THE 'WORCESTER' ON 12 FEBRUARY 1942

flown down from Scotland to Coltishall, but had been delayed there waiting for a fighter escort from Manston, and for technicians to come from North Coates _ on snowy roads _ to prime their torpedoes, by which time it was almost dark. Further air strikes, by both British and Germans, now milling around in scores, were aimed at all five destroyers but missed. Naturally the day left some of the Navy bitter against the RAF, but the confusion was great on both sides. An air battle as deadly and chaotic as the naval engagement below was going on. Captain Wright wrote in his report;

> "The mixture of aircraft in our vicinity was extraordinary...In the course of the action we sighted Hampdens, Halifaxes, Beauforts, Wellingtons, Manchesters, Whirlwinds, Spitfires, Dorniers, Me 110s, Me 109s, FW 190s, Junkers 88s, Junkers 87s and He 111s".*

The Whirlwinds, incidentally, had been sent via Manston to escort Pizey, but could not find him.

---

*ADM 1/12459

BATTLE WITH GIANTS

Over the next two hours thirty-nine Bomber Command aircraft aimed bombs at the German fleet. They sank the route-marking trawler VP 1302 and damaged the steam torpedo boats *Jaguar* and T 13 (which went into Rotterdam for repairs), but did not hit the big ships. More than two hundred other bombers had taken off but could not find their targets in the murk. However a few performed one useful task (as it turned out) by mining the channel especially swept for the runaways off Borkum, the existence of which had been discovered only two days before by the "Ultra" codebreakers at Bletchley Park. Coastal Command had torpedo and bomber planes at North Coates and Bircham Newton, but having been delayed by snow on their runways, these were no more successful than Bomber Command's.

At first *Worcester* appeared certain to sink. Her captain, Lt-Cdr Coats, gave the order "Prepare to abandon" but intended to save the ship if possible. In the prevailing confusion his words were misinterpreted by some of the crew, who abandoned their posts and began to lower lifeboats and even to jump into the sea. He had to shout at them through a loudhailer that the destroyer could be saved. Pizey and Coats conferred and decided that *Worcester* could regain Harwich without assistance. Although her water supply had leaked out, she restarted her engines on seawater, and managed a speed of eight knots, while the steering seemed workable.

The four other destroyers rushed back to HMS *Badger* in order to get *Worcester*'s wounded to Shotley hospital and reload with torpedoes in the hope that there was still time to catch the straggling *Scharnhorst*. Regaining Parkeston Quay by 2000, they disembarked the wounded and were then tended by as many maintenance personnel as could be found, working by floodlights in emergency disregard for the blackout. As soon as they left next morning, however, a signal came that all enemy warships were now back in port.

Meanwhile, four of the Hunt-class destroyers hastened to meet *Worcester* and escort her back to harbour. The Admiralty ordered the exposure of the Orfordness Light to guide her. During the night she buried some of her dead at sea. Of her crew of 130 the majority were casualties _ twenty-three dead or missing and at least forty-five wounded. Sixteen *Worcester* gravestones can still be seen side by side at Shotley Cemetary. Just after dawn, still on her own power, *Worcester* limped in past Landguard Point to the cheers of servicemen lining both banks of the estuary. As soon as she berthed at Parkeston the Salvage Department set to work to keep her afloat. She was later towed off for full repairs at Chatham, and returned to her Harwich flotilla in May.

The Nore Command won more awards that February day than on any other. Pizey was knighted, Coats and two other destroyer captains won the DSO, and six DSCs and sixteen DSMs were given.

The German "Channel Dash" ("Operation Cerberus", they called it), was, however, a blow to British morale which brought discredit to many; even, for a time, Churchill himself. Vice-Admiral Binney, of the Admiralty, took part in the investigation which found no one overall cause of the failure. The RAF, including RDF, on the Channel Coast was blamed for not immediately spotting the German air buildup over the ships as they approached the Dover Strait at dawn. The Admiralty, however, had never thought that the enemy would run such a dangerous bottleneck at such an obvious and high-alert time as daybreak. RDF jamming, delays in sending and decoding signals, and in shifting aircraft from their normal stations to bases within range of the enemy, and the weather, were all blamed but might have been allowed for in advance.

Eventually it emerged that the Germans had not in any case had quite the triumph supposed. Not only *Scharnhorst*, but after the action near the Hook both the other big ships as well, had been damaged _ on those Bomber Command mines off Borkum. All three needed many months' repair, during which they were no threat to the extremely hard-pressed Allied convoys in the Arctic and Atlantic. The RAF took satisfaction that the mines concerned had been laid by them.

THE ACTION AGAINST THE GERMAN CRUISERS... THE COST

LEFT: The grave of Lt-Cdr Esmonde at Gillingham.
BELOW: Graves of men killed on the Harwich destroyer *Worcester*, at Shotley.

MORE HEAVY AIR ATTACKS ON PORTS

The more northerly East Coast ports were again badly blitzed in 1942 and 1943.

London Road, Lowestoft, after the lethal attack of 13 Jan, 1942 *(Ford Jenkins).*

The Southcoates Lane area of Hull after 19-20 May, 1942. *(Hull Daily Mail)*

Hope Street, Grimsby, after the raid of 13 July, 1943, which had been heavier than all the town's previous attacks put together. *(M Smith)*

12
FOUR YEARS OF AIR WAR

With the exception of two "Gruppen" of KG 4, and II/KG 40*, in Holland, the Luftwaffe bombers pulled out of Western Europe in the spring of 1941 to take part in the Balkan and then the Russian campaigns. The Blitz on Britain, in the sense of heavy and continual air raids, therefore died away.

The RAF had been preparing for a second and fiercer Battle of Britain at that juncture, for until Hitler attacked Stalin it was believed that he might invade Britain that summer. The main fighter stations all had satellite airfields, where planes could be dispersed to avoid bombing or landed in emergencies. On the RDF front the equivalent was the "Buried Reserve" CH stations, which were outside the site perimeter fences, had smaller (120-foot) T and R towers (one of each), and entirely underground rooms. Burying the Intermediate CH as a reserve once Final was working had been first suggested in October 1939, and next August an additional Buried Reserve chain was suggested for the whole East Coast. Stenigot was then built as a prototype. By the spring of 1941 all the others had been completed underground, but when the Luftwaffe went to Russia the RAF suggested abandoning them. The Air Ministry overruled it for the superbly bureaucratic reason that so much money and time had been spent on the sites, and so much equipment with no other use manufactured for them, that it was better to finish them! In fact work was slow to restart, for the MRUs (see Chapter 6) were on hand. The Buried Reserves were finally completed in the autumn of 1942, using shortwave aerials transferred from the unused towers of main stations.

IFF (Identification Friend or Foe) Marks I and II (also see Chapter 6) had been invaluable but with increasing Allied air activity threatened to choke the CH receiver scopes. In December 1942, after months of testing under the codename "Mark IIG", Mark III came on a separate, shorter wavelength (1.64 metres), in the form of coded pulses like Morse, and was automatically switched on and off in the aircraft by a ground control called the *Interrogator*. Every CH station had it, though not the CHLs and CDs. The IFF terminology has been given wrongly by some authors: the correct name for the radio device on the plane which the Interrogator activated was the *Transponder*, and the receiver on the ground which read its signals was

---

*The "4" and "40" here are the *Geschwader* (literally "squadron") numbers, though a Geschwader mustered up to a hundred combat aircraft. The "II" is the *Gruppe* number, a Gruppe consisting of about one third that number. So I refer to three Gruppen of about one hundred planes in all.

the *Responser*. If she wished to identify an oncoming plane a CH receiver operator now merely flipped the Interrogator switch, or got a colleague to do so, and a blip would pulsate for a few seconds on a separate trace, instead of every arriving aircraft half swamping the trace on which enemies had to be detected.

From early in 1943 the CH stations were equipped with new receivers of the RF8 or R 3103 type. Many new refinements were fitted to these. AJIJ (Anti-Jamming Intentional Jitter) randomly varied pulse-timing to dodge jamming. Time-bases were variable and radial (ran round the scope instead of straight across), so that more accurate tracking could be done at different ranges. The ERM (Electric Rangemarker) now fed the Uniselector Converter automatically by a light-sensitive device near the scope, without the operator setting dials. If required a second trace could be switched on above the first, and on this the IFF Mark III blips appeared.

By 1942 there were four types of RDF station on the East Coast _ CH for general early warning, CHL for detection of ships and lowflying planes, GCI for detailed tracking of night raiders and direction of British night fighters, and CHEL (CD or CM) for extra-low-level detection. On the whole these various stations were not on the same sites, the exception being Bawdsey, which had CH, CHL and CD. Many stations took on work in addition to their basic roles. West Beckham and some others monitored and jammed the enemy's "Knickebein" bomber-navigation beams. In 1941 and 1942 Great Bromley was the HQ and monitoring station for "Gee", the first British radar-guided bomber-navigation system: Stenigot and later Canewdon were "Gee" "slave" stations. Trimingham, a clifftop CD station, was also the "Cat" station for the RAF's second radar bomber-guidance system, "Oboe" _ the other station, "Mouse", was at Walmer in Kent.

Even without these extras, which came under Bomber Command, East Coast radar had come to absorb considerable man (and woman) power. 75 Wing, which controlled all defensive radar from the Isle of Wight to Dunwich, had 5,800 personnel when expanded in the middle of 1943. An average East Coast CH station had about 130 RAF and WAAF personnel, eighty infantrymen for local security and defence, and fifty AA gunners, though from henceforth these Army contingents were cut back and taken over by the RAF Regiment. A CHL station averaged seventy RAF and WAAF personnel, and a GCI forty-four.

FOUR YEARS OF AIR WAR

First the RAF night fighters had been slow Blenheims and small Hurricanes; then came powerful (but, if power was lost, rock-heavy) cannon-firing Beaufighters and over-large American-derived Havocs; but by 1943 the ultimate had appeared in the form of De Havilland's fast "Wooden Wooden" Mosquito. In the spring of that year seven GCI-guided Mosquito night fighter squadrons, with 140 aircraft, were guarding the Thames Estuary and eastern approach to London: No 25 at Coltishall, 29 and 488 (New Zealand) at Bradwell Bay, 85 and 96 at West Malling, 157 at Hunsdon, and 410 (Canadian) at Castle Camps. Each night, from dusk till dawn, a squadron would patrol its "beat" with pairs of fighters working in relays; for two hours each pair would circle until alerted by a GCI, this radar having been forewarned by a CH. The fighter pilot's "oppo" or observer would then switch on his AI, and expect to see a blip appear as the GCI guided them towards their quarry: but only in a minority of cases was contact made, and, in turn, only a minority of contacts meant an enemy shot down.

By 1942 the AA defences had been thickened. The heavy batteries at the harbours were linked by others on the coastline in between _ at, for example, Foulness and Clacton, making a continuous barrage along the coast. Small naval bases like Burnham-on-Crouch and Brightlingsea, and the non-naval seaside towns, received four or eight Bofors light guns each, where there had been only the odd machine gun previously.

But the spectacular innovation were the seven steel AA platforms placed out in the Thames Estuary _ the Maunsell Forts (named after their designer). Four were manned by the Navy and Royal Marines, with five officers and 153 ratings on each, of whom fifty or so were ashore on leave at any one time. These were Roughs and Sunkhead Towers, off Harwich, and under its FOIC, and Tongue Sand and Knock John Towers, off the North Kent coast and under the Extended Defences Officer, Sheerness. The trawlers *Strathmaree* and *Strathelliott* were the respective tenders. Each of these naval forts rested on two sixty-foot hollow legs, in which the crews lived, and carried a Type 273 (10-cm) radar set, two 3.7-inch and two Bofors guns. They were built by Sir Alexander Gibb and Partners, at Red Lion Wharf, Gravesend, fitted at Tilbury, and towed out and sunk in place by London tugs, escorted by Sheerness Harbour Defence MLs. They were operational by the spring of 1942. The other three forts, built it situ between mid and late 1943, were Army property, and were called Great Nore, Red Sand and

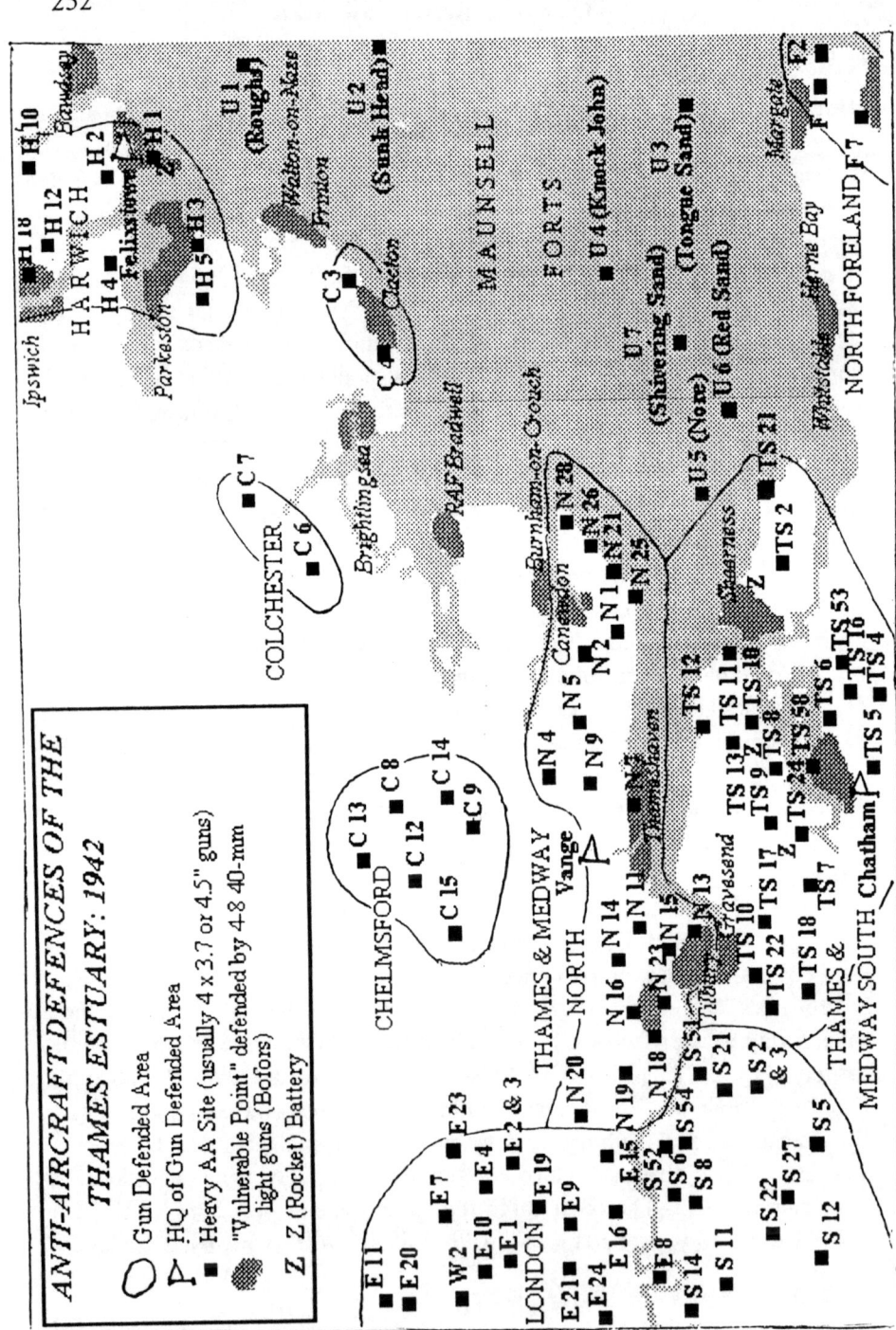

FOUR YEARS OF AIR WAR

Shivering Sand Forts. They lay nearer the Thames mouth; indeed Great Nore occupied the position of the Nore Light Vessel. Each was enormous, consisting of seven towers mounted on four legs apiece and linked by catwalks; of the seven four mounted 3.7-inch guns, one a Bofors, one a searchlight, and one the gunnery control gear. Roughs Fort alone engaged ninety-six enemy planes and fired 1,784 3.7-inch and 1,217 Bofors rounds, claiming six planes and six flying bombs. On one occasion Tongue Sand Fort even engaged and claimed an E-boat.

The East Coast Blitz receded northwards, away from London, in the early summer of 1941. By late summer the Luftwaffe rarely came overland. In the last five months of that year no one was killed by bombing at Chatham, Harwich, Ipswich, Lowestoft, or Yarmouth, and the same was true at Hull for the last four months. The few small attacks on Yarmouth and Lowestoft seem mainly to have been overspill from the still serious raids on shipping which I mentioned in Chapter 10.

There were exceptions to this. On the Sunday morning of 24 August 1941 a Ju 88, flying at little more than the height of the transmitter towers, put some heavy bombs onto the lane leading to Great Bromley CH and "Gee" station before the defences had been alerted. A visiting official reported that the PBX telephone switchboard had been too tied up with routine calls to hear the warning. A PAC was then fired and British fighters gave chase, and apparently it was their bullets which went through the side of a cottage and killed an elderly couple, an incident on which all the official records are silent. In the early hours of 12 October several planes attempted a raid on Ipswich: two bombed just south of the town centre, while others went far astray.

Late that year the upsurge of minelaying in the Thames Estuary may explain the rash of mine explosions on land in Essex, though one suspects an attempt to hit RDF stations. "There is no earthly reason why the enemy should worry to attack this place", wrote Captain Dane, the local RNO, after six mines had fallen on or near Burnham-on-Crouch within three days that November, blasting the mine control tower, breaking hundreds of windows (including those of his yacht-club HQ), felling an electricity pylon, and blacking out the town*. Could Canewdon CH have been the objective? On the night of 27-28 November two mines fell on farmland two miles west of

---

*PRO ADM 199/251.

the Great Bromley equivalent.

On the night of 22 January 1942 some minelaying planes came very near Harwich. One shot up the barrage balloons, another dropped a mine in the approach channel, and a third was said to have crashed in the sea after the trawlers *Exhayne, Spina* and *Warwing* fired on it from east of the Cork Lightship. This "kill" was confirmed when Landguard Fort reported a fire on the water a mile out, and a few days later wreckage and oxygen cylinders, uncorroded and with German lettering, were washed up at Harwich Hard.

The enemy's bomber strength was now reviving somewhat. The Do 217s of KG 2 complemented and then replaced the He 111s of KG 4 in Holland. Later the Ju 88s of KG 6 arrived in Belgium and Northern France. From now on the Luftwaffe mostly carried 500-kilogram (half-ton) bombs instead of the varied loads of the main Blitz. In early 1942 there was no attempt to bomb London, Chatham, Sheerness, the Southend convoy anchorage, or Harwich, but the daylight Luftwaffe anti-shipping strikes in Yarmouth Sub-Command extended to some small (mostly one-plane) attacks on the nearby ports and naval bases. And some of these were terrifying.

On the afternoon of 13 January, in spite of (or perhaps because of) evacuation, rationing, the earlier air raids, and a snow storm outside, hundreds of Lowestoft civilians and off-duty service people were crowded into the shops and café on the east side of London Road North. No alarm had been sounded when four 500-kg bombs entered this scene: a Do 217 had come in low and hidden by snow flurries. Hundreds of people were buried in the debris, some for twenty-four hours. Three hundred troops were brought in to help dig them out; Private John Scott, of the 7th Borderers, won the George Medal for his heroic efforts. Wild rumours circulated, with attempts by the authorities to play down the incident _ our friend the Intelligence Officer of 54 Division (see Chapter 4) seemed to believe that no one had been killed at all! The final death toll was seventy, with over a hundred injured, making this the worst single bombing incident in East Anglia. Fifteen more Lowestoft civilians died in another unheralded raid only ten days later. On 18 February eight more were killed at Rampart Street, Yarmouth. And on the 21st another Do 217, repeating the previous tactics, made a shallow diving attack on HMS *Royal Arthur*, the huge naval training camp at Ingoldmells (Skegness), under cover of a snow shower. The camp cinema and ninety former Butlins' chalets were destroyed and a crater ninety feet wide appeared. Since hundreds of men were nearby and had ignored the alarm it is surprising that only four were killed.

East Coast civilians were outraged by the official refusal to permit "crash warnings" _ sounding the sirens when the Civil Defence HQs had given no notice of a raid, yet planes were seen approaching with the naked eye. The authorities believed that this practice would continually trigger false alarms and needless panics, since approaching RAF planes would often be taken for enemy _ and work and morale would suffer. Understandably civilians thought that the constant low-level, opportunist, attacks came quicker than the authorities could notify, and that the lack of impromptu local warnings was depriving people of time to shelter and condemning many to death. Surely anyone spotting approaching enemy planes should be allowed to run to the nearest siren and get it sounded? In the end crash warnings were allowed.

In April Norwich suffered two "Baedecker" raids in retaliation for "Bomber" Harris's fire raids on Lubeck and Rostock. These were the only mass raids on East Anglia throughout the war (i.e, ones involving over fifty planes), unless one includes the daylight strikes on fighter aerodromes during the Battle of Britain. As a result of the Norwich raids not only that city but also Ipswich and Chelmsford received balloon barrages and heavy AA guns.

Neither Hull nor Grimsby had been raided since 1941, but their turn now came again. On the night of 13/14 April one plane bombed Hull and killed four civilians, while two more hit Grimsby and killed thirteen _ the worst raid the former "capital" of British fishing had so far experienced. On the night of 19/20 May Hull took its first mass raid since the main Blitz. About twenty planes hit the city, while another seventy bombed around it. Alexandra Dock and Southcoates Lane were much damaged, and though the death toll of ten was surprisingly low the authorities reported a severe drop in public morale.

In the early hours of 30 May some scattered bombing around the Humber missed Hull, but three raiders hit Yarmouth and killed four people. Lt Freeman RNVR and Seaman Turner won the MBE and BEM respectively for putting out a fire *on top of* one of the naval oil tanks. An unexploded 1000-kg "Hermann" was defused on the beach, and   today stands in front of the Maritime Museum.

Against Ipswich a big, Baedecker-scale, raid, said to involve more than thirty planes, was mounted on the night of 1/2 June. Ipswich could have suffered as much as Norwich five weeks earlier if the bombing had not been largely shifted onto the heathlands to the east by "Starfish" decoy fires at Bucklesham (where eight "Starfish" men paid with their lives) and Shottisham. Most of the rural parishes between the Orwell and Deben Estuaries received 1000, 500, or 250-kg HE, phosphorous, or incendiary bombs in a night of terror. One bombload on the south-eastern edge of Ipswich killed another five civilians.

King's Lynn was a market town and small port with scant strategic significance, yet ended the war with the fourth highest air raid death toll in East Anglia (seventy-five) _ higher than Harwich's. For this a raid on 12 June 1942 was mainly responsible; bombs fell on the Eagle Hotel and nearby buildings in the town centre, and forty-two people died.

On the night of 24/25 June, in addition to taking two salvoes of 500-kg HEs, the northern part of Yarmouth was smothered with incendiaries. There were fires throughout the three hundred acres between Vauxhall Station, the Hospital, North Denes Road and Regent Street. St Nicholas's, the largest parish church in England, had a vulnerable oak roof and only members of the Boys' Brigade as firewatchers. It was completely gutted. The stonework of the pillars inside was so damaged as to resemble charred wood, and the clock on the tower was stopped at the time of the bombing, commemorating it for the next twenty years till the church was restored.

On 12 July HMS *Minos II*, the Lowestoft Coastal Forces base in Hamilton Dock, was attacked. The base commander's launch was sunk, MGBs 14 and 15 were wrecked and two more boats damaged, some dockside buildings were demolished, and there were five casualties, one fatal. At the same time another plane bombed Yarmouth bus depot.

In one week in late July Withernsea, Skegness, Sheringham, Cromer and Yarmouth were all bombed in daylight by single planes. Altogether thirty-seven people were killed. The naval HQ at Yarmouth was damaged without loss of life. The worst incident was at harmless Withernsea on the 24th, when one of two bombs, perhaps aimed at the nearby station, exploded in Queen Street and killed at least fifteen. Meanwhile one small night raid actually did a little strategic damage: on 22 July a load of incendiaries burned some oil and damaged a disused seaplane in a hangar at Felixstowe Dock. It was the only time in 1942 that bombs fell on Harwich Harbour area.

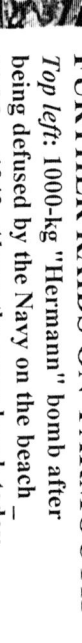

FURTHER RAIDS ON YARMOUTH

Top left: 1000-kg "Hermann" bomb after being defused by the Navy on the beach 30 May, 1942. *Above*: the same bomb today. *Left*: Southtown Maltings after a mine explosion on 18 March, 1943.

(Box)

**THE RAID ON YARMOUTH
OF 25 JUNE 1942**

This page: the shell of St Nicholas's Church, burned out by incendiaries.

Facing page (top to bottom):
Lacon's Brewery, destroyed by the same hu shower of incendiaries; a postwar reminder; bomb damage in Middlegate Street, probably most bombed thoroughfare in East Anglia. *(B*

DESTROYED BY FIRE
DURING AN AIR RAID
25th JUNE, 1942
REBUILT 1948

BURIED RESERVE CH (radar) STATION AT GREAT BROMLEY (photographed in 1989).
Top: Concrete hatch and ventilation shafts of the receiver site.
Bottom: Base of the dismantled transmitter site, with the old main transmitter site and one surviving (though altered) 358-foot steel tower in the background.

FOUR YEARS OF AIR WAR

The Lowestoft AA gunners claimed some successes that year. On 30 July Heavy AA Sites H1 and H2 each declared that they had brought a bomber down in the sea: one was said to be off Southwold, where bodies were later washed ashore, and another certainly crashed halfway back to the Dutch coast. An almost unprecedented tally of six German bombers were shot down near the ·East ı coast that moonlit night, all en route to Liverpool: the others crashed near Hearty Knoll, off Yarmouth, at Salthouse (Norfolk) and in the Thames Estuary. For the next few months the enemy preferred to send only a small handful of bombers to each target.

Colchester had taken very few raids in the main Blitz. It had a small port at the Hythe and a famous garrison district, but its real strategic significance lay in the Paxman factory, which made many of the engines for British submarines and landing craft. Its final death toll would have been very low if it had not been for a stray bomb on Severall's mental hospital on the northern edge of town on 11 August 1942, which killed thirty-eight patients. It might not be a pacifist cliché to ask whether the victims or their killers had been the least sane.

Most of Ipswich's bombs seemed to fall on its industrial, Nacton, or south-eastern, side. On the night of 25 August a direct hit on a shelter there killed twelve civilians.

In this same part of the world Great Bromley RDF station believed itself a target. Night after night that month the staff plotted a single German plane, flying straight towards it from Holland, circling overhead, and then flying back home, always without bombing. On the 26th/27th a larger, menacing, raid, turned back off the Naze (its scheduled target had been Colchester). On 15-16 September two or three Do 217s bombed Ipswich and just outside it. And then, on the following night, six planes came in low over the Orwell, circled Colchester, and bombed, mainly with the new "firepot" giant phosphorous incendiaries. Four of the raiders struck round the edges of Colchester without killing anyone, while within half a mile of Great Bromley "AMES" barns, hedges and haystacks blazed. Probably Paxman's had been the intended target.

On 27/28 of that month four planes staged a much more concentrated raid on King's Lynn Docks, without causing deaths or strategic damage.

Then came another phase of the nasty little opportunist daylight attacks which had characterised the winter and late July. One plane descending through low cloud killed eight civilians at Chapel Road, Colchester, on 28 September. On 19 October many such attacks were made, in the most widespread raid of 1942. Bombs fell at Southend (killing two people), Colchester, Little Oakley (near Dovercourt), Cranfield's Maltings at Ipswich, Snape (near Aldeburgh), Needham Market, Kessingland (just south of Lowestoft _ two more killed), Yarmouth, Cromer (two dead) and Wainfleet. A Czech with a Bren gun brought down a Ju 88 at Oulton, near Lowestoft. Three days later thirteen (mainly soldiers) were killed by a single bomb in Orford's picturesque square, once the haunt of Watson Watt and co. On 6 November a Do 217 bombed two shipyards and a malthouse on the north side of Oulton Broad, killing one man and destroying the redundant MGB 19 on the slip at Leo Robinson's Yard. Eleven died at nearby Aldeburgh on 15 December, including soldiers but also a ninety-year-old civilian who had refused to leave his armchair for the family Morrison shelter (splinter and blast-proof cage under the table). And on the morning of 22 December eight civilians died when one plane bombed Albion Road, off Yarmouth sea front, from above a Scotch mist: one woman was hideously burned by a phosphor bomb. The AA claimed to have shot down the perpetrator.

These "tip and run" daylight raids continued into early 1943. On 6 January the Harwich Fixed Defences were strafed by one plane, which, however, failed to release its bombs until it was over Ramsey _ a few civilians and artillerymen were wounded by bullets. Six days later another bomber killed four residents of Heybridge, the small port adjoining Maldon. On the 18th and 30th there were similar attacks on Margate, which between them killed six people.

On the night of 17 January 1943 Do 217s and Ju 88s gave London its first serious air raid since the main Blitz. Only rather scant damage was done, including a fire at a wharf in Upper Thames Street in the City and three small bombs on Deptford Power Station. Several of the raiders were intercepted by British fighters, among them 85 Squadron, which downed three, one falling in the sea off Bradwell to the squadron CO, Wing Commander Raphael. 85 was undoubtedly the élite night fighter squadron of this period. In 1941 it had converted to night fighting at what its then commander Peter Townsend called "dismal Gravesend", though it still had its

FOUR YEARS OF AIR WAR

Hurricanes. Later it had moved to Hunsdon (in Hertfordshire near the Essex border at Harlow), and had re-equipped with Havocs and then Mosquitos. Its aircrew now included the top-scoring duo Cunningham and Rawnsley and Flight Lt Bunting.

Late in 1942 the South Coast _ as far up as Canterbury _ had been raided by Focke-Wulf FW 190s from the two Jagdgeschwadern ("Hunt Squadrons") in Northern France, each fighter rigged to carry one 500-kg bomb. Flying as close to sea level as they could, they were, of course, below CH and CHL detection, but, moreover, could not be spotted by the existing CHEL (CM) radar until within five minutes of the coast, a shorter time than it took to ready the defences. In daylight on 20 January all these FW 190s struck far inland _ at the same area of London as the night raid three days earlier. A school at Lewisham was direct-hit, while a bomb hit the nearby Greenwich Royal Naval College and killed one officer _ the Nore Command's first air raid casualty of the year.

On 17 February FW 190s made their first East Coast attack, bombing Clacton and killing one child _ the rationale for raiding the town must have been the large Light AA school at Butlin's camp. On 13 March six of them dumped their bombs on the fields of the Dengie Peninsula instead of their nearby objective RAF Bradwell Bay, whereupon 331 Norwegian Squadron Spitfires pursued and claimed to have shot them all down in the sea. (This was the occasion when the sailing barge *Alaric* was strafed). Next day they raided Frinton and Walton, killing two soldiers and six civilians. Ten days later they were down in Kent, delivering their most lethal attack; fifty people were killed by their bombing and strafing of Ashford.

Meanwhile, on 3-4 March, over a hundred Do 217s and Ju 88s crossed the Essex coast and bombed London, Chelmsford, and other places. One derailed a Liverpool Street-Colchester train at Mountnessing (near Chelmsford) and killed two. Another hit Gravesend, where one person died and the Everard senior barge skipper Uglow lost the roof of his house, and several salvoes of assorted bombs fell on Southend. More exploded at No 1 Basin at Chatham Dockyard and killed five _ the only mid-war air raid deaths in the Medway Towns. This was the night of the dreadful panic at Bethnal Green Underground Station, in which 178 people were trampled to death. At the start of the raid Shoeburyness Heavy AA Site N1 brought down a Ju 88 at Burnham-on-Crouch, and at the end Clacton C3 site shot another one down in the sea.

On the night of 15 March some of the same raiders attempted the Luftwaffe's first major attack on Grimsby, the Nore Command's largest minesweeping base. Due, perhaps, to two "Starfish" decoys, not one bomb hit the town. Moreover five planes were claimed by the fighters and AA: five Germans were captured from two of them, including a pair brought in by ground staff from North Coates airfield.

Early on 18 March, in a last example of the single-plane daylight raid, eleven young women died at Yarmouth when bombs struck the Wrens' quarters in Queens Road. The local AA claimed to have downed the bomber. That night, coincidentally, a mine blasted a riverfront maltings at Gorleston, and many HEs and incendiaries fell on Oulton and the north-west side of Lowestoft _ these incidents were part of a large failed raid on Norwich.

On 4 April another thirty enemy planes came in on the Essex approach. One bombed Thameshaven, killing four oil refinery workers; the rest mined the Estuary (and over the next few days probably caused the loss of SS *Josefina Thorden* and *Dynamo* in the Sunk area. Sunkhead Fort claimed two of the raiders shot down and Roughs one.

85 Squadron shot down two Do 217s over Essex early on 15 April 1943 (at Layer Bretton and Little Clacton). The raider's main target had been the Hoffmann's ball bearing factory at Chelmsford, at which over a hundred bombs fell. But an equal bombload struck the rural area between Ramsey and Thorpe-le-Soken, just south-west of Harwich, and close to the Bramble Island explosives works. After a strawstack on Holland's Farm (Beaumont) had caught fire Great Oakley found itself ringed by ten planeloads of blazing incendiaries, "firepots" and phosphor bombs. While Chelmsford was attacked again a month later one bomber was brought down on Bawdsey village, after at least three planes had struck at or near Ipswich.

Meanwhile the FW 190s, reorganised into a single Gruppe called II/SKG 10*, struck fiercely at the East Anglian coast. On 7 May, at Yarmouth, seven of them killed twelve people in the vicinity of Vauxhall and Southtown Stations. When dropped from such low altitude heavy bombs often bounced in dramatic fashion, and on this occasion one ricocheted a quarter of a mile right over Vauxhall Station. Simultaneously another eight FW 190s bombed and strafed such villages north of town as Caister, Hemsby and Winterton. Four days later nineteen or twenty of these planes were back,

---

*SKG="Schnellkampfgeschwader" (fast combat squadron).

FOUR YEARS OF AIR WAR

bombing the northern outskirts of Yarmouth, far from the Navy, but well populated by the Army. The ATS (Auxiliary Territorial Service, or Woman's Army) quarters were hit and twenty-six girls died, only two months after the bombing of the Wrens' accommodation. In all forty-nine people were killed that day at Yarmouth, its worst of the war. Some of the raiders strafed the same villages north of town, plus Ormesby, Filby, California and others.

On the following, misty, morning eight Focke-Wulfs raided Lowestoft at "rooftop" level and killed six people and wounded twelve. The brunt of the attack fell on the Patrol Service gunnery training trawlers *Strathgarry* and *Shova*; Seaman James Swann on the former won the DSM for facing the raiders with a machine-gun while four of his shipmates were wounded (one fatally) around him. Twenty of these planes returned at dusk and repeated the performance. 500-kg HEs struck the Outer Harbour, the Gasworks and the High Street area. A bomb at Corton Road bounced 150 yards. Thirty-three more people were killed and fifty-five wounded. In the High Street a Patrol Service stoker saved the life of a Wren at the cost of his own by throwing himself on top of her as a pub collapsed onto them.

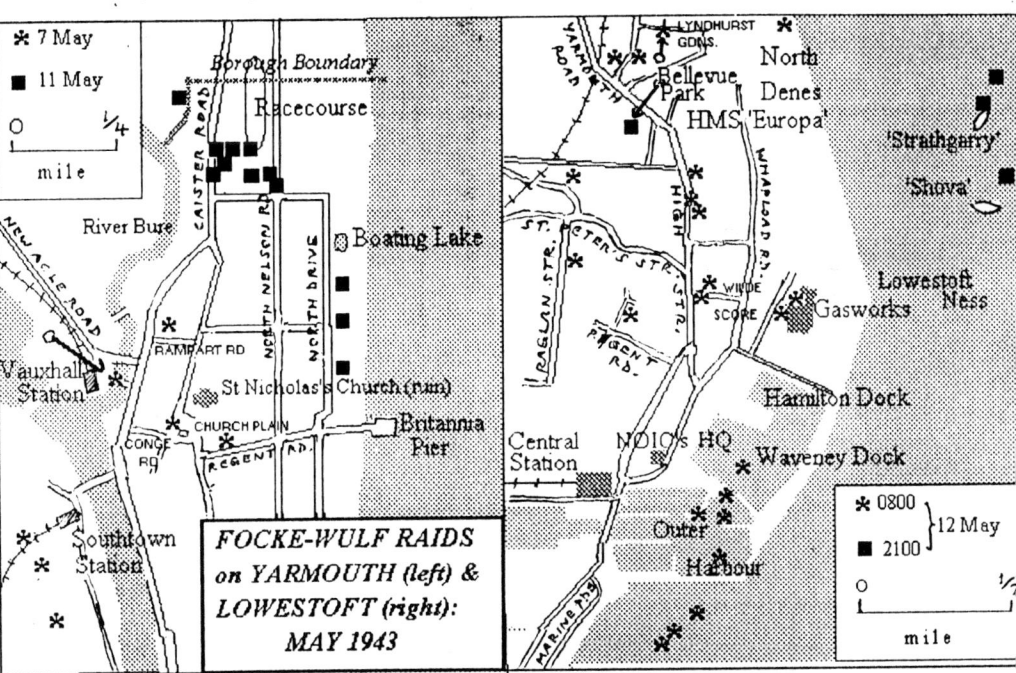

FOCKE-WULF RAIDS on YARMOUTH (left) & LOWESTOFT (right): MAY 1943

FOUR YEARS OF AIR WAR

At dusk on the 15th it was the turn of Southwold and Felixstowe _ barrage balloons apparently deterred the attackers from their primary target of Harwich. Ten people were killed at Southwold and six wounded at Felixstowe Ferry, the gravel-fringed hamlet opposite Bawdsey. Offshore Roughs Fort and the Harwich guardship *Queen Empress* fired back, each claiming one (though apparently the same) raider, which *Balmoral*, another guardship, saw go into the sea. On the 30th the FW 190s made their second attack on Frinton and Walton-on-Naze. At the former one bomb landed at the seaward end of Connaught Avenue, the smart main street, and another wedged itself in the girders of the water tower (by the station). At Walton the Police Station and Catholic Church were destroyed, and four people were killed. On 1 June the target was Margate. While the fighters scrambled from nearby Manston ten civilians died and a solid Victorian church was utterly caved in by a single bomb.

At dawn next day II/SKG 10 made the last of these forays. Again giving up on Harwich, they bombed the Ipswich Dock area, as well as Felixstowe and Bawdsey. Ransome and Rapiers' were hit, while at Felixstowe one bomb missed a gun emplacement by yards and another landed on Brackenbury Beach, bounced up over the sixty-foot cliff, and came to earth in a road, all without exploding. Eleven people were killed and fifteen wounded at Ipswich, and at Bawdsey an RAF corporal also died. One raider was destroyed when it struck an Ipswich dock crane.

The FW 190s continued to roam the North Sea on defensive and night bombing missions. Short of fuel, one such had already been forced to land at Manston on 20 May. On the night of 22 June another crashed in the Medway immediately above Rochester Bridge, smashing up some sailing barges in the process. On 8 September Cunningham and Rawnsley claimed another one off Aldeburgh, as the local Coast Artillery and Coastguard confirmed. (Cunningham was by now 85 Squadron's commander, in place of Raphael, who had become CO at Manston).

After the FW 190 scare in the south, the focus of activity briefly moved up to the Humber. With fewer air raid casualties so far than the much smaller borough of Harwich, Grimsby had come to be regarded as proverbially lucky, especially compared to Hull just up the estuary. But on the night of 13-14 June it suffered a stunning attack with incendiaries and anti-personal bombs. 332 separate fires were counted, especially around the

FOUR YEARS OF AIR WAR

Fish Dock. But the worst menace was the "butterfly" anti-personal bomblets, first seen at Ipswich nearly three years before. 754 unexploded specimens were found, but thousands more were dropped. They lodged in trees, gutters and even on the rooves of buses, and detonated when moved, even slightly. Unknowing civilians were being killed and grievously injured by them well into the next day. So widespread was the bombload that nearly every premises in the town had to be searched.

On the night of 23/24 June Hull was hit, with much scattered damage but no serious casualties. On 13/14 July it took a more serious raid by at least twenty planes. Twenty-six people were killed, and of the several "Hermanns" dropped was found intact in Victoria Dock and defused by the Navy. The same night sixty-nine fires were started in the town centre, station, and Cleethorpes-boundary areas of Grimsby: burned, half-buried and rotten fish by the Docks made a stench that had to be smelt to be credited. 111 people died at Grimsby and Cleethorpes in these two summer raids, suddenly bumping up their total air raid death toll to 140. For their work on those two nights thirteen officers and men of the Army's 3rd Bomb Disposal Company won George Medals, more than were awarded in connection with any other raids on Britain throughout the war.

II/KG 40, which had attacked Chelmsford from Holland in the spring, meanwhile re-equipped with Me 410s in place of Do 217s, moved to Épinoy near Cambrai (France), and was incorporated in KG 2. The night Hull and Grimsby had their last major raid Bunting of 85 Squadron downed the RAF's first Me 410 (from KG 2) in the sea off Felixstowe. Seventeen days later a Felixstowe rescue launch found the body of one Franz Linzler, presumably a crewman of this plane _ his gravestone can still be seen in Felixstowe Cemetary. On 23 August Flight Lt Howitt, of this same squadron (he had claimed the Little Clacton Do 217) shot down at Chelmondiston, near Shotley, the first Me 410 to succumb to the defences on land _ its observer was captured alive.

Very early on 28 September one bomber killed five people on the eastern edge of Ipswich.

Yarmouth and Lowestoft escaped what could have been the worst of all their raids late on 23 October, when twelve thousand incendiaries and fifty HEs turned the fields between them into a lake of fire. There must be local people who still have the little four-pointed spikes they picked up that night _ "crowsfeet" designed by the Germans to puncture the tyres of fire engines and military vehicles. The concentrated inaccuracy of this raid must have been due to a decoy or bent "Knickebein". It may have been intended to disorganise the Navy's Coastal Forces at Yarmouth and thereby help facilitate the big E-boat raid which took place next night. After repeated pleas this port, and Lowestoft, at last received some barrage balloons that December. Ironically neither was raided more than once subsequently, and without loss of life.

The enemy had begun to try to blind the East Coast radar with a new form of jamming _ "Duppel" (his equivalent of the RAF's "Window"), in which thousands of false echoes were created by showering the sky with strips of metal foil. This was evident in a raid on Ipswich on the night of 3/4 November. Twenty raiders close together gave Walton CHL the impression

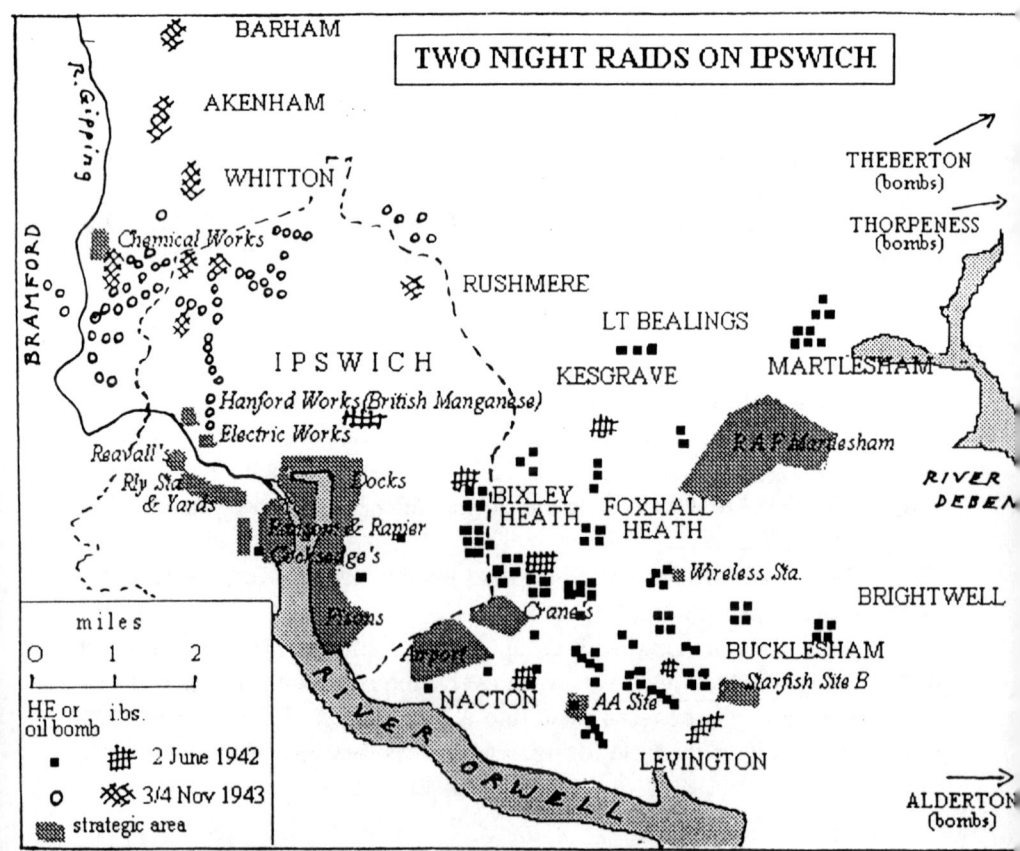

FOUR YEARS OF AIR WAR

that they were a scattered force of two hundred, equal to the whole German bomber strength in the West at the time! Most of the bombs fell in the northwestern part of the town, where two people were killed, and at adjacent Bramford, though there were nine more deaths at Rushmere, just outside the borough on the north-east. The bombers got away without loss. Countless metal strips were gathered up by the Felixstowe police. Three nights later there was a smaller such operation against Norwich. During this a III/KG 2 Do 217 was brought down at Gillingham, near Beccles, by the AA guns at Burgh Castle, just inland from Gorleston.

On the evening of 10 December Flying Officer Schultz of 410 Canadian Squadron claimed no fewer than three more Do 217s over the sea off Clacton during a raid which was scheduled for Chelmsford, but diverted mainly to the new US 9th Airforce bases in North Essex. One German corpse was later found at Foulness, a second off Harwich. One raider wandered as far south as Westcliff, where it killed three civilians.

More than doubling their strength with four new Kampfgeschwadern, the Germans began their "Baby Blitz" on London on 21 January 1944. They had two new types of bomber _ the Ju 188, and the He 177.

Unknown to the defenders, one of the first already lay entombed in the mud of Kirton Creek, a muddy saltwater channel north of Felixstowe. Early on 16 October Squadron Leader Maguire and Flying Officer Jones, of 85 Squadron, had accounted for it, but it was thought at the time to be an Me 410, and down off Clacton, though its four crew had been captured at Hemley, near the real crash site. The wreckage, including an unexploded "Hermann", was to be unearthed in 1988, having lain undetected for forty-five years.

The other new plane, the He 177, was the first and only Luftwaffe heavy bomber, with a bombload of five or six tons to the two of previous types, and lifted by two huge propellers each driven by a pair of engines.

Had these German forces faced the defences of 1940, they might have achieved all they hoped, but instead most of their bombing was wildly inaccurate, and "Baby Blitz" meant so many Luftwaffe losses to nightfighters it was more like "Baby Battle of Britain". However "Düppel" did confuse the defence initially. On the night of 13 February, for instance, all the Thames Estuary radar was affected, though the bombing, mainly with incendiaries, was so scattered it extended as far out as Felixstowe. On 14/15 March the metal foil, at its peak, blanked out all radar in a vast area covering London, Surrey, Kent, the whole Thames Estuary, and nearly all East Anglia. Nevertheless 410 Squadron claimed a Ju 88 and a Ju 188, and 488 Squadron shot down another Ju 188 at Great Leighs, near Chelmsford. A week later a Ju 88 was brought down near Southend airfield, with all its crew dead, while from another, felled next night at Great Wakering, there were three prisoners.

During these raids most of the East Coast towns received their last (conventional) bombs. At Colchester there were bad fires in the St Botolph's area. At Clacton incendiaries fell through the roof of the Odeon Cinema during a showing. A whole planeload of oil, phosphorous and incendiary bombs fell north-east/south-west across Brightlingsea without harming life and limb. Huts were burned in the Army camps at Dovercourt and Felixstowe. Southend took more incendiaries from one plane than Yarmouth had endured in its fire raid in April 1941. Two people were killed at Gillingham, but, up the Medway, Strood was unlucky enough to lose twenty-seven lives from three raids.

On 18 April three more bombers were shot down: the one at Little Walden (Essex) turned out to be an He 177. The same night, in a rare incident, a Ju 88 voluntarily landed at Bradwell Bay airfield.

Coincidentally, this seemed to set a precedent: another German deserter landed a training variant of the Me 109 at Herringfleet, near Lowestoft, on 15 May, and another Ju 88 was captured on Woodbridge emergency landing strip on 13 July, though it had landed in error (a nightfighter, it carried a "Lichtenstein" AI radar of much interest to the Allies).

Meanwhile two big raids on Hull, comparable in scale to those of 1941, had been planned. They indicate the complete failure, and also mark the virtual end, of the Luftwaffe piloted-aircraft bombing of Britain. In the first raid, on 17/18 March, only one bombload struck Hull, causing twelve deaths. In the second, on the night of 20/21 April, *not one of the 130 planes sent found the city*, and the only problem for the defences was the temporary elimination of Dimlington radar station by a power cut.

This was just as well. Since 1940 the bombing of Hull had destroyed or permanently wrecked one building in twenty, caused some degree of damage to nearly every remaining premises, and killed nearly 1200 people.

FOUR YEARS OF AIR WAR

The "North East Coast town", as the media had been constrained to call it, rightly commemorated its sufferings, but it was not as badly hit as Yarmouth, with one building in nine destroyed, or Lowestoft, where the death toll of 266 equates to one in 150 of the peacetime population, compared with a figure of one in 260 at Hull. By contrast the Medway towns, Sheerness, Harwich, and for most of the time Grimsby, had been lucky.

At first light on 13 June, 1944, one week after "D-Day", the Gravesend Mosquito Wing was landing at base after patrolling over Normandy. Some officers standing by the runway heard a strange, croaking, engine, almost like a motor bike's, coming up from the south. Over the aerodrome hurtled a flying object with no engines or propellers on its small wings but with a streak of flame at its tail. As they watched in silence the engine suddenly cut out and the flying object glided on towards the bank of the Thames at Swanscombe, whence a heavy explosion was then heard. The Gravesend officers had seen and heard the very first of the German V1s, flying bombs, "doodlebugs" or (in RAF parlance) "divers" to be fired towards London. Since they were launched from the Pas de Calais, they crossed the Dover area, and not the East Coast, but many ended up in this area after swerving off course to the right. Several fell in the sea off Harwich at the end of the month, and the first to reach Suffolk struck Woolverstone on 16 June. The V1s were launched "blind" at the general London area, and any specific damage was fortuitous. In July the London Docks took many hits. One bomb missed the upper walkway of Tower Bridge by a few feet before crashing into the Upper Pool off the City. On the 4th a small tug, *Naja*, was sunk at Wapping, along with the sizeable merchantman *Fort McPherson*, in Victoria Dock, and a small tanker was destroyed off Beckton. From his "NAB" (naval auxiliary boat) *Water Gipsy*, down river, A P Herbert "could see the little lights (of V1 exhausts) appearing far off, like fireflies, over the Kentish hills", as every armed craft in the river fired every weapon. On shore many hundreds of fatalities were again being inflicted on London. Elsewhere, ten people died at Dartford and eight at Southend that August, and an enormous explosion was narrowly averted when Wrabness Mine Depot was near-missed.

Early in the campaign the various balloon barrages were taken down so that they could be formed into one great screen south-east of London. A lull ensued while the Germans, who were being beaten in Normandy, evacuated their equipment to Holland. From there the second V-Bomb campaign opened in September. The V2 rocket now joined the V1. Nothing could be done to intercept this newcomer, but to stop the flying bombs Army AA Command shifted hundreds of guns from the South to the East Coast, to form "Diver Strip", an AA "freefire" zone into which Allied aircraft could not venture, and stretching from North Kent to Yarmouth. Nearly every coastal village in this belt had a heavy AA battery, and the number of such guns there rose from three hundred to 1100, with an average of ten to the mile. The existing "GORs" (Gun Operations Rooms) at Yarmouth, Felixstowe, Vange (near Tilbury) and Chatham were joined by ones at Theberton, Saxmundham and Orford, Thorpe-le-Soken, Burnham-on-Crouch and Southend. Each was linked to several radar stations and AA batteries. The Harwich frigate *Caicos* was fitted with additional 10-cm radar and stationed near the Outer Gabbard sandbank to provide early warning and fighter direction.

With all the radar on the East Coast, it was possible for the flak to shoot up the bombs through fog, cloud and darkness. Outside the "Strip" more fell to fighters. Harwich and the Medway naval towns were very much on the front line. Many an officer on a ship's bridge said he had felt the blast of a V1 jet. No serious damage was caused at any naval base, though eight civilians were killed at Rochester on 8 November, and two days later three V1s exploded close to Harwich _ one on HMS *Ganges'* playing fields, one off the Old Shipyard, and one in the harbour mouth. Five civilians were killed in two incidents at Ipswich at this period. Sometimes, from one place, half a dozen "divers" could be heard exploding in quick succession, for most were being brought down by the flak. All were being launched, not from ground ramps, but from He 111s flying out over the North Sea. That Christmas Eve these planes ventured almost to the Humber to loose sixty V1s on Manchester, being tracked by the North Norfolk radar.

As with earlier types of bomb, many V1s landed unexploded, especially on mud or soft ground. A new Army Bomb Disposal Company was based at Thorpeness to deal with such incidents all along the East Anglian coast. It dug out one bomb from the Bawdsey foreshore. Captain Hunt came from London to supervise it in recovering another, intact, from swampy ground at Capel Farm, alongside Woodbridge airfield.

The direct route of the V2s ran just south of Harwich, Clacton and

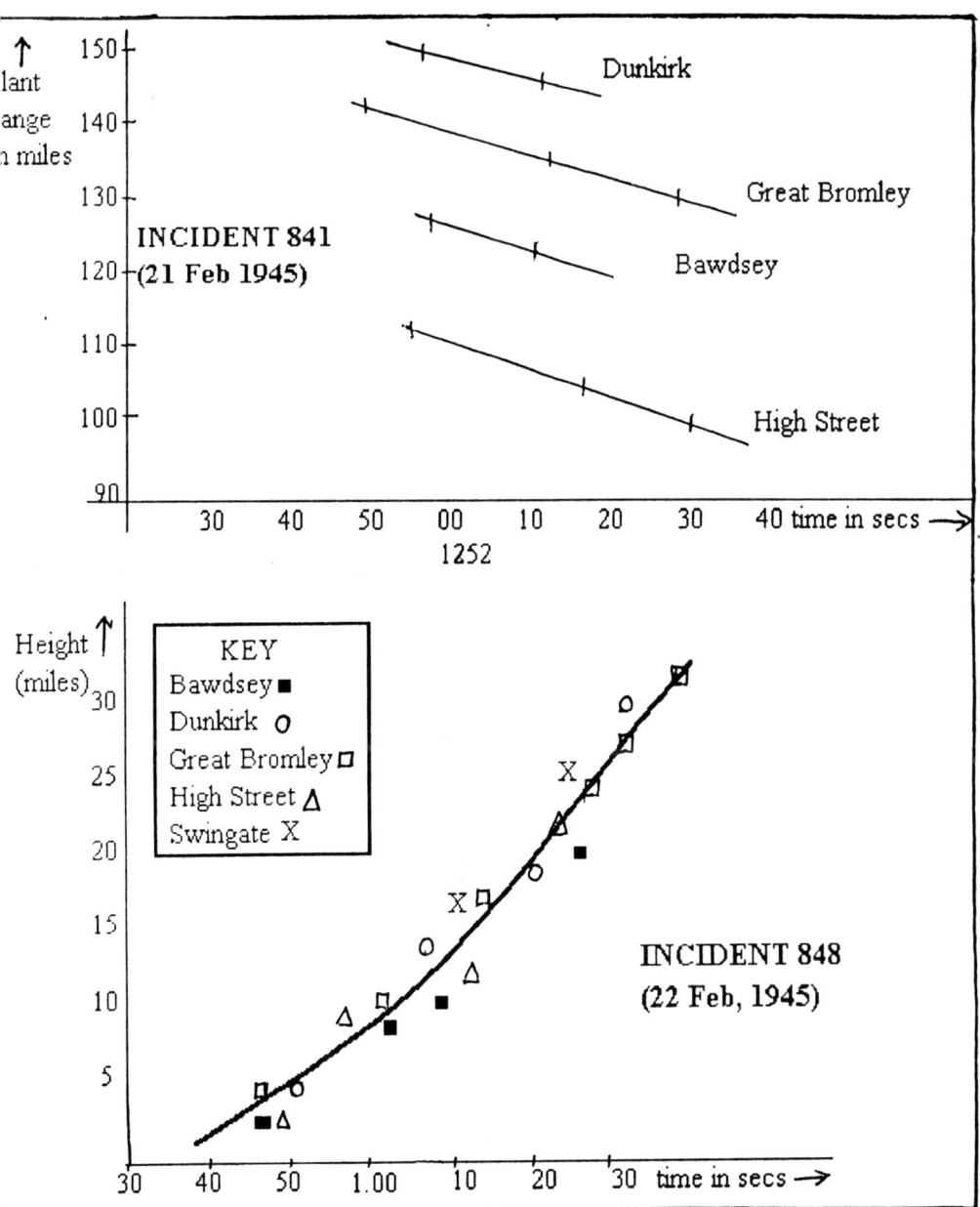

PLOTS OF V2 LAUNCHING TRAJECTORIES MADE BY EAST COAST RADAR STATIONS _ RANGES (above) and HEIGHTS (below). EACH MARKER REPRESENTS ONE "OSWALD" PHOTO.

Brightlingsea, and right over Burnham-on-Crouch. Detection equipment was shifted from South Coast radar stations to five facing east; High Street, Bawdsey, Great Bromley, Dunkirk and Swingate (Dover). This comprised "Oswald", which took long-exposure photographs of the radar blips caused by the rockets before they rose above the radar "ceiling" into the upper atmosphere, and "Willie" (only at Bawdsey) which made a continuous cine film. But in fact any civilian in North East Essex could, on clear mornings, spot the silver vapour trails pointing up into the pink eastern sky. However promptly a "Big Ben" (code for V2) was spotted no more than four minutes elapsed before it landed, so giving warning was impossible _ the purpose of the tracking was to pinpoint the launching sites in Holland.

V2s were normally undetectable once over the East Coast, but a number malfunctioned and crashed or blew up locally. On 10 October one exploded many miles above Harwich, and another over Brightlingsea on 22 March 1945: fragments showered down without doing serious damage. One rocket bored into the mud only sixty yards to seaward of Southend Pier, and, though the warhead exploded, the engine unit was thrown clear and was dug out. Another exploded against the cliff face at Clacton, just west of the Pier, and blasted windows, doors and tiles off the Grand Hotel. A third blew up on Bradwell aerodrome. The only unexploded one was dug out at Paglesham, on the River Roach. At one brief period several V2s hit Norfolk, after Norwich had become a target. On 12 January 1945 one destroyed houses and the railway line at Trimley St Mary, and on 18 February another killed two civilians at Rochester. Inland there were some terrible tragedies, such as at Chelmsford just before Christmas (1944), when forty girls were killed by a direct hit on the Hoffmann's factory.

Air war deaths at this period were not all due to the Germans' "wonder weapons". On the night of 23 June 1944 a Soesterberg reconnaissance Ju 188 crashed in Rendlesham Forest, near Woodbridge, killing all but one of its five crew. On 12 August Joseph Kennedy Junior USN, son of a former American ambassador to Britain and brother of a future President, was killed along with his co-pilot when their Liberator bomber blew up over Blythburgh on the Suffolk coast. Based at Fersfield and loaded with explosives, the plane was being expended on a test for "Operation Aphrodite", the deliberate crashing of remote-controlled Allied bombers onto V1 and other enemy sites _ but in this case the payload

FOUR YEARS OF AIR WAR

detonated before the crew could bail out. On 7 November a Fortress from Thorpe Abbots (Norfolk) was also blown up in mid air by its bombs, though it was on a routine raid. A chunk of fuselage, containing two bodies, struck the Coastguard cottages in Langer Road, Felixstowe, and killed three RAF Regiment men who were billeted there. And on 3-4 March 1945 the Luftwaffe made its last conventional raid over Eastern England: "Intruder" night fighters gained an unprecedented, but isolated and now irrelevant, victory over the Lincolnshire and Yorkshire airfields, and nine civilians were killed by a stray bomb on Ipswich.

There were a few even stranger incidents. Why did a few conventional German HE bombs fall at Southwold on the nights of both 14 and 15 October 1944, at a period otherwise bereft of such raids? Why were V2-like vapour trails seen by some off-duty policemen near Grimsby, beyond the range of those missiles? The answer may lie in the German Arado 234 high-altitude jets, which, it later transpired, probed the East Coast in search of the Allied invasion craft _ the only *piloted* enemy jets to come into British airspace.

The V-Bomb campaign peaked in February 1945, but rapidly petered out in March. The 29th brought its last day. In the early hours flak brought down a V1 in the sea off Dovercourt, the tail falling on land. Those which went over that town soon after 9.30 that morning were the last to fall on England, the final one crashing near Sittingbourne. And the destruction of the V1 at Orfordness at 12.43 marked the final offensive act of the Luftwaffe against the United Kingdom. Never had there been more soldiers, gunfire, and heavy explosions, on the East Coast, than in the previous six months, but the local flak and fighters had saved untold further deaths in London. Altogether 912 V-Weapons had crashed in Essex alone, of which 511 had been flying bombs and 401 rockets.

When that first V-Weapon had exploded by the river near Gravesend one of the RAF officers on the airfield is supposed to have turned to another and said: "From now on nations will have to be very polite to one another".

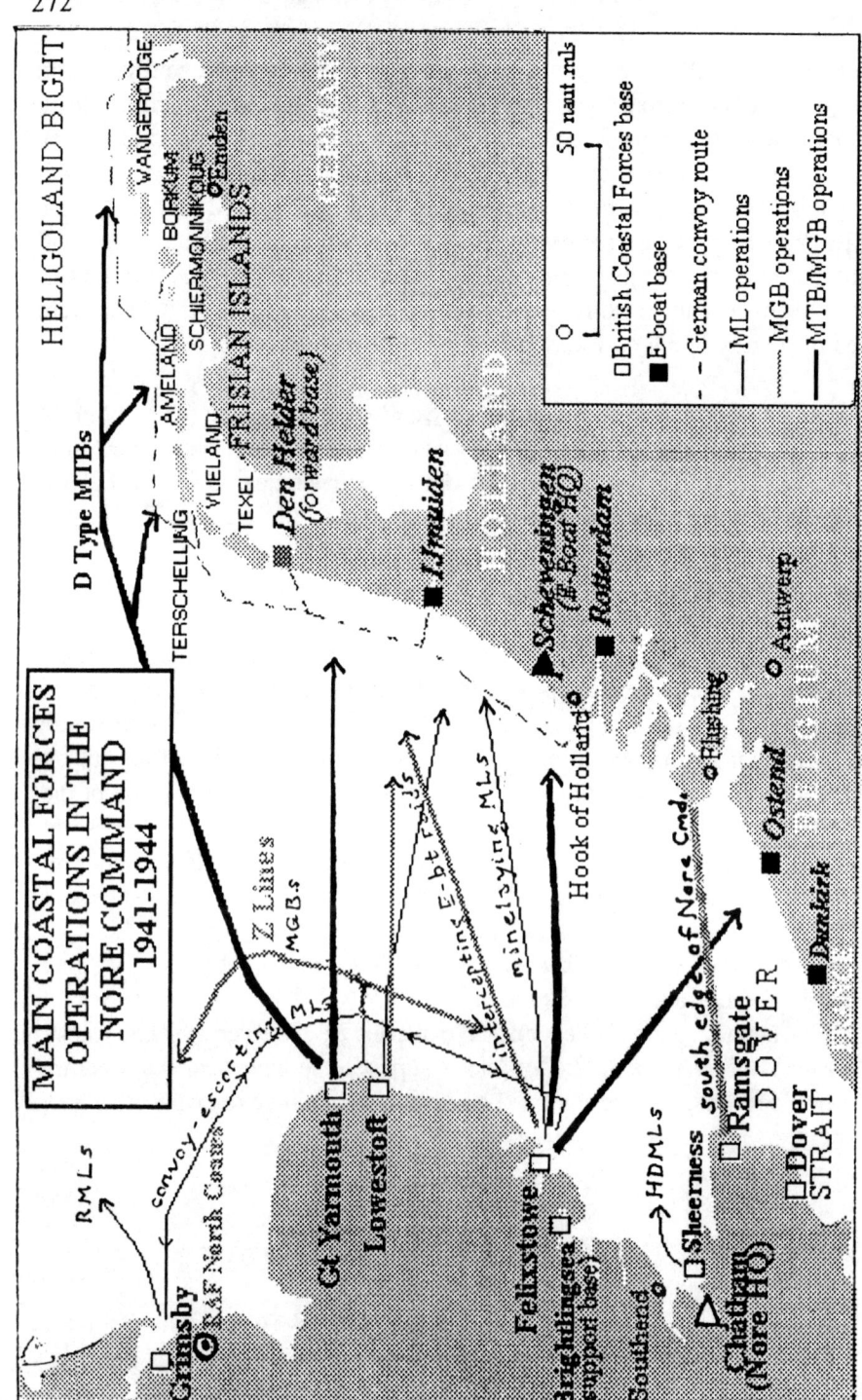

13
BEEHIVE, MANTIS & MIDGE

One day in the New Year of 1940 the youthful and virile roar of unfamiliar engines drowned out the elderly chugging of trawlers, drifters and tugs in Harwich Harbour. Lt-Cdr C M Donner's 1st Motor Torpedo Boat Flotilla arrived after a voyage from the "Med", through the French canals, and via Portsmouth. His boats were refitted at Parkeston, while the trawler *Vulcan* berthed at Felixstowe Quay, to serve as his depot and HQ ship. This was the only flotilla of MTBs, or combat motor craft of any type, then in the Royal Navy, the many CMBs (coastal motor boats) and MLs (motor launches) of the Great War having been scrapped in the '20s.

At first the North Sea seemed to offer it little prospect of action. Donner's ten boats were put to training and even used as "trotboats". Their furthrest venture was on 20 April, when they rescued the crew of the mined merchantman *Hawnby* near Knock John Buoy, and landed them at Ramsgate.

But the Germans soon invaded the Low Countries. In late April and early May two more MTB flotillas, 3rd (Lt Cole) and 10th (Lt Anderson) arrived, making a total of sixteen boats. Four MASBs (Motor Anti-Submarine Boats) also appeared. In Chapter 3 I described the exploits of both types of craft in the Dutch and Dunkirk evacuations.

The inadequacy of *Vulcan* as a depot for three flotillas, and the overcrowding at HMS *Badger*, prompted the establishment of HMS *Beehive* in July. All the MTBs berthed in the southern half of Felixstowe Dock. Since the northern half continued as a grain wharf (Marriage's Mill was there), 19th century sailing barges jostled, incongruously, with modern power boats. *Beehive* also acquired the northernmost part of the RAF station, where one of the hangars was used for servicing boats, which were landed by the massive hammerhead crane formerly used for lifting seaplanes. Lt E M Thorpe was *Beehive*'s first CO, but after a fortnight Cdr R H McBean DSO DSC (a CMB hero of the Allied war against Lenin's Bolsheviks), took over, remaining until July 1941, whereupon Cdr T Kerr was in charge for all but the last few weeks of war. *Beehive* eventually numbered up to 1200 officers and ratings, though till the autumn of 1944 about eight hundred was more usual. Its organisation and atmosphere resembled those of an RAF rather than a naval base. Of a breed similar to fighter pilots, its officers spoke of "parties" rather than battles.*Only half their work was regular patrolling, the rest being special attacks. Off duty they lived in comfortable Felixstowe

---

*...and called each other by nicknames, like "Tubby" (Cambridge), "Boffin" (Campbell), "Bussy" (Carr), "Harpy" (Lloyd), and the famous "Hitch" (Hichens).

houses (the ratings mostly inhabited the RAF barracks). They were usually nocturnal warriors, though briefing began in the afternoon and debriefing did not end till daylight. Because of the maintenance needs of the highly temperamental boats operational crews were almost outnumbered by base staff.

Felixstowe was not then, as now, a huge seaport. Bleak marshland flanked the small dock area, and larger RAF base, on either side. *Beehive*'s main social haunt was the weatherboarded Little Ships Hotel, facing Harwich, where landlord Powell was the host, and in the air raid shelter of which the King had taken refuge while visiting the base, and Landguard Fort, in July 1940. In the small and sedate town officers frequented the Ordnance Hotel, and ratings the more boisterous Cavendish. The RAF base included a NAAFI and a small theatre. After patrols the seagoing officers liked to give their men their tots of rum and put them ashore, and to socialise on one given boat (each took a turn) over a bottle or two of gin. They even talked politics on these occasions (they were RNVR and not professional sailors!) _ according to Lt-Cdr Hichens the gist was anti-party, anti-big capitalism, pro-Soviet (not until 1941 presumably?) and anti-trade union, all at the same time!

The 1st Flotilla MTBs, sixty-footers built by the British Power Boat Company in 1936, were of limited value. Their top speed of 27 knots was much less than that of the E-boats. Their guns were eight quadrupally-mounted Lewises, while their torpedo-launching gear was extraordinarily awkward:

> "In those days some of the MTBs carried their topedoes in the engine room, and released them by dropping them out astern. This required a portable outrigger protruding over the transom to guide the torpedo clear of the boat"*

When Lt G J Mannooch's three MTBs, accompanying the Harwich destroyers *Malcolm* and *Verity* off Holland on 13 August 1940, had *Beehive*'s first opportunity of sinking an enemy vessel, they missed it. They could not work their torpedoes quickly enough to catch the German trawler which steamed right past them, and Mannooch's desperate ramming of another target resulted only his MTB being towed home with bedding stuffed in a massive hole in her bows. The seventy-foot Vosper and seventy-five-foot

---

*Peter Scott (see Bibliography)

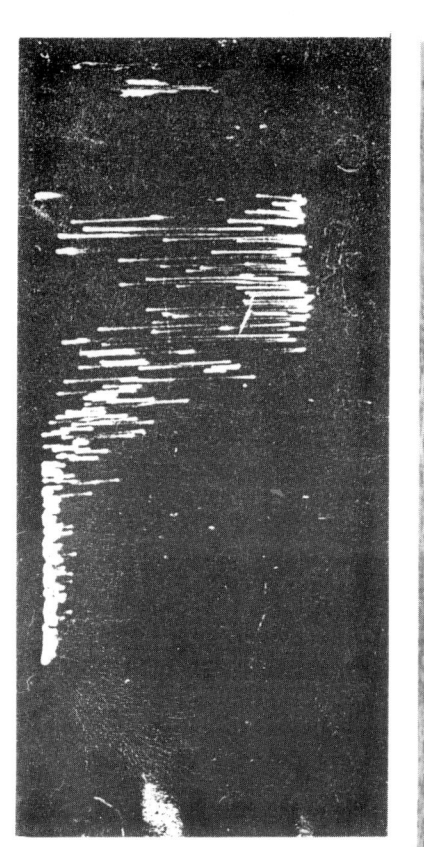

Left: Roughs Fort being placed. Note the 3.7" & Bofors guns, & the radar. *(IWM)*
Below: Shivering Sand Fort. *(Rotherham)*
Below Left: The scope (screen) at Great Bromley CH station during the RAF 1000-bomber raid on Cologne, 31 May 1942. *Below Right:* Royal Engineers recovering the engine of the V2 which fell 60 yards from Southend Pier.
(Herbert)

HMS BEEHIVE, **FELIXSTOWE BASIN, 1942 _ MTBs preparing for operations.**
(Scott)

BEEHIVE, MANTIS & MIDGE

Thornycroft boats of 3rd and 10th Flotillas, and of the former's successor, the 4th, had proper torpedo tubes but were little faster. The practice of combining Felixstowe MTBs with Harwich destroyers was soon stopped owing to the protests of the later, who feared that at night their consorts' roaring engines would betray them to the enemy.

Four of the Felixstowe MTBs were especially to the fore at this period; 14 (Lt E Hamilton-Hill RNR), 15 (Lt J A Eardley-Wilmot), 16 (Lt P F S Gould) and 17 (Lt R I J Faulkner). On 1 September they went to the rescue of the ill-fated 20th Destroyer Flotilla off the Texel (see Chapter 4). A week later 14, 15 and 17 became the first MTBs to claim sinkings when they fired torpedoes at German shipping (thought to be invasion craft) off Ostend, while Harwich destroyers fired shells and the RAF bombed the port. Next day air reconnaissance spotted three wrecks, though which British fighting arm had sunk them was unknown.

On 11 October, however, there was a certain victory. Three more *Beehive* MTBs, 22, 31 and 32, using Dover as a forward base, sank two German trawlers off Calais and captured thirty-four crewmen. But retribution soon followed. On 24 September, when 14, 15, 16 and 17 were returning to Felixstowe past 53 Buoy, 15 was mined and abandoned. On 21 October MTB 17 was also lost by mine near Ostend, and ten days later 16 was sunk (and 22 damaged) by mines in Barrow Deep.

Not until December was there another success. In thick mist near Flushing Lt R A Ellis's MTB 32, leading 29 and 31, suddenly came upon an enemy merchant ship. At almost pointblank range Lt C A James's MTB 29 torpedoed and sank this target. For one such victory there were countless nights of danger and hardship but no action. Ellis described the typical MTB patrol thus;

"...all night on the bridge, feeling ones way through the sandbanks and wrecks, ones eyes glued to the binoculars searching every inch of water, keyed up for instant action, and never seeing a sign of a single object, whether landmark, buoy, wreck or ship".*

The German equivalent of the MTB was the "Schnellboot" (fast boat), termed by the British the "E-boat" ("E" simply meant "enemy"). An E-boat (i.e, an "S-Boot") displaced almost one hundred tons, carried two 20-mm

---
*quoted by Scott.

cannon as well as torpedo tubes, was capable of thirty-nine knots speed, and had a crew of twenty or so. The British never devised a fully satisfactory answer to her, and their own boats were inferior in practically every way. She was bigger, and therefore roomier, more stable, more heavily armed, and less likely to sink. Yet she was also faster and of lower silhouette. Her great diesel engines were admittedly noisy, yet less flammable, and were switched off in favour of a "quiet motor" when she needed to hide. Therefore, although the E-boats in the North Sea were never more than fifty strong, and were always outnumbered, they compelled the Royal Navy to keep disproportionately large forces on the East Coast till the very end of the war.

At first the British did not know the exact layout and features of E-boats, since, unlike the German big ships, they had not visited foreign waters before the war, and now operated largely by night. Those who fought them were supposed to report on their appearance, though the only description many could offer was "a dirty white colour" (in actuality a matt silver night camouflage). However, Lt-Cdr Hichens' story that the Admiralty had overlooked detailed commercial advertisements published by the E-boat builders (Lürssen's) in the prewar *Jane's Fighting Ships* is probably apocryphal.

The E-boat officers, like those of the Luftwaffe and U-Boats, were keen and courageous. Already Birnbacher, Klug, Feldt, Mirbach and others bore the "Ritterkreuz" (Knight's Cross, or higher order of the Iron Cross). But, to risk a truism, they were not on our side. Even if not Nazis as such, they were of course German nationalists and sons of nationalists who believed in a Reich great on land and sea.

According to former AB Bridge, Secretary of the Coastal Forces' Veterans' (Ratings') Association:
> "In books the E-boats seem to take the blame for everything, but in fact we didn't meet them that often _ our worst enemies were really the German armed trawlers. The flak trawlers off Scheveningen were the most formidable: a Luftwaffe officer had made them into a floating battery, and had beefed them up with concrete and armour plate. They pumped out a terrible amount of fire and were very hard to sink".

Their Ijmuiden equivalents were tellingly known as "The Four Horsemen of the Apocalypse".

BEEHIVE, MANTIS & MIDGE

The Germans called their armed trawlers "V" ("Vorposten", or "Outpost") Boats, and used them both as an offshore patrol and as escorts for the convoys* which brought metals and timber down to the Low Countries (for transhipment to Germany) from Scandinavia, and took coal in the opposite direction. Other escorts included the so-called M-boats (minesweepers), T-boats (steam torpedo boats), R-boats (ML/MMSs), and the occasional Z-boat (destroyer)+. Because the enemy convoys were much smaller and less frequent than our own their merchantmen were outnumbered by escorts which often literally surrounded them. Yet because they were for long the only enemy warships to bring the war to this side of the North Sea it was the E-boats which caught the imagination.

In not untypical style the British, lacking a single antidote, planned to respond with three types of motor boat. The relatively slow-moving MTB tried to torpedo German coastal shipping, and those warships which interfered. The faster MGB (Motor Gunboat) was being designed specifically to hunt the E-boats and destroy them by gunfire. And the ML (Motor Launch), slowest of the trio, was built partly to shield the East Coast convoys from the raiders. For lightness and speed of construction all were made mainly of wood. In November 1940 they were put under a single command for fitting-out, personnel, supply and training purposes _ Coastal Forces. The head of this, Rear-Admiral Kekewich ("RACF"), was at first based at Portland, but in 1941 moved to Wendover Court, in the unlikely setting of Golder's Green, London. He was not in charge of operations _ on the East Coast the C-in-C Nore was responsible and briefed the boat officers via their base commanders, an arrangement which was inevitable for defensive work, and undesirable for offensive.

In spite of their technical advantages the E-boats seldom sought battle with Coastal Forces. Their typical, and effective, guerrilla tactic was to concentrate on merchant-ship targets and give their pursuers the slip. Not till 1942 could Coastal Forces genuinely claim to have deprived the enemy of an E-boat.

---

*Many of the merchant ships involved were from the Danish Maersk Line (still prominent today); oddly it also had vessels in Allied service.
+German minesweepers were numbered, with "M" prefixes, likewise with R-boats. One class each of steam torpedo boats and destroyers bore T and Z prefixes respectively, and numbers. Appendix Q gives the bases of some of these craft at one moment of the War.

BEEHIVE, MANTIS & MIDGE

In September 1940 the E-boats first effectively raided an East Coast convoy _ off Norfolk. In response Lt-Cdr W G Everett's 1st ML Flotilla was brought to Yarmouth. HMS *Midge* was established as a separate base for Coastal Forces the next January. Subsequently 13th, followed by 12th, ML Flotilla, also arrived there, along with 5th MTB Flotilla. 11th ML Flotilla came to Lowestoft that spring, and a separate Coastal Forces base was started there in August _ *Minos II*. At the same time the first flotilla of HDMLs (Harbour Defence MLs), numbered from 1001, arrived at Sheerness _ these were scaled-down, short-range versions of the ML for, in this case, guarding the Thames mouth. One ML each also went to Grimsby, Yarmouth, Lowestoft, Harwich and Sheerness as command boats for the Captains M/S.

The Yarmouth and Lowestoft MLs worked in pairs, shuttling between the Humber and Harwich (and vice versa) as convoy escorts. They kept station on the seaward side of convoys, halfway along. If E-boats appeared they fired their 3-pdrs (surplus saluting guns from old warships) and machine guns, and stood by to rescue survivors. Yarmouth's 1st Flotilla, made up of A-class vessels, lost two boats from mines at an early date, both near Chequer Shoal Buoy just outside the Humber. ML 109 sank with three dead, including her captain Lt Kirk RNVR, on 30 October 1940. ML 111 (Lt Hoadley RNVR) sank with two missing on 25 November. 109 was the first of all MLs to be lost. The briefing about "QZs" (minefields) the two officers had been given at Yarmouth was, to say the least, casual. In late 1941 the four survivors of this flotilla, now renamed the 51st, were based at Felixstowe and for the rest of the war were used to mine the Dutch coast. They were the oldest MLs in service.

Lowestoft's 6th ML Flotilla was especially prominent in rescue. Sub-Lt Williams's ML 150 saved four Merchant Navy crews in three voyages in late November and early December 1941. On 24 November, helped by Sub-Lt Steele's ML 152, she saved injured men from near the edge of a fire, three hundred yards long and fifty feet high, fuelled by oil from the sinking *Virgilia*. Leaning over the side, Motor Mechanic Caffrey held up an unconscious man in near-freezing water for twenty minutes because he was too heavy to lift, and he and Steele were near to collapse by the time all the survivors had beeb taken on. In mid-1942 the first of the purpose-built RMLs (Rescue MLs) arrived at Grimsby _ standard B-types with deckhouse sickbays astern instead of depth charges or mines. By then there were also six

BEEHIVE, MANTIS & MIDGE

flotillas of standard MLs in the Nore Command _ one each at Yarmouth and Lowestoft, and two each at Felixstowe and Grimsby, plus the Sheerness HDML flotilla. This totalled sixty-eight MLs of all types.

Now that the U-Boats had left the North Sea, there was little use for Asdic and depth-charge-equipped MASBs. 5, 6 and 7 were turned into MACs (Motor Attendant Craft) with the same numbers and used for rescue and salvage duties. The MGBs were now building, but in March 1941, as a stopgap the remaining MASBs were equipped with guns and gathered at *Minos II* and *Beehive* as 5th and 6th MGB Flotillas. These conversions were MGBs in name only, quite unfit for tackling E-boats. They were each armed with one Oerlikon 20-mm cannon or one quadruple .303 aircraft-type machine gun turret. The MASB had only been a twin-screw, twenty-knot version of the triple-screw British Power Boat MTB, and even when adapted were incapable of successful pursuit.

Nevertheless 6th Flotilla's Senior Officer, Lt Howes, did his best. Night after night his MGBs went to a point midway between the main E-boat lair at Ijmuiden and their main hunting ground off Yarmouth, and lay listening, engines stopped. After two indecisive brushes with the raiders he was determined to catch them, and on 24 June drove his boats far beyond their planned maximum speed and kept up the pursuit, and a torrent of fire, for almost an hour before his five quarries escaped. By then his MGBs had practically white-hot guns and engines.

6th Flotilla's next mission, soon afterwards, was an air-sea rescue search off Cromer. Lts Richards and Hichens found five men from a Hampden bomber. Hichens later related how he found one airman who had survived the crash but was drowned in the foot of water in the bottom of his dinghy when he slid down into it owing to exhaustion and loss of blood. Richards had come up with four cheerful survivors and asked about this fifth man, to be told his foully trivial fate.

Whatever the state of the sea MGBs (and MTBs) were required to rush out at top speed on air-sea rescue missions, since, apart from a very few RAF launches, the appointed rescue boats were capable only of inshore work. The self-inflicted punishment of 6th MGB Flotilla was such that at any one time half its craft were under repair at James's Shipyard, Brightlingsea. Four had to be sent there after a single air-sea rescue trip in August.

At that point Howes was succeeded by one of his boat commanders, Lt Robert Hichens, a charismatic and genial Cornish solicitor and amateur sailor and racing driver, hobbies not unconnected with his present work. The first RNVR officer ever to command a flotilla, he soon proved himself the outstanding figure in Coastal Forces, a mixture of amateur enthusiasm and professional calculation and skill.

In October Hichens was re-equipped with the first of the purpose-built MGBs, forty-knot seventy-footers built by British Power Boat and up to E-boat standards at least in speed and armament, if not in such other vital aspects as engine reliability. In the early hours of 20 November Hichens, Lt L G R Campbell and Lt G B Bailey, all three RNVR, took their boats halfway to the Hook of Holland in order to intercept the E-boats which had just wrought havoc among FS 50 off Yarmouth (see Chapter 10). The MGBs switched off their engines and listened for the enemy as usual. Five raiders then appeared but fled into the darkness before they could be chased. Hichens delivered a burst of fire at one but then his guns jammed. The MGBs dallied until first light, when again they heard engines. Heading in their direction, they found S 41, the slayer of SS *Waldinge*, sinking and abandoned. She had been crippled by an accidental collision, and the engine noise just heard had come from another E-boat rescuing her crew. The MGB men boarded the vessel and recovered such trophies as a portrait of Hitler and a half-eaten sausage, but she was sinking too fast to tow home. Hichens returned to Felixstowe flying the White Ensign over the Swastika. Meanwhile another 2nd Flotilla E-boat had been badly damaged by 19 Squadron Spitfires from Coltishall _ the first time the RAF hit an E-boat at sea.

Coastal Forces now sent many more MGBs to the two bases which looked straight out onto E-boat Alley _ Lowestoft and Yarmouth. The two new Yarmouth flotillas, 12th and 16th, consisted of Fairmile C Types. These were MLs of the 313-335 series which had been reclassified because of their supercharged engines and superior armament. They were larger and more seaworthy than previous MGBs, though much slower than E-boats. Yarmouth Sub-Command Coastal Forces set up standing night patrols (each codenamed "QE", plus a number) to seaward of the convoy route.

On the night of 14/15 March, 1942, three groups of E-boats came to raid FN 55 and FS 49. Half of 4th Flotilla headed for Southwold waters

BEEHIVE, MANTIS & MIDGE

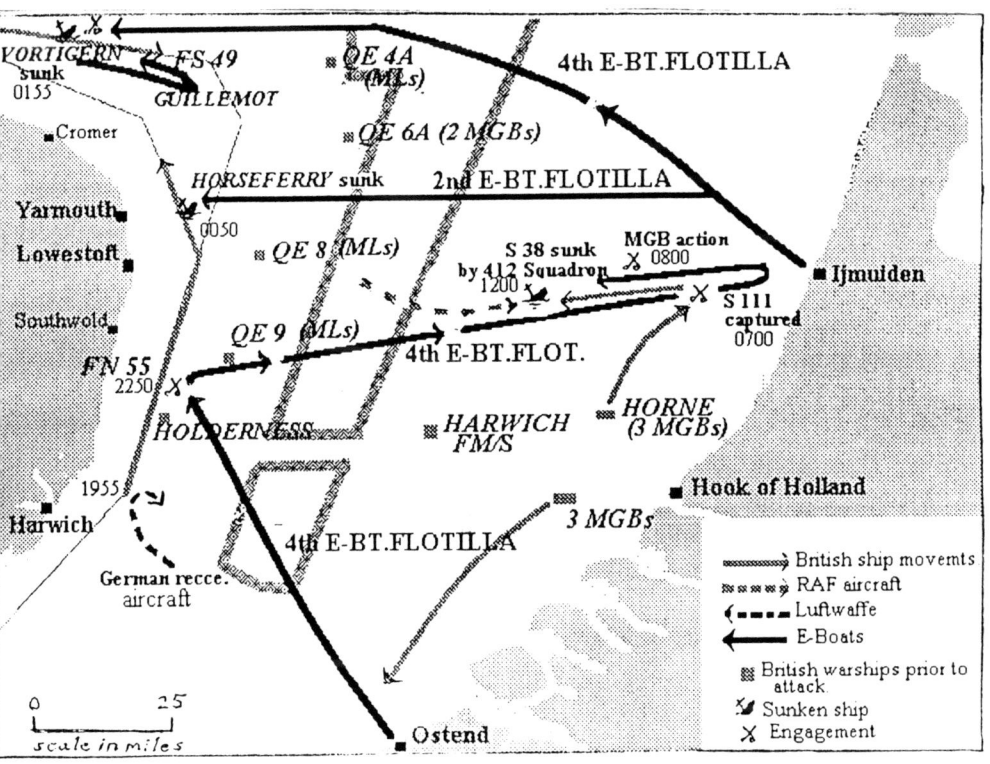

from Ostend, having transferred there to make the voyage in the three hours between darkness and the arrival of the convoy. 2nd Flotilla, and the other half of 4th, left Ijmuiden to raid off Yarmouth and Cromer respectively. Each group went into action against the two converging convoys. First the Rosyth escort destroyer *Wallace* and the Sheerness standing-patrol destroyers *Holderness* and *Pytchley*, with FN 55, briefly clashed with the Ostend group, before it withdrew into a smokescreen. Then 2nd Flotilla sank SS *Horseferry*, leaving her seven survivors to be rescued by the stalwart Lowestoft ML 151. Then 4th Flotilla sank FS 49's Rosyth escort destroyer *Vortigern* with dire loss of life (see Chapter 10). On their way in and out the raiders by-passed three slow "QE" units of Lowestoft MGBs and Yarmouth MLs.

But coincidentally two more MGB units, each of three boats, were off the Hook of Holland to prevent German warships from attacking Harwich fleet minesweepers then clearing the "QZS 403" minefield which the enemy had laid east of Gap E in 1940. One unit, Lt J B R Horne's little Lowestoft-based 7th Flotilla, was sent to intercept the returning Ijmuiden groups. The other, C Types from Yarmouth's 16th Flotilla, was sent to do likewise off Ostend.

In fact *all three* groups returned to Ijmuiden. S 111, from the Ostend group, had been damaged off Southwold and fell behind. At daybreak Horne's MGB 88, with 87 and 91, disabled, surrounded and boarded her twenty miles short of her destination. In a surreal moment the E-boat men saved the officer who had come to demand their surrender when he slipped and nearly fell overboard. The victory was almost precisely reversed when MGB 91 developed engine trouble herself, fell behind the other two MGBs, and was overtaken by S 111's four companions, which had doubled back to find her. The three MGBs poured out a smokescreen until a kindly fog came down and blanketed everybody. Horne cast S 111 and her dead adrift, but brought her survivors into Lowestoft, fallen in on MGB 88's deck _ they were led ashore blindfolded. Five wounded were treated in Lowestoft hospital while the others were held in the Police Station until troops arrived to collect them. In view of the enemy's racial theories it is interesting that of the nine prisoners five had Slavic names. Captain Stoker, the NOIC, came and toured the victorious MGB in Hamilton Dock. MGB 91 had been so badly shot up that she was feared sunk, but at last she limped into harbour with six wounded, three of them seriously.

Meanwhile four RAF fighter squadrons (19, 137, 412 and 616) had taken off from Coltishall and Matlask to cover the rescue of ship survivors and to find S 111 and her would-be rescuers. Just before noon Wing Commander Hanks led 412 (Canadian) Squadron in a diving attack on these E-boats. According to some sources S 111 had by now been scuttled, but one E-boat (possibly she, or perhaps S 38) was seen to catch fire astern, and later a 137 Squadron Whirlwind spotted wreckage and floating dead.

That night and morning had certainly entered the records: the worst loss of life on an East Coast warship, the first E-boat captured in combat and then sunk from the air. These two British successes had only been possible because for a change the enemy were still out at daybreak. They were not typical: for instance no Coastal Forces boat *sank* an E-boat that year, and the many night air searches _ e.g. those by 53 (Coastal Command) Squadron from North Coates _ were all fruitless.

COASTAL FORCES HEROES

Right: Felixstowe, early 1943_ Lt-Cdr Hichens RNVR (left) and Lt-Cdr Dickens RN.
(IWM)

Below: Great Yarmouth, Sept, 1943 _officers of Lt-Cdr D G Bradford's flotilla after their attack on the *Strasbourg*. L to R; Lt W Harrop RNVR, Lt C S Claydon RNVR, Lt P C Wilkinson RNVR, Lt-Cdr D G Bradford DSC RNR, Lt D G Dowling RNVR, Lt J A N Whitby RNVR *(Scott)*

15 MARCH 1942
ABOVE: E-boat S 111 being towed to Lowestoft by 7th MGB Flotilla. *(Scott)*
BELOW: Prisoners from this E-boat being led ashore at Hamilton Dock, Lowestoft.   *(Ford Jenkins)*

BEEHIVE, MANTIS & MIDGE

4th E-boat flotilla continued to work from Ostend, and that spring concentrated on contact minelaying between Orfordness and Lowestoft, a tactic the Germans had not used for over a year. On 20 April it was one such operation which sank two merchantmen and damaged the destroyer *Cotswold* (see Chapter 10) in Harwich Sub-Command. Hichens and four of his MGBs were off Ostend to stop a second such foray the very next night. In the ensuing action no German craft was lost, but Hichen's boat was very lucky to survive after she was hit by thirteen shells, and five casualties, one of them fatal, had been sustained For his efforts Hichens received the DSO.

He and his 6th Flotilla moved to the Channel for a short spell, but then came round to Lowestoft, as two smaller flotillas numbered 6th and 8th. With them came 21st MTB Flotilla, of forty-knot Vosper boats, under the command of Lt Peter Dickens. This officer had made his name in the *Belgia* rescue the previous year, when first officer on *Cotswold*. His turn to be rescued came when E-boats mined his destroyer, and it was then that he met Hichens. Their partnership in 1942 and 1943 was not merely social, however , but of tactical importance. Dickens (a future admiral) was the great grandson of the novelist and had inherited some of his imagination. He had been given the task of marrying the MTBs and MGBs, ineffective separately, for a new joint offensive against the enemy's Dutch coast shipping, in response to the E-boat depradations in the "Alley". He and Hichens began to work out scientific tactics which were later copied throughout Coastal Forces. His ruses were legendary: on being flashed a coded challenge by an enemy ship, he would flash the same signal to one of her companions, obtain the answer, and relay it to the first vessel in time to satisfy her.

At this time the QE patrols gave way to the Z Lines. In consequence of this and the proposed Dickens-Hichens offensive Lowestoft Coastal Forces base (which was rechristened *Mantis*), had more MGBs than anywhere else in the country _ thirty-seven, in four flotillas. Many were lamentably slow: had they been faster so many would not have been necessary. But Yarmouth and Lowestoft MGBs did now begin to see action. That September those on E-boat-intercepting and convoy-raiding missions, and the E-boats themselves, began to put to sea on the same nights. This happened on the 10th, when Horne's 7th Flotilla left for the Dutch convoy route with Dickens's MTBs, and 16th Flotilla went near to Ijmuiden to trap E-boats on their return from an expected raid on the "Alley". HMS *Midge*'s C-Type MGB 335 suffered the same fate as S 111 while intercepting returning E-boats off Ijmuiden: 16th Flotilla's Senior Officer, Lt E M Thorpe, won the DSO for rescuing her crew from amid the enemy's fire. And on 30 September the joint offensive chalked up its first success: Dickens's MTBs sank the German motor ship *Thule* and a "V -Boot" trawler near the Texel, though Lt M T C Sadler RNVR was killed on MGB 18.

That autumn Hichens and Dickens moved down to Felixstowe. This brought the real blooding of HMS *Beehive*, and some furious and instructive action. But the joint offensive was hardly going well. On 3 October MGB 78 failed to return from "an offensive patrol": Lt Duncan DSC (a Canadian) and his whole crew of fifteen (one of them a Dutchman) perished.

Three nights later a combined attack brought costly failure. MTBs 29, 30, 69, 70 and 241, and MGBs 75 and 76 (with Hichens aboard), left Felixstowe in response to intelligence from Dover to intercept the *Komet* (otherwise "Raider B") a disguised enemy commerce-raider which had already made one fantastic voyage round half the world and, like *Scharnhorst* and *Gneisenau*, was attempting to run the Dover Strait, though in the opposite direction. Off Blankenberge Hichens battled with E-boats and R-Boats (German MLs) escorting the raider. But MTBs 29 and 30 collided, and the former, commanded by the New Zealander Lt Tattersfield, sank with all ten crew. An E-boat was said to have caught fire and blown up. Meanwhile both MGBs were badly damaged: 75 was holed underwater and had a man seriously wounded, and 76's petrol tanks caught fire. *Komet* got through to the Channel, and though the enemy lost four R-Boats, they all seem to have been sunk by mines, not MTBs or MGBs. At daybreak, as the battered Felixstowe force passed 54A Buoy on its way home, MGB 76 suddenly burst into flames again _ the earlier fire had not been completely dowsed after all. The blaze killed a motor mechanic and forced the abandonment of the boat. Hichens and his crew escaped in a life raft. As they paddled for safety the MGB blew up: a blazing fuel slick spread across the water and stopped short of them by yards. The glare was seen by MTBs 61 and 64, which rescued Hichens' party and landed them at *Beehive*.

On 9 November Dickens and two MGBs torpedoed a three-thousand-ton collier off Terschelling, but she jettisoned her cargo and reached Emden. Off Ijmuiden, on 18 December, four *Beehive* MTBs, working with four *Midge* MGBs, were deprived of a convoy by the weather, and MTB 30,

BEEHIVE, MANTIS & MIDGE

which had survived the *Komet* action, was sunk by a mine with four dead.

Exactly one month later, however, Dickens and five MTBs pulled off another victory by torpedoing and sinking a merchantman and a "V -Boot" without British casualties. Since the North Coates Beaufighters had just sunk their first ship (a modest Dutch tug) off the Hook there was now a feeling that at last the British were carrying the war to the other side of the North Sea. As a further step in coordinating the various motor boat bases and flotillas in the Nore Command a Coastal Forces staff was set up at Chatham in February 1943, with planning, gunnery and intelligence officers and Captain H T Armstrong DSC DSO in charge. That year the strength of Coastal Forces in his Command rose to over 130 boats in twenty flotillas.

On the night of 27/28 February, Hichens' flotilla, together with *Beehive* MTBs, went to within half a mile of the Hook of Holland harbour piers to attack a German convoy as it entered the Nieuwe Waterweg. MTB 72's Sub-Lt G R Price RNVR was killed (and later buried at Felixstowe). MGB 79 was sunk with nine dead. Hichens stopped to rescue the survivors, but as a rope was thrown to Lt David James RNVR, Hichens was subjected to a hail of enemy fire and had to accelerate, dragging James astern. This officer lost his grip, and was run over by another MGB, which pushed him so deep underwater he nearly drowned, though thereby he missed the deadly propellers. Picked up by the Germans, James later escaped, and crossed Europe posing as a fictitious Bulgarian naval officer wittily named Bugerov. (Subsequently he became an MP...and Loch Ness Monster hunter).

That March was costly for the Germans.

On the 5th RAF fighter-bombers, flying from Coltishall, caught the enemy still outside Ijmuiden at dawn, and sank S 70 and 75.

Then Lt-Cdr Gemmel's *Midge*-based 58th MTB flotilla made its first successful raids on enemy convoys north of the Dutch Frisian Islands. It was composed of the big new Fairmile D-Types, which had the bulk to carry torpedo tubes *and* sizeable guns *and* sufficient fuel to reach round the north-west "corner" of Holland. However it did lose one MTB on the 10th of that month _ Lt F W Carr's 622. One of her crew, Stoker Rose, was captured, and after bullying and brainwashing "volunteered" for the "Legion of St George", the British SS unit being formed in Germany.

During a raid on a British convoy early on the 20th S 119 collided with S 114 and had to be abandoned and blown up _ her wreckage was found

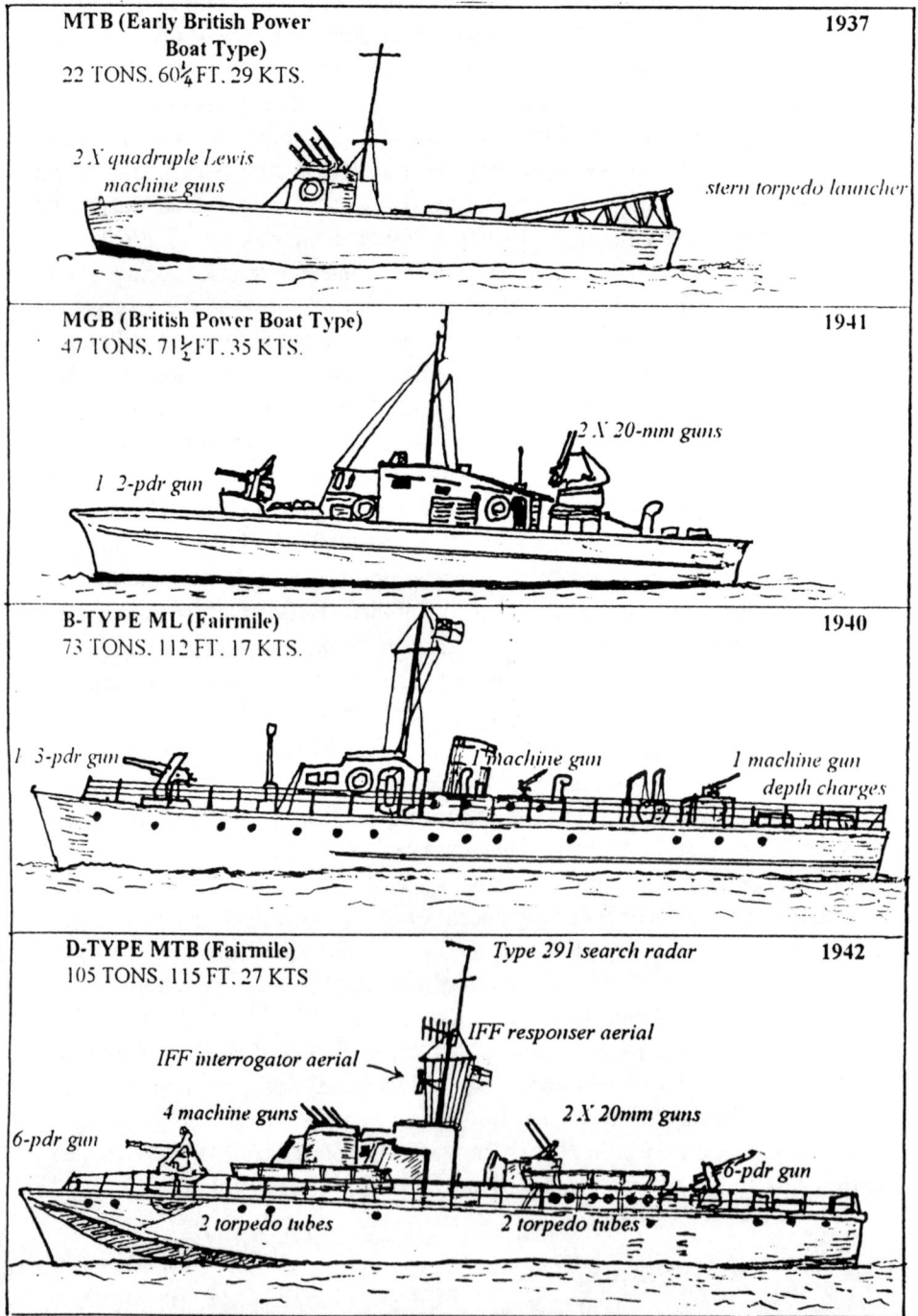

BEEHIVE, MANTIS & MIDGE

by *Mantis*'s MGB 20.

And on the 29th RNR Lt Donald Bradford's C-Type MGB, from *Midge*, sank S 29 by ramming after the two craft had shot each other to a shambles at a range of forty yards. Bradford was the most aggressive officer at Yarmouth. Most certainly a "man of action", his background included the Merchant Navy, the Bolivian Army during the Chaco War, the International Brigades in the Spanish Civil War (he was wounded in both conflicts), and escape from a Vichy French prison in West Africa. Later promoted Lieutenant-Commander and Senior Officer of the new D-Type 55th Flotilla, he had sharks' teeth painted on its bows.

By now Hichens had used up eight of his nine lives. On 12 April his legendary luck came to an end. In command of four MGBs escorting Lowestoft MLs on a minelaying operation off Scheveningen, he was not on his usual boat, MGB 77, because she was refitting, but had instead embarked on 112. With him on her bridge was her commander _ Lt Sidebottom RNVR, and two "guests", one from the RAF and the other from the Fleet Air Arm, but both (absurdly) named Edwards. As the British force engaged a German flak trawler and a schuyt a single short cannon burst hit MGB 112's bridge. Sidebottom and his first officer were badly wounded, and Hichens was killed instantly. The two Edwardses took charge and the boat regained *Beehive*. It had been Hichens's fourteenth action and 148th patrol. As a hero not only of *Beehive* and the MGBs (which he had pioneered), but of Coastal Forces and

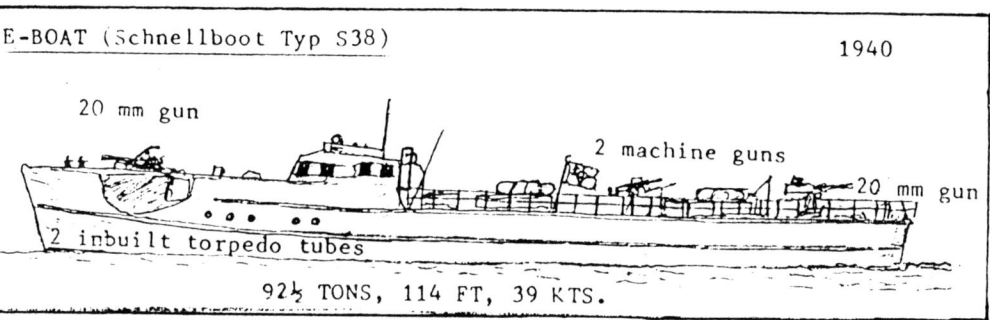

above & facing page...
COMBAT MOTOR CRAFT OF THE TWO SIDES
(to scale; dates are those of introduction of the class)

the whole RNVR, he was one of the few junior officers to achieve national fame. The BBC had even come down to Felixstowe and interviewed him on his boat. His book *We Fought Them in Gunboats* was posthumously published, with a foreword from his FOIC (and distant relation) Rear-Admiral Rogers. He left a wife and two young children. His grave may still be seen in Felixstowe Cemetary.

Lt-Cdr Dickens remained Felixstowe-based until his promotion and transfer that summer. His 21st MTB Flotilla, and Lt-Cdr Trelawny's 11th, achieved mounting success. The North Coates Beaufighters had forced the German convoys to take refuge by day and sail only at night _ and this meant more targets for Coastal Forces. A week after Hichens' death Trelawny* led an attack in which two merchantmen were sunk off the Hook. On 13 May four MTBs, commanded by Hartley, MacDonald, Ohlenschlager and Dickens himself, sank two minesweepers in the same area:"Up went the target in a terrific sheet of flame, the firing ceased as if it had been turned off with a tap, and she appeared to break in two."+

On 24 July, on an eerie phosphorescent sea, seven craft led by Dickens and Trelawny fought an unprecedented three-hour action off Ijmuiden.Dickens' MTB 225 was hit by one large shell without serious casualties. Lt Neill's MTB 223 was struck by another which killed two men and set her ablaze: all the extinguishers were used to no avail and it was only after a desperate struggle with seawater that the fire was put out. A "VP-Boat" was seen to sink, probably from Sub-Lt Lee's torpedoes.

Trelawny had his narrowest escape on 14 October, when his MTB 356 was sunk. His report gives the flavour of the time in full measure:
> Last October my crowd were operating off Scheveningen, when we ran into a patrol, the very patrol we had been told to avoid. We wanted to save our fish for another customer, so we retired, closely pursued by a lot of hot metal. One of these objects had our number on it, for there was suddenly the most enormous explosion just behind me, the boat skidded like a police car on the films, and we began to sink rapidly by the stern. We had been hit on the small of the back by a four-inch brick, and had suffered very severe damage. There was nothing we could do for the poor old girl, and the Hun, elated by his success, was coming up rapidly, preceded by a hail of fire from everything he could bring to bear. So we

---

*the same Trelawny returned to Felixstowe in the 1970s as manager of the container port.   +quoted by Scott (see Bibliography).

yelled to the next boat, commanded by Lt Peter Magnus, who had seen our plight and stopped: he brought his boat to bear alongside us and we transferred, with only three casualties and hardly a wet foot.*

On the night of 9-10 December his boats fought perhaps the longest-ever action by Coastal Forces, against a typically small but heavily escorted German convoy of three merchant ships, eight trawlers and several R-Boats. He himself claimed one merchantman sunk by torpedo: "There was one really big fellow spitting tracer at us along his entire length, so we closed in and let him have it".*

Meanwhile *Mantis* and *Midge* had not been inactive. On 19 September Bradford led a mixed MTB and MGB force to the Dutch shore near Ijmuiden, where they torpedoed and wrecked the grounded 17,000-ton German-controlled liner *Strasbourg*. (She was later finished off by the North Coates aircraft). Five nights later came the unique sinking of an E-boat by two Lowestoft Z-Line MLs, described in Chapter 10. But Coastal Forces in Yarmouth Sub-Command fought their fiercest, and most successful, battle in the early hours of 25 October, and this I must now describe.

That night the Z Lines were occupied by various two-boat units from *Midge* (Yarmouth). RNVR Lt R H Marshall's Unit Y, D-Types from 17th MGB Flotilla, was at Z 16 _ off Winterton, and near to the Harwich patrol destroyer *Mackay* (Lt-Cdr J H Eaden DSC). RNVR Lts J A Caulfield and P N Edge had V (12th MGB Flotilla C-Types) and R (17th Flotilla D-Types) at Z 55 and 56 respectively _ off Happisburgh. They and the two MLs of Unit S, at Z 22, were near another Harwich destroyer, the famous *Worcester* (Lt J A H Hamer). FN 1160 and FS 1164 were moving through the Alley, with 21D (Sheerness) Flotilla escorting. On them twenty-eight E-boats from 2, 4, 6 and 8 Flotillas, gathered at Ijmuiden for the occasion, attempted a raid second only in size to the operation a month earlier. But this time the Germans brought torpedoes, not mines.

The destroyers and MGBs, all of which were engaged, completely shielded the convoys. The Sheerness destroyer *Pytchley* repelled the first probe, north-east of Sheringham Light Float, at a quarter to midnight. Responding to radar and hydrophone, Units V and R sped off in that direction, keeping between the enemy and FN 1160, and drove off more

---

*quoted by Scott.

raiders. 6th E-boat Flotilla got through to the outer convoy route but found only the Lowestoft patrol trawler *William Stephen*: at 0110 S 74 torpedoed and sank her, killing five crewmen and capturing fifteen. Meanwhile *Worcester* and *Mackay* drove off the two divisions into which Korvettenkapitän Lützow's 4th E-boat Flotilla had split. Covering the damaged S 63, which later sank, Lützow withdrew, but Unit Y was sent to intercept him north-east of Smith's Knoll. Around 0200 it shot up S 88, killing Lützow and two of his crew, crippling two engines, and setting the boat afire. Marshall's MGB 607 then rammed a second E-boat* amidships at almost full speed and sank her, though at the cost to himself of five dead and six wounded. Abandoned, S 88 blew up in a two-hundred-foot column of burning debris. Lt Lightoller's MGB 603 rescued her nineteen survivors, who had been blowing whistles, shouting and flashing torches in the water. She took MGB 607 in tow for Yarmouth, breaking off at one stage to chase more E-boats in vain.

10 MTB Flotilla's Units E and J, waiting in Hamilton Dock, Lowestoft, had torn out of harbour and RCNVR Lt C A Burk's J (MTBs 439 and 442) intercepted another enemy flotilla near Brown Ridge. In a wild melée Burk's first officer was killed and the E-boats regained Ijmuiden. Nonetheless the night's score was an unprecedented three E-boats sunk.

According to Gerald Pawle the British success was due to a new type of starshell fired on the same ammunition belts as the Oerlikon rounds. Weight for weight they had thirteen times as much candle power as the old ones. Not only did they illuminate the enemy but, being hyper-flammable, rapidly destroyed wood and thin metal. Even their inventor was amazed by their success.

Other technical developments were by now afoot. Hichens had experimentally mounted small torpedo tubes on his MGB early in 1943, and there had been a similar project with Lowestoft MLs back in 1941. Now, with the big D-Types, it was found possible to mount both guns, including 2- and even 6-pdrs, and torpedo tubes, on the same boats. Though this reduced their speed and overcrowded them with as many as thirty-three crew each, it gave them E-boat-style versatility. At the end of 1943 the distinction between MTBs and MGBs was dropped, and the term "MGB" was dropped. Coastal Forces had been using the rather ineffective short-range Type 286 RDF since August 1941. Now Type 291, a 10-cm radar capable of searching out E-

---

*given in Volkmar Kühn's list as S 172, but this must be wrong as she was not built until later.

boats up to eight miles away, became standard on all Nore MTBs, with the invasion of Occupied Europe officially in mind. The set was housed on the lower (navigation) deck of the bridge, and the aerial used both for transmission and reception was a rotating "Yagi" with four dipoles on the masthead. Below were IFF Interrogator and "Responder". (See sketch on Page 286).

S 74 was soon punished for sinking *William Stephen*. Returning from the "Alley" raid of 3/4 November (see Chapter 10) she was sunk off the Texel by 254 Squadron (North Coates) Beaufighters. That same night, though, and nearby, Bradford had MGB 606 sunk under him and nine of his crew killed, though he was rescued and brought back to *Midge*.

The motor-boat fighting in this Sub-Command continued into 1944. Intercepting E-boats near Brown Ridge on 15 February Lt "Blondie" Leaf DSC, Senior Officer of *Mantis*'s 10th MTB Flotilla, was killed on MTB 455, along with three of his crew. Leaf was then probably the longest-serving Coastal Forces boat commander in the Nore Command, having been in the original Felixstowe MGB flotilla, and served at Lowestoft for two and a half years. Lt-Cdr D N E McCowen's 53rd Flotilla was now based at Yarmouth. On 6 March, having sunk a German coaster and probably also an R-Boat and a merchantman off Ijmuiden, it came under heavy fire: among those killed was Lt Wickham, the Nore Coastal Forces Gunnery Officer, who was on board one MTB. McCowen went on to torment the enemy off Normandy and then, in the last few weeks of war, to command HMS *Beehive*.

Immingham became the base for some unusual Coastal Forces vessels when five craft built as large MGBs were converted into fast cargo boats and used to import 360 tons of high-quality ball bearings from Lysekil, near Gothenburg, Sweden. During the dark winter nights of 1943-4 *Gay Corsair, Gay Viking, Hopewell, Nonsuch* and *Master Standfast* made nine voyages each, in spite of some obstruction by Swedish port officials. *Master Standfast* was captured just outside Swedish territorial waters on 2 November.

Surprisingly there had been very little attempt to bomb the E-boats in harbour. Late in 1941 the RAF had again bombed Ostend, but, as in 1940, in order to prevent the enemy mounting landings in Britain from there _ it

BEEHIVE, MANTIS & MIDGE

was not yet an E-boat base. Though the RAF and the US Eighth Air Force attacked Ijmuiden, Rotterdam and Ostend in 1942 and 1943, power stations and industries had been the targets. (Ijmuiden, for instance, had the only steelworks in Holland).

In March, 1944, during the air campaign softening up the Western Continent for invasion, the Allies made one big joint attempt to knock out the Ijmuiden E-boat base _ partly to reduce a distraction on their left flank, partly to divert the Germans' attention from Normandy. On the night of the 25th RAF 2 Group attacked the Dutch port's AA sites, especially those on the little island in the harbour entrance. Next day a huge raid was delivered on the E-boat base by 373 Marauders of the US Ninth Air Force, flying from Earl's Colne, Great Saling, Dunmow and elsewhere in Essex. The aerial reconnaissance pictures taken after the attack show a cratered moonscape on the open land south-west of the harbour, but in avoiding the town the bombers had also mostly (just) missed the base. The enemy's old concrete E- and R-boat shelters had been wrecked, and in the Herring Harbour in front of them S 93 and 129 had been destroyed. But the Germans had anticipated the

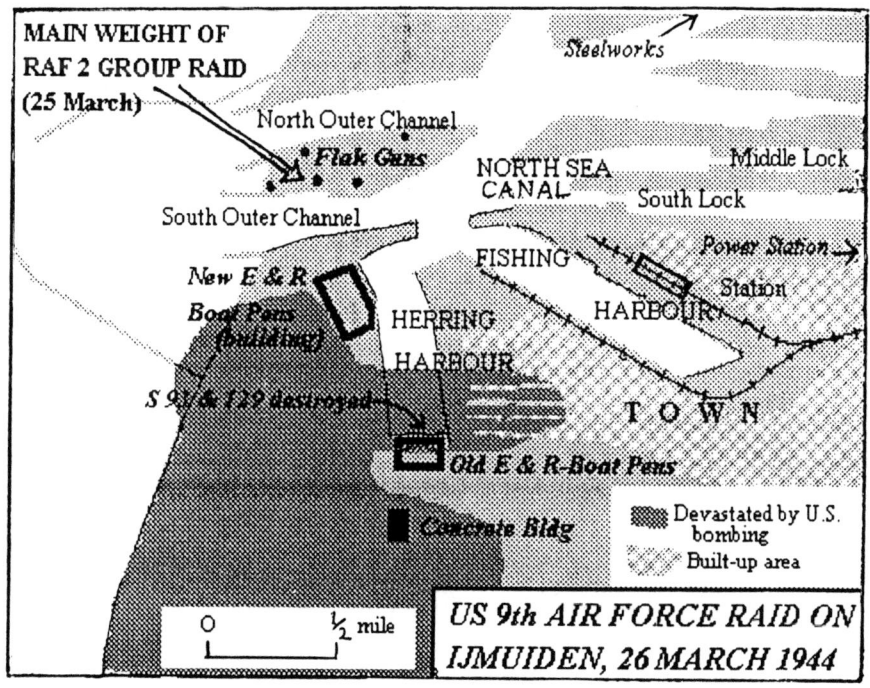

danger, and much stronger shelters, like those of the Atlantic U-Boats, were already under construction. Soon after this raid the Ijmuiden E-boats found safety in these.

In the spring of 1944 many of the Yarmouth and Lowestoft MTBs shifted to the Channel for the build-up to Normandy, and many of the E-boats went too. This meant a lull in the North Sea motor boat war. The period from September 1944 to April 1945 saw the final showdown between Nore Command Coastal Forces and Dutch-based E-boats, but I shall leave this till my last chapter. Meanwhile, as some measure of the East Coast Coastal Forces' activity, these are the enemy vessels claimed by HMS *Beehive* to the end of the war: fourteen merchantmen, eleven flak trawlers, one unidentified escort craft, three large T-class torpedo boats, one M-class minesweeper, and five or six E-boats _ total thirty-five or six. (In fact the real number of sinkings was lower). Felixstowe's own boats had lost sixteen of their number, and since late 1942 alone it had carried out 4,080 individual sorties.

In addition to the Nore Command's operational Coastal Forces bases, an important supporting role was played by Brightlingsea. First, it was from 1941 responsible for the equipping and trials of all MLs (and from 1942 other Coastal Forces craft) built between the Thames and Humber inclusive. From an HQ at the Manor House Captain J P Farquharson and a shore staff of up to thirty inspected new boats, summoned crews from drafting bases, provided their temporary billets, supervised trials of craft, fitted Asdic, supplied all non-technical stores, and arranged for visiting personnel to fit weapons, radio and radar. Most of the fitting out was done at Aldous's Shipyard, Brightlingsea, but Brooke Marine, Oulton Broad, was used for boats built at the northern yards. Second, Brightlingsea was the main repair base for North Sea and Dover Coastal Forces craft . The successive engineering officers in charge were Lt-Cdrs(E) Kellaway and Griffiths (both RNVR). Until 1944 the repair staff was only about fourteen naval personnel plus shipyard workers, but then expanded to over forty. By then the number of Coastal Forces boats in harbour for equipping, refitting or repair was as high as twenty-four at one time.

Of course these did not fight the Germans, but on 5 March, 1943,

HMS *BEEHIVE*, FELIXSTOWE
Above: Two early Vosper-type MTBs under repair in one of the former RAF hangars.
Below: A Wren driving one of 6th MGB Flotilla's boats out of a hangar towards the harbour. *(both photos IWM)*

Above: MTB 233's engines being removed for overhaul at James & Stone's Shipyard, Brightlingsea, in 1943. A motor minesweeper, a line of *Helder* landing craft, and the St Osyth Stone Martello Tower in the background. *(Gray)*

Below: The wreck of the destroyer *Gipsy* being refloated early in 1940. The two towers on the horizon are Harwich High Lighthouse and Church. *(GPU)*

three sailors died at Brightlingsea when MTB 667's crew, sleeping on board, were overcome by gas leaking from an engine fire extinguisher. Two of the victims are buried at All Saints' Churchyard. MTB 667 went on to be an "ace" boat in the Mediterranean.

There was also a small Coastal Forces office at Ipswich, where an RLO (Repair Liaison Officer), Lt Snoxell RNVR, coordinated the work of the various repair and refit yards (including those at Brightlingsea), so that boats could be finished as soon as possible.

The war of the MTBs and MGBs was the only aspect of the Second World War in the North Sea to leave a lasting impression on the public mind. This is in part due to the books written by Hichens and Scott. But there is undoubtedly a whole series of fascinating further reasons. This was a British naval *offensive* _ one of the few. Also, it came to have a predominantly amateur (RNVR) character _ yet the amateurs had the fastest boats in the Navy. The image of the dashing amateur was somehow mixed up with a youthful middle-class camaraderie, with crisp yacht-club and public-school accents. At the time (even more than today) most people would have felt this if they had seen Hichens and Dickens park their sports cars (red and blue respectively) by Felixstowe Dock and walk into the Little Ships' Hotel for gin with their fellow-officers. Yet these were no younger or "posher" than many other naval officers, and the RNVR were just as common on minesweepers and landing craft. In any case most Coastal Forces' personnel were socially humble conscript ratings, not gentleman adventurers.

14
SHIP RESCUE AND SALVAGE

Saving stricken ships and sailors from the North Sea was as much a part of the Nore Command's contribution to national defence as minesweeping, escort or patrol. Unlike on the oceans, on the East Coast the shallow water and proximity of the shipping lanes to the shore made rescue of both ship and crew possible in many cases. More than humanitarian considerations were involved: one out of three ships disabled by the enemy were saved to work another day.

The relevant operations fall into three kinds: the rescue of sailors, the rescue of sinking or crippled ships, and the salvage of sunken ones.

For the firstnamed only the peacetime RNLI (Royal National Lifeboat Institution) was for long available. Its part-time civilian volunteers manned stations at Margate, Southend, Clacton, Walton, Aldeburgh, Southwold (this one until 1940 only), Lowestoft, Gorleston, Caister, Cromer, Sheringham, Wells, Skegness, Spurn Point and Bridlington. Lifeboats were not needed to rescue from enemy-damaged ships in convoy, since the escorts were much closer at hand: usually they were launched for ships sailing independently, or for convoy stragglers. More often out for ditched aircraft than anything else, they were in this case usually beaten to the scene by RAF or naval rescue launches. The "eyes" of the RNLI (and later rescue services) were the Coastguards. There was one of their permanent stations every seven or eight miles on average, with about twice that number of temporary night posts _ manned by civilian volunteers. The Coastguard HQs on the East Coast were at Yarmouth and Walton-on-Naze. At this period most lifeboats and Coastguard posts possessed neither radio nor radar, today standard equipment. Both civilian services came under the orders of the local naval FOICs or NOICs.

The most celebrated wartime lifeboatman was Henry Blogg, senior coxswain at Cromer (where there were, in fact, two boats). Already the holder of rescue medals dating back to the *First* World War, in the Second he and his crew saved more seamen (over four hundred) than any other lifeboatmen.

They rescued the twenty-four crew of the Greek merchant ship *Mount Ida* soon after the declaration of war, and thirty more from the Italian *Traviata*, a magnetic mine casualty, on 4 January 1940. On 6 August 1941 FS 69 came to grief in a disaster as bad as anything inflicted by E-boats in

SHIP RESCUE & SALVAGE

those waters. Six merchant ships, including one French and one Estonian, followed the off-course Harwich escort trawler *Agate* onto Haisborough Sands, and were then torn apart by a storm as ferocious as it was unseasonal. Blogg's *H F Bailey* saved eighty-eight lives in repeated perilous trips, sailing right on top of a half-submerged wreck in one instance: meanwhile another thirty-one had been rescued by the second Cromer lifeboat and the one from Gorleston, and still more by the Harwich A/S trawler *Bassett*. Blogg won the BEM for this exploit.

The following month he won praise from the Admiralty Salvage Department for taking out firemen and Yarmouth-based salvagers to the burning wreck of SS *Teddington*, torpedoed by an E-boat (see Page 215). Next 27 October he saved forty-four more men from another storm victim, *English Trader*, aground on Hammond Knoll. He and some of his crew were thrown overboard during the rescue, and the signalman was drowned. In 1942, in recognition of his whole career to date Blogg was awarded the George Cross, the highest honour ever won by the RNLI. He was then seventy-one years old. In retirement after the war he is said to have taken no interest in anything on land, but pined away gazing out to sea.

Robert Cross, of the isolated post at Spurn Head, was almost a northern equivalent. His first and most dangerous wartime mission was the rescue of nine men from the trawler *Garth* on 12 February 1940: the gale, the near-flooding of his lieboat, and his sixty-eight years did not daunt him, and he received the George Medal.

The Caister boat saved the crew of the M/S trawler *Charles Boyes*, mined two days before the beginning of the Dunkirk Evacuation: two of her own crew lost their footing and drowned. The Gorleston boat, *Louise Stephens*, landed the survivors of the mined Norwegian SS *Deodata* and the Greek *Konstantinos Hadjupikios* in October 1939. Aldeburgh's *Abdy Beauclerk* rescued seventy-four oil-stained men, several of them injured, from the very first of the magnetic mine victims, SS *Magdapur*, on 10 September 1939. She saved twenty-four more from the French *Phryne* a fortnight later. On 27 February she saved the three crew of the sailing barge *Martinet* (one of them the noted skipper Bob Roberts), sunk by a gale in Hollesley Bay.

The Frinton-Walton lifeboat, usually *EMED*, rescued from the sailing barges *Esterel* and *Yampa* (14 October 1939) and *Martha* (19

January 1941). She also towed in a boatload of Japanese from *Terukuni Maru* on 21 November 1939, and the mine-damaged barge *Maria* on 9 July 1943. At Clacton the *Edward Z Dresden* was deprived of her base when the pier was mined and partly demolished by uninformed Army engineers as an anti-invasion measure in 1940. From August till November, until her station was repaired, she worked from Brightlingsea. In November she saved the seven crew of the mined coaster *Ability*. On 6 April 1943 Frank Castle, one of her crew, was drowned along with the two stubborn men she had come to save while he was on board their Battersea rubble barge *Tam O'Shanter* trying to get them to leave. The incident happened near Wallet Spitway Buoy. On other occasions the Clacton boat towed the sailing barges *Glenmore* and *Thalatta* to safety, and landed the thirteen crew of a stranded Harwich LL drifter. It was mostly into Brightlingsea Creek that the Clacton or Walton boats towed damaged vessels.

The Southend lifeboat, *Greater London*, put out sixty-six times and saved over three hundred men. Among others, she rescued from *Aridity*, *Dagenham*, *Letchworth* and *Winkfield*, and during three stormy days in December 1940 saved the crews of six London and Ipswich sailing barges. The Dunkirk operations of the Essex and Suffolk lifeboats have already been mentioned.

On the convoy route escorting warships saved many times the number picked up by the RNLI. Though the Lowestoft MLs must again be mentioned, Harwich-based craft were most prominent in this. For example, the A/S trawler *Kingston Olivine* (Lt F W Lewis RANVR)* rescued no fewer than 105 men from three merchant ships within a month in March-April 1942 — *Frumenton* off Southwold, *Cressdene* off Aldeburgh, and *Chatwood* near the Dudgeon. Those saved were not necessarily very cooperative or grateful. On 10 October 1941 the Greek grain ship *Kyma*, whose degaussing did not work, was mined in convoy near the Humber Lightship. Two of the crew abandoned ship in a boat with a bottle of whisky, and were found drifting, drunk, and not attempting to row, by the destroyer *Quantock*, whose captain confiscated the alcohol. The other twenty-five crew were taken off the ship by *Kingston Olivine*, including six injured, who were transferred to *Mahseer*. While the trawler crew were vainly trying to tow the *Kyma*, her survivors were below decks looting their rescuers' alcohol: after they had started fighting one had to be locked up. On shore at Harwich

---

*Royal Australian Navy Volunteer Reserve.

SHIP RESCUE & SALVAGE

Quantock's captain solemnly returned the whisky bottle he had confiscated earlier in the day. When Lombard-Hobson's corvette *Guillemot* towed the mine-damaged *Nicholaos Piangos* into the Humber at this same period, he found her Asiatic crew so panicky that he had to hold them at gunpoint to stop them abandoning ship.
 A great many sailors owed their lives to these Harwich corvettes. *Pintail* saved the crew of the *Amelia Lauro* and *Puffin* that of the *Scotia*. *Shearwater* rescued from *Stad Maastricht*, *Exmoor* and *Polgarth*, and towed *Quorn* to safety. *Sheldrake* saved *Artemisia's* mainly Chinese crew, and later towed *Largo* to Harwich. *Widgeon* rescued from *Hornchurch*, *Cormead* and *Aruba*. The NCSO at HMS *Badger*, whose responsibility this was, took care of 994 shipwreck survivors between 1939 and 1945.

 The towing to safety of damaged ships was the responsibility of the naval Rescue Tugs, and the raising and provisional repair of those already sunk of the Admiralty Salvage Department. In practice the two branches worked as one, for tugs were needed in most salvage operations and vessels to be towed often needed preliminary pumping and patching. The PLA salvaged in the River Thames and Sheerness Dockyard in the southern Outer Estuary, with the assistance of the Southend tugs when needed. Harwich had charge of the Brightlingsea-Lowestoft coastline. Hull, with (from 1941) a forward base at Yarmouth, was responsible for Lowestoft-Flamborough Head. Operationally the tugs and salvage craft came under the London, Southend, Harwich and Humber NCSOs.
 The salvage craft carried an extraordinary range of equipment. The most common items were: centrifugal pumps, suction hoses and strainers, electric generators, dynamos, electric cables, copper flex, steam pipes, oxy-acetylene torches, air compressors, underwater cutting gear, exploders, bolt-firing guns, screwing machines, patching timber and cement, hawsers, hoists, fastening ribbons, wedges, strops, clamps, towing lines, collision mats, telephone lines, toolkits and diving gear!
 The usual salvage method was to tow the stricken ship into a harbour or onto a sandbank where she could be beached, patched with timber, metal or concrete, pumped out, refloated, and towed to a repair yard. Each merchant ship provisionally repaired in harbour had to be inspected by a representative of Lloyds before proceeding on her way. many salvage

SHIP RESCUE & SALVAGE

operations involved underwater work by divers, who were required to make damage inspections and sometimes to clear cables or debris from ships' screws.

Apart from one officer in charge and his assistant, and a few administrative personnel, who were Royal Navy or RNR, salvage bases were staffed by civilians. Their ambiguous status, as neither servicemen nor war industry workers, made them liable to the call-up. On occasion officers had to protest loudly to hang on to them. As Lt-Cdr Scurr, of Harwich, pointed out; "This work is very exacting and is of a highly specialised nature, and it would be a very serious matter if the men were taken away at random".* Some of the less skilled salvagers were local men, often unemployed labourers or seamen hired on a temporary basis for particular operations. Civil contractors were brought in to finish off some jobs.

The rescue tugs were also, apart from the odd naval signaller, crewed by civilians, though with "T 124" status. Most tugs came to their war bases complete with their peacetime crews. The tugmasters were fiercely proud both of their skill and their independence, insisting on working in their own way, free from the by no means expert interference of naval officers. Almost as much rescue and salvage work as that of the designated rescue tugs was done by some of the smaller harbour tugs which served Royal and Merchant Navy alike from the Thames ports, Harwich, and the Humber. Tugs with names ending in *ia* came from the Gravesend firm of William Watkins. All the *Saints* originated from the Great Western Railway's Welsh ports. The *Suns* came from W H J Alexander, another Thames firm. *Bessie* and *Lady Brassey* were the property of the Dover Harbour Board, and *Stronghold* belonged to the Ipswich Dock Company.

On the Thames Captain Brooke's PLA Salvage Department used numbered lighters with winches on their bows. Shallowness of water, nearness of the Docks and the abundance of tugs made their life relatively easy. Two ships raised were *Halo* from off Barking and *Kinnaird Head* from off Southend. The PLA also patched and pumped dozens of bombed ships in the London Docks, and towed away and cut up the AA paddler *Helvelyn*.

Sheerness Dockyard salvaged many wrecks between the Medway and Barrow Deep, such as *Dixcove*, *Winkfield* and *Till*. It was also the base for the wreck disposal ship *Colchester* (formerly the Harwich ferry SS *Felixstowe*), which cleared unsalvable and dangerous wrecks with explosives.

---

*Harwich Salvage Records (PRO ADM 199/1805).

SHIP RESCUE & SALVAGE

From there too a survey of wrecks in formerly mined areas, like the dreaded Tongue "QZ", was carried out in 1943, so that these could be disposed of by Trinity House after the war. From Sheerness the rescue tug *Mammoth* regularly escorted the Channel convoys, though her attempt on 5 June 1941 to stop the mined A/S trawler *Ash* from sinking ended rather disgracefully when her pumping hoses burst because they had perished. *St Clears* was the other *Wildfire* rescue tug in the earlier part of the war.

    The Hull ("Eastern Area") Salvage Base had its office in Nelson Street and its depot at No 34 Shed, River Pier. In 1941 a section moved to Yarmouth to deal with the many wrecks in that area; it was based at the Nelson Garage and the ABC Wharf. The Hull department started with the requisitioned local vessel *Cité de Londres*; in 1941 *Nessus* was the salvage ship. Until she was mined that year the rescue tug was *St Cyrus*. At Yarmouth the rescue tugs at this period were *Norman*, later renamed *Diversion*, and *Krooman*. The first major Hull rescue was of the tanker *San Delfino* on 28 December 1939. The SS *Cree* was saved by continuous pumping on 26 April 1940 and towed to Hull. While being worked on in the Would on 26 January 1941 *Meriones* was bombed and sunk, and the same happened to *Ethel Radcliffe* in April. SS *Kaida*, off Yarmouth Beach, was a similar victim, while *Fleet Tender C* was being salvaged off Sheringham when sunk by an E-boat that June. *Essex Lance* was one of the bigger vessels saved off Cromer. On 14 October 1942 the E-boat victims *Lysland* and *George Balfour* were towed from the South East Dudgeon to the Humber and Yarmouth respectively, though the second ship was in two pieces. Between 1940 and 1944 the Hull/Yarmouth Rescue and Salvage Departments took part in 214 major and minor operations.

    On his own initiative Cdr Heaton, the Lowestoft Minesweeping Officer, salvaged the bombed 4,363-ton *Royal Crown* at Covehithe in the bitter winter of 1940. Equipment and supplies had to be dragged across clifftop snowdrifts and then lowered to the shore on breeches buoys. The damaged ship was nearly sunk in a gale, and held up with two thousand lumps of timber, sheets of canvas, okum, and coatings of red lead. By 27 February she was safe, and left for repair on the Tyne. A year later she was sunk in the Atlantic by the *Gneisenau*.

    Harwich was the leading Salvage (and Rescue Tugs) base on the East Coast, and the best documented. As a general illustration of all the

SHIP RESCUE & SALVAGE

bases, I shall therefore describe its work in more detail.

Its office was initially in the Alexandra Hotel, Dovercourt, and then at 41B Church Street, Harwich, but from late 1940 it was located alongside Rescue Tugs in the old Great Eastern Railway Hotel on Harwich Quay. It took over the Train Ferry Berth and one berth and a shed at Parkeston in mid-1940.

Three large salvage vessels were permanently based at Badger: *Forde* (Captain Trodden) _ a converted Isle of Wight ferry, *Freija* (Captain Austin and later Goddard), and *Foremost 18*. They bore pwerful cranes and winches with cables up to nine inches thick, capable of strains of several hundred tons. Assisting them were the small motor boats *Jeff, Mutt* and *Salvage Prince*, and later the converted trawlers *Dapper* and *Wrangler* joined. At any one time up to five radio-equipped rescue tugs were present, ranging from thirty years old to brand new. *Muria*, in October 1939, was the first to arrive. Her most notable peacetime assignment had been to tow the *Cutty Sark* up to Greenwich. Her master, Captain Walker, was William Watkins' senior master. Subsequent arrivals were *Caroline Moller, St Olaves, Kenia, St Mellons, Nubia* and *Lady Brassey*. Late in 1941 three tugs seized from the French appeared: *Attentif, Champion* and (from Sheerness) *Mammoth*, a 954-tonner which had towed Atlantic liners at peacetime Cherbourg. From late 1942 to early 1945 *Kenia, Krooman* and the first two French boats were the regulars, but *St Clears, Seaman, Superman* and the ex-American *Sea Giant* sometimes helped. Of the many small harbour tugs the best-known were *Bessie* and *Stronghold*. The former, captained by W H Lydamore, served at Harwich for all but the first few months of war and took part in more rescue and salvage work than any other tug except *Kenia*, whose master was W C Hoiles.

The last group of rescue tugs to make their Harwich debut were the big purpose-built Admiralty fleet tugs which arrived in January 1945. They carried unprecedentedly high-powered engines and, in contrast to all but a couple of the older tugs, armaments, including at least one 3-inch and two 20-mm AA guns apiece. *Bustler* and *Growler* were each 1,120 tons and 205 feet in length, the American-built *Director, Emulous, Freedom* and *Justice* 1360 tons and 165 feet. They were, absurdly, bigger than many of the ships they were required to tow. Manpower shortage made it hard to crew them. The men provided were mostly young and completely inexperienced. Not

SALVAGE & RESCUE TUGS AT HARWICH

ABOVE: The *Freija* salvaging debris from HMS *Gipsy*'s bows off RAF Felixstowe (late 1942). Felixstowe Dock, Little Ships Hotel, hammerhead crane and moored MGBs on the left, and barrage balloons overhead.
BELOW: Tug *Kenia* in Harwich Harbour, March 1943. In the background two Woolverstone-based tank landing craft contrast with a sailing barge.   *(IWM)*

RESCUE TUGS AT HARWICH
ABOVE: The Sheerness-based ex-Cherbourg tug *Mammouth* off the Harwich Salvage and Rescue Tugs Headquarters (formerly Great Eastern Railway Hotel)
BELOW: The ex-American rescue tug *Sea Giant* off HMS Ganges, Shotley. *(IWM)*

SHIP RESCUE & SALVAGE

surprsingly *Growler* ran aground on one of her first missions, towing a floating dock from Yarmouth up the Orwell to Ipswich. She had to be pulled clear by the humble *Bessie*.

The slow and lightly armed tugs and salvage craft ran considerable risks at sea. On 7 November 1940 *Muria* was bombed and sunk with all hands near the North Foreland. She had been bound for Ramsgate to refit, and her crew were looking forward to an unusually long leave. *Caroline Moller* was sunk near Sheringham by an E-boat torpedo on 7 October 1942, with the loss of sixteen of her thirty crew.

The Harwich salvage vessels and associated tugs took part in almost one hundred major and about 150 minor operations. By far the most active were *Forde* and *Kenia* (each about thirty major operations) and *Bessie* (twenty).

The first and longest salvage conducted by HMS *Badger* was the marathon operation on *Gipsy*, the destroyer mined and blown in two right in the harbour entrance. In the winter of 1939-40 Harwich sailors had removed such valuable items as the compass binnacles and ship's bell, and an Admiralty team had cleared the wreck from the shipping channel aboard hired PLA lighters. At low tide thick steel hawsers had been fixed to the wreck and pulled taut by winches mounted on massive floats lying alongside. With the rise of the tide each half of the ship had cleared the bottom and been towed to the edge of the channel and run aground, the fore section on the Felixstowe side and the stern on the Harwich. Temporarily afloat and quite unscarred at either end, the destroyer looked, to the layman, almost as if she could somehow be joined together and made as good as new. Indeed it was at this juncture that the press published misleading photographs of the wreck and claimed that *Gipsy* was completely salvaged. In reality she was never salvaged intact _ merely broken up f or scrap and cleared from the harbour. a process which took several more years.

HMS *Badger*'s Salvage Department started work on the wreck on 24 June 1940. *Forde, Wrangler* and *Bessie* hauled the stern afloat after many attempts, and in August beached it right in front of Harwich Church. This part, containing most of the ship's machinery, was of considerable value to the Admiralty. The shafts and other engine parts were removed for new ships. The condenser was stripped out for its copper, then very scarce in war industry. The stores were also landed, including a great deal of Navy rum which had, however, been spoilt. The hulk remained in position until after the war, for though its steel was valuable, its breaking up would have taken too much manpower. In August 1942 investigations began on the fore part, on the Felixstowe side. It was then blown up. According to Captain Lydamore of *Bessie,* the explosion was a cullinary boon for HMS *Beehive,* for it brought shoals of dead fish to the surface. *Freija* and *Foremost 18* salved the debris, a process not completed until 1944. The stern section was finally patched up and towed away to the breakers in 1945.

During the mines crisis of late 1939 and early 1940 there was only one rescue tug at Harwich, and no organised Salvage Department. The tug *Muria* went out on 30 January to help the *Highwave,* bombed near Kentish Knock. Captain Walker put out twice but each time turned back because of near gale-force winds. Meanwhile the Walton lifeboat had approached the crippled ship but been told that she would not be needed as *Muria* was expected. In the event *Highwave* sank with several of her crew. There were complaints via the Admiralty to Rear-Admiral Harris, who admitted that Walker had "lost his nerve", but "due to a fall on the ice at Parkeston", and sent him on a week's leave.

During their Dunkirk operations the newly arrived *Forde* and *Bessie* were called to SS *Fulham IV,* a collier bombed in convoy. They found her ready to founder from three bomb holes which ran clean through from top to bottom. They rescued the crew and towed her to Shotley Point. The subsequent repair and refloating was very speedily accomplished owing to the help of a technician called Cox, who had just been sent from the Admiralty. This man had much prewar experience in civilian salvage, and saved a week's work on *Fulham IV* by using a bolt-driving gun, a device which HMS *Badger* promptly christened the "Cox Gun".

By contrast, few of the ships sunk that summer and autumn proved salvable. In nine cases the Salvage Department surveyed the wrecks and winched off their 12-pdr guns. At the beginning of August six wrecks (*Clan Monroe, Gipsy, City of Canberra, Montrose, Westavon** and *Whitshed*) were being worked on simultaneously, and *Forde* had gear aboard four vessels. Her work on *Westavon,* which put to sea under her own power only twelve days after being hit by four bombs, and on *City of Canberra,* whose crew she rescued and which she patched up within four days in the choppy waters of Hollesley Bay, was particularly skilful. Another ship saved in August was

---

*Westavon had been bombed due east of Bawdsey. She was finally sunk on 30 May, 1941, by mine in the Barrow Deep.

SHIP RESCUE & SALVAGE

the tanker *Oiltrader*, bombed on the 11th. When found she was ablaze and drifting east of the convoy route. The trawler *Thomas Leeds* rescued her crew and put out the fires. *Muria* and *St Olaves* then towed her to a point near Felixstowe Pier and anchored her. *Forde* kept her afloat by pumping while she was patched up. All was conducted in the teeth of a north-westerly gale. While the debris was being cleared from *Oiltrader*'s stern, which had been crumpled by a direct bomb hit, the corpse of a seaman gunner was found. Now seaworthy, the tanker was towed to Gravesend by *Muria* and *Fairplay I* on 16 August. In 1941 she was bombed and sunk off Yarmouth.

The vain mission to the *Dungeness*, a Lowestoft patrol trawler bombed off Happisburgh Lighthouse on 15 November 1940, was one of the most hazardous undertaken by *Forde*. At the outset the weather was so bad that she had to take refuge at Yarmouth, Lt-Cdr Scurr going ahead by car to survey the wreck. Upon leaving for Harwich on the 21st *Forde* was machine-gunned by a German aircraft.

The minesweeper *Fitzroy* was the first successful operation of 1941. Having been mined she was towed in by the tug *Stronghold* and minesweeper *Gossamer*, and berthed near Harwich Guard Buoy. She had to be put under guard after being looted. Patched up at Parkeston, she was towed to London.

Perhaps the most dramatic rescue operation in Harwich area was that of the Swedish freighter *Belgia*, bombed near the Sunk Light on 26 January 1941. That night the Harwich destroyer *Cotswold* closed astern of her to rescue survivors. In spite of the swell, the darkness, and the fierce blaze, Lt Dickens, the destroyer's first officer (and future MTB commander), accompanied by two ratings, jumped from bow to stern, searched the wreck, and brought off twenty of her twenty-six crew. *Cotswold* then towed the *Belgia* to Frinton Beach and ran her aground five hundred yards south-west of Walton Pier at 1230 the following morning. The Walton lifeboat, *EMED*, put out with a Harwich salvage party led by Lt Whittle and equipped with pumps. They fought the fire for five hours and finally dowsed it, though the merchant ship was left with her whole deck buckled and only the blackened hull of her superstructure. The salvagers went on board to survey, but the lifeboat had to land them when the weather worsened. On 30 January *Kenia*, *St Mellons* and *EMED* tried unsuccessfully to tow the ship off the beach. This was finally achieved by the two Harwich tugs on 14 February, and *Belgia* was brought to harbour and beached at Bloody Point, Shotley, to be patched up and towed away a week later. Dickens and the Walton lifeboat were officially praised by the FOIC.

Among several other bombed vessels salvaged by HMS *Badger* in 1941 was the LL drifter *Jeannie Leask*, sunk at Brightlingsea in March. Her immediate salvage was imperative because she was blocking one of Aldous's slipways and preventing the launching of an ML. *Forde* raised the drifter, packed her hull with empty oil drums, and on these towed her to Rowhedge, where she was repaired _ to re-enter service with HMS *Nemo* in January 1942.

The next major operation could hardly have been more conveniently situated for the Salvage Department, for it was deal with the victims of the April air raid at Trinity Pier, Harwich, right next to *Forde*'s berth and almost in front of the GER Hotel. The paddle minesweeper *Marmion* lay partly underwater from a gaping hole in her starboard bow, against the east side of the pier, facing north. The drifter *Darcy Cooper*, outside her, had been blown clean in two, the bow lying on its side as much as sixty feet from the stern section. Lt-Cdr McPhee, the Salvage Officer, conducted a survey on 11 April, which led to an argument with Cdr Boxall, of *Queen Empress*, about the latter's crew removing equipment from the *Marmion*. An Admiralty salvage official then came and took charge. Work started on the morning of 13 April, with twenty-one men, including divers from *Forde* and *Freija*, and three pump hands sent from Harwich Labour Exchange. While the divers were below a German plane dropped bombs three-quarters of a mile away in the harbour, and a diver was concussed by the blast from the AA guns of *Princess Elizabeth*, moored at the Passenger Pier nearby. After six weeks work *Marmion* was refloated and towed to Pin Mill, on the Orwell, by *Kenia*, and thence to Tilbury. *Freija*, *Salvage Prince* and *Stronghold* meanwhile dragged the remains of *Darcy Cooper* further inshore to free the approach to the piers on either side. A steel company later broke her up where she lay.

Another long operation which began in 1941 was that on the Norwegian collier *Skagerrak*, which had been mined and blown in two in the Orwell. Having been surveyed and declared unsalvable, she was gradually cut up for scrap. At one time or another most of Harwich's salvage craft worked on her, while her clearance was finished by Harwich Lighters Ltd in 1944. In 1943 she was fouled by the Colchester grain barge *Castanet*, about to enter Felixstowe Dock. When *Stronghold* towed off the new casualty, the

SHIP RESCUE & SALVAGE

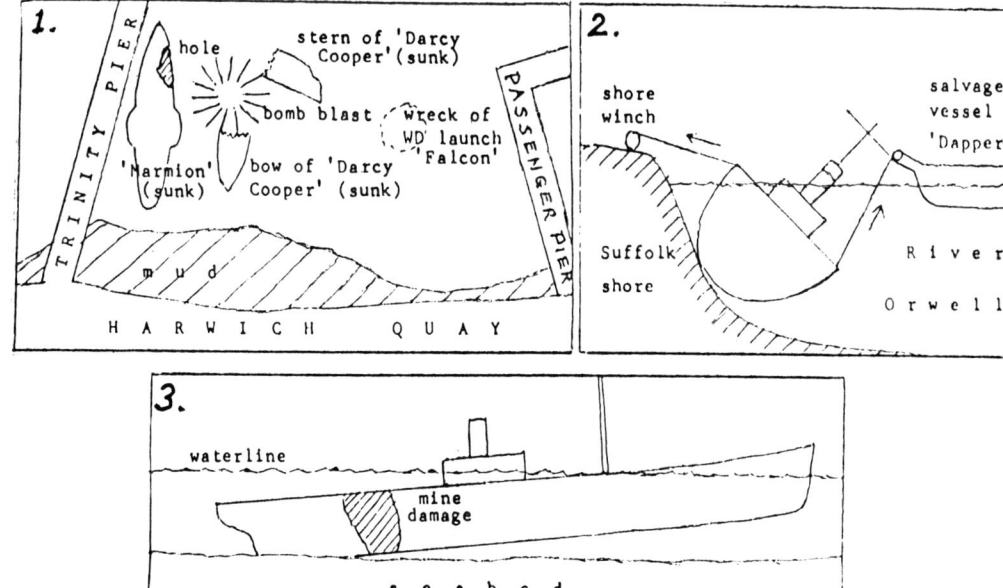

SALVAGE PROBLEMS AT HARWICH:
1.'Marmion' & 'Darcy Cooper'   2.'Portia'   3.'Swynfleet'

latter simply sank. Four salvage craft and the *Bessie* were therefore required in another tricky operation. *Castanet* was dragged onto Trimley Beach on two wires, pumped out, and then towed to Pin Mill.

One of the neatest pieces of salvage work by HMS *Badger* was on another Norwegian collier, *Bestum*, sunk by bombing on Cork Spit in November 1941. The ship had been holed by a near miss, but, lodged in the hold was a second, unexploded, bomb. This was removed by *Badger*'s bomb disposal squad, though not until after the salvagers had already started work. One thousand tons of coal were saved and taken to Ipswich by SS *Wyetown*. Working from *Forde* and the drifters *Sailor King* and *Shila*, the salvagers made *Bestum* seaworthy in nine days, whereupon *Kenia* and *Lady Brassey*, with two AA paddler escorts, towed her to the Thames.

Another impressive success, this time of the rescue tugs, was the *Eastwood* operation on Christmas Eve 1941. That collier had been mined and

SHIP RESCUE & SALVAGE

sunk near the Aldeburgh Light Float, but was refloated and towed into Harwich in pitch darkness, out of a mine-infested area, by *Kenia, Champion, Stronghold* and *Forde*. Two more mine victims, *Largo* and *Scottish Musician*, were rescued from only a few miles further north on 6 January 1942 in a simultaneous operation involving four tugs and the *Forde*.

Nothing, however, could be done to save the collier *Swynfleet*, mined close to Landguard Point. SS *Norbritt* removed some of her cargo, while salvagers saved the guns and started patching. But gales drove the wreck deeper and deeper into the mud, and the salvagers were called away to six other operations before they finally gave up.

The Salvage Department was twice summoned to help the destroyer *Worcester _ Forde* and *Salvage Prince* after her horrific encounter with *Gneisenau* and *Prinz Eugen*, and *Kenia, Krooman, Champion, Dapper, Bessie* and *Stronghold* when she was mine-damaged on 23 December 1943. Captain Lydamore, of *Bessie*, found her captain most apologetic about disturbing the tugs on Christmas Eve, and invited him on board for a drink.

One minor operation of 1942 which intrigued Lydamore was the salvage of the trawler *Portia*, which had gone too near the left bank of the Orwell while on her way to Ipswich, and heeled over and sank. She was righted by two winches, one on shore to starboard and one on *Dapper* to port. *Bessie* then towed her, submerged, to Parkeston, where she was pumped out. Her wheelhouse had been torn off but she was still in working order and steamed to a London dockyard without assistance.

While engaged on the *Swynfleet* wreck on 20 April *Dapper* received the following signal from the FOIC: "Proceed immediately at full speed to the assistance of *Cotswold* in position $52°5'N, 1°50'E$." The salvage vessel, together with *Salvage Prince, Bessie, Kenia and Superman* towed the mined destroyer sternfirst to Shotley Spit, where she was beached. Salvage proved to be no light task. *Cotswold* was in an appalling state, all her decks buckled, leaks everywhere, and full of foul oil. When plugged and refloated, she was shifted to Parkeston Quay for further repair, and then towed to Chatham, where her recommissioning took until September 1943.

The most difficult rescue or salvage operation of 1943 was that on the Finnish tanker *Josefina Thorden*, which was blown in two by a mine near Sunk Head Fort on 6 April. No fewer than seven Harwich tugs were involved in the attempt to save her. On being towed the after half sank. The fore

SHIP RESCUE & SALVAGE

section, having been lightened by the discharge of some of its oil, was towed to Shellhaven, though not before it had been stranded on a sandbank and rescued for a second time.

Most of the operations of 1944 and 1945 were minor. But on 5 February 1944 Harwich rescue tugs saved one of the largest warships to pass through local waters when they towed to Sheerness the escort aircraft carrier *Slinger*, of 11,400 tons, which had been mined off Lowestoft. The hardest job of 1944 was the patching and towing of BYMS 2040, almost broken apart in a collision with the corvette *Camelia* near Roughs.

The numerous minor operations each year of the war included the towing-off of grounded ships, the inspection of underwater damage caused by collisions, and the disentangling of boom or minesweeping wire from screws. *Bessie* pulled off the Do 17 which had landed on Erwarton mudflats and towed it on floats to RAF Felixstowe, where it was landed by the hammerhead crane. She similarly handled an RAF Wellington bomber which had crashlanded on the Orwell foreshore opposite Pin Mill on 13 July 1943. In February 1945 *Forde* raised an American Flying Fortress, containing seven corpses, from the River Deben.

15
DOCKYARDS AND SHIPYARDS

The Nore Command area contained no great shipyards (the two on the Medway aside) like those on the Clyde or Tyne. No ship built on the Thames or Humber, or at points in between, displaced more than one thousand tons, and the great majority were much smaller. And only on the Thames, Medway and Humber were there dockyards capable of *repairing* ships of more than this size.

The biggest and oldest naval dockyard on the East Coast of England was Chatham, and it is the inevitable starting point for this chapter. Chatham Dockyard was established originally by Elizabeth I, and refounded on its present site by Charles II. It sprawled along the right bank of the Medway below the town, and thence right across the big bend in the river. The site covered little short of one square mile. The older part of it, an extraordinary-looking jumble of Georgian and Victorian buildings, lay nearest to Chatham Town along the river. Here were the Admiral's office, roads with quaint names like "Tinker's Alley", four big dry docks, a picturesque 18th century clock tower, two square ponds for swelling timber, and eight wet docks covered by huge glass-rooved sheds. To the north, in the more modern extension, three large basins ran en-echelon from two locks on the seaward side in the east to the west shore below the old docks. Five more dry docks branched from No 1 (the westernmost) Basin. Each of the nine Chatham dry docks was large enough for a destroyer. To the north, occupying most of the western part of St Mary's "Island", were the huge workshops known as "The Factory", where ships' engines, other machinery, and armaments, were repaired or readied for fitting.

The civilian workforce rose to twelve thousand, up to a sixth of them women. Many of those enrolled prewar had taken an examination, famous in the Medway Towns, on the results of which they had been appointed to apprenticeships in particular trades (electricians were at "the top of the tree"), but now much untrained, so-called "dilute" labour was employed. The Superintendant was a Vice-Admiral _ Danby until 1942, and then Grace.

Chatham had built battleships, cruisers and sloops in the 19th century. Since 1900 it had specialised in submarine-building and warship repairs and refits, though for some reason one light cruiser, the *Euryalus* (5,450 tons) was built there, on Slip 8, as late as 1939. During the Second World War the submarines *Tigris, Torbay, Umpire, Una, Splendid,*

DOCKYARDS & SHIPYARDS

Sportsman, Tradewind, Trenchant, Shallimar, Turpin and *Thermopylae* were built on Slip 7. *Torbay* became famous, and had a captain who won the VC. In July 1941 *Umpire* was sunk in a collision with the Harwich trawler *Peter Hendricks* off Cromer on her way from Chatham to Scotland, with the loss of twenty-two lives, including that of a Dockyard electrical inspector. The submarine had been with an FN convoy, and the trawler had been escorting an FS. Like two polite but absent-minded people in a narrow corridor, they had seen each other at the last moment but swerved in the same direction. Among the rescued were the captain, Lt-Cdr Wingfield, and Lt Young RNVR, formerly of the Harwich-based H 28. Young, who later blamed himself for not shutting off the ventilation ducts in the submarine, made a desperate escape from the fully submerged wreck, but of the three men who came out of a tiny hatchway with him only one also survived. Apparently the Dockyard official got stuck in the escape chamber, thereby ending several lives besides his own.

Two sloops, two mooring vessels and two Admiralty floating docks were also completed at wartime Chatham. The ships refitted and repaired included numerous light cruisers, destroyers, corvettes and minesweepers from as far away as Scapa Flow, but mainly from Sheerness and Harwich _ the latter had no dry dock of its own. As a typical example, the following warships were refitting or repairing at Chatham in May 1940: the heavy cruiser *London*, the light cruiser *Ajax* (repairing after the Battle of the River Plate), the cruiser minelayer *Adventure* (see Page 16), and the destroyers *Verdun, Wolfhound* and *Sardonyx*. *

The cruisers attracted some attention from the Luftwaffe. In the September 1940 air raids some bombs fell close to the *Ajax*. When the *Arethusa* was in dry dock she still manned, and fired, her heavy AA guns. On 9 February 1941, as the light cruiser *Neptune* came up Barrow Deep, en route to the yard from Scapa, she was slightly damaged by bombs from one Do 17, and the sizeable (though unsuccessful) raid on Chatham twelve days later may have been occasioned by her presence.

Yet, as I said in Chapter Seven, the Dockyard enjoyed unusual luck during five years of intermittent bombing. Here was the closest permanent naval installation to the Luftwaffe bases, obvious from the air, and a

---

*The Dockyard is now open to the public, but only the older part. Without greypainted warships, barrage balloons overhead, and the clanging and humming of the workshops, little of its wartime atmosphere can be sensed, though the Covered Slips are worth the visit.

convenient secondary target for bombers unable to reach London. It was too big to have been put out of action, but more serious bombing could have killed hundreds of skilled workers and immobilised thousands of tons of naval shipping. The nearest the Germans came to causing serious damage was on 3 December 1940, when they got one bomb on "The Factory" and killed five workers. In all ninety-two HE bombs hit the yard, killing fifteen and injuring 107 workers. And work was continually interrupted by Red Alerts, which sent everyone scurrying like ants into the dozens of shelters.

Sheerness Dockyard, also familiar to Pepys and Nelson in its earlier guise, was second in size to Chatham, with three tidal basins, five dry docks (one for submarines) and up to four thousand civilian workers. In addition to warship repairs, it salvaged merchantmen in the Estuary and provided the shore site of HMS *Wildfire*. The Dockyard Superintendant doubled as Commodore-in-Charge, Sheerness.

The Dockland reaches of the Thames in London had been a great shipbuilding centre in the 19th century, when Brunel's *Great Eastern* was launched at Millwall. Since then it had seen the repair and routine maintenance of merchant vessels, work which continued in support of the East Coast convoys after 1939. From that year the Port of London became a major fitting-out centre for the war equipment installed on both merchantmen and warships, as well as a repair base for the latter. The DEMS (Defensive Equipping of Merchant Ships) section was a naval organisation which fitted guns on cargo vessels. Dealing with up to fifty ships a month, it supplied weapons from 12-pdrs to 6-inch. Acting Captain H M Garrett had his office at the Albert Dock until bombed out in September 1940 _ he then moved to Newell Street, Limehouse. The DEMS depots were at Tilbury and Southend. Equivalent work on naval vessels was supervised by a FOGO (Fitting Out Gunnery Officer) for light armaments and a FOGMO (Fitting Out and Mounting Guns Officer) for heavy, at Gravesend. Tilbury was the degausssing station for the southern part of the Nore Command.

The main private shipyards on the Lower Thames were Green and Silley Weir (of Albert Dock, Blackwall and Tilbury), Harland and Wolff (the Belfast firm, but with branches at North Woolwich and Tilbury), J Russell and Co (Canning Town), the London Graving Dock Co (Poplar and Tilbury), the General Steam Navigation Co (Deptford _ also a large shipping firm and the owners of the "Eagle" paddle steamers), and the Tilbury Dredging and

DOCKYARDS & SHIPYARDS

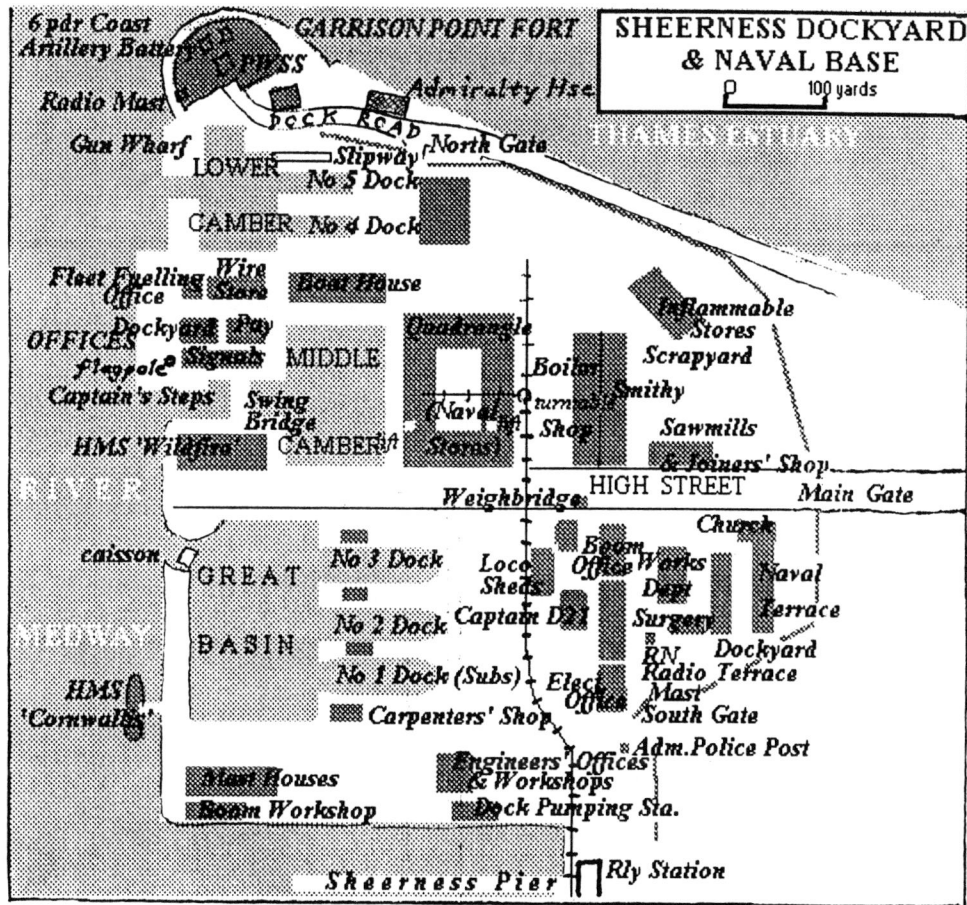

Contracting Co (Gravesend). Apart from repairs on merchant and naval vessels, these yards were employed from 1942 constructing major landing craft, mostly LCTs (landing craft tank) _ Green and Silley Weir built sixteen of these, Russell's fifteen, and Harland and Wolff twelve. Several smaller firms in the area turned out LCMs (landing craft mechanised), the largest type of minor landing craft. The two biggest engineering projects on the wartime Thames were the building of the Maunsell Forts at Gravesend and of the ferroconcrete Mulberry Harbour units in the drained-out East India and Surrey Docks.

DOCKYARDS & SHIPYARDS

The lesser Nore Command harbours specialised in building coastal motor craft. Five classes of small warship were involved _ the Motor Minesweeper, Motor Fishing Vessel (usually a harbour tender), Motor Torpedo Boat, Motor Gunboat and Motor Launch (including her smaller derivative the Harbour Defence ML). All were of under 140 feet in length and 260 tons (particulars may be found in Appendix H). They were built mainly of wood for speed and cheapness, and to minimise the magnetic mine risk. Thirty-four small shipyards were contracted to build them from early in 1940 onwards: these clustered on the Thames above London, in Essex and North Kent, in the Lowestoft-Broads area, and on the Humber. In peacetime they had been builders and repairers of fishing boats, harbour craft and pleasure yachts. The largest were equipped to work in steel (hence the name "ironworks"), and had at one time constructed coasters and barges. At some yards the majority of workers had been seasonal _ taken on in spring and moving on to professional yacht-crewing in summer and fishing in autumn. With the wartime contracts the workforces swelled fivefold with men, women and boys, all without shipbuilding experience and many without trades. The small yards became the biggest civilian employers at the smaller East Coast harbour towns, employing about twelve thousand in all.

Those nearest the sea also undertook refits and repairs, as opposed to the mere maintenance carried out by the naval bases themselves. Supervision of building was entrusted to "Principal Boat Overseers", independent of the private companies and responsible to the Admiralty Construction Department at Bath. Repairs came under "Emergency Repair Overseers" _ or Principal EROS as the ones at the bigger centres were called. Fitting out, including installation of weapons, and trials, were carried out by naval personnel.

The smaller types of MTB and MGB were designed by private companies and built at only two East Coast yards _ Thornycrofts of Hampton and Vospers' Wivenhoe branch, apart from some MTBs built under licence at Aldous's Brightlingsea, early in the war. MMSs, MFVs and HDMLs were of Admiralty design but were built by groups of shipbuilders under the guidance of "parent" yards. All MLs proper, the larger MTBs and MGBs (after 1942), and also some types of small landing craft and harbour launch, emanated from the Fairmile company. So called after the district in Cobham, Surrey, where its owner Captain Macklin lived and had his head office, this had an exclusive contract with the Admiralty. It manufactured

DOCKYARDS & SHIPYARDS

blueprints, keels, bulkheads and "stringers" (longitudinal frame strips) at a factory in Gillingham while various small firms, including a former bell foundary and a former wire netting works, made fuel tanks, rudders, propellers and shafts, and engines were imported from the Hall Scott and Packard companies in America. All these parts were collected at a central store at Brentford, Middlesex, and then supplied to the small shipyards _ twenty-three in the Nore Command area alone _ to be assembled, clad with timber, and turned into complete craft.

Only a dozen of the A-type Fairmile MLs were built, since their sleek hulls made them rather unstable at sea, and their high-powered engines were unnecessary for convoy escorting. The round-bilged ("fatter-bottomed") and slower B-type became the standard ML, and some six hundred were built. Their usual work was coastal convoy-escorting at home and abroad: they therefore carried Asdic and depth charges against U-Boats. The B-types in the late 400s and early 500s were Rescue Launches, and a few in the 200s were used as senior officers' launches. Some A and B types were fitted for minelaying, after MTBs had been used for the purpose. The name "Motor Launch" was misleading, for these were "young ships", as large as small coasters or ocean yachts, and capable of running alongside convoys for two hundred miles in the worst of seas. Fairmile C-types (numbered in the low 300s) were basically A-types with supercharged engines and stern exhaust vents instead of funnels ; they were employed (mainly in Yarmouth Sub-Command) as MGBs. The D-types, slightly larger and still more powerful vessels (numbered in the 600s and 700s) were equipped originally as MTBs or MGBs, but eventually combined both functions. Equipping and trials of all Fairmile craft were supervised by Coastal Forces' officers _ the four "Captains ML", one of whom ran the Nore Command area from an office in Chatham and later Brightlingsea. (See Page 294).

The other naval craft produced at the thirty-four small yards included minor landing craft, minesweeping skids, and ships' boats (ranging from the thirty-two-foot cutters for cruisers to the sixteen-foot rowing boats for drifters). There was also a large production for the RAF. The HSLs (High-Speed Air-Sea Rescue Launches) were comparable in size, speed and range to the earlier MTBs and MGBs, and designed by the same firms, were sub-contracted. The sixty-foot Air-Sea Rescue Pinnace was a vessel of only half this speed and range, employed in "backwaters" like the Irish Sea, Bristol

DOCKYARDS & SHIPYARDS

Channel and Wash. The same hull, with lower-powered engines, was used as a trotboat between flying boats and shore. The 52½-foot steam pinnace, an old design revived to save scarce imported oil, served the same purpose. And the forty-foot ST (Seaplane Tender) was also used as an air-sea rescue boat, for instance at Sheerness and Wells on the East Coast. Many yards also made airborne lifeboats _ long wooden dinghies fitted with engines, sails and all kind of comforts, to be dropped to ditched airmen from rescue planes. In 1944 there were even orders from the Army; many thousands of pontoons were supplied for bridging the rivers and canals of the Continent after the Normandy Invasion. At some places two types of Ministry of War Transport cargo vessel were built; the 130-160-ton VICs (Victualling Inshore Coasters) and the two-three hundred-ton *Empire* coasters, both of simple design and quick construction.

It is now hard to credit that 105 small warships, including ninety-seven for Coastal Forces, were built on the Thames *above* Central London. The Admiralty yard furthrest upstream, James Taylor, built twelve MLs at the unlikely setting of Chertsey, eighty miles from the sea. Yet even further up, 110 miles from Southend, RAF launches were built by Meakes of Marlow. At Hampton were Thornycrofts, a pioneer MTB builder today merged with Vospers.

Toughs of Teddington had only a dozen workers at the start of war, and had built nothing longer than thirty feet. Property of the same family from about 1820 until today*, this firm had once repaired tugs and barges at Battersea. In 1940 it was the starting-point for many of the Dunkirk small boats. Being near the Fairmile head office, Toughs launched the first B-type ML (113), C-type (316) and D-type (601). ML 113 was laid down before Dunkirk, while a shed was being put up around her. She featured in the Amy Johnson rescue bid (see my next chapter). Toughs later assembled Fairmile H-type landing craft, with platforms for "blinding lights", primitive lasers never installed because of the Geneva Convention. The yard also built the pinnace for the naval cable ship *Alert*, firefloats for the London fire brigades (very soon used to fight the huge Blitz fires along the Thames), canoes for the Pantellaria landings, and six submersible "chariots" for Commando raids, one

---

*Toughs are still in business. When I visited the owner there a few years ago he told me the workforce was down to nine. The yard has often featured in films and TV programmes about Dunkirk, and has also specialised in building the boats used in James Bond and other films.

ABOVE: Amy Johnson, in romantic 1930s pose.

LEFT: The Gillingham grave of Lt-Cdr Fletcher, who lost his life in the Thames Estuary attempting to save Amy Johnson. He had already been singled out for his courage in taking his Sheerness-based balloon trawler through German shelling in the Dover Strait. Another heroic Lt-Cdr, Esmonde, of *Scharnhorst* and *Gneisenau* fame, is buried a few feet away.

THE COLNE SHIPYARDS

ALDOUS SUCCESSORS', BRIGHTLINGSEA, 1942
(from top left) 1) ML 559 being planked in the main shed; 2) LCMs under construction; 3) Looking out from the Boatbuilding Shed across the Creek, with HMS *Helder*'s paddle steamer *Duchess of Rothesay* in the distance. 4) MTB 22 (left), formerly the 4th Flotilla Senior Officer's boat, and an RAF pinnace, at one of the jetties.   *(Motor Boat and Yachting magazine)*

Above: THE COLNE SHIPYARDS: MMSs on the stocks at Wivenhoe Shipyard (*Essex County Standard*) and RAF steam pinnace from James & Stone's, Brightlingsea, whose supervisor, Harold Warren, is on the stern. (*Gray*)
Below Left: Lady Fullerton launching *Motor Minesweeper 1* at Richards' Ironworks, Lowestoft (March 1941)
(*Ford Jenkins*)

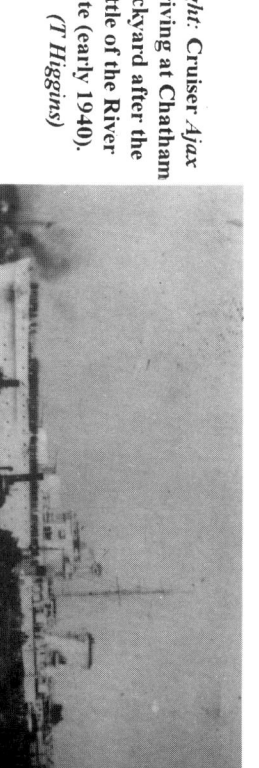

Right: Cruiser *Ajax* arriving at Chatham Dockyard after the Battle of the River Plate (early 1940).
(*T Higgins*)

Above: **HDML** off the Promenade, Brighlingsea, in 19— heading towards a supply barge. *(Ashcro—*

Other Photos
TOUGHS' YARD, TEDDINGTON
(in order):
1) The first B-type ML, 113, being launched in the spring of 1940.
2) The first D-type MGB, 601, under construction, late in 1941.
3) The same boat on trials down-river. She went into operation at Dover and was soon shot up.
4) Aerial view of the yard, 1944: showing numerous MTBs, harbour launches, supply barges and (bottom left, four minesweeping skids). South is towards the right. *(Tough Brothers)*

AIR-SEA RESCUE HIGH-SPEED LAUNCHES AT GORLESTON

Above: HSL 108 in the hands of the German Navy at Wilhelmshaven _ July 1941. Note labelling of the machine-gun turrets and the "V-Boat" (naval trawler) in the background.

Left: HSL 2706 on fire and sinking after being strafed by American fighters in March 1944.

(RAF Museum)

DOCKYARDS & SHIPYARDS

of which went to the Far East, where her crew were captured and shot by the Japanese. Craft repaired included the American-built MGBs 100 and 101. The workforce was 220 in 1944. HE bombs once fell just above the yard by the weir, and on three occasions incendiaries were smothered or shovelled into the Thames.

A few miles down-river Kris Cruisers of Isleworth (the site, now hard to see as associated with the Royal Navy, borders St Margaret's Road) assembled MTB 2001, prototype of a Fairmile F-class which was never built. Watercraft of East Molesey built HDMLs, and Walton Yacht Works RAF HSLs.

The shipyards of North Kent put together forty-nine naval motor craft. Sheerness Dockyard supplied four MLs. Other builders were Sittingbourne Shipbuilding (HDMLs), New Medway SPC, of Rochester (MFVs), Anderson Rigden and Perkins, of Whitstable (HDMLs and MFVs), and James Pollock of Faversham (large landing craft). Ridham Dockyard, on the Swale, was a busy repair yard for naval tugs and barges: nearby, on 4 October 1940, the tug *Sirdar*, coming in for repair, disappeared in the same mysterious way as the trawler *Staunton* (see Page 85) _ either a bomb or an acoustic mine was to blame. On the Medway were slipways famous, not in the shipbuilding, but the aircraft, industry. At Strood, opposite Rochester Castle, Shorts had launched the luxurious Empire flying boats and (until manufacture moved to Belfast) the Sunderland U-Boat hunters.

Across the Thames in Essex the twelve shipyards built no fewer than 195 small naval vessels, two-thirds for Coastal Forces. The biggest single yard was Aldous Successors of Brightlingsea. This was a public company formed in 1934 after the folding of the century-old family firm of Aldous's, on the same site. The controlling interest was held by a South London businessman named Wild, who owned three notable vintage steam yachts, *Heartsease, Medea* and *Tamesis*. Aldous's was used also as the equipping dockyard of the Captain ML, and also by HMS *Nemo*, whose offices lay on its south-west corner. There were three main slips (one steam-powered), and a large double shed which was a surplus RAF hangar from Biggin Hill. The yard covered fifteen acres and had up to 660 workers. It built all four types of Fairmile launch (A,B,C and D), including the first RML (492) and the MGB (318) which was used for running secret agents into France. It designed the LCP(S), a small wooden landing craft, and built 128 other

DOCKYARDS & SHIPYARDS

minor landing craft, ninety-one boats for the RAF, and over 4,600 Army pontoons. James's and Stone's, the two small yards below the Hard, were little used till many small naval craft came to the locality in 1940. They started to repair the Felixstowe Coastal Forces boats in 1941. MTBs 22 and 29 spent most of 1941 and 1942 being reconstructed at James's, though the first was downgraded to a target boat and the second was almost immediately lost attempting to intercept the *Komet*. Apart from refitting and repairing over five hundred small craft (a similar number to Aldous's), the two yards, which were merged in 1942, built diesel and steam pinnaces for the RAF and 132 ships' boats and life rafts. There were 150 workers.

Up the Colne at Wivenhoe two pre-war shipyards lay near-derelict in 1939. The upper one, Husk's, was taken over by Vospers of Portsmouth, and between 1942 and 1944 built fifteen MTBs in the late 300s series as well as Mulberry Harbour caissons. The workforce rose to 225. The lower site, Wivenhoe Shipyard, was merged with Rowhedge Ironworks across the river, and built MMSs and MFVs, plus two torpedo-recovery vessels ordered by Turkey in 1939 but bought up by the Admiralty _ and decoy submarines. The workforce reached 350. This yard had the only dry dock between Lowestoft and Sheerness.

Rowhedge Ironworks' speciality had always been small steam vessels. One of its craft, the *Brightlingsea*, built in 1926, has, on and off ever since, been a Harwich-Felixstowe ferry, though during the war was HMS *Badger*'s destroyer tender. Rowhedge's wartime production included three VICs, three *Empire* coasters, six MFVs and the patrol yacht *Umbriel*, based at Lowestoft. It built three of the RAF rescue HSLs based at Grimsby, and forty steam pinnaces _ it was the parent yard for this craft. The RNLI boat later named *Guide* went straight from this yard to Dunkirk. The main landmark at Rowhedge was the sailing barque *Cap Pilar*, which lay on the mud after being towed up from Aldous's, where the outbreak of war had found her refitting after her famous round-the-world voyage.

On the Blackwater were J Sadd's, a Maldon shipyard once known for building sailing barges, and Cardnell Brothers, at the obscure creek village of Maylandsea, and with a workforce of only ninety. They built MTBs, MLs and MFVs in slow and craftsmanlike fashion. On the Crouch, overlooked by the Canewdon RDF towers, were William King of Burnham and, on the opposite bank, the Wallesea Island Yacht Station. They produced D-type

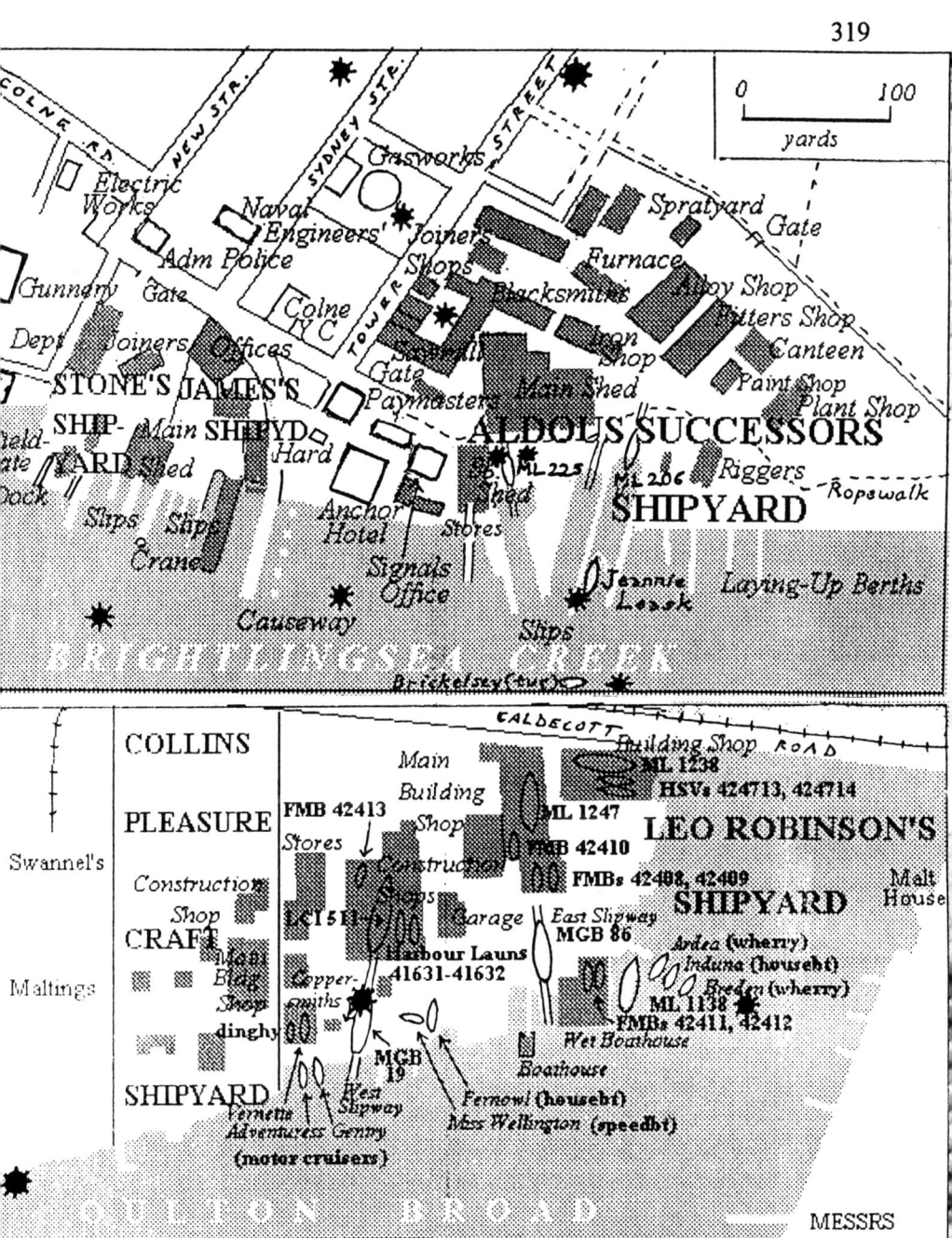

SHIPYARDS AT BRIGHTLINGSEA & OULTON BROAD
showing vessels present and bombs dropped during air raids

MTBs and MLs, and later repaired many minor landing craft for the nearby Combined Operations base. Johnson and Jago, of Leigh-on-Sea, was the country's largest ML builder, with an output of thirty-five. Austin's of East Ham was the only shipyard in Metropolitan Essex to build for Coastal Forces.

Lowestoft was the biggest single centre for motor-craft construction on the East Coast, with as many as six shipyards, plus three small boatyards, lining the strip of water known as Oulton Broad above Carlton Bridge, and Lake Lothing below. Their combined production of naval motor vessels alone was 182. Richards' Ironworks lies (it still exists) off Horn Hill on the south bank opposite the station. It was the parent yard for MMSs, No 1 being launched there early in 1941 by Lady Fullerton, wife of the Yarmouth FOIC. Five *Empire* Coasters were also built there. It can lay claim to being the only British shipyard raided by the Italian airforce! (See Page 155). On a separate site the firm built the first of the larger MFVs, and twenty-four altogether. Richards was also much used for fitting and repairing naval drifters, in continuation of prewar work on Lowestoft fishing vessels. It equipped the first flotilla of mine recovery drifters at the end of 1939. By late 1940 the labour force was 580.

Brooke Marine's address was Oulton Broad, though it fronted Lake Lothing. Founded in 1874, the firm had pioneered fast motor craft, and built RAF HSLs in the 1930s. After 1939 it built MLs, D-type MTBs and minor landing craft, and was also used for fitting out other Fairmile vessels built in the area. Leo Robinson, just "upstream" on Oulton Broad, was one such builder, together with the small Collins Pleasurecraft yard next door. Robinson's workforce was no more than 150, but it also built HDMLs, MMSs, MFVs, RAF steam pinnaces and small fast motor boats. Across the Broad East Anglian Constructors and G Overy were MFV builders; the former also made MMSs.

Inland on the Norfolk Broads three small pleasure-boat building firms between them built ten MLs, eighteen HDMLs and two Landing Craft Support: they were Herbert Woods of Potter Heigham, H J Percival of Horning, and Graham Bunn of Wroxham _ three enduring centres of Broads sailing and tourism. As on the Thames above London, the narrow rivers forced sideways launching, and so low were some of the local bridges that masts could not be erected till the boats got down to Lowestoft. Yarmouth

DOCKYARDS & SHIPYARDS

built no combat warships. Woods acquired a site which built a few MFVs there, and Fellows and Co assembled minor landing craft and did repairs. Nearby, on the Gorleston bank of the Yare, was the firm rather mysteriously named "Crabtree 1931". In spite of having a very small site, being hit in three separate air raids, and having never more than eighty-three workers, it built two *Empire* coasters and twelve VICs, and in 1941 alone repaired or serviced over three hundred naval, 107 merchant and twenty Trinity House vessels.

On the Humber and its tributaries 265 naval vessels were constructed, and another 402 converted from civilian uses. The majority of both were trawlers, following the peacetime tradition. Those constructed were based on a 1935 prototype, the *Bassett* (which had become a Harwich A/S vessel), and were all just over five hundred tons and 160 feet, with one 4-inch gun on each A/S ship and one 3-inch on each M/S. The classes included the Tree, Military, Dance, Fish, Hills and Round Table, but the great bulk were Isles, with romantic Gaelic or Norse names like *Mull*, *Benbecula* and *Lindisfarne*, plus the more prosaic *Foulness*, *Grain* and *Sheppey*. Cook, Walton and Gemmel, of Beverley, built the most (seventy-four), at a rate of more than two a month over the whole war. That firm's largest projects were, however, two 925-ton, 205-foot, Flower-class corvettes, *Azalea* and *Begonia*, both built in the summer of 1940, and the largest vessels built outside Chatham Dockyard in the Nore Command area. Cochrane's of Selby built forty trawlers, thirty *Empire* coasters and twenty-seven rescue tugs. Goole Shipbuilding was a smaller trawler and coaster builder. Four mooring and boom vessels also started life there. J Harker of Knottingley and D Dunston of Thorne built *Empires* and VICs. The Hull firm of Holmes engined most of the craft built by all these yards.

All these Yorkshire yards were astonishingly far upstream for their size of vessels _ Selby was fifty miles from the sea, and Knottingley, on the Dutch River Canal, fifty-five. Beverley vessels had to reach open water at Hull via a mere rivulet named the Beck and the River Hull. Five torpedo-recovery vessels originated from Gainsborough, up the Trent.

Strangely, the smaller Humber naval craft were built beside deeper water on the estuary itself. Doig's, just outside the Grimsby Royal Docks, was the only Coastal Forces builder in the area. With Humphrey and Smith, nearby, and Clapson's, in the junction of Barton Creek and the Humber, it also built MMSs and MFVs. At Clapson's some were built, without stocks or slipway, in a drainage channel and pulled out into the river through the mud! Pearson's of Hull, D E Scarr of Goole and Henry Scarr of Hessle, were other small local builders.

The Humber docks were the biggest fitting-out base on the East Coast after London/Tilbury. The DEMS section armed about a thousand merchantmen at Hull and four hundred at Grimsby and Immingham. The Humber was also the Nore Command's main radar-fitting base. One officer, helped by a few civilians, originally ran this, though eventually there were four officers, seven radio mechanics, and two civilians. The work was done at all three Humber naval bases. In all 319 warships were equipped, including ninety destroyers and fifty fleet minesweepers. The Amos Smith Dock, off Albert Dock, Hull, was the major repair yard on the Humber, and handled both destroyers and merchant ships. The other important Hull yard was Brigham and Cowan's, between the east end of King George V Dock and Hedon Road. Both firms suffered extensive damage in the Blitz, but work was hardly delayed because so much of it had been sub-contracted to smaller firms scattered all along the waterfront. The Humber ERO was an Engineer *Rear-Admiral*, J P Foster.

The East Coast shipyards were very odd mixtures. There were old-time craftsmen expert with adze and timber who had never used electric light, and specialists in power engines and electronics. Most of the yards have long been closed, though many of their buildings remain, rusting and rotting, but somehow atmospheric in their dereliction.

16
AIR-SEA RESCUE

On the afternoon of 25 July 1943, between two horrendous RAF fire raids on Hamburg, the US Eighth Airforce bombed the same target and reported several of its B 17 Flying Fortress bombers missing over the North Sea. Wing-Commander Corry DFC, commander of 279 (long-range air-sea rescue) Squadron, took off from Bircham Newton in a Hudson to look for an American dinghy reported sixty-five miles north of Ameland, in the Frisian Islands. En route, off Cromer, he saw a Fortress in the sea, with the crew clambering down over the wings and into their dinghies. He circled and dropped a wooden airborne lifeboat on parachutes. Meanwhile another Hudson was calling all HSLs on 500 k/cs, and one came out from Gorleston and saved the whole crew. The plane overflew the scene at low altitude and snapped photographs in which the squadron took great pride. Some twenty miles west a third Hudson spotted two more dinghies, and two Walrus amphibian biplanes, from 278 Squadron at Matlask, near Sheringham, put down and rescued eight more Americans. Other Hudsons had flown on to the waters off Ameland, and began to circle the crew of the original Fortress sought by Corry. But then a Danish fishing boat, "beyond her prescribed limits" (in the official phrase) approached and took on the Americans. The location was right in the heart of the North Sea, about a hundred miles from the Yorkshire and Dutch coasts. Two Gorleston HSLs sped out to the area and intercepted the fishing boat before she could regain Danish (i.e, German-controlled) waters. The Americans were taken home by one launch, while the Danish vessel* was "arrested" and brought in by the other. Meanwhile another HSL had saved the commander of RAF 611 Squadron ninety miles east of Yarmouth. And about the same time MTB 621, from Yarmouth, found the two survivors of a German Me 110 shot down near Den Helder while intercepting the withdrawing B 17s. Altogether twenty-nine airmen had been saved in one of the major "victories" of what had now become a very professional air-sea rescue service. But it had taken four years to get this far...

On the eve of the Second World War there was only one air-sea rescue base on the East Coast _ Felixstowe. The early-pattern HSLs there were intended more as standby boats for the seaplanes taking off, landing and doing trials near that base, than as a general rescue service for the North Sea. Another launch was found for Grimsby at the outbreak of war, but otherwise

---

*her crew were the five Danes mentioned on Page 52.

AIR-SEA RESCUE

the only rescue craft on the East Coast in the first year of hostilities were the civilian lifeboats, slow, badly-equipped and limited in range as these were. One useful backup that was already available was the RAF's chain of "fixer stations", which could locate planes making "Mayday" calls to within a few miles by means of directionfinding aerials. The East Anglian fixer stations (each with one small mast and a handful of staff) were at Barton Bendish (near Downham Market, Norfolk), Shropham (near Attleborough, Norfolk), Stowupland (near Stowmarket), Duxford (near Cambridge), Debden (two stations for different frequencies, near Saffron Walden), and Wix (near Harwich).

The Royal Navy largely stood in for the RAF in rescue matters when the Battle of Britain first brought the issue to a head. The huge Auxiliary Patrol had a boat within a few miles of any location in Coastal waters, and the Felixstowe MTBs were on hand to rush ashore airmen rescued by the slower craft, and to rescue out to sea (for instance, see Pages 143 and 279).

The Navy it was who also provided the ARBs (Air-Sea Rescue Boats). In Autumn 1940, with the Battle of Britain almost over, one or two requisitioned speedboats or motor yachts were crewed by the RNPS and sent to each naval harbour from Grimsby to Ramsgate. ARBs were from twenty to seventy feet long (mostly about forty) and had crews of from two to four. Most carried short-range R/T sets. A naval officer (e.g, Cdr Campbell at Brightlingsea) was in charge at each base, and organised training, weapons, and communications _ with, for example, Auxiliary Patrol, RAF, Coastguards, RNLI, Observer Corps and ambulances. ARBs usually relied on the Auxiliary Patrol to make initial rescues. Since they liaised with MTBs, and were a force of supposed "fast boats", they were counted as part of Coastal Forces.

For its part, the RAF set up an Air-Sea Rescue Directorate early next year which issued rubber dinghies, emergency ration packs, flourescent dyes, etc, to pilots, and supervised their rescue training. It sent a flight of Lysander light aircraft to Martlesham Heath airfield to spot wrecks and airmen in the sea. In August 1941 the RAF assumed a more direct and active role. Coastal Command was put in overall charge of naval as well as RAF boats _ in the Nore area this meant 16 Group. Air-Sea Rescue Directorate, spotter planes, HSLs and ARBs came under the single umbrella of the Directorate of Air Safety. Henceforth naval air-sea rescue officers were given

AIR-SEA RESCUE

daily orders about "states" to adopt _ I meant boats at sea at waiting positions; II some at sea, some in harbour; III in harbour ready to go instantly; IV in harbour at normal readiness. The Air Ministry contracted shipyards to build the 60-foot, 17-knot pinnaces, though MGB and MTB construction meant that as yet no more HSLs could be ordered. Slightly faster craft were available in the now redundant MASBs, which were supplied to Grimsby, Yarmouth and Ramsgate, where they supplanted the ARBs.

Some early amphibious raiding launches, called "R-boats", were also marginally faster than the original ARBs, and from their base at Brightlingsea some were distributed as a stopgap _ two each to Yarmouth, Harwich and Sheerness, while two remained at their home base. Sheerness and Grimsby had started a system of air-sea rescue floats. These were small rafts, equipped with food, medical supplies and Very lights, placed at intervals in the Outer Thames Estuary and off the Humber. The idea was for "ditched" airmen to swim to them, climb aboard, and signal for rescue.* The two Sheerness R-boats (Nos 101 and 104) serviced and inspected the Thames floats. Sub-Lt Sulman told me that on one occasion he took out an Air Ministry official, whose haughty demeanour soon changed as the sea affected his stomach. On 7 August 1941 he saved no fewer than seventeen men _ survivors of MMS 39, which was blown up right in front of him at Longsand Head.

The biggest advance of this period was, however, in air search. From late in 1941 277 Squadron, with HQ at Gravesend, operated three flights over South Eastern waters, including "A" Flight at Martlesham. This had Lysanders for spotting, Walruses for longer-range search and actual rescuing and Defiants (obsolete fighters) for protection. "A" Flight frequented Brightlingsea for training and practice purposes in conjunction with the local ARBs. On 12 July 1942 one of its Walruses crashed there _ three of the crew were saved by ARB 1, while the pilot, strapped to his seat, drowned. (When the plane was towed in he was found still sitting upright at the controls). Walruses rescued in reasonably calm seas, but constantly found it impossible to take off when laden with survivors, and had to be towed in. On 21 January 1943 one rescued a German FW 190 pilot (involved in the raid on London mentioned on Page 259) eighteen miles north-east of Manston, and on 31 May found one of his compatriots in the same area _ he had been afloat for

---

*The Germans had invented these: on 7 November 1940 one was found by the Royal Navy only forty miles due east of Felixstowe.

two days since the FW 190 raid on Walton and Frinton.

The most dramatic week in 277 Squadron "A" Flight's history was perhaps one towards the end of June 1943. On the morning of the 22nd Warrant Officer Boddy and Sergeant Campbell circled nine American bomber crewmen thirty miles east of Felixstowe and guided that base's HSL 2562 to the rescue. Early that afternoon Flight Lt Brown sent out two Walruses and two Spitfire escorts to search for seven more Americans east of Kentish Knock. The Martlesham planes combed the sea to within sight of the Dutch coast before spotting the airmen. The Walruses put down as the Spitfires circled overhead. Warrant Officer Greenfield took three survivors onto his plane and took off for base, but Flight Sgt Ormiston, with the other four, found their weight and the waves stopped him taking off. As Ormiston struggled with the controls two FW 190s appeared and tangled with Boddy's and Warrant Officer Hesselyn's Spitfires _ he thought he saw one of the Germans "splash" before the battle was broken off in the fading light. Ormiston now attempted to taxi the Walrus towards England. It rocked alarmingly in the heaving sea and fifteen-foot waves broke in front of the cockpit window. At 2 a.m. next morning fuel ran out and the plane shuddered to a halt. It now seemed in imminent danger of breaking up, and Ormiston and his comrades evacuated onto a Felixstowe HSL which now showed up. He regained Felixstowe at 1630, after a round trip of sixteen hours! Meanwhile the tide had beached his Walrus, surprisingly in one piece, on Gunfleet Sand. Flight Lt Brown and a salvage party went out in an HSL in the hope of saving it, and met the Harwich destroyer *Mackay* towing it in. In spite of multiple damage, the deceptively flimsy-looking plane was declared repairable. As for Ormiston, after a day's rest he was ready to fly again, and as early as 25 June dropped a dinghy for six 15 Squadron (Stirling) crewmen and guided in the Felixstowe launches to rescue them.

278 Squadron set up at Matlask (near Sheringham) in 1943, and a year later relieved 277 at Martlesham, though the HQ and another flight went to Bradwell Bay. By then it flew Ansons and Warwicks.

279 Squadron was formed at Bircham Newton at the end of 1941 and started operations next January. For the rest of the war it flew Hudson IIIs, American-built planes previously used as passenger liners and bombers. Its duties were long-range air-sea rescue search (i.e, beyond the range of 277 and 278 Squadrons), and the dropping of ration packs and airborne lifeboats.

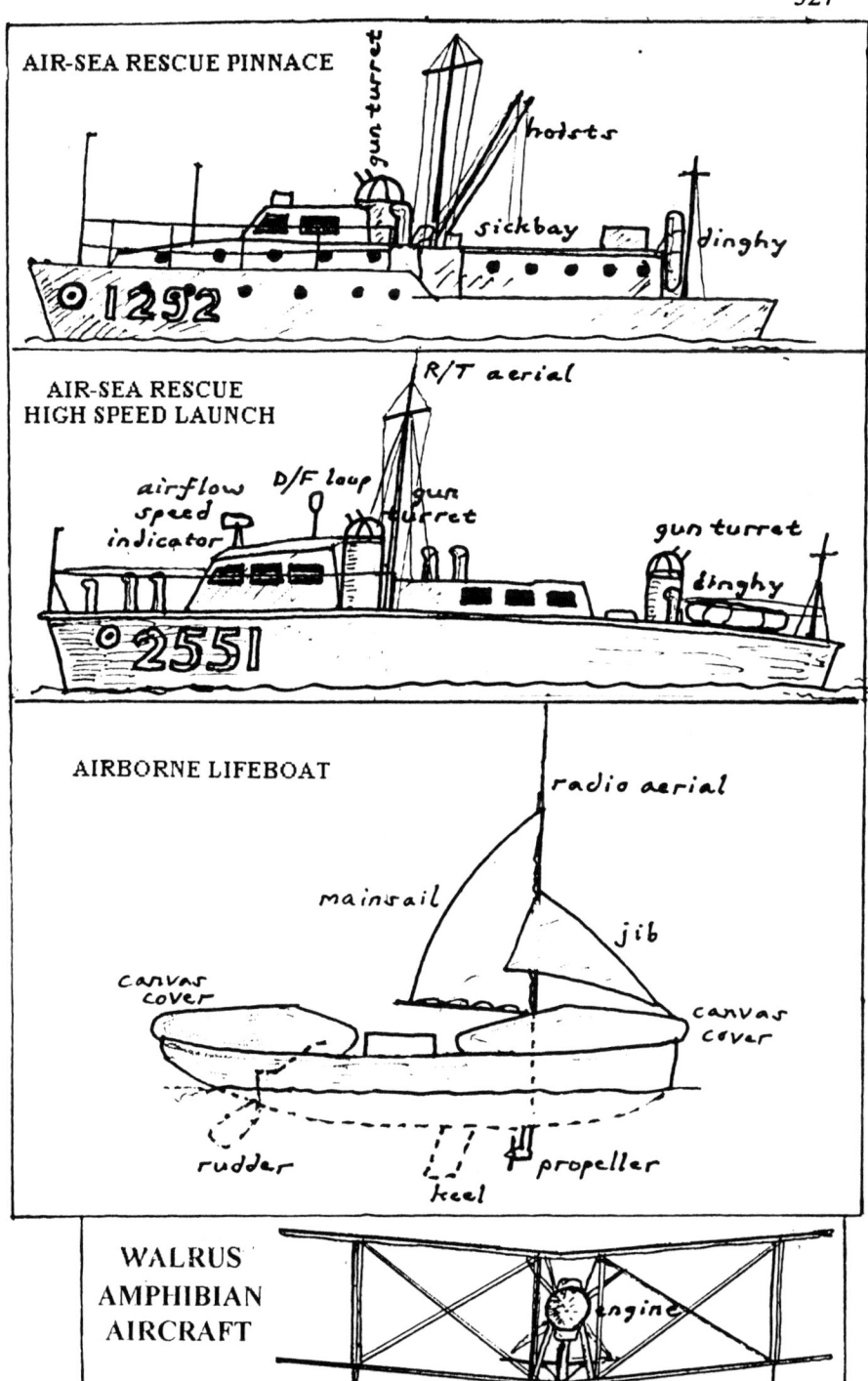

AIR-SEA RESCUE ORGANISATION

50 mls

Legend:
- ■ RAF or RN rescue boats
- ■ RNLI station
- ⊙ RAF seaplane or search a/c
- ○ Coastguard station
- △ RAF fixer base
- ⚑ RAF W/T or R/T station
- —— Approx boundary of rescue base's op/zone
- + Rescue in text (& date)

HELIGOLAND BIGHT

BORKUM + 31/3/45
AMELAND
VLIELAND
TEXEL
TERSCHELLING
Den Helder ⊙ + 10/10/44
IJmuiden ⊙ + 25/7/43
HOLLAND
RIVER MAAS
RIVER SCHELDT
OSTEND (from 10/44)

+ 29/5/44
+ 26/7/43
+ 21/1/44
+ 9/7/41
+ 12/10/44
+ 17/9/44
+ 22/7/43

GRIMSBY / GORLESTON / LOWESTOFT / FELIXSTOWE / RAMSGATE (zones)

BRIDLINGTON
BRID.
Hornsea
Withernsea
Kilnsea
Spurn
GRIMSBY
Mablethorpe
Chapel Pt
STRUBBY
Skegness
WELLS
Hunstanton
BIRCHAM NEWTON
Sheringham
Cromer
Mundesley
Palling
Winterton
Caister
Gt Yarmouth
GORLESTON
Corton
LOWESTOFT
Covehithe
Southwold
Dunwich
Sizewell
Aldeburgh
Orfordness + 17/9/44
MARTLESHAM
Walton-on-Naze
FELIXSTOWE
Foulness
BOXTED
BRIGHTLINGSEA
Clacton
BRADWELL BAY
SHEERNESS
Reculver + 18/8/43 RAMSGATE
Margate
HERNE BAY
Southend
Gravesend
Egypt Bay
Sheerness
Duxford
Bawdsey
Debden
Foxton
Bawdish
Pulham
Coltishall
MATLASK

AIR-SEA RESCUE

279 lost its first plane on 13 February 1942, but otherwise its first few months were uneventful, consisting mainly of the aerial inspection of rescue floats. Its first rescue came on 4 May, when it found an RAF dinghy and dropped a "Lindholme" (dinghy with rations and medicines), to the visible joy of the five or six airmen below, to whom the Hudson later guided two HSLs. On 2 June another 279 Squadron Hudson, while searching and dropping a Lindholme, was attacked by two Me 109s. The pilot took violent evasive action but his plane was repeatedly hit astern and both the other crew were wounded, though they continued to fire back until the enemy disappeared _ the rear gunner claimed one destroyed. The Hudson landed at Eastchurch with a jammed rudder and over a hundred holes in the fuselage. The rear gunner was wounded in the side, leg and back, and the observer in the stomach and mouth.

From now on the squadron was very stretched _ for instance on 26 July, supporting the Gorleston rescue on Page 323, it flew ten Hudsons, some twice. Nevertheless from about a year later it was even busier. Some pressure was taken off it by the new 280 Squadron, which operated Warwicks (adapted Wellingtons) from Detling, Bircham Newton and Strubby (Lincolnshire) successively, together with Thornaby (near Middlesbrough).

Control of these two Coastal Command squadrons was exercised principally through the W/T station at Pulham (Norfolk), site of the old British airship base. There was an air-sea rescue R/T mast next door at Colegate End. The USAAF had a chain of fixer stations for its own rescue purposes, with an HQ at Saffron Walden.

Until 1945 the Americans had no floatplanes in England. From May 1944 they flew one air-sea rescue spotting and covering force, 5 Emergency Rescue Squadron, of Thunderbolts, from Boxted*(north of Colchester) and later Halesworth (near Lowestoft). On 8 March 1945 two of its planes collided and fell into Fritton Lake, behind Lowestoft (they have since been recovered by aviation enthusiasts). Soon after this incident US Catalina flying-boats arrived at Halesworth as a direct rescue unit, with some B 17 Fortresses as lifeboat-droppers. On the rough seas off the Frisians two "Cats" came to grief on 30 March. As they lay helpless and sinking on the water one was shot up by an enemy jet aircraft. Both crews were rescued by Yarmouth RMLs, one after four days.

In 1943, as the Allied air offensive mounted, and the air-sea rescue

---

*also home to the highest-scoring US fighter group, the 56th. Actually at Langham, the airfield was named after the nearby Boxted to avoid confusion with RAF Langham in Norfolk.

got into their stride, the Air Ministry kept pace at sea by commissioning a new and second wave of HSLs, numbered in the 2000s to distinguish them from the old HSLs (in the 100s) and the pinnaces (in the 1000s). Grimsby, Gorleston, Lowestoft and Felixstowe received these superior craft, which worked in conjunction with naval RMLs from 1942 at Grimsby and Yarmouth and from 1944 at Felixstowe. Apart from these latter craft, air-sea rescue was now almost exclusively an RAF affair.

An HSL varied from sixty-three to seventy-three feet long (according to type), was capable of up to thirty-four knots, and carried a crew of ten or eleven. In all these respects she resembled the naval MGB. She was armed with perspex gun turrets like those on bomber planes. Most HSLs built after No.198 had slightly convex decks (again like some MGBs), earning them the nickname "whalebacks". Astern each had a rubber dinghy and a small sickbay. HSLs by now carried IFF devices to distinguish themselves from E-boats, and D/F radio loops to pick up the distress signals from the small hand-cranked transmitters of aircraft dinghies.

In mid-1941 there had only been six or seven HSLs throughout the Nore area, and at Ramsgate, and there were still only ten a year later. By 1945, however, the number had swollen to thirty-five. Once available in larger numbers, at the end of 1943, they adopted a system of "rendezvous" or standing patrol positions at sea, and during big Allied air raids lay along the bombers' outward and return routes, often within sight of the enemy coast and over a hundred miles from base. Their speed, numbers and range significantly improved on the proportion of ditched airmen saved, though the figure of seventy percent given in some sources is an exaggeration.

It might be assumed that the HSL crews were merely pushed into the job because they were not up to flying, or else were men who had gone into it to avoid combat, but in fact most were volunteers from the ground staff of the RAF, who might otherwise have passed the war in much less demanding duties ashore. The majority were new to the sea and the horrors of what was in effect frontline service, but "Once you'd been sick you were alright for the rest of the trip" (as one veteran told me), and the obvious and utter gratitude of the rescued, of whatever nationality, gave many HSL men a profound sense of meaning.

During the war some seven thousand airmen aboard 1,500 planes ditched in the Nore Command, and about one third were rescued. This

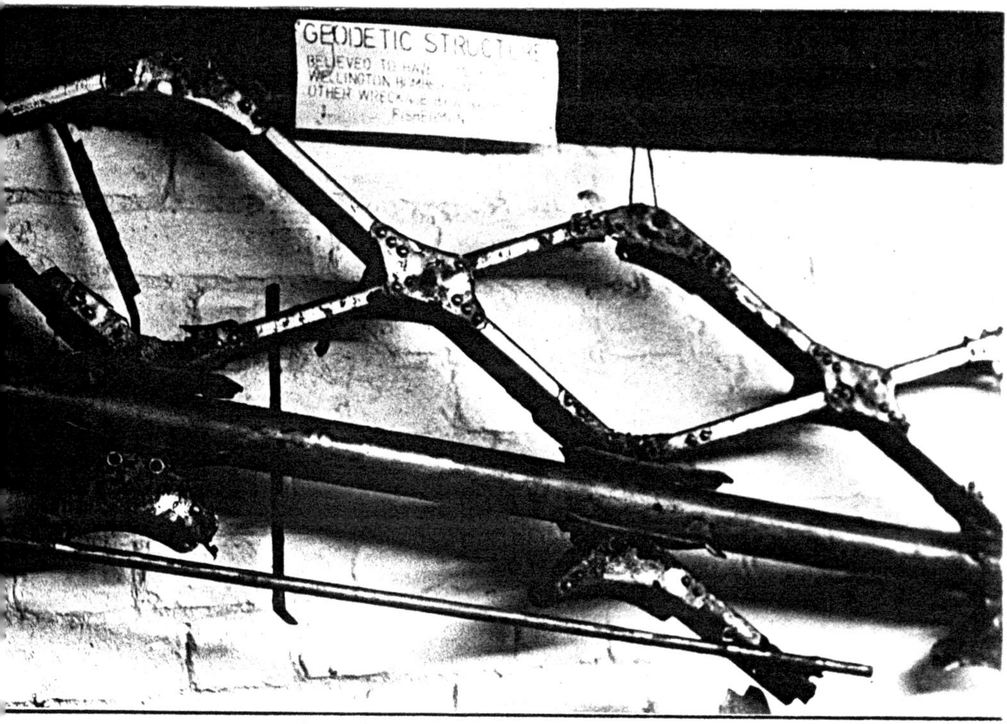

ABOVE: Section of airframe from the 305 (Polish) Squadron, Syerston-based Wellington which crashed off Clacton on 25 June, 1941, while raiding Boulogne. *(East Essex Aviation Museum, Point Clear)*
BELOW: Airborne lifeboat hull, and Lindholme dinghy. *(RAF Museum)*

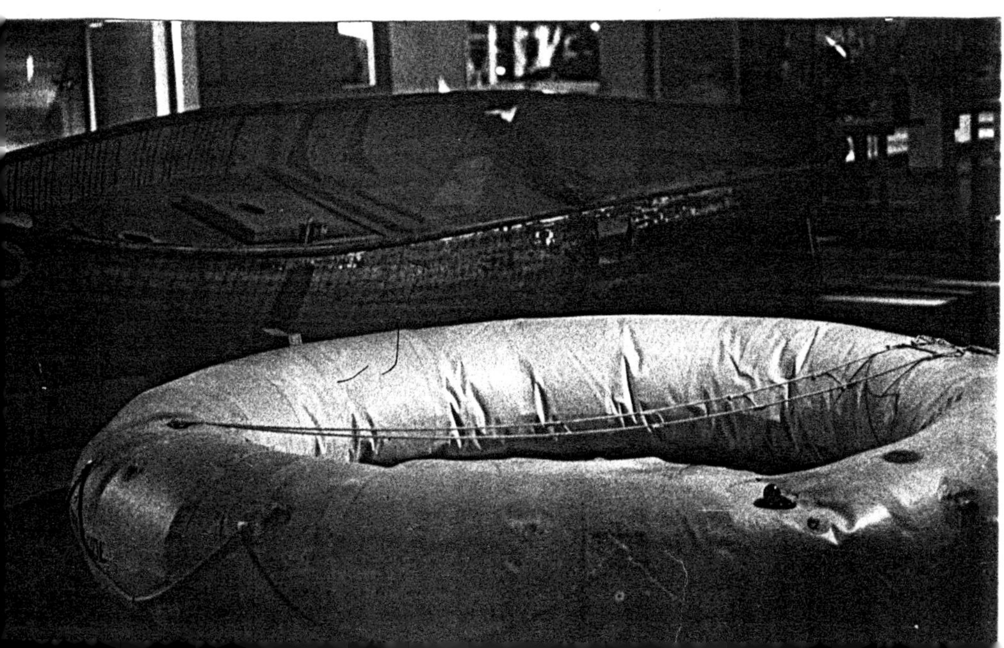

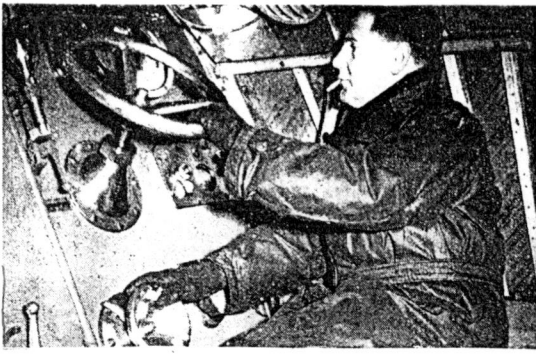

THE EAST ANGLIAN
LIFEBOATS, 1939-40

TOP LEFT: A Cromer crew running through the streets in response to a call. On 22 July 1942 German bombs fell near this spot and damaged the church and houses.
TOP RIGHT: Beaumont Derby, chief engineer of the Gorleston boat, *Louise Stephens*, at the controls.
BELOW LEFT: Cromer boat being launched.
BELOW RIGHT: An Aldeburgh boat landing survivors of SS *Magdapur*, 10 Sep, 1939.   *(Topical)*

AIR-SEA RESCUE

command, lying between Britain and Germany, saw more rescues than all other British home waters put together. The number of searches exceeded planes ditched by a factor of two or three to one, since so many were false alarms _ the distressed aircraft landed on the Continent, or reached the RAF coastal airfields of Manston or Bradwell Bay, or the huge emergency crash-strips at Carnaby (Yorkshire) or Woodbridge (Suffolk). On average there were three searches a day in the Nore Command, in addition to regular patrols. By 1944 up to forty aircraft were involved in a single search, apart from other planes on their normal missions which helped by circling wrecks and providing defensive cover.

Incidentally the RAF had its *land* rescue services, based with crash tenders, fire engines and ambulances at airfields, or, where there were none, radar stations. At Woodbridge, in particular, large teams of emergency personnel waited around the vast concrete strip day and night, listening for the faltering engines of British and American bombers. Many hundreds of Allied aircraft forcelanded in the Eastern Counties, not only on airfields but at almost every village up to ten or twenty miles inland. In remote places, often on pitchblack (blacked-out) nights, many a funeral pyre burned, frequently with an eerie silence after the initial explosion. Skywatchers ashore and afloat saw trails of smoke and flame, and planes descending with pieces of wing, tail and fuselage shot away. Some three hundred machines fell into the Thames Estuary alone. Half a century on the debris continues to be found.

The northernmost air-sea rescue base in the Nore Command was the minor one at Bridlington, where Lawrence of Arabia, in his 1930s RAF guise, had tested a prototype of the HSL. It covered the coastal sector from Flamborough Head to Withernsea, and carried out ten rescues, totalling forty-five personnel (apart from dead). An odd phenomenon was very evident here _ the way in which two rescues would occur in close succession, a long gap would ensue, then there would be two more rescues, etc. The first two rescues happened in December 1940 a few days after the base was started, the third not until August 1941, to be followed by the fourth that same month. The fifth and sixth rescues were both in September 1941, and the seventh and eighth in late July 1942. The original Bridlington boat was the single ARB *Stardust*. RAF 21 Marine Craft Unit, which replaced her in

1941, consisted initially of Seaplane Tender 439, and from 1942 Pinnaces 1285 and 1292, and later 270 (or 357), with 1501. In charge for most of the war was Warrant Officer E Gallimore.

An RAF rescue unit, eventually numbered 22, was located at the Grimsby Royal Dock from the outbreak of war, on account of the 4 and 5 Bomber Group bases nearby. Initially it consisted only of HSL 111. On 2 July 1940 she found Leutnant Schrooten, Unteroffizier Soest, and Oberfeldwebel Warms, the crew of an He 115 which had been raiding Hartlepools. The rescue location was given as "NLGR 0943" _ that is, just off Bridlington*. Flying Officer Bowen was then in charge, but later Squadron Leader Syme took over. Late in 1940 the base was boosted to five vessels with naval ARBs, but these proved of little use and in 1941 the unit consisted of two HSLs (141 and 144). The number of these was up to three by 1942 (131, 139 and 141), with three naval MASBs (25, 26 and 29). That June 60th RML Flotilla replaced the MASBs (with 492, 498, 499, 512, 515 and 517). By the latter part of the war the MCU comprised six HSLs _ 124, 125 and 157 of the older type, and 2572, 2574 and 2578 of the new.

The first MASB rescue was from a Wellington off Spurn Point on 16 January 1942, though the three airmen were actually taken from the sea by the paddle ship HMS *Goatfell*. On 30 June 1942 RML 517 saved a complete seven-man Lancaster crew in the same area, and 498 and 512 saved four Wellington crewmen eight days later.

One of the most hectic days for Grimsby was 21 January 1944. Helped by relays of search aircraft, totalling thirty-nine, two RMLs braved heavy seas and 547 took on four live men and one dead from a 578 Squadron Halifax forty-four miles east of Flamborough Head. The weather that day was so bad that a second operation, centred on a 76 Squadron Halifax down twenty-eight miles off Skegness, disastrously miscarried. Eight Grimsby HSLs and RMLs and forty-nine planes could not find any of the bomber crew and two Halifaxes circling their ditched companion also crashed without survivors.

Not all Grimsby operations were so difficult. One of the swiftest was on 16 April 1944, when a 550 Squadron Lancaster, descending towards Killingholme, crashed into the Humber off North Coates, only a few miles south-east of 22 MCU's base. HSL 2574 saved all eight crew, including two injured men, within minutes.

---

*See map on facing page. In this code, mainly used by RAF Coastal Command, NL meant 51°North, and GR 0°East. It took me some time to "break" it!

333

U	V SHEET R		W	**MILITARY GRID**	different from the civilian Ordnance Survey Grid, this worked on the basis of lettered 100-km squares. It was used by the Army, RAF Fighter Cmd & Royal Observer Corps.
	SHEET W				
A	B		C	D	E
F	G	■ H 215679 H		J	K
L	M	■ N0150 N		O	P
Q	R		S	T	U

```
0°   0°30'   1°   1°30'   2°   2°30'   3°   3°30'   4°   4°30'   5°   5°30'   6°   6°30'   7°
```

-54°——NL

-53°30'

■ 53 45N/1 18E or YZGR 4518

-53°——YZ

-52°30'

-52°——ZJ

CODED LATITUDE & LONGITUDE
In plain form along top & left of chart, and in Coastal Command's standard code along bottom & right. In the code a random pair of letters stood for degrees latitude & a second for longitude. The minutes were paired at the end, uncoded.

-51°30' ■ 51 35N/1 19E or FDCE 3529

-51°——FD

GR | CE | WT | TA | JK | UB | VA | XG

Map Codes Used by Air-Sea Rescue & Other British Forces, 1939-45

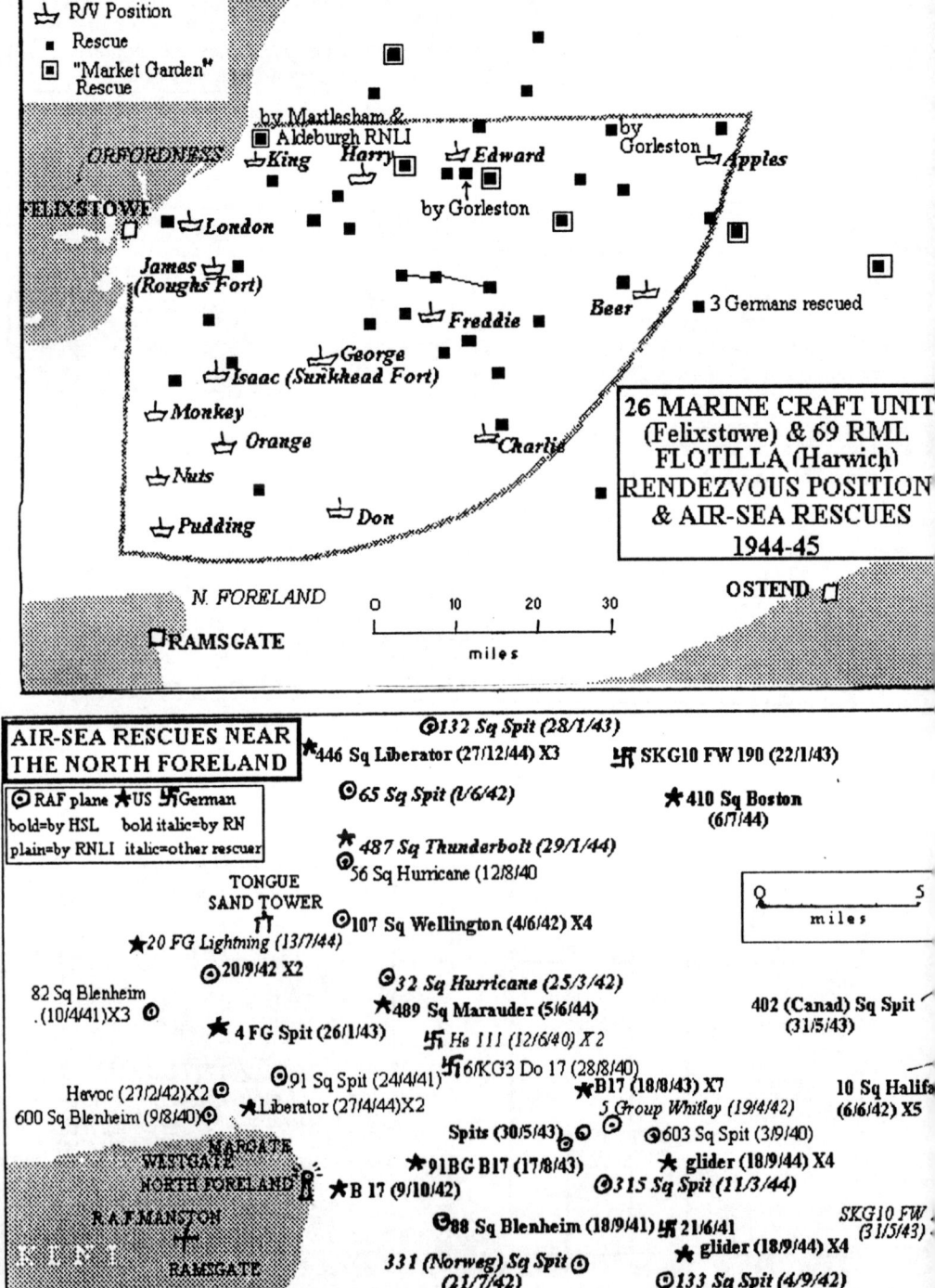

AIR-SEA RESCUE

The Skegness lifeboat sometimes searched for crashed aircrew inshore, where it stood a chance of getting to the scene before Grimsby. An early mission was on 27 October 1940, when it saved one of four airmen only half a mile off the local pier. On the morning of 20 July 1941 it put out for a Hampden bomber which ditched just south of the pier on a test flight, and recovered two live men and one dead. It rescued three more, under the guidance of a 278 Squadron (Matlask) Anson, on 27 July 1943. Early in 1941 an unsavoury episode occurred there. Squadron Leader Guy Gibson, later the "Dambusters" leader but then a 29 Squadron night fighter pilot, came to the town with the Lincolnshire Chief Constable to inspect the body of an He 111 pilot Gibson had shot down off the pier. Recovered and brought to the mortuary, it was headless. Gibson had heard that the airman's Iron Cross and personal effects had been found, but on claiming them for posting to the German's family, found they had been looted.

At Wells, near the northernmost point of Norfolk, the RAF's 23 MCU was based from early in 1942 to April 1944. It comprised only Seaplane Tenders 349 and 350 and Pinnace 1241. Its personnel billeted ashore in a disused cinema, the "Ostrich House", and the old lifeboat house. As far as I can trace, 23 MCU rescued no one at all! The only moment of excitement occurred when a Seaplane Tender sank at her moorings in a storm, to be raised next day. The Wells lifeboat rescued two injured bomber crewmen in July and September 1942, but both later died in hospital.

Along the coast the Sheringham and Cromer lifeboats were often out for ditched airmen, in addition to their famous exploits in rescuing seamen. By a fluke most of the airmen saved were Poles (serving with the RAF). A Cromer boat landed six from the trawler *Strathgarry* on 27 June 1941, and the *Foresters' Centenary*, of Sheringham, rescued five from a Wellington that November and six from a Halifax the following October. *H F Bailey*, Blogg's boat, found five British Wellington crewmen close to her base on 26 July 1943. The Caister lifeboat towed in a 278 Squadron Walrus and the American pilot it had just rescued on 22 June 1943.

The most active air-sea rescue base in the world was certainly that at Gorleston, opposite Yarmouth, where the crews billeted ashore in the Cliff Hotel and the boats moored in the Yare opposite the naval oil tanks. Thence and from Lowestoft the RAF ran a single unit (MCU 24). In 1941 there were two ARBs at each place and HSL 112 at Gorleston. In 1942 the latter operated two HSLs (124 and 130), and three ARBs, while at Lowestoft there were two or three naval MASBs (1, 25 and 33) and one or two ARBs. On 7 March 1941 a Gorleston launch rescued two Germans from a Do 17 downed by a Yarmouth Harbour Bofors; the third crewman was drowned and the fourth, the pilot, swam ashore and was captured by the Coast Artillery. That 19 May a Lowestoft ARB rescued the one survivor from the Me 110 which had just bombed the local PWSS.

Flight Lt Arnold was in charge of 24 MCU at the busiest period. From the outset, with its HSLs, Gorleston made valiant attempts to rescue as far out as the Dutch coast, even within view of the enemy ashore. June 1942 saw a surge of activity, with rescues on the 5th (by Lowestoft), 9th, 10th, 26th and 30th _ all much helped by 279 Squadron, Bircham Newton. The base had the very rare experience of rescuing German *naval* personnel on 25 October 1943, when an HSL brought in four E-boat survivors from the battle in the "Alley" described in Chapter Thirteen. On 9 March 1944 24 MCU carried out no fewer than four rescues in one day. HSL 158 saved ten Flying Fortress crew from an airborne lifeboat just dropped by 279 Squadron. RML 514* saved another such crew nearby. HSL 2679 found two survivors and a body eighty-five miles east of Yarmouth. And RML 498 saved a fighter pilot fifty-five miles off Southwold. All twenty-three airmen were American.

By now Gorleston's range extended into Heligoland Bight. Many Allied bombers had always come down there, as it offered the shortest overland route to and from Hamburg and Berlin. On 19 May 1944 a Fortress of 100 Bombardment Group (Thorpe Abbotts, Norfolk) was seen by accompanying bombers ditching seventy-four miles north of the German Frisian island of Borkum. In spite of air searches by thirty-nine planes in relays the crew were only spotted again twenty-four hours later. 280 Squadron dropped an airborne lifeboat and a message to steer West-South-West. HSL 2551, coming on through a now dark and choppy sea, saw one of the periodic light flashes from the survivors' torches and took all ten aboard just before one in the morning on 21 May. As an indication of how busy Gorleston now was, over the next eight days it carried out four more rescues, including two near the Frisians. At midnight on 29th/30th, thirty-eight miles off Terschelling, HSL 185 found a Fortress crew only one mile from the position supplied by the fixer stations, proof of how valuable these still were. The most forlorn survivors were brought back by HSL 2679 on 10 October _

---

*subsequently commanded by Lt Patrick Troughton RNVR, later the actor.

AIR-SEA RESCUE

the two Langham Torbeau crewmen concerned had been afloat for over a week, having drifted a full hundred miles from near Ameland to near Den Helder.

Gorleston regularly operated thirteen HSLs in 1944 and 1945, and at one time as many as sixteen, in addition to four more at Lowestoft, and eight Yarmouth RMLs. More airmen were landed at Gorleston and Yarmouth than any other three bases put together. In all over eight hundred were saved, including 538 from the start of 1944 onwards. The number landed by the RAF alone just topped three hundred in 1944.

Three Gorleston RAF rescue launches were lost, and dramatically.

The first, Flying Officer Jackman's HSL 108, hitherto Felixstowe-based, was captured by the Germans on 1 July 1941, while unsuccessfully searching for a Hampden off the Texel. The launch had been strafed by two He 115s, and a W/T operator had died from a bullet in the chest. Jackman had then "broken the rules" and used his R/T, which could easily be monitored in nearby Holland. A German seaplane with red crosses came down and captured him and his crew, and a trawler towed in his launch. The prisoners were flown to Schipol and then moved to Stalag Luft III prison camp in Silesia, also shortly to be the home of the fighter heroes Tuck and Bader. Meanwhile the Hampden crew suffered just as grim an ordeal. For nine days they drifted in their dinghy, vainly signalling to passing aircraft and rescue launches with mirrors, enduring a storm, and trying to survive on thirty-six Horlicks tablets, a pint and a half of water and a bar of chocolate. At first they played a game in which the winner was he who held his head underwater longest. When one player saw a mine right under the dinghy they abandoned it. They were resigning themselves to death when another Gorleston launch found them.

On 3 March 1944, halfway between Harwich and the Hook, Flying Officer Mitchell's HSL 2706 was five times shot up by American Thunderbolt fighters, ironically while waiting to rescue along the return route for a US Eighth Airforce bombing mission. The launch was reduced to a blazing charnel house, with only three men alive; one, Leading Aircraftman/Gunner Anderson, had pulled a wounded comrade out of the burning wheelhouse (for which many thought he should have been decorated). Guided by another Thunderbolt, Pilot Officer Herrick's HSL 2679 desperately roared to the scene (Mitchell was a personal friend) and rescued the survivors, of whom one died while Herrick was holding and talking to him. Mitchell was among those lost.

On 29 June 1944 Flying Officer Lindsay's HSL 2551 (mentioned above) went to a point twenty-five miles off Ijmuiden (one unofficial source says three miles) and saved ten (the same source says eight) Flying Fortress survivors. On turning back she was assailed by German aircraft (variously described as Ju 88s, Me 210s, or Me 410s). She caught fire and was abandoned as three other HSLs came to help. Lindsay, a corporal, two Leading Aircraftmen and two Americans lost their lives; the rest were saved by HSLs 158 and 184. At the Z Line these were met by a Walrus, with two American medical officers on board, and by HSL 2679, with an RN surgeon. Lindsay, forty-three years old and from a drab business job, was a man of very different temperament and background from some of the airmen and naval officers who had lost their lives in the North Sea, but he was much respected, and his funeral was the occasion for a wider tribute. An HSL carried his body out from Gorleston, surrounded by flowers and by naval, RAF and USAAF officers, and escorted by seven other HSLs and RMLs. As he was put into the sea three B 17s flew over and dropped wreaths.

Further south down the coast, the Aldeburgh lifeboats put out many times for airmen, especially in the Battle of Britain. On 19 August one picked up a 66 Squadron (Coltishall) Spitfire pilot, but he died on board. On 11 November the two boats found wreckage from one of the Italian planes supposedly raiding Harwich, and six days later saved the crew of one of the Me 110s which had attacked Felixstowe Dock. On 30 January 1941 one lifeboat was machine-gunned, though not hit, while being hauled up Aldeburgh's shingle beach. This lifeboat rescued nine Americans off Thorpeness on 12 May 1944, and on 18 September five were saved right off the town from one of the gliders bound for the Allied airborne landings in Holland _ one by a lifeboat and four by a cooperating Martlesham Walrus.

RAF Felixstowe, with 26 MCU, was the oldest air-sea rescue base on the East Coast, and second in achievement to Gorleston. It originated as far back as the First World War with the flying boat base which looked across Harwich Harbour. For the first half of the Second World War it operated one, two or three HSLs (old type) _ 108, 112, 125 and 141 inter alia. On 18 May 1942 an HSL landed one of the two Spitfire pilots who had collided over the North East Gunfleet _ he had been picked up by the

AIR-SEA RESCUE

Sheerness trawler *Constant Friends*, while the other man crashlanded at Frinton. The early hours of 5 June 1942 saw the sort of rescue which was still very rare at this period; Flying Officer Greenway's HSL 125 ventured almost as far as the enemy-held Maas delta to save six Leeming-based 10 (Bomber) Squadron aircrew. HSL 134, on the same search, was fired on by an E-boat.

Not all of those brought back by Felixstowe were airmen. On 15 November 1942 an HSL saved eleven merchant seamen from SS *Linwood*, which had strayed from a convoy in fog and been mined. On 17 April 1943 another saved eleven from SS *Dynamo*, mined near B8 Buoy. On 4 August one picked up a corpse from the Ipswich trawler *Red Gauntlet*, and on 25 September brought ashore four survivors from the *Franc Tireur* _ both ships had been torpedoed by E-boats. 16 December 1942 saw HSL 118 called out in connection with a famous raid: 2 Bomber Group's Ventura attack on Philip's Factory, Eindhoven. The Felixstowe launch brought in four Australian crew originally saved by the Harwich trawler *Strathmaree* near the Shipwash.

In the spring of 1943 the new "2000" HSLs arrived and Felixstowe began its stream of rescues. The first, by HSL 2558, was of three survivors of a British 180 Squadron (Foulsham, Norfolk) Mitchell bomber, returning from Flushing and down near B8 Buoy. Like Gorleston, from now on 26 MCU saved from several crashes a month, and since these were mostly of U.S. Fortresses, this meant nine or ten men at a time. The number of HSLs was four by late 1943, six in the New Year of 1944, and eight by mid-year, when 69th RML Flotilla of four also joined. Felixstowe adopted standing patrol positions, occupying sixteen points in all, and covering a fan-shaped area with a "rim" running from the North Foreland to a point halfway between Orfordness and the Hook of Holland. The base saved over 180 airmen in 1944, out of a whole-war total of some 260 (fifty-six aircrew rescues). In the last two years the great bulk were Americans, but on 12 October 1944 RML 550 (Lt Shepperd RNVR) saved three grateful and talkative Germans. The peak came between 17 and 21 September, during "Operation Market Garden", the Allied airborne invasion of Holland. In those four days Felixstowe HSLs and RMLs carried out eight rescues, of sixty-two airmen and soldiers. They rescued from two of the four Allied gliders down in the sea on the first lift, three launches taking eighteen survivors from one. A third glider rescue was carried out by Yarmouth RML 498 so close to the Dutch coast that German shore batteries fired at her.

A few ARBs worked from Harwich in 1941 _ one with the superb name of *King Duck*. They seem to have rescued on three occasions _ from a fighter down off Landguard Point on 19 February, a small trainer aircraft in a similiar location on 7 July, and from a Wellington bomber in the Orwell off Trimley on 28 August _ an odd location, since it was inland from the harbour.

The air-sea rescue base at Brightlingsea was unique in being an old-style naval ARB set-up throughout _ no RMLs or RAF launches ever operated there, though Aldous's Shipyard was a centre for building and equipping them. Begun with a single ARB (*Aro*) in 1940, by 1941 the base had four. Numbers then fluctuated above and below this figure, settling at eight for two years (1942-44), and then fell to five. Most of the personnel were from the locality, and, having served on the river patrol yachts, were retained for their local knowledge at the suggestion of Cdr Campbell. Only between 1941 and 1943 was there a specialist air-sea rescue officer, Lt Warren RNVR. The boats, simply numbered ARBs 1-8 (though they also had names) included the launch from Sir Tom Sopwith's magnificent ocean yacht *Philante* and some leftovers from Lt-Cdr Corke's "T-Boat Flotilla" (see next chapter). In April 1941 one, *Miss Virginia* (ARB 2) was lost in rough weather. From 1942 the base kept one boat waiting at sea at each of "rendezvous" positions A (Colne entrance), B (Wallet Spitway Buoy) and C (West Buxey Buoy, by the Crouch entrance), with a fourth at "first degree" (instant readiness) in harbour and a fifth at normal readiness. In harbour the crews used the yacht *Terminist*, peacetime property of a German doctor (now interned) as a floating base.

The Brightlingsea boats carried out some eighteen live rescues of twenty-eight airmen, plus about as many involving sailors, mainly from barges, but also from SS *Folda* and the Trinity House Vessel *Strathearn*. The total number of searches was about 175. The airspace off Brightlingsea was widely used because of the Dengie Flats strafing range, because the Essex estuaries were a bomber mustering-point, and because of Bradwell Bay aerodrome.

The most famous pilot landed at Brightlingsea (on 21 June 1941) was Stanford Tuck, the "ace" commander of 257 Squadron, Coltishall.

AIR-SEA RESCUE AT BRIGHTLINGSEA
Photos show ARBs 2, 4, 8 ("WD 65", to her port, is the patrol boat *Kongoni*, now crewed by the Army), the Clacton lifeboat, while operating from Brightlingsea *(left)*, and the Blenheim which was towed into the Creek in Sept, 1941. *(Ashcroft, White & Gray)*

Above: Personnel of the Brightlingsea ARBs (Top left is P O Hazell White, mentioned on P. 86). Half-hidden in the middle of the group is one of the Martlesham Walrus pilots.   *(White)*
Below: St Osyth Stone Point Aviation Museum _wreck of the Mustang (P 51) fighter flown by Lt King USAAF, which crashed off Clacton Pier on 13 January 1945. *(E.Essex Aviation Soc.)*

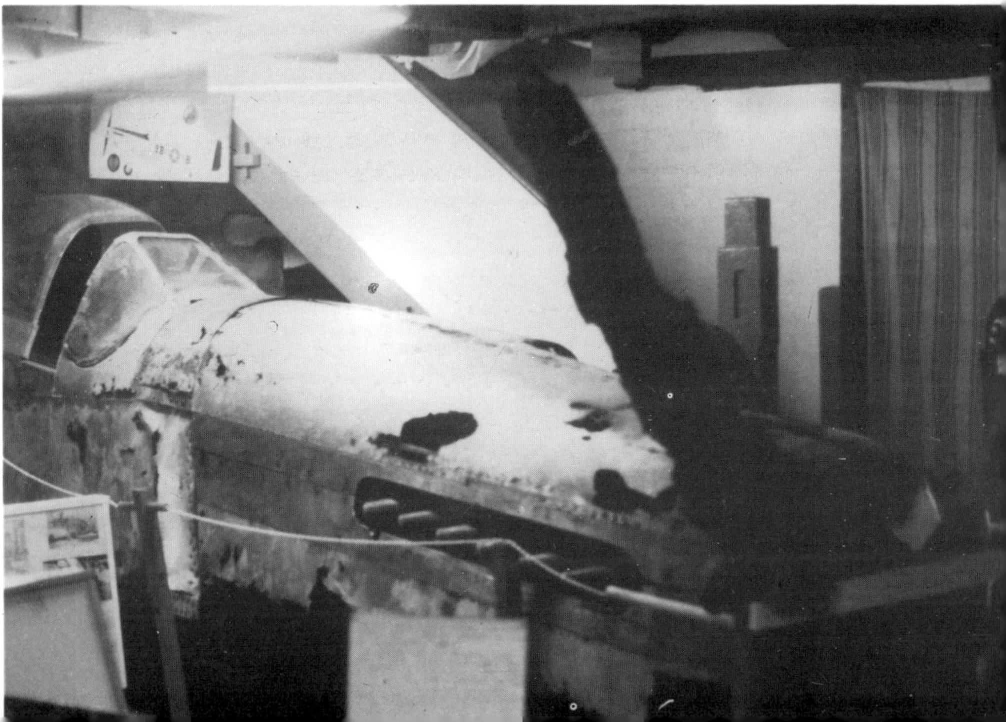

AIR-SEA RESCUE

having been jumped by three Me 109s over the Belgian coast and claimed two of them, he abandoned his Hurricane off Clacton. Air searches failed to find him, but all the time he was on board a Gravesend coal barge coming up the Wallet to Colchester _ the crew had abused him as a German and pointed a gun at him, but then atoned by priming him with beer. ARB 2 then arrived and took him off to the Hard. Twice in 1941 British bomber crews were saved _ that of a 58 Squadron Whitley (minus one missing) on 30 August (the examination yacht made the initial rescue), and from a 139 Squadron Blenheim which bellylanded on Gunfleeet Sand during a test flight on 16 September. On the second occasion the base also towed the wreck into Brightlingsea Creek, though saltwater corrosion made it unsalvable. A Canadian (403 Squadron) Spitfire pilot was rescued after being shot down down in the air battle over *Scharnhorst* and *Gneisenau*.

A rather remarkable rescue was that of a Ju 88 crewman on 20 April 1943. Having flown over from Holland at very high altitude to photograph Chelmsford after the raid on it a few days previously, he was shot down out of a perfect spring sky by two Norwegian Spitfires from North Weald. ARB 7 was guided to him, as far offshore as Longsand, by a Martlesham Walrus which had taken him to be dead but then seen him wave one arm. On several other occasions German bomber crews were fished out dead, and on 10 September 1942 a Ju 88, corpses and all, was towed into the Colne and run aground. A Martlesham Walrus pilot put down to lend a hand and was given ammunition as souvenirs. Certainly some unusual bodies were brought ashore here. On the night of 17 December 1943 the boats found three in *civilian* clothes near the wreck of a 138 Squadron Halifax down off Tollesbury in a storm. They were secret agents of SOE on their way to Poland. 138 Squadron lost four other Halifaxes that night, one of which bellylanded in the Deben Estuary after slicing off the tip of a Bawdsey radar receiver tower. In September 1944 HMS *Nemo* landed as many as twenty-six drowned U.S.101 Airborne Division paratroops from a 9th Airforce Dakota crashed in Raysand Channel en route to Eindhoven. The first live American to be saved had been a Spitfire pilot from one of the "Eagle" Squadrons, formed of pre-Pearl Harbor volunteers to the RAF. This was perhaps not a true air-sea rescue, as the plane had come down close to Foulness and men on land had already helped the pilot ashore when the boat arrived to ferry him to Brightlingsea.

AIR-SEA RESCUE

The ARBs were often called out to look for Mosquitos crashed off Bradwell on takeoff or landing, yet rarely found more than a wreck or dead body. On 5 March 1945 they were prevented from saving two injured men in a 157 Squadron Mosquito because it was imbedded in the impassible Blackwater mud _ they had to watch the tide slowly swamp the plane and hear the cries from the cockpit gradually die away*. Coincidentally, only two nights later they were able to save a crew from the same squadron, down near St Peter's Chapel. On 5 April 1944 a boat landed a dead Mosquito navigator found by the local LL drifter *Marie Elena*. He had died needlessly, because his pilot had not joined him and bailed out, but crashlanded his flak-damaged plane on the Bradwell runway and survived.

The NOIC Brightlingsea was also in overall charge of the Walton and Clacton lifeboats. *EMED*, of Walton, put out twenty-four times for crashed aircraft, but saved no one, though on 30 May 1943 she found the body of an FW 190 pilot shot down by the local light flak while raiding the town. At Clacton *J B Proudfoot* saved one Polish airman on 25 June 1941 (of his comrades one bailed out on land, one was landed dead at Brightlingsea, and the rest were washed ashore dead _ their Wellington had been raiding Boulogne). Clacton rescued only one other airman, an American Mustang pilot who ditched near the Pier on 13 January 1945, but he died in the boat. A local aviation society has researched his story and feature it in a small air museum housed in Stone Point Martello Tower.

Sheerness was an early ARB base, with from two to four boats, plus air-sea rescue floats. In May 1942 it was upgraded to 31 MCU, with RAF Seaplane Tenders 443 and 444. Because Allied aircraft systematically avoided the Thames mouth owing to barrage balloons this unit was not a busy one. That 9 September it landed two dead crewmen from a 23 Squadron (Bradwell) Mosquito, though they had originally been found by the Sheerness patrol drifter *Lord Keith* near B6A Buoy. On 27 August 1943 Sheerness at last achieved a live rescue _ of ten USAAF Fortress crewmen from two dinghies off the Medway. On 4 October ten more were taken from *Lord Keith*, and five were ferried from another drifter on 3 March 1944. A U.S. Lightning pilot was saved in the same way on 13 April near B5 Buoy. ST 444 was called out to Knock John on 12 May to land nine Fortress crewmen saved by the Fort's boat. By now 31 MCU comprised four STs. Leaving aside some early ARB work, the Sheerness RAF rescue craft performed only

---

*The ground staff at Donna Nook, the North Coates "satellite" field, had had the same experience with a crew trapped in a marshpool beside the Humber.

AIR-SEA RESCUE

five air-sea rescues, totalling thirty-six men.

The most famous pilot to ditch in the Sheerness zone was Amy Johnson, the flying heroine of the 1930s. Now an Air Transport Auxiliary pilot, she crashed by East Knock John Buoy, about twelve miles off both Foulness and Reculver, while ferrying an Oxford on the cold and blustery 5 January 1941. A passing CE convoy, with the American reporter Drew Middleton coincidentally on the lookout from a ship, saw the crash, and (according to Middleton and others) a parachute drop out seconds before. The escort warships searched. The balloon vessel *Haslemere* stopped near a floating survivor who was seen and heard to be a woman: seamen reached out astern and nearly touched her, but she did not move, and then a wave lifted the stern and made it fall violently, after which the woman was nowhere to be seen. Meanwhile the crew thought they saw a second survivor further away. *Haslemere*'s captain, Lt-Cdr W Fletcher RN , most courageously stripped and swam through the bone-chilling sea. He was seen to grab the person, then let go. Lt Loasby's ML 113 came up, found only Fletcher, and pulled him out of the water unconscious with shock and exposure: he never came round, and died on shore later*. Then the Sheerness destroyer *Berkeley* found wreckage and two kitbags, which contained papers belonging to Miss Johnson, and further north the Brightlingsea patrol drifter *Young Jacob* fished out a piece of wing fabric bearing part of her plane's identification number.

Rumours soon flew. Miss Johnson had taken off alone; who, then, was the second person in the sea? Was he a man friend, stowed away or secretly picked up en route? The more prosaic explanation, which for obvious reasons Fletcher could not verify, was that "he" was merely another floating kitbag or piece of wreckage. Had the aviatrix been shot down by the Germans, who had just been raiding another convoy close by? (see Page 103). Was this a deliberate act of spite? If so were the British authorities covering it up to protect the morale of a sentimental public? But the Germans would hardly have been able to identify the plane as Amy Johnson's, and British propaganda would surely have blamed the enemy if it could. A recent writer+ has more convincingly suggested that she had engine trouble and, deceived by the Thames floating barrage balloons visible above the unbroken blanket of low cloud, thought she must be only just outside London, and therefore come down for a crash landing, not realising till too late that there

---

*his grave may be seen at Gillingham, only a few yards from Lt-Cdr Esmonde's. Even before this he had won official praise for courage in facing German long-range shelling in the Dover Strait.   +R Conyers Nesbit.

AIR-SEA RESCUE

was only sea underneath. Her body was not among the many washed ashore during the war _ unusual as she had bailed out. And why such an experienced pilot was over the East Coast, and had been airborne for four hours, when flying from Lancashire to Oxfordshire (a two-hour journey at most) remains a mystery. The theory she was on some secret mission is certainly absurd: there is no evidence of a female civilian pilot flying on one, especially not in daylight, and above all not in an Oxford. Her one-glamorous life had come to be marred by marital breakdown and depression: might she have reached Oxfordshire, been overcome by despair, and flown on to the nearest sea to die where she might not be rescued and no one else would be endangered by the crash*? Might this explain why she had not tried to swim towards *Haslemere*? But those who were last to see her detected no inkling of this, and why had she parachuted and called for help? She might have been too injured, shocked, or cold, to swim. Her solicitor, William Crocker, received little Admiralty help when he tried to investigate her death, being, for example, refused permission to visit Brightlingsea to interview *Young Jacob*'s skipper and look at the piece of wing. But in 1941 the Essex coast was a high-security area owing to the continued fear of German invasion, and Crocker eventually did get his permission in 1942, though admittedly the skipper turned out to have been transferred to Ulster and the wing fabric had disappeared!

Herne Bay, on the North Kent coast, was the smallest of all the Nore Command air-sea rescue bases, with just the single *civilian*-manned ARB *Dandy*. Its existence was justified mainly by the nearby Reculver bombing range, where 617 ("Dambuster") Squadron first tested Barnes Wallis's "bouncing bomb" in 1943. Two rescues have been documented. On 27 November 1941 *Dandy* saved five from a Wellington bomber only a quarter of a mile from Herne Bay, and on 25 January 1943 she picked up Flight Lt E P Wood, who ditched his fighter on the way back from a raid on Flushing.

Margate's lifeboat, on the north-east corner of Kent, was more prominent in air-sea rescue than any other. On 12 August 1940 she landed Pilot Officer Geoffrey Page, of 56 Squadron (North Weald), after he had been found in the sea by a fishing smack. As since often told, he had bailed out with face and hands so terribly burned that the skin had peeled off like parchment. He had lost his trousers and one shoe, and when he grabbed his brandy flask a wave knocked it from his grasp. He had to swim for his

---

*her sister had committed suicide, though this may not be relevant.

AIR-SEA RESCUE

life, because his Mae West had been burned. His long fightback to health began in Margate Hospital. On 28 August the lifeboat and two small boats rescued the four crew of a German bomber. 3 September saw her save a badly burned Flight Lt Richard Hillary, the literary battle of Britain pilot. On 10 April 1941 she saved the three crew of an 82 Squadron Blenheim, and a fortnight later a 91 Squadron Spitfire pilot. 27 February 1942 marked her rescue of a Havoc crew only one and a half miles from her station.

Ramsgate, though in Dover Command, conducted many rescues on the southern edge of Nore Command. Northwards its zone stretched round to the Tongue and Kentish Knock. From early in 1941 it operated older-type HSLs. In 1942 it had three of these, plus a MAC, and one or two ARBs. Eventually the naval unit alone consisted of eight MASBs. On 18 July 1941 an HSL rescued three airmen near Tongue Sand, and on 17 September a Spitfire pilot thirteen miles out from North Foreland. On 1 June 1942 the MAC saved Pilot Oficer Richards, an Australian from 65 Squadron at Great Sampford (Essex), who was worsted by an FW 190 returning over the Kentish Knock from raiding Margate. Three days later one of the MASBs picked up the four crew of a 107 Squadron Boston eight miles north of the North Foreland; they had been bombing Dunkirk from West Raynham in Norfolk. And on 6 June 1942 HSL 127 ventured to a point fifteen miles off Blankenberge to save the five survivors of a 149 Squadron Stirling which had been returning to Mildenhall from the Ruhr.

On 22 January 1943 a German was rescued from the Kentish Knock by HSL 169 _ apparently another FW 190 pilot from the raid on London mentioned previously. Four days later an American, Second Lt Brock, was saved only a few miles off Margate _ he was from the Eighth Airforce's 4th Fighter Group, based at Debden in Essex. On 17 August two of the "Eighth"'s B 17s crashed in the sea off Kent after the famous and costly raid on the Schweinfurt ball-bearing factory deep in Germany. HSL 127 rescued Lt Lockhart and the remaining nine of his crew only two and a half miles east-north-east of the North Foreland, and next morning towed in a Walrus and the seven Americans it had found six miles out from the first crash. During the first phase of "Market Garden", on 17 September 1944, HSL 2549 rescued six more Americans from a glider between the West Hinder and Dunkirk. And in the Dover Strait there were many more Ramsgate rescues, but these are beyond my purview.

17
TO THE FAR SHORE

On 6 June 1944 over four thousand Allied ships and major landing craft put 130,000 troops onto the beaches of Normandy, and opened the long-awaited "Second Front" against Germany. About one eighth of this force, in itself a considerable armada, was called "Force L" and had left from East Coast ports. For the branch of the Navy known as "Combined Operations" this D-Day was the culmination of almost four years of preparation. Combined Operations had always been based mainly on the Channel coast, but it had East Coast connections as well.

These went back to the summer of 1940. Churchill was urging the Admiralty and War Office to cooperate in sending commando-type troops across to raid occupied Europe from small landing craft, thereby stirring up resistance among the conquered peoples, forcing the enemy to disperse his troops, and instilling the offensive spirit into our own services. Eight flotillas of naval "raiding craft", in addition to Commando or "Special Service" Army units, were planned. Two naval officers, Cdrs Hornby and Donovan, toured the East Coast looking for a suitable base for one such flotilla, to be employed in raiding between Calais and the Texel, and in August visited Brightlingsea. Captain Henniker-Heaton told them that his base was under capacity (at that time it accommodated only the Auxiliary Patrol), and that rather than going to the trouble of starting a new base, the Navy might send him their proposed raiding unit. 7th Raiding or Landing Craft Flotilla was formed at Hull in September, with Lt-Cdr Charles Corke RNVR in charge, and arrived at Brightlingsea in October after a rough and perilous voyage.

The flotilla had nine boats _ T 10-14, 16-18 and 21. "T" stood for "taxi boat", because the nine were water-taxis from New York Harbour, bought by the U.S.Government and sent to England along with other early aid. But any idea that their luxurious origins made them effective landing craft was soon dispelled. According to Sub-Lt(E) Hollick, commander of T 16 and engineer for the flotilla, they were worn out, completely neglected and unsuitable craft. Almost every one had a distinct type of engine (of obsolete model), making maintenance difficult. There were no radios or navigation lights, and the only armament on each boat was a Hotchkiss machine-gun with a tendency to jam once it opened fire. and a dozen hand grenades kept in a box.

If anyone envisaged the "Raiding Flotilla" setting out on cut-and-

TO THE FAR SHORE

thrust expeditions to Holland he was disappointed. For a start, whatever Churchill's impatience, the Forces insisted on putting the boats and their crews through a long period of working up and training _ of which most time was, in reality, spent at Stone's Shipyard, tinkering with unreliable engines and mending the propellers, which stuck out below the sterns and constantly fouled the foreshore. During the winter of 1940-41 7th Flotilla provided sea training for Commandos temporarily based in the Alresford Creek area of Brightlingsea and at Creeksea, Burnham-on-Crouch, where the Commando pioneer Lt-Col Laycock was based for a time.

In May 1941 nine "Eurekas" or "R-Boats" (no connection with the German warship) replaced three of Corke's T-Boats, and the combined force was split into two flotillas, 7th and 8th. The former spent that summer doing air-sea rescue duty at various places. Later the remaining T-Boats were downgraded to local harbour launches or ARBs, and all the "Eurekas" became a single 7th Flotilla.

Corke had long tried to get his unit away from Brightlingsea, where there was insufficient room for his men, accommodation was scattered and costly, discipline hard to maintain, mustering unpunctual, and "security...practically non-existent"(!) He offered a plan for a Combined Ops base at Alresford Grange, but his superiors overruled this as they envisaged a much larger base at Point Clear and St Osyth Stone, on the south side of Brightlingsea Creek. An officer visited this area on 1 April 1942 and it was then requisitioned and named HMS *Helder*, apparently in honour of the Dutch seaport.

Corke and his flotilla moved to the English Channel in July, and from Newhaven took part in the Dieppe Raid in August. Corke lost his life in that abortive and costly affair, and is today commemorated by a wall plaque at the Colne Yacht Club at Brightlingsea.

I do not suppose many will have heard of "Operation Consular" _ the transfer that year, via Southend, of nearly five hundred trawlers and drifters, 164 tugs, and over a thousand dumb barges, from Northern and Eastern ports to the Channel. The intention must have been to deceive the enemy into thinking that another Dieppe was planned, thereby diverting him from the Mediterranean. Most of the shipping involved was returned in 1943.

HMS *Helder* did not amount to much for its first year. During the summer of 1942 it had no boats, save for a few under repair. The first drafts spent their time doing PT, playing ball games (to the delight of some sports-minded officers), "square-bashing", listening to talks, and even practicing sea formations _ minus boats _ on the tarmac! Catering and hygiene were primitive. At first potatoes were boiled in their string bags, peel and dirt and all. Later the base made some medical history when Surgeon-Lt Aucutt diagnosed the first home-contacted case of malaria for two decades (he blamed water and sewage). The base was still dependent on *Nemo* across the Creek for engineering, medical and other services. During late 1942 and the first half of 1943 Cdr Voelcker, formerly Plans Officer at the Nore, was in charge.

Meanwhile, in October 1942, Combined Ops started HMS *Westcliff*, a shore training and accommodation base. It expanded to include all the empty hotels and houses between the station, Manor Road and Crowthorne Avenue, Westcliff, plus huts on the seafront used as galleys. Officers were based in the Grosvenor Hotel. Cdr Tollemache, and then Cdr Poignard, were in charge.

Major landing craft, e.g. LCTs, began to train in the Stour and Orwell, and early in 1943 a new base, HMS *Woolverstone*, was established at the village of the same name, just below Ipswich. (Its Orwellside site, the intriguingly named Cat House Landing*, is now Harwich Yacht Club). In March plans to expand this and also to base major landing craft at *Helder* were debated, but it was instead decided to make the latter a minor landing craft training centre, and to downgrade *Woolverstone* to a repair and loading base. In July *Woolverstone*'s Captain Brookfield and most of his shore staff moved to *Helder*. The minor landing craft were those which the big invasion ships were to carry across to an enemy coast and lower into the sea for the actual landings. They were of four main types; LCAs (landing craft assault), LCPs (personnel), LCMs (mechanised _ for small tanks), and LCVs (vehicle), and were crewed by from three to six men each. Five flotillas, each of about a dozen craft, went to *Helder*. The old PMS *Duchess of Rothesay*, minus engines, was moored in Brightlingsea Creek as a base for their guards.

The engineers used Stone Point Martello Tower as an HQ, and parts of the Brightlingsea shipyards as offices and a maintenance base. The Point Clear chalets provided trainees' accommodation. Two landing barge oilers, two landing barge engineering (for repairs afloat) and two harbour launches were laid on. Captain Lord Mountbatten, then head of Combined Operations,

---

*legend has it that a stuffed cat used to be displayed in the window of a nearby house as a signal to smugglers.

visited the base at this point.

Meanwhile Tilbury was becoming the East Coast's main LST (landing ship tank) base, and in September 1943 Captain W S Harman established HMS *St Clement* as their shore HQ. U.S. Navy LSTS came under its command, berthing and drawing their supplies from Convoys Wharf, up-river at Deptford. One LST displaced either 1,600 or 3,600 tons according to type, and could carry up to thirty tanks and half a dozen minor landing craft. Across the Estuary the LCIs (major infantry landing craft) were based near Sheerness at Queenborough (alongside *St Tudno* minesweeper base), and their shore office took the name HMS *Wildfire III*.

Harwich (Parkeston Quay) became another LST base, under *Woolverstone's* command. Early in 1944 there were seventeen of these big square-ended vessels on the Stour_ nine of them US Navy, plus the 4,200-ton super-LSTs *Bachaquero, Misoa* and *Tasajera*. And Combined Operations were spreading north. At Boston, on the little-frequented Wash, the tiny base called HMS *Arbella* became home to a dozen or so LCTs. At Lake Lothing, Lowestoft, HMS *Mylodon* was set up as an operational LCT base, with shore accommodation in an old silk factory (today the site of the Pye factory) and berths at Yarmouth and Gorleston as well as locally.

A little *Westcliff* minor landing craft training had been going on for a time on the Crouch, when at the end of 1943 Burnham was elevated to the status of HMS *St Matthew*, and the whole of HMS *Effingham*, the Dartmouth minor landing craft training base, was transferred to it, including six flotillas of boats. The old Creeksea Commando camp, much enlarged, formed the accommodation. The arrangements were unusual: once a very minor dependency of London or Southend, Burnham was now a major base in its own right, yet its RNO, Captain Dane, remained in charge. The base took its name from a requisitioned yacht, the *St Matthew*: it also had a sea training yacht called *Iona III*, a storage barge, and about a dozen miscellaneous launches and boats for supply, ferrying, river patrol and other purposes. Early in 1944 *St Matthew* began concentrating on training officers, leaving all ratings to *Helder*.

By now the LCAs, since they were to spearhead invasions, were manned by Royal Marines, so that up to a third of the personnel at the Essex training bases consisted of them. Lt Badlan DSC RM, a hero of Dieppe, was in charge of *Helder's* sea training. Another Marine, Lt-Col Edds, veteran of

TO THE FAR SHORE

Narvik, transferred from *Helder* to be in charge at *Woolverstone*.

Both *St Matthew* and *Helder* confined themselves to initial, not combat, training. Trainees practiced embarkation, loading, formation steering, and beaching. But visiting troops were routinely carried to get each service used to the other and for added realism. For some reason the "rides" even extended to the USAAF, the Home Guard, and the Royal Observer Corps. Guns, jeeps and Bren carriers were taken on board at hards on Mersea Island, Tollesbury and elsewhere, and beaching took place mainly around Colne Point and Bradwell, where the mines and beach obstacles had been cleared. "Coming alongside" had to be practiced, the vessel in question being the iron Finnish ship *Alestor*, moored at Bradwell as a base for the Army river patrol. Everyone was also taken aboard this vessel on the grounds that it was essential for the men, some of whom had hardly seen the sea in their lives before, to know the main features of a sizeable ship, albeit a sailing barque built in 1874! New hards were laid down at Steeple Stone and Stansgate, with fuel and storage compounds attached, for major landing craft, such as LCTs, which frequented the Blackwater on exercises.

By 1944 there were 1,300 personnel at *Helder*, 1,500 at *St Matthew*, and over six thousand (including seven hundred Wrens) at *Westcliff*. The area from Holehaven to Bradwell was now so populated by Combined Ops that it became a separate Sub-Command, under the NOIC Southend, who was upgraded to Commodore-in-Charge.

The MP for Maldon, the now notorious Tom Driberg, lived at Bradwell and took it on himself to speak up for the conscripts at these Essex bases. In April 1944 a *Helder* Marine complained to him about being given pack drill for insubordination, a punishment by then illegal in the services. As a result there was a correspondence involving people as exalted as the C-in-C Home Fleet and First Lord of the Admiralty, but Captain Brookfield brushed the matter aside by saying that the man had merely been given parade drill while wearing hius normal kit and ration pack.

All the East Coast landing-craft activity served a strange secondary purpose _ reinforcing the German belief that the main Allied invasion of Europe would come across the North Sea and not over the Channel. Enemy Intelligence was populating East Anglia with American and British combat divisions, corps and even armies which either inhabited South and South-West England or did not exist, partly because a bogus Allied radio network

TO THE FAR SHORE

was deliberately feeding German "Y" (they called it "B") in Holland with signals emanating from the fictitious "FUSAG" (First U.S.Army Group).

East Anglia was not without real troops at this period, of course. The thinly populated Suffolk coast was much used for infantry and tank training. An area around Dunwich was torn up by the special amphibious, flamethrowing and mine-clearing tanks of 79 Armoured Division. On the other side of Southwold an area of seven square miles, including the villages of Uggeshall, Frostenden and South Cove, was evacuated to provide another training area. And if the U.S.Army was not present, the U.S.Army *Air Force* was _ with nearly a hundred airfields, five thousand bomber, fighter and transport aircraft, and over two hundred thousand men, in the Eastern Counties.

Neither the Brightlingsea "Raiding Flotillas", nor the later and much larger naval and Army forces on the East Coast, ever did cross to the Dutch Coast or the Calais region. When Allied clandestine operations were mounted into Holland by sea, Coastal Forces was utilised. I have been able to piece together an account of these obscure and fascinating missions by combining the recent autobiographies of various Dutchmen with bits and pieces from the British Admiralty and RAF records.

As early as October 1940 a Felixstowe MTB (number unknown) crept very close to the shore at Renasse, a Dutch village on the island of Schouwen, lowered a dinghy, landed a Dutch agent, and took off another. The agent embarked was making his second escape from Holland, having reached Lowestoft from Scheveningen in the very same dinghy the previous July. (See Page 50). As she turned for home the MTB was chased and hit by a German patrol boat: an officer and a rating were wounded and the Dutchman fired back with a machine gun, though his claim to have sunk an E-boat has no foundation.

The reader may recall from Chapter Three that a wave of Dutch escapers reached the English East Coast by sea in 1941. Working with British Intelligence, some of these men devised and took part in a daring plan to infiltrate Holland, link up with the local Resistance, and gather information, and called "Contact Holland". In charge were the British SIS (Secret Intelligence Service) Colonel Euan Rabagliati and the Dutch escaper Erik Hazelhoff Roelfzema. Their first infiltration missions were launched from Felixstowe, where the participants waited incognito at the Felix Hotel _ until one almost compromised himself by dropping a Luger pistol onto the dancefloor. The C-Type MGB 320 (commanded by Lt P G Loasby DSC, earlier involved in the attempt to save Amy Johnson) was employed. She had to sneak the agents across on nights with faint moonlight and moderate, though not calm, sea. Only late-autumn and winter nights were possible, because she had to come and go under cover of darkness, yet not land or pick up men between midnight and 4 a.m, the time of the German curfew and beach patrols. The proposed landing place was certainly audacious, being the unmined beach at Scheveningen, the seaside district of The Hague, almost in front of the Palace Hotel, HQ of German Coastal Defences in Western Europe. To blend in with the prosperous (and perhaps collaborationist!) restaurant and hotel patrons on the seafront the agents were clad in evening dress! The MGB was to come in towards the coast on one engine at low power, then put her passengers into a dinghy. The initial operation was codenamed "Table", and Hazelhoff Roelfzema came along in person. After six failed attempts, when the weather was too rough, the first man, Peter Tazelaar, was landed in the early hours of 23 November 1941. MGB 320 had worked from Yarmouth on this occasion, and when she approached base Hazelhoff found Rabagliati waiting in the mist at the tip of North Pier. On 9 December the second agent, Willem van der Reyden, was landed.

Occasionally Dutch agents had to be brought back. Unlike in France this seems to have been attempted by air in only one early instance. On 15 October 1940, in the unsubtly named "Operation Windmill", Cdr Schaper's Dutch Fokker Tviii-W floatplane flew from Felixstowe to pick up naval Lt Van Hamel and two friends from Tjeuke Lake, twenty miles south of Leeuwarden* in Friesland. But the would-be escapers had been betrayed by a farmer's wife who thought they were stealing from her husband's eel traps, and when the plane put down on the dark and foggy lake it had to fight a gun battle with Germans ashore and on boats. It escaped with forty bullet holes but without the agents.+ Of these one was shot by the Germans at their execution place in Scheveningen sand dunes, another turned traitor and was later executed by the Dutch.

On 17 January 1942 MGB 320 (now commanded by Lt Hall) was sent to Scheveningen to take off a party of Dutchmen who included Dr Beckman, Deputy Premier-Designate in Queen Wilhelmina's government in

---

*the birthplace of Mata Hari, appropriately.   +incidentally Schaper and his plane had already made one escape from Holland to Felixstowe _ the previous May.

TO THE FAR SHORE

exile. She went to Katwijk (about ten miles north) by mistake, while Beckman was arrested on Scheveningen Beach (he later died in Dachau). Having refuelled at HMS *Beehive* MGB 320 got to Scheveningen next night, unaware of events ashore. Hazelhoff and Lt Goodfellow, the First Officer, waited for hours in a tiny boat in sub-zero temperatures, drenched with surf which froze their clothes as stiff as boards, only yards from the spot where Beckman had hidden. In a desperate attempt to find out what was wrong Hazelhoff did the unbelievable. Clad in borrowed Royal Navy uniform (which he hoped would be taken for German and accorded respect), he walked up the beach and into the town's main square, where he tried to telephone a shore agent, after looking up the number in the book! He failed to get through because his obsolete prewar coins fell uselessly out of the slot. By now a sinister onlooker had appeared and stood between him and the beach. As Hazelhoff left the booth the watcher shone a torch in his face. Levelling a pistol under his coat, Hazelhoff walked straight by unmolested, reached the shore, and boarded Goodfellow's boat!

Not surprisingly Scheveningen was now abandoned as a landfall in favour of Katwijk, Noordwijk and elsewhere. Several more agents were taken across via Felixstowe and Yarmouth. For instance, on 11 March, another Yarmouth MGB, 325 (Lt P Williams RNVR), took over two men, but on the beach they and the MGB's Lt C Elwell were captured. Early on 9 April Jan de Haas was put ashore at Castricum, just north of Ijmuiden, with an "S Phone", a new type of secret agent's radio set. But he too was seized, together with all subsequent agents*. All the rendezvous points had been betrayed by van der Reyden and his wireless operator, who had been captured and "turned"+. This "Englandspiel" ploy crippled the Allied cause in Holland for the middle part of the war. As one result MGB 320 was no longer required to land agents.

However her last mission was memorable. In August 1942, operating from Felixstowe again, she nearly met her end. She had just landed Jonkheer Ernst de Jonge at Noordwijk when a German rocket flare lit up the seafront and boat as bright as day. The MGB fought a tracer battle with Germans on the roof and balcony of the Huis ter Duin Hotel. Escaping to sea, she was surrounded by E-boats which tried to spot her silhouette against each others' lights. Narrowly threading her way out, and only just in time to avoid daybreak, she eventually regained HMS *Beehive*.

*One prisoner was Van Rietschoten, mentioned on Page 52. +Van der Reyden settled in Norfolk after the war. The other man was savagely maltreated and murdered by the SS in the quarry near Mauthausen concentration camp, where most of the "Englandspiel" prisoners died.

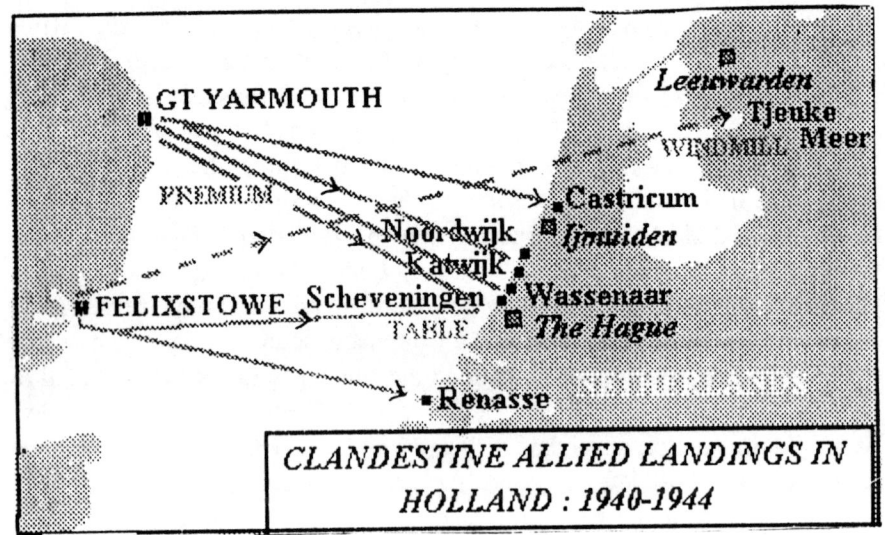

CLANDESTINE ALLIED LANDINGS IN HOLLAND : 1940-1944

In London Hazelhoff and Goodfellow were awarded Holland's highest decoration, the MWO (Military William's Order) by Queen Wilhelmina. Goodfellow was the first Briton to receive it since Wellington at Waterloo.

Meanwhile the realm of Combined Ops (Commando and landing-craft) raids was the Channel, but on the night of 24 February 1944 one small, and disastrous, operation, called "Premium", was mounted from Great Yarmouth at Wassenaar, on the dunes immediately north of Scheveningen. Seven Frenchmen of 10 (Inter-Allied) Commando were taken over in MTB 682, escorted by five more boats of Lt-Cdr Bradford's famous flotilla, and landed via a dory. They were to link up with the Dutch Resistance and return for re-embarkation before first light, but none returned, and after the war they were found buried in a Dutch cemetery. No shooting had been heard by the MTBs when they landed, though the Frenchmen were silhouetted by enemy flares. Bradford had been ordered back before dawn, and bad weather was given as the reason why the Navy was not sent back to try another rendezvous next night. Some mystery still surrounds the episode.

The plans for "Operation Neptune", the naval side of the Normandy Invasion, located the Combined Operations fleet called "Force L" in the Nore Command. This was charged with carrying 7th Armoured Division (the

TO THE FAR SHORE

"Desert Rats"), part of 51st Highland Division, and the HQs of 1st and 30th Corps, to the invasion beachheads as the immediate follow-up to the D-Day landings, to arrive on "D+1". Force L's HQ was at St Felix's, in peacetime a girls' boarding school, at Southwold. There a large administrative staff spent months devising, amending and issuing the orders which made up a book as big as a telephone directory. They planned ship-loading, convoy mustering and routing, timetabling and security. The landing craft were divided into three fleets; L1 at Harwich, L2 at Lowestoft, L3 on the Thames and Medway.

The Nore Command, especially Harwich, was now reinforced by several Flower-class corvettes and American-built Captain-class frigates from Western Approaches _ in case U-Boats returned to the area to interfere with Force L. *Byron* was the first frigate to arrive at Harwich since the early 19th century, the classification having been long extinct in the Royal Navy.

On 1 April 1944 the whole East Coast from Margate to the Wash and ten miles inland was closed to all outside civilians save some on official business. All servicemen's mail from inside this zone was read by censors. For security reasons neither the naval nor army invasion forces moved to the embarkation ports until the last moment, though both were fully equipped and at the ports themselves hundreds of preparations were being made, ranging from the collection of food and fuel to the construction of roads, vehicle parks, and accommodation camps. In May L2, made up of fifty-three LCTs of "H" and "V" Squadrons, moved from Lowestoft and Yarmouth/Gorleston to the Orwell, where HMS *Woolverstone* temporarily took charge of it. To deceive any enemy reconnaissance planes, it was replaced along Lake Lothing and the Yare by huge canvas dummies (codenamed "bigbobs", and part of the "Operation Quicksilver" deception plan). L1 and L2 sheltered beneath a much strengthened Harwich-Ipswich AA barrage, for the GDA's (Gun Defended Area's) seven heavy AA sites had been supplemented with additional ones at Ramsey (H6), Erwarton (H7), Trimley St Martin (H8), North Felixstowe (H9) and Kesgrave (H11). At the same time L3's U.S.Navy commanding officer, Captain Shaw, moved his HQ to the Pier Hotel, Southend.

On the 31st 21,000 troops and 3,600 vehicles moved in convoy to the outskirts of the loading ports _ Tilbury for the HQ, infantry and support units of 7th Armoured Division, and for 151 Highland Brigade, Felixstowe

TO THE FAR SHORE

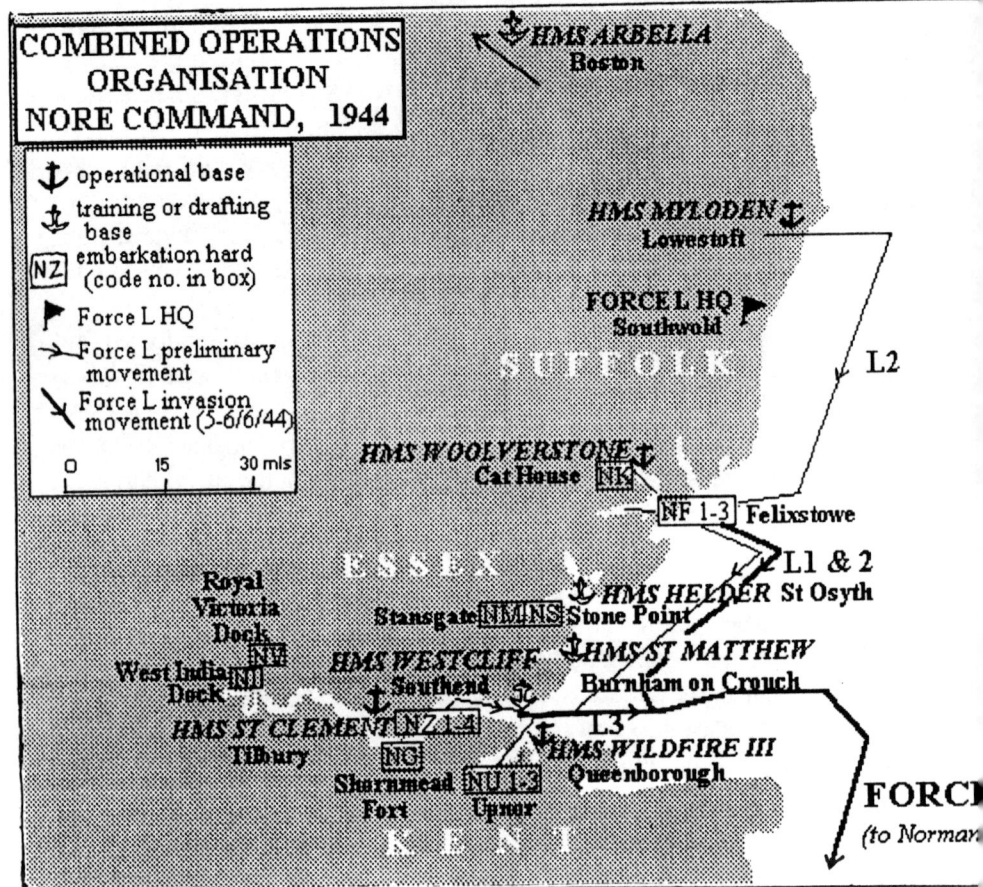

and Ipswich for 1st and 30th Corps HQs and the 22nd Armoured Brigade of 7th Armoured Division. Thousands of locally-based troops, Home Guards and Special Constables were on duty along much of the East Coast for traffic control and security. L2 took on 22nd Armoured Brigade's two hundred tanks and 1,600 men at Ipswich Docks. For mustering purposes it was now termed "Sailing Group 1". L1, the Harwich fleet, split in two. The twelve available British LSTs loaded 1st and 30th Corps vehicles, guns and personnel at Felixstowe. They were now Sailing Group 2. Eight American LSTs left to join the other thirty U.S.Navy LSTs at Tilbury, forming Sailing Group 3 (under Captain Shaw USN). L3's three British LSTs, *Bachaquero*, *Misoa* and *Tasajera*, also loaded at Tilbury, were Sailing Group 4. And its

TO THE FAR SHORE

nineteeen LCIs on the Medway, and loaded at Upnor, opposite Chatham Dockyard, were Sailing Group 5. Some of the LSTs in each group carried a minor landing craft on deck for ferrying purposes, but otherwise these craft were not to go from the East Coast.

By 5 June the cavernous invasion craft had been filled and their huge doors shut, and they had taken on defensive balloons at Tilbury and RAF Felixstowe. They were all ready to leave that morning, but bad weather forced a twenty-four hour postponement, during which they rocked uncomfortably in the swell and the troops grew edgy and then weary. The eastern skies were anxiously scanned for German reconnaissance planes, but none came, for not only was enemy overflying now rare, but low cloud blanketed the whole coast.

That night the inland districts of East Anglia shook to the roar of RAF Bomber Command planes heading south to bomb Normandy, followed at dawn, and nearer to the coast, by the U.S.Eighth and Ninth Airforces. Early that morning, while the main invasion armada was closing the beaches, Force L Sailing Groups 1 and 2 left Harwich Harbour. They comprised sixty-five major landing craft and ships, escorted by the familiar local destroyers *Montrose*, *Vivacious*, *Whitshed* and *Cotswold*, corvettes *Borage*, *Clematis*, *Loosestrife* and *Mignonette*, A/S trawlers *Damsay*, *Fairsay* and *Gairsay*, seven MLs, and many minesweeepers, including a BYMS flotilla down from Yarmouth. Two hours later Sailing Groups 3, 4 and 5 left the Southend anchorage, comprising another sixty-five landing ships and craft, with sixty-six London merchant ships (mainly stacked with vehicles) and three cable ships, escorted by the destroyer *Meynell*, frigates *Chelmer* and *Halstead*, corvettes *Camelia*, *Charlock*, *Narcissis*, *Gardenia* and *Oxlip*, and twenty Queenborough MMSs.

Simultaneously more dummy landing craft were assembled in woodlands around the Stour, Orwell and Thames and set afloat, to feed the enemy suspicion that the Pas de Calais might yet be invaded from Eastern England.

Harwich corvette, Coastal Forces', RAF Coastal and Fighter Command patrols formed a shield across the approach to the English coast from Ostend and Ijmuiden, since there were five operational (8th Flotilla) E-boats at the former and six (6th Flotilla) at the latter. Gorleston, Felixstowe and Ramsgate air-sea rescue craft stationed themselves underneath the air cover at new patrol positions all along the enemy-held coast.

Force L at last united late that morning at B2 Buoy, by Knock John Fort, and with its grand total of some 280 vessels, steered for the Dover Strait. As it sailed on that night hundreds more bombers thundered overhead. On the following morning it discharged its troops and tanks onto a beachhead already in Allied hands.

For the next three months the Harwich and Sheerness destroyers, fleet minesweepers, corvettes and frigates remained in the invasion area under the effective control of "ANCXF" (Allied Naval Command Expeditionary Forces) at Portsmouth. This period of the East Coast sea war saw less fighting than any other, but a huge flow of shipping to Normandy. From long before D-Day shipping and stores had been pouring into the Port of London under the control of the "TURCO" ("Turn-Round Combined Operations") organisation. Five thousand supply and other vessels* were to leave there for the invasion area during the Battle of Normandy, including 170 LBVs (Landing Barge Vehicle) from Tilbury and the huge floating concrete boxes of "Mulberry Harbour", which were towed round from the London Docks to an assembly base at Richborough and then taken across to Arromanches. Tilbury was also in charge of "PLUTO" ("Pipeline under the Ocean"), for pumping oil from Hampshire straight to Normandy; it was shipped round in sections and then joined and laid on the bed of the Channel. Till it was ready scores of "Esso" trawlers, previously gathered at the Humber, Yarmouth and Southend, had ferried across fuel in drums.

Combined Operations, which on D-Day had as many craft and personnel as the whole Navy of 1938, could now be run down. It was not abolished, as fresh amphibious landings were planned for the Pacific and considered for Holland. For the rest of the war many of the landing craft were employed ferrying supplies, reinforcements, casualties and prisoners. HMS *Helder* was paid off in the autumn, and the site, like *Westcliff*, was then used to house the naval parties earmarked for administering the Dutch seaports once they had been captured. *St Matthew* continued. *Woolverstone* carried on as a depot and repair base and absorbed *Bunting* (Ipswich), which the Auxiliary Patrol had now left. Seventy LCTs were laid up at King's Lynn, Lowestoft and Woolverstone.

---

*Few were lost en route, but there was one notable exception. On "D+4" (the fourth day after D-Day), the American Liberty Ship *Richard Montgomery* ran onto Sheerness Middle Sand and sank. She and her thousands of tons of ammunition still lie (unexploded!) in the mud just two miles off Sheerness.

18
THE LAST ELEVEN MONTHS

In September 1944, having lost the Battle of Normandy, the Germans fell back right across France and Belgium within a matter of days. The seaward end of the Western Front shifted to the Low Countries, facing East Anglia. On 17 September and successive days hundreds of Allied aircraft and gliders flew over the Colne-Blackwater mouth and Orfordness, for Arnhem and the other Dutch bridges, but this attempt to deal Germany the death blow failed, and the line stabilised with the enemy still entrenched along the Reich western border and in Northern and Western Holland. (See map on Page 362). The Allies next succeeded in clearing the Scheldt Estuary and opening up Antwerp as their main supply base in Western Europe. The German Navy in Holland prepared for a desperate last offensive to cut this vital route. These events were the background to a new campaign in the southern North Sea, quiet for many months.

The warships which had left Harwich and Sheerness for the Channel on D-Day returned. 16th Destroyer Flotilla, of Harwich, commanded by Captain J S Salter, reached a peak strength of twenty-eight vessels by the end of the year, including frigates as well as destroyers. 6th and 7th Minesweeper Flotillas, and 1st Corvette Flotilla (the "Ducks") were again with HMS *Badger*. By that date there were seventeen MTB and twelve ML flotillas in the Nore Command. At maximum nearly eighty Coastal Forces' boats were based at both Yarmouth and Lowestoft, and sixty at Felixstowe, though in each case several were temporarily elsewhere. 8th MTB Flotilla (Felixstowe) was Polish: 29th (Felixstowe) and 65th (Yarmouth) were Canadian, and 54th (Yarmouth) was Norwegian. Sheerness became a major Coastal Forces' base for the first time, with three ML flotillas, one for minesweeping and two for anti-E-boat work. The number of naval craft at Sheerness and Queenborough (not counting landing craft) exceeded 270 at its peak.

A medium bomber squadron, 415 (Canadian) had now become part of 16 Group Coastal Command, and, with successor formations, was based at Bircham Newton. Their Wellingtons tracked German vessels with ASV Mark III (10-cm) radar and PPI, and guided in the frigates and MTBs by R/T and copious flares. From North Coates and Langham six RAF (including three "Anzac") squadrons were raiding enemy shipping in the Heligoland Bight, and often sinking three or four vessels on a single mission.

The German Navy no longer had any operational major surface

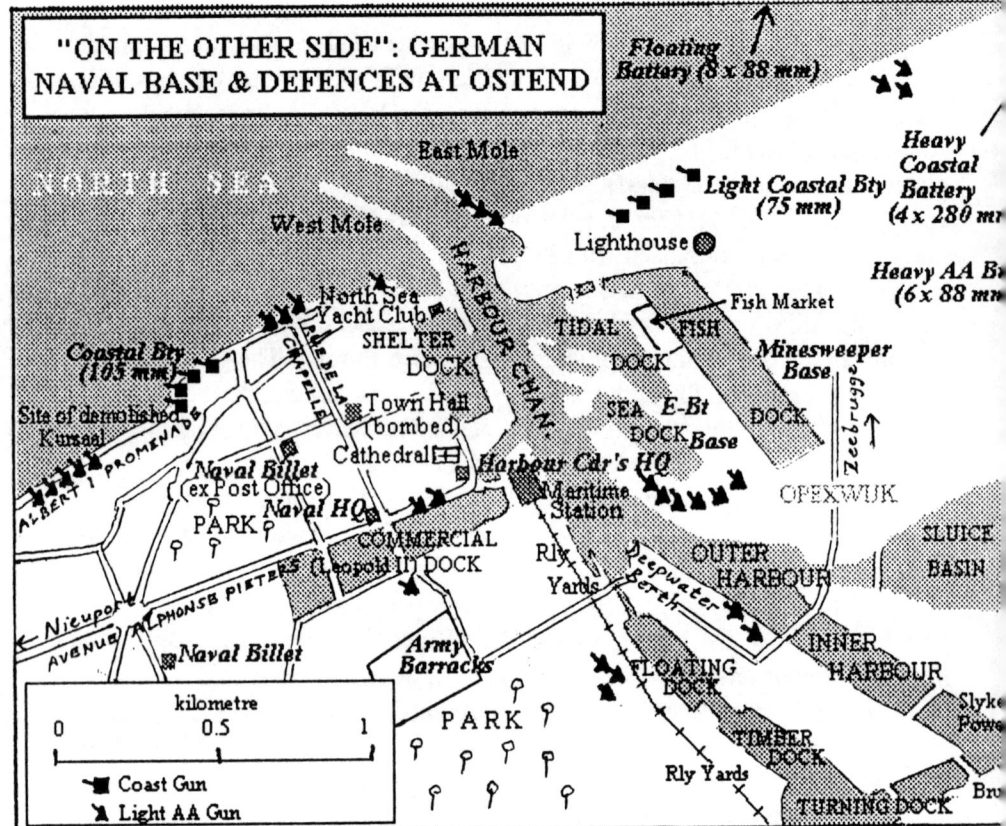

vessels, nor the direct assistance of the enfeebled Luftwaffe, but turned to a fleet of small craft _ E-boats, midget-submarines called "Biber" ("beavers") and "Seehunde" ("seadogs"), and explosive motor boats called "EMBs" in English and "Linsen" in German. Nore warships, with larger craft now working in company with Coastal Forces boats, carried out nightly battle with these opponents.

One German North Sea naval base, Ostend, fell to the Allies on 9 September 1944, denying the Germans their last E-boat lair south-west of Rotterdam. The bombing of both sides had inflicted remarkably similar damage and casualties to that suffered by Lowestoft, Yarmouth or Hull, but there had been hardly any air raids for over two years.* However the retreating enemy had sunk some twenty-six ships, tugs and barges as

---

*the most recent, apparently an accidental offloading of bombs by the RAF, had been on 31 March, and, in killing thirty-six civilians, had been the heaviest since May 1940.

THE LAST ELEVEN MONTHS

blockships in the harbour mouth and various docks, and, by detonating 150 land-mines, turned every quayside into piles of rubble, thereby preventing ships from being unloaded. The seaward approach had also been mined: while the Harwich MMSs were sweeping it on 19 September the Captain M/S's vessel, ML 216, was badly damaged and later sank. But rapid work by British and Canadian engineers reopened the port within five weeks. Ostend became a Royal Navy base, with a Commodore-in-Charge and a plot room, and the Belgian coast came under an "Ostend Sub-Command" within the Nore Command. A mobile Coastal Forces' base, under Captain Brind (formerly of HMS *Midge*), MMSs, and a unit of RAF HSLs, appeared there. It was from Ostend that Commandos sailed to storm the island of Walcheren, from which the enemy commanded the Scheldt entrance, on 1 November 1944. A sheer freak accident did cause a setback at Ostend, however. In a "St Valentine's Day Massacre" on 14 February 1945 a chance explosion and fire in the Shelter Dock (nowadays, appropriately, the Montgomery Dock) in front of the old town destroyed *thirteen* MTBs and killed sixty-three sailors _ in addition to thirty Belgian civilian casualties.

Although every other port in Belgium and Northern France had been liberated, thirty miles west of Ostend the Germans clung until the very end of the war to Dunkirk _ in view of events in 1940 certainly an ironic twist. They supplied their isolated garrison by night _ from the air (by parachute), and by means of hired Dutch trawlers (until their crews refused to go, even for danger money), and E-boats. 10th E-boat Flotilla was on such a mission when intercepted late on the night of 18 September 1944. Two new D-type MTBs from Lt-Cdr Wilkie's Lowestoft-based 64th Flotilla _ 724 (Lt J F Humphreys RNVR) and 728 (Lt F N Thomson RNVR), accompanied by the Harwich frigate *Stayner* _ sank three of the E-boats (S 183, 200 and 702), and captured sixty prisoners. One was the flotilla commander, Kapitanleutnant Karl Müller, a holder of the Knight's Cross who had sunk SS *Groenlo* off Suffolk three years earlier. Here was a victory to rank alongside that on the Yarmouth Z Lines the year before. The occasion was marred for HMS *Mantis* only by the shooting-up of MTB 728 by 724 in mistake for an E-boat.

Yet the Germans were still capable of putting up formidable opposition. Enemy convoys had rarely ventured round the Dutch coast since 1943, mostly starting from, or terminating at, Emden (in spite of the bombing

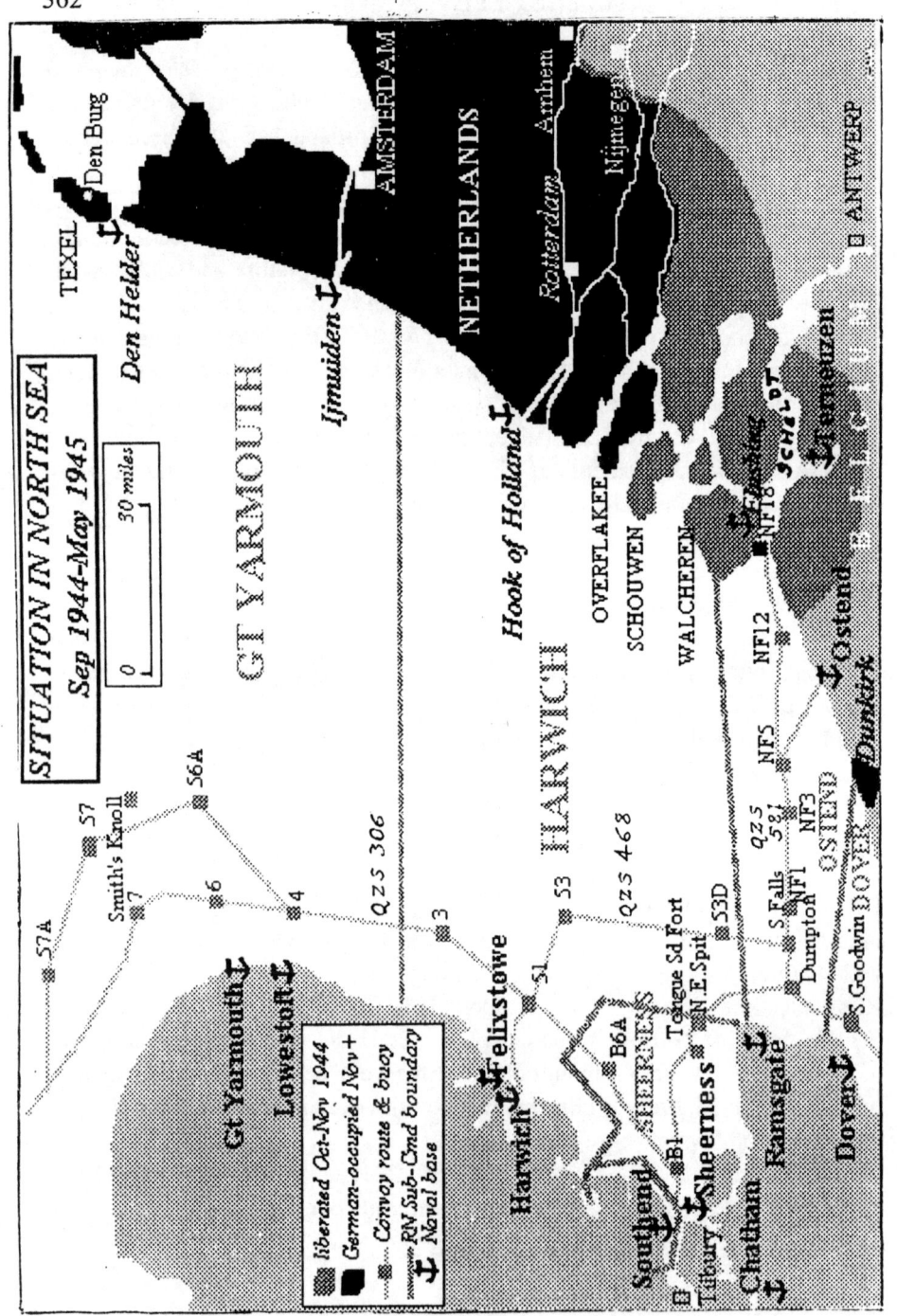

THE LAST ELEVEN MONTHS

there), but on the night of 1 October 1944 one was reported to have left Rotterdam for the north, and was said to include troopships. Lt F W Bourne and five MTBs of his 11th Flotilla therefore left Felixstowe to catch it as it reached Ijmuiden. It turned out to consist of some eighteen ships, and as usual two-thirds were warships. In a ferocious battle MTBs 347 and 360 were both hit by large-calibre shells and sank, with nine dead and six wounded in all. The Germans had several vessels torpedoed and shot up, but whether any sank remained unconfirmed.

After the German Army had been cleared from its banks, a huge minesweeping effort was needed to make the Scheldt Estuary navigable. Two forces of fleet and motor minesweepers, drawn from many bases, were based at Sheerness (Force A, up to 112 craft) and Harwich (Force B, up to fifty). The task was complicated and prolonged by enemy pressure or "oyster" mines, which were susceptible to the increased water pressure caused by the hulls of ships overhead and were quite immune to normal sweeping methods _ depthcharging was one expedient. The Harwich frigates *Duff* and *Dakins* were both mine-damaged off the Scheldt in the last month of 1944. On 25 November the first Antwerp-bound convoy left Southend, steering via the NF (North Foreland) series of buoys along the new QZS 581 parallel to the Belgian coast. A month later regular London-Antwerp convoys, codenamed "TAM"s, began, with the Sheerness 21st Destroyer Flotilla as their main escort. Thirty-five LCTs operated a continuous Army ferry service from Tilbury to Antwerp and Ostend. A Continental passenger ferry service from Parkeston was also revived, in the form of the Antwerp leave ships *Empire Parkeston* (a captured German vessel), *Lady of Man*, and the prewar *Vienna*. Shipping from Harwich reached QZS 581 by cutting across on QZS 468 (formerly 117), past 53 Buoy, to South Falls. Another fruit of victories on the Continent was the return of Channel-routed *ocean* convoys to the Thames (codenamed ONAs and UCs).

The Allied land offensive had stalled through increased enemy resistance, yet another of this war's harsh winters (snow was settling a week before Christmas), and the unexpectedly slow development of the Antwerp supply base. Overhead growled the V-bombs, which were being aimed in thousands at the two termini of the Scheldt route, London and Antwerp (in a few months three times as many people were killed at the latter than at Hull throughout the war).

THE LAST ELEVEN MONTHS

From Rotterdam and Ijmuiden the German Navy's small craft attempted in vain to close the Scheldt. The Admiralty had been expecting some of the naval "secret weapons", from what the enemy called the "K Flotillas", for some time. Some had been in action a few weeks earlier off Normany, but even before that, on 20 March 1944, the Harwich coast artillery had opened up on "three suspicious low objects", thought to be "W-Boats" (a generic British term for enemy midget U-Boats, human torpedoes, and "Linsen" motor boats), but no sign of wreckage had been seen. On 2 November a "Marder" human torpedo sank a British A/S trawler off Ostend. On the 29th a "Biber" midget-submarine was captured east of the Kentish Knock _ it was found on the surface with its operator dead from petrol fumes.* This one man craft, complete with a little conning tower and two torpedoes strapped alongside, was barely thirty feet long, or one quarter the length of a British ML. The daring+ of the lone 'Biber' men was to accomplish little: though hundreds of these tiny U-Boats were built, they were lost in droves from rough seas and accidental fires (their petrol engines were highly unsafe), and most never saw action.

But the Dutch-based E-boats were more numerous in the last six months of war than they had ever been, and only lack of fuel eventually stopped them. At the end of 1944 2nd, 4th, 5th, 9th and 10th Flotillas _ up to fifty E-boats (though several were out of action) were based at Den Helder, Ijmuiden and Rotterdam, shifting from one to the other for various missions. The Royal Navy now had enough well-armed and radar-equipped craft to patrol QZS 581 more thoroughly than any shipping route had ever been. On the night of 22/23 December the Harwich destroyer *Walpole* and frigates *Curzon, Riou* and *Torrington*, together with Ostend MTBs, were therefore able to corner three E-boats near the East Hinder and saturate these unfortunates with 2-pdr and Oerlikon fire. All three (plus a non-existent fourth) were claimed sank _ in fact one got away and S 185 and 192 were lost. But there *were* Allied losses on this Scheldt route, totalling twenty ships in the six months November 1944-April 1945 inclusive.

On 13/14 January 1945 and the succeeding night the E-boats carried out their biggest single operation since 1943, sowing mines in many scattered parts of the Nore Command. From Harwich the destroyer *Cotswold*, corvette

---

*having been tested at Chatham Dockyard, this may nowadays be seen in the Imperial war Museum, Lambeth.
+On the night of 12/13 January 1945 some even went up the River Waal and into Allied territory in an attempt to blow up the Nijmegen Bridge.

MINOR LANDING CRAFT TRAINING IN BRIGHTLINGSEA CREEK
Upper photo: Officers of the original 7th Raiding Craft Flotilla. L to R; Sub-Lt(E) Hollick, Sub-Lt Liley, Lt Treadwell, Lt-Cdr Corke, Sub-Lt Foreman (all RNVR) *(Hollick)*
Lower: LCAs from HMS *Helder* moored at James & Stone's Shipyard, Brightlingsea, in June 1944. (Mersea Island in the distance). *(Gray)*

Above: **HDML 1383 in Harwich Harbour, with frigate** *Curzon* **in the background.**
(IWM)

Below: **German "Biber" midget U-Boat captured off the North Foreland in Nov, 1944.** *(IWM)*

THE LAST ELEVEN MONTHS

Guillemot and frigates *Curzon* and *Seymour* were all engaged. Two sizeable merchantmen were sunk _ the Dutch *Lisetta* close to Margate and the *Dalemoor* in the Dudgeon area, on the edge of Humber Sub-Command. Two more later went down near the Dudgeon _ the Norwegian SS *Carrier* on the 19th, and the Grimsby trawler *Arley* on 3 February.

In the early hours of both 16 and 23 January the E-boats came right up to the Thames Estuary for the first time, and on both nights were engaged at five miles range by the AA guns of Tongue Sand Fort firing at low elevation by radar _ also unprecedented. On the first occasion LST 415 was torpedoed, though not sunk, with six dead _ and another rating was later killed when some of her ammunition exploded as it was being unloaded at Tilbury. On the second the Fort claimed a sinking, though German sources maintain that S 199 was sunk by a collision with HMS *Mantis*'s MTB 495, not an artillery shell: eighteen Germans were captured and taken to Chatham. *Guillemot* and *Seymour* had also been in this battle.

Soon there was another unusual incident. On the 24th ML 153 claimed to have sunk a midget U-Boat off Yarmouth: three days later a Trinity House vessel found a lieutenant and a petty officer, the entire crew of "Seehund" 303, on Scroby Sands (only two miles offshore), and the local HSL 2507 brought them in to base. That same night minelaying E-boats came near to Orfordness without causing sinkings.

The enemy now threw a full-sized U-Boat into this campaign, for the first time in nearly five years. U 245 shuttled back and forth between Heligoland, the lonely island fortress off the Elbe mouth, and NF 1 Buoy, twenty miles off Ramsgate, sinking a large merchantman on 6 February and an LST on the 22nd.

On this second night E-boats staged their first successful torpedo raid on an East Coast (in this case FS) convoy for a year, sinking two colliers, *Goodwood* and *Blacktoft*, near Smith's Knoll.

The following day, the 23rd, saw one striking victory for each side. Off Walcheren the Sheerness-based 32 ML Flotilla destroyed three "Biber"s (and a fourth succumbed to Army guns on Walcheren). And near the Dudgeon the French destroyer *La Combattante* was sunk by an underwater explosion, and with the heavy loss of sixty-five lives, making it the worst marine incident in the Nore Command since 1942.*Attributed at the time to one of the E-boat mines which had recently sank three other ships nearby, *La*

---

*Those lost included Capitaine de Corvette J Pepin-Lehalleur and two British signallers. 117 survivors crowded onto MTBs 763 and 770.

THE LAST ELEVEN MONTHS

Combattante's sinking was later discovered to have been due to a torpedo from Leutnant-zur-See Sparbrodt's Ijmuiden-based "Seehund". This was (though quite coincidentally) a revenge victory for the German Navy, and former U-Boat chief, Admiral Dönitz, since the French destroyer had taken his son's life when she sank two E-boats in the Channel the year before.

Five nights later the Harwich (16th Flotilla) destroyer *Cotswold* and frigate *Seymour* once again intercepted E-boats off Ostend, and sank S 220, capturing her whole crew of twenty-six.

In the concrete pens at their Dutch bases the E-boats were in practice immune from normal bombs, for the Allied Air Forces calculated that destroying these shelters would take hundreds of direct hits, eroding them bit by bit and taking too many bombers away from their other duties. Only one Allied squadron, the RAF's famous 617 (the "Dambusters"), based at Woodhall Spa (between Lincoln and Boston) was equipped to attack these pens, and it was mostly preoccupied with V-bomb sites, finishing off the *Tirpitz*, and targets in Germany. In daylight, on 24 August, and 15 and 29 December, 1944, however, it raided Ijmuiden _ and on the third occasion also Waalhaven, Rotterdam: each time about twenty Lancasters dropped one $5\frac{1}{2}$-ton "Tallboy" bomb apiece. Only the 15 December raid was effective. At Ijmuiden lumps of concrete collapsed over the entrances of four of the ten pens, another, fifteen-foot, hole was punched through the roof, and S 193 was wrecked. At Waalhaven the central and southern sections of the shelter building were heavily damaged and a section of roof forty yards long caved in. But it was later learned that 9 and 10 E-boat Flotillas had abandoned Waalhaven in November, dispersing to various unobvious spots along the Rotterdam river and canal system.

On 14 and 21 March 1945 the US Eighth Airforce lent a hand, raiding the Ijmuiden pens with rocket-boosted three-ton "Disney" bombs. This port was again heavily bombed by the RAF early in April (up to fifty-five planes at a time), but the target was less the E-boat pens than shipping outside, which the Germans seem to be planning to use as blockships in the event of the Allies reaching and trying to use the harbour.

At sea, between 12 and 15 March, the Germans lost at least a dozen midget submarines (four of them to Felixstowe MTBs) and three Linsen in suicidal raids on the Scheldt. That month midget U-boats and E-boats both raided close to the East Coast of England, and off Suffolk the first ships were

THE LAST ELEVEN MONTHS

lost since before Normandy. The merchantman *Taber Park* was torpedoed by a "Seehund" twelve miles off Southwold on 12 March, with twenty-eight dead. On the night of 19 March E-boats sank two cargo ships, the *Rogate* and *Crichtown*, off Corton and Aldeburgh respectively, killing twenty-two merchant seamen. They also mined around H2 Buoy, off the Humber. Three nights later, during a repeat of this second operation, S 181 and 203 were sunk and Korvettenkapitän Opdenhoff, commanding 2nd E-boat Flotilla, was killed by strafing Mosquitos: it was he who had nearly sunk Mountbatten's destroyer *Kelly* five years earlier. On the 23rd a "Seehund" sank SS *Newlands* off Westgate (Kent), the nearest any U-boat ever came to the

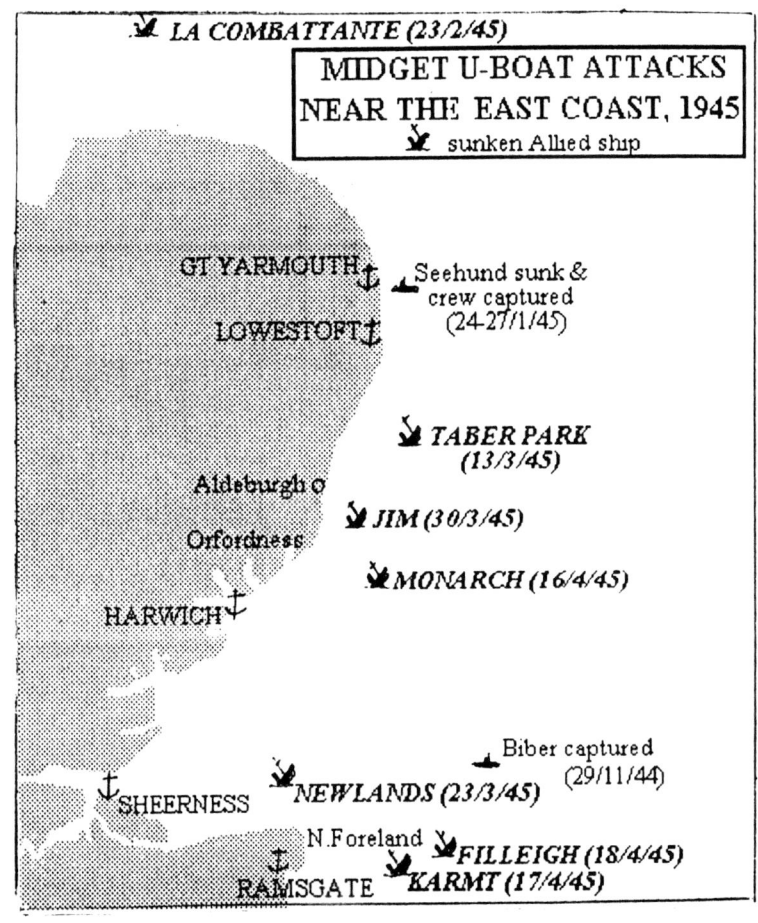

THE LAST ELEVEN MONTHS

Thames. On the 30th *Jim*, another small cargo vessel, was sunk near the Aldeburgh Light Float by the same type of raider. Four days earlier, near the Scheldt, another one had so badly damaged the Harwich corvette *Puffin* below the waterline that it proved easier to scrap than repair her.

As late as April the E-boats and small U-boats continued to strike at the Scheldt and East Coast routes. On the 6th, at Smith's Knoll, HMS *Midge*'s MTB 5001 was sunk by an E-boat, while 494 collided with another, overturned, and drowned all but three of her crew. But on the other side S 176, 177, 202 and 703 all sank as a result of collisions with each other or British boats: they seem to have indulged in a desperate spate of ramming. In the last year or two of war the Germans had built more E-boats than ever before (the same was true of U-boats, planes and tanks), but they were now losing them at an unprecedented rate. Total wartime E-boat losses in the

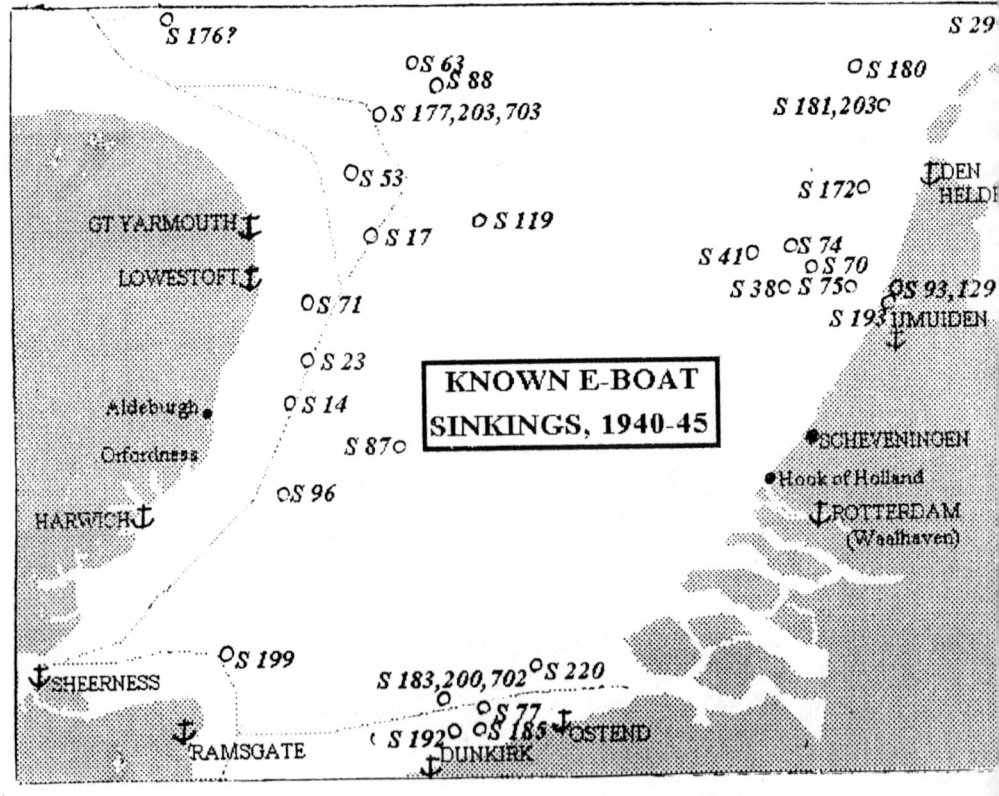

THE LAST ELEVEN MONTHS

North Sea were about thirty-six _ the same number as British Coastal Forces' losses. Of these E-boats fifteen were sunk near the East Coast of England. Of the thirty-six fourteen were lost to gunfire, ten to air attack, nine to ramming or collisions, two to mines and one to capture.

The Germans struck their last blows towards the English coast with small submarines. A handful of small, modern, turbo-electric, Type XXIII U-Boats, intermediate in size between full-sized raiders and the midgets, and designed to operate round the British Isles, had just entered service. On 16 April the first of these, U 2324, approached the Shipwash area, off Felixstowe. She torpedoed, and blew in half, the British cable ship *Monarch*, which, along with her attendant barge *Leslie*, had just arrived at Harwich to restore a telephone link between Suffolk and Holland. Three men were lost and the remaining sixty-eight rescued by RML 544 _ constituting over half of all those saved by Felixstowe's 69th RML Flotilla. The wreck sank after the minesweeper *Jasper* had made a brief bid to tow it. This was the final sinking on the East Coast proper, though over the next two days three large Allied merchantmen were lost on QZS 581, one to a mine, one to a midget U-Boat, and one to another Type XXIII. Yet all these losses made scarely a dent in British maritime power.

And already the armies of the Western Allies were thrusting into the heart of Germany on supplies the bulk of which had come via Antwerp. Without that port such a decisive offensive might not have been possible. The Nore Command, in opening and safeguarding the Scheldt route, had therefore struck its most effective blow of either world war.

For some time the East Coast had had the happy feeling that the war was receding from it, like a thunderstorm fading into the distance. Since the end of 1944 Army units other than AA had been packing up and moving out _ for instance the Dutch Brigade at Harwich, and the Czechs at Southend, had gone to fight on the Continent. The Home Guard had disbanded that December, each member handing in his greatcoat, helmet and rifle, and receiving a letter of thanks "from the King". Some beaches were re-opened to the public, as the huge job of clearing mines, obstacles and barbed wire began. Early in 1945 inshore pleasure sailing was permitted in some areas. In April no more V-weapons came over, and the mighty AA at last fell silent.

But some dramatic signs of the desperation "on the other side" were

THE LAST ELEVEN MONTHS

now being seen at East Coast ports. On 10 April sixteen Dutchmen and four Soviet Georgians came into Yarmouth on the *Joan Hodshon*, the lifeboat from Den Burg, on the Dutch island of Texel, off Den Helder. They told a nightmare story. Texel was garrisoned by Georgians who had been captured from Stalin's Red Army, served as allies of Germany, but recently mutinied. For five nights and days there had been savage slaughter, as the rebels killed their German officers, the Wehrmacht poured 1,800 artillery shells onto the island and the SS stormed in to massacre the surviving Georgians and several of their Dutch sympathisers. Some 1,500 people, of three nationalities, had died. Escaping the mayhem, sixteen local Dutch Resistence men, led by one van der Kooi, and four of the Georgians, had taken out the lifeboat, hoping to use a radio to ask England for help. When the set refused to function, they had steered the boat all the way over to the coast just east of Cromer. Van der Kooi had swum ashore to contact the authorities, and the Navy had then escorted the *Joan Hodshon* into port. The story did not have a pretty ending, for the desperate pleas of the refugees, and of the Dutch leaders in England, did not move the Allies to mount any relief expedition to Texel (to be fair, it would in any case have been too late).

Meanwhile there were rumours that the Germans were about to seize the Danish fishing fleet in order to help evacuate their isolated garrison in Norway, and from 8 April the Esbjerg "Freedom Committee" began to organise their escape to the Dogger Bank, whence Grimsby MLs brought them into the Humber. In the first two or three weeks only a few arrived, but then it seemed that the whole Danish fleet was swarming over _ some were still coming in when Germany surrendered. The Danes seemed keener to trade than to join the Allies, for they brought tons of fish, the profits from which were spent on cigarettes, alcohol and cocoa in the Grimsby shops.

With the major German industrial towns encircled and captured that month, the RAF night bombing offensive was called off. The fifteen hundred Lancasters and Halifaxes in Yorkshire, Lincolnshire and the Fen Country were seen over the East Coast in broad daylight, flying out to new objectives just across the North Sea. On the 18th nearly a thousand of them dropped over 4,400 tons of bombs on Heligoland, and a week later about half that number bombed the Frisian island of Wangerooge _ in avenging the losses suffered by Bomber Command over "the Bight" in 1939 the strategic aim was to eliminate the enemy radar stations and "W-Boat" bases across the sea

THE LAST ELEVEN MONTHS

approaches to the Weser and Elbe. In two days two tiny islands (each containable several times over within Canvey or Mersea) received a greater weight of bombs than that recorded in the whole of East Anglia throughout the war! Bremen and Hamburg received their last raids on the same scale, to soften them up for capture by Montgomery's troops.

Since the end of 1944, to serve their war effort, and in retaliation against local strikers and resisters, the Germans had stripped Holland of transport and food. That winter 18,000 Netherlanders had died of hunger and cold, and people had been eating tulip bulbs. On the last day of April, the day Hitler killed himself, the Allies and the German garrison in Holland agreed to a truce, and to the mass air-dropping of food by the British _ the operation Bomber Command called "Manna". The same planes were then shifted to "Operation Exodus", the airlifting to England of sick prisoners from the liberated Nazi camps.

With the Dutch truce and the fall of the German North Sea ports the remaining enemy shipping, merchant and naval, retreated to the Baltic. On 3 and 4 May the North Coates Beaufighters rampaged up the Kattegat and Belts, sinking five U-Boats among other craft.

On the English East Coast an atmosphere of winding-down and anti-climax was already obvious when news was received on 5 May that the German armed forces in Holland and Denmark as well as North West Germany had surrendered to Montgomery on Lüneburg Heath. Three days later came "VE Day", the overall German surrender in Europe. A carnival mood spread, and everywhere, regulations or not, blackout curtains were torn down and pub licensing hours went by the board.

The following day the Sheerness, Harwich and Yarmouth minesweepers left to clear channels to the Dutch ports. The latter were first entered from the landward side, by British and Canadian troops and naval officers. Crowds of emaciated but cheering Dutch civilians, clutching orange and Union Jack flags, flowers, and some of the rations that had just been air-dropped, thronged the streets. At the bases from which the Germans had for five years raided the East Coast of England the scene was grim and desolate. Amsterdam's Schipol Airport, and the other airfields, were littered with abandoned and burned out planes and vehicles. At Rotterdam a mass of E-boats lay silent, but under German guard, in the huge Waalhaven basin, while, opposite, a weed-choked desolation marked the city centre bombed

THE LAST ELEVEN MONTHS

by the Luftwaffe in 1940. At the Hook the W/T station stood empty, and had evidently been looted. At Ijmuiden there was no sign of the E-boats with which it had been more identified than any other German base, though three "Seehunde" were lashed to a quayside. Beside the Herring Harbour the Allied visitors marvelled at the vast bomb craters and acres of rubble around the concrete E-boat pens, which stood remarkably intact.

On Sunday 13 May there were big combined service parades at all the East Coast naval towns, followed by church thanksgiving services and municipal tea parties. That afternoon the public were gathering on Harwich and Felixstowe sea fronts. Lt-Cdr Hodder DSC RNVR, Senior Officer of HMS *Beehive* MTBs, led in ten of his craft escorting two E-boats. Aboard the MTBs were many famous Coastal Forces officers, such as Lt-Cdr Peter Scott, son of the Antarctic explorer, and writer, broadcaster and ornithologist. Aboard the E-boats, which had come from Rotterdam and been met at South Falls, were Admiral Bräuning (commanding the German Navy in Holland), Korvettenkapitän Fimmen (commanding 4th E-boat Flotilla), and Korvettenkapitän Rebensburg (Operations Officer at the E-boats' Scheveningen HQ, and in command of S 104 when she sank *War Mehtar* off Yarmouth three and a half years before). They had come to surrender charts of the German North Sea minefields, as stipulated by Admiral Tovey, C-in-C Nore. Bräuning was said to be curt, scowling, but punctiliously correct. Peter Scott wrote:

> "With some difficulty we persuaded the Germans to fall their crews in on deck as they entered harbour, where a great crowd of spectators was assembled on all the piers and jetties. The E-boats berthed alongside Hodder's boat, a manoeuvre which, with their large screws and considerable astern power, was carried out at most spectacular speed in the small basin".*

The Coastal Forces campaign had ended where it began _ in Felixstowe Dock. Bräuning was introduced to Beehive's Senior Officer, Lt-Cdr McCowen RNVR. Rear-Admiral Watson, the Harwich FOIC, had sent his "barge", the motor-boat *London Pride*, and this ferried the German officers across to Parkeston, where they handed over their charts. Later one of the E-boats, and a captured Linsen towed in on 11 June, were opened to the public

---

*Scott.

Left: **Shotley naval cemetary, looking towards the Orwell. Most of the dead here are from Harwich warships.**

Below Left: **Admiral Bräuning's E-boat arriving at Felixstowe Basin from Rotterdam (13 May 1945) _ Harwich in the left distance and Shotley on the right.** *(IWM)*

FELIXSTOWE BASIN, 13 MAY 1945
Above: Admiral Bräuning boarding the *London Pride*, the FOIC Harwich's "barge", for his journey over to Parkeston. Note British Power Boat MTBs in the background. *(HMS Dauntless Collection)*
Below: The E-boat which had brought Bräuning and his party lying alongside a British D-Type MTB (right). *(IWM)*

THE LAST ELEVEN MONTHS

at Felixstowe, while a U-Boat came up to London and another E-boat was exhibited at Lowestoft.

The armed forces took another year and a half to disappear from the East Coast, or to retreat back to the bases they had populated before 1939. Naval FOICs were downgraded to NOICs and NOICs to RNOs. Plot rooms closed. Redundant warships were laid up at Harwich in a Reserve Fleet. Such light craft as the Coastal Forces' motor boats, landing craft, and MMSs, had not been intended to be permanent additions to the Fleet, and were soon paid off or scrapped. Names like *Badger, Beehive* and *Beaver* forever vanished. The many small shipyards, like those at Burnham, Brightlingsea and Oulton Broad, continued to build and equip vessels for operations against Japan, such as the D-type MTBs converted into Long-Range Air-Sea Rescue Launches, but then began to revert to civilian work. The Humber and East Anglian fishing fleets returned and found rich catches after six years of underfishing. Half the airfields and radar stations closed, though some remained for many years on the reserve, with their great towers, bunkers and runways apparently permanent features of the landscape. The one great and urgent naval operation was mine clearance _ for which a huge fleet led by the Harwich FOIC (turned NOIC) Captain T W Marsh, was largely responsible. There were ten times as many mines (of both sides) to be swept in peacetime as were swept throughout the war, and for years anyone in charge of a North Sea vessel of any size carried minefield charts as a life and death precaution. But if a host of memories and visual reminders lingered on, the reality of war itself evaporated as quickly and completely as a dream.

Unfortunately within a generation most of the peacetime assets of the same coast were fast fading as well. Economic and technological changes have done to the London Docks, the shipyards, the fishing fleets, the sailing barges, the paddle steamers and the lightships, what the Ju 88s and the E-boats failed to do.

The East Coast's part in the Second World War was not particularly well documented, nor is it well remembered today. The story contains a great deal of humdrum routine, such as garrison duty and minesweeping, while what was spectacular by local standards cannot compete with the dramatic highlights selected by historians and the media from a *world* conflict. There

THE LAST ELEVEN MONTHS

was a gap between the memories of local civilians and those of the wartime service "guests". Many of the former were evacuated and only saw the first part of the East Coast war: others spent their war away with the forces. Conversely, practically all the wartime armed forces' residents left for distant homes shortly after the coming of peace. However much we may find battle and violent death credible in faraway places, they seem hard to conjure up when looking at the now peaceful coast of East Anglia. Did a ship, along with most of her crew, really sink there? Did a divebombing raid really happen here?

Most assuredly they did, and much else besides. There was almost daily (or, more usually, nightly) German air and naval activity against this coast. On average, for every day of the war, three aircraft dropped mines, two dropped bombs, and two (from both sides) crashed. A daily average of eight people, service and civilian, Allied and Axis, died. Two ships were lost a week. In the first half of the war these rates were far higher.

Yet, as an air and naval war, it had nearly all been strangely impersonal. Except when German airmen or sailors were captured the defenders never came face to face with their attackers. Even those paid to do so had only vague ideas about the shape of E-boats or particular types of German aircraft. No enemy soldier set foot on this coast, nor (for years) did any Allied soldier go the opposite way.

It was largely, though not entirely, a nocturnal war. From their beds or air-raid shelters the civilians heard the German bombers drone in and out, as well as our own. They heard the bombs and "ack-ack" thumping round the harbours. The same sounds awed the troops trudging the beaches and marshes in readiness for invaders, as they watched the eerie starshells and gunflashes from convoys fighting E-boats. Dawn brought gaping ruins in seaport towns, smoking crashed aeroplanes in the fields, leaning shipwrecks on the sea lanes.

If inky, blacked-out darkness was one universal local memory, another was biting, face-numbing, wind. It tore the North Sea into the ridges over which MTBs and air-sea rescue launches staggered, and which frightened Lt-Cdr Hichens more than the Germans. It beat rain or sleet onto ships' bridges and aircraft cockpit windows, and into gun embrasures. In the towering radar pylons it truly howled. It warned of more shipwrecks, barrage balloons torn loose, and vile stomachs for those forced to go to sea in it.

THE LAST ELEVEN MONTHS

So much for the physical setting: what of the human? Two kinds of person, both rare today, populate the historical imagination or the memory _ the RNVR gentleman-amateur officer, fresh from public school and yacht club, and the weather-beaten native fisherman, accustomed from boyhood to his Hull trawler. But this is misleading. There were also professional officers (though increasingly rare on this coast as the war progressed). Americans, Canadians, Australians, New Zealanders, Frenchmen, Dutchmen, Belgians, Norwegians, Poles and Czechs, and a few others even more exotic came to bandy such Anglicisms as "Yarmouth" or "Southend". And ashore and on the ground (though never afloat or in the air) were hordes of uniformed girls of all classes _ Wrens, WAAFs and ATS, the middle-class ones mostly at typewriters, radio sets or radar "scopes", the daughters of workers mostly cooking or cleaning. But the great majority of those who served here were male, working-class landlubbers, as unaccustomed to trawlers as to yachts. Within, and less frequently between, these categories there was camaraderie, for which this war is justly famous. Yet often this tended to have its "duration": to a surprising degree people as well as ships "passed in the night".

What had it all been for? Thousands of Britons and Allies had been rescued from the Germans, or from the sea. Invasion, in so far as it had ever been intended, was blocked both by sea and air. London and its surrounding war industries had been supplied. Sailors had been trained, and warships from submarines and corvettes to motor launches and rowing boats had been built, fitted or repaired _ and these had contributed to victory all over the world. No great battle had been wholly encompassed within the North Sea, but it had seen a large part of the mine and E-boat war, the Battle of Britain, the Blitz, and the invasion of Europe. This was a place where victory was forged.

APPENDIX A

NORE COMMAND NAVAL BASES

Sub-Command	Base Name	Date F'ded	Status Senior Officer	Location	Main Duties
NORE	Pembroke	1891	C-in-C Nore	Chatham	ACHQ, Dockyard, Personnel Depot
	Wildfire	1900	Cdre-in-C Sheerness	Sheerness	Destroyers, AP, Thames Defences, Dockyard
	Wildfire IV/ St Tudno	1939	Captain M/S	Queenboro	M/S
	Wildfire III	1943		Queenboro	CO
			RNO	Margate-Herne Bay-Whitstable	
	Duke			Gt Malvern	training
LONDON	Pembroke IV/ Yeoman	1939	FOIC London	London	AP, NCS, DEMS
	Pembroke III	1939		London	WRNS drafting
	Tower	1941	SOAP	London	AP
	Gordon	1941	Captain M/S	Gravesend	M/S
	St Clement	1943		Tilbury	CO
	Copra	1943		Chelsea	CO drafting
(SOUTHEND 1944-45 only)	Leigh	1941	NOIC & NCSO (Cdre-in-C, 1944-5)	Southend	NCS
	St Matthew	1943	RNO from 1939	Burnham	CO training
	Westcliff	1942		Westcliff	CO training
HARWICH	Badger	1939	FOIC Harwich	Parkeston	destroyers, subs, M/S
		1942	SNO	Harwich Town	NCS, harbour defence
	Epping	1941	Captain M/S	Parkeston	M/S
	Ganges	1899		Shotley	training
	Beehive	1940		Felixstowe	CF
	Bunting	1940	SOAP	Ipswich	AP
	Nemo	1940	NOIC (+RNO Frinton)	Brightlingsea	AP, ML equipping
	Helder	1942		St Osyth/ B'sea Creek	CO training
	Woolverstone	1942		Woolverstone	CO
			RNO	Aldeburgh-Felixstowe	river patrol
YARMOUTH	Watchful	1939	FOIC Yarmouth (from 1940)	Yarmouth	

	Name	Year	Role	Location	Type
	Miranda	1940	Captain M/S	Yarmouth	M/S
	Midge	1940		Yarmouth	CF
	Minos	1940	NOIC	Lowestoft	AP, M/S
	Martello	1941	Captain M/S & P	Lowestoft	AP, MS
	Minos IV/ 'Mantis	1941		Lowestoft	CF
	Pembroke X/ Europa	1939		Lowestoft	RNPS Depot
	Myloden	1943		Lowestoft	CO
			RNOs	Southwold	
				Wroxham	Broads Patrol
				Cromer	
				Hunstanton	
				King's Lynn	
HUMBER	*Beaver*	1939	FOIC Humber	Hull/Immingham	destroyers (1939-40), AP, M/S, NCS, MLs
	Beaver II	1939	NOIC (till 1940)	Grimsby/Immingham	
	Beaver III	1941		Immingham	CF
	Royal Arthur	1939		Ingoldmells (Skegness)	training
	Arbella	1943	RNO from 1939	Boston	AP, CO
			RNOs	Mablethorpe	
				Bridlington	

ABBREVIATIONS

AP=Auxiliary Patrol
CF=Coastal Forces
Cdre-in-C=Commodore-in-Charge
C-in-C=Commander-in-Chief
CO=Combined Operations
FOIC=Flag Officer in Charge
M/S=Minesweeping
NCS(O)=Naval Control Service (Officer)
NOIC=Naval Officer in Charge
P=Patrol
RNO=Resident Naval Officer
SOAP=Senior Officer Auxiliary Patrol

APPENDIX B
SENIOR OFFICERS OF NORE COMMAND BASES

C-IN-C NORE (CHATHAM)
Adm Sir H Brownrigg KBE CB DSO -12/39
Adm Sir R P-E-E Drax KCB DSO   12/39-3/41
Vice-Adm Sir G Lyon KCB   3/41-7/43
Adm of the Fleet Sir J Tovey
CGB KCB KBE DSO   7/43

CDRE-IN-C, SHEERNESS
Rear-Adm H R Marrack DSC (ret)   12/39-1/41
Rear-Adm J A Scott (ret)   1/41-10/42
Vice-Adm G A Taylor CMG CVO   10/42-

CAPTAIN M/S, SHEERNESS
Cap L C P Tudeney DSO DSC   11/39-6/41
Cap F S Smith   6/41-10/42
Acting Cap H G Hopper   10/42-7/45

SO, QUEENBOROUGH COMBINED OPS BASE
Cdr T Hughes DSC RNR   8/43-

FOIC LONDON
Rear-Adm E B Boyle VC (ret)   9/39-2/42
Rear-Adm Sir M Dunbar-Smith VC
KCB (ret)   2/42-7/45

SO, LONDON AP BASE
Cap A M Coleman DSC   6/40-

SO GRAVESEND
Cdr C S LOckhart 3/41-

SO TILBURY COMBINED OPS BASE
Cap W S Harman (ret)   9/43-

NOIC SOUTHEND (Cdre-in-C from 1/44)
Cap E H Martin   8/39-12/40
Cap J F Champion DSO (ret)   12/40-7/41
Cao R S Goff DSO   7-10/41
Cap J P Champion DSO (ret)   10/41-9/45

SO, COMBINED OPS BASE, WESTCLIFF
Cdr H D Tollemache   10/42-2/43
Cap G A Poignard (ret)   2/43-5/45

RNO, BURNHAM-ON CROUCH (& SO, Combined Ops Base, from 11/43)
Cap G R Dane (ret)   6/40-5/45

NOIC BRIGHTLINGSEA (& RNO Frinton & Captain ML from 11/43)
Vice-Adm G Campbell VC (ret)   6/40-7/40
Cap A Henniker-Heaton (ret)   7/40-5/42
Cap J P Farquharson DSO OBE (ret)5/42
Cap C C Bell   5-12/42
Cap J P Landon   12/42-5/45
Lt-Cdr Nosworthy (RNO)   5-9/45

SO, COMBINED OPS, B'SEA-ST OSYTH
Lt-Cdr P J Britten   7-9/42
Cdr V J Voelker   9/42-7/43
Cap E W Brookfield (ret)   7/43-9/44

FOIC HARWICH
Rear-Adm C F Harris   3/39-5/40
Acting Cdre F W H Goolden   5-7/40
Rear-Adm C F Harris   7/40-1/41
Rear-Adm F W H Goolden   1/41-2/42
Rear-Adm H H Rogers MVO OBE   2/42-3/44
Vice-Adm H T Baillie-Grohman CB   3-7/44
Rear-Adm F B Watson CBE DSO   7/44-7/45
Cap T W Marsh (NOIC)   7/45-10/46

SO, SHOTLEY TRAINING ESTABLISHMENT
Cap F W H Goolden   -5/40
Cap W H G Fallowfield   5/40-5/44
Cap G L D Gibbs   5/44-7/45

CAP M/S, HARWICH
Cdr C Coppinger DSC   8-12/39
Cdre C H G Benson DSO (ret)   12/39-3/40
Cdr H C Heaton (ret)   3/40-2/41
Cap D P Evans   2/41-10/42
Cap T W Marsh   10/42-5/45

SO AP, IPSWICH
Lt-Cdr G B Anderton RNVR	7-9/40
Cdr A J Cubison DSC	9/40-4/41
Acting Cdr L K Perrin RNVR	4/41-10/44

SO, WOOLVERSTONE COMBINED OPS BASE
Cap F W H Brookfield (ret)	12/42-7/43
Cap S E Holder (ret)	10-12/43
Cap R P Selby	12/43-3/44
Lt-Col W F Edds OBE RM	3-12/44

SO, FELIXSTOWE COASTAL FORCES BASE
Lt E M Thorpe	7/40
Cdr R H McBean DSO DSC	7/40-7/41
Cdr T Kerr OBE	7/41-3/45
Lt-Cdr D H E McCowen RNVR	3-7/45

NOIC LOWESTOFT
Cdr A L Sanders	7/40
Cap H H G D Stoker DSO	7/40-7/42
Rear-Adm G H Knowles DSO	7/42-1/45
Cap J Figgins CBE	1-2/45

SO, LOWESTOFT RNPS DEPOT
Cdre B H Piercey	9/39-4/41
Cdre D de Pass	4/41-3/44
Cdre R G Duke (ret)	3/44-6/45

CAPTAIN M/S (& P) LOWESTOFT
Lt-Cdr D R C Hodson	8/40-2/41
Lt-Cdr E C Hulton	2-4/41
Cdr A J Cubison DSC	4/41-7/42

SO, LOWESTOFT COASTAL FORCES BASE
Cap K M B L Barnard (ret)	8/41-5/45

SO, LOWESTOFT COMBINED OPS BASE
Lt-Cdr C O Pallin RNVR	10/43-10/44

FOIC, GT YARMOUTH
Adm Sir E Fullerton DSO KB MA	7/40-4/42
Vice-Adm A J L Murray	4-12/42
Adm Sir D B N North	12/42-7/45

SO, GT YARMOUTH COASTAL FORCES
Cdr E R Lewis DSO DSC	2-11/41
Cdr M A Brind (ret)	11/41-5/44
Lt-Cdr W D F B Muspratt	5-6/44
Cdr A C G Jolley (act, ret)	6/44-7/45

CAP M/S, GT YARMOUTH
Acting Cap St J Cronyn DSO	7/40-2/42
Cap C S B Swinley DSO DSC	2/42-7/4

SO, SKEGNESS TRAINING ESTABLISHM
Rear-Adm F A Buckley CB (ret)	9/39-9/43
Cap E Rotherham (ret)	9/43-6/4

RNO, BOSTON
Cap C C B Vacher DSO	10/40-3/
Lt-Cdr J Chacroft-Ancotts DSC	3/41-1/4
Cap K N Humphreys	1/44-1/4
Cap S E Holder (ret)	1-2/45

FOIC HUMBER
Rear-Adm A F Pridham CB	9/39-10/
Vice-Adm R V Holt CB DSC MVO (ret)	10/40-10
Rear-Adm C M Graham CB	10/42-7/

SO, IMMINGHAM & HULL
Cdr H Walker (ret)	11/39-4/
Cdr E L D Bartley (ret)	4/41-?

CAPTAIN M/S, GRIMSBY
Cap W Bardwell DSO MVO (ret)	12/40-

APPENDIX C
NAVAL VESSELS IN THE NORE COMMAND, 22 JUNE 1941*

CHATHAM

Monitor *Erebus*	Gunboat *Locust*	8 River Patrol Boats

SHEERNESS

21st Destroyer Flotilla	*Campbell, Cattistock, Cottesmore, Garth, Hambledon, Holderness, Mendip, Vanessa, Vesper, Vesper, Vivacious*
Convoy Leader	*Van Meerlant*
AA Paddle Ships	*Aristocrat, Balmoral, Goatfell, Golden Eagle, Jeannie Downs, Queen Eagle, Royal Eagle, Scawfell*
AA Ship	*BV 18*
Aux. Patrol MFVs	*Fezzara, Frieda, Marcelle Pierre, Ocean's Gift, Oscar Angelo, President Herriot*
Harbour Defence Drifters	*Constant Friends, Ocean Retriever, Ocean Toiler, Ocean Treasure, Peacemaker, Phyllis Rose, Receptive*
105th ML Flotilla	(HD)MLs 1001, 1010, 1021, 1024
Boomgate Vessels	*BVs 1, 2, 5, 10, Arrest, Coronatia, Fieldgate, Moorgate, Natal II*
Boom Defence Vessels	*Buckingham, Colline, Sarba*
Boom Tugs	*Kelpy, Kestrel*
Examination Vessels	*Danube V, Kaverne, St Katherine*
Air-Sea Rescue Boats	*Jamarna, Miss Littlehampton, Springtime, White Wings*
Channel Mobile Balloon Barrage	*Astral, Fratton, Gatinais, Haslemere, Pinguoin, Pintade, Sambur + Mammouth* (attached rescue tug) & 1 motor boat
Thames & Medway Balloons	35 drifters & barges

QUEENBOROUGH

Captain M/S's Boat	ML 221 Depot Ship *St Tudno*
M/S Trawler Group 2	*Force, Rudilais, Sovenus*
″ 3	*Bernard Shaw, Milford Prince, Wardour*
″ 17 (part)	*Earl Essex, Staunch*
″ 30	*Hermine, Peter Carey, St Olive, Windward Ho*
″ 120	*Arctic Hunter, Emilion, Saturn, Sunlight*
″ 121	*Ben Glas, Fentonian, Sanson, Tocsin*
″ 122	*Elsie cam, Liberia, Lylian, Malacolite*
″ 123	*Delphinus, Lucienne Jeanne*
M/S Drifters	*Arcady, Boy Philip, Devon County, Egeria, Forerunner, Gilt Edge, Girl Nancy, Monarda, Renascent, Solstice, Tilly Duff, Vernal, Welcome Home*
Motor Minesweepers	1, 8, 19, 39, 40

*includes warships out of action; excludes civilian-manned harbour craft.

Echo-Sounding Yacht	*Alouette II*
M/S Attendant Craft	MAC 1, *Seamaster*

HERNE BAY

Air-Sea Rescue Boat	*Dandy*

TOWER PIER, LONDON

River Patrol	10 motor boats

GRAVESEND

M/S Group 124 (LL tugs)	*Salvo, Servitor, Shako, Solitaire*		
LL Drifters	*Consolidation, Rosebud*		
M/S Skid-Towing Drifter	*Ascona*		
M/S Skid-Towing Launches	*Collette, General N, Girl Pat, Lichen, New Prince of Wales, Plumer*		
M/S Skid-Towing Tugs	*Ambi, Ansay, Bass, Isleworth Lion, Exertion, Roden, Seaby*		
Motor Minesweepers	14, 15, 16, 17		
Bomb Disposal Craft	*Bill Adams*	Echo-Sounding Yacht	*Myris*
Naval Control Service	2 launches		

GREENHITHE

River Patrol Depot Ship	*Worcester*	River Patrol	14 motor boats
Repair Craft	*Melissa*		

CLIFFE

River Patrol	5 motor boats

DAGENHAM

River Patrol	6 motor boats	Local Defence	*Josefina Ford*

TILBURY

River Patrol	9 motor boats	Repair Craft	*Thames Britain*
Mobile Wiping Drifter	*Ocean Guide*	4 DEMS motor boats	
2 Barrage Balloon Motor Bts	1 mine-searching launch		

HOLEHAVEN

7 River Patrol Boats	10 tugs

SOUTHEND

Naval Control Service	drifters *Lord Anson, Ocean Lover*, MFVs *Basil George, De Hoop* + 8 tugs, 1 steam launch, 1 motor boat

BURNHAM-ON-CROUCH

River Patrol	5 motor boats

BRIGHTLINGSEA

Aux.Patrol Drifters	*Eadwine, Evening Primrose, John Alfred, Lord Keith, Lord St Vincent, Reids, Restart, Rig, Silver Dawn, True Friend*
River Patrol	23 motor boats
Examination Yachts	*Giroflée, Laureate*
LL Drifters	*Jeannie Leask, Marie Elena*
Mine Recovery Drifters	*Fisher Boy, Jacketa, Sailor King*
Echo-Sounding Yacht	*Bystander*
Firefloat/Tug	*Portreeve*
Air-Sea Rescue Boats	*Aro, Eclipse, Primrose*
Accommodation Yachts	*Terminist, Aerolite*
3 Harbour	launches
Raiding Craft	T 10-18, 21, R 83, 84, 99, 101, 102, 104, 159, 160

HARWICH (& Parkeston Quay)

16th Destroyer Flotilla	*Cotswold, Eglinton, Quorn, Walpole, Whitshed, Windsor, Worcester*
1st A/S Strikg Force(Corvettes)	*Kittiwake, Mallard, Puffin, Sheldrake*
2nd A/S Striking Force	*Guillemot, Shearwater, Widgeon*
Small Attached Destroyer	*La Melpomene*
4th (Auxiliary) M/S Flotilla	*Albury, Elgin, Fitzroy, Kellett, Lydd, Pangbourne, Saltash, Sutton*
Minelayer	*Plover*
A/S Trawler Group 1	*Bassett, Sapphire, Turquoise*
" 11	*Lady Philomena, Sword Dance, Tango*
" 18	*Elsie Rykens, Neil Mackay, Paul Rykens, Peter Hendricks*
" 19	*Agate, Greenfly, Kingston Olivine, Lord Plender*
M/S Depot Ship	*Epping*
Captain M/S's Boat	ML 216
Paddle Minesweepers	*Duchess of Fife, Princess Elizabeth, Queen Empress*
30th M/S (Danlaying) Flotilla	*Shila, Shova, Signa, Silva, Spina*
M/S Trawler Group 4	*Carena, Caswell, Stella Leonis, Stella Rigel*
" 5	*Edwardian, Firefly, Lord Melchett, Red Gauntlet*
" 56	*Berberis, Marconi, Stour, Tehana*
" 58	*Edward Walmsley, Thomas Leeds, Tranio*
" 81	*Patti*
" 116	*Earl Kitchener, Raymont, Warwing, William Stephen*
" 117	*Etruscan, Exhayne*
" 119	*Avola, Charles Vaillant, Rosemonde, Tornado*
LL Drifters	*Sea Holly, Sweet Promise*

Torpedo Recovery Drifters	*Ocean Scout, Sun beam II*
Examination Drifters	*Dunedin, Hilda Cooper, H M Stephen*
3 Harbour Defence Launches	3 Harbour Duty Craft
Salvage Vessels	*Forde, Freija, Foremost 18, Dapper, Wrangler, Jeff, Mutt*
Rescue Tugs	*Kenia, St Mellons*

IPSWICH

Aux.Patrol Depot Yacht	*Freelance*
Aux.Patrol Trawlers	*Avalon, Destinn, Doonie Braes, Flandre, Gava, George Adgell, Jacinta, King's Grey, Liddock, Mary D Hastie, Norland, Strathelliott, Typhoon, Vidonia, Vindelicia, Warstar*
Aux.Patrol Drifters	*Mare, Nairnside, Sarah Hyde*
River Patrol	11 motor boats
6th ML Flotilla	MLs 145, 146, 147, 148, 149, 150, 151, 152

FELIXSTOWE

1st MTB Flotilla	MTBs 14, 17, 18
4th MTB Flotilla	MTBs 22, 28, 29, 32, 34
6th MGB Flotilla	MGBs 58, 59, 60, 61, 62, 63, 64, 65
Boom Defence Trawlers	*Alida, Astros, Ocean Eddy, Tunisian*
Boom Defence Tenders	4 light craft
Air-Sea Rescue	RAF HSLs 108, 124, 125, ARB *Roffen*
Barrage Balloon Vessels	22 miscellaneous

LOWESTOFT

M/S & P Depot Yacht	*Martello* Captain M/S & P's Boat ML 253
M/S Trawler Group 7	*Euclase, Lowther, Menslade, Osako*
" 8	*Ben Brachie, Ben Roy, King Emperor*
" 9	*Craigmillar, Star of Pentland, Sunspot*
" 80	*Moravia*
" 83	*Galvani, Glen Kidston* M/S Motor Yacht *Sunflower IV*
Aux. Patrol Trawlers	*Commander Holbrook, Commander Naismith, Controller, Evesham, Flying Admiral, Fort Rose, Helvetia, Niblick, Oystermouth Castle, Philippe, River Spey, Rugby, Semnos, Simpson, Strathgarry, Strath Maree, Strath Rannoch*
Aux. Patrol Drifter	*Aurilia*
Aux. Patrol Yachts	*Gula, Reurga, Umbriel*
River Patrol	8 motor boats
Examination Drifters	*Caprice, Woodbridge*
ARBs	*Diana III, Quicksilver*
5th MGB Flotilla	MGBs 16, 17, 18, 19, 20, 21

11th ML Flotilla MLs 187, 189, 190, 191, 193, 194, 214, 230

GT YARMOUTH

Captain M/S's Ship (Barge)	*Mehalah*
M/S Trawler Group 10	*Arkwright, Ben Erne, Milford Prince, Milford Queen*
" 11	*Contender, Irvana, Nogi, Solon*
" 13	*Blighty, Charles Doran, Clothilde, Cotsmuir*
" 14	*Cardiff Castle, Epines, Star of Orkney, Their Merit*
" 15	*Avon Stream, Madden, Princess Mary, Tamara*
" 31	*Bracon Moor, Carisbrook, Curtana, George Robb*
" 115	*Hartensia, Marano, Nadine, Orizaba, Valesca*
Unattached M/S Trawlers	*Cape Melville, Feasible, Silver Crest*
LL Drifters	*Genius, Golden News, Margaret Hyde*
Minesweepers' Tender	*Waldemar*
Aux. Patrol MFV	*Hektor Frans* Attendant MFV *Blangy*
Mobile Wiping Vessels	*Mon Plaisir, Rose Haugh*
Examination Drifters	*Millwater, Sir E P Wills, Ventose*
Air-Sea Rescue Craft	*Fast Lady, Theleba,* RAF HSL 112
5th MTB Flotilla	MTBs 42, 43, 44, 45, 46, 47, 48
1st ML Flotilla	MLs 100, 105, 106, 108, 110, 207, 222, 224
13th ML Flotilla	MLs 195, 196, 197, 198, 200, 201, 202, 204

WROXHAM (& Broads)

Broads & River Patrol 26 River Patrol Boats

BOSTON

Wash Patrol *Ouzel, Ro-Beda, Wing Cliffe*

GRIMSBY (& Immingham)

Minelayer	*Teviot Bank*
M/S Depot Ship	*Colonsay* Captain M/S's Boats *ML 211, Ombra*
Mine Destructor Ships	*Borde, Corfield*
M/S Trawler Group 16	*Alafoss, Loch Eribol, Loch Leven, Wellsbach*
" 17	*Kurd, Loch Alsh, Solomon*
" 20	*Elbury, Goth, Negro*
" 21	*British, Erith, Seamist, Withernsea*
" 40	*Akranes, Almadine, Sandringham*
" 72	*Courser, Meror, Rose of England*
" 110	*Ben Meidie, Rolls Royce, Varenis, War Duke*
" 111	*Cayrian, Gwenllian, Remexo, Strathborve*
" 112	*Aiglon, Bracon Dene, D W Fitzgerald, Recone*
" 113	*Drummer Boy, Fazenta, Kestonia*
Ungrouped M/S Trawler	*Laurel*

LL Drifters *Ben Tarbert, Castle Bay, George D Irvine, Ocean Lux, Rose Hilda*
Skid & Bottom-Sweep Drifters *Benarchie, Justifier, Silver Seas*
LL Maintenance Yacht *Sheila*
M/S Attendant Craft MAC 6   Echo-Sounding yacht *Alicia*
Aux. Patrol Depot Ship *Royal Charter*
Aux. Patrol Craft *Ampulla, Corcyra, Eroica, Everton, Foamcrest, Jennifer, Loch Moidart, Louis Botha, Mirabelle, Monique, Camille, Orvieto, Sangarus, Sheraton, Tartan, Tartarin, Tumby, Warland*
Harbour Defence Patrol Craft 2 Motor Boats
Examination Drifters *Arlette, Belton, Ferryman, Flixton, River Leven*
MFVs (Harbour Duties) *Alex Gabrielle, Jordaens, Better Hope, Chancellor, Clara, Enterprise, Peggy, Precision, Premier, Triumph*
Salvage Vessel *Nessus*   Netlayer *Pecheur*
Boom Defence Trawlers *Barslake, Basuto, Caliban, Count, Northlyn, Okino, William Hannam*
Boom Tenders 3 Motor Boats
Barrage Balloon Vessels 9 Drifters + 1 servicing craft
Air-Sea Rescue RAF HSLs 141. 144

APPENDIX D
EXAMPLE OF HARBOUR CRAFT AT A NORE COMMAND NAVAL BASE _ HARWICH, SEPT 1941

Vessel's Name	Vessel Type	Duties	Crew
London Pride	motor launch	Admiral's barge	3 RNPS
Ocean Scout	drifter	corvette tender	7 civilians
Sunbeam II	drifter	fleet M/S tender	7 civilians
Brightlingsea	ferry boat	destroyer tender	8 cvns (2 crews)
Willa	drifter	RNR (trawler) tender	?
Lorry	motor boat	HMS Beehive's boat	3 RN
Madeline	drifter	victualling tender	RNPS
Epping	motor boat	harbour ferry/trotboat	8 cvns (2 crews)
Plover	launch	Shotley boat	8 cvns (2 crews)
Beryl	motor boat	trotboat	3 civilians
Edme	motor boat	Ipswich launch	2 civilians
Lady Packard	motor boat	harbour launch	8 cvns (2 crews)
Pinmill	motor boat	Shotley Officer of Works Boat	2 civilians
Jeannie Mckintosh	drifter	for barge towing	9 civilians
C III	barge	storeship	2 civilians
Fraternity	barge	ammunition	2 civilians
Whitemay	diesel barge	oiler	4 civilians
Brown	dumb barge	ammunition	2 civilians
Gift	"	"	"
Mallou	diesel barge	"	4 civilians
Cormorant	motor boat	water	4 civilians
Ramore	motor boat	despatch boat	3 RNPS
Georgia III	launch	hospital boat	"
Ivy League	launch	general harbour duty	"
Mollie	launch	"	"
Steam Pinnace 141		Examination Service	11 cvns (shifts)
Steam Pinnace 674		NCSO's boat	"
Kenia, Bessie, Stronghold, Bheestie	tugs		civilians

APPENDIX E
TYPES OF GERMAN MINE LAID ON THE EAST COAST*

British designation+	German designation	basic type	laying method	charge in lbs.	attachmts	approx date of introdctn.
GA (Type A)	LMA (I)	ground	air or surface	650		Sep 1939
GB (Type B)	LMB (I)	"	"	1500		Dec 1939
GC (Type C)	LMB (II,III)	"	"	1500		Mar 1940
GD (Type D)	LMA (II,III)	"	"	650		Mar 1940
unidentified	RMA	ground	surface	1817		Sep 1939
"	RMH	"	"	1938		"
GG (Type G)	BM 1000	"	air(no para)	1550		May 1941
GM (Type M)	BMC	contact	surface	110	4 horns	Oct 1940
GO (Type O)	SMA	moored influence	U-Boat or surface	750		?
GP (Type P)	LMF	"	air	620		Aug 1941
GQ (Type Q)	FMC	contact	surface	90	5 horns	?
GR (Type R)	UMB	"	"	65/90	3-5 horns	?
GS (Type S)	TMB	ground	U-Boat	945/1230		Sep 1939
GT (Type T)	TMA	moored influence	U-Boat	460		Aug 1941
GU (Type U)	EMB	contact	surface	?	horns	Oct 1939
GV (Type V)	EMF	"	"	660	6 horns + antenna	Oct 1939
GW (Type W)	EMA	"	"	150	4 horns	July 1940
GX (Type X)	EMD	"	"	330	4/5 horns	Sep 1939
	EMD mit Ant.	"	"	"	4 horns + antenna	"
GY (Type Y)	EMC I	"	"	660	7 horns	"
GY*(" Y*)	EMC II	"	"	550	6 horns	?
GZ (Type Z)	EM?	"	"	180?	6 horns	Sep 1939
	Sp Boje C & D	explosive conical float	"	$1^{3}/_{4}$		Oct 1940

*ADM 199/129, 213/62   +The prefix stood for "German". Type GG was thus the same as Type G. Mines were also classified according to firing mechanism, as follows: "blue"=normal polarity magnetic (introduced Sept. 1939), "red"=reversed polarity magnetic (Apr. 1940), "blue-red"=bipolar magnetic (June 1940), "green"=acoustic (October 1940). Note also "Type DM" (Type D magnetic), "Type CAM" (Type C acoustic-magnetic), etc.

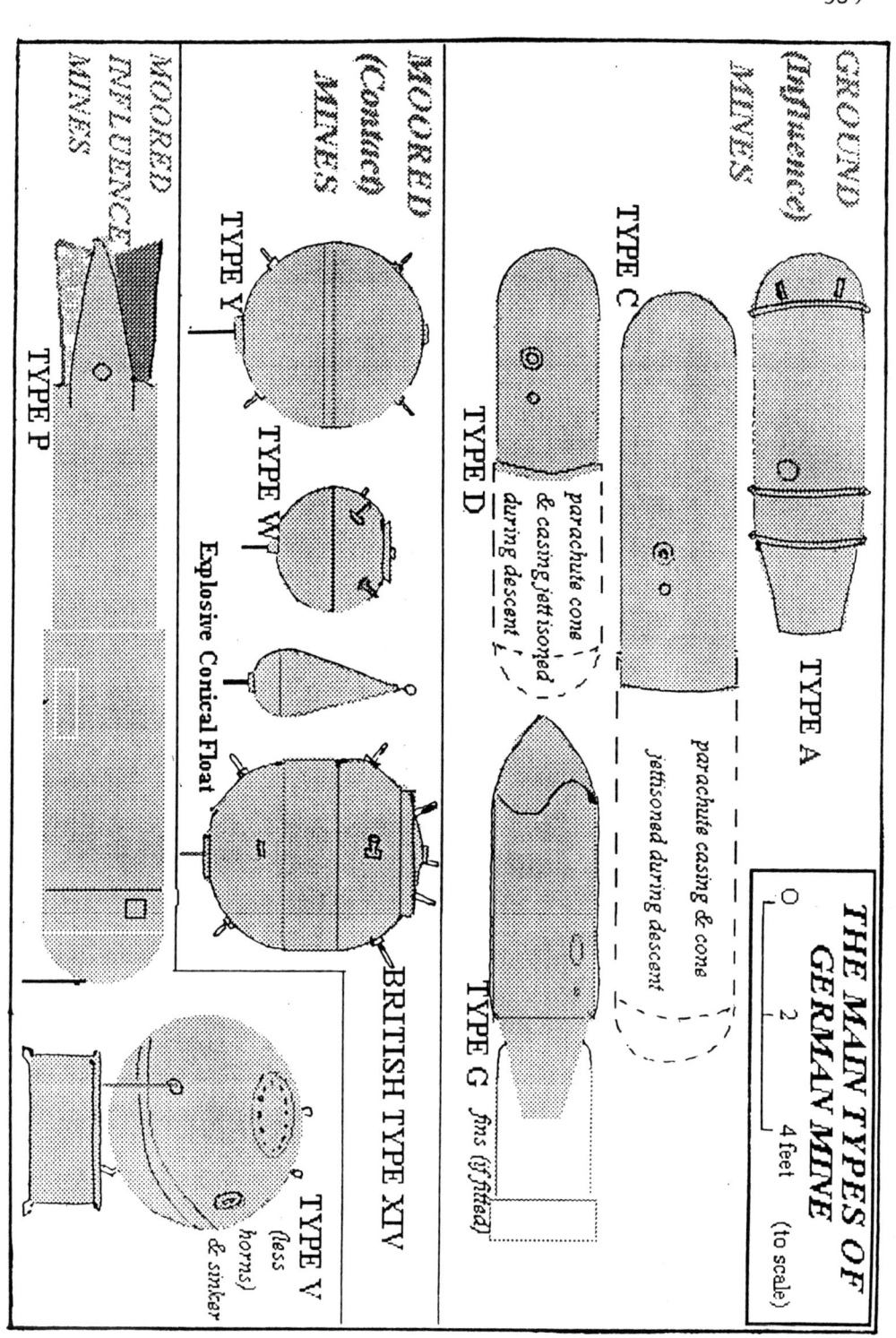

APPENDIX F
COMPOSITION OF AN EAST COAST CONVOY
FS 91 (January 1941)

PORT COLUMN				STARBOARD COLUMN			
Ship	GRT	cargo	destinatn.	Ship	GRT	cargo	destinatn.
POZNAN(Polish)	2017	coal	London	ARDENZA	933	copper	London
EGEE	2666	coal	London	DONA FLORA	1179	coal	London
BESTUM(Norw)	2215	timber	London	PARIS	1508	coal	London
DAGNY (Swed)	809	coal	London	CHRISTIAN KROGH	1192	coal	London
STANHOPE	2336	coal	London	MIERVALDIS	1265	coal	London
SWIFT	936	general	London	LWOW(Polish)	1409	general	London
KILDRUMMY	628	general	London	KODGE	536	general	London
DUNVEGAN HD	639	coal	Sheerness	THE SULTAN	823	spelter*	London
MANO	1418	coal	Ipswich	SOLLUND(Nor)	941	phosphates	Ipswich
SPIND(Norw)	2128	timber	Hull	MORLAIX (Fr)	420	grain	Ipswich
HEIEN(Norw)	995	pit props	Immingham	THYRA(Norw)	1655	pulp	Grimsby
LONDON II	1266	zinc	W Hartepl	BROUGHTY	504	general	Hull
MORAY FIRTH	540	ballast	Tyne	LEWANT(Pol)	1923	ballast	Tyne
				EASTERN COAST	1233	general	Tyne

APPENDIX G
ALLEGED CODE OF THE GERMAN PARACHUTISTS & FIFTH COLUMNISTS+

A	enemy attack	⌐ ⌐ ⌐	enemy on our right
b	enemy ready to attack	U	support necessary
N	attack beaten off	↑	ready to attack
I I	battery ready to fire	⼋	change target
ロ	encircled	⌐ ⌐ ⌐	enemy on our left
V V	effective firing	П	ammunition needed

*zinc ore.   +from War Diary of 18th Division, Norfolk (June 1940)

APPENDIX H
TYPES OF WARSHIP BASED ON THE EAST COAST

TYPE	DISPLCMT	LENGTH (feet)	MAX SPD SPEED(kts)	MAIN ARMT.	COMPLT.	MAIN DUTIES
cruiser	9100	591	32	12 x 6", TTs	700	invasion defence
monitor	7200	405	12	2 x 15"	315	"
lt cruiser	5200	506	32	6 x 6", TTs	450	"
AA cruiser	4200	451	29	8 X 4" AA	400	convoy AA escort
ESCORT DESTROYERS:						
Scott	1530	332	36.5	2-3 x 4.7"	164-183	flotilla leaders
V/W	1100	312	34	4 x 4"or 6pdr	125-134	convoy escort
Hunt	907-1087	264	25	4 x 4" AA or 5 x 2 pdr	146-168	"
FLEET DESTROYERS:						
A, B. E. F. G, H. I. J. K. Tribal	1350-1870	323-377	35-36	4-8 x 4.7", TTs	140-190	blockade & invasion patrol
Sloop	990-1190	266-282	16.5	2-4 x 4 or 4.7"	100	convoy escort
CORVETTES:						
Kingfisher	510-580	234-43	20	1 x 4"	60	convoy rescue
Flower	925	190	16	1 x 4"	85	Force L escort
frigate	1300	306	26	3 x 3" AA	200	anti-E-boat
SUBMARINES:						
S-class	670	209	15	1 x 3", TTs	40	raiding, recce.
H-class	410	171	13	TTs	30	"
minesweeper	590-875	162-245	16	2-3 X 3"/4"AA	60-85	Oropesa M/S
paddle ship*	300-700	120-200	10-15	1 x 12 pdr. AA	35-40	AA cover or M/S
trawler	200-650	140-164	12	1 x 3",12 pdr,4"	19-35	A/S, M/S, AP,
drifter	50-150	75-100	9	1 x 6 pdr, 3 pdr	12-16	exam.boom,M/R
yacht	25-90	40-80	10-20	1 x 6 pdr or 20 mm	4--13	AP, exam
ARB	5-60	20-70	12-27	rifles	2-4	air-sea rescue
MTB (stand)	22-47	60-73	25-39	2-4 TTs, MGs	9-13	raiding
" (D-Type)	95-105	115	27.5-31	4 TTs,1 x 2pdr	14-33	raiding, anti-E-bt
MGB(stand)	24-47	69-78	23-42	1 x 2pdr/20mm	12	anti-E-boat
" (C-Type)	72	110	26.5	2 x 2 pdr	16	anti-E-boat
A-Type ML	57	110	25	1 x 3 pdr	16-18	convoy escort,
B-Type ML	72	112	18			rescue, minelayg.

HDML	54	72	11.5	1 x 1 pdr	10	harbour defence	
MASB,MAC	19-23	60-70	23-25	MGs,depth chs.	9	anti-U-Bt, rescue	
LST	1625-3065	327-345	10-13	up to 12 pdr	86-104		
LCT	226-513	151-203	8-13.5	2 x 2 pdr,20 mm	12-13		
LCI	234	158	14	4 x 20 mm	24	D-Day invasion	
LCA, LCM,	9-50	41-50	7.5-10	MGs (mortars	3-6	(& training)	
LCP, LCV,etc.				on LCAs)			
LB	100-200	100-200	6-7	MGs	6 (24 on LBE)	D-Day supply barge	
MMS(stand)	165	119	11	MGs	20	LL & SA M/S	
" (later)	225	140	10	2 x 20 mm	21	"	
BYMS	207	135	14	1 x 3" AA	30	"	
MFV	50-200	64-97	7-9	MGs	4-11	harbour duties	

ABBREVIATIONS

AA anti-aircraft guns
AP Auxiliary patrol
ARB air-sea rescue boat (naval)
A/S anti-submarine
BYMS British Yard Minesweeper
HDML Harbour Defence Motor Launch
LBE Landing Barge Engineering
LCA Landing Craft Assault
LCI Lanidng Craft Infantry
LCM Landing Craft Mechanised
LCP Landing Craft Personnel
LCT Landing Craft Tank
LCV Landing Craft VBehicle
LST Landing Ship tank
HDML Harbour Defence Motor Launch
MASB Motor Anti-Submarine Boat
MFV Motor Fishing Vessel
MG Machine Gun (s)
MGB Motor Gunboat
ML (Fairmile) Motor Launch
MMS Motor Minesweeper
M/S Minesweeping
MTB Motor Torpedo Boat
TT Torpedo Tubes

APPENDIX I
SHIPS SUNK IN THE ENGLISH COASTAL WATERS OF NORE COMMAND*, 1939-45

Facts given are (in order): date, name of vessel, nationality (if other than British), gross registered tonnage (for merchant ships) or displacement (warships), cause of loss. For locations see maps. Warships given in capital letters.

Abbreviations: AC=air crash   B=bombed   Belg=Belgian   C=collision   D=Danish
Dut=Dutch   Est=Estonian   ET=E-boat torpedo   F=fire   Fin=Finnish
Fr=French   G=gunfire   Gk=Greek   Ital=Italian   Jap=Japanese
Lat=Latvian   M=mined   Nor=Norwegian   Pol=Polish   R=rammed
Sal=salvaged   SB=sailing barge   St=storm   Swe=Swedish   UT=U-Boat torpedo   Yug=Yugoslav.

1939

Sep: 10 Goodwood 2796 M; Magdapur 8641 M; 20 Phryne (Fr) 2660 M.

Oct: 14 Esterel (SB, sal), 67 St; Yampa (SB) 69 St; 17 Capitaine Edmund Laborie (Fr) 3087 M; 19 Deodata (Nor) 3295 M; 21 Orsa 1478 M; 22 Whitemantle 1692 M; 24 Konstantinos Hadjupikios (Gk) 5962 M; 29 Varanghelm 3618 M; 30 Juno (Dut) 1241 M.

Nov: 3 Canada (Dut) 11108 M; 4 Sig 1542 M; 13 BLANCHE (Harwich destroyer) 1360 M; Ponzano 1346 M; Matra 8003 M; 15 Woodlawn 794 M; 18 Blackhill 2492 M; Simon Bolivar (Dut) 8309 M; Carica Milica (Yug) 6371 M; 19 Rhuys (Fr) 2921 M; B O Borjesson (Swe) 1586 M; Torchbearer 1267 M; Grazia (Ital) 5857 M; 20 MASTIFF (Sheerness M/S trawler) 520 M; 21 Terukuni Maru (Jap) 11930 M; Geraldus 2495 M; GIPSY (Harwich destroyer) 1335 M; 22 Lowland 794 M; 23 Hookwood 1537 M; 24 Mangalore 8886 M; 26 Pilsudski (Pol) 14294 M; 27 Spaardam (Dut) 8857 M; 28 Rubislaw 1041 M; 29 Ionian 3114 M; 30 Sheaf Crest 2730 M.

Dec: 1 Greta (Fin) 1563 M; Dalryan 4558 M; Realf (Nor) 8083 M; 2 San Calisto 8010 M; 4 Horsted 1670 UT; 6 Parabos 3455 M; WASHINGTON (Yarmouth M/S trawler) M; 8 Corea 751 M; 10 Willowpool 4815 M; 12 Marwick Head 496 M; King Egbert 4535 M; 15 Ursus (Swe) 1499 M; Pearl (FV) 198 B; 19 City of Kobe 4373 M; 28 San Delfino (sal) 8072 M; 31 Box Hill 5677 M.

1940

Jan: 6 Eta (FV) 81 M; 7 Townsley 2888 M; 9 Oakgrove 1985 B; 10 Upminster 1013 B; 11 Keynes 1706 B; Croxton (FV) 195 B; 12 Granta 2719 M; VALDORA (Yarmouth M/S trawler) 251 B; Hammond Knoll Light Vessel B; 14 Traviata (Ital) 5123 M; 15 Newhaven (FV) 162 M; 16 Josephine Charlotte (Belg) 3310 M; 17 Asteria

---

including Humber area but excluding Dover. Excludes ships sunk and salvaged in London Docks.

(Gk) 3313 M; GRENVILLE (Harwich destroyer) 1485 M; 23 Onto 1333 M; 26 Herbert (SB,sal) 49 St; 29 Stanburn 2881 B; Tautmila (Lat, sal) ? B; E Dudgeon Light Vessel B; 30 Vareda 7216 B; Highwave 1178 B; Royal Crown 4363 (sal) B.

Feb: 2 British Councillor 7048 UT; Portelet 1064 M; 13 British Triumph 8501 M; 14 Giorgio Ohlsen (Ital) 5694 M; 17 Baron Ailsa 3658 M; 18 Ameland (Dut) 4537 ET; 23 BENVOLIO (Grimsby M/S trawler) 352 ; 24 Clan Morrison 5936 M; Jevington Court 4544 M; 29 Maria Rosa (Ital) 4211 M.

Mar: 1 Mirella (Ital) 5340 M; 9 Amelia Lauro (Ital, sal) 5335 B; Chevychase 2719 M; 11 Niritos (Gk) 3854 M; Halifax (FV) 165 M; Gardenia 3745 M; 16 MAIDA (Harwich M/S drifter) 107 M; 17 Capitaine Augustine (Fr) 3137 M; 18 Tino Primo (Ital) 4853 M; 28 Burgos (Nor) 3219 M.

Apr: 1 Walsingham (FV) ? C; 12 Velocitos (Dut) 197 M; 20 Hawnby 5580 M; 24 Stokesley 1149 M; 25 Margam Abbey 2490 M; 30 DUNOON (Yarmouth M/S) 710 M.

May: 10 Henry Woodall 625 M; 19 PRINCESS VICTORIA (Immingham minelayer) 2197 M; 22 Teaser (FV) 9 M; CHARLES BOYES 275 (Yarmouth M/S trawler) 275 M.

June: 1 Slasher (FV) 195 M; OCEAN LASSIE (Harwich examination drifter) 41 M; 4 EMILE DESCHAMPS (French M/S) 349 M; 5 Sweep II 145 M; 8 Hardingham 5415 M; 9 Empire Commerce 3857 M; 12 SISAPON (Harwich M/S trawler) 326 M; 14 MYRTLE (Sheerness A/S trawler) 550 M; 19 Golden Grain (SB, sal) 101 AC.

July: 3 Bijou (SB) 98 B; 4 Remembrance (FV) 7 M; 10 Waterloo 1905 M; 12 Hornchurch 2162 B; 15 Heworth 2855 B, Zbaraz (Pol) 2088 B; 24 FLEMING (Harwich M/S trawler) 356 B; 26 Haytor 1189 M; 27 STAUNTON (Brightlingsea AP trawler) 283 M; Westavon (sal) 2842 B; WREN (Harwich destroyer) 1120 B; 30 Clan Monroe 5952 M; Moidart 1262 M; 31 City of Canberra (sal) 7843 M.

Aug: 1-17 City of Brisbane 8006 B(x 2); 2 CAPE FINISTERRE (Harwich A/S trawler) 591 B; Wychwood 2974 M; 4 DRUMMER (Brightlingsea AP trawler) 297 M; 5 RIVER CLYDE (Harwich M/S trawler) 276 M; 11 EDWARDIAN (Sheerness M/S trawler, sal) 348 B; 12 WHITEMAY (Harwich oil barge) 79 C; 12 TAMARISK 540, PYROPE 295 (Sheerness M/S trawlers) B; 15 Brixton 1557 M; 16 Birmingham 5309 M; 21 KYLEMORE (Yarmouth netlayer) 319 B; 27 WHITE FOX II (Brightlingsea AP yacht) 23 F; 30 SH3 (hopper, sal) 389 B.

Sep: 4 Nieuwland (Dut) 1075 ET; Corbrook 1729 ET; New Lambton 2709 ET; Joseph Swan 1571 ET; Fulham IV 1562 ET; 7 Stad Alkmaer (Dut) 5750 ET; 7 Salacon (FV) 21 M; PLA tug ? 45 B; 9 DERVISH (Grimsby M/S trawler) 346 M; Minnie de Larrinaga 5049 B; 12 Gothic 2444 M; 20 Thames Balloon Lighter ? M; 24 MTB 15 (Felixstowe) 2: M; LOCH INVER (Ipswich AP trawler) 356 ET.

Oct: 4 Sirdar (tug) 34 M?; 5 Adaptity 372 M; 6 SCOTCH THISTLE (Lowestoft mine recovery drifter) 84 St; 9 SEA KING (Grimsby M/S trawler) 321 M; 11 AISHA (Grimsb AP yacht) 177 M; Thyra II (sal) 1088 M; Till (sal) 367 M; 12 RESOLVO (Sheerness M/ trawler) 231 M; 13 DANUBE III (Sheerness examination tug) 234 M; Reculver (Trinity House tender) 683 M; 15 Frankrig (Dan) 1361 M; MISTLETOE (Grimsby AP yacht) ? M; 17 Albatross (FV) 15 M; DUNDALK (Harwich M/S) 710 M; Hauxley 1505 ET; 19 VELIA (Ipswich AP trawler) 290 M; VENETIA (Sheerness destroyer) 1120 M; Aridity

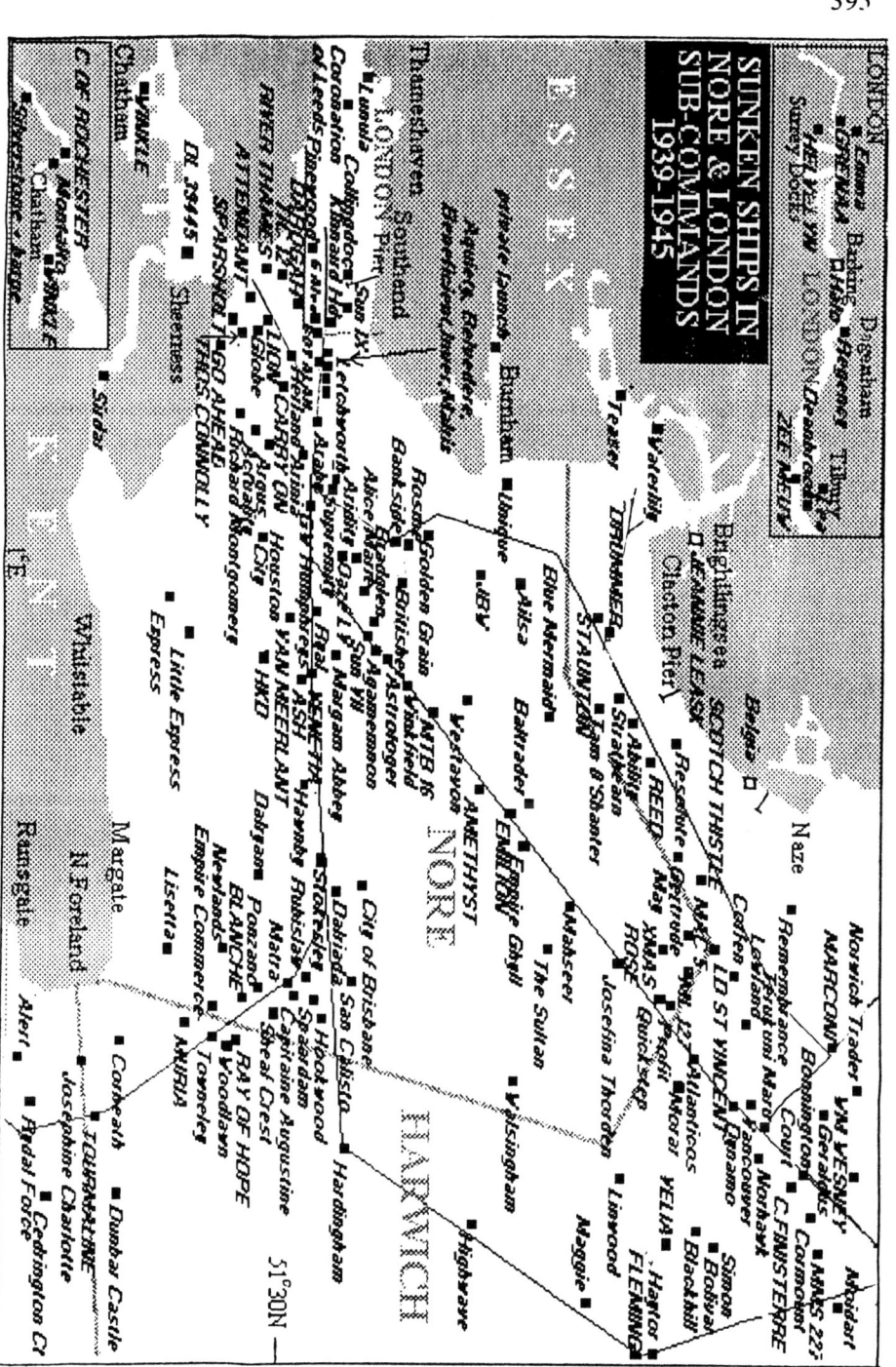

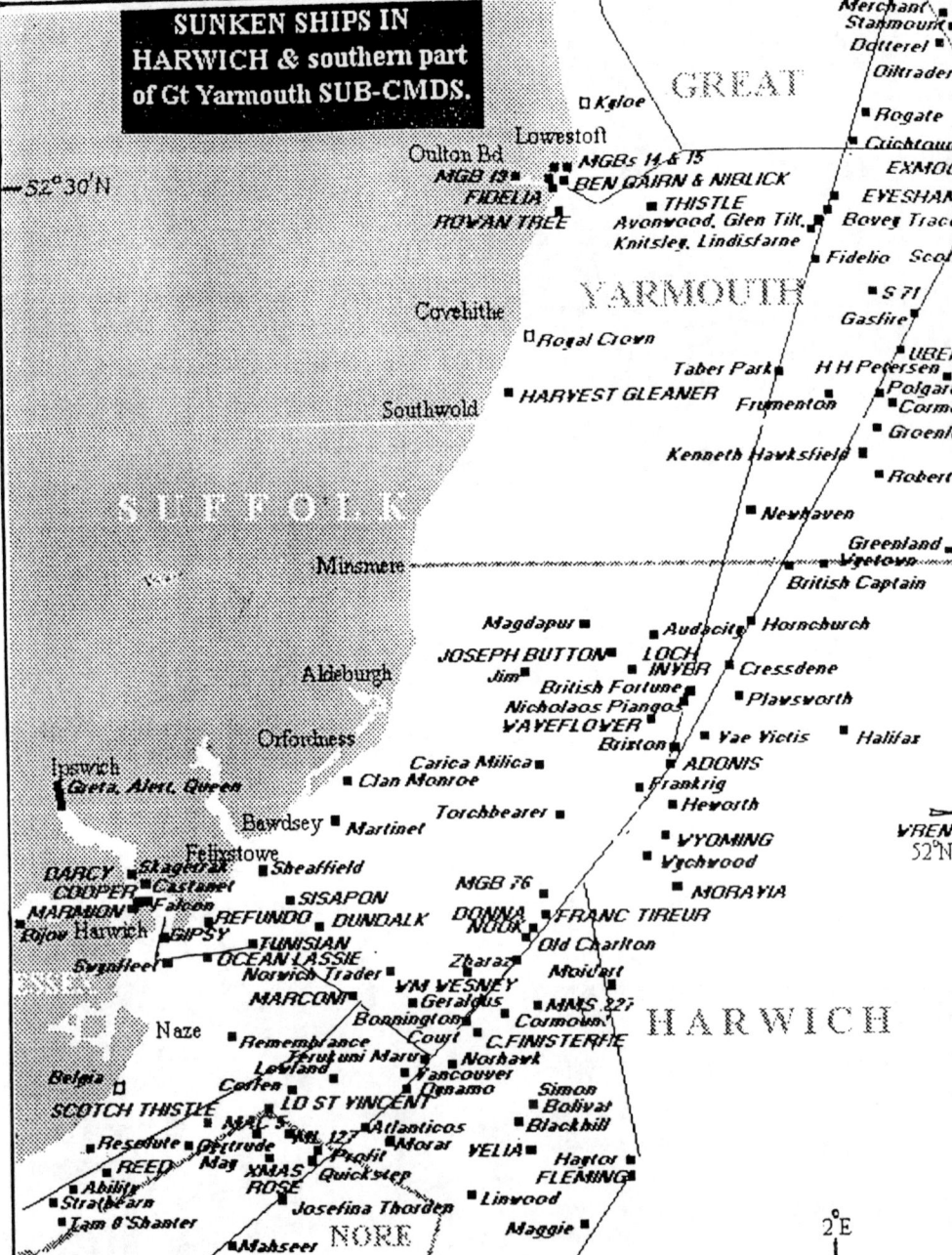

336 M; 21 WAVEFLOWER 368, JOSEPH BUTTON 290 (Harwich M/S trawlers) M; Houston City 4935 M; 25 Windsor 322, Carlton 207 (FVs) M; 28 Sagacity 490 M; HARVEST GLEANER (Lowestoft AP drifter) 96 B; Sheaf Field 2719 M; G W Humphreys 1500 M; ML 109 (Yarmouth) 57 M; MTB 16 (Felixstowe) 22 M.
Nov: 1 East Oaze Light Vessel B; TILBURYNESS (Sheerness M/S trawler) 279 B; Letchworth 1317 B; 2 Lea 168, Deanbrook 149 (PLA tugs) M; 7 Astrologer 1673 B; MURIA (Harwich rescue tug) 192 B; REED (Brightlingsea AP drifter) 99 M; WILLIAM WESNEY (Harwich M/S trawler) 364 M; Herland 2645 M; 8 Agamemnon (Dut) 1390 B; Actuosity ? M; Baltrader 1699 M; 11 STELLA ORION (Sheerness M/S trawler) 417 M; 12 Argus (Trinity House tender) 661 M; 14 RISTANGO (Sheerness boom trawler) 178 M; Buoyant 300 M; 15 Guardsman (tug) 120 M; 15 Blue Galleon 712 B; DUNGENESS (Lowestoft MP Trawler) 264 B; Amenity 279 M; 16 Dagenham (sal) 2178 M; 18 Ability 293 M; 19 AMETHYST (Sheerness A/S trawler) 627 M; Folda (sal) 1165 B; S 14 (E-boat) 92 R; FONTENOY (Lowestoft M/S trawler) 276 B; XMAS ROSE (Brightlingsea AP drifter) 96 M; 22 ML 127 (from Lowestoft builders) 73 M; 23 Ryal 367 M; GAEL (Grimsby AP yacht) 101 M; Thomas M 310 M; Alice Marie 2208 M; 25 ML 111 (Yarmouth) 57 M; KENNYMORE (Sheerness M/S trawler) 255 M; CONQUISTADOR (Sheerness M/S trawler) 224 C; 28 MANX PRINCE (Grimsby M/S trawler) 221 M; 29 CALVERTON (Grimsby M/S trawler) 214 C; CHESTNUT (Sheerness M/S trawler) 530 M.
Dec: 6 Supremity 554 M; Glencoe (SB) ?,St; 7 CORTINA (Grimsby M/S trawler) 213 C; 8 Actuality 311 M; 11 CAPRICORNUS (Sheerness M/S trawler) 219 M; 15 N C Monberg 230 ET; 17 CARRY ON (Sheerness balloon drifter) 93 M; THOMAS CONNOLLY (Sheerness boom trawler) 290 M; Inver 1543 M, Malrix 703 M; Beneficient 2944 M; Aquiety 370 M; Belvedere 809 M; 18 REFUNDO (Harwich M/S trawler) 258 M; 19 Arinia 8024 M; 21 Sun IX (tug) 196 M; TIC 12 (barge) 118 M; River Thames (tug) 88 M; 24 PELTON (Lowestoft M/S trawler) 358 ET; 25 Stad Maastricht (Dut) 6552 ET; 26 MTB 29 (Felixstowe, sal) 20 C; MAC 5 (Harwich) 18 M; TRUE ACCORD (Lowestoft AP drifter) 92 C; 27 Araby 4936 M; Kinnaird Head (sal) 449 M.

1941
Jan: 1 ATTENDANT (Sheerness oiler) 1016 M; 3 NEW SPRAY (Sheerness balloon drifter) 70 M; Pinewood 2466 M; 6 LION (Sheerness balloon barge-towing tug) 87 M; 7 H H Petersen (Danish) 975 M; 8 Strathearn (Trinity House tender) 683 M; 16 Spirality (sal) 360 C; 16 DESIREE (Yarmouth M/S trawler) 212 C; 19 Martha (SB) ? St; 20 Bonnington Court 4909 B; 22 LUDA LADY (Grimsby M/S trawler) 234 M; ST CYRUS (Hull rescue tug) 860 M; 23 S 14? (E-boat) G; 24 Corheath 1096 M; 25 OCEAN GAIN (Harwich wiping drifter, sal) 77 C; Meriones (sal) 7557 B; Belgia (Swe. sal) 1568 B; 27 DAROGAH (Sheerness M/S trawler) 221 M.
Feb: 2 The Sultan 824 B; 4 Gwynwood 1177 M; 5 TOURMALINE (Harwich A/S trawler) 641 B; 6 Thomas Deas (FV) 276 M; 8 Angularity 501 ET; 10 BOY ALAN (Sheerness M/S drifter) 109 C; 12 SEA ROAMER (Brightlingsea AP yacht) 23 F; 12

MTB 41 (Felixstowe) 33 M; 18 BONNY HEATHER (Harwich harbour launch) ? F; 19 Algarve 1355 ET; 22 Hull motor barge + lighter ? M; 25 EXMOOR (Harwich destroyer) ET; Minorca 1123 ET; Globe (SB) 46 M; 27 REMILLO (Grimsby AP trawler) 266 M; Martinet (SB) 99 St; Old Charlton 1562 B.

Mar: 1 ST DONATS (Grimsby M/S trawler) 349 C; 3 COBBERS (Lowestoft AP trawler) 275 B; 6 Silverstone (tug) ? + dumb barge M; Mexico (Nor) 3107 M; 7 Flashlight 934 B; Sun VII (tug) 202 M; DHOON (Harwich M/S trawler, sal) 325 B; 7/8 Dotterel 1385 ET. Kenton 1047 (driven ashore by E-boats), Boulderpool 4805 ET; Togston 1547 ET; Corduff 2345 ET; Norman Queen 957 ET; Rye 1048 ET; 12 Essex Lance 6625 (sal) N; Trevethoe 6507 ET; 14 Artemisia 6507 B; 14 Herport 2633 M; 17 Cormead 2842 B; 18 Daphne (Nor) 1950 ET; 20 Lindenhall (sal) 5248 B; Telesfora de Larrinaga (sal) 5780 B; Charlight (tug) ? B; Nailsea Meadow (sal) 4962 B; 8 PLA lighters ? B; HELVELYN (Sheerness paddle AA ship) 642 B; Joan Margaret (FV) 25 M; GLOAMING (Grimsby net vessel) 21 M; 21 Halo (sal) 2365 M; 22 JEANNIE LEASK (Brightlingsea M/S drifter, sal) 95 B; Dashwood 2154 M; 29 Grenaa (Nor) 1262 M; Emma (SB) 81 M; Kimberley (FV) 190 B; Oiltrader 5550 M; 31 LORD SELBORNE (Grimsby M/S trawler) 247 M.

Apr: 2 Fermain 759 M; 3 BAHRAM (Grimsby harbour defence bt) 72 M; Salvus (Nor) 4815 B; 6 Glenfinlas (sal) 7572 B; 8 Ahamo 8621 M; 9 Lunula 6363 M; Persia (tug, sal) 165 M; MARMION (Harwich paddle M/S, sal) 409 B; DARCY COOPER (Harwich examination drifter) 126 B; Falcon (Army launch) ? B; 10 Greta, Queen (firefloats) ? B; 11 OTHELLO (Grimsby boom trawler) 201 M; YORKSHIRE BELLE (Grimsby boom yacht) 56 M; 16 Aquila (tug) + 5 Hull lighters B; Profit (Nor) 1608 B; 17 Effra 1446 ET; Nereus (Dut) 1298 ET; Ethel Radcliffe (sal) 5700 ET; Montalto 623 B; 20 MISS VIRGINIA (Brightlingsea ARB) ? St; 22 Coronation of Leeds (barge) 87 M; Regency (tug) 200 M; 26 Murdock (sal) 336 ?; 28 Ambrose Fleming 1555 ET.

May: 1 WINKLE (Chatham dockyard boat) ? M; Sitona 1100 B; Trajan (Nor) 1300 B; 4 Royston 2722 B; BEN GAIRN (Lowestoft AP trawler) 234 M; NIBLICK (Lowestoft AP trawler) 255 M; 5 FIDELIA (Lowestoft block trawler) ? B; 7 SUSARIAN (Grimsby M/S trawler) 261 B; Waterlily (FV(12 B; Shamley (barge) + 12 Hull lighters & 1 LNER launch ? B; 8 THISTLE (Lowestoft examination drifter) 79 M; Thistle (FV) ? M; Welcome Home (FV) 38 B; JUSTIFIER (Grimsby M/S drifter, sal) 93 B; SILICIA (Grimsby M/S trawler) 250 M; UBERTY (Lowestoft AP drifter) 93 B; 9 QUEENWORTH (Grimsby mine destructor ship) 2047 B; 11 GYPSY (London AP accommodation yacht) 261 B; 12 Fowberry Tower 4500 B; 14 M A WEST (Yarmouth examination drifter) 96 B; 19 Winkfield (sal) 5279 M; Dixcove (sal) 3790 M; CITY OF ROCHESTER (Sheerness paddle M/S) 194 B; 27 EVESHAM (Lowestoft AP trawler) 239 B; Westavon 2842 M.

June: 3-4 FLEET TENDER C ? St & ET; 4 VAN MEERLANT (Sheerness AA convoy leader) ? M; 5 Lavinia (FV) 73 B; DIESEL LAUNCH 39445 (Sheerness) ? M; ASH (Sheerness M/S trawler) 530 M; 10 Royal Scot 1444 M; PINTAIL (Harwich corvette) 580 M; 13 KING HENRY (Lowestoft block trawler) 162 B; 15 Audacious (FV) 7 M; 18 Doris II (FV) 6 M; 21 Cormount (sal) 2841 B; Schieland (Dut) 2250 B; Kenneth Hawksfield 1546 M; Gasfire 2972 B; 22 Skum (Nor, sal) 1304 B; 23 NOGI (Yarmouth M/S trawler) 299 B; Hull Trader 717 ET; Trelissic 5625 ET; Dashwood 2154 B; 26 TRANIO Harwich

M/S trawler) 275 B; 27 FORCE (Sheerness M/S trawler) 327 B; Montferland (Dut) 6790 B; 28 Barhill 4972 B.
July: 1 DEVON COUNTY (Sheerness M/S drifter) 86 M; ELECTRA II (Lowestoft AP trawler, sal) B; 2 Homefire 1200 B; 3 Rosme (SB) 67 M; RECEPTIVE (Sheerness AP drifter) 86 M; 4 AKRANES (Grimsby M/S trawler) 358 B; 7 LORD ST VINCENT (Brightlingsea AP drifter) 115 M; 9 Blue Mermaid (SB) ?9 M; private launch in River Crouch ? M; 13 Collingdoc 1780 M; 19 UMPIRE (Chatham-built submarine) 540 C; 23 Omfleet (barge) + 2 Hull lighters ? M.
Aug: 5 Deerwood 1914 St; Gallois (Fr) 2687 St; Oakshott 1241 St; Aberhill 1516 St; Paddy Hendly (sal) ? St; Taat (Est) 1334 St; 6 AGATE (Harwich A/S trawler) 627 St; 7 MMS 39 (Sheerness) 165 M; 9 Cordene 2345 B; 12 Express FV 16 M; 16 NESS POINT (Lowestoft tug) 85 B; 19 Golden Grain (SB) 101 M; 20 Czestochowa (Pol) 1970 ET; 22 TONBRIDGE (Yarmouth netlayer) 683 B; 24 Skagerrak (Nor) 1283 M.
Sep: 6 STRATHBORVE (Grimsby M/S trawler) 216 M; 7 Ophir II (FV) 213 M; 7 Duncarron 478 ET; Eikhaug (Nor) 1430 ET; Marcrest 4224 B; 8 CORFIELD (Grimsby mine destructor ship) 1791 M; 15 Birtley 2873 M; 15 Pontfield 8300 M; 17 Teddington 4762 ET; 19 Glen Alva (FV) 6 M; Prestatyn Rose (sal) 1151 M; Bradglen 4741 M; 20 MARCONI (Harwich M/S trawler) 322 C; 21 Vancouver 5729 M; 23 Vechstroom (Dut) 845 B; 26 British Prince 4979 M.
Oct: 10 Kyma (Gk) 3958 M; 11 Icemaid (sal) 1964 M; 12 Roy 1768 ET; Glynn 1134 B; 13 Chevington 1357 ET; 14 FORERUNNER (Sheerness M/S drifter) 92 M; 17 Lingfield 1002 C; 18 Empire Ghyll 2011 M; Mahseer 7911 M; 24 EMILION (Sheerness M/S trawler) 201 M; 27 Friesland (Dut) 2600 B; Antiope 4545 B; 31 Nicholaos Piangos (Gk) 4499 B; British Fortune 4696 B.
Nov: 2 Brynmill 743 B; Marie Dawn 2157 B; 3 OUZEL (Boston AP yacht) ? M; 4 Britisher (SB) 68 M; 8 MONARDA (Sheerness M/S trawler) St; 12 FRANCOLIN (Yarmouth M/S trawler) 322 B, 15 Corhampton 2495 B; 17 Bovey Tracey 1212 B; 18 GO AHEAD (Sheerness balloon drifter) 100 C; 19-20 Waldinge 2462 ET; Aruba 1159 ET; WAR MEHTAR (Harwich oiler) 5502 (grt) ET; 21 ROWAN TREE (Lowestoft M/S drifter) 91 C; 22 Bestum (Nor, sal) 2215 B; 24 Virgilia 5723 ET; 26 Groenlo (Dut) 1984 ET; 29-30 Asperity 699 ET; Cormarsh 2848 ET, Empire Newcomen 2840 ET.
Dec: 2 British Captain 6968 M; 6 Greenland 1281 M; 7 Welsh Prince 5150 M; 8 Fireglow 1261 M; Lord Shrewsbury (FV) 167 M; 12 Dromore Castle 5242 M; 21 Ben Macdhui 6870 M; 22 Stephanos Chandris (Gk) 6060 M; 23 Leopold III (Belg) 2902 M; Rokos Vergotris (Gk) 5640 ET; 24 Merchant 4615 M; Stanmount 4468 M; Eastwood (sal) 1550 M; 25 Cormead 2848 M; 26 HENRIETTE (Grimsby trawler) 261 M; 27 J B Paddon 700 M.

1942
Jan: 1 Kentwood 2180 M; 3 Corfen 1848 M; 4 Robert 1272 M; 6 Norwich Trader 217 M; VIMIERA (Rosyth destroyer) 1120 M; 12 Quickstep 2722 M; 16 IRVANA (Yarmouth M/S trawler) 276 B; 19 HKD (also called Kathleen, SB) ? M; 25 Swynfleet 1168 M; 30 LOCH ALSH (Grimsby M/S trawler) 385 B.

Feb: CAPE SPARTEL (Grimsby M/S trawler) 346 B; CLOUGHTON WYKE (Yarmouth M/S trawler 324 B; 18 WARLAND (Grimsby AP trawler) 214 B; 19 S 53 (E-boat) 92 G; 21 Atlanticos (Gk) 5446 M; 28 Thyra (Swe) 1796 M.
Mar: 1 Audacity 589 M; Polgarth 794 M; 3 Frumenton 6675 M; 11 Horseferry 961 ET; 13 SPARSHOLT (Sheerness boom mooring lighter) 104 M; 15 VORTIGERN (Rosyth destroyer) 1120 ET; 16 Cressdene 4270 M.
Apr: 1 Robert W Pomeroy 1750 M; SOLOMON (Grimsby M/S trawler) 357 M; 12 Scotia (Swe) ? M; 20 Vae Victis (Belg) 1829 M; Plawsworth 1489 M; 23 Chatwood 2767 M; 26 THORA (Grimsby balloon drifter) 37 C.
May: 4 Little Express (FV) 9 M; 5 Unique (SB) 51 M; 16 Arduity 304 M; 27 FITZROY (Yarmouth M/S) 710 M.
June: 17 Maggie (FV) 6 M; 19 Dalriada 973 M.
July: 9 TUNISIAN (Felixstowe boom trawler) 238 M; 12 MGBs 14 & 15 (Lowestoft) 31 B.
Aug: 25 Kyloe (sal) 2820 M.
Sep: —
Oct: 6 MGB 76 (Felixstowe) 47 G; CAROLINE MOLLER (Harwich rescue tug) 444 ET; ML 339 (Yarmouth) 72 ET; Sheaf Water 2730 ET; Ightham 1337 M; Ilse 2874 ET; Jessie Maersk 1972 ET; 14 Lysland (Nor) 1335 ET; George Balfour (sal) 1570 ET.
Nov: 6 MGB 19 (Lowestoft) 31 B; Fidelio (Nor) 1843 ET; 15 Linwood 992 M.
Dec: Avonwood 1056 ET; Lindisfarne 999 ET; Knitsley 2272 ET; Glen Tilt 871 ET; Bankside (SB) ? M; 27 Gertrude May (SB) 72 M.

1943

Jan: 8 Bolbec 1345 M; 13 Ailsa (SB) 67 M; 14 Wyetown 624 M; Resolute (SB) 76 M.
Feb: 8 Pacific ? M; 17 S 71 (E-boat) 92 G; 27 Castanet (SB) 79 C.
Mar: 3 PREMIER (Grimsby MFV) 22 C; 4 Sjofra (Nor) 619 M; 14 MORAVIA (Yarmouth M/S trawler) 306 M; 19 Glendalough 868 M.
Apr: 6 Tam O'Shanter (SB) 48 St; Josefina Thorden (Fin) 6620 M; 15 ADONIS (Harwich A/S trawler) 1004 ET; 17 Dynamo 809 M.
May: 31 Catford 1568 M.
June: 22 Wouldham Court (SB) ? AC.
July: 15 JBW (SB) 72 M.
Aug: 5 RED GAUNTLET (Ipswich AP trawler) 388 ET.
Sep: 21 ZEE MEEUW (Gravesend M/S drifter) 100 C; OCEAN RETRIEVER (Sheerness harbour defence drifter) 95 M; 25 FRANC TIREUR (Ipswich AP trawler) 314 ET; DONNA NOOK (Ipswich AP trawler) 307 C; S 96 (E-boat) 92 R.
Oct: 3 MEROR (Grimsby M/S trawler) 250 M; 25 WILLIAM STEPHEN (Lowestoft AP trawler) 235 M; S 88 & S 63 (E-boats) 92 G.
Nov: 4 British Progress 4581 ET; 13 Cormount 2841 M; 28 Morar 1507 M.

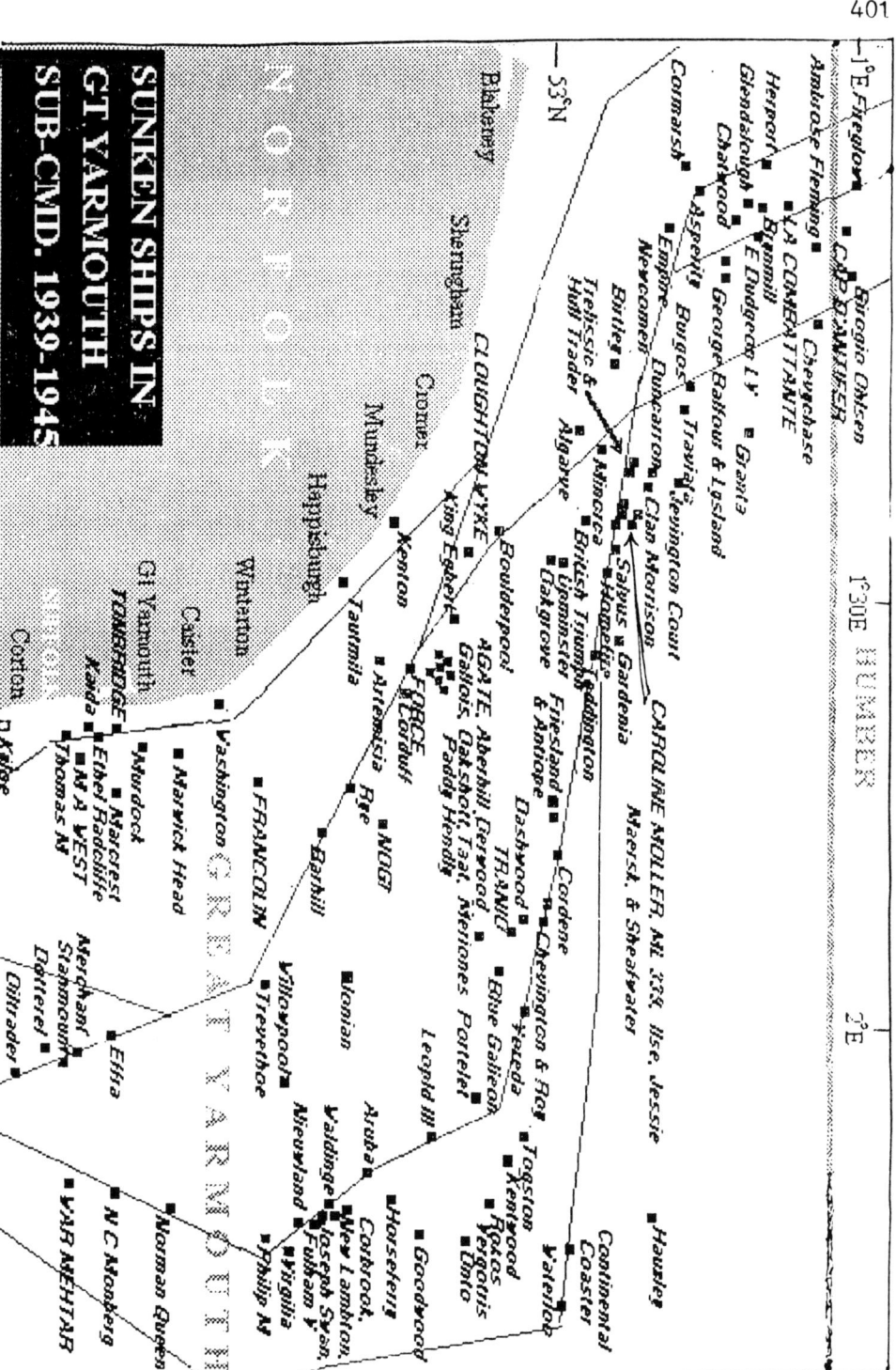

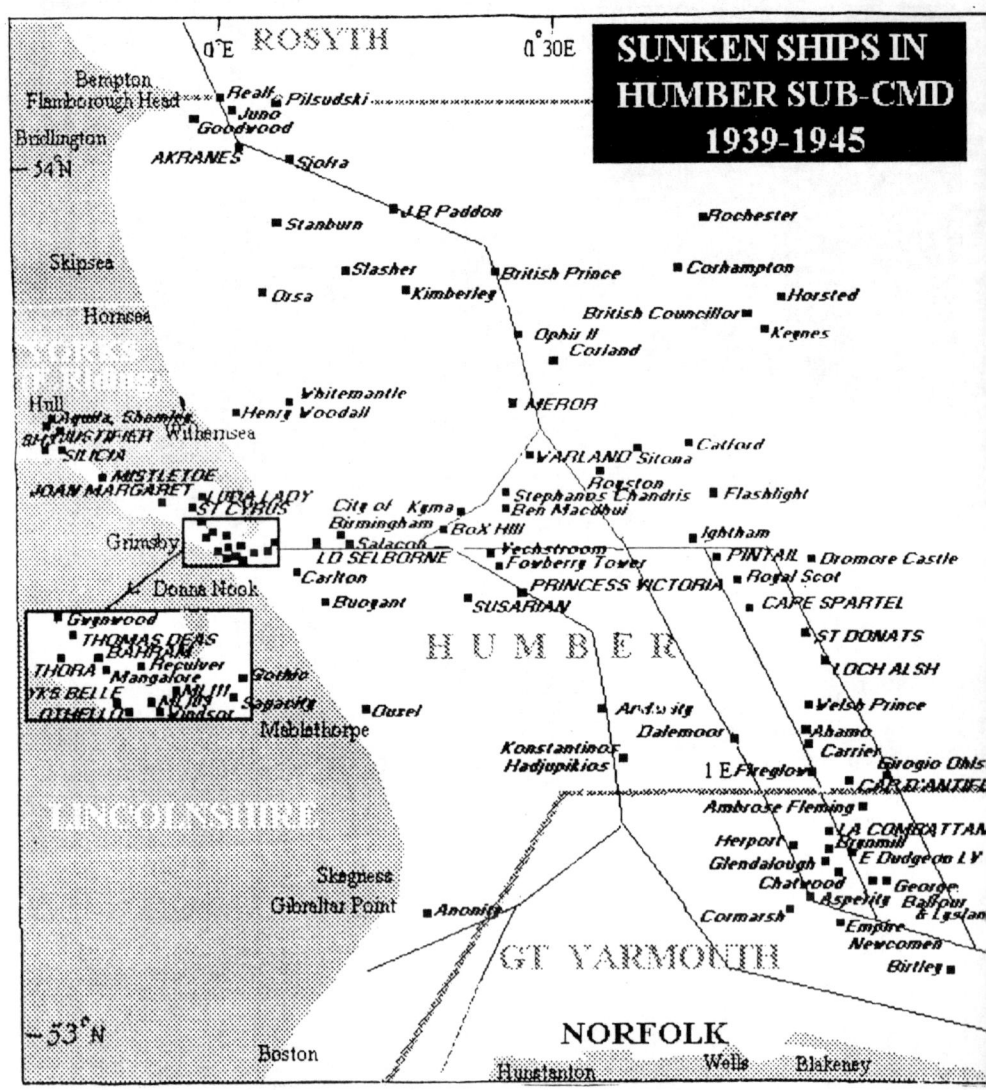

Dec: 21 Norhawk (Nor) 6080 M.

1944
Jan: 16 LCT 1029 (Boston) 200 ?; 20 LCV 716 (sal) 7 leaked.
Feb: 13 CAP D'ANTIFER (Grimsby AP trawler) 294 ET; 24; Philipp M 2085 ET; 25 dumb barge ? st.
Mar & Apr: __
May: 20 WYOMING (Ipswich AP trawler) 302 M; MMS 227 (Harwich, Dut) 165 M; BYMS 2040 (sal) 215 C.
June: 4 Clearpool ? St; Richard Montgomery (USA), 9000 St.
July: 4 Naja (tug) B (V1); 27 Rochester (FV) ? C.
Aug: 18 MTB 93 (Felixstowe) 47 C.
Sep: __
Oct: 30 LCT 936 (Lowestoft) 200 St.
Nov: __ 29 "BIBER" MIDGET U-BOAT 6 occupant suffocated.
Dec: __

1945
Jan: 15 Dalemoor 5835 M; Lisetta 2580 M; 19 Carrier (Nor) 3056 M; 24 SEEHUND 303 15 depth charged.
Feb: 3 ARLEY (Grimsby M/S trawler) 304 M; 22 Goodwood 2788 ET; Blacktoft 1109 ET; 23 LA COMBATTANTE (Sheerness destroyer, Fr) 1087 UT; 25 Aquarius (FV) 187 M.
Mar: 2 Excelsior (dumb barge) ? St; 13 Taber Park 2878 UT; 19 Crichtoun 1097 ET; Rogate 2871 ET; 23 Newlands 1556 UT; 30 Jim 823 UT.
Apr: 6 MTB 5001 105 E-Bt G; MTB 494 37 R; S 202, 703 (E-boats) 92 R; 12 Falmouth (FV) 165 M; 16 Monarch (cable ship) 1150 UT; 28 Dinorah (FV) 192 M.
May: __

APPENDIX J.
LOSSES OF NORE COMMAND NAVAL BASES
(throughout North Sea)

The losses given are from all causes. The personnel losses are deaths, and therefore exclude injured and captured _ they are minimum figures and approximations, and ma therefore be a few short of the real total in each case.

Immingham	2 destroyers, 1 minelayer (+ 350 personnel)
Grimsby	2 mine destructor ships, 25 trawlers and drifters, 3 yachts, 1 tug (+ 2! personnel)
Skegness (training camp)	12 personnel
Boston	1 patrol yacht, 1 landing craft tank (+ 7 personnel)
Gt Yarmouth	2 netlayers, 2 auxiliary minesweepers, 10 trawlers and drifters, 7 MT 1 MGB, 3 MLs, 3 RAF air-sea rescue launches, (+195 personnel)
Lowestoft	17 trawlers and drifters, 1 tug, 3 MTBs, 5 MGBs, 1 LCT, 1 harbour launch. (+ 145 personnel)
Felixstowe	11 MTBs, 5 MGBs, 1 trawler (+ 93 personnel)
Ipswich	6 trawlers (+70 personnel)
Shotley (training base)	10 personnel
Harwich	5 destroyers, 2 submarines, 2 corvettes, 1 auxiliary minesweeper, 2 paddle minesweepers, 1 oiler, 1 motor minesweeper, 1 ML, 1 MAC, 1! trawlers and drifters (+ 660 personnel)
Brightlingsea	5 trawlers and drifters, 2 patrol yachts, 1 air-sea rescue boat (+ 53 personnel)
Burnham-on-Crouch	1 person known.
London	1 accommodation yacht, 1 trawler, 1 LST (+ 35 personnel)
Chatham	1 submarine (in transit from dockyard), 1 ML (in transit to dockyard), dockyard boat (+75 personnel)
Sheerness	1 destroyer, 1 gunboat, 1 convoy leader, 1 AA paddle ship, 1 motor minesweeper, 1 oiler, 1 tug, 1 mooring lighter, 1 base launch, 27 trawlers and drifters (+ 320 personnel)

TOTAL SHIPS LOST: 200; PERSONNEL at least 2147.
Figures exclude losses of ships and men from other Commands (e.g. Rosyth) in transit through the Nore Command.

APPENDIX K — BOMBING OF NAVAL-BASE TOWNS*

Figures refer to raids within municipal boundaries, official harbour areas, and in the sea within 2 miles & nearer to the town than to any other shore locality, except in the cases of Hull, Grimsby and Sheerness, where nos. of bombs & mines dropped in the adjacent estuaries are unknown (for comparison purposes add about 15% to the respective totals). London not included, & I have not been able to trace figures for Immingham.

	Raids	Bombs				Casualties		Damage to Bldgs		
		HE	IB	Mines	Other	Killed	Injured	Destr.	Bad	Slight
HULL	72	1,264	15,000	122	35 phos, 74 butterfly	1,062	c3,000	4,354	15,378	66,983
GRIMSBY & Cleethorpes	43	233	7,300	4	2,500 butterfly, 26 firepot, 101 phos	148	c250	400	600	5,000
SKEGNESS & Ingoldmells	30	140	c400		7 firepot	11	80	101	120	?
GT YARMOUTH	126	1,070	9,060	10	10 firepot, 10 phos.	217	588	1,836	2,016	19,840
LOWESTOFT	83	681	4,644	6	7 phos, 7 firepot, 5 V1	266	690	578	c 13,000	
IPSWICH	48	316	906	2	310 butterfly, 15 firepot, 9 oil, 2 V1	78	407	c180	c5,500	
FELIXSTOWE	47	327	1,200	5	27 V1s	7	42	29	71	789
HARWICH & Parkeston	62	446	1,305	4	1 oil, 5 V1s, 1 V2	23	100	47	127	1,186
BRIGHTLINGSEA	12	34	2,380	2	4 oil, 4 phos, 2 V2s	2	21	10		274
SOUTHEND	85	567	12,454	13	185 butterfly, 22 phos 5 oil, 5 V1s, 2 V2s.	62	370	c350	c900	14,000
TILBURY DOCKS AREA	40	165	1622	2	4 firepot, 1 phos	21	c100	c200	c600	c3,000
SHEERNESS & Queenboro	22	c100	1240	3	1 firepot, 1 phos. 2 oil, 1 V1, 1 V2	2	10	80	220	1,500
MEDWAY TOWNS	78	838	4778	9	13 firepot, 32 phos. 8 oil, 6 V1, 1 V2	201	570	c800	c2,500	15,000

*bombing at some non-harbour coastal towns was heavier than in the cases above; for instance Clacton received over 200 HE and 5,000 incendiary bombs in 56 separate attacks (not counting V-Bombs), and some 100 buildings were destroyed and 5,000 damaged.

APPENDIX L
AIR RAID FATALITIES ON THE EAST COAST

These figures include Services personnel as well as civilians. They include persons killed while defusing bombs and air-dropped mines, but exclude those killed on ships at sea, by ships setting off mines, by AA shells, and by German anti-minesweeping floats. Deaths in the Greater London Civil Defence Region were only a few short of 30, 000. <u>Civilian</u> *deaths in the whole No 4 (Cambridge) Civil Defence Region (covering all of East Anglia, Essex outside Greater London, and Hertfordshire) were 2108.*

Bridlington	26	Kirby	1
Withernsea	15	Walton-Frinton	15
Easington	2	Clacton (Holland-on-Sea)	17
Hull	1200	Brightlingsea	2
Hessle	1	Colchester	54
Goole	3	Heybridge	4
Immingham	17?	Burnham-on-Crouch	6
Grimsby (+Cleethorpes)	148	Paglesham	1
Skegness (+Ingoldmells)	11	Southend (+Westcliff-Leigh-	
Boston	20	Shoebury)	62
King's Lynn	75	Hadleigh (Essex)	2
Hunstanton	3	Thurrock (Urban District,	
Sheringham	14	including Thameshaven,	
Cromer	19	Tilbury & Grays)	131
Happisburgh	2	Dartford	59
Winterton	2	Greenhithe	7
Caister	2	Gravesend	36
Gt Yarmouth (+Gorleston)	217	Northfleet	41
Lowestoft	270	Hoo	1
Kessingland	3	Rochester & Strood	95
Southwold	10	Chatham	58
Aldeburgh	11	Gillingham	53
Orford	13	Sheerness	2
RAF Bawdsey	6	RAF Eastchurch	20
Melton	1	Oare	3
Martlesham	3	Sittingbourne	27
Felixstowe	7	Faversham	9
Levington	1	Whitstable	9
Nacton	2	Herne Bay	4
Ipswich	78	Margate	35
Harwich (+Dovercourt)	21		
Parkeston	2		

APPENDIX M
GERMAN AIRCRAFT CLAIMED BY HARWICH DEFENCES OR CRASHED IN THEIR AREA*

Date	Time	Type	Unit	Cause of Loss	Crash Site	Evidence of Crash
19/6/40	0113	He 111	KG4	25 Sq Blenheim	sea off Fort Brackenbury	seen from shore
14/9/40	1530	He 111	2?KG 126	257 Sq Hurricane	Harkstead	wreck found
12/10/40	2004	Ju 88	KG 30?	accident	sea off Doverct.	wreck found
16/10/40	2221	He 111	II/KG26	balloon	Shotley Spit	wreck found
18/10/40	2100	bomber		Bawdsey LAA	"Brightlingsea"	false claim?
21/10/40	0020	Do 17	1/Ku Fl 126	abandoned in flight	Erwarton	wreck found
27/10/40	1817	Do 17	KG 76	Nacton HAA Site 1112 LMG	Holbrook	wreck found
27/10/40	1825	Do 17	III/KG 77	17 Sq Hurricane	4000x S Landguard Point	2 bodies washed up, Hollesley Bay
29/10/40	0110	He 111	9/KG 53	Harwich HAA	off Parkeston	crew POW
18/2/41	0400			HAA Sites H3 (Dovercourt) & H4 (Shotley)	in sea	unconfirmed
18/2/41	0400			HAA Sites H1 (Landguard) & H3 (Dovercourt)	in sea	unconfirmed
12/5/41	0144	Ju 88		Martlesham & Bawdsey LAA	sea off Bawdsey	wreckage seen
19/5/41	2348	He 111		HMS *Princess Elizabeth*	2 mls NE Cork LV	body found
22/1/42	0930	bomber		HMTs *Exhayne, Spina, Warwing*	off Cork LV	debris ashore at Harwich
14/3/42	2017	He 111	KG 4	paddle AA ship	Landguard 6000x 150°	seen from shore
26/8/42	2230	Ju 88	1/KG 77	HAA Site H1 (Landguard)	out to sea	German records
14/5/43	0210	Do 217	6/KG 2	Bawdsey LAA Site 2	Bawdsey	wreck found

*within 8 miles of Landguard Fort. See Page 126 for map of Harwich AA defences.

date				scale of raid			
15/5/43	2205	FW 190	SKG 10	Roughs Tower & Queen Empress	9,500x 104° Landguard		seen by R.N.
30/5/43	1730	FW 190	SKG 10	Naze LAA Site L1	2.5 mls S of Walton Pier		body recovered by RNLI
2/6/43	0530	FW 190	SKG 10	collision with dock crane	Orwell at Ipswich		wreckage found
13/7/43		Me 410	V/KG2	85 Sq Mosquito	5 mls Bawdsey		body found
23/8/43	0134	Me 410	16/KG2	85 Sq Mosquito	Clelmondiston		observer POW
22/10/43	1948			HAA Site H3 (Dovercourt)	in sea		*Shearwater* saw crash
13/1/44	1946	Me 410?	V/KG2?	HAA Sites H2 (Trimley) & H5 (Lt Oakley)	Cork LV		seen from shore
23/2/44	0015	Ju 88	KG 6	HAA Sites H1 (Landguard), H2 (Trimley), & H5 (Lt Oakley)	Buxey Sand		wreckage found & 2 bodies recovered by ARB.

APPENDIX N
AN EXAMPLE OF LUFTWAFFE BOMBING ACCURACY
–THE EIGHT LARGEST RAIDS ON HULL*

date	scale of raid	tons of HE & mines on city	% of HE & mines on city
18/19 March 1941	316 tons HE & mines, 77,040 IB	49.75	12.65
7/8 May 1941	110 tons HE & mines, 9,648 IB	46	41
8/9 May 1941	167 tons HE & mines, 19,440 IB	75.9	45.45
17/18 July 1941	174 tons HE & mines, 5802 IB	35.85	20.6
22/23 Oct 1941	45 aircraft	0	0
19/20 May 1942	150 tons	23	22
17-18 Mar 1944	118 aircraft	1.05	1
20-21 April 1944	131 aircraft	0	0

*RAF Fighter Command History (PRO AIR 41/17, 49) + Geraghty.

APPENDIX O
COASTAL FORCES CRAFT IN THE NORE COMMAND – SEPT.1943

base	flotilla	boats
GT YARMOUTH (HMS *Midge*)	31 MTB	617, 621, 624, 628, 632, 650, 652, 668, 671, 682
	59 MTB	705 (697, 700-703, 706, 710 to join on completion)
	12 MGB	313, 315, 320, 321, 327, 333
	16 MGB	319, 323, 325, 331, 332, 334
	17 MGB	603-7, 609, 610, 612
	13 ML	196-198, 200-202, 204, 294
	19 ML	217, 236, 243, 250
	60 RML	492, 496, 498, 499, 512, 514, 515, 517
		53 boats
LOWESTOFT (HMS *Mantis*)	10 MTB	438-445
	22 MTB	83, 88, 92, 222, 230, 238, 245, 347
	32 MGB	689, 693, 694
	7 MGB	82-89, 91
	2 ML	112-114, 116, 117, 119, 120, 171
	6 ML	145-152
		44 boats
FELIXSTOWE (HMS *Beehive*)	4 MTB	22, 31, 32, 34 (mostly paid off)
	11 MTB	348-352, 355, 356, 360
	21 MTB	223-225, 232, 234, 241, 244
	6 MGB	58-65, 67
	51 ML	100, 105, 106, 110
		33 boats
SHEERNESS (HMS *Wildfire*)	105 HDML	1001, 1024
		2 boats

all boats given at home bases, though several craft, and some others from outside the Command, were equipping, refitting or repairing at Brightlingsea.

APPENDIX P
AIR-SEA RESCUE CRAFT IN THE NORE COMMAND _ SEPT.1943

base	unit/flotilla	craft
BRIDLINGTON	21 MCU (RAF)	Pinnaces 1285, 1292, ST 439
GRIMSBY	RN	Harbour Launches 304 (steam), 4002, 41107 (diesel)
	22 MCU (RAF)	HSLs 2503, 2559, 2560, 2579, 2594, 2677
WELLS	23 MCU (RAF)	STs 349, 350, Pinnace 1241
GT YARMOUTH/	24 MCU (RAF)	HSLs 185, 2550, 2551, 2506, 2570, 2707
GORLESTON	60 RML (RN)	RMLs 492, 496, 498, 499, 512, 514, 515, 517
LOWESTOFT	24 MCU (RAF)	HSLs 195, 2501, 2502
	RN HMS *Europa*	3 ARBs for training
FELIXSTOWE	26 MCU (RAF)	HSLs 2555, 2557, 2558, 2562
BRIGHTLINGSEA	RN	ARBs *Patrician* (1), *Eclipse* (2), *Aro* (3), T 21 (4), *Mike*/T 16 (5), T 10 (6), T 11 (7), *Romany* (8)
SHEERNESS	31 MCU (RAF)	STs 443, 444
HERNE BAY	RN civilians	ARB *Dandy*
RAMSGATE	32 MCU (RAF)	HSLs 127, 149, 169, 178
(Dover Command)	RN	MASBs 23-29, 31-33, 38 (all temporarily at Dover).

APPENDIX Q
GERMAN NAVY IN SOUTHERN NORTH SEA : NOV, 1941

WESERMUNDE: *8th & 11th VP-Boat Flotillas (24 escort and flak trawlers)*
DEN HELDER: *13th & part of 31st Minesweeper Flotillas (22 M-Class sweepers)*
IJMUIDEN: *2nd and part of 4th E-Boat Flotillas (18 E-Boats)*
ROTTERDAM: *5th Torpedo Boat Flotilla (6 Large Steam Torpedo Boats)*
14th Minesweeper Flotilla (8 M-Class sweepers)
1st R-Boat Flotilla (16 motor minesweeping & escort craft)
34th Minesweeper Flotilla (7 M-Class sweepers)
13th VP-Boat Flotilla (12 escort and flak trawlers)
FLUSHING: *part of 32nd Minesweeper Flotilla (about 12 M-Class sweepers)*
OSTEND: *18th VP-Boat Flotilla (12 escort and flak trawlers)*
DUNKIRK: *36th Minesweeping Flotilla (15 M-Class sweepers).*

SOURCES & ACKNOWLEDGMENTS

OFFICIAL RECORDS
This book is very largely based on the analysis and cross-checking of Public Record Office documents in London. I can claim to have ransacked most of what relates to the wartime East Coast (in its land, sea and air dimensions) since the relevant files began to emerge from the "Thirty Year Rule" in 1972 (and fortunately most of the "One Hundred Year Rule" papers have since been reclassified and made public as well). On all these I gratefully acknowledge Crown Copyright.

Admiralty (PRO code ADM)
1 (Miscellaneous):
   for my purposes mainly reports of awards for bravery in naval actions and mine   disposal (Chs 5, 7, 10, 11, 12, 18), on base manpower and organisation (Ch 8), and on Boards of Inquiry (used in most full descriptions of warship sinkings, in Chs 2, 4, 5, 10).
53 (Warship Logs)
   used to establish precise warship movements in the period to May 1940 (Chs 1-   3), but thereafter only a few specimens have been preserved.
104 (Alphabetical Register of Ratings' Deaths...giving Place, Date, Ship or Base, and Cause) was occasionally used, but can only yield information if one knows the names of particular ratings first.
116 (Vice-Admiral Binney Manpower Inquiries, 1943)
   ...for Nore Command bases; in Ch 8 took the guesswork out of determining how   many personnel were assigned to each major duty, at least at that juncture of the war.
179 (Navy Lists)
   ...give names, ranks and dates of appointment of RN, RNR, RNVR, RM and WRNS officers on all ships and at all bases; printed every other month for most of the war (but contain much inaccuracy and misleading data). Used in Ch 8 and Appendix A, mainly.
187 ("Pink Lists"= Locations of Major Warships)
   ...span the whole war period and include all Nore Command bases; printed weekly). Used in all naval chapters.
189 (HMS *Vernon* Technical Histories)
   ...cover British and German mines and sweeping gear. Used in Chs 1 and 2 and Appendix E.
199 (operational records):
   Nore Command War Diaries and War History, Dover Command War Diaries, First Lord's Daily Events Summaries, Trade Division History, Southend Base History, and East Coast and Channel Convoy Reports(all naval chapters); Reports of Air Attacks on Ships, Convoys and Naval Bases, German Minelaying and British Minesweeping, and British Losses from Mines (Chs 5 and 10); Invasion Precautions (Ch 3); Dunkirk Evacuation (Ch 3); Coastal Forces Actions (Ch 13); E-Boat Raids (Chs 5, 10, 13, 18); Harwich Salvage Dept (Ch 14); Awards (Chs 3, 4, 5 and 8); Operation "Outward" and Reports of Harwich-based Submarines (Ch 9) ;
Routing and Navigational Instructions (Ch 1).
208 ("Red Lists"=Locations of Minor Warships)
   issued on same basis as Pink Lists (ADM 187). Used in all naval chapters and for Appendix B.
209 ("Blue Lists"=Locations of Warships Under Construction), for Ch 15.
210 ("Green Lists"=Locations of Landing Craft),
   ....issued from 1942 onwards. Used in Ch 17.
213 (HMS *Vernon*)
   62 includes particulars of German mines. Used in Chs 5 and 10 and Appendix E.
223 (Intelligence "Acqaints")

SOURCES & ACKNOWLEDGMENTS

....frequently relate to the Nore Command, but rarely give precise information. Of some use in each naval chapter.
239 (includes useful charts). Used in Ch 1.
Other official maritime records researched includes those of Combined Operations (separately filed at the PRO under DEFE _ Ministry of Defence), used in Ch 17, the Naval Historical Branch's Dockyard Reports, for Ch 15, Lloyd's Lists (for particulars of civilian vessels in all naval chapters), and the reports of the RNLI and Coastguards at Clacton and Walton (mainly for parts of Chs 14 and 16).

Air Ministry (AIR and AVIA)
AIR 2 and particularly AVIA 7 (mostly on radar technicalia).
    The basis of much of Ch 6, but also used in Chs 2 and 10 and 11.
AIR 13 Harwich & Sheerness Barrage Balloon Squadrons.
AIR 15 Air-Sea Rescue Monthly & Weekly Reports.
AIR 20 Air-Sea Rescue Maps (an impressionistic source only).
AIR 24 Bomber Command Operational Record & Intelligence Reports.
AIR 25 (Group), 26 (Wing), 27 (Squadron), 28 (Station) and 29 (Independent Flight and Marine Craft Unit).Were used in connection with the air combat sections of Chs 1, 5, 7, 10, 11, and 12, and the air-sea rescue in Ch 16. The Signals' Group and Wings were used for Chs 6 and 11.
AIR 40 Air Intelligence Reports.
AIR 41 Fighter Command History (6 vols).
AIR 50 RAF and USAAF Combat Reports.
Other official air records included the Air Historical Branch's Air Crash Card Index and the reports of the Royal Observer Corps at Colchester.

War Office (WO)
166 (War Diaries)
    consulted for scores of units, ranging from corps to battalion, and including AA and Coast Artillery, though for some reason only the formations in East Anglia kept fully informative records.
192 and 199 (additional Coast Artillery records).
    My Army sources mostly relate to Ch 4, but were also important in 6 and helped in researching inshore naval actions and air crashes mentioned in Chs 5, 7, 10, 11 and 16.

Civil Defence (HO)
182-4 (Air Raid Reports by Regions), 192 and 199 (Air Raid Damage Reports), 198 (Bomb Census) and 202 (Air Raid Regional Summaries) _ very patchy and limited sources. Much more useful air raid records were filed locally, and I consulted those of Essex (Chelmsford and Southend) and Suffolk (Ipswich) County Record Offices, Harwich Civil Defence Controller Bernard, and Felixstowe Police Inspector H C Rush's War Incidents Diary. The booklets by Jenkins (Lowestoft), Box (Yarmouth) and Geraghty (Hull) must rank as quasi-official air raid sources (see Bibliography).

NEWSPAPERS & MAGAZINES
Owing to the censorship and paper shortage these were of very scant value, for the most part. After consulting several of the East Anglian coastal papers (*Essex County Standard, Essex Telegraph,*

SOURCES & ACKNOWLEDGMENTS

East Essex Gazette, Harwich and Dovercourt Standard, East Anglian Daily Times and *Eastern Daily Press*) I gave up on those for the rest of the region. The 1939-40 issues of *The War Illustrated* provided some material for Chs 1 and 2, however. Articles by C R Elliott in 1960s issues of the *East Anglian Magazine, Suffolk Mercury* and *Air Pictorial* gave me some of my earliest pointers to the Italian air raids. During the 1970s and 80s the following were good enough to publish appeals for information from me: *Chatham News, East Anglian Daily Times, East Anglian Magazine, Essex Countryside, Essex County Standard, Grimsby Telegraph, Holderness Gazette, Hull Daily Mail, Navy News, Sheerness Times Guardian.* I was also allowed to go through back numbers of *Motor Boat and Yachting* by that magazine's editor.

PHOTOGRAPHS
Apart from those owned by private individuals or published, I made use of the Port of London Authority's collection, some at the Public Record Office, and above all those of the Imperial War Museum (where I was once briefly employed) and the RAF Museum.

CEMETERIES
A little-known, very incomplete, but sometimes valuable source of information on the local sea war is literally engraved in tablets of stone. Commonwealth War Graves Commission stones are scattered in churchyards and cemeteries all along the coast, though the two largest groups are at Woodlawns' Cemetary, Gillingham, and Shotley Churchyard.

WARTIME EYE WITNESSES
The following list (contemporary service ranks where appropriate) includes only those whose recollections helped shape some part of my text, or who provided photographs.
AB G Ashcroft and Mrs Ashcroft, Surg-Lt W H Aucutt RNVR, AB J Bailey, 2nd Officer M R Bammant WRNS, Lt(E) K H Barette (RNVR), AB T M F Bernard, Sub-Lt E J Bland RNVR, ABS L Bridge, Lt W H G Brunt RNVR, E A Cummings, Miss N Dalton, 3rd Officer D W Dowding WRNS, Mr and Mrs E H Foynes, Lt R D Franks RN, Writer J French RN, AB R A Gammon, G Gray, Lt R C Green RNVR, Lt-Cdt M W Griffiths GM RNVR, Sgt C Hesketh, AB T Higgins, Sub-Lt(E) W E Hollick RNVR, Lt D E P Howard RNVR (now Lord Strathcona), Lt D E J Hunt RNVR, Miss E King, Lt J B S Laine RNVR, Lt-Cdr S Lombard-Hobson RN, W H Lydamore, Ord Teleg H G Marshall, Surg-Lt J Nixon RNVR, Pay-Lt L C Pegg RNVR, D Pigg, Lt A N Piper RNVR, C Posner, Mrs Raspin, Lt H Rackham RNVR, Lt B Ridley RN, G E Rotherham, Sub-Lt R A Ruegg RNVR, Inspector H C Rush, AC F E Shute, AB T Stockdale, Sub-Lt D J D Sulman RNVR, AB G F Syratt, Ord Teleg W Tyler, Lt(Elect) E E F W Usher RNVR, Signaller W K Webster, PO H White.

OTHER PERSONAL ACKNOWLEDGMENTS
Mrs O Barber, R Bostock, P F Brookes, Mrs B W Burrow, J Catton, W Clayton, S Cox, A R Crane, C R Elliott, W Gadd, N Hostyn, J E Hudgens, J Jefferies, P Jenkins, D Johnson, G Kinsey, P Long, H Lord, M Middlebrook, Mrs A Miller, P G Oxley, D Scarles, B Taylor, C Tooke, R Tough, A Wakeling, A Werner.

I must also record my thanks to the late Sir Peter Scott and his secretary June White for trying to chase a thorny copyright problem on my behalf.

SOURCES & ACKNOWLEDGMENTS

BIBLIOGRAPHY

C Babington Smith; *Amy Johnson* (Collins, 1967)
L M Bates; *Thames on Fire* (Dalton's, 1985)
C Bekker; *Luftwaffe War Diaries* (Corgi, 1964)
H Benham; *Essex at War* (Essex County Standard, 1945) _ on the Colchester area.
Bommen op Belge, 1940-1945 (Belgian Civil Defence Organisation) _ for effects of Allied air raids on the Belgian coast. (Also articles and booklets by O Vilain, P Cocle & "Haril", & from *Ter Cuere Bredene, Jaarboek 1985* _ all on Ostend during the war.)
E G Bowen; *Radar Days* (Hilger, 1987) on early radar research on the Suffolk coast.
M J F Bowyer; *Airfields of East Anglia* (Patrick Stephens, 1979)
 Air Raid (Patrick Stephens, 1986)
C G Box; *Great Yarmouth, Frontline Town* (Gt Yarmouth Corporation, 1945)
C Brann; *Little Ships of Dunkirk* (Collectors' Books, 1990)
P Brickhill; *Reach for the Sky* (Collins, 1954) on Douglas Bader.
British Merchant Shipping Losses (official list, HMSO, 1947)
P Brooks; *Coastal Towns at War* (Poppyland, 1988) _ on Cromer & Sheringham.
R Douglas Brown; *East Anglia 1939, 1940, 1941, 1943* (Daltons', successive vols, 1980-91)
Bryant, B; *Submarine Command* (Kimber, 1958) _ includes the Harwich submarines.
F G G Carr; *The Sailing Barges* (1967) _ has a chapter on their wartime work.
W S Churchill; *The Second World War, Vol I* (Cassell's, 1952)
B Collier; *Defence of the United Kingdom* (HMSO, 1957)
R Collier; *The Sands of Dunkirk* (Collins, 1961)
G C Connell; *Valiant Quartet* (Kimber, 1979)_ on the Humber-based AA cruisers.
B Cooper; *The Battle of the Torpedo Boats* (MacDonald & Janes, 1971)_ MTBs, E-Boats, etc.
 The E-Boat Threat (do, 1976)
C Cruickshank; *Deception in World War 2* (Oxford U P, 1988) _ Normandy Invasion deception schemes.
L Deighton; *Fighter* (Jonathan Cape, 1977) _ features Bawdsey.
P Dickens, Adm Sir; *Night Action* (1974) _ on East Coast Coastal Forces operations.
A D Divine; *Dunkirk* (Faber, 1957) _ still the best source on Operation "Dynamo".
L Forrester; *Fly For Your Life* (Frederick Muller, 1956) _ on Sq Ldr R S Tuck.
H Friedhoff; *Requiem for the Resistance* (Bloomsbury, 1988) _ features Dutch escapers and secret agents.
J P Foynes; *Under the White Ensign: Brightlingsea & the Sea War of 1939-1945* (privately, 1993) _ a detailed account of HMSs *Nemo & Helder*.
T Geraghty; *A North East Coast Town* (Hull Corporation, 1951) _ on the Hull Blitz
G Gibson; *Enemy Coast Ahead* (Pan, 1946) _ includes local night fighter episodes.
C Goodey & J Rose; *HMS Europa* (RNPS Association, 1977) _ brief pamphlet on the Navy at Lowestoft.
E Hazelhoff Roelfzema; *Soldier of Orange* (Sphere, 1982) _ same topic as Friedhoff.
Sir A P Herbert; *The War Story of Southend Pier* (Southend Corporation, 1945) *Independent Member* (Methuen, 1951) _ includes the Thames auxiliary patrol.
Lt-Cdr R P Hichens, *We Fought Them in Gunboats* (Michael Joseph, 1944) _ on the Felixstowe MGBs.
H Hitchman and P Driver; HMS *Badger* (privately printed, 1985) _ a vague outline of a few

SOURCES & ACKNOWLEDGMENTS

aspects of wartime Harwich.
H J Hunt; *Bombs & Booby Traps* (Romsey Medal Centre, 1986) _ includes local bomb disposal.
Ford Jenkins; *Lowestoft, Port War* (Lowestoft Corporation, 1945).
A Jobson; *The Felixstowe Story* _ has a chapter on the war years.
D E Johnson; *East Anglia at War, 1939-45* (Jarrold's, 1978) _ mainly on Clacton area.
J C Jones; *From the Forecastle to the Messdeck* (Book Guild, 1987) _ first hand account of the 20th Destroyer Flotilla disaster of 31 August 1940, but ships' names are muddled.
Prof. R V Jones; *Most Secret War* (Hamish Hamilton, 1978) _ of some relevance to local radar.
T Jones; *Hearts of Oak* (Bodley Head, 1984) _ includes HMS *Ganges*.
N Kelso; *Errors of Judgment _ SOE's Disaster in the Netherlands, 1941-44* (Robert Hale, 1988) _ on same topic as Friedhoff & Hazelhoff Roelfzema.
W King; *The Stick & The Stars* (1957) _ includes the Harwich submarines.
G Kinsey; *Bawdsey, Birth of the Beam* (Daltons', 1983)
V Kühn; *Schnellboote im Einsatz, 1939-45* (Motorbuch Verlag, Stuttgart, 1986) _ has brief sections on the North Sea E-boats.
J Lambert; *The Fairmile D* (Conway Maritime, 1985)_ on the MGBs and MTB of this type.
D Lampe; *The Last Ditch* (Cassell, 1966) _ on the secret guerilla army.
H T Lenton & J J Colledge, *Warships of World War II* (Ian Allan, 1964)
S Lombard-Hobson, *A Sailor's War* (Butler & Tanner, 1983) _ includes the Harwich corvettes.
P Lund & H Ludlam; *Out Sweeps* (Foulsham, 1972) _ on minesweeping.
I McLachlan, *Final Flights* (Patrick Stephens, 1989) _ includes unusual local air crashes.
R Malster; *Saved from the Sea* and *Wreck & Rescue on the Essex Coast* (1968, David & Charles) _ on the East Anglian lifeboats, including chapters on the war years.
F K Mason, *Battle over Britain* (McWhirter, 1969) _ on the Battle of Britain.
N Monsarrat; *Three Corvettes* (Cassell, 1943-4, 3 vols).
R Convers Nesbitt; *The Strike Wings* (Kimber, 1984) _ on the North Coates Beaufighters and Langham Mosquitos.
Failed to Return (Patrick Stephens, 1988) _ includes the Amy Johnson crash.
O Olsen; *Two Eggs on my Plate* (Allen & Unwin, 1952)_ on one escape from Norway.
R O'Neill; *The Suicide Squadrons* (Salamander, 1981) _ includes the midget U-Boats.
G Pawle; *The Secret War* (Companion Book Club, 1958) _ on unusual naval weapons.
W D Pereira; *Boat in the Blue* (1985) _ brief remarks on air-sea rescue at Lowestoft.
G D Pilborough; *The History of RAF Marine Craft* (Canimpex) _ features some Gorleston HSL rescues in detail.
R Plummer; *The Ships that Saved an Army* (Patrick Stephens, 1990) _ on Dunkirk.
J D Porter; *Fiasco; the Breakout of the German Battleships* (1970) _ on the *Scharnhorst & Gneisenau* episode.
A Price; *The Hardest Day* (Arms & Armour, 1979) _ on the air battle of 18 August, 1940.
W G Ramsey; *The Battle of Britain, Then & Now* (*After the Battle* Magazine, 1986)
C F Rawnsley & R Wright; *Night Fighter* (Collins, 1957)
A Robinson; *Night Fighter* (Ian Allan, 1988)
RAF Fighter Squadrons of the Battle of Britain (Arms & Armour, 1987)
J Röhwer; *Chronology of the War at Sea* (Ian Allan, 2 vols, 1971) _ from the German side.
A Rootes; *Frontline County* (Robert Hale, 1980_ on wartime Kent.

SOURCES & ACKNOWLEDGMENTS

S Roskill; *The War at Sea* (HMSO, 3 vols. 1954) _ the official history.

General G Santoro; *Stralcio dell' Opera Aeronautica Italiana nella II Guerra Mondiale* (Vol I) includes the local CAI raids.

D Scarles; *Raiders Overhead* (1976) _ an unpublished typescript in Gt Yarmouth Library, similar to Box.

Lt-Cdr P Scott; *The Battle of the Narrow Seas* (Country Life, 1945) _ the best account of the Coastal Forces campaign.

Rr-Adm G W G Simpson; *Periscope View* (Macmillan, 1972) _ as Bryant.

M Smith; *Blitz on Grimsby* (Humberside Leisure Services, 1983).

P Smith; *Wild Swan* (Kimber, 1983) _ mentions this destroyer's time at Harwich in 1940.

B L Summers; *HMS Ganges* (HMS Ganges, 1966).

P Townsend; *Duel of Eagles* _ including author's time at Martlesham Heath in 1940.

J F Turner; *The Bader Wing* (Midas, 1981).

D E Walker; *Adventure in Diamonds* (Evans Bros, 1955) _ on the party landed at IJmuiden from *Walpole* on 12 May 1940.

N Wallington; *Firemen at War* (David & Charles, 1981) _ includes Thames firefloats.

O Warner; *Lifeboats* (Cassell, 1974) _ includes the Cromer and Spurn RNLI.

R Willson; *Red Alert* (privately, 1984) _ on King's Lynn air raids.

E Young; *One of Our Submarines* (Rupert Hart-Davies, 1952) _ as Simpson.

H van der Zee; *The Hunger Winter* (Jill Norman & Hobhouse, 1983) _ includes the Texel Mutiny and the situation in Holland in the final months of war.

INDEX*

AA artillery, 126-7, 198, 268
AA cruisers, 6
Aalborg, 143
Abbots, L/S J W, 161
Abdy Beauclerk (see Aldeburgh lifeboat)
Ability, 298
Abukir, 47
ACHILLE, 201
Adaptity 96
ADMIRAL SCHEER, 205
ADVENTURE, 16, 311
Affriani, Sgt.Plt, 154
Agamemnon, 96
AGATE, 297
AI radar, 226, 251
AIGLON, 107
Ailsa, 231
Air-sea rescue (RAF):
  High Speed Launches ,315, 318, 323, 330, 361
  Pinnaces, 315, 325
  Floats, 325
AKRANES, 213
AJAX, 311
Alaric, 231, 259
Aldeburgh, 93, 97, 110, 154, 217, 223, 258
Aldeburgh Lifeboats, 48,154,297-8
Aldbrough, 137
Aldie, 46
Aldous Successors' Shipyard (Brightlingsea), 30, 158, 294, 306, 314, 317-8, 340
Aldridge, ABS S, 39
Alert (cable ship), 185
Alert.(THV), 316
Alestor, 350
Alexander, Skipper J S, RNR, 105 213
Alexander, W H J, Ltd, 300
ALFREDIAN, 221
ALGERINE-class M/S, 231
Alice Marie, 99
Alioth, 103
Allard, Fl Sgt S, 87, 90
Alresford (Essex), 347
Althorne, 67
AMAZONE, 201
Ambrose Fleming, 115
AMBUSCADE, 83
Ameland, 323
Amelia Lauro, 13, 60, 299
AMESs, 117, 123

AMETHYST, 99
AMRE (see Bawdsey)
Amsterdam, 38
Amsterdam, 238
Andalsnes, 35
Anderson, Lt, 273
Anderson, Rigden & Perkins,317
Ansons, 12
Antiope, 215
Antwerp, 206, 359
ANZAC Strike Wing, 209, 360
"Aphrodite", Operation, 270
Aquiety, 101
Arado Ar-234s, 271
ARBs, 324-5; No 2, 325, No 3 231
ARBELLA, HMS, 195, 349
Archangel, 238
Ardenza, 215
ARDROSSAN, 236
ARETHUSA (cruiser), 36, 37, 311
Arethusa (TS), 55
Argus, 99
ARGYLLSHIRE, 47
Aridity, 298
Arinia, 101
ARLEY, 365
Armitage, Lt, RNVR, 150, 228
Amos & Smith, 322
Armstrong, Cap H T, 285
Army (British):
  Bomb Disposal Coys, 263, 268
  Corps:*I* 355-6; *II* 68; *XI* 67; *XXX* 355-6
  Divisions: *1st* 68; *1st London* 68, 72; *7 Armoured* 354, 356; *15th (Scots)* 67; *18th* 68, 72; *51st* 355; *54th* 79, 210, 254; *55th* 68; *79th (Armoured)* 351
Arnhem, 359
ARO, 340
ARP, 128
Artemisia, 106, 158
Artillery, 66, 67, 69
  German long-range....155
Aruba, 216, 299
Asdic, 60, 94, 315
ASH, 301
Ashford (Kent), 259
Ashmore, Lt RNVR, 110
Asperity, 216-7
A/S trawlers, 7, 321
Astrologer, 95
ASV radar, 132

ATTENTIF, 302
Atlanticos, 219
ATS, 161
Aubrey, Lt-Cdr. 16
AUCKLAND, 10
Aucutt, Surg-Lt W H, RNVR, 348
AURORA, 77
Austin, Capt, 302
Austins' (East Ham), 320
Auxiliary Patrol, 57-59, 74, 82, 93, 180, 324
Ave Maria, 53
AZALEA, 321

Babington, Sub-Lt, RNVR, 150
"Baby Blitz", 265-7
BACHAQUERO, 349, 356
Bader, Sq Ldr D S, 87, 88, 91
BADGER, HMS, 2, 373 (also see Harwich, Parkeston Quay)
BAHRAM, 108
Bailey, Lt G B, RNVR, 280
Bainbridge-Bell, L H, 117
Baldwin, CPO, 21
Balloon Barrages, 19, 91 (mobile), 127, 187, 255, 264, 267
BALMORAL, 221, 262
BANGOR-class M/S, 231
Bankside, 231
Barbara Jean, 46
Bard Hill, 131, 226, 232
Bardwell, Cap. W S, 107
Barette, Lt(E) K H, RNVR, 99
Barking, 60, 149, 300
Barr, Sub-Lt, RNVR, 110
Barrow Deep LV, 143
Barton Bendish, 324
Barton on Humber, 321
BASILISK, 16
BASSETT, 297, 321
Bätge, Kplt von, 215, 229
Bawdsey, 25, 80, 90, 97, 117, 118, 121, 125, 126, 129, 130, 135, 137, 151, 167, 226, 232, 234, 244, 250, 260, 262, 268, 270, 341
Beachy Head CD radar, 241
Beacon, 185
Beacon Hill (Harwich), 66
Beamish, Gp Cap V, 142, 241
Beatrice Maud, 44
Beatrix, Princess, 37
Beatty, Lt-Cdr Earl, 6
Beaufighters, 133, 208-9, 371

4-17

Ships in italics & warships in capital italics. Officers RN unless otherwise indicated.

INDEX

Beaumont, 151, 260
BEAVER & BEAVER II, HMSs, 195, 373 (see also Humber)
Beccles, 137
Beckton, 147, 267
BEDOUIN, 53
BEEHIVE, HMS, 61, 187, 273, 275,294,373(& see Felixstowe)
BEGONIA, 321
Belgia, 104, 283, 305
Belgian Brigade, 79
Belot, Cap, 201
Belvedere, 101
Benacre CD radar, 232-3
BENBECULA, 321
Beneficient, 101
BEN GAIRN, 163
Ben Macdhu, 217
Bennett, Cdre, 177
BERBERIS, 90
Berger, Kapt, 21
BERKELEY, 113-4, 343
Bernard, Prince, 37
Bernard C M F, 17
Berstead, 155
Bessie......300, 302-4, 307-8
Bestum, 215, 307
Bethnal Green, 259
Beverley, 321
Beverley Rural Dist, 164
Bey, Kplt, 20, 31
"Biber" (U-Bt), 360, 364
Bickford, Capt J G, 36, 75-6
Bickford, Lt E O, 199, 200-1
Biggin Hill, RAF, 242, 317
Bijou, 137, 231
Binney, Adm Sir T H, 197, 248
Bircham Newton, RAF, 7, 12, 24, 207-9, 247, 323, 329, 336, 359
BIRKJA, 40
BIRMINGHAM, 36, 56
Birnbacher, Kplt, 92, 103, 113, 114, 276
Blackford, Gp Cap, 71
Blacktoft, 105
Blackwall, 312
Blackwater, River, 59, 60, 78, 128, 141, 198
Blake, CPO J, 105
Blakeney, 49
BLANCHE, 16
Blankenberge, 284, 345
Blatchford, Fl.Lt, 152, 154
Bleed Hill, 226

Blenheims, 12, 75, 132, 205, 250
Bletchley Park, 247
Blockade, Allied, 13
Blogg, H, 296, 335
Blue Mermaid, 213, 231, 238
BLYSKAWICA, 10, 13, 47
Blyth (Northumberld), 3, 104, 113, 199
Blythburgh, 270
BOADICEA, 10, 19
Boddy, Wt.Off, 326
Bofors guns, 127, 251-3
Bomber Command (RAF), 205, 241, 247, 293, 370-1
Bonnington Court, 103
Bonser, Capt, 17
Bonte, Kapt, 20
Booms, 8-9, 60
BORDE, 26, 29
Borderers, 7th, 254
Borkum, 26, 247-8
Bostock, 46
Boston (Lincs), 59,195,214,342
Boulderpool, 114
Boulogne, 40, 49, 206, 209, 342
Bourne, Lt F W, RNVR, 363
Bouvier d'Yvoire, Cap, 50
Bovey Trace, 215
Bowen, E G, 117, 132
Bowerman, Cdr H G, 37
Bowles, Cdr G T, 21
Bowles, Cpl, 105
Box, Cf Const C G, 72, 160
Boxall, Cdr, 306
Boxted (Essex), 329
Boyd, Wg-Cdr, 241
Boyle, Rr-Adm E C, 2, 180, 182
Brackenbury Fort, 66, 198, 262
Bradfield (Essex), 128
Bradfield,Lt-Cdr D,RNVR, 287,354
Bradwell (Essex), 133, 231, 251, 258-9, 266, 331, 342, 350
Braintree, 135
Bramble Island, 137, 260
Bramford, 265
Brancaster, 49
Brantham, 137
Brauchitsch, Hauptmann, 91
Brauning, Adm, 372
Bredfield, 155
Bremen, 371
Bremen, 200
Brentford (Middx), 315

Bridge, ABS L, 276
Bridlington, 9, 33, 53, 59, 213, 296, 331-2. Air raids,137,141, 145, 168
Brielle, 52
Brigham & Cowan, 322
Brightlingsea, 28, 30, 33, 45, 59, 60, 71, 84-6, 99, 104, 105, 128, 146, 166, 174, 176, 183, 188-90, 219, 222, 231, 252, 294-5, 298-9, 305, 317-8, 325, 340-4, 347, 373
Air raids, 137, 139, 158, 266, 270
Brinkley, C,118
Brind, Cap M R, 361
BRINLO, 40
Britannia IV, 45
British Captain, 217
British Councillor,9
Britisher, 231
British Fortune, 215
British Triumph, 31
Broads, Norfolk, 194-5, 314, 320
Broadstairs, 51
Brock, Lt, USAAF, 345
Bromswell, 154
Brooke Marine Shipyard, 99,167, 294
Brookes, Captain, 300
Brooke, Rr-Adm Sir B, 180
Brookfield, Cap, 348, 350
Brooks' (Mistley), 137
Brown, Fl.Lt, 326
Brown, Percy, 52
Brown, Seaman S L, 11
Brownrigg, Adm Sir H, 2
Bruges, 238
Brundle, 194
Brunton, Lt RNR, 95
Bryant, Cdr B J, 199, 201, 204
Brynmill, 215
Buchanan, Lt-Cdr RAN (ret), 49
Büchting, Oblt-z-S H, 113
Bucklesham, 256
Buckley, Lt P N, 199
Buckley, Rr-Adm F A, 195
Bucks, 5th, 56
BUNTING, HMS, 61, 187, 358
Burgh Castle, 265
Burgos, 31
Burgwal R F, 51
Buried Reserve CH, 249
Burk, Lt C A, RCNVR, 291

INDEX

Burnham-on-Crouch, 45, 251, 253, 268, 270, 318, 347, 349, 373
   Air raids on, 149, 253
BURZA, 13, 19, 40
BUSTLER, 302
BYMSs, 232
BYMS 2040, 309
BYRON, 355

Cabby, 46
Caffrey, MM, 278
Caister, 12, 23, 104, 115, 260
   Lifeboat, 296, 355
Calais, 40, 53, 77, 78, 135, 206, 275, 346
CALCUTTA, 43, 55
California (Norfolk), 261
Callaghan, J, 192
CALYPSO, 201
Cambrai, 142
Cambridge, 118, 129, 136, 139
CAMELIA, 309
Cameronians, 10th, 68
CAMPBELL, 94, 216, 239, 44-5
Campbell, Cdr C D, RNVR, 189, 324
Campbell, V-Adm G, 189
Campbell, Lt L G R, RNVR, 280
Campbell, Sgt, RAF, 326
Canada, 17
Canewdon, 118, 121, 125, 130, 132, 135, 146, 244, 250, 253
Canning Town, 312
Canvey Island, 26, 45, 60
CAP D'ANTIFER, 237
CAPE SPARTEL, 220
CAP FINISTERRE, 88, 90
Cap Pilar, 318
Cap Gris Nez, 156
CAPRICORNUS, 99
CARDIFF, 143
Cardwell, Mrs N, 137
CARENA, 53, 88, 235
Carnaby, RAF, 331
CAROLINE MOLLER, 229, 302-3
Carr, Lt F W, RNVR, 285
Carrier, 365
CARRY ON, 101
CASABLANCA, 201
Castle Camps, RAF, 133, 251
Castle, F, 298
Castanet, 231, 306-7
Castricum, 353
CASWELL, 221

Catalina aircraft, 329
Catherine Hawksfield, 105
CATTISTOCK, 243
Caulfield, Lt J A, RNVR, 289
CAYRIAN, 107
CD radar, 226, 232, 237, 250
"Cerberus", Operation, 248
CH(radar), 117-125, 250
CHAMPION, 302, 308
Champion, Cap J P, 182
Champion de Crespigny, Cdr F P, 184
Channel convoys, 3, 92, 363
Chaplin, Det.Con. L, 53
Chapman, PO, 219
Chapple, Lt-Cdr C W A, 107
CHARLES BOYES, 297
CHARLOCK, 357
Chatham, 1, 2, 30, 33, 36, 37, 78, 99, 117, 126, 136, 139, 142, 225-6, 248, 268, 285, 365
   Air raids, 145-8, 150, 155-7, 253-4, 259
   Dockyard, 308, 310-2
Chatwood, 298
Checcucci, Lt, 113
CHEL radar (see CD)
CHELMER, 357
Chelmondiston, 263
Chelmondsleigh, 45
Chelmsford, air raids, 259-60, 263, 270, 341
Chertsey, 341
Chièvres, 157
Chiswick, 45
CHL (radar), 29, 94, 121, 126, 226
Christie, Fl.Lt., 208
Churchill, Winston, 19, 79, 145, 248, 346-7
Chrysolite, 11
Ciliax, Admiral, 241, 245
CIRCE, 201
CITE DE LONDRES, 301
City of Brisbane, 90
City of Canberra, 84, 304
City of Kobe, 23
CITY OF ROCHESTER, 167
Clacton, 32, 33, 46, 49, 55, 63, 96, 104, 108, 110, 136, 137, 198, 217, 251, 341-2
   Air raids on; 141, 143, 149, 151, 153, 156, 158, 259, 266
   Holiday Camp.....1, 8
   Lifeboat........17, 46, 296, 298

Clan Forbes, 143
Clan Monroe, 83, 164, 304
Clapsons', 321
Cleethorpes, 196, 263
CLEMATIS, 357
Cley, 136
Cliff, Lt, RANVR, 212
CLOUGHTON WYKE, 220
CM radar (see CD)
Coalhouse Fort, 64
Coastal Command, RAF, 116, 176, 198
Coastal Forces, Ch 13 passim, 324
Coast Artillery:
   327 Battery, 56
   Regts: *514*, 106; *515*, 63; *518*, 20; *544*, *546*, *547*, *548* & *572*, 64
Coastguards, 296, 324
Coats, Cdr, 215, 247-8
COBBERS, 105
Cochranes', 321
Cockley, Lt J P R, RNR, 93
CODRINGTON, 13, 37, 47
Coity Castle, 103
COLCHESTER, 300
Colchester, 138, 141, 162, 238
   Air raids, 257-8, 266
   Essex County Hospital, 17
Cole, Lt-Cdr A, 38, 273
Colegate End, 329
Coleman, Cdr A M, 180, 187
Coleman C A (MN), 11
Collins Pleasurecraft, 320
Colne Point, 156, 350
Colne, River, 59, 60, 78, 128, 146, 341
Coltishall, RAF, 87, 162, 246, 251, 282, 285
Conder, Cdr E R, 63
COMBATTANTE, *LA*, 365-6
Combined Operations, Ch 17
Commandos, 346-7, 361
COMO, 60
Conical Floats (German), 97, 108-9
Coningsby, RAF, 208
Consolidated Fisheries, 58
CONSTANT FRIENDS, 339
"Consular", Operation, 347
Constant Nymph, 45
Continental Coaster, 93
Cook, Walton & Gemmel, 321
Coombes, Lt A C D, RNR, 228

INDEX

Copperas Wood, 127
Corbrook, 92
Cordeaux, Cdr, 29, 43
Corduff, 113
Corea, 24
CORFIELD, 214
Corhampton, 215
Corke,Lt-Cdr C L,RNVR, 340,347
Cork LV,
Cormarsh, 216
Cormead, 299
Cormount, 212, 236
CORNWALLIS, 60
Coronation of Leeds, 162
Corringham, 161
CORSAIR, 292
Corton, 101, 111, 113, 115, 157, 167, 224, 228, 230, 367
Coryton, 147
Cory, William, Ltd, 238
Cory, Wg-Cdr, 323
Corvettes, Harwich-based, 6, 40,299, 357, 359
COSSACK, 13
COTSWOLD, 104, 216, 223, 237, 283, 305, 308, 357, 364, 366
COTTESMORE, 243
Coulen, Cap W K E, 196
Covehithe, 12, 51, 301
Cox, Mr, 304
Coxyde, 152
Cozens, L/S A A, 161
Crabtree, 1931, 321
Craig, Lt-Cdr D L, 98
Crane's Factory, 163
Creasy, Capt G E, 31, 37, 55
Cree, 301
Creeksea, 146, 347
Cressdene, 298
Crichtoun, 367
Cromer, 24, 31, 47, 63, 66, 88, 106, 114, 139, 212, 215, 222, 236, 311,323, 370
 Air raids, 137, 256, 258
 lifeboats, 11, 114, 206, 223, 296, 335
"Crash Warnings", 255
"Cromwell", 77
Cronyn, Cap St J, 194
Cross, R, 297
Crossley, Lt-Cdr N J, 19
Crouch, Lt-Cdr R J H, 74
Crouch, River, 59, 60, 183, 318
Croydon Airport, 130

Cruiser Squadrons: *2nd*, 36; *18th*, 56; *20th*, 6
Cubison, Lt-Cdr A J, 28, 61, 163, 187, 191
Cunningham, Fl.Lt J, 259, 262
Curtayne, Lt W J, RNVR, 98
CURZON, 364-5
CYCLOPS, 136, 199, 202
Czech Brigade, 79, 369
Czestochowa, 215
Czernin, Plt. Off. Count, 155

DAKINS, 363
Daalen Waters, R F, 51
Dab II, 45
Dagenham, 149, 159, 162, 180
Dagenham, 298
Dalewood, 215
DAMSAY, 357
Danby, Vc-Adm, 344
Danckwerts, Sub-Lt, RNVR, 150
Dane, Cap, 182, 253, 349
Dann, Pt.Off, 208
DANUBE III, 97
Daphne, 115
DAPPER, 302, 308
DARCY COOPER, 160, 306-7
Darrell's Battery, 63, 67
Dartford, 162, 267
Deal, 152
Deanbrook, 98
Debden, RAF, 87, 91, 117, 129, 133, 143, 146, 150, 152, 324, 345
Deben, River, 78, 309, 341
Dechaineux, Cdr E F V,RAN, 115
Degaussing, 24-25D
De Haas, J, 353
DEMS, 312
Dengie, 198, 217, 226, 232, 259, 340
Den Helder, 37, 39, 204, 207, 323, 364
De Jonge E, 353
Deodata 297
De Pass, Cdre D,192
Deptford, 159, 258, 312, 349
Destroyer Flotillas: *1st*,13, 18, 35, 55; *5th*, 13, 35, 56, 195; *7th*,13, 35; *8th*, 56; *16th*, 56, 93, 239, 241, 359;*18th*, 56, 94; *20th*, 14, 36, 56, 74, 275; *21st*, 56, 92, 93, 98, 179, 222, 239, 289, 363

Destroyer patrols, 56
Detling, RAF, 7,142,146,156,329
DEVON COUNTY, 212
Dickens, Lt-Cdr P,283-5, 288, 305-6
Digby, RAF, 133
Dimlington, 266
DIRECTOR, 302
Discovery II, 185
Ditcham, Mids.F RNR, 222
DIVERSION, 301
Dixcove, 300
Doig's Shipyard, 321
Divoy, L, 52
Docking, RAF, 198, 208
Domburg, 40, 135
Donna Nook, RAF, 198, 208
DONNA NOOK, 235
Donner, Lt-Cdr C M, 278
Donnet, M, 52
DORIS, 201
Dornier Do 217s, 219
Dotterel, 38, 113
Dover, 2, 41, 47, 48, 211, 211, 241,244, 267,270,275,284,300
 Air raids, 152, 155, 157, 161, 163
 CH Station, 118,125,129,152 155,157,161,163,185,198
Dovercourt, 53,106,137, 01,302
 Air raids on,155,163,266,271
 Hospital, 218
Dover Strait, 91, 226, 239, 248, 345
Dowding, ACM Sir H, 119
Downs (Ramsgate), 29, 40
Drax, Adm Sir R P E E, 12, 36, 77, 98, 143, 178
Drayton (Norfolk), 135
Driberg, T, MP, 350
Driffield, RAF, 143
Drifters, 58
Dromore Castle, 217
Dronkers, 53
DUCHESS OF ROTHESAY, 348
"Ducks" (see Corvettes)
Dudley, Surg-Rr-Adm, 177
DUFF, 363
Duke, Cdre R G, 192
Dunbar-Naismith, Rr-Adm Sir M, 180
Duncan, Lt G F RCNVR, 284
Duncarron, 214
DUNGENESS, 305

INDEX

Dunkirk (France), 66, 78, 83, 206, 318, 345, 361
Dunkirk (Kent) CH Station, 118, 121, 142,232, 244, 270
Dunkirk Evacuation, 41-49, 87, 92, 339
Dunmow, Great, 293
DUNOON, 29
Dunwich, 224, 350
CHL, 109, 126, 141, 166, 250
"Duppel" jamming, 264-5
Dutch Brigade, 79, 369
DWI, 26, 30
Dynamo, 260
Dynamo, Operation (see Dunkirk Evacuation)

Eaden, Lt-Cdr J H, 289
EAGER, 105
Eagle Ships, 29, 43, 150, 179, 312
Eagle Squadrons, 341
Eardley-Wilmot, Lt J A, 275
Earl's Colne, 293
Easington (Yorks), 237
Eastchurch, RAF, 83, 142, 146, 168, 198, 329
East Coast Convoys, 2-8, & Chs 5 & 10 passim, 181-2
East Dudgeon LV, 11
East Mersea, 128, 130
Eastwood, 307
E-boats, 36, 63, 80, 82, 93-4, 97, 110-5, 116, 209-18, 222-3, 227, 229, 234, 237-8, 264, 275-7, 293, 301, 303, 353, 367, 369, 372
Flotillas: *1st*, 113; *2nd*, 112,115, 216-7, 229, 234, 280, 289,367; *3rd*, 113; *4th*, 215, 217, 222-3, 229, 234, 243; 280-1, 283, 289, 291; *6th*, 234, 243, 289, 291, 357; *8th*, 236-7, 289, 357; *9th*, 366; *10th*, 261, 366
EC convoys, 3
Edds, Lt-Col W F, 349
EDWARDIAN, 91
Edwards, Lt-Cdr R, 228
Edward Z Dresden (see Clacton lifeboat)
EDWINA, 93
Eecklo, 152
Effra, 115
Edge, Lt P N, RNVR, 289
EGLINTON, 51, 243

EGRET, 96
Eikhaug, 215
Eindhoven, 339, 341
Ellingworth, CPO, 149
Ellis, Lt R A, 275
Elmsett, 110
Emden, 77, 204, 206-7
EMDEN, 205
Emma, 59, 231
EMED, 46, 297, 305-6, 342
ÉMILE DESCHAMPS, 49
Empire coasters, 316,318,320-1
Empire Ghyll, 216
Empire Newcomen, 216
Empire Parkeston, 363
Empire Sound, 155
Empson, Lt K, RNVR, 99
EMULOUS, 302
Ena, 44
Endenburg, K van, 50
"Englandvaarder", 50-4
English Trader, 297
Epinoy, 263
EPPING, HMS, 84, 183
EREBUS, 77, 79
ERICH GEISE, 24
Erith, 44
Erpr. Gr. 210, 88, 142, 167
EROs, 314
Erwarton, 151, 355
Esbjerg, 370
ESK, 14, 36, 74
Esmeralda, 228
Esmonde, Lt-Cdr(A) E, 241
Essex County Divison, 78
Essex Lance, 301
Esterel, 297
Ethel Everard, 46
Ethel Radcliffe, 115, 164, 301
EUCLASE, 84, 221
EUROPA, HMS, 57, 155, 191
EURYLUS, 310
EVENING PRIMROSE, 27, 59
Everards Ltd, 231, 238
Everett, Lt-Cdr W G, 278
EVESHAM, 158
Examination Service, 59, 103, 182, 184-5
EXHAYNE, 254
EXMOOR, 110-111, 299
"Exodus", Operation....371
EXPRESS, 14, 36, 74-5
Express, 228
Eyke, 33

FABIA, 16
Fairlight CD radar, 241
Fairmile Company, 314-5
Fairplay I, 305
FAIRSAY, 357
Falcon, 160
Fallowfield, Cap W H G, 187
Farquharson, Cap J P, 294
Farringdon, Lt-Cdr, 243
Faulkner, Lt R I J, 275
Faversham, 317
Feldt, Kaplt K, 112, 276
Felixstowe, 19, 32, 36. 38-9, 55, 61, 65, 73, 75, 87,88, 90, 92,96, 108,117, 128,136, 143,187, 198, 219-21,227-9,231,235,243,263, 265, 267, 271, 273-4. 294, 303, 318, 324, 326, 330, 338-9, 351, 353. 355, 359, 366, 369, 372
Air raids, 153, 155, 157, 158. 160, 166, 256, 266
RAF, 40, 309, 352
FELIXSTOWE, 8, 360
Fellows & Co, 321
Fersfield, 270
FIDELIA, 163
Fidelio, 229
Fields, Gracie, 200
Fifeshire, 57
Filby, 261
Fimmen, K.Kap K, 372
FIREFLY, 221
Fireglow, 106
FISHER BOY, 104, 228
FITZGERALD (DIW), 107
FITZROY, 49, 228, 305
Fixed Defences, 61-66
Flamborough Head, 2, 11, 331
Fleet Air Arm Squadrons: *812*, 75, 207; *819*, 237; *825*, 241-2
FLEET TENDER C, 301
Fleetwood, 57
FLEMING, 89, 90
Fletcher, Lt-Cdr W, RNR, 343
Flushing, 37, 207, 275, 344
FN Convoys (See East Coast Convoys)
Focke-Wulf FW 190s, 231,259-62, 326
FOGMO & FOGO, 312
Folda, 340
Folkestone, 44
FORCE, 212

INDEX

FORDE, 48, 302-9
FOREMOST 18, 302, 304
Foreness CHL, 29, 126, 133, 135
Foulness, 95, 100, 104, 109, 128, 133, 143, 146, 149, 152, 182-3, 198, 251, 265, 341, 343
Foulsham, RAF, 339
Fowberry Tower, 106
Francis & Gilders, 238
FRANCOLIN, 215, 221
FRANC TIREUR, 163, 235-6, 339
Frankrig, 97
Franks, Lt R, 19
Frating, 132
FREDERIKA LENSEN, 60
FREEDOM, 302
Freeman, Lt RNVR, 255
FREIJA, 302, 304, 306
"Freya" (Gm radar), 135, 205
Friesland, 215
Frinton, 51, 71, 103, 104, 131, 217, 305
  Air raids, 137, 259, 262
Frisian Islands, 285, 323
Fritton, 305
Frohlieb, Oblt. K, 104
Frostenden, 351
Froud, Cdr P, 185
Frumenton, 219, 298
FS convoys (see East Coast Convoys)
Fulham IV, 87, 304
Fulham V, 92
Fullerton, Adm Sir E, 61, 194
Fullerton, Lady, 320
FYLDEA, 221

GAIRSAY, 357
GALATEA, 36, 37, 56, 77
Gallimore, Wt.Off E, 352
GALVANI, 104
GANGES (Shotley), 47, 55, 174, 186, 268
GARDENIA, 357
Gardner, Lt M, RNVR, 98
Garland, Lt H, RNVR, 105
Garrett, Act.Cap H M, 312
Garrett, Paym.Lt-Cdr H, 42
Garrison Point Fort, 65, 66, 179
GARTH, 75, 216, 229
Garth, 297
Gasfire, 93
Gas, Light & Coke Co, 238
GAY VIKING, 292

GCI radar, 226, 250-1
"Gee", 250
Gemmel, Lt-Cdr K, RNVR, 285
Gernet, Oblt, von, 114
Georg. von, Lt z S, 235
George Balfour, 97, 229, 301
GEORGE ROBB, 106
Georgians, 370
Gertrude May, 231, 238
Gibb, Sir Alexander, 251
Gibson, Flt Lt Guy, 133, 335
Giel, W A, 50
Gill, 3rd Off. WRNS, 234
Gillingham (Kent), 43, 137, 177, 242
  Air raids on, 146,148,160,266
Gillingham (Norfolk), 265
Giorgio Ohlsen, 31
GIPSY, 10, 19, 303
GIROFLEE, 85
Gleave, Wg Cdr T, 242
Glencoe, 83
Glenfinlas, 106
Glenmore, 298
Glenny, Lt, 22
GLOAMING, 107
Globe, 231
GLOWWORM, 16
GNEISENAU, 239,245,301,308
GOATFELL, 159, 332
Goddard, Cap, 302
Goff, Cap R S, 182
GOLDEN EAGLE, 48
Golden Grain, 231
Golder's Green, 277
Goldhanger, 152
Goodfellow, Lt R, RNVR, 353
Goodwood, 9
Goolden, Rr-Adm F W H, 161, 186
Goole, shipbuilding, 321-2
GORDON, HMS, 180
Gorleston, 106, 194, 211, 227, 243
  Air raids, 145, 160, 168
  Air-sea rescue, 321, 323, 325-8
  lifeboat, 11, 49, 296-7
GOSSAMER, 305
Gould, Lt P F S, 39, 275
Grace, Vc-Adm, 310
Grace Darling, 45
GRAFTON, 47
Grain,148, 156; Fort, 64
Graham Bunn, 320
Gravelines, 155, 242
Gravesend, 22, 26, 133, 180, 300,

312-3
  Air raids, 156, 159, 168, 251 258-9, 267
Grays, 148, 156
Great Bentley, 128
Great Bromley CH Sta, 118, 121, 123, 124, 129-32, 145, 232, 244, 250, 253, 257
GREATER LONDON (see Southend lifeboat)
Great Leighs, 266
Great Nore Fort, 251
Great Saling, 293
Great Sampford, 345
Great Wakering, 266
GREENFLY, 87
Greenhithe, 180
Grenaa, 159
Greening, Lt-Cdr C W, 38
Green, Silley Weir, 312-3
Greenway, Fl.Off, 339
Greenwich RN College, 27, 259
GRENVILLE, 31
GREYHOUND, 47
GRIFFIN, 37
Griffiths, Lt-Cdr M W, RNVR, 99
Griffiths, Lt-Cdr(E) J P K, RNVR, 294
Grimsby, 12, 26, 37, 57, 58, 86, 195, 197, 205, 214, 216, 219-221, 237, 271, 278, 318, 321-2, 324-5, 330, 332, 370
  Air raids, 137, 142, 155, 157, 254, 260, 262-3
GRIVE, 46
GROM, 10, 13
GROWLER, 302-3
GRUNLO, 40
GUILLEMOT, 106,213,222-3,298, 365
GURKHA, 10
Gwynwood, 107
GYPSY, 166

H 28, 205, 311
H 34, 74
Haabet, 53
Haddiscoe Bridge, 195
Hadow, Cdr P H, 76
Haigh, Prof, 27
Haisborough Sands, 92, 296
HALCYON, 87
HALCYON Class M/S, 25
Halesworth, 329

INDEX

ıll, Cap J B E, 40
ıll, Seaman, 105
ılo, 159, 300
ılsey, Cap T E, 36, 113, 115
ıMBLEDON, 52, 75, 216, 229, 243
ımburg, air raids, 323, 371
ımer, Lt J A H, 289
ımford Water, 60
ımilton, Lt, RNVR, 110
ımilton Dock, Lowestoft, 191, 291
ımilton-Hill, Lt E, RNR, 275
ıMMOND, 11, 25
ımmond Knoll LV, 11
ımond, Cdr, 107
ımpston Hill, 133
ımpton, 314, 316
ımpton Court, 45
ınks, Wg Cdr, 282
ınnah, Sgt J, RAF, 206
ıppisburgh, 10, 66, 108, 126
ırdcastle, Lt-Cdr, 177
ırker, Lt-Cdr I W G, 90
ırker, J, 321
ırkstead, 150, 357
ırland & Wolff, 312-3
ırlingvliet, 50
ırmer-Elliott, Lt S F, RNVR, 48
ARRIER, 87
ırris, Rear-Adm C F, 2,10,19,61, 78, 127, 128, 185, 304
ırtmann, Kplt, 20
ırwich, 2, 6, 8, 13, 17, 18, 26, 30, 1, 36-8, 40, 46, 48, 50, 55,56,60, 68, 77-9, 83-4, 87, 91-3, 95-8, 103-6, 108, 110, 113, 117, 127-8, 132-3, 176, 183-7, 194-5, 199, 212, 214-5, 218-20, 222-4, 226-8, 230, 232, 234-9, 243, 251, 253-4, 256, 262, 265, 268, 273, 278, 281, 289, 298-300, 311, 325, 340, 349, 355-7, 359, 363, 371-3
Air raids, 136-9,141-3,147,150-5, 157, 160, 162-3, 166-7, 258, 267, 268, 270
Fixed Defences, 63-67
Harwich Quay, 302
RN Sub-Cmd, 61, 182, 229, 237
Salvage, 301-9
ASLEMERE, 343
asse, Lt, 167
ıuxley 93

HAVOCK, 37
Havocs, 251, 259
Haward, Lt G H S, 199
HAWFINCH, 78
Haytor, 83-4
Hazelhoff Roelfzema, E, 351
HDMLs, 314
"Headache",116, 222, 227, 230
Heartsease, 317
Heaton, Cdr, 301
Heber-Percy, Lt-Cdr D J L, 108
HEEMSKERK, 40
Heinkel He 177s, 265
HEKLA, 98
Helder, 221
HELDER, HMS, 197, 347-50, 358
Heligoland, 201, 365, 370
Heligoland Bight, 200-1, 205, 336
Hellyers (Hull), 58
Helmswell, RAF, 127
HELVELYN, 159, 300
Helyer, O, 197
Henley, 265
Hemsby, 260
Henniker-Heaton, Cap A, 61, 84, 346
Henry Woodall, 34
Herbert, 230
Herbert, PO A P, MP, 100, 267
Herbert Woods, 320-1
Heriot, Lt H S, RNVR, 102
Herland, 98
Herne Bay, 344
Herrick, Plt.Off, 337
Herringfleet, 266
Hessle, 322
Hesselyn, Wt.Off, 326
Heworth, 88
Heybridge, 145, 258
H F Bailey, 297, 335
Hichens, Lt-Cdr R P, RNVR, 224, 274, 276, 279-80, 283-4, 287, 345
Higgins, ABS T, 35-6
Highland Lt Infantry, 70
High Street (Darsham), CH Sta, 118, 129, 130-2, 135
Highwave, 12, 304
Hillary, Fl.Lt R, 345
Hilda Jean, 46
Hine, Lt-Cdr J P W, 47
HKD, 231
Hoadley, Lt, RNVR, 278
Hodder, Lt-Cdr, RNVR, 372

Hoiles, W C, 302
HOLDERNESS, 222-3,236,243,281
Holderness Rural Dist, 164
Holbrook, 152
Holehaven, 26, 60, 78, 180
Holland-on-Sea, 67, 136
Hollesley Bay, 297, 230, 304
Hollick, Sub-Lt(E) W, RNVR, 346
Holman projectors, 58
Holmes Ltd, 321
Holt, V-Adm R V, 196
Home Guard, 71, 369
Honington, RAF, 205
Hook of Holland, 38, 39, 52, 281, 285, 339, 372
HOPEWELL, 292
Hopton, 232-3
Horlocks (of Mistley), 238
Hornchurch, 88, 299
Hornchurch, RAF, 146, 149
Horne, Lt J B R, RNVR, 282-3
Horning, 163, 320
Horseferry, 281
Horsham St Faith, RAF, 54
Howard, Ensign, USN, 228
Howes, Lt-Cdr P, 279
Howitt, Fl.Lt, 263
HSLs (see RAF launches)
Hudson, Cap R, 29
Hudsons(aircraft),208,323,326,329
Hudsons (Hull), 58
Hughes, Surg-Lt, RNVR, 111
Hull, 8, 57, 58, 107, 192, 195-7
   Air raids, 138, 141, 145, 158-160,163,167-8, 255, 262-3, 266
   Salvage Dept, 299, 301
   Shipyards, 321-2
Hull Trader, 212
Humber, 17, 20, 35, 37, 40, 52, 59, 66, 75, 78, 94, 97, 99, 106, 195-7, 219, 255, 262, 268, 294, 299, 300, 301, 310, 321-2, 358, 367
   Sub-Command (RN), 60, 218, 220, 224, 226, 229, 237, 278, 365
Humphreys, Cap K N, 195
Humphreys, Lt J W, RNVR, 361
Humphrey & Smith, 321
Hunsdon, RAF, 133, 251, 259
Hunt, Cap, 268
Hurlingham, 45
Hurricane fighters, 259
Husks' Shipyard, 318
HUSSAR, 136
HYDROGRAAF, 232

INDEX

Hydrophones, 94
HYPERION, 38

IFF, 130, 249, 292
IFRU, 125
IJmuiden, 37, 38, 207, 281-2, 284, 288-9, 293, 357, 362-3, 366, 372
Ilse, 229
Immingham, 13, 56, 74, 108, 195, 197, 225, 227, 237, 292, 322
Ingoldmells, 145, 195, 254
INDRABARAH, 199
INTER, 101
IONA III, 349
Ipswich, 44, 46, 61, 63, 97, 112, 130, 187, 212, 214-5, 219, 234-5, 237, 298, 303, 307-8, 356, 358
  Air raids, 137, 149, 155,158, 160-1, 166-7, 253, 255-60, 262-5, 268, 271
Irene, Princess, 37
IRMA, 182
IRENA-I, 219, 221
Isleworth, 317
Italian air raids, 151-5
IVANHOE, 14, 43, 74-6

Jackman, FLOff, 337
JAGUAR (Br destr), 47
JAGUAR (Gm torp-bt), 247
James, Lt C A, 275
James, Lt D, RNVR, 285
James & Stone, B'sea, 279, 318
James L Maguire, 18
James Pollock, 317
Jamming, RDF, 133-5, 241, 244, 264-6
JASPER, 369
JAVELIN, 47, 75
Jaywick, 71
J R Proudfoot, 342
JIW, 231
JEANNIE LEASK, 158, 306
JEFF, 302
Jenkins, Lt E J M, RNVR, 213
Jepson's Shipyard, 161
JERSEY, 24
JG 26, 166
Jim, 368
Joan Hodson, 370
Joan Margaret, 108
Johnson, Amy, 343-4

Johnson & Jago, 370
Jones, FLOff, 265
Jones, Prof R V, 71, 119
Josefina Thorden, 233, 259, 308
Joseph Button, 98
Joseph Swan, 92
Junkers Ju 188s, 265
JULES VERNE, 201
Juno, SS, 17
JUNO HMS, 24
JUPITER, 75
JUSTICE, 302
JUSTIFIER, 164
"J" Watch, 133

Kanda, 301
Kango Hammer, 99
Katwijk, 353
Keesom H W, 50
Kekewich, Rr-Adm Sir P, 277
Kellaway, Lt-Cdr(E) J, RNVR, 294
KELLY, 36, 75
Kelly, Lt J P, RNVR, 83
Kennade, Kplt F, 113
KENIA, 95, 302, 305-8
Kenley, RAF, 241
Kennedy, Lt J, USN, 270
KENNYMORE, 99
Kentish Knock LV, 12
Kenton, 114
Kerr, Cdr, 273
Kerr, Lt-Cdr, 225
Kesgrave, 355
Kessingland, 258
Kew, 45
Keynes, 11
KG (German bomber force): 2,142, 254; 3, 143; 4, 82, 249, 254; 6, 244; 30, 82; 40, 249
Kidd, Surg-Lt, 219
Killingholme, 136, 197, 332
King, 45
King, Lt W, 202, 204
KING ALFRED (RNVR base), 42
KING DUCK, 340
King Egbert, 24
King Henr, 168
King's Lynn, 59
  Air raids, 158, 167-8, 256-7
KINGSTON OLIVINE, 216, 220, 298
"Kipper patrols", 12
Kirk, Lt, RNVR, 278
Kirnwood, 91
Kirton (Suffolk), 265

Kirton-in-Lindsay, RAF, 133
Kitcat, Cdr, 243
Klein E, 50
Klug, Lt z S B, 92, 101, 113, 276
Knock Deep, 91
Knock John Fort, 251, 342, 358
Knottingley, 321
Knowles, Rr-Adm G H, 282
KOMET, 284
Konstantinos Hadjupikios, 297
Kris Cruisers, 317
KROOMAN, 302, 308
Kuntz, Oblt, 106
KYLEMORE, 91
Kyloe, 224
Kyma, 298

L 23 & 26, 204
L, Force, 354-8
Lady Brassey, 300, 302, 307
Lady of Man, 363
Lady Rosebery, 44
LADY SHIRLEY, 93
Laine, Lt J N B, RNVR, 59
Lampard, Lt-Cdr R T, 110
Lampe, D, 73
Landguard Fort, 18, 19, 63-4, 136, 152, 187, 254
Landguard Peninsula, 84, 150, 210, 219, 221, 228, 247, 340
Landing Craft, Chs 14 & 17 passim
Langenhoe, 152
Langham (Norfolk), 198, 207, 209
Langley, Lt M A, 204
Langtoft, 133
La Panne, 48
Largo, 218, 308
Larnder, H, 25
LARWOOD, 12, 35
Lawrence, T E, 331
Layer Breton, 260
Lazzari, Sgt Plt, 154
Lea, 98
Leaf, Lt E D W, RNVR, 52, 292
LEBERECHT MAASS, 14
LEDA, 50, 75
Lee, Sub-Lt, 288
Lees, Cap. (TH) W J, 11
Legapi, Cap, 13
LEIGH, HMS, 182
Leigh-on-Sea, 45, 318
LEIPZIG, 200
Leo Robinson's, 320
Letchworth, 95, 298

INDEX

Levington, 67
Lewis, Lt-Cdr E R. 160, 194
Lewis, Lt F W. RANVR. 298
Lewis. Lt-Cdr R, 21. 27
Leysdown, 212
Lightoller,Lt F R.RNVR, 45, 160. 291
Lightships, Air Attacks on, 11-3. 90, 95, 103
Lincolnshire Division, 78
Lindemann, H. 167
Lindenhall, 159
Lindholme dinghy. 329
LINDISFARNE, 321
Lindsay, Pt.Off G. 338
Linsen. 360, 364-5
Linwood, 339
Linzler. F. 263
Lisetta. 365
Little Clacton, 156, 260
Little Express, 228
Little Oakley, 258
Little Walden. 266
LL Sweep, 27, 30, 31, 109
Lloyd. Captain, RA, 20
Loasby, Lt P G, RNVR. 343. 352
LOCH ALSH, 219
LOCH INVER, 93
Lockhart, Cdr C S, 180
Lockhart, Lt, USAAF. 345
LOCUST. 43, 56
Loftus. Gunner. 105
Lombard-Hobson, Lt-Cdr S. 185. 222-3, 299
London:
 Blitz, 139, 141, 145, 147-9. 156,159,162,166,259,267
 Port, 2, 3, 82. 148, 180, 312
 Sub-Command (RN), 2, 180
LONDONDERRY, 13
LOOSESTRIFE, 357
LORD KEITH, 219, 222, 342
LORD SELBORNE, 108
LORD ST VINCENT. 105, 213
Louise Stephens (see Gorleston lifeboat)
Lovelock, Lt RNVR, 44
Lowestoft, 10, 20, 48, 49, 51, 55, 57, 59. 61, 79, 82, 84, 87, 92. 103-5, 109-10, 113, 115, 129. 190, 192, 194, 195, 209, 211, 215, 221, 228-9, 233-4, 253-4,256,257,278-83,291-2, 294, 298-9,301,305,309,314, 318.

349,351, 355, 359, 361, 373
Air raids, 137-9,141,145,150, 154-7,162-4,167-8,261,263
Lowestoft Steam Drifters Co. 58
"Lucid", Operation, 78
Lucy Lawers (see Aldeburgh lifebt)
Luftflotte 2, 142
Luftkorps IX, 100
LUNULA, 161
Lutjens, Kont.Adm, 17
Lützow, K.kap, 291
Lydamore, W H. 302. 304, 308
Lyon, V-Adm Sir G. 239, 241
Lysekil. 292
Lysland, 301

Mablethorpe, 33, 60, 195. 197, 214-5
MAC 5. 103
MacDonald. Lt G J, RNZNVR. 288
Mack, Cap P J. 13
MACKAY. 241, 242-5, 289, 291. 326
Macklin, Cap, 314
MackenZie, Lt-Cdr, RNR, 219
Magdapur. 9, 16, 297
Maggie, 228
Magnus, Lt P, RNVR, 289
Maguire, Sq Ldr, 265
Mahoney, Lt(E), 76
Mahseer. 216, 298
MAIDA, 32
Maidstone. 168
Ma Joi, 45
Malan. Sq Ldr A. 136, 142
MALCOLM. 36, 38, 39, 56
Maldon, 71, 128, 146, 149, 318
Malines, 44n
MALLARD, 10, 95, 229
Malrix, 101
MAMMOUTH, 301
"Manna", Operation, 371
Mannooch, Lt G J, 274
Manston, RAF, 7, 26, 91, 117, 133, 137, 142, 145, 207, 331
MANTIS. HMS. 191, 283
Marder, 364
Marchioness, 45
Margaret Mary, 45
Margate, 26, 28. 49, 55, 57, 91, 136, 145, 198, 217, 355
 Air raids, 258, 262
 Lifeboat. 49, 61, 296, 344-5

Marie Dawn, 215
MARIE ELENA. 342
Mark, W J, 17
MARMION, 28, 48, 160, 306-7
Marrack, Rr-Adm H R (ret).2
Marsayru, 45
Marsh, Cap T W. 184. 373
Marshall, Ord Tel H G. 192
Marshall,Lt R H, RNVR.289,291
Marson, Lt-Cdr. 164
MARTELLO. HMS. 61, 163, 191
Martello Towers. 59, 78, 129
Martinet, 297
Martlesham Heath. RAF, 7. 87. 96, 117, 132, 142-3, 152, 166-7, 324, 326, 341
Marwick Head, 23
Mary Scott (see Southwold lifebt)
MASBs, 55, 273, 279, 325, 345
MASB 6, 47
Massey Shaw, 45
MASTER STANDFAST. 292
MASTIFF. 6, 21
Matlask, RAF. 282,323, 326, 335
Maton, Cdr R F P. 21
Matra, 16
Matukura, Capt, 18
Maunsell Forts, 232, 251, 313
MAX SCHULTZ, 14
May, A J. 45
May, Cap A S, 20
Mayer, Oblt, 114
Maylandsea, 318
McBean, Cdr R H. 273
McCowen,Lt-Cdr D N E.RNVR.292
McGregor, Sq Ldr, 44
Meakes of Marlow. 316
McPhee, Lt-Cdr R D, 306
MEDEA, 317
Medway, 78. 310
 Fixed Defences, 64, 66
 Oil Depot (see Port Victoria)
MEDWAY QUEEN. 43
Mead, Lt RNVR, 46
MEHALAH, 194
Melsbroeck, 151
MENDIP. 222
Meriones, 301
Merkert, Fwbl. 221
MEROR, 237
Mersea Island, 198, 350
Merson, Skipper J, RNR, 99
Metecalfe, Sub-Lt, RNVR, 93
Methil, 3

INDEX

MEYNELL, 50, 243, 357
MFVs, 314
MGBs, 116, 224, 233, 277
 14, 15.256; 20, 287; 75, 76,78,
 284; 77, 112, 287; 79, 285;
 87, 88, 91, 282; 89, 52; 100 &
 101, 317; 312, 320, 352; 603,
 607, 291.
Flotillas: 5th, 278; 6th, 278-80,
 283; 7th, 282-3; 12th, 279,
 289; 16th, 279, 282-3; 17th
 289; 55th, 287
Michielsen K, 50
Mid Barrow LV, 95
MIDGE, HMS, 194, 278 (see also
 Yarmouth)
MIGNONETTE, 357
Mildenhall, RAF, 205, 345
MILFORD QUEEN, 106
Miller, Lt J B P, RNVR, 156
Mines & Minefields, British
 Controlled,78; East Coast, 14,
 Observation, 60, 78; Offensive,
 207, 229
Mines & Minefields, German,
 108, 230;
 Acoustic, 96, 99, 100, 107
 Contact, 17, 22, 223-4, Land,
 149; Magnetic, 9, 22, & Ch 2
 passim; Type A, 22, 32; B 22,
 32; C & D, 32; G, 109; P, T
 & V, 214
Mine Destructor Ships, 30
Mine Recovery Vessels, 28, 61, 99
Minesweeping, 25-31, 84-5, 218,
 363; Chs 2, 5 & 10 passim.
M/S Flotillas:
 4th,231; 7th,231; 9th, 231,239;
 12th, 28, 48, 84; 13th, 239;
 18th, 231; 139th, 232
Minnie de Larrinaga, 148
Minorca, 111
MINOS, HMS, 61, 117, 190 (&
 see Lowestoft)
MINOS II, HMS, 256, 278
Minotaur, 45
Minsmere River, 60
MIRANDA, HMS, 194
Mirbach, Lt z S Freiherr G von,
 113, 115, 276
MISOA, 349, 356
MISS VIRGINIA, 340
Mistley, 130, 137
Mitchell, Fl.Off., 337

MLs, 99, 277, 315, 317, 359
ML 113, 343; 127, 99; 153, 365;
 180, 106; 195, 160; 211, 164;
 216, 316; 253, 216; 339, 229
Captain ML, 315, 317
ML Flotillas: 1st, 278; 6th, 130;
 11 & 12th, 278; 13th, 160, 187;
 32nd, 365; 51st, 278
MMSs, 109, 232
MMS 39, 213, 325; 227, 237;
 553, 216
Moidart, 83
Molde, 35
Moldenhauer, Fwbl, 12
Monarch, 369
MONARDA, 44, 46
Monsarrat, Lt N, RNVR, 186,
 213, 223
Montalto, 162
Mont Couple, 135
Montdidier, 143
Montferland, 212
MONTROSE, 90, 304, 357
Morar, 236
MORAVIA, 233
More, Cap G I S, 187
Mortlake, 45
MOSQUITO, 43
Mosquito aircraft, 251, 259, 267
Mould, Lt I S, RANVR, 150, 228
Mountbatten, Capt Lord L, 13,
 36, 75, 195, 348
Mount Ida, 296
Mountnessing, 259
MRUs, 131, 249
MTBS, 36, 96, 205, 277, 283,
 291, 324, 329
MTB 14,75, 275; 15, 75, 275, 284;
 16, 39, 75, 275; 17, 75, 275;
 22, 39, 275, 318; 24, 39; 29, 75,
 275, 318; 30,75; 31, 275; 32, 95,
 275; 61, 64, 69, 70, 241, 284;
 223 & 225, 288; 347 & 360, 361;
 439 & 442, 291; 445, 292; 495,
 365; 621, 323; 622, 285; 667, 295;
 682, 354; 724 & 728, 361; 734,
 209; 2001, 317; 5001, 368
MTB Flotillas;
 1st, 273-4; 3rd, 273; 5th, 278;
 8th, 359; 10th, 273, 292; 11th,
 288; 21st, 283, 288; 29th, 359;
 53rd, 292; 54th, 359; 58th, 285;
 64th, 361; 65th, 359
Mucking Flats, 22

Muggeridge, Malcolm, 43
Mulberry harbours, 313, 317
MULL, 321
Muller, Lt z S K, 99, 361
Mundesley, 113
Mundon, 147
MURIA, 89, 95, 302-5
MUTT, 302
MWSSs, 60
MYLODEN, HMS, 349
MYRTLE, 16

Naasen, 52
Nacton, 152, 163, 166
NADINE, 105
Naja, 267
NARCISSUS, 357
Nautilus, 52
Naval Control Service, 175, 182,
 184, 195, 225, 299
Naze (Essex), 18,80,198,214,234
N C Monberg, 103
Neatishead, 133
Needham Market, 258
Neill, Lt T, RNVR, 288
NEMO, HMS, 61, 188, 197 (& see
 Brightlingsea)
NEPTUNE, 311
Nereus, 115
NESS POINT, 168
NESSUS, 301
Newcastle, 112, 214
New Lambton, 92
Newlands, 105, 367
NEW PRINCE OF WALES, 26, 44
NIBLICK, 163
Nicholaos Piangos, 215, 299
Nicholson, Cdr H St L, 38
Nicholson, Cdre, 177
Nickson, Sub-Lt, 228
Niet, J M De, 50
Nieuwlands, 92
NIGER, 10
Niritos, 31
NONSUCH, 292
Noordwijk, 353
Norbritt, 308
Nore Command, 2, 179
 (passim in sea war chapters)
 C-in-C, 175
Nore LV, 253
Norfolk Division, 78
Norhawk, 236
NORLAND, 221

INDEX

NORMAN, 301
Norman Queen, 115
North Coates, RAF. 75, 198, 207, 209, 246-7, 260, 282, 285, 288, 292, 332, 359, 371
Northfleet, 143
North Foreland, 110,135,226,232, 339, 345
North Shoebury, 146
North Weald, RAF. 91, 132, 142-3, 145-6, 152, 341, 344
Norway, Campaign in, 35-36, 201
Norwich, air raids, 87, 136, 167, 227, 255, 265, 270
Norwich Trader, 218
Nunes, F van, 50
NÜRNBERG, 200

Oakfield, 78
Oakgrove, 11
Oaze LV, 95
OCEAN LASSIE, 83
Ohlenschlager, Lt V, RNVR, 288
Oiltrader, 91, 305
Oldstairs (Kent), 211
Olivier, Lt G D, RNVR, 45
Olsen, O, 53
ONA, 187
Onto, 23
Opdenhoff, K Kap H, 367
Ore, River, 60, 80
Orford, 118, 136, 232, 258, 268
Orfordness, 20, 52, 80, 87-8, 101, 117, 136, 139, 141, 154, 198, 215, 233, 235, 237, 242, 271, 339, 359, 365
ORIOLE, 28, 48
ORIZABA, 105
Ormesby, 194, 261
Ormiston, Fl.Sgt, 326
OROPESA Sweep, 25
ORPHÉE, 201
Orsett,149
Orwell, River, 127-8, 306-7, 309, 340, 348, 358
Ostend, 41, 47, 77, 79,109, 206-7, 223, 275, 281, 283, 292-3, 357, 360-1, 363-4, 366
OTHELLO, 108
Oulton, 163, 258
Oulton Broad, 99, 166, 191, 195, 258, 294, 328, 373
Out Newton, 237
"Outward", Operation, 209-11

Ouvry, Lt-Cdr J G D, 21
OUZEL, 214
Overy, G, 320
Owles, Lt-Cdr G H F, 91
OXLIP, 357
PACs, 58, 106
Page, Plt.Off G, 344
Paglesham, 270
Pakefield, 50, 156, 162, 166
Parker, C D, 49
Parkeston Quay, 9, 17, 19, 37-8, 48, 53, 55, 83, 127-8, 157, 160, 162-3, 183,185, 199,201,203-5, 217, 223, 235-6, 247-8, 273, 308, 349
Parkinson, Sub-Lt R, 39
Parry, Cdr C R L, 90
PASTEUR, 201
Pathfinder, 185
Patrol Service, RN, 57, 191-2
Pawle, G, 291
Pearl, 11
Pearsons', 322
Peck, Skipper, RNR, 104
Pelagia, 46
PELICAN, 8
Pelloe, 2nd Off, WRNS, 234
PEMBROKE, HMS, 2, 174, 179
(& see Chatham)
PEMBROKE III, HMS, 180
PEMBROKE IV, HMS, 2, 180
PEMBROKE X, HMS, 191
Percival, H J, 320
PETER HENDRICKS, 311
Peteri Brothers, 52
Peterson, Cdr, 27
Phaedra, 14
Philante, 340
Philip M, 237
Philip, Prince, Lt, 223
Phillips, Cap G, 204
Phillips, Lt-Cdr H B, RNR, 191
Phryne, 297
Pickering & Haldane's, 58
Piercey, Cdre B H, 192
Pilsudski, 20
Pin Mill, 306-7, 309
PINTAIL, 13, 95, 108, 299
Pinto, Col O, 53
Pizey, Cap C T M, 239-48
Plawsworth, 223
PLM 14, 93
Plomer, Lt J, RCNVR, 104
Plotting, Ship, 225

PLOVER, 78
PLUTO, 358
Poignard, Cap G A, 348
Point Clear, 71, 341
Polgarth, 299
Polgrange, 87
Pollard, Lt-Cdr, 187
Pomona, 8
Ponzano, 16
Popp, Lt z S, 93
Portelet, 23
PORTIA, 307-8
Port Victoria, 40, 148, 179
Potter Heigham, 194
"Premium", Operation, 354
PRESIDENT, HMS, 174, 180
Preston, Adm Sir L, 41
Price, Sub-Lt G R, RNVR, 285
Price, Lt J W G, RNR, 105
Pridham, Rr-Adm A F, 2
PRINCESS ELIZABETH, 167,306
Princess Juliana, 37
Prins Willem van Oranje, 37
PRINZ EUGEN, 239-48, 308
"Probestick", Operation, 234
PTEROMYS, 182
Puckle, Fl.Off, F, 92
PUFFIN, 10, 83, 103, 114-5, 236, 299, 368
Pulham, 329
Purfleet, 147
PWSSs, 59, 225
Pyefleet, 147
PYROPE, 91
PYTCHLEY, 113-4, 221-3, 236, 243, 281

"QE" patrols, 116, 283
"Q" sites, 128
QUANTOCK, 105, 298
Queen, 46
Queenborough, 179, 349, 357
QUEEN EAGLE, 43, 166
QUEEN EMPRESS, 84
QUEEN OF THE CHANNEL, 43
"Quicksilver",Operation, 355,359
Quilters (Bawdsey), 118
Quisiana, 45
QUORN, 216, 223, 243
QZSs, 3, 20, 90

Rabagliatti, Col E, 351
Rabagliatti, Fl.Lt, 153
RAF: Bomber Command, 205-7
Coastal Command (16 Group),7

INDEX

176, 207-9, 226, 324, 359
Fighter Command, 7, 207
Group, 60 (Signals), 131
Rescue Launches, Ch 16 passim
RAF Launch 108, 331, 338; *111*,
332; *112*, 338; *124*, 332; *125*, 332,
338-9; *127*, 345; *134, 135 & 139*
332, 339; *141*, 338; *144 & 151*
339; *158*, 336, 338; *169*, 345;
184, 338; *2507*, 365; *2549*, 345;
2551, 336, 338; *2558*, 339;
2572, 2574 & 2578, 332; *2679*,
336-8; *2706*, 337
Squadrons:
9, 205; *17*, 87-8, 91, 96; *19*, 280,
282; *25*, 132, 251; *29*, 251; *42*,
245; *44*, 127; *46*, 9, 152-4; *53*,
282; *56*...344; *66*...338; *72*, 242;
74, 10, 91; *82*, 345; *85*, 91, 251,
258, 263, 265; *96*, 251; *107 &
110*, 205; *121*, 242; *137*, 282;
138, 341; *139*, 341; *144*, 127;
149, 205; *180*, 339; *242*, 87, 207;
254, 292; *257*, 96, 340; *277*,
325-6; *278*, 326; *279*, 326, 329,
336; *280*, 329; *401 (Canad)*, 242;
403 (Canad), 341; *407 (Canad)*,
208; *410 (Canad)* 251; *412
(Canad)*, 282; *415 (Canad)*, 359;
488 (NZ), 251; *611*, 323; *616*,
282; *617*, 344, 366; 80 Wing, 135
Raiding Craft Flotillas, 346
Rainham (Kent), 155
Ramsgate, 16, 18, 41, 49, 81, 217,
273, 303, 324, 330, 345
Ramsay, V-Adm Sir B, 2, 41, 241-2
Ramsey (Essex), 258, 260, 355
Ransome & Rapier, 161
Raphael, Wg Cdr, 258, 262
Raversyde, 152
Rawnsley, Fl.Sgt F, 259, 262
R-Boats (British), 325, 347
R-Boats (German), 209, 277, 284, 293
RDF, 10, 94, 116-126, 129-35, 226-7,
233, 241, 250, 268, 291
Rebensburg, Lt z S, 216, 372
RECEPTIVE, 213
Reculver, 52, 84, 343-4
Reculver, 11, 97
Red Alerts, 139
RED GAUNTLET, 234, 339
Red Sand Fort, 251
REED, 99
Reed, Bombardier H, 212

Reed, L/S W R, 222
REIDS, 99, 105
Rees, Captain D E, 114
Regency, 162
REMILLO, 107
RENASCENT, 45-6
Rendlesham, 270
Renown, 45
Rescue Launches, RAF (see RAF)
Rescue Tugs, RN, 299
Resolute, 231
Ribe, 53
Richards, Lt G D K, RNVR, 279
Richards' Ironworks, 109, 320
Richborough, 358
Richmond, 45
Ridham Dock, 317
Rietschoten, van, 52, 353n
RIOU, 364
Ritchie, J D, 180
RIVER CLYDE, 83
RLOs, 295
RMLs, 315, 332
RML 498, 336; *514*, 336;
544, 369
RML Flotillas:
60th, 332; *69th*, 339, 369
RMS parties, 33, 109, 229
RNLI, 324
RNR, 174
RNVR, 174, 236, 295
Roberts, Bob, 297
Robbins, Ernest, 58
Rochester, 44,
air raids, 143, 148, 150, 158,
160, 162, 230, 262, 268,
270, 317
Rochford, RAF, 133, 142, 146, 166
Rogate, 367
Rogers, Rr-Adm H H, 288
Rokos Vergotris, 216
Rolfe, Lt-Cdr, 222
ROLLS ROYCE, 107
Rose, L, 161
Rose, Stoker, 285
ROSE HILDA, 30
Roslea, 201
Rosme, 213, 231
Rosyth, 2, 6, 47, 53, 199, 201
Rosyth Escort Force, 6, 183
Rotterdam, 38, 52, 363-4, 366
Rowe, A P, 25, 118
Rowhedge, 46, 306, 318
Roy, 215

Royal Crown, 12
Royal Daffodil, 48
ROYAL EAGLE, 95
Royal Marines, 66, 78, 177
Royal Observer Corps, 128-9
Royal Scot, 108
Royston, 106
Rubensdorffer, Hptm, 88, 90, 142-3
RUBIS, 201
Ruck-Keene, Captain Sir P, 202
Rushmere (Ipswich), 265
Russell, J, & Co, 312-3
Ryal, 99
Ryan, Cap R C F, 185
Ryan, Lt-Cdr R J H, 149
Ryder searchlights, 78-9
Rye, 113

Sadler, Lt M T C, RNVR, 284
Sadd's Shipyard, 318
Saffron Walden, 329
S-Boats (=E-boats):
S 18, 21, 22, 92; *23*, 94; *27 & 28*,
113; *29*, 113, 115, 287; *30*,
112; *31*, 114; *38*, 282; *33*, 93;
53, 92, 222; *59*, 103; *70 & 75*,
283; *71*, 229; *74*, 292; *93 & 12*
293; *104*, 216, 222; *111*, 282;
114 & 119, 285; *176 & 177*, 36
199, 365; *193*, 366; *202*, 368;
220, 366. *703*, 368
ST ACHILLEUS, 47
ST CLEARS, 301-2
ST CYRUS, 107
St Denis, 38, 238
St Margaret's, 241
ST MATTHEW, HMS, 349-50, 35
ST MELLONS, 305
ST OLAVES, 89, 302, 305
St Olaves, 194
St Osyth, 128, 137, 197, 347
ST TUDNO, 179, 183
St Valéry, 207
Sailing barges, 230-1
SAILOR KING, 307
Sale, Mr, 148
SALMON, 199, 200
SALTASH, 75
Saltend Oil Depot, 136-7
Salter, Cap J S, 359
Salthous, 257
Salvadori, Sgt Plt, 154
Salvage Depts;
Harwich, 248, 301-9

INDEX

Hull/Yarmouth, 301
PLA, 300
Sheerness, 300-1
SALVAGE PRINCE, 302, 306, 308
SALVO, 30, 95
Sanders, J, 11
SAPPHIRE, 89
SARAWARA, 85
"Satan" bombs, 168
Saxmundham, 64, 268
Scarr (Shipbuilders), 322
Schaper, Cdr, RNN, 352
SCHARNHORST, 239-45
Scheldt, River, 75, 359-63
Scheveningen, 28, 351-2
Schieland, 212
SCHIFF II, 31
Schipol, 104, 371
Schouwen, 104, 351
Schrooten, Lt, 332
Scole (Suffolk), 135
Scott, Lt-Cdr P, RNVR, 372
Scott, Pte J, 254
Scottish Musician, 218, 308
Scratby, 34
Scurr, Lt-Cdr F, 305
SEA GIANT, 302
SEA KING, 213
SEALION, 199-201
SEAMAN, 302
"Sealion", Operation, 80-1, 206
Seaplane Tenders, 316
Sea Roamer, 45
Seasalter, 229
Seasalter, 45
Seddon, Lt R F, RNVR, 236
"Seehunde", 360, 365, 367, 372
Selby, 321
SELKIRK, 10, 163
SEYMOUR, 365-6
SPAN, 201
SHALIMAR, 311
SHARK, 199, 202
Shaw, Cap, USN, 356
Sheafwater, 229
SHEARWATER, 103, 111, 219, 224
Sheerness, 2, 19, 20, 27, 30, 36, 37
  40-5, 50, 52, 55-8, 65, 77, 91-6,
  99, 100, 113, 126-8, 166, 174,
  178-9, 189, 200, 213-4, 217,219,
  222-3, 226, 229, 236, 239, 242,
  251, 254, 267, 278,281, 289,309,
  311, 316, 325, 339, 342-3, 359,
  363, 365, 371

Air raids, 142, 148, 150, 156
  Dockyard, 78, 178-9, 299, 312-3,
    317
  RN Sub-Cmd, 95, 99, 218, 224,
    237, 256,
SHELDRAKE, 99, 113-4, 299
Shellhaven, 147, 214, 233, 309
Shepperd, Lt, RNVR, 303
Sheringham, 24, 49, 91, 112, 136,
  141, 167, 229, 303 Lifebt...335
SHILA, 307
Shingle Street, 80, 164, 228
Shivering Sand Fort, 253
Shoebury, 90, 136
Shoeburyness, 20, 21, 90, 198, 217,
  259
Shotley, 143, 150, 155, 161, 174,
  186, 199, 224, 263, 305
Sickquarters, 247
Shottisham, 256
SHOVA, 261
Shropham, 324
Shrublands Camp, 180
Shuttlewood, Mr, 22
SIBYLLE, LA, 201
Sidebottom, Lt D C, RNVR, 287
SILICIA, 164
Silverstone, 158
Simeon, S S B, 187
Simon Bolivar, 17
Simspon, Cdr G W G, 200
Sirdar, 317
Sittingbourne, 44, 168, 271, 317
Sizewell, 52, 135
Skagerrak, 201-2
Skagerrak, 214, 231, 306
Skegness, 214, 254, 256, 296
  Lifeboat, 335
Skids, M/S, 26
Slaughter, Lt-Cdr J E, 199
SLINGER, 309
Smith, FLt C D S, 132
Snape, 258
SNAPPER, 199, 202
Snoxell, Lt F H, RNVR, 295
Soest, Unt.Off., 332
SOLON, 52
Somerleyton, 194
Southby, Sir A, MP, 12
South Cove, 349
SOUTHDOWN, 185, 243
Southend, 3, 19-21, 44, 49, 55, 67,
  79, 96, 100-1, 126, 180-2, 212,
  254, 268, 299, 355, 358, 363

air raids, 136, 143, 145-6,
  149, 156-7, 167, 258-9, 266-7,
  270
SOUTHEND BRITANNIA, 26, 45
Southend lifeboat, 44, 296
Southern Express, 136
South Fambridge, 147
Southwold, 10, 51, 56, 94, 223,
  227, 229, 233-4, 257, 280, 355,
  367
  bombed, 145, 262, 271
  lifeboat, 48, 296, 298
Spaardam, 16
Spalding, 137
SPEEDWELL, 87
SPHENE, 89
SPINA, 254
SPLENDID, 310
SPORTSMAN, 311
Spurn Point, 221, 237, 332;
  lifebt, 296
Stad Alkmaer, 92
Stad Maastricht, 103, 299
Stanburn, 11
Stanmount, 217
Stanford-le-Hope, 161
Stanmore, RAF, 125, 129, 130, 241,
  244
STARDUST, 331
"Starfish" decoys, 256
Starshells, 94, 115, 291
Statendam, 38
STAUNTON, 85-6
Staxton Wold CH Sta, 118
Steadman, Mr, 148
STELLA CARINA, 98
STELLA LEONIS, 90
Stempel, Lt z S N von, 234
Stempel CH Sta, 118, 250
Stephanos Chandris, 217
STERLET, 199, 202
Stock Church, 100
Stoke Holy Cross CH Sta, 129, 132
Stoker, Captain H H G D, 190
Stoker, Mrs, 194
Stone Point, St Osyth, 347
Stone's Shipyard, B'sea, 158, 347
Stour, River, 128
Stow Maries, 147
Stowupland, 324
Strasbourg, 289
STRATHBORVE, 106
Strathearn, 108, 185, 340
STRATHELLIOTT, 251

INDEX

STRATHGARRY, 261, 335
STRATHMAREE, 251, 339
Stronghold, 300, 302, 305-6, 308
Strood (Kent), 150, 317
Strubby, RAF, 198, 329
Stukas, 91-2, 96
Submarines, British;
   3rd Flotilla, 199-202
   H-class, 202-5
   (and see Chatham)
Sudbourne, 198
Sulman, Sub-Lt D J D, RNVR, 325
Sultan, The, 105
SUN tugs, 101, 181
Sundowner, 45
SUNFISH, 199, 201
Sunk Head Fort, 236, 251, 260
Sunk LV, 90
SUPERMAN, 222, 302, 308
Swale, 217, 317
Swann, Ord Seaman J, 261
Swanscombe, 267
Swayne, Cdr, 187
Sweep II, 83
Swift, Lt D H, 32
Swinley, Cap C, 194
Swynfleet, 8, 219, 307-8
Sylt, 26
Syme, Sq Ldr, 332

T 13 (German torp-bt), 247
T 124, Form. 42, 57, 174, 300
Taber Park, 367
"Table", Operation, 352
TAMARISK, 91
Tamesis, 317
Tam O'Shanter, 231, 298
Tamzine, 49
TASAJERA, 349, 356
Tattersfield, Lt, RNZVR, 284
Tautmila, 11
Taylor, James, 316
Taylor, Rr-Adm A H, 43
Tazelaar, P, 352
T-Boats (British), 340, 346-7
Teddington, 45, 316
Teddington, 215, 297
Teaser, 34
Tennant, Cap W, 43
TERMINIST, 340
Terrington, 158
Terschelling, 204, 284
Terukuni Maru, 18, 298
Tester, Sq Ldr J A, 132

TEVIOT BANK, 79
Texel, 74, 208, 275, 284, 337, 346, 370
Teynham, Cap Lord, 180
Thalatta, 298
Thames Fixed Defences, 63
Thameshaven, 60, 126
   air raids, 136,141,147,161-2,260
Thames Pilot Cutter 6, 96
Thames, River, 59,60,78,176,180
   187,294, 299, 307, 310
Theberton, 268
THEIR MERIT, 157
Theobald, Cap F O A, 191
THERMOPYLAE, 311
THETIS, 201
Thomas, Lt J O, RNVR, 236
THOMAS BARTLETT, 49
THOMAS CONNOLLY, 101
Thomas Deas, 107
THOMAS LEEDS, 98, 305
Thomson, Lt F N, RNVR, 361
Thornycrofts', 314, 316
Thorp, Sub-Lt, RNVR, 110
Thorpe Abbotts, 271
Thorpe, Lt E M, 273, 284
Thorpe-le-Soken, 52, 128, 260, 268
Thorpeness, 52, 87, 232, 234, 237, 268, 338
THREE KINGS, 218
Thule, 284
TIGRIS, 310
Tibbenham, Fl.Off, 133
Tilbury, 8, 44, 98, 126, 180, 306, 312, 349, 356-8, 363, 365
   air raids, 143, 146
TILBURYNESS, 95
Till, 300
TIRPITZ, 207
Tollemache, Cdr.H D, 342
Tollesbury, 34, 67, 228, 341. 350
Tollesbury, 44
TONBRIDGE, 168
Tongue LV, 16
Tongue Sand Fort, 251, 253
TORBAY, 310-11
TORRINGTON, 364
Tough's Shipyard, 45, 316
TOURMALINE, 110
Tovey, Adm Sir J, 372
TOWER, HMS, 180
Tower Bridge (London), 267
Townsend, Sq Ldr P, 87-8, 91, 142, 218

TRADEWIND, 311
Train Ferries *1-3* (LNER), 8, 238
Tramecourt, 143
TRANIO, 212
Traviata, 296
Trawlers, RN, 57-8
Trelawny, Lt-Cdr I C, RNVR, 288
Trelissic, 212
TRENCHANT, 311
Trevethoe, 115
Trimingham, 226-7, 232, 250
Trimley, 127, 151, 270, 340, 355
Trinder, T, 45
Trinity House, 12, 185, 321
Triton, 185
Trodden, Cap, 302
Trotter, W P, 45
Troup, Cdr, 43
Tuck, Sq Ldr R S, 142, 152, 154, 213, 340
Tudor, Cap, 114
TUNISIAN, 228
Turner, Seaman, 162, 255
TURPIN, 311
TURQUOISE, 90, 110

U-Boats, 209, 238, 369
U *12, 13*, 9; *15*, 9, 20; *19*, 20; *36* 200; *40*, 9; *56*, 23; *58*, 20; *59 &* 60, 23; *2324*, 369
UBERTY, 164
Uggeshall, 351
Uglow, W, 231, 259
UJ 126, 204
ULM, 32, 202
"Ultra", 247
UMBRIEL, 318
Upminster, 11
UMPIRE, 310-11
Unwin, Lt-Cdr, 221-2
Upnor, 357
Ursel, 152
USAAF, 200
   8th A F, 323, 329, 357, 366
   9th A F, 293, 357

Vacher, Cdr C B, 195
Vae Victis, 223
VALOROUS, 8, 88, 214
Vancouver, 214
Van der Kooi, K, 370
Van der Veen, 50
VAN DER ZAAN, 78
Vanguard, 45

INDEX

Vange, 268
VANITY, 53
Van Hamel, Lt. RNN, 352
VAN MEERLANT, 108
Van Rensaluer, 37
V-bombs, 267-71, 369
Vearncombe, ABS, 21
Veendam, 38
VEGA, 40, 99
VELIA, 97
VENEMOUS, 88
VERDUN, 95, 216
VERNON, HMS, 20, 27-8, 33, 61, 84, 99, 100, 149, 156, 188, 228
VERSATILE, 113
VESPER, 216, 239
VICs, 316, 321
"Victor", Operation, 79
VIDONIA, 89
Vienna, 363
Viking (WD launch), 19
Viking, 45
VIMIERA, 219
VIMY, 40, 43
VINDELICIA, 50
VIRGILIA, 216, 278
VIVACIOUS, 239, 243, 245, 357
VIVIEN, 92
Vivien, Rr-Adm J P, 6
Vlaardingen, 75
Voelcker, Cdr V J, 348
Voorspuiy, Cap, 17
Voreda, 12
VORTIGERN, 96, 222-3, 281
Vospers Ltd, 314, 316, 318
VP-Boats, 277
Vrede, Rr-Adm, RNN, 39
VULCAN, 273

WAAFs, 125, 198
Waalhaven, 366
Waddley, Sub-Lt, RNVR, 107
Wainfleet, 198, 258
WAKEFUL, 112
Walcheren, 361
Walcot, 11
Waldinge, 216, 280
Waldringfield, 133
Walker, Cap, 302, 304
WALLACE, 105, 281
Wallesea Island, 318
Walmer, 250
WALPOLE, 37, 241, 244, 364

Walrus aircraft, 323, 325
Walton CHL Sta, 29, 126, 244, 264
Walton & Frinton lifeboat, 17, 46, 296-8, 304, 342
Walton-on-Naze, 32, 46, 79, 131-2, 146, 156, 296
Walton (Felixstowe), 166
Walton Yachtworks (Surrey), 317
Wandle, 229
Wangerooge, 370
Wanklyn, Lt M D, 204
Wapping, 267
Ward, Lt-Col H, 19
Warden Point, 232
WARDOUR, 51
WARLAND, 221
WAR MEHTAR, 216
Warms, Oberfdwl, 332
War Nizam, 78
Warren, Lt R T, RNVR, 340
War Signal Stas, 78
WARWING, 254
Wash, 136, 195, 316, 355
WASP, HMS, 2
Wassenaar, 358
WATCHFUL, HMS, 194
WATCHMAN, 95
WATER GIPSY, 267
Waters, Elsie & Doris, 191
Watkins, William, 302
Watson, Rr-Adm F B, 372
Wattisham, RAF, 205
WAVEFLOWER, 32, 98
WAVERLEY, 48
Waxham, 211
Weeley, 73
Wells (Norfolk), 49, 87, 215, 316 lifeboat, 335
WELLSBACH, 221
Westavon, 8, 304
West Beckham CH Sta, 24, 71, 118, 130, 135, 250
Westcliff, 265
WESTCLIFF, HMS, 348-50, 358
Westgate, 367
West Malling, RAF, 133
West Mersea, 71, 152, 173, 228
West Raynham, RAF, 345
WESTMINSTER, 216
WESTON, 9
Whalers, RN, 58
Whirlwind aircraft, 246, 282
White, Lt A J R, RNVR, 222

White, PO H, 86
WHITLEY, 10
Whitney-Straight, Sq Ldr, 207
WHITSHED, 83, 113-4, 241, 243, 304, 357
Whitstable, 100, 143, 228-9, 232, 317
Whittle, Lt, 305
Whittle, Lt-Cdr, 182
Wickham, Lt D T, 292
Widdington, RAF, 127
WIDGEON, 48, 88, 97, 216
"Wikinger", Operation, 14
Wild, J, 317
WILDFIRE, HMS, 2, 174, 179, 312 (also see Sheerness)
WILDFIRE II, HMS, 179
WILDFIRE III, HMS, 349
WILD SWAN, 38
Wilhelmina, Queen, 38, 354
Wilhelmshaven, 205, 207
Wilkins, A J, 117
Will Everard, 231
Williams, Sub-Lt, 278
William King Shipyard, 318
WILLIAM STEPHEN, 291
William Watkins Ltd, 300
WILLIAM WESNEY, 14, 98
WINCHESTER, 96
"Windmill", Operation, 352
Wingfield, Lt-Cdr M, 311
Winkfield, 298, 300
Winterton, 114, 226-7, 229, 230, 260, 289
"Wiping", 25
Withernsea, 9, 34, 221, 237, 256, 331
Wivenhoe shipyards, 204, 314, 318
WIVERN, 25, 88
Wix, 324
WOLSEY, 216
Woltjer, 50
Wood, Dr, 22
Wood, Lt E P, 344
Woodbridge, 154, 266, 268, 270, 331
Woolverstone, 267
WOOLVERSTONE, HMS, 348, 355, 358
Woolwich, 22, 149
WORCESTER, 113-5, 215, 236, 241-7, 289, 291
Worlingworth, 149
Wotton, Cap J V, 22
Would, 91, 113, 301

INDEX

Wouldham Court, 231
Wrabness
  bombed, 145, 147, 151, 267
  Mine Depot, 127, 187
WRANGLER, 302-3
WREN, 90
Wright, Cap J P, 241, 243, 246
WRNS, 174, 180, 191
Wroxham, 194, 320
WVS, 194
Wyetown, 307
WYOMING, 237
Wyton (Hunts), RAF, 137

XMAS ROSE, 99

"Y" Service, 116, 227, 234, 237
Yampa, 297
Yarmouth, Great, 10-13, 33, 49, 53, 55, 57-9, 63, 74, 78-9, 82, 84,91, 93, 95, 97, 99, 101, 105, 113, 117, 128, 185, 192-5, 198, 210-2, 215-6, 218-9, 221-2, 22-6, 228-9, 234, 243, 268, 278-81, 283, 289, 291, 294, 296-7, 299, 303, 305, 323, 330, 336, 353, 355, 358-9, 365, 371
  Air raids, 138-9,141,151-2, 157-8, 160, 162-4, 166, 168, 253-8, 260-1, 263, 267

RN Sub-Cmd, 60, 139
Salvage Dept, 297, 301
Shipyards, 320-1
YEOMAN, HMS, 180
YORKSHIRE BELLE, 108
Young, Sub-Lt E, RNVR, 204, 311
YOUNG JACOB, 334

Zbaraz, 88
Zeebrugge, 40, 207
Zeppelins, 113
Z Lines, 224, 233-4, 283, 289
"Z" rockets, 127
Zwarte Zee, 40
Zymalkowski, Kaplt F, 234, 237